Course   MGMT 59000
PURDUE UNIVERSITY

http://create.mheducation.com

ISBN-10: 1308536518   ISBN-13: 9781308536514

Contents

Credits

1

Intercorporate Acquisitions and Investments in Other Entities

KRAFT'S ACQUISITION OF CADBURY

In recent years, as well as during the past several decades, the business world has witnessed many corporate acquisitions and combinations, often involving some of the world's largest and best-known companies. Some of these combinations have captured public attention because of the personalities involved, the daring strategies employed, and the huge sums of money at stake. On February 2, 2010, Kraft Foods Inc. finalized a deal to *acquire* Cadbury PLC for $18.5 billion, forming the second-largest confectionery, food, and beverage company in the world. At the time of the acquisition, Cadbury's net assets were worth only around $4.6 billion. This highly visible transaction was merely the next step in more than a century of regular acquisitions.

In 1903, James L. Kraft started selling cheese door to door from the back of a horse-drawn wagon. Although not immediately successful, he continued operations and was eventually joined by four of his brothers in 1909. By 1914, Kraft & Bros. Company (later Kraft Foods Inc.) had opened its first cheese manufacturing plant and, in 1916, patented a new process for pasteurizing cheese, making the cheese resistant to spoilage and allowing it to be transported over long distances. In 1937, Kraft launched its well-known macaroni and cheese dinners.

Philip Morris acquired General Foods in 1985 and Kraft in 1988. A year later, General Foods and Kraft were *merged* to form Kraft General Foods Inc., which was renamed Kraft Foods Inc. in 1995. In 2000, Philip Morris acquired Nabisco Holdings and began integrating Nabisco and Kraft. In August 2008, the Post Cereal portion of Kraft was *split off* and *merged* with Ralcorp Holdings. The remaining portion of Kraft Foods Inc. is the company that took part in the 2010 acquisition of Cadbury PLC. Of course, this is only half of the story as Cadbury's history includes a unique journey as well. It took 104 years and dozens of *mergers* and *acquisitions* for Cadbury to grow into the company acquired by Kraft in 2010.

In August 2012, a mere two and a half years after acquiring Cadbury, Kraft's board of directors approved a *spin-off* of several of its businesses, including Cadbury. This *spin-off* would separate the high-growth global snack business from the North American grocery business ($18 billion in annual sales), which is focused in more mature markets. Analysts predicted that this *spin-off* would allow Kraft to separate two very distinct businesses that face different opportunities and challenges.

Accordingly, Kraft Foods Inc. was *split* into two separate companies, Kraft Foods Group and Mondelēz International on October 1, 2012. The Kraft Foods Group includes the U.S. and Canadian grocery operations of the Kraft food family including brands like Cheez Whiz, Cool Whip, Jell-O, Kraft Macaroni & Cheese, Oscar Mayer, and Velveeta. Mondelēz International includes brands such as Cadbury, Chips Ahoy!, Nabisco, Oreo, Tang, Teddy Grahams, and Wheat Thins. Mondelēz includes nine brands that generate over $1 billion in revenue annually and Kraft Foods includes 10 brands with over $500 million in annual revenue. With the *division* into two companies complete, each can now focus on its own distinct strategies. For example on July 1, 2013,

Kraft Food Groups *created* two new business units, a meals and desserts unit and an enhancers and snack nuts unit.

The business world is complex and frequent business combinations will continue to increase the complex nature of the business environment in the future. An understanding of the accounting treatment of mergers, acquisitions, and other intercorporate investments is an invaluable asset in our ever-changing markets. This chapter introduces the key concepts associated with business combinations.

LEARNING OBJECTIVES

When you finish studying this chapter, you should be able to:

LO 1-1 Understand and explain the reasons for and different methods of business expansion, the types of organizational structures, and the types of acquisitions.

LO 1-2 Understand the development of standards related to acquisition accounting over time.

LO 1-3 Make calculations and prepare journal entries for the creation of a business entity.

LO 1-4 Understand and explain the differences between different forms of business combinations.

LO 1-5 Make calculations and business combination journal entries in the presence of a differential, goodwill, or a bargain purchase element.

LO 1-6 Understand additional considerations associated with business combinations.

AN INTRODUCTION TO COMPLEX BUSINESS STRUCTURES

LO 1-1

Understand and explain the reasons for and different methods of business expansion, the types of organizational structures, and the types of acquisitions.

The business environment in the United States is perhaps the most dynamic and vibrant in the world, characterized by rapid change and exceptional complexity. In this environment, regulators and standard setters such as the Securities and Exchange Commission (SEC), the Financial Accounting Standards Board (FASB), and the Public Company Accounting Oversight Board (PCAOB) are scrambling to respond to the rapid-paced changes in a manner that ensures the continued usefulness of accounting reports to reflect economic reality. A number of accounting and reporting issues arise when two or more companies join under common ownership or a company creates a complex organizational structure involving new financing or operating entities. The first 10 chapters of this text focus on a number of these issues. Chapter 1 lays the foundation by describing some of the factors that have led to corporate expansion and some of the types of complex organizational structures and relationships that have evolved. Then it describes the accounting and reporting issues related to formal business combinations. Chapter 2 focuses on investments in the common stock of other companies. It also introduces basic concepts associated with the preparation of *consolidated financial statements* that portray the related companies as if they were actually a single entity. The next eight chapters systematically explain additional details related to the preparation and use of consolidated financial statements.

Enterprise Expansion

Most business enterprises seek to expand over time in order to survive and become profitable. Both the owners and managers of a business enterprise have an interest in seeing a company grow in size. Increased size often allows economies of scale in both production and distribution. By expanding into new markets or acquiring other companies already in those markets, companies can develop new earning potential and those in cyclical industries can add greater stability to earnings through diversification. For example, in 1997, Boeing, a company very strong in commercial aviation, acquired McDonnell Douglas, a company weak in commercial aviation but very strong in military aviation and other defense and space applications. In the early 2000s when orders for commercial air-liners plummeted following a precipitous decline in air travel, increased defense spending helped level out Boeing's earnings.

Business Objectives

Complex organizational structures often evolve to help achieve a business's objectives, such as increasing profitability or reducing risk. For example, many companies establish subsidiaries to conduct certain business activities. A ***subsidiary*** is a corporation that another corporation, referred to as a ***parent company,*** controls, usually through majority ownership of its common stock. Because a subsidiary is a separate legal entity, the parent's risk associated with the subsidiary's activities is limited. There are many reasons for creating or acquiring a subsidiary. For example, companies often transfer their receivables to subsidiaries or special-purpose entities that use the receivables as collateral for bonds issued to other entities (securitization). External parties may hold partial or complete ownership of those entities, allowing the transferring company (i.e., the parent that originally held the receivables) to share its risk associated with the receivables. In some situations, companies can realize tax benefits by conducting certain activities through a separate entity. Bank of America, for example, established a subsidiary to which it transferred bank-originated loans and was able to save $418 million in quarterly taxes.[1]

Frequency of Business Combinations

Very few major companies function as single legal entities in our modern business environment. Virtually all major companies have at least one subsidiary, with more than a few broadly diversified companies having several hundred subsidiaries. In some cases, subsidiaries are created internally to separately incorporate part of the ongoing operations previously conducted within the parent company. Other subsidiaries are acquired externally through business combinations.

Business combinations are a continuing and frequent part of the business environment. For example, a merger boom occurred in the 1960s. This period was characterized by frantic and, in some cases, disorganized merger binges, resulting in creation of a large number of conglomerates, or companies operating in many different industries. Because many of the resulting companies lacked coherence in their operations, they often were less successful than anticipated, and many of the acquisitions of the 1960s have since been sold or abandoned. In the 1980s, the number of business combinations again increased. That period saw many leveraged buyouts or LBOs (when an acquiring company borrows the funds to buy another company), but the resulting debt plagued many of those companies for many years.

Through much of the 1990s, merger activity was fueled by a new phenomenon, the use of *private equity* money. Rather than the traditional merger activity that typically involves one publicly held company acquiring another, groups of investors—such as wealthy individuals, pension and endowment funds, and mutual funds—pooled their money to make acquisitions. Most of these acquisitions did not result in lasting ownership relationships, with the private equity companies usually attempting to realize a return by selling their investments after a relatively short holding period.

The number of business combinations through the 1990s dwarfed previous merger booms, with all records for merger activity shattered. This pace continued into the new century, with a record-setting $3.3 trillion in deals closed in 2000.[2] However, with the downturn in the economy in the early 2000s, the number of mergers declined significantly. Many companies put their expansion plans on hold, and a number of the mergers that did occur were aimed at survival.

---

[1] "PNC Shakes Up Banking Sector; Investors Exit," *The Wall Street Journal,* January 30, 2002, p. C2.

[2] Dennis K. Berman and Jason Singer, "Big Mergers Are Making a Comeback as Companies, Investors Seek Growth," *The Wall Street Journal,* November 5, 2005, p. A1.

Toward the middle of 2003, merger activity again increased and accelerated significantly through the middle of the decade. During one period of less than 100 hours in 2006, "around $110 billion in acquisition deals were sealed worldwide in sectors ranging from natural gas, to copper, to mouthwash to steel, linking investors and industrialists from India, to Canada, to Luxembourg to the U.S."[3]

FYI

Historically, mergers have come in waves as indicated by the following summary:

Period	Name	Facet
1897–1904	First Wave	Horizontal mergers
1916–1929	Second Wave	Vertical mergers
1965–1969	Third Wave	Diversified conglomerate mergers
1981–1989	Fourth Wave	Congeneric mergers; hostile takeovers; corporate raiding, LBOs
1992–2000	Fifth Wave	Cross-border mergers
2003–2008	Sixth Wave	Shareholder activism, private equity, LBOs
2010–2014	Seventh Wave	Global expansion

Sources: Martin Lipton, "Merger Waves in the 19th, 20th and 21st Centuries," *The Davies Lecture*, York University, September 14, 2006."
Michael J. De La Merced and Jeffrey Cane, "Confident Deal Makers Pulled Out Checkbooks in 2010," *The New York Times*, January 3, 2011.

This activity was slowed dramatically by the credit crunch of 2007–2008. Nevertheless, business combinations have increased dramatically in the postcrisis period and will continue to be an important business activity into the foreseeable future.

Aside from private equity acquisitions, business combinations have been common in telecommunications, defense, banking and financial services, information technology, energy and natural resources, entertainment, pharmaceuticals, and manufacturing. Some of the world's largest companies and best-known names have been involved in recent major acquisitions, such as Procter & Gamble, Gillette, Citigroup, Bank of America, AT&T, Whirlpool, Sprint, Verizon, Adobe Systems, Chrysler, Daimler, ConocoPhillips, BP, and ExxonMobil.

Ethical Considerations

Acquisitions can sometimes lead to ethical challenges for managers. Corporate managers are often rewarded with higher salaries as their companies increase in size. In addition, prestige frequently increases with the size of a company and with a reputation for the successful acquisition of other companies. As a result, corporate managers often find it personally advantageous to increase company size. For instance, Bernard Ebbers started his telecommunications career as the head of a small discount long-distance telephone service company and built it into one of the world's largest corporations, WorldCom. In the process, Ebbers became well known for his acquisition prowess and grew tremendously wealthy—until WorldCom was racked by accounting scandals and declared bankruptcy and Ebbers was sentenced to prison in 2003.

Acquisitions and complex organizational structures have sometimes been used to manipulate financial reporting with the aim of enhancing or enriching managers. Many major corporations, taking advantage of loopholes or laxness in financial reporting requirements, have used subsidiaries or other entities to borrow large amounts of money without reporting the debt on their balance sheets. Some companies have created special entities that have then been used to manipulate profits.

The term *special-purpose entity* has become well known in recent years because of the egregious abuse of these entities by companies such as Enron. A *special-purpose entity* (SPE) is, in general, a financing vehicle that is not a substantive operating entity, usually one created for a single specified purpose. An SPE may be in the form of a corporation, trust, or partnership. Enron, one of the world's largest companies prior to its collapse in 2001, established many SPEs, at least some of which were intended to manipulate financial reporting. Some of Enron's SPEs apparently were created primarily to hide debt, and others were used to create fictional transactions or to convert borrowings into reported revenues. The FASB has since clarified the rules around the accounting for SPEs to avoid this issue.

Accounting for mergers and acquisitions is also an area that can lend itself to manipulation. Arthur Levitt, former chairman of the SEC, referred to some of the accounting

[3] Dennis K. Berman and Jason Singer, "Blizzard of Deals Heralds an Era of Megamergers," *The Wall Street Journal*, June 27, 2006, p. A1.

practices that have been used in accounting for mergers and acquisitions as "creative acquisition accounting" or "merger magic." For example, an approach used by many companies in accounting for their acquisitions was to assign a large portion of the purchase price of an acquired company to its in-process research and development, immediately expensing the full amount and freeing financial reporting in future periods from the burden of those costs. The FASB has since eliminated this practice.

The scandals and massive accounting failures at companies such as Enron, WorldCom, and Tyco—causing creditors, investors, employees, and others to suffer heavy losses—focused considerable attention on weaknesses in accounting and the accounting profession. In the past several years, Congress, the SEC, and the FASB have taken actions to strengthen the financial reporting process and to clarify the accounting rules relating to special entities and to acquisitions. However, the frequency and size of business combinations, the complexity of accounting, and the potential impact on financial statements of the accounting methods employed mean that the issues surrounding the accounting for business combinations are still of critical importance.

BUSINESS EXPANSION AND FORMS OF ORGANIZATIONAL STRUCTURE

Historically, businesses have expanded by internal growth through new product development and expansion of existing product lines into new markets. In recent decades, however, many companies have chosen to expand by combining with or acquiring other companies. Either approach may lead to a change in organizational structure.

Internal Expansion: Creating a Business Entity

As companies expand from within, they often find it advantageous to conduct their expanded operations through new subsidiaries or other entities such as partnerships, joint ventures, or special entities. In most of these situations, an identifiable segment of the company's existing assets is transferred to the new entity (Subsidiary), and in exchange, the transferring company (Parent) receives equity ownership.

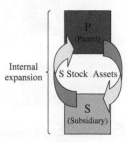

Companies may be motivated to establish new subsidiaries or other entities for a variety of reasons. Broadly diversified companies may place unrelated operations in separate subsidiaries to establish clear lines of control and facilitate the evaluation of operating results. In some cases, an entity that specializes in a particular type of activity or has its operations in a particular country may qualify for special tax incentives. Of particular importance in some industries is the fact that a separate legal entity may be permitted to operate in a regulatory environment without subjecting the entire entity to regulatory control. Also, by creating a separate legal entity, a parent company may be able to protect itself from exposing the entire company's assets to legal liability that may stem from a new product line or entry into a higher-risk form of business activity.

Companies also might establish new subsidiaries or other entities, not as a means of expansion, but as a means of disposing of a portion of their existing operations through outright sale or a transfer of ownership to existing shareholders or others. In some cases, companies have used this approach to dispose of a segment of operations that no longer fits well with the overall

6   Chapter 1   *Intercorporate Acquisitions and Investments in Other Entities*

FYI

In October of 2012 Kraft spun off its $32 billion snack business in order to better focus on its grocery business and other strategic goals.

mission of the company. In other cases, this approach has been used as a means of disposing of unprofitable operations or to gain regulatory or shareholder approval of a proposed merger with another company. A *spin-off* occurs when the ownership of a newly created or existing subsidiary is distributed to the parent's stockholders without the stockholders surrendering any of their stock in the parent company. Thus, the company divests itself of the subsidiary because it is owned by the company's shareholders after the spin-off.

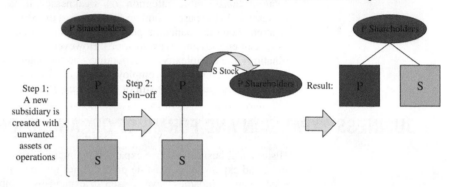

A *split-off* occurs when the subsidiary's shares are exchanged for shares of the parent, thereby leading to a reduction in the parent company's outstanding shares. Although the two divestiture types are similar, the split-off could result in one set of the former parent shareholders exchanging their shares for those of the divested subsidiary.

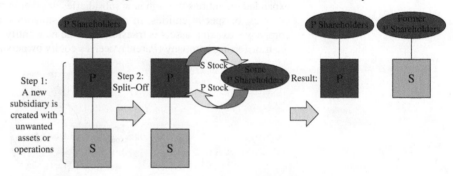

External Expansion: Business Combinations

Many times companies find that entry into new product areas or geographic regions is more easily accomplished by acquiring or combining with other companies than through internal expansion. For example, SBC Communications, a major telecommunications company and one of the "Baby Bells," significantly increased its service area by combining with Pacific Telesis and Ameritech, later acquiring AT&T (and adopting its name), and subsequently combining with BellSouth. Similarly, because the state of Florida has traditionally been very reluctant to issue new bank charters, bank corporations wishing to establish operations in Florida have had to acquire an existing bank to obtain a charter in the state.

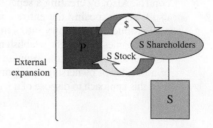

A business can be defined as an organization or enterprise engaged in providing goods or services to customers. However, a business doesn't necessarily have to be a separate legal entity. A ***business combination*** occurs when ". . . an acquirer obtains control of one or more businesses."[4] The diagram on the preceding page illustrates a typical acquisition. The concept of ***control*** relates to the ability to direct policies and management. Traditionally, control over a company has been gained by acquiring a majority of the company's common stock. However, the diversity of financial and operating arrangements employed in recent years also raises the possibility of gaining control with less than majority ownership or, in some cases, with no ownership at all through other contractual arrangements.

> **FYI**
>
> On April 2, 2012, Zynga Inc. purchased its previously leased corporate headquarters building located in San Francisco, California, to support the overall growth of its business. In accordance with **ASC 805**, "Business Combinations," Zynga accounted for the building purchase as a business combination even though it wasn't a stand-alone legal entity because (it argued) the building met the definition of a business.

The types of business combinations found in today's business environment and the terms of the combination agreements are as diverse as the firms involved. Companies enter into various types of formal and informal arrangements that may have at least some of the characteristics of a business combination. Most companies tend to avoid recording informal agreements on their books because of the potential difficulty of enforcing them. In fact, some types of informal arrangements, such as those aimed at fixing prices or apportioning potential customers, are illegal. Formal agreements generally are enforceable and are more likely to be recognized on the books of the participants.

Organizational Structure and Financial Reporting

When companies expand or change organizational structure by acquiring other companies or through internal division, the new structure must be examined to determine the appropriate financial reporting procedures. Several approaches are possible, depending on the circumstances:

1. **Merger** A merger is a business combination in which the acquired business's assets and liabilities are combined with those of the acquiring company. Thus, two companies are merged into a single entity. In essence, the acquiring company "swallows" the acquired business.

2. **Controlling ownership** A business combination in which the acquired company remains as a separate legal entity with a majority of its common stock owned by the purchasing company leads to a parent–subsidiary relationship. Accounting standards normally require that the financial statements of the parent and subsidiary be consolidated for general-purpose reporting so the companies appear as a single entity. The treatment is the same if the subsidiary is created rather than purchased. The treatment is also the same when the other entity is unincorporated and the investor company has control and majority ownership.[5]

3. **Noncontrolling ownership** The purchase of a less-than-majority interest in another corporation does not usually result in a business combination or controlling situation. A similar situation arises when a company creates another entity and holds less than a controlling position in it or purchases a less-than-controlling interest in an existing partnership. In its financial statements, the investor company reports its interest in the investee as an investment with the specific method of accounting (cost method, equity method, consolidation) dictated by the circumstances.

4. **Other beneficial interest** One company may have a beneficial interest in another entity even without a direct ownership interest. The beneficial interest may be defined by the agreement establishing the entity or by an operating or financing agreement. When the beneficial interest is based on contractual arrangements instead of majority stock

---

[4] **ASC 805-10-65-1.**

[5] Majority ownership is generally a sufficient but not a necessary condition for the indicated treatment. Unlike the corporate case, percentage ownership does not fully describe the nature of a beneficial interest in a partnership. Investments in partnerships are discussed in later chapters.

ownership, the reporting rules may be complex and depend on the circumstances. In general, a company that has the ability to make decisions significantly affecting the results of another entity's activities or is expected to receive a majority of the other entity's profits and losses is considered to be that entity's ***primary beneficiary.*** Normally, that entity's financial statements would be consolidated with those of the primary beneficiary.

These different situations, and the related accounting and reporting procedures, are discussed throughout the first 10 chapters of the text. The primary focus is on the first three situations, especially the purchase of all or part of another company's stock. The discussion of the fourth situation in Chapter 3 is limited because of its complexity and the diversity of these contractual arrangements.

THE DEVELOPMENT OF ACCOUNTING FOR BUSINESS COMBINATIONS

LO 1-2

Understand the development of standards related to acquisition accounting over time.

For more than half a century, accounting for business combinations remained largely unchanged. Two methods of accounting for business combinations, *the purchase method* and the ***pooling-of-interests method,*** were acceptable during that time. However, major changes in accounting for business combinations have occurred over the past 15 years. First, the FASB eliminated the pooling-of-interests method in 2001, leaving only a single method, purchase accounting. Then, in 2007, the FASB issued the revised standard (**ASC 805**) that replaced the purchase method with the *acquisition method,* which is now the only acceptable method of accounting for business combinations.

Although all business combinations must now be accounted for using the acquisition method, many companies' financial statements will continue to include the effects of previous business combinations recorded using the pooling-of-interests and purchase methods. Thus, a general understanding of these methods can be helpful.

The idea behind a pooling of interests was that no change in ownership had actually occurred in the business combination, often a questionable premise. Based on this idea, the book values of the combining companies were carried forward to the combined company and no revaluations to fair value were made. Managers often preferred pooling accounting because it did not result in asset write-ups or goodwill that might burden future earnings with additional depreciation or write-offs. Also, reporting practices often made acquisitions appear better than they would have appeared if purchase accounting had been used.

Purchase accounting treated the purchase of a business much like the purchase of any asset. The acquired company was recorded based on the purchase price that the acquirer paid. Individual assets and liabilities of the acquired company were valued at their fair values, and the difference between the total purchase price and the fair value of the net identifiable assets acquired was recorded as goodwill. All direct costs of bringing about and consummating the combination were included in the total purchase price.

Acquisition accounting is consistent with the FASB's intention to move accounting in general more toward recognizing fair values. Under acquisition accounting, the acquirer in a business combination, in effect, values the acquired company based on the fair value of the consideration given in the combination and the fair value of any noncontrolling interest not acquired by the acquirer.

ACCOUNTING FOR INTERNAL EXPANSION: CREATING BUSINESS ENTITIES [6]

LO 1-3

Make calculations and prepare journal entries for the creation of a business entity.

Companies that choose to conduct a portion of their operations through separate business entities usually do so through corporate subsidiaries, corporate joint ventures, or partnerships. The ongoing accounting and reporting for investments in corporate joint ventures and subsidiaries are discussed in Chapters 2 through 10. This section discusses the origination of these entities when the parent or investor creates them rather than purchases an interest in an existing corporation or partnership.

---

[6] To view a video explanation of this topic, visit advancedstudyguide.com.

Advanced
StudyGuide
.com

When a company transfers assets or operations to another entity that it has created, a vast number of variations in the types of entities and the types of agreements between the creating company and the created entity are possible. Accordingly, it is impossible to establish a single set of rules and procedures that will suffice in all situations. We focus on the most straightforward and common cases in which the transferring company creates a subsidiary or partnership that it owns and controls, including cases in which the company intends to transfer ownership to its stockholders through a spin-off or split-off. In simple cases, the company transfers assets, and perhaps liabilities, to an entity that the company has created and controls and in which it holds majority ownership. The company transfers assets and liabilities to the created entity at book value, and the transferring company recognizes an ownership interest in the newly created entity equal to the book value of the net assets transferred. Recognition of fair values of the assets transferred in excess of their carrying values on the books of the transferring company normally is not appropriate in the absence of an arm's-length transaction. Thus, no gains or losses are recognized on the transfer by the transferring company. However, if the value of an asset transferred to a newly created entity has been impaired prior to the transfer and its fair value is less than the carrying value on the transferring company's books, the transferring company should recognize an impairment loss and transfer the asset to the new entity at the lower fair value.

FYI

An "arm's-length transaction" is one in which the parties are completely independent of one another so that they act in their personal best interests or to maximize their own wealth. Thus, there is no chance of collusion between them.

The created entity begins accounting for the transferred assets and liabilities in the normal manner based on their book values at the time of transfer. Subsequent financial reporting involves consolidating the created entity's financial statements with those of the parent company. Overall, the consolidated financial statements appear the same as if the transfer had not taken place.

As an illustration of a created entity, assume that Allen Company creates a subsidiary, Blaine Company, and transfers the following assets to Blaine in exchange for all 100,000 shares of Blaine's $2 par common stock:

Item	Cost	Book Value
Cash		$ 70,000
Inventory	$ 50,000	50,000
Land	75,000	75,000
Building	100,000	80,000
Equipment	250,000	160,000
		$435,000

Allen records the transfer with the following entry:[7]

(1)			
Investment in Blaine Company Common Stock		435,000	
Accumulated Depreciation, Building		20,000	
Accumulated Depreciation, Equipment		90,000	
Cash			70,000
Inventory			50,000
Land			75,000
Building			100,000
Equipment			250,000

Record the creation of Blaine Company.

[7] Journal entries used in the text to illustrate the various accounting procedures are numbered sequentially within individual chapters for easy reference. Each journal entry number appears only once in a chapter.

Blaine Company records the transfer of assets and the issuance of stock (at the book value of the assets) as follows:

(2)	Cash	70,000	
	Inventory	50,000	
	Land	75,000	
	Building	100,000	
	Equipment	250,000	
	Accumulated Depreciation, Building		20,000
	Accumulated Depreciation, Equipment		90,000
	Common Stock, $2 par		200,000
	Additional Paid-In Capital		235,000

Record the receipt of assets and the issuance of $2 par common stock.

ACCOUNTING FOR EXTERNAL EXPANSION: BUSINESS COMBINATIONS

LO 1-4

Understand and explain the differences between different forms of business combinations.

Advanced StudyGuide .com

A business combination occurs when one party acquires control over one or more businesses. This usually involves two or more separate businesses being joined together under common control. The acquirer may obtain control by paying cash, transferring other assets, issuing debt, or issuing stock. In rare cases, the acquirer might obtain control by agreement or through other means without an exchange taking place. Business combinations can take one of several different forms and can be effected in different ways.

Legal Forms of Business Combinations

Figure 1–1 illustrates the three primary legal forms of business combinations. A *statutory merger* is a type of business combination in which only one of the combining companies survives and the other loses its separate identity. The acquired company's assets and liabilities are transferred to the acquiring company, and the acquired company is dissolved, or *liquidated*. The operations of the previously separate companies are carried on in a single legal entity following the merger.

A *statutory consolidation* is a business combination in which both combining companies are dissolved and the assets and liabilities of both companies are transferred to a newly created corporation. The operations of the previously separate companies are carried on in a single legal entity, and neither of the combining companies remains in existence after a statutory consolidation. In many situations, however, the resulting corporation is new in form only, and in substance it actually is one of the combining companies reincorporated with a new name.

A *stock acquisition* occurs when one company acquires the voting shares of another company and the two companies continue to operate as separate, but related, legal entities. Because neither of the combining companies is liquidated, the acquiring company accounts for its ownership interest in the other company as an investment. In a stock acquisition, the acquiring company need not acquire all the other company's stock to gain control. The relationship that is created in a stock acquisition is referred to as a *parent–subsidiary relationship*. A *parent company* is one that controls another company, referred to as a *subsidiary*, usually through majority ownership of common stock. For general-purpose financial reporting, a parent company and its subsidiaries present consolidated financial statements that appear largely as if the companies had actually merged into one.

Sometimes a new corporation is created by two (or more) companies to become their common *holding company*, a special case of a stock acquisition. Assuming the shareholders of the two companies approve of the creation of the new holding company, they will exchange their shares in the existing companies for shares of the newly created holding company. The holding company becomes the parent company and the existing companies become the subsidiaries.

FIGURE 1–1
Legal Forms of Business
Combinations

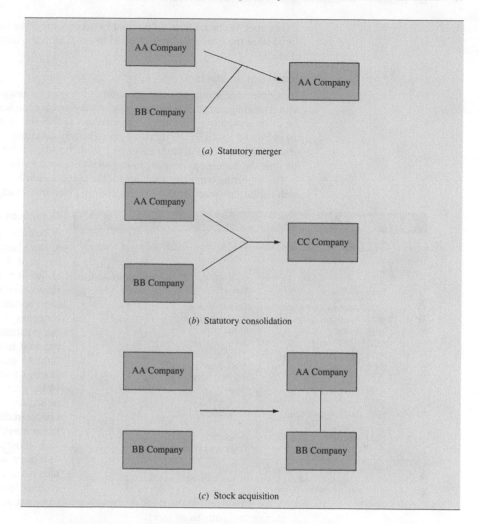

(*a*) Statutory merger

(*b*) Statutory consolidation

(*c*) Stock acquisition

The legal form of a business combination, the substance of the combination agreement, and the circumstances surrounding the combination all affect how the combination is recorded initially and the accounting and reporting procedures used subsequent to the combination.

Methods of Effecting Business Combinations

Business combinations can be characterized as either friendly or unfriendly. In a friendly combination, the managements of the companies involved come to an agreement on the terms of the combination and recommend approval by the stockholders. Such combinations usually are effected in a single transaction involving an exchange of assets or voting shares. In an unfriendly combination, or "hostile takeover," the managements of the companies involved are unable to agree on the terms of a combination, and the management of one of the companies makes a ***tender offer*** directly to the shareholders of the other company to buy their stock at a specified price. A tender offer invites the shareholders of the other company to "tender," or exchange, their shares for securities or assets of the acquiring company. If sufficient shares are tendered, the acquiring company gains voting control of the other company and can install its own management by exercising its voting rights.

The specific procedures to be used in accounting for a business combination depend on whether the combination is effected through an acquisition of assets or an acquisition of stock.

Acquisition of Assets

Sometimes one company acquires another company's assets through direct negotiations with its management. The agreement also may involve the acquiring company's assuming the other company's liabilities. Combinations of this sort normally take form (*a*) or form (*b*) in Figure 1–1. The selling company generally distributes to its stockholders the assets or securities received in the combination from the acquiring company and liquidates, leaving only the acquiring company as the surviving legal entity.

The acquiring company accounts for the combination by recording each asset acquired, each liability assumed, and the consideration given in exchange at fair value.

STOP & THINK

Can you name the 10 largest and best-known North American merger and acquisition transactions? They've all happened in your lifetime!

Rank	Year	Acquirer	Target	Transaction Value (in bil. USD)
1	2000	America Online Inc.	Time Warner Inc.	164.7
2	1999	Pfizer Inc.	Warner-Lambert Co.	89.2
3	1998	Exxon Corp.	Mobil Corp.	78.9
4	2006	AT&T Inc.	BellSouth Corp.	72.7
5	1998	Travelers Group Inc.	Citicorp	72.6
6	2001	Comcast Corp.	AT&T Broadband & Internet Services	72.0
7	2009	Pfizer Inc.	Wyeth Corp.	67.3
8	1998	SBC Communications Inc.	Ameritech Corp.	62.6
9	1998	NationsBank Corp., Charlotte, NC	BankAmerica Corp.	61.6
10	1999	Vodafone Group PLC	AirTouch Communications Inc.	60.3

Source: Institute of Mergers, Acquisitions and Alliances.

Acquisition of Stock

A business combination effected through a stock acquisition does not necessarily have to involve the acquisition of all of a company's outstanding voting shares. For one company to gain control over another through stock ownership, a majority (i.e., more than 50 percent) of the outstanding voting shares usually is required unless other factors lead to the acquirer gaining control. The total of the shares of an acquired company not held by the controlling shareholder is called the **noncontrolling interest.** In the past, the noncontrolling interest was referred to as the **minority interest.**

In those cases when control of another company is acquired and both companies remain in existence as separate legal entities following the business combination, the investment in the stock of the acquired company is recorded on the books of the acquiring company as an asset.

Valuation of Business Entities

All parties involved in a business combination must believe they have an opportunity to benefit before they will agree to participate. Determining whether a particular combination proposal is advantageous can be difficult. Both the value of a company's assets and its future earning potential are important in assessing the value of the company. Tax laws also influence investment decisions. For example, the existence of accumulated net operating losses that can be used under U.S. tax law to shelter future income from taxes increases the value of a potential acquiree.

Value of Individual Assets and Liabilities

The value of a company's individual assets and liabilities is usually determined by appraisal. For some items, the value may be determined with relative ease, such as investments that are traded actively in the securities markets or short-term receivables or payables. For other items, the appraisal may be much more subjective, such as the value of land located in an area where few recent sales have occurred. In addition, certain intangibles typically are not reported on the balance sheet. For example, the costs of developing new ideas, new products, and new production methods normally are expensed as research and development costs in the period incurred.

Current liabilities are often viewed as having fair values equal to their book values because they will be paid at face amount within a short time. Long-term liabilities, however, must be valued based on current interest rates if different from the effective rates at the issue dates of the liabilities. For example, if $100,000 of 10-year, 6 percent bonds, paying interest annually, had been issued at par three years ago, and the current market rate of interest for the same type of security is 10 percent, the value of the liability currently is computed as follows:

Present value for 7 years at 10% of principal payment of $100,000	$51,316
Present value at 10% of 7 interest payments of $6,000	29,211
Present value of bond	$80,527

Although accurate assessments of the value of assets and liabilities may be difficult, they form an important part of the overall determination of the value of an enterprise.

Value of Potential Earnings

In many cases, assets operated together as a group have a value that exceeds the sum of their individual values (i.e., there is unrecorded goodwill). This "going-concern value" makes it desirable to operate the assets as an ongoing entity rather than sell them individually. A company's earning power as an ongoing enterprise is of obvious importance in valuing that company.

There are different approaches to measuring the value of a company's future earnings. Sometimes companies are valued based on a multiple of their current earnings. For example, if Bargain Company reports earnings of $35,000 for the current year, the company's value based on a multiple of 10 times current earnings is $350,000. The appropriate multiple to use is a matter of judgment and is based on factors such as the riskiness and variability of the earnings and the anticipated degree of growth.

Another method of valuing a company is to compute the present value of the anticipated future net cash flows generated by the company. This requires assessing the amount and timing of future cash flows and discounting them back to the present value at the discount rate determined to be appropriate for the type of enterprise. For example, if Bargain Company is expected to generate cash flows of $35,000 for each of the next 25 years, the present value of the firm at a discount rate of 10 percent is $317,696. Estimating the potential for future earnings requires numerous assumptions and estimates. Not surprisingly, the buyer and seller often have difficulty agreeing on the value of a company's expected earnings.

Valuation of Consideration Exchanged

When one company acquires another, the acquiring company must place a value on the consideration given in the exchange. Little difficulty is encountered when the acquiring company gives cash in an acquisition, but valuation may be more difficult when the acquiring company gives securities, particularly new untraded securities or securities with unusual features. For example, General Motors completed an acquisition a number of years ago by issuing a new Series B common stock that paid dividends based on subsequent earnings of the acquired company rather than on the earnings of General Motors as a whole. Some companies have issued non-interest-bearing bonds (zero coupon bonds), which have a fair value sufficiently below par value to compensate the holder for interest. Other companies have issued various types of convertible securities. Unless these securities, or others that are considered equivalent, are being traded in the market, estimates of their value must be made. The approach generally followed is to use the value of some similar security with a determinable market value and adjust for the estimated value of the differences in the features of the two securities.

ACQUISITION ACCOUNTING

LO 1-5

Make calculations and business combination journal entries in the presence of a differential, goodwill, or a bargain purchase element.

Advanced
StudyGuide
.com

Current standards require the use of the ***acquisition method*** of accounting for business combinations. Under the acquisition method, the acquirer recognizes all assets acquired and liabilities assumed in a business combination and measures them at their acquisition-date fair values. If less than 100 percent of the acquiree is acquired, the noncontrolling interest also is measured at its acquisition-date fair value. If the acquiring company already had an ownership interest in the acquiree, that investment is also measured at its acquisition-date fair value. Note that a business combination does not affect the amounts at which the other assets and liabilities of the acquirer are valued.

Fair Value Measurements

Because accounting for business combinations is now based on fair values, the measurement of fair values takes on added importance. The acquirer must value at fair value (1) the consideration it exchanges in a business combination, (2) each of the individual identifiable assets and liabilities acquired, (3) any noncontrolling interest in the acquiree, and (4) any interest already held in the acquiree. Normally, a business combination involves an arm's-length exchange between two unrelated parties. The value of the consideration given in the exchange is usually the best measure of the value received and, therefore, reflects the value of the acquirer's interest in the acquiree.[8]

Applying the Acquisition Method

For all business combinations, an acquirer must be identified, and that party is the one gaining control over the other. In addition, an acquisition date must be determined. That date is usually the closing date when the exchange transaction actually occurs. However, in rare cases control may be acquired on a different date or without an exchange, so the circumstances must be examined to determine precisely when the acquirer gains control.

Under the acquisition method, the full acquisition-date fair values of the individual assets acquired, both tangible and intangible, and liabilities assumed in a business combination are recognized by the consolidated entity. This is true regardless of the percentage ownership acquired by the controlling entity. If the acquirer acquires all of the assets and liabilities of the acquiree in a merger, these assets and liabilities are recorded on the books of the acquiring company at their acquisition-date fair values. If the acquiring company acquires partial ownership of the acquiree in a stock acquisition, the assets acquired and liabilities assumed appear at their full acquisition-date fair values in a consolidated balance sheet prepared immediately after the combination.

All costs of bringing about and consummating a business combination are charged to an acquisition expense as incurred. Examples of traceable costs include finders' fees, consulting fees, travel costs, and so on. The costs of issuing equity securities used to acquire the acquiree are treated in the same manner as stock issues costs are normally treated, as a reduction in the paid-in capital associated with the securities.

Goodwill

Conceptually, *goodwill* as it relates to business combinations consists of all those intangible factors that allow a business to earn above-average profits. From an accounting perspective, the FASB has stated that **goodwill** "is an asset representing the future economic benefits arising from other assets acquired in a business combination that are not individually identified and separately recognized" (**ASC 805-10-65-1**). An asset is considered to

---

[8] However, the FASB decided in **ASC 805** to focus directly on the value of the consideration given rather than just using it to impute a fair value for the acquiree as a whole. In some cases, the value of the consideration given may be difficult to determine, or there may be no exchange, and valuation is better based on the value of the acquirer's interest in the acquiree or other valuation techniques. **ASC 820** provides a framework for applying fair value measurements in accounting.

be *identifiable,* and therefore must be separately recognized, if it is separable (can be separated from the business) or arises from a contractual or other right.

Under the acquisition method, an acquirer measures and recognizes goodwill from a business combination based on the difference between the total fair value of the acquired company and the fair value of its net identifiable assets. However, the FASB decided, for several reasons, not to focus directly on the total fair value of the acquiree, but rather on the components that provide an indication of that fair value.

The fair value of the consideration given is compared with the acquisition-date fair value of the acquiree's net identifiable assets, and any excess is *goodwill.*

As an example of the computation of goodwill, assume that Albert Company acquires all of the assets of Zanfor Company for $400,000 when the fair value of Zanfor's net identifiable assets is $380,000. Goodwill is recognized for the $20,000 difference between the total consideration given and the fair value of the net identifiable assets acquired. If, instead of an acquisition of assets, Albert acquires 75 percent of the common stock of Zanfor for $300,000, and the fair value of the noncontrolling interest is $100,000, goodwill is computed as follows:

Fair value of consideration given by Albert	$300,000
+ Fair value of noncontrolling interest	100,000
Total fair value of Zanfor Company	$400,000
− Fair value of net identifiable assets acquired	(380,000)
Goodwill	$ 20,000

Note that the total amount of goodwill is not affected by whether 100 percent of the acquiree or less than that is acquired. However, the fair value of the noncontrolling interest does have an effect on the amount of goodwill recognized. In the example given, the fair values of the controlling and noncontrolling interests are proportional (each is valued at an amount equal to its proportionate ownership share of the total) and imply a total fair value of the acquired company of $400,000. This is frequently the case and will always be assumed throughout the text unless indicated otherwise. However, that may not always be the case in practice. Situations might arise in a stock acquisition, for example, where the per-share value of the controlling interest is higher than that of the noncontrolling interest because of a premium associated with gaining control.

Combination Effected through the Acquisition of Net Assets

Advanced
StudyGuide
.com

When one company acquires all the net assets of another in a business combination, the acquirer records on its books the individual assets acquired and liabilities assumed in the combination and the consideration given in exchange. Each identifiable asset and liability acquired is recorded by the acquirer at its acquisition-date fair value. The acquiring company records any excess of the fair value of the consideration exchanged over the fair value of the acquiree's net identifiable assets as goodwill.

To illustrate the application of the acquisition method of accounting to a business combination effected through the acquisition of the acquiree's net assets, assume that Point Corporation acquires all of the assets and assumes all of the liabilities of Sharp Company in a statutory merger by issuing 10,000 shares of $10 par common stock to Sharp. The shares issued have a total market value of $610,000. Point incurs legal and appraisal fees of $40,000 in connection with the combination and stock issue costs of $25,000. Figure 1–2 shows the book values and fair values of Sharp's individual assets and liabilities on the date of combination.

16   Chapter 1   *Intercorporate Acquisitions and Investments in Other Entities*

FIGURE 1–2

Sharp Company Balance Sheet Information, December 31, 20X0

Assets, Liabilities & Equities	Book Value	Fair Value
Cash & Receivables	$ 45,000	$ 45,000
Inventory	65,000	75,000
Land	40,000	70,000
Buildings & Equipment	400,000	350,000
Accumulated Depreciation	(150,000)	
Patent		80,000
Total Assets	$400,000	$620,000
Current Liabilities	$100,000	110,000
Common Stock ($5 par)	100,000	
Additional Paid-In Capital	50,000	
Retained Earnings	150,000	
Total Liabilities & Equities	$400,000	
Fair Value of Net Assets		$510,000

The relationships among the fair value of the consideration exchanged, the fair value of Sharp's net assets, and the book value of Sharp's net assets are illustrated in the following diagram:

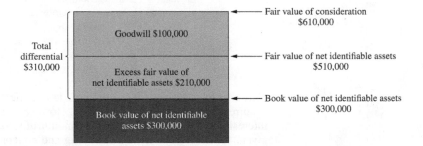

The total difference at the acquisition date between the fair value of the consideration exchanged and the book value of the net identifiable assets acquired is referred to as the **differential.** In more complex situations, the differential is equal to the difference between (1) the acquisition-date fair value of the consideration transferred by the acquirer, plus the acquisition-date fair value of any equity interest in the acquiree previously held by the acquirer, plus the fair value of any noncontrolling interest in the acquiree and (2) the acquisition-date book values of the identifiable assets acquired and liabilities assumed.

In the Point/Sharp merger, the total differential of $310,000 reflects the difference between the total fair value of the shares issued by Point and the carrying amount of Sharp's net assets reflected on its books at the date of combination. A portion of that difference ($210,000) is attributable to the increased value of Sharp's net assets over book value. The remainder of the difference ($100,000) is considered to be goodwill.

The $40,000 of acquisition costs incurred by Point in carrying out the acquisition are expensed as incurred:

(3)	Acquisition Expense	40,000	
	Cash		40,000

Record costs related to acquisition of Sharp Company.

Portions of the $25,000 of stock issue costs related to the shares issued to acquire Sharp may be incurred at various times. To facilitate accumulating these amounts before recording the combination, Point may record them in a separate temporary "suspense" account as incurred:

(4)	Deferred Stock Issue Costs	25,000	
	Cash		25,000

Record costs related to issuance of common stock.

On the date of combination, Point records the acquisition of Sharp with the following entry:

(5)	Cash and Receivables	45,000	
	Inventory	75,000	
	Land	70,000	
	Buildings and Equipment	350,000	
	Patent	80,000	
	Goodwill	100,000	
	Current Liabilities		110,000
	Common Stock		100,000
	Additional Paid-In Capital		485,000
	Deferred Stock Issue Costs		25,000

Record acquisition of Sharp Company.

Entry (5) records all of Sharp's individual assets and liabilities, both tangible and intangible, on Point's books at their fair values on the date of combination. The fair value of Sharp's net assets recorded is $510,000 ($620,000 − $110,000). The $100,000 difference between the fair value of the shares given by Point ($610,000) and the fair value of Sharp's net assets is recorded as goodwill.

In recording the business combination, Sharp's book values are not relevant to Point; only the fair values are recorded. Because a change in ownership has occurred, the basis of accounting used by the acquired company is not relevant to the acquirer. Consistent with this view, accumulated depreciation recorded by Sharp on its buildings and equipment is not relevant to Point and is not recorded. (Note that this is different from the way depreciable assets for an internally created subsidiary were handled previously.)

The stock issue costs are treated as a reduction in the proceeds received from the issuance of the stock. Thus, these costs are removed from the temporary account with a credit and decrease to Additional Paid-In Capital. Point records the $610,000 of stock issued at its value minus the stock issue costs, or $585,000. Of this amount, the $100,000 par value is recorded in the Common Stock account and the remainder in Additional Paid-In Capital.

Entries Recorded by Acquired Company

On the date of the combination, Sharp records the following entry to recognize receipt of the Point shares and the transfer of all individual assets and liabilities to Point:

(6)	Investment in Point Stock	610,000	
	Current Liabilities	100,000	
	Accumulated Depreciation	150,000	
	Cash and Receivables		45,000
	Inventory		65,000
	Land		40,000
	Buildings and Equipment		400,000
	Gain on Sale of Net Assets		310,000

Record transfer of assets to Point Corporation.

Sharp recognizes the fair value of Point Corporation shares at the time of the exchange and records a gain of $310,000. The distribution of Point shares to Sharp shareholders and the liquidation of Sharp are recorded on Sharp's books with the following entry:

(7)			
	Common Stock	100,000	
	Additional Paid-In Capital	50,000	
	Retained Earnings	150,000	
	Gain on Sale of Net Assets	310,000	
	Investment in Point Stock		610,000

Record distribution of Point Corporation stock.

Subsequent Accounting for Goodwill by Acquirer

The acquirer records goodwill arising in a merger as the difference between the fair value of the consideration exchanged and the fair value of the identifiable net assets acquired, as illustrated in entry (5). Once the acquirer records goodwill, it must be accounted for in accordance with **ASC 350.** Goodwill is carried forward at the originally recorded amount unless it is determined to be impaired. Goodwill must be reported as a separate line item in the balance sheet. A goodwill impairment loss that occurs subsequent to recording goodwill must be reported as a separate line item within income from continuing operations in the income statement unless the loss relates to discontinued operations, in which case the loss is reported within the discontinued operations section.

Goodwill must be tested for impairment at least annually, at the same time each year, and more frequently if events that are likely to impair the value of the goodwill occur. The process of testing goodwill for impairment is complex. It involves examining potential goodwill impairment by each of the company's reporting units, where a reporting unit is an operating segment[9] or a component of an operating segment that is a business for which management regularly reviews financial information from that component. When goodwill arises in a business combination, it must be assigned to individual reporting units. The goodwill is assigned to units that are expected to benefit from the combination, even if no other assets or liabilities of the acquired company are assigned to those units. To test for goodwill impairment, the fair value of the reporting unit is compared with its carrying amount. If the fair value of the reporting unit exceeds its carrying amount, the goodwill of that reporting unit is considered unimpaired. On the other hand, if the carrying amount of the reporting unit exceeds its fair value, an impairment of the reporting unit's goodwill is implied.

The amount of the reporting unit's goodwill impairment is measured as the excess of the carrying amount of the unit's goodwill over the implied value of its goodwill. The implied value of its goodwill is determined as the excess of the fair value of the reporting unit as a whole over the fair value of its net assets excluding goodwill.[10]

As an example of goodwill impairment, assume that Reporting Unit A is assigned $100,000 of goodwill arising from a recent business combination. The following assets and liabilities are assigned to Reporting Unit A:

[9] An operating segment is defined in **ASC 280-10-50.** Whereas U.S. GAAP assigns goodwill to reporting units, IFRS assigns goodwill to cash-generating units (GCU).

[10] The one-step impairment test for goodwill under IFRS is slightly different. The recoverable amount of the cash-generating unit (GCU) is compared with its carrying amount. Any impairment loss is recognized in operating results as the excess of the carrying amount over the recoverable amount. Impairment losses are recognized in operating results. If the impairment loss exceeds the book value of goodwill, the loss is allocated first to goodwill and then on a pro rata basis to the other assets of the CGU.

Item	Carrying Amount	Fair Value
Cash and Receivables	$ 50,000	$ 50,000
Inventory	80,000	90,000
Equipment	120,000	150,000
Goodwill	100,000	
Total Assets	$350,000	$290,000
Current Payables	(10,000)	(10,000)
Net Assets	$340,000	$280,000

By summing the carrying amounts of the assets and subtracting the carrying amount of the payables, the carrying amount of the reporting unit, including the goodwill, is determined to be $340,000. If the fair value of the reporting unit is estimated to be $360,000, (or any number greater than the carrying amount) there is no evidence of goodwill impairment. On the other hand, if the fair value of the reporting unit is estimated to be $320,000, a second comparison must be made to determine the amount of any impairment loss because the fair value of the reporting unit is lower than its carrying amount. The implied value of Reporting Unit A's goodwill is then determined by deducting the $280,000 fair value of the net assets, excluding goodwill, from the unit's $320,000 fair value. The $40,000 difference ($320,000 − $280,000) represents Reporting Unit A's implied goodwill. The impairment loss is measured as the excess of the carrying amount of the unit's goodwill ($100,000) over the implied value of the goodwill ($40,000), or $60,000. This goodwill impairment loss is combined with any impairment losses from other reporting units to determine the total goodwill impairment loss to be reported by the company as a whole. Goodwill is written down by the amount of the impairment loss. Once written down, goodwill may not be written up for subsequent recoveries.

Bargain Purchase*

Occasionally, the fair value of the consideration given in a business combination, along with the fair value of any equity interest in the acquiree already held and the fair value of any noncontrolling interest in the acquiree, may be less than the fair value of the acquiree's net identifiable assets, resulting in a *bargain purchase.* This might occur, for example, with a forced sale.

When a bargain purchase occurs (rarely), the acquirer must take steps to ensure that all acquisition-date valuations are appropriate. If they are, the acquirer recognizes a gain at the date of acquisition for the excess of the amount of the net identifiable assets acquired and liabilities assumed as valued under **ASC 805,** usually at fair value, over the sum of the fair value of the consideration given in the exchange, the fair value of any equity interest in the acquiree held by the acquirer at the date of acquisition, and the fair value of any noncontrolling interest. Along with the amount of the gain, companies must disclose the operating segment where the gain is reported and the factors that led to the gain.

To illustrate accounting for a bargain purchase, assume that in the previous example of Point and Sharp, Point is able to acquire Sharp for $500,000 cash even though the fair value of Sharp's net identifiable assets is estimated to be $510,000. In this simple bargain-purchase case without an equity interest already held or a noncontrolling interest, the fair value of Sharp's net identifiable assets exceeds the consideration exchanged by Point, and, accordingly, a $10,000 gain attributable to Point is recognized.

FYI

On September 22, 2008, at the climax of the global financial crisis, Barclays Bank PLC completed the bargain purchase acquisition of Lehman Brothers' North American businesses. Lehman Brothers was a former U.S.-based investment bank. Barclays is an international banking and financial services firm based in London. Barclays recorded a significant gain on bargain purchase at the time of this acquisition:

		In 1000s of USD
Net Assets Acquired		$6,098[a]
Cash Paid	1,541	
Attributable Costs	75	
Obligation to Be Settled in Shares	301	
Less: Total Consideration		1,917
Gain on Bargain Purchase		$4,181

[a]Selected Information from Barclays Bank PLC Annual Report 2008 Note 40(a), translated to U.S.$ using the GBPUSD Spot Rate 9/22/08 of 1.8483£/$.

---

* See Chapter 4 for a more detailed discussion of this topic.

In accounting for the bargain purchase (for cash) on Point's books, the following entry replaces previous entry (5):

(8)			
	Cash and Receivables	45,000	
	Inventory	75,000	
	Land	70,000	
	Buildings and Equipment	350,000	
	Patent	80,000	
	Cash		500,000
	Current Liabilities		110,000
	Gain on Bargain Purchase of Sharp Company		10,000

Record acquisition of Sharp Company.

Combination Effected through Acquisition of Stock

Many business combinations are effected by acquiring the voting stock of another company rather than by acquiring its net assets. When a business combination is effected through a stock acquisition, the acquiree may lose its separate identity and be merged into the acquiring company or it may continue to operate as a separate company. If the acquired company is liquidated and its assets and liabilities are transferred to the acquirer, the dollar amounts recorded are identical to those in entry (5).

If the acquired company continues to exist, the acquirer records an investment in the common stock of the acquiree rather than its individual assets and liabilities. The acquirer records its investment in the acquiree's common stock at the total fair value of the consideration given in exchange. For example, if Point Corporation (a) exchanges 10,000 shares of its stock with a total market value of $610,000 for all of Sharp Company's shares and (b) incurs merger costs of $40,000 and stock issue costs of $25,000, Point records the following entries upon receipt of the Sharp stock:

(9)			
	Acquisition Expense	40,000	
	Deferred Stock Issue Costs	25,000	
	Cash		65,000

Record merger and stock issue costs related to acquisition of Sharp Company.

(10)			
	Investment in Sharp Stock	610,000	
	Common Stock		100,000
	Additional Paid-In Capital		485,000
	Deferred Stock Issue Costs		25,000

Record acquisition of Sharp Company stock.

The details of the accounting and reporting procedures for intercorporate investments in common stock when the acquiree continues in existence are discussed in the next nine chapters.

Financial Reporting Subsequent to a Business Combination

Financial statements prepared subsequent to a business combination reflect the combined entity beginning on the date of combination going forward to the end of the fiscal period. When a combination occurs during a fiscal period, income earned by the acquiree prior to the combination is not reported in the income of the combined enterprise. If the combined company presents comparative financial statements that include statements for periods before the combination, those statements include only the activities and financial position of the acquiring company, not those of the combined entity or the acquiree.

To illustrate financial reporting subsequent to a business combination, assume the following information for Point Corporation and Sharp Company:

	20X0	20X1
Point Corporation:		
Separate Income (excluding any income from Sharp)	$300,000	$300,000
Shares Outstanding, December 31	30,000	40,000
Sharp Company:		
Net Income	$ 60,000	$ 60,000

Point Corporation acquires all of Sharp Company's stock at book value on January 1, 20X1, by issuing 10,000 shares of common stock. Subsequently, Point Corporation presents comparative financial statements for the years 20X0 and 20X1. The net income and earnings per share (EPS) that Point presents in its comparative financial statements for the two years are as follows:

20X0:	
Net Income	$300,000
Earnings per Share ($300,000/30,000 shares)	$10.00
20X1:	
Net Income ($300,000 + $60,000)	$360,000
Earnings per Share ($360,000/40,000 shares)	$9.00

If Point Corporation had acquired Sharp Company in the middle of 20X1 instead of at the beginning, Point would include only Sharp's earnings subsequent to acquisition in its 20X1 income statement. If Sharp earned $25,000 in 20X1 before acquisition by Point and $35,000 after the combination, Point would report total net income for 20X1 of $335,000 ($300,000 + $35,000). Note that if the shares are issued in the middle of the year to effect the acquisition, the weighted-average shares used in the EPS calculation would change as well.

ADDITIONAL CONSIDERATIONS IN ACCOUNTING FOR BUSINESS COMBINATIONS

LO 1-6

Understand additional considerations associated with business combinations.

ASC 805 includes a number of requirements relating to specific items or aspects encountered in business combinations. A discussion of the more common situations follows.

Uncertainty in Business Combinations

Uncertainty affects much of accounting measurement but is especially prevalent in business combinations. Although uncertainty relates to many aspects of business combinations, three aspects of accounting for business combinations deserve particular attention: the measurement period, contingent consideration, and acquiree contingencies.

Measurement Period

One type of uncertainty in business combinations arises from numerous required fair value measurements. Because the acquirer may not have sufficient information available immediately to properly ascertain fair values, **ASC 805** allows for a period of time, called the *measurement period,* to acquire the necessary information. The measurement period ends once the acquirer obtains the necessary information about the facts as of the acquisition date, but may not exceed one year beyond the acquisition date.

Assets that have been provisionally recorded as of the acquisition date are retrospectively adjusted in value during the measurement period for new information that clarifies the acquisition-date value. Usually, the offsetting entry is to goodwill. Retrospective adjustments may not be made for changes in value that occur subsequent to the acquisition date, even when those changes occur during the measurement period.

As an illustration, assume that Blaine Company acquires land in a business combination and provisionally records the land at its estimated fair value of $100,000. During the measurement period, Blaine receives a reliable appraisal that the land was worth $110,000 at the acquisition date. Subsequently, during the same accounting period, a change in the zoning of a neighboring parcel of land reduces the value of the land acquired by Blaine to $75,000. Blaine records the clarification of the acquisition-date fair value of the land and the subsequent impairment of value with the following entries:

(11)	Land	10,000	
	Goodwill		10,000
	Adjust acquisition-date value of land acquired in business combination.		

(12)	Impairment Loss	35,000	
	Land		35,000
	Recognize decline in value of land held.		

Contingent Consideration

Sometimes the consideration exchanged by the acquirer in a business combination is not fixed in amount, but rather is contingent on future events. For example, the acquiree and acquirer may enter into a *contingent-share agreement* whereby, in addition to an initial issuance of shares, the acquirer may agree to issue a certain number of additional shares for each percentage point by which the earnings number exceeds a set amount over the next five years. Thus, total consideration exchanged in the business combination is not known within the measurement period because the number of shares to be issued is dependent on future events.

ASC 805 requires contingent consideration in a business combination to be valued at fair value as of the acquisition date (and classified as either a liability or equity). The right to require the return of consideration given that it is dependent on future events is classified as an asset. Contingent consideration classified as an asset or liability is remeasured each period to fair value and the change is recognized in income.[11] Contingent consideration classified as equity is not remeasured.

Acquiree Contingencies

Certain contingencies may relate to an acquiree in a business combination, such as pending lawsuits or loan guarantees made by the acquiree. Certainly, the acquirer considers such contingencies when entering into an acquisition agreement, and the accounting must also consider such contingencies. Under **ASC 805,** the acquirer must recognize all contingencies that arise from contractual rights or obligations and other contingencies if it is more likely than not that they meet the definition of an asset or liability at the acquisition date. The acquirer records these contingencies at acquisition-date fair value.

For all acquired contingencies, the acquirer should provide a description of each, disclose the amount recognized at the acquisition date, and describe the estimated range of possible undiscounted outcomes. Subsequently, the acquirer should disclose changes in the amounts recognized and in the range of possible outcomes. Note that the accounting for acquiree contingencies is no different from the accounting for any other contingency.

In-Process Research and Development

In normal operations, research and development costs are required to be expensed as incurred except under certain limited conditions. When a company acquires valuable ongoing research and development projects from an acquiree in a business combination,

---

[11] The treatment of contingent consideration under IFRS is slightly different. Although contingent consideration classified as an asset or liability will likely be a financial instrument measured at fair value with gains or losses recognized in profit or loss, if the asset or liability is not a financial instrument, it is accounted for in accordance with the standard provisions for that class of asset or liability (i.e., not necessarily at fair value).

a question arises as to whether these should be recorded as assets. The FASB concluded in **ASC 805** that these projects are assets and should be recorded at their acquisition-date fair values, even if they have no alternative use. These projects should be classified as having indefinite lives and, therefore, should not be amortized until completed and brought to market. They should be tested for impairment in accordance with current standards. Projects that are subsequently abandoned are written off when abandoned. Subsequent expenditures for the previously acquired research and development projects would normally be expensed as incurred.

Noncontrolling Equity Held Prior to Combination

In some cases, an acquirer may hold an equity interest in an acquiree prior to obtaining control through a business combination. The total amount of the acquirer's investment in the acquiree subsequent to the combination is equal to the acquisition-date fair value of the equity interest previously held and the fair value of the consideration given in the business combination. For example, if Lemon Company held 10 percent of Aide Company's stock with a fair value of $500,000 and Lemon acquired the remaining shares of Aide for $4,500,000 cash, Lemon's total investment is considered to be $5,000,000.

An acquirer that held an equity position in an acquiree immediately prior to the acquisition date must revalue that equity position to its fair value at the acquisition date and recognize a gain or loss on the revaluation. Suppose that Lemon's 10 percent investment in Aide has a book value of $300,000 and fair value of $500,000 at the date Lemon acquires the remaining 90 percent of Aide's stock. Lemon revalues its original investment in Aide to its $500,000 fair value and recognizes a $200,000 gain on the revaluation at the date it acquires the remaining shares of Aide. Lemon records the following entries on its books in connection with the acquisition of Aide:

(13)	Investment in Aide Company Stock	200,000	
	Gain on revaluation of Aide Company Stock		200,000

Revalue Aide Company stock to fair value at date of business combination.

(14)	Investment in Aide Company Stock	4,500,000	
	Cash		4,500,000

Acquire controlling interest in Aide Company.

SUMMARY OF KEY CONCEPTS

Business combinations and complex organizational structures are an important part of the global business scene. Many companies add organizational components by creating new corporations or partnerships through which to carry out a portion of their operations. In other cases, companies may enter into business combinations to acquire other companies through which to further their objectives.

When a company creates another corporation or a partnership through a transfer of assets, the book values of those assets are transferred to the new entity and no gain or loss is recognized. The creating company and the new entity will combine their financial statements for general-purpose financial reporting to appear as if they were a single company as long as the creating company continues to control the new entity.

A business combination occurs when an acquirer obtains control of one or more other businesses. The three legal forms of business combination that are commonly found are (*a*) statutory mergers in which the acquiree loses its separate identity and the acquirer continues with the assets and liabilities of both companies; (*b*) statutory consolidations in which both combining companies join to form a new company; and (*c*) stock acquisitions in which both combining companies maintain their separate identities, with the acquirer owning the stock of the acquiree.

ASC 805 requires that the acquisition method be used to account for business combinations. Under the acquisition method, all of the assets acquired and liabilities assumed by the acquirer in a business combination are valued at their fair values. The excess of the sum of the fair value of the acquirer's consideration transferred, the fair value of any equity interest in the acquiree already held, and the fair value of any noncontrolling interest in the acquiree over the fair value of the net identifiable assets acquired is goodwill. In subsequent financial statements, goodwill must be reported separately. Goodwill is not amortized, but it must be tested for impairment at least annually. If goodwill is impaired, it is written down to its new fair value and a loss recognized for the amount of the impairment. If the fair value of the consideration transferred by the acquirer in a business combination, along with the fair value of an equity interest already held, and the noncontrolling interest is less than the fair value of the acquiree's net identifiable assets, a situation referred to as a bargain purchase, the difference is recognized as a gain attributable to the acquirer.

All costs associated with a business combination are expensed as incurred. Any stock issue costs incurred in connection with a business combination are treated as a reduction in paid-in capital. A business combination is given effect as of the acquisition date for subsequent financial reporting.

KEY TERMS

acquisition method, *14*	liquidated, *10*	primary beneficiary, *8*
bargain purchase, *19*	measurement period, *21*	special-purpose entity, *4*
business combination, *7*	minority interest, *12*	spin-off, *6*
consolidated financial	noncontrolling interest, *12*	split-off, *6*
statements, *2*	parent company, *3*	statutory consolidation, *10*
control, *7*	parent–subsidiary	statutory merger, *10*
differential, *16*	relationship, *10*	stock acquisition, *10*
goodwill, *14*	pooling-of-interests	subsidiary, *3*
holding company, *10*	method, *8*	tender offer, *11*

QUESTIONS

LO 1-1 | **Q1-1** | What types of circumstances would encourage management to establish a complex organizational structure?

LO 1-1 | **Q1-2** | How would the decision to dispose of a segment of operations using a split-off rather than a spin-off impact the financial statements of the company making the distribution?

LO 1-1 | **Q1-3** | Why did companies such as Enron find the use of special-purpose entities to be advantageous?

LO 1-4 | **Q1-4** | Describe each of the three legal forms that a business combination might take.

LO 1-1 | **Q1-5** | When does a noncontrolling interest arise in a business combination?

LO 1-5 | **Q1-6** | How is the amount reported as goodwill determined under the acquisition method?

LO 1-5 | **Q1-7** | What impact does the level of ownership have on the amount of goodwill reported under the acquisition method?

LO 1-5 | **Q1-8** | What is a differential?

LO 1-5 | **Q1-9** | When a business combination occurs after the beginning of the year, the income earned by the acquired company between the beginning of the year and the date of combination is excluded from the net income reported by the combined entity for the year. Why?

LO 1-5 | **Q1-10** | What is the maximum balance in retained earnings that can be reported by the combined entity immediately following a business combination?

LO 1-5 | **Q1-11** | How is the amount of additional paid-in capital determined when recording a business combination?

LO 1-5 | **Q1-12** | Which of the costs incurred in completing a business combination are capitalized under the acquisition method?

LO 1-5 | **Q1-13** | Which of the costs incurred in completing a business combination should be treated as a reduction of additional paid-in capital?

LO 1-5 | **Q1-14** | When is goodwill considered impaired following a business combination?

LO 1-5   **Q1-15**   When does a bargain purchase occur?

LO 1-6   **Q1-16**   Within the measurement period following a business combination, the acquisition-date fair value of buildings acquired is determined to be less than initially recorded. How is the reduction in value recognized?

LO 1-6   **Q1-17**   P Company reports its 10,000 shares of S Company at $40 per share. P Company then purchases an additional 60,000 shares of S Company for $65 each and gains control of S Company. What must be done with respect to the valuation of the shares previously owned?

CASES

LO 1-2, 1-5   **C1-1**   **Assignment of Acquisition Costs**

Research   Troy Company notified Kline Company's shareholders that it was interested in purchasing controlling ownership of Kline and offered to exchange one share of Troy's common stock for each share of Kline Company submitted by July 31, 20X7. At the time of the offer, Troy's shares were trading for $35 per share and Kline's shares were trading at $28. Troy acquired all of the shares of Kline prior to December 31, 20X7, and transferred Kline's assets and liabilities to its books. In addition to issuing its shares, Troy paid a finder's fee of $200,000, stock registration and audit fees of $60,000, legal fees of $90,000 for transferring Kline's assets and liabilities to Troy, and $370,000 in legal fees to settle litigation brought by Kline's shareholders who alleged that the offering price was below the per-share fair value of Kline's net assets.

Required

Troy Company's vice president of finance has asked you to review the current accounting literature, including authoritative pronouncements, and prepare a memo reporting the required treatment of the additional costs at the time Kline Company was acquired. Support your recommendations with citations and quotations from the authoritative financial reporting standards or other literature.

LO 1-1, 1-3   **C1-2**   **Evaluation of Merger**

Research   One company may acquire another for a number of different reasons. The acquisition often has a significant impact on the financial statements. In 2005, 3M Corporation acquired CUNO Incorporated. Obtain a copy of the 3M 10-K filing for 2005. The 10-K reports the annual results for a company and is often available on the Investor Relations section of a company's website. It is also available on the SEC's website at www.sec.gov.

Required

Use the 10-K for 2005 to find the answers to the following questions about 3M's acquisition of CUNO Inc. (*Hint:* You can search for the term CUNO once you have accessed the 10-K online.)

a. Provide at least one reason why 3M acquired CUNO.

b. How was the acquisition funded?

c. What was the impact of the CUNO acquisition on net accounts receivable?

d. What was the impact of the CUNO acquisition on inventories?

LO 1-4   **C1-3**   **Business Combinations**

Analysis   A merger boom comparable to those of the 1960s and mid-1980s occurred in the 1990s and into the new century. The merger activity of the 1960s was associated with increasing stock prices and heavy use of pooling-of-interests accounting. The mid-1980s activity was associated with a number of leveraged buyouts and acquisitions involving junk bonds. Merger activity in the early 1990s, on the other hand, appeared to involve primarily purchases with cash and standard debt instruments. By the mid-1990s, however, many business combinations were being effected through exchanges of stock. In the first decade of the new century, the nature of many business acquisitions changed, and by late 2008, the merger boom had slowed dramatically.

a. Which factors do you believe were the most prominent in encouraging business combinations in the 1990s? Which of these was the most important? Explain why.

b. Why were so many of the business combinations in the middle and late 1990s effected through exchanges of stock?

c. What factors had a heavy influence on mergers during the mid-2000s? How did many of the business combinations of this period differ from earlier combinations? Why did the merger boom slow so dramatically late in 2008 and in 2009?

d. If a major review of the tax laws were undertaken, would it be wise or unwise public policy to establish greater tax incentives for corporate mergers? Propose three incentives that might be used.

e. If the FASB were interested in encouraging more mergers, what action should it take with regard to revising or eliminating existing accounting standards? Explain.

LO 1-5

Research

C1-4 Determination of Goodwill Impairment

Plush Corporation purchased 100 percent of Common Corporation's common stock on January 1, 20X3, and paid $450,000. The fair value of Common's identifiable net assets at that date was $430,000. By the end of 20X5, the fair value of Common, which Plush considers to be a reporting unit, had increased to $485,000; however, Plush's external auditor made a passing comment to the company's chief accountant that Plush might need to recognize impairment of goodwill on one or more of its investments.

Required

Prepare a memo to Plush's chief accountant indicating the tests used in determining whether goodwill has been impaired. Include in your discussion one or more possible conditions under which Plush might be required to recognize impairment of goodwill on its investment in Common Corporation. In preparing your memo, review the current accounting literature, including authoritative pronouncements of the FASB and other appropriate bodies. Support your discussion with citations and quotations from the applicable literature.

LO 1-1

Analysis

C1-5 Risks Associated with Acquisitions

Not all business combinations are successful, and many entail substantial risk. Acquiring another company may involve a number of different types of risk. Obtain a copy of the 10-K report for Google Inc. for the year ended December 31, 2006, available at the SEC's website (www.sec.gov). The report also can be accessed through Yahoo! Finance or the company's Investor Relations page.

Required

On page 21 of the 10-K report, Google provides information to investors about its motivation for acquiring companies and the possible risks associated with such acquisitions. Briefly discuss the risks that Google sees inherent in potential acquisitions.

LO 1-1

Communication

C1-6 Numbers Game

Arthur Levitt's speech, "The Numbers Game," is available on the SEC's website at www.sec.gov/news/speech/speecharchive/1998/spch220.txt. Read the speech, and then answer the following questions.

Required

a. Briefly explain what motivations Levitt discusses for earnings management.

b. What specific techniques for earnings management does Levitt discuss?

c. According to Levitt, why is the issue of earnings management important?

LO 1-1, 1-4

Research

C1-7 MCI: A Succession of Mergers

MCI WorldCom Inc. (later MCI), was known as a high-flying company, having had its roots in a small local company and rising to one of the world's largest communications giants. The company's spectacular growth was accomplished through a string of business combinations. However, not all went as planned, and MCI is no longer an independent company.

Required

Provide a brief history of, and indicate subsequent events related to, MCI WorldCom. Include in your discussion the following:

a. Trace the major acquisitions leading to MCI WorldCom and indicate the type of consideration used in the acquisitions.

b. Who is Bernard Ebbers, and where is he now?

c. What happened to MCI WorldCom, and where is it now?

| LO 1-4 | **C1-8** | **Leveraged Buyouts** |

Analysis

A type of acquisition that was not discussed in the chapter is the *leveraged buyout.* Many experts argue that a leveraged buyout (LBO) is not a type of business combination but rather just a restructuring of ownership. Yet some would see an LBO as having many of the characteristics of a business combination. The number of LBOs in recent years has grown dramatically and, therefore, accounting for these transactions is of increased importance.

Required

a. What is a leveraged buyout? How does an LBO compare with a management buyout (MBO)?

b. What authoritative pronouncements, if any, deal with leveraged buyouts?

c. Is a leveraged buyout a type of business combination? Explain.

d. What is the major issue in determining the proper basis for an interest in a company purchased through a leveraged buyout?

EXERCISES

| LO 1-1, 1-3, 1-5 | **E1-1** | **Multiple-Choice Questions on Complex Organizations** |

Select the correct answer for each of the following questions.

1. Growth in the complexity of the U.S. business environment

   a. Has led to increased use of partnerships to avoid legal liability.

   b. Has led to increasingly complex organizational structures as management has attempted to achieve its business objectives.

   c. Has encouraged companies to reduce the number of operating divisions and product lines so they may better control those they retain.

   d. Has had no particular impact on the organizational structures or the way in which companies are managed.

2. Which of the following is *not* an appropriate reason for establishing a subsidiary?

   a. The parent wishes to protect existing operations by shifting new activities with greater risk to a newly created subsidiary.

   b. The parent wishes to avoid subjecting all of its operations to regulatory control by establishing a subsidiary that focuses its operations in regulated industries.

   c. The parent wishes to reduce its taxes by establishing a subsidiary that focuses its operations in areas where special tax benefits are available.

   d. The parent wishes to be able to increase its reported sales by transferring products to the subsidiary at the end of the fiscal year.

3. Which of the following actions is likely to result in recording goodwill on Randolph Company's books?

   a. Randolph acquires Penn Corporation in a business combination recorded as a merger.

   b. Randolph acquires a majority of Penn's common stock in a business combination and continues to operate it as a subsidiary.

   c. Randolph distributes ownership of a newly created subsidiary in a distribution considered to be a spin-off.

   d. Randolph distributes ownership of a newly created subsidiary in a distribution considered to be a split-off.

4. When an existing company creates a new subsidiary and transfers a portion of its assets and liabilities to the new entity

   a. The new entity records both the assets and liabilities it received at fair values.

   b. The new entity records both the assets and liabilities it received at the carrying values of the original company.

   c. The original company records a gain or loss on the difference between its carrying values and the fair values of the assets transferred to the new entity.

   d. The original company records the difference between the carrying values and the fair values of the assets transferred to the new entity as goodwill.

5. When a company assigns goodwill to a reporting unit acquired in a business combination, it must record an impairment loss if

   a. The fair value of the net identifiable assets held by a reporting unit decreases.

   b. The fair value of the reporting unit decreases.

   c. The carrying value of the reporting unit is less than the fair value of the reporting unit.

   d. The fair value of the reporting unit is less than its carrying value and the carrying value of goodwill is more than the implied value of its goodwill.

LO 1-2, 1-5 **E1-2** **Multiple-Choice Questions on Recording Business Combinations [AICPA Adapted]**
Select the correct answer for each of the following questions.

1. Goodwill represents the excess of the sum of the fair value of the (1) consideration given, (2) shares already owned, and (3) the noncontrolling interest over the

   a. Sum of the fair values assigned to identifiable assets acquired less liabilities assumed.

   b. Sum of the fair values assigned to tangible assets acquired less liabilities assumed.

   c. Sum of the fair values assigned to intangible assets acquired less liabilities assumed.

   d. Book value of an acquired company.

2. In a business combination, costs of registering equity securities to be issued by the acquiring company are a(n)

   a. Expense of the combined company for the period in which the costs were incurred.

   b. Direct addition to stockholders' equity of the combined company.

   c. Reduction of the recorded value of the securities.

   d. Addition to goodwill.

3. Which of the following is the appropriate basis for valuing fixed assets acquired in a business combination carried out by exchanging cash for common stock?

   a. Historical cost.

   b. Book value.

   c. Cost plus any excess of purchase price over book value of assets acquired.

   d. Fair value.

4. In a business combination in which an acquiring company purchases 100 percent of the outstanding common stock of another company, if the fair value of the net identifiable assets acquired exceeds the fair value of the consideration given. The excess should be reported as a

   a. Deferred credit.

   b. Reduction of the values assigned to current assets and a deferred credit for any unallocated portion.

   c. Pro rata reduction of the values assigned to current and noncurrent assets and a deferred credit for any unallocated portion.

   d. No answer listed is correct.

5. A and B Companies have been operating separately for five years. Each company has a minimal amount of liabilities and a simple capital structure consisting solely of voting common stock. In exchange for 40 percent of its voting stock A Company, acquires 80 percent of the common stock of B Company. This is a "tax-free" stock-for-stock exchange for tax purposes. B Company's identifiable assets have a total net fair market value of $800,000 and a total net book value of $580,000. The fair market value of the A stock used in the exchange is $700,000, and the fair value of the noncontrolling interest is $175,000. The goodwill reported following the acquisition would be

   a. Zero.

   b. $60,000.

   c. $75,000.

   d. $295,000.

LO 1-2, 1-5 **E1-3** **Multiple-Choice Questions on Reported Balances [AICPA Adapted]**
Select the correct answer for each of the following questions.

1. On December 31, 20X3, Saxe Corporation was merged into Poe Corporation. In the business combination, Poe issued 200,000 shares of its $10 par common stock, with a market price of

$18 a share, for all of Saxe's common stock. The stockholders' equity section of each company's balance sheet immediately before the combination was:

	Poe	Saxe
Common Stock	$3,000,000	$1,500,000
Additional Paid-In Capital	1,300,000	150,000
Retained Earnings	2,500,000	850,000
	$6,800,000	$2,500,000

In the December 31, 20X3, combined balance sheet, additional paid-in capital should be reported at

a. $950,000.

b. $1,300,000.

c. $1,450,000.

d. $2,900,000.

2. On January 1, 20X1, Rolan Corporation issued 10,000 shares of common stock in exchange for all of Sandin Corporation's outstanding stock. Condensed balance sheets of Rolan and Sandin immediately before the combination follow:

	Rolan	Sandin
Total Assets	$1,000,000	$500,000
Liabilities	$ 300,000	$150,000
Common Stock ($10 par)	200,000	100,000
Retained Earnings	500,000	250,000
Total Liabilities & Equities	$1,000,000	$500,000

Rolan's common stock had a market price of $60 per share on January 1, 20X1. The market price of Sandin's stock was not readily determinable. The fair value of Sandin's net identifiable assets was determined to be $570,000. Rolan's investment in Sandin's stock will be stated in Rolan's balance sheet immediately after the combination in the amount of

a. $350,000.

b. $500,000.

c. $570,000.

d. $600,000.

3. On April 1, 20X2, Jack Company paid $800,000 for all of Ann Corporation's issued and outstanding common stock. Ann's recorded assets and liabilities on April 1, 20X2, were as follows:

Cash	$ 80,000
Inventory	240,000
Property & Equipment (net of accumulated depreciation of $320,000)	480,000
Liabilities	(180,000)

On April 1, 20X2, Ann's inventory was determined to have a fair value of $190,000, and the property and equipment had a fair value of $560,000. What is the amount of goodwill resulting from the business combination?

a. $0.

b. $50,000.

c. $150,000.

d. $180,000.

4. Action Corporation issued nonvoting preferred stock with a fair market value of $4,000,000 in exchange for all the outstanding common stock of Master Corporation. On the date of the exchange, Master had tangible net assets with a book value of $2,000,000 and a fair value of $2,500,000. In addition, Action issued preferred stock valued at $400,000 to an individual as a finder's fee in arranging the transaction. As a result of this transaction, Action should record an increase in net assets of

    a. $2,000,000.

    b. $2,500,000.

    c. $4,000,000.

    d. $4,400,000.

LO 1-2, 1-5   **E1-4**   **Multiple-Choice Questions Involving Account Balances**

Select the correct answer for each of the following questions.

1. Topper Company established a subsidiary and transferred equipment with a fair value of $72,000 to the subsidiary. Topper had purchased the equipment with ten-year expected life of four years earlier for $100,000 and has used straight-line depreciation with no expected residual value. At the time of the transfer, the subsidiary should record

    a. Equipment at $72,000 and no accumulated depreciation.

    b. Equipment at $60,000 and no accumulated depreciation.

    c. Equipment at $100,000 and accumulated depreciation of $40,000.

    d. Equipment at $120,000 and accumulated depreciation of $48,000.

2. Lead Corporation established a new subsidiary and transferred to it assets with a cost of $90,000 and a book value of $75,000. The assets had a fair value of $100,000 at the time of transfer. The transfer will result in

    a. A reduction of net assets reported by Lead Corporation of $90,000.

    b. A reduction of net assets reported by Lead Corporation of $75,000.

    c. No change in the reported net assets of Lead Corporation.

    d. An increase in the net assets reported by Lead Corporation of $25,000.

3. Tear Company, a newly established subsidiary of Stern Corporation, received assets with an original cost of $260,000, a fair value of $200,000, and a book value of $140,000 from the parent in exchange for 7,000 shares of Tear's $8 par value common stock. Tear should record

    a. Additional paid-in capital of $0.

    b. Additional paid-in capital of $84,000.

    c. Additional paid-in capital of $144,000.

    d. Additional paid-in capital of $204,000.

4. Grout Company reports assets with a carrying value of $420,000 (including goodwill with a carrying value of $35,000) assigned to an identifiable reporting unit purchased at the end of the prior year. The fair value of the net assets held by the reporting unit is currently $350,000, and the fair value of the reporting unit is $395,000. At the end of the current period, Grout should report goodwill of

    a. $45,000.

    b. $35,000.

    c. $25,000.

    d. $10,000.

5. Twill Company has a reporting unit with the fair value of its net identifiable assets of $500,000. The carrying value of the reporting unit's net assets on Twill's books is $575,000, which includes $90,000 of goodwill. The fair value of the reporting unit is $560,000. Twill should report impairment of goodwill of

    a. $60,000.

    b. $30,000.

    c. $15,000.

    d. $0.

LO 1-3

E1-5   Asset Transfer to Subsidiary

Pale Company was established on January 1, 20X1. Along with other assets, it immediately purchased land for $80,000, a building for $240,000, and equipment for $90,000. On January 1, 20X5, Pale transferred these assets, cash of $21,000, and inventory costing $37,000 to a newly created subsidiary, Bright Company, in exchange for 10,000 shares of Bright's $6 par value stock. Pale uses straight-line depreciation and useful lives of 40 years and 10 years for the building and equipment, respectively, with no estimated residual values.

Required

a. Give the journal entry that Pale recorded when it transferred the assets to Bright.

b. Give the journal entry that Bright recorded for the receipt of assets and issuance of common stock to Pale.

LO 1-3

E1-6   Creation of New Subsidiary

Lester Company transferred the following assets to a newly created subsidiary, Mumby Corporation, in exchange for 40,000 shares of its $3 par value stock:

	Cost	Book Value
Cash	$ 40,000	$ 40,000
Accounts Receivable	75,000	68,000
Inventory	50,000	50,000
Land	35,000	35,000
Buildings	160,000	125,000
Equipment	240,000	180,000

Required

a. Give the journal entry in which Lester recorded the transfer of assets to Mumby Corporation.

b. Give the journal entry in which Mumby recorded the receipt of assets and issuance of common stock to Lester.

LO 1-2, 1-3

E1-7   Balance Sheet Totals of Parent Company

Foster Corporation established Kline Company as a wholly owned subsidiary. Foster reported the following balance sheet amounts immediately before and after it transferred assets and accounts payable to Kline Company in exchange for 4,000 shares of $12 par value common stock:

	Amount Reported			
	Before Transfer		After Transfer	
Cash		$ 40,000		$ 25,000
Accounts Receivable		65,000		41,000
Inventory		30,000		21,000
Investment in Kline Company				66,000
Land		15,000		12,000
Depreciable Assets	$180,000		$115,000	
Accumulated Depreciation	75,000	105,000	47,000	68,000
Total Assets		$255,000		$233,000
Accounts Payable		$ 40,000		$ 18,000
Bonds Payable		80,000		80,000
Common Stock		60,000		60,000
Retained Earnings		75,000		75,000
Total Liabilities & Equities		$255,000		$233,000

Required

a. Give the journal entry that Foster recorded when it transferred its assets and accounts payable to Kline.

b. Give the journal entry that Kline recorded upon receipt of the assets and accounts payable from Foster.

LO 1-2, 1-5   **E1-8**   **Acquisition of Net Assets**

Sun Corporation concluded the fair value of Tender Company was $60,000 and paid that amount to acquire its net assets. Tender reported assets with a book value of $55,000 and fair value of $71,000 and liabilities with a book value and fair value of $20,000 on the date of combination. Sun also paid $4,000 to a search firm for finder's fees related to the acquisition.

Required

Give the journal entries to be made by Sun to record its investment in Tender and its payment of the finder's fees.

LO 1-5   **E1-9**   **Reporting Goodwill**

Samper Company reported the book value of its net assets at $160,000 when Public Corporation acquired 100 percent of its voting stock for cash. The fair value of Samper's net assets was determined to be $190,000 on that date.

Required

Determine the amount of goodwill to be reported in consolidated financial statements presented immediately following the combination and the amount at which Public will record its investment in Samper if the amount paid by Public is

a. $310,000.

b. $196,000.

c. $150,000.

LO 1-5   **E1-10**   **Stock Acquisition**

McDermott Corporation has been in the midst of a major expansion program. Much of its growth had been internal, but in 20X1 McDermott decided to continue its expansion through the acquisition of other companies. The first company acquired was Tippy Inc., a small manufacturer of inertial guidance systems for aircraft and missiles. On June 10, 20X1, McDermott issued 17,000 shares of its $25 par common stock for all 40,000 of Tippy's $10 par common shares. At the date of combination, Tippy reported additional paid-in capital of $100,000 and retained earnings of $350,000. McDermott's stock was selling for $58 per share immediately prior to the combination. Subsequent to the combination, Tippy operated as a subsidiary of McDermott.

Required

Present the journal entry or entries that McDermott would make to record the business combination with Tippy.

LO 1-5   **E1-11**   **Balances Reported Following Combination**

Elm Corporation and Maple Company have announced terms of an exchange agreement under which Elm will issue 8,000 shares of its $10 par value common stock to acquire all of Maple Company's assets. Elm shares currently are trading at $50, and Maple $5 par value shares are trading at $18 each. Historical cost and fair value balance sheet data on January 1, 20X2, are as follows:

	Elm Corporation		Maple Company	
Balance Sheet Item	**Book Value**	**Fair Value**	**Book Value**	**Fair Value**
Cash & Receivables	$150,000	$150,000	$ 40,000	$ 40,000
Land	100,000	170,000	50,000	85,000
Buildings & Equipment (net)	300,000	400,000	160,000	230,000
Total Assets	$550,000	$720,000	$250,000	$355,000
Common Stock	$200,000		$100,000	
Additional Paid-In Capital	20,000		10,000	
Retained Earnings	330,000		140,000	
Total Equities	$550,000		$250,000	

Required

What amount will be reported immediately following the business combination for each of the following items in the combined company's balance sheet?

a. Common Stock.

b. Cash and Receivables.

c. Land.

d. Buildings and Equipment (net).

e. Goodwill.

f. Additional Paid-In Capital.

g. Retained Earnings.

LO 1-5

E1-12 Goodwill Recognition

Spur Corporation reported the following balance sheet amounts on December 31, 20X1:

Balance Sheet Item	Historical Cost	Fair Value
Cash & Receivables	$ 50,000	$ 40,000
Inventory	100,000	150,000
Land	40,000	30,000
Plant & Equipment	400,000	350,000
Less: Accumulated Depreciation	(150,000)	
Patent		130,000
Total Assets	$440,000	$700,000
Accounts Payable	$ 80,000	$ 85,000
Common Stock	200,000	
Additional Paid-In Capital	20,000	
Retained Earnings	140,000	
Total Liabilities & Equities	$440,000	

Required

Blanket acquired Spur Corporation's assets and liabilities for $670,000 cash on December 31, 20X1. Give the entry that Blanket made to record the purchase.

LO 1-5

E1-13 Acquisition Using Debentures

Fortune Corporation used debentures with a par value of $625,000 to acquire 100 percent of Sorden Company's net assets on January 1, 20X2. On that date, the fair value of the bonds issued by Fortune was $608,000. The following balance sheet data were reported by Sorden:

Balance Sheet Item	Historical Cost	Fair Value
Cash & Receivables	$ 55,000	$ 50,000
Inventory	105,000	200,000
Land	60,000	100,000
Plant & Equipment	400,000	300,000
Less: Accumulated Depreciation	(150,000)	
Goodwill	10,000	
Total Assets	$480,000	$650,000
Accounts Payable	$ 50,000	$ 50,000
Common Stock	100,000	
Additional Paid-In Capital	60,000	
Retained Earnings	270,000	
Total Liabilities & Equities	$480,000	

Required

Give the journal entry that Fortune recorded at the time of exchange.

LO 1-5

E1-14 Bargain Purchase

Using the data presented in E1-13, determine the amount Fortune Corporation would record as a gain on bargain purchase and prepare the journal entry Fortune would record at the time of the exchange if Fortune issued bonds with a par value of $580,000 and a fair value of $564,000 in completing the acquisition of Sorden.

LO 1-5

E1-15 Impairment of Goodwill

Mesa Corporation purchased Kwick Company's net assets and assigned goodwill of $80,000 to Reporting Division K. The following assets and liabilities are assigned to Reporting Division K:

	Carrying Amount	Fair Value
Cash	$ 14,000	$ 14,000
Inventory	56,000	71,000
Equipment	170,000	190,000
Goodwill	80,000	
Accounts Payable	30,000	30,000

Required

Determine the amount of goodwill to be reported for Division K and the amount of goodwill impairment to be recognized, if any, if Division K's fair value is determined to be

a. $340,000.

b. $280,000.

c. $260,000.

LO 1-5

E1-16 Assignment of Goodwill

Double Corporation acquired all of the common stock of Simple Company for $450,000 on January 1, 20X4. On that date, Simple's identifiable net assets had a fair value of $390,000. The assets acquired in the purchase of Simple are considered to be a separate reporting unit of Double. The carrying value of Double's investment at December 31, 20X4, is $500,000.

Required

Determine the amount of goodwill impairment, if any, that should be recognized at December 31, 20X4, if the fair value of the net assets (excluding goodwill) at that date is $440,000 and the fair value of the reporting unit is determined to be

a. $530,000.

b. $485,000.

c. $450,000.

LO 1-5

Advanced
StudyGuide
.com

E1-17 Goodwill Assigned to Reporting Units

Groft Company purchased Strobe Company's net assets and assigned them to four separate reporting units. Total goodwill of $186,000 is assigned to the reporting units as indicated:

	Reporting Unit			
	A	B	C	D
Carrying value of investment	$700,000	$330,000	$380,000	$520,000
Goodwill included in carrying value	60,000	48,000	28,000	50,000
Fair value of net identifiable assets at year-end	600,000	300,000	400,000	500,000
Fair value of reporting unit at year-end	690,000	335,000	370,000	585,000

Required

Determine the amount of goodwill that Groft should report at year-end. Show how you computed it.

LO 1-5   **E1-18**   **Goodwill Measurement**

Washer Company has a reporting unit resulting from an earlier business combination. The reporting unit's current assets and liabilities are

	Carrying Amount	Fair Value
Cash	$ 30,000	$ 30,000
Inventory	70,000	100,000
Land	30,000	60,000
Buildings	210,000	230,000
Equipment	160,000	170,000
Goodwill	150,000	
Notes Payable	100,000	100,000

Required

Determine the amount of goodwill to be reported and the amount of goodwill impairment, if any, if the fair value of the reporting unit is determined to be

a. $580,000.

b. $540,000.

c. $500,000.

d. $460,000.

LO 1-5   **E1-19**   **Computation of Fair Value**

Grant Company acquired all of Bedford Corporation's assets and liabilities on January 1, 20X2, in a business combination. At that date, Bedford reported assets with a book value of $624,000 and liabilities of $356,000. Grant noted that Bedford had $40,000 of capitalized research and development costs on its books at the acquisition date that did not appear to be of value. Grant also determined that patents developed by Bedford had a fair value of $120,000 but had not been recorded by Bedford. Except for buildings and equipment, Grant determined the fair value of all other assets and liabilities reported by Bedford approximated the recorded amounts. In recording the transfer of assets and liabilities to its books, Grant recorded goodwill of $93,000. Grant paid $517,000 to acquire Bedford's assets and liabilities. If the book value of Bedford's buildings and equipment was $341,000 at the date of acquisition, what was their fair value?

LO 1-5   **E1-20**   **Computation of Shares Issued and Goodwill**

Advanced
StudyGuide
.com

Dunyain Company acquired Allsap Corporation on January 1, 20X1, through an exchange of common shares. All of Allsap's assets and liabilities were immediately transferred to Dunyain, which reported total par value of shares outstanding of $218,400 and $327,600 and additional paid-in capital of $370,000 and $650,800 immediately before and after the business combination, respectively.

Required

a. Assuming that Dunyain's common stock had a market value of $25 per share at the time of exchange, what number of shares was issued?

b. What is the par value per share of Dunyain's common stock?

c. Assuming that Allsap's identifiable assets had a fair value of $476,000 and its liabilities had a fair value of $120,000, what amount of goodwill did Dunyain record at the time of the business combination?

LO 1-5   **E1-21**   **Combined Balance Sheet**

The following balance sheets were prepared for Adam Corporation and Best Company on January 1, 20X2, just before they entered into a business combination:

Item	Adam Corporation		Best Company	
	Book Value	Fair Value	Book Value	Fair Value
Cash & Receivables	$150,000	$150,000	$ 90,000	$ 90,000
Inventory	300,000	380,000	70,000	160,000
Buildings & Equipment	600,000	430,000	250,000	240,000
Less: Accumulated Depreciation	(250,000)		(80,000)	
Total Assets	$800,000	$960,000	$330,000	$490,000
Accounts Payable	$ 75,000	$ 75,000	$ 50,000	$ 50,000
Notes Payable	200,000	215,000	30,000	35,000
Common Stock:				
$8 par value	180,000			
$6 par value			90,000	
Additional Paid-In Capital	140,000		55,000	
Retained Earnings	205,000		105,000	
Total Liabilities & Equities	$800,000		$330,000	

Adam acquired all of Best Company's assets and liabilities on January 1, 20X2, in exchange for its common shares. Adam issued 8,000 shares of stock to complete the business combination.

Required
Prepare a balance sheet of the combined company immediately following the acquisition, assuming Adam's shares were trading at $60 each.

LO 1-5 **E1-22 Recording a Business Combination**
The following financial statement information was prepared for Blue Corporation and Sparse Company at December 31, 20X2:

	Balance Sheets December 31, 20X2			
	Blue Corporation		Sparse Company	
Cash		$ 140,000		$ 70,000
Accounts Receivable		170,000		110,000
Inventory		250,000		180,000
Land		80,000		100,000
Buildings & Equipment	$ 680,000		$ 450,000	
Less: Accumulated Depreciation	(320,000)	360,000	(230,000)	220,000
Goodwill		70,000		20,000
Total Assets		$1,070,000		$700,000
Accounts Payable		$ 70,000		$195,000
Bonds Payable		320,000		100,000
Bond Premium				10,000
Common Stock		120,000		150,000
Additional Paid-In Capital		170,000		60,000
Retained Earnings		390,000		185,000
Total Liabilities & Equities		$1,070,000		$700,000

Blue and Sparse agreed to combine as of January 1, 20X3. To effect the merger, Blue paid finder's fees of $30,000 and legal fees of $24,000. Blue also paid $15,000 of audit fees related to the issuance of stock, stock registration fees of $8,000, and stock listing application fees of $6,000.

At January 1, 20X3, book values of Sparse Company's assets and liabilities approximated market value except for inventory with a market value of $200,000, buildings and equipment with a market value of $350,000, and bonds payable with a market value of $105,000. All assets and liabilities were immediately recorded on Blue's books.

Required
Give all journal entries that Blue recorded assuming Blue issued 40,000 shares of $8 par value common stock to acquire all of Sparse's assets and liabilities in a business combination. Blue common stock was trading at $14 per share on January 1, 20X3.

LO 1-5   **E1-23**   **Reporting Income**

On July 1, 20X2, Alan Enterprises merged with Cherry Corporation through an exchange of stock and the subsequent liquidation of Cherry. Alan issued 200,000 shares of its stock to effect the combination. The book values of Cherry's assets and liabilities were equal to their fair values at the date of combination, and the value of the shares exchanged was equal to Cherry's book value. Information relating to income for the companies is as follows:

	20X1	Jan. 1–June 30, 20X2	July 1–Dec. 31, 20X2
Net Income:			
Alan Enterprises	$4,460,000	$2,500,000	$3,528,000
Cherry Corporation	1,300,000	692,000	—

Alan Enterprises had 1,000,000 shares of stock outstanding prior to the combination. Remember that when calculating earnings per share (EPS) for the year of the combination, the shares issued in the combination were not outstanding for the entire year.

Required
Compute the net income and earnings-per-share amounts that would be reported in Alan's 20X2 comparative income statements for both 20X2 and 20X1.

PROBLEMS

LO 1-3   **P1-24**   **Assets and Accounts Payable Transferred to Subsidiary**

Tab Corporation decided to establish Collon Company as a wholly owned subsidiary by transferring some of its existing assets and liabilities to the new entity. In exchange, Collon issued Tab 30,000 shares of $6 par value common stock. The following information is provided on the assets and accounts payable transferred:

	Cost	Book Value	Fair Value
Cash	$ 25,000	$ 25,000	$ 25,000
Inventory	70,000	70,000	70,000
Land	60,000	60,000	90,000
Buildings	170,000	130,000	240,000
Equipment	90,000	80,000	105,000
Accounts Payable	45,000	45,000	45,000

Required
a. Give the journal entry that Tab recorded for the transfer of assets and accounts payable to Collon.

b. Give the journal entry that Collon recorded for the receipt of assets and accounts payable from Tab.

LO 1-3   **P1-25**   **Creation of New Subsidiary**

Eagle Corporation established a subsidiary to enter into a new line of business considered to be substantially more risky than Eagle's current business. Eagle transferred the following assets and accounts payable to Sand Corporation in exchange for 5,000 shares of $10 par value stock of Sand:

	Cost	Book Value
Cash	$ 30,000	$ 30,000
Accounts Receivable	45,000	40,000
Inventory	60,000	60,000
Land	20,000	20,000
Buildings & Equipment	300,000	260,000
Accounts Payable	10,000	10,000

Required

a. Give the journal entry that Eagle recorded for the transfer of assets and accounts payable to Sand.

b. Give the journal entry that Sand recorded for receipt of the assets and accounts payable from Eagle.

LO 1-3   **P1-26**   **Incomplete Data on Creation of Subsidiary**

Thumb Company created New Company as a wholly owned subsidiary by transferring assets and accounts payable to New in exchange for its common stock. New recorded the following entry when it received the assets and accounts payable:

Cash	3,000	
Accounts Receivable	16,000	
Inventory	27,000	
Land	9,000	
Buildings	70,000	
Equipment	60,000	
Accounts Payable		14,000
Accumulated Depreciation—Buildings		21,000
Accumulated Depreciation—Equipment		12,000
Common Stock		40,000
Additional Paid-In Capital		98,000

Required

a. What was Thumb's book value of the total assets (not net assets) transferred to New Company?

b. What amount did Thumb report as its investment in New after the transfer?

c. What number of shares of $5 par value stock did New issue to Thumb?

d. What impact did the transfer of assets and accounts payable have on the amount reported by Thumb as total assets?

e. What impact did the transfer of assets and accounts payable have on the amount that Thumb and the consolidated entity reported as shares outstanding?

LO 1-5   **P1-27**   **Acquisition in Multiple Steps**

Deal Corporation issued 4,000 shares of its $10 par value stock with a market value of $85,000 to acquire 85 percent ownership of Mead Company on August 31, 20X3. Mead's fair value was determined to be $100,000 on that date. Deal had earlier purchased 15 percent of Mead's shares for $9,000 and used the cost method in accounting for its investment in Mead. Deal also paid appraisal fees of $3,500 and stock issue costs of $2,000 incurred in completing the acquisition of the additional shares.

Required

Give the journal entries to be recorded by Deal in completing the acquisition of the additional shares of Mead.

LO 1-5   **P1-28**   **Journal Entries to Record a Business Combination**

On January 1, 20X2, Frost Company acquired all of TKK Corporation's assets and liabilities by issuing 24,000 shares of its $4 par value common stock. At that date, Frost shares were selling at

$22 per share. Historical cost and fair value balance sheet data for TKK at the time of acquisition were as follows:

Balance Sheet Item	Historical Cost	Fair Value
Cash & Receivables	$ 28,000	$ 28,000
Inventory	94,000	122,000
Buildings & Equipment	600,000	470,000
Less: Accumulated Depreciation	(240,000)	
Total Assets	$ 482,000	$ 620,000
Accounts Payable	$ 41,000	$ 41,000
Notes Payable	65,000	63,000
Common Stock ($10 par value)	160,000	
Retained Earnings	216,000	
Total Liabilities & Equities	$ 482,000	

Frost paid legal fees for the transfer of assets and liabilities of $14,000. Frost also paid audit fees of $21,000 and listing application fees of $7,000, both related to the issuance of new shares.

Required

Prepare the journal entries made by Frost to record the business combination.

LO 1-5

P1-29   ### Recording Business Combinations

Flint Corporation exchanged shares of its $2 par common stock for all of Mark Company's assets and liabilities in a planned merger. Immediately prior to the combination, Mark's assets and liabilities were as follows:

Assets	
Cash & Equivalents	$ 41,000
Accounts Receivable	73,000
Inventory	144,000
Land	200,000
Buildings	1,520,000
Equipment	638,000
Accumulated Depreciation	(431,000)
Total Assets	$2,185,000

Liabilities & Equities	
Accounts Payable	$ 35,000
Short-Term Notes Payable	50,000
Bonds Payable	500,000
Common Stock ($10 par)	1,000,000
Additional Paid-In Capital	325,000
Retained Earnings	275,000
Total Liabilities & Equities	$2,185,000

Immediately prior to the combination, Flint reported $250,000 additional paid-in capital and $1,350,000 retained earnings. The fair values of Mark's assets and liabilities were equal to their book values on the date of combination except that Mark's buildings were worth $1,500,000 and its equipment was worth $300,000. Costs associated with planning and completing the business combination totaled $38,000, and stock issue costs totaled $22,000. The market value of Flint's stock at the date of combination was $4 per share.

Required

Prepare the journal entries that would appear on Flint's books to record the combination if Flint issued 450,000 shares.

P1-30 **Business Combination with Goodwill**

Anchor Corporation paid cash of $178,000 to acquire Zink Company's net assets on February 1, 20X3. The balance sheet data for the two companies and fair value information for Zink immediately before the business combination were:

Balance Sheet Item	Anchor Corporation Book Value	Zink Company Book Value	Zink Company Fair Value
Cash	$ 240,000	$ 20,000	$ 20,000
Accounts Receivable	140,000	35,000	35,000
Inventory	170,000	30,000	50,000
Patents	80,000	40,000	60,000
Buildings & Equipment	380,000	310,000	150,000
Less: Accumulated Depreciation	(190,000)	(200,000)	
Total Assets	$ 820,000	$ 235,000	$315,000
Accounts Payable	$ 85,000	$ 55,000	$ 55,000
Notes Payable	150,000	120,000	120,000
Common Stock:			
$10 par value	200,000		
$6 par value		18,000	
Additional Paid-In Capital	160,000	10,000	
Retained Earnings	225,000	32,000	
Total Liabilities & Equities	$ 820,000	$ 235,000	

Required

a. Give the journal entry recorded by Anchor Corporation when it acquired Zink's net assets.

b. Prepare a balance sheet for Anchor immediately following the acquisition.

c. Give the journal entry to be recorded by Anchor if it acquires all of Zink's common stock (instead of Zink's net assets) for $178,000.

P1-31 **Bargain Purchase**

Bower Company purchased Lark Corporation's net assets on January 3, 20X2, for $625,000 cash. In addition, Bower incurred $5,000 of direct costs in consummating the combination. At the time of acquisition, Lark reported the following historical cost and current market data:

Balance Sheet Item	Book Value	Fair Value
Cash & Receivables	$ 50,000	$ 50,000
Inventory	100,000	150,000
Buildings & Equipment (net)	200,000	300,000
Patent	—	200,000
Total Assets	$350,000	$700,000
Accounts Payable	$ 30,000	$ 30,000
Common Stock	100,000	
Additional Paid-In Capital	80,000	
Retained Earnings	140,000	
Total Liabilities & Equities	$350,000	

Required

Give the journal entry or entries with which Bower recorded its acquisition of Lark's net assets.

P1-32 **Computation of Account Balances**

Aspro Division is considered to be an individual reporting unit of Tabor Company. Tabor acquired the division by issuing 100,000 shares of its common stock with a market price of $7.60 each. Tabor management was able to identify assets with fair values of $810,000 and liabilities of

$190,000 at the date of acquisition. At the end of the first year, the reporting unit had assets with a fair value of $950,000, and the fair value of the reporting entity was $930,000. Tabor's accountants concluded it must recognize impairment of goodwill in the amount of $30,000 at the end of the first year.

Required

a. Determine the fair value of the reporting unit's liabilities at the end of the first year. Show your computation.

b. If the reporting unit's liabilities at the end of the period had been $70,000, what would the fair value of the reporting unit have to have been to avoid recognizing an impairment of goodwill? Show your computation.

LO 1-5   **P1-33**   **Goodwill Assigned to Multiple Reporting Units**

The fair values of assets and liabilities held by three reporting units and other information related to the reporting units owned by Rover Company are as follows:

	Reporting Unit		
	A	**B**	**C**
Cash & Receivables	$ 30,000	$ 80,000	$ 20,000
Inventory	60,000	100,000	40,000
Land	20,000	30,000	10,000
Buildings	100,000	150,000	80,000
Equipment	140,000	90,000	50,000
Accounts Payable	40,000	60,000	10,000
Fair Value of Reporting Unit	400,000	440,000	265,000
Carrying Value of Investment	420,000	500,000	290,000
Goodwill Included in Carrying Value	70,000	80,000	40,000

Required

a. Determine the amount of goodwill that Rover should report in its current financial statements.

b. Determine the amount, if any, that Rover should report as impairment of goodwill for the current period.

LO 1-5   **P1-34**   **Journal Entries**

On January 1, 20X3, PURE Products Corporation issued 12,000 shares of its $10 par value stock to acquire the net assets of Light Steel Company. Underlying book value and fair value information for the balance sheet items of Light Steel at the time of acquisition follow:

Balance Sheet Item	Book Value	Fair Value
Cash	$ 60,000	$ 60,000
Accounts Receivable	100,000	100,000
Inventory (LIFO basis)	60,000	115,000
Land	50,000	70,000
Buildings & Equipment	400,000	350,000
Less: Accumulated Depreciation	(150,000)	—
Total Assets	$ 520,000	$695,000
Accounts Payable	$ 10,000	$ 10,000
Bonds Payable	200,000	180,000
Common Stock ($5 par value)	150,000	
Additional Paid-In Capital	70,000	
Retained Earnings	90,000	
Total Liabilities & Equities	$ 520,000	

Light Steel shares were selling at $18 and PURE Products shares were selling at $50 just before the merger announcement. Additional cash payments made by PURE Products in completing the acquisition were

Finder's fee paid to firm that located Light Steel	$10,000
Audit fee for stock issued by PURE Products	3,000
Stock registration fee for new shares of PURE Products	5,000
Legal fees paid to assist in transfer of net assets	9,000
Cost of SEC registration of PURE Products shares	1,000

Required

Prepare all journal entries to record the business combination on PURE Products' books.

LO 1-5

P1-35 Purchase at More than Book Value

Ramrod Manufacturing acquired all the assets and liabilities of Stafford Industries on January 1, 20X2, in exchange for 4,000 shares of Ramrod's $20 par value common stock. Balance sheet data for both companies just before the merger are given as follows:

Balance Sheet Items	Ramrod Manufacturing Book Value	Ramrod Manufacturing Fair Value	Stafford Industries Book Value	Stafford Industries Fair Value
Cash	$ 70,000	$ 70,000	$ 30,000	$ 30,000
Accounts Receivable	100,000	100,000	60,000	60,000
Inventory	200,000	375,000	100,000	160,000
Land	50,000	80,000	40,000	30,000
Buildings & Equipment	600,000 }	540,000	400,000 }	350,000
Less: Accumulated Depreciation	(250,000) }		(150,000) }	
Total Assets	$ 770,000	$1,165,000	$ 480,000	$630,000
Accounts Payable	$ 50,000	$ 50,000	$ 10,000	$ 10,000
Bonds Payable	300,000	310,000	150,000	145,000
Common Stock:				
$20 par value	200,000			
$5 par value			100,000	
Additional Paid-In Capital	40,000		20,000	
Retained Earnings	180,000		200,000	
Total Liabilities & Equities	$ 770,000		$ 480,000	

Ramrod shares were selling for $150 on the date of acquisition.

Required

Prepare the following:

a. Journal entries to record the acquisition on Ramrod's books.

b. A balance sheet for the combined enterprise immediately following the business combination.

LO 1-5

P1-36 Business Combination

Following are the balance sheets of Boogie Musical Corporation and Toot-Toot Tuba Company as of December 31, 20X5.

BOOGIE MUSICAL CORPORATION
Balance Sheet
December 31, 20X5

Assets		Liabilities & Equities	
Cash	$ 23,000	Accounts Payable	$ 48,000
Accounts Receivable	85,000	Notes Payable	65,000
Allowance for Uncollectible Accounts	(1,200)	Mortgage Payable	200,000

(continued)

Inventory	192,000	Bonds Payable	200,000
Plant & Equipment	980,000	Capital Stock ($10 par)	500,000
Accumulated Depreciation	(160,000)	Premium on Capital Stock	1,000
Other Assets	14,000	Retained Earnings	118,800
Total Assets	$1,132,800	Total Liabilities & Equities	$1,132,800

TOOT-TOOT TUBA COMPANY
Balance Sheet
December 31, 20X5

Assets		Liabilities & Equities	
Cash	$ 300	Accounts Payable	$ 8,200
Accounts Receivable	17,000	Notes Payable	10,000
Allowance for Uncollectible Accounts	(600)	Mortgage Payable	50,000
Inventory	78,500	Bonds Payable	100,000
Plant & Equipment	451,000	Capital Stock ($50 par)	100,000
Accumulated Depreciation	(225,000)	Premium on Capital Stock	150,000
Other Assets	25,800	Retained Earnings	(71,200)
Total Assets	$347,000	Total Liabilities & Equities	$347,000

In preparation for a possible business combination, a team of experts from Boogie Musical made a thorough examination and audit of Toot-Toot Tuba. They found that Toot-Toot's assets and liabilities were correctly stated except that they estimated uncollectible accounts at $1,400. The experts also estimated the market value of the inventory at $35,000 and the market value of the plant and equipment at $500,000. The business combination took place on January 1, 20X6, and on that date Boogie Musical acquired all the assets and liabilities of Toot-Toot Tuba. On that date, Boogie's common stock was selling for $55 per share.

Required
Record the combination on Boogie's books assuming that Boogie issued 9,000 of its $10 par common shares in exchange for Toot-Toot's assets and liabilities.

LO 1-5　　**P1-37**　### Combined Balance Sheet
Bilge Pumpworks and Seaworthy Rope Company agreed to merge on January 1, 20X3. On the date of the merger agreement, the companies reported the following data:

Balance Sheet Items	Bilge Pumpworks		Seaworthy Rope Company	
	Book Value	Fair Value	Book Value	Fair Value
Cash & Receivables	$ 90,000	$ 90,000	$ 20,000	$ 20,000
Inventory	100,000	150,000	30,000	42,000
Land	100,000	140,000	10,000	15,000
Plant & Equipment	400,000	300,000	200,000	140,000
Less: Accumulated Depreciation	(150,000) }		(80,000) }	
Total Assets	$ 540,000	$680,000	$180,000	$217,000
Current Liabilities	$ 80,000	$ 80,000	$ 20,000	$ 20,000
Capital Stock	200,000		20,000	
Capital in Excess of Par Value	20,000		5,000	
Retained Earnings	240,000		135,000	
Total Liabilities & Equities	$ 540,000		$180,000	

Bilge Pumpworks has 10,000 shares of its $20 par value shares outstanding on January 1, 20X3, and Seaworthy has 4,000 shares of $5 par value stock outstanding. The market values of the shares are $300 and $50, respectively.

Required

a. Bilge issues 700 shares of stock in exchange for all of Seaworthy's net assets. Prepare a balance sheet for the combined entity immediately following the merger.

b. Prepare the stockholders' equity section of the combined company's balance sheet, assuming Bilge acquires all of Seaworthy's net assets by issuing

1. 1,100 shares of common.
2. 1,800 shares of common.
3. 3,000 shares of common.

LO 1-5   **P1-38**   **Incomplete Data**

On January 1, 20X2, End Corporation acquired all of Cork Corporation's assets and liabilities by issuing shares of its common stock. Partial balance sheet data for the companies prior to the business combination and immediately following the combination are as follows:

	End Corp. Book Value	Cork Corp. Book Value	Combined Entity
Cash	$ 40,000	$ 10,000	$ 50,000
Accounts Receivable	60,000	30,000	88,000
Inventory	50,000	35,000	96,000
Buildings & Equipment (net)	300,000	110,000	430,000
Goodwill			?
Total Assets	$450,000	$185,000	$?
Accounts Payable	$ 32,000	$ 14,000	$ 46,000
Bonds Payable	150,000	70,000	220,000
Bond Premium	6,000		6,000
Common Stock, $5 par	100,000	40,000	126,000
Additional Paid-In Capital	65,000	28,000	247,000
Retained Earnings	97,000	33,000	?
Total Liabilities & Equities	$450,000	$185,000	$?

Required

a. What number of shares did End issue to acquire Cork's assets and liabilities?

b. What was the total market value of the shares issued by End?

c. What was the fair value of the inventory held by Cork at the date of combination?

d. What was the fair value of the identifiable net assets held by Cork at the date of combination?

e. What amount of goodwill, if any, will be reported by the combined entity immediately following the combination?

f. What balance in retained earnings will the combined entity report immediately following the combination?

g. If the depreciable assets held by Cork had an average remaining life of 10 years at the date of acquisition, what amount of depreciation expense will be reported on those assets in 20X2?

Advanced
StudyGuide
.com

LO 1-5   **P1-39**   **Incomplete Data Following Purchase**

On January 1, 20X1, Alpha Corporation acquired all of Bravo Company's assets and liabilities by issuing shares of its $3 par value stock to the owners of Bravo Company in a business combination. Alpha also made a cash payment to Banker Corporation for stock issue costs. Partial balance sheet data for Alpha and Bravo, before the cash payment and issuance of shares, and a combined balance sheet following the business combination are as follows:

	Alpha Corporation	Bravo Company		Combined Entity
	Book Value	Book Value	Fair Value	
Cash	$ 65,000	$ 15,000	$ 15,000	$ 56,000
Accounts Receivable	105,000	30,000	30,000	135,000
Inventory	210,000	90,000	?	320,000
Buildings & Equipment (net)	400,000	210,000	293,000	693,000
Goodwill				?
Total Assets	$780,000	$345,000	$448,000	$?
Accounts Payable	$ 56,000	$ 22,000	$ 22,000	$ 78,000
Bonds Payable	200,000	120,000	120,000	320,000
Common Stock	96,000	70,000		117,000
Additional Paid-In Capital	234,000	42,000		553,000
Retained Earnings	194,000	91,000		?
Total Liabilities & Equities	$780,000	$345,000		$?

Required

a. What number of its $5 par value shares did Bravo have outstanding at January 1, 20X1?

b. Assuming that all of Bravo's shares were issued when the company was started, what was the price per share received at the time of issue?

c. How many shares of Alpha were issued at the date of combination?

d. What amount of cash did Alpha pay as stock issue costs?

e. What was the total market value of Alpha's shares issued at the date of combination?

f. What was the fair value of Bravo's inventory at the date of combination?

g. What was the fair value of Bravo's net assets at the date of combination?

h. What amount of goodwill, if any, will be reported in the combined balance sheet following the combination?

LO 1-5

P1-40 ### Comprehensive Business Combination

Bigtime Industries Inc. entered into a business combination agreement with Hydrolized Chemical Corporation (HCC) to ensure an uninterrupted supply of key raw materials and to realize certain economies from combining the operating processes and the marketing efforts of the two companies. Under the terms of the agreement, Bigtime issued 180,000 shares of its $1 par common stock in exchange for all of HCC's assets and liabilities. The Bigtime shares then were distributed to HCC's shareholders, and HCC was liquidated.

Immediately prior to the combination, HCC's balance sheet appeared as follows, with fair values also indicated:

	Book Values	Fair Values
Assets		
Cash	$ 28,000	$ 28,000
Accounts Receivable	258,000	251,500
Less: Allowance for Bad Debts	(6,500)	
Inventory	381,000	395,000
Long-Term Investments	150,000	175,000
Land	55,000	100,000
Rolling Stock	130,000	63,000
Plant & Equipment	2,425,000	2,500,000
Less: Accumulated Depreciation	(614,000)	
Patents	125,000	500,000
Special Licenses	95,800	100,000
Total Assets	$3,027,300	$4,112,500

(continued)

	Book Values	Fair Values
Liabilities		
Current Payables	$ 137,200	$ 137,200
Mortgages Payable	500,000	520,000
Equipment Trust Notes	100,000	95,000
Debentures Payable	1,000,000	950,000
Less: Discount on Debentures	(40,000)	
Total Liabilities	$1,697,200	$1,702,200
Stockholders' Equity		
Common Stock ($5 par)	600,000	
Additional Paid-In Capital from Common Stock	500,000	
Additional Paid-In Capital from		
Retirement of Preferred Stock	22,000	
Retained Earnings	220,100	
Less: Treasury Stock (1,500 shares)	(12,000)	
Total Liabilities & Equity	$3,027,300	

Immediately prior to the combination, Bigtime's common stock was selling for $14 per share. Bigtime incurred direct costs of $135,000 in arranging the business combination and $42,000 of costs associated with registering and issuing the common stock used in the combination.

Required

a. Prepare all journal entries that Bigtime should have entered on its books to record the business combination.

b. Present all journal entries that should have been entered on HCC's books to record the combination and the distribution of the stock received.

2 Reporting Intercorporate Investments and Consolidation of Wholly Owned Subsidiaries with No Differential

BERKSHIRE HATHAWAY'S MANY INVESTMENTS

As of this writing (February 2014), Warren Buffett is the fourth-richest man in the world, worth a staggering $58.5 billion. He is also the chairman, CEO, and primary shareholder of Berkshire Hathaway Inc. Over the past 48 years, Berkshire has grown at an average rate of 19.7 percent annually. Warren Buffett has achieved this success through his unparalleled business sense regarding investments and acquisitions of other companies.

Berkshire Hathaway was originally a textile manufacturing company. In 1962, Warren Buffett and his partners began buying large blocks of Berkshire stock. Within five years, Buffett began expanding into the insurance industry, and in 1985 the last of Berkshire's textile operations was shut down. In the late 1970s, Berkshire began acquiring stock in GEICO insurance and in January 1996 bought GEICO outright. While Berkshire has extensive insurance holdings, it has not focused its investment activities solely on insurance. Since Buffett took the helm in the 1960s, Berkshire has made many acquisitions. Look at the list of selected Berkshire holdings as of the end of 2013 (on the next page). Do you recognize any of these companies?

Each item in Berkshire's portfolio has to be accounted for individually. For example, Comdisco Holdings and Graham Holdings Company are accounted for as equity method investments, while Walmart and American Express are classified as available-for-sale investments. Berkshire consolidates the fully owned companies such as Wesco Financial and See's Candies. In addition, companies like GEICO have many subsidiaries of their own. As you can imagine, accounting for investments at Berkshire can be very complex. This chapter focuses on issues related to the accounting for investments.

BERKSHIRE HATHAWAY INC.

BERKSHIRE HATHAWAY SELECTED HOLDINGS (AS OF 12/31/2013)		
Examples of fully owned subsidiaries:		
Benjamin Moore & Co.		
Dairy Queen		
GEICO		
Fruit of the Loom		
H.J. Heinz Company		
See's Candies		
The Pampered Chef Ltd.		
15 largest partially owned companies:	**% Owned**	**Market Value**
DIRECTV	4.2	$ 1,536
American Express Company	14.2	13,756
Exxon Mobil Corp.	0.9	4,162
International Business Machines Corporation	6.3	12,778
Moody's Corporation	11.5	1,936
Munich Re Group	11.2	4,415
Phillips 66	3.4	1,594
Sanofi	1.7	2,354
Tesco PLC	3.7	1,666
The Coca-Cola Company	9.1	16,524
The Goldman Sachs Group Inc.	2.8	2,315
Procter & Gamble Co.	1.9	4,272
U.S. Bancorp	5.3	3,883
Wal-Mart Stores Inc.	1.8	4,470
Wells Fargo & Company	9.2	21,950

Material is copyrighted and used with permission of the author.

LEARNING OBJECTIVES

When you finish studying this chapter, you should be able to:

LO 2-1   Understand and explain how ownership and control can influence the accounting for investments in common stock.

LO 2-2   Prepare journal entries using the cost method of accounting for investments.

LO 2-3   Prepare journal entries using the equity method of accounting for investments.

LO 2-4   Understand and explain differences between the cost and equity methods.

LO 2-5   Prepare journal entries using the fair value option.

LO 2-6   Make calculations and prepare basic consolidation entries for a simple consolidation.

LO 2-7   Prepare a consolidation worksheet.

ACCOUNTING FOR INVESTMENTS IN COMMON STOCK

LO 2-1

Understand and explain how ownership and control can influence the accounting for investments in common stock.

Companies acquire ownership interests in other companies for a variety of reasons. For example, some companies invest in other companies simply to earn a favorable return by taking advantage of the future earnings potential of their investees. Other reasons for acquiring interests in other entities include (1) gaining voting control, (2) entering new product markets by purchasing companies already established in those areas, (3) ensuring a supply of raw materials or other production inputs, (4) ensuring a customer for production output, (5) gaining economies associated with greater size, (6) diversifying operations, (7) obtaining new technology, (8) lessening competition, and (9) limiting risk.

The method used to account for investments in common stock depends, in part, on the level of influence or control that the investor is able to exercise over the investee. The investment will normally be reported on the investor's balance sheet using the cost method (adjusted to market value, if appropriate), the equity method, or the fair value option. Note that, while use of the cost or equity method is dictated by the level of influence, the investor can elect the fair value option in place of either method. However, if the investor company acquires more than 50 percent of the investee's voting shares, it is required to consolidate the investee company, in which case, the investment account would not appear on the consolidated balance sheet. Essentially, consolidation replaces the investment account with all of the detail on the subsidiary's balance sheet. Figure 2–1 summarizes how the reporting of intercorporate investments in common stock changes with the investor's level of ownership and influence.

The *cost method* is used for reporting investments in equity securities when both consolidation and equity-method reporting are inappropriate. If cost-method equity securities have readily determinable fair values, they must be adjusted to market value at year-end under **ASC 320-10-30-2.**[1] Under the cost method, the investor recognizes income from the investment when the income is distributed by the investee as dividends.

The *equity method* is required for external reporting when the investor exercises *significant influence* over the operating and financial policies of the investee and consolidation is not appropriate. This method is used most often when one company holds 20 percent or more of another company's common stock. Under the equity method, the investor recognizes income from the investment as the investee earns the income. Instead of combining the individual assets, liabilities, revenues, and expenses of the investee with those of the investor, as in consolidation, the investment is reported as one line in the investor's balance sheet, and income recognized from the investee is reported as one line in the investor's income statement. The investment represents the investor's share of the investee's net assets, and the income recognized is the investor's share of the investee's net income.

For financial reporting, consolidated financial statements that include both the investor and the investee must be presented if the investor can exercise *control* over the investee. *Consolidation* involves combining for financial reporting the individual assets, liabilities, revenues, and expenses of two or more related companies as if they were part of a single company. This process includes the elimination of all intercompany ownership and activities. Consolidation normally is appropriate when one company, referred to as the *parent,* controls another company, referred to as a *subsidiary.* We discuss the specific requirements for consolidation later in this chapter. A subsidiary that is not consolidated with the parent is referred to as an *unconsolidated subsidiary* and is shown as an

FIGURE 2–1
Financial Reporting Basis by Level of Common Stock Ownership

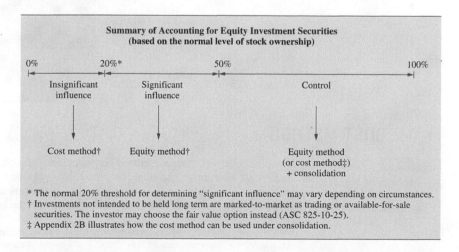

* The normal 20% threshold for determining "significant influence" may vary depending on circumstances.
† Investments not intended to be held long term are marked-to-market as trading or available-for-sale securities. The investor may choose the fair value option instead (ASC 825-10-25).
‡ Appendix 2B illustrates how the cost method can be used under consolidation.

[1] Because the provisions of **ASC 320-10-30-2** are normally discussed in Intermediate Accounting, detailed coverage is not provided here. Note, however, that equity investments accounted for using the cost method are accounted for as discussed in this chapter, with the provisions of **ASC 320-10-30-2** applied as end-of-period adjustments. **ASC 320-10-30-2** is not applicable to equity-method investments.

investment on the parent's balance sheet. Under current accounting standards, most subsidiaries are consolidated. When intercorporate investments are consolidated for financial reporting, the investment and related income accounts are eliminated in preparing the consolidated financial statements. Nevertheless, the parent must still account for the investments on its books. Parent companies have the choice of accounting for investments in consolidated subsidiaries on their books using the cost or equity method.[2]

Under the fair value option (**ASC 825-10-25**), companies have the choice of using traditional methods, such as the cost and equity methods, to report financial assets and liabilities of unconsolidated subsidiaries, or they can elect to report some or all of their financial assets and liabilities at fair value. Under the fair value option, intercorporate investments in common stock are remeasured to fair value at the end of each period, and the unrealized gain or loss is recognized in income. The fair value option does not apply to intercorporate investments that must be consolidated.

This chapter follows Figure 2–1 in summarizing the accounting for investments in other companies. It first discusses the cost and equity methods of accounting for investments. It then summarizes the fair value option. Finally, it introduces the preparation of consolidated financial statements using the most simple consolidation scenario (when a subsidiary is wholly owned and it is either created or purchased for an amount exactly equal to the book value of the subsidiary's net assets). Since consolidation is a major topic of this textbook, we use a building block approach to our coverage of consolidation in Chapters 2 through 5. Chapter 3 explains how the basic consolidation process changes when the parent company owns less than 100 percent of the subsidiary. Chapter 4 shows how the consolidation process differs when the parent company acquires 100 percent of a subsidiary for an amount greater (or less) than the book value of the subsidiary's net assets. Finally, Chapter 5 presents the most complex consolidation scenario (where the parent owns less than 100 percent of the subsidiary's outstanding voting stock and the acquisition price is not equal to the book value of the subsidiary's net assets). Chapters 6 through 10 delve into asset transfers among members of the same consolidated group of companies and additional details related to consolidation.

Summary of Consolidation Coverage in Chapters 2–5

	Wholly Owned Subsidiary	Partially Owned Subsidiary
Investment = Book value	Chapter 2	Chapter 3
Investment > Book value	Chapter 4	Chapter 5

THE COST METHOD

LO 2-2

Prepare journal entries using the cost method of accounting for investments.

Intercorporate investments reported on the balance sheet using the cost method are carried by the investor at historical cost, or at market value if the security is considered to be "marketable." Income is recorded by the investor as dividends are declared by the investee. The cost method is used when the investor lacks the ability either to control

---

[2] The cost method is also used frequently in practice for consolidated investments since (as explained later in this chapter) the investment account is eliminated in the consolidated financial statements. While both the cost and the equity methods are acceptable in accounting for a consolidated subsidiary, we advocate the use of the equity method because it ensures that the parent company's books accurately reflect everything on the subsidiary's books. Conceptually, the use of the equity method is a useful way to understand the notion of consolidating a controlled subsidiary because the investment account is simply replaced by the detail on the subsidiary's balance sheet.

or to exercise significant influence over the investee. The inability of an investor to exercise either control or significant influence over an investee may result from the size of the investment, usually at common stock ownership levels of less than 20 percent. In some situations, other factors, such as the existence of a majority shareholder, prevent the investor from exercising significant influence regardless of the size of the investment. (See Appendix 2A for a discussion of additional factors that may influence the use of the cost or equity methods.)

Accounting Procedures under the Cost Method

The cost method is consistent with the treatment normally accorded noncurrent assets. At the time of purchase, the investor records its investment in common stock at the total cost incurred in making the purchase. Subsequently, the carrying amount of the investment remains unchanged under the cost method; the investment continues to be carried at its original cost until it is sold. Income from the investment is recognized by the investor as dividends are declared by the investee. Once the investee declares a dividend, the investor has a legal claim against the investee for a proportionate share of the dividend, and realization of the income is considered certain enough to be recognized. Recognition of investment income before a dividend declaration is considered inappropriate because the investee's income is not available to the owners until a dividend is declared.

To illustrate the cost method, assume that ABC Company purchases 20 percent of XYZ Company's common stock for $100,000 at the beginning of the year but does not gain significant influence over XYZ. During the year, XYZ has net income of $60,000 and declares dividends of $20,000. Assuming the dividend is paid later, ABC Company records the following entries relating to its investment in XYZ:

(1)	Investment in XYZ Company Stock	100,000	
	Cash		100,000
	Record purchase of XYZ Company stock.		

(2)	Dividends Receivable	4,000	
	Dividend Income		4,000
	Record dividend declared by XYZ Company ($20,000 $\times$ 0.20).		

Note that ABC records only its share of XYZ's distributed earnings and makes no entry for the undistributed portion. The carrying amount of the investment is still the original cost of $100,000.

Declaration of Dividends in Excess of Earnings since Acquisition

A special treatment is required under the cost method in situations in which an investor holds common stock in a company that declares dividends in excess of the cumulative income it has earned since the investor acquired its stock. The dividends received are viewed first as representing earnings of the investee from the purchase date of the investment to the dividend declaration date. All dividends declared by the investee in excess of its earnings since acquisition by the investor are viewed by the investor as *liquidating dividends.* The investor's share of these liquidating dividends is treated as a return of capital, and the investment account balance is reduced by that amount. Blocks of an investee's stock acquired at different times should be treated separately for purposes of computing liquidating dividends.

Liquidating Dividends Example

To illustrate the computation of liquidating dividends received by the investor, assume that Investor Company purchases 10 percent of the common stock of Investee Company on January 2, 20X1. The annual income and dividends of Investee, the amount of dividend income recognized by Investor each year under the cost method, and the reduction of the carrying amount of Investor's investment in Investee when appropriate are as follows:

	Investee Company			Investor Company		
Year	Net Income	Dividends	Cumulative Undistributed Income	Cash Received	Dividend Income	Reduction of Investment
20X1	$100,000	$ 70,000	$30,000	$ 7,000	$ 7,000	
20X2	100,000	120,000	10,000	12,000	12,000	
20X3	100,000	120,000	0	12,000	11,000	$1,000
20X4	100,000	120,000	0	12,000	10,000	2,000
20X5	100,000	70,000	30,000	7,000	7,000	

Investor Company records its 10 percent share of Investee's dividend as income in 20X1 because the income of Investee exceeds its dividend. In 20X2, Investee's dividend exceeds earnings for the year, but the cumulative dividends declared since January 2, 20X1, the date Investor acquired Investee's stock, do not exceed Investee's earnings since that date. Hence, Investor again records its 10 percent share of the dividend as income. By the end of 20X3, dividends declared by Investee since January 2, 20X1, total $310,000 while Investee's income since that date totals only $300,000. Thus, from Investor's point of view, $10,000 of the 20X3 dividend represents a return of capital while the remaining $110,000 represents a distribution of earnings. Investor's share of each amount is 10 percent. The entry to record the 20X3 dividend on Investor's books is:

(3)	Cash	12,000	
	Investment in Investee		1,000
	Dividend Income		11,000

Record receipt of 20X3 dividend from Investee.
$12,000 = $120,000 × 0.10.
$1,000 = ($310,000 − $300,000) + 0.10.
$11,000 = ($120,000 − $10,000) + 0.10.

Once the investor has recorded a liquidating dividend, the comparison in future periods between cumulative earnings and dividends of the investee should be based on the date of the last liquidating dividend rather than the date the investor acquired the investee's stock. In this example, Investor Company records liquidating dividends in 20X3 and 20X4. In years after 20X4, Investor compares earnings and dividends of Investee from the date of the most recent liquidating dividend in 20X4 rather than comparing from January 2, 20X1. Investor considers the entire dividend paid in 20X5 to be a distribution of earnings.

Acquisition at Interim Date

The acquisition of an investment at a date other than the beginning or end of a fiscal period generally does not create any major problems when the cost method is used to account for the investment. The only potential difficulty involves determining whether some part of the payment received by the investor is a liquidating dividend when the investee declares a dividend soon after the investor purchases stock in the investee. In this situation, the investor must estimate the amount of the investee's earnings for the portion of the period during which the investor held the investee's stock and may record dividend income only on that portion.

Advanced Financial Accounting, 11th Edition

53

Chapter 2 *Reporting Intercorporate Investments and Consolidation of Wholly Owned Subsidiaries with No Differential* **53**

Changes in the Number of Shares Held

Changes in the number of investment shares resulting from stock dividends, stock splits, or reverse splits receive no formal recognition in the accounts of the investor. The carrying value of the investment before the stock dividend or split becomes the carrying amount of the new, higher or lower number of shares. Purchases and sales of shares, of course, do require journal entries but do not result in any unusual difficulties under the cost method.

Purchases of Additional Shares

The purchase of additional shares of a company already held is recorded at cost in the same way as an initial purchase of shares. The investor's new percentage ownership of the investee then is calculated, and other evidence, if available, is evaluated to determine whether the total investment still should be carried at cost or if the investor should switch to the equity method. When the additional shares give the investor the ability to exercise significant influence over the investee, the equity method should be applied retroactively from the date of the original investment, as illustrated later in this chapter.

Sales of Shares

If a company sells all or part of an intercorporate investment in stock, the transaction is accounted for in the same manner as the sale of any other noncurrent asset. A gain or loss on the sale is recognized for the difference between the proceeds received and the carrying amount of the investment sold.

If shares of the stock have been purchased at more than one price, a determination must be made at the time of sale as to which of the shares have been sold. The specific shares sold may be identified through segregation, numbered stock certificates, or other means. When specific identification is impractical, either a FIFO or weighted-average cost flow assumption may be used. However, the weighted-average method seldom is used in practice because it is not acceptable for tax purposes.

THE EQUITY METHOD

LO 2-3

Prepare journal entries using the equity method of accounting for investments.

The equity method of accounting for intercorporate investments in common stock is intended to reflect the investor's changing equity or interest in the investee. This method is a rather curious one in that the balance in the investment account generally does not reflect either cost or market value, and it does not necessarily represent a pro rata share of the investee's book value. Instead, the investment is recorded at the initial purchase price and adjusted each period for the investor's share of the investee's profits or losses and the dividends declared by the investee.

Use of the Equity Method

ASC 323-10-30 requires that the equity method be used for reporting investments in common stock of the following:

1. Corporate joint ventures. A ***corporate joint venture*** is a corporation owned and operated by a small group of businesses, none of which owns a majority of the joint venture's common stock.
2. Companies in which the investor's voting stock interest gives the investor the "ability to exercise significant influence over operating and financial policies" of that company.

The second condition is the broader of the two and establishes the "significant influence" criterion. Because assessing the degree of influence may be difficult in some cases, **ASC 323-10-15** establishes a 20 percent rule. In the absence of evidence to the contrary, an investor holding 20 percent or more of an investee's voting stock is presumed to have the ability to exercise significant influence over the investee. On the other hand, an investor holding less than 20 percent of an investee's voting stock is presumed not to have the ability to exercise significant influence in the absence of evidence to the contrary.

In most cases, an investment of 20 percent or more in another company's voting stock is reported under the equity method. Notice, however, that the 20 percent rule does not apply if other evidence is available that provides a better indication of the ability or inability of the investor to significantly influence the investee.

Regardless of the level of ownership, the equity method is not appropriate if the investor's influence is limited by circumstances other than stock ownership, such as the existence of a majority shareholder (i.e., two owners with a 25/75 split) or severe restrictions placed on the availability of a foreign investee's earnings or assets by a foreign government.

Investor's Equity in the Investee

Under the equity method, the investor records its investment at the original cost. This amount is adjusted periodically for changes in the investee's stockholders' equity occasioned by the investee's profits, losses, and dividend declarations. The effect of the investee's income, losses, and dividends on the investor's investment account and other accounts can be summarized as follows:

Reported by Investee	Effect on Investor's Accounts
Net income	Record income from investment Increase investment account
Net loss	Record loss from investment Decrease investment account
Dividend declaration	Record asset (cash or receivable) Decrease investment account

Recognition of Income

Under the equity method, the investor's income statement includes the investor's proportionate share of the investee's income or loss each period. The carrying amount of the investment is adjusted by the same amount to reflect the change in the net assets of the investee resulting from the investee's income.

To illustrate, assume that ABC Company acquires significant influence over XYZ Company by purchasing 20 percent of XYZ's common stock for $100,000 at the beginning of the year.

| (4) | Investment in XYZ Company Stock | 100,000 | |
| | Cash | | 100,000 |

Record purchase of XYZ Company stock.

XYZ reports income of $60,000 for the year. ABC records its 20 percent share of XYZ's income ($12,000) in an account called "Income from XYZ Company" as follows:

| (5) | Investment in XYZ Company Stock | 12,000 | |
| | Income from XYZ Company | | 12,000 |

Record income from XYZ Company ($60,000 × 0.20).

This entry may be referred to as the ***equity accrual*** and normally is made as an adjusting entry at the end of the period. If the investee reports a loss for the period, the investor recognizes its share of the loss and reduces the carrying amount of the investment by that amount.

Because of the ability to exercise significant influence over the policies of the investee, realization of income from the investment is considered to be sufficiently ensured to warrant recognition by the investor as the investee earns the income. This differs from the case in which the investor does not have the ability to significantly influence the investee and the investment must be reported using the cost method; in that case, income from the investment is recognized only upon declaration of a dividend by the investee.

Recognition of Dividends

Dividends from an investment are not recognized as income under the equity method because the investor's share of the investee's income is recognized as the investee earns it. Instead, the investee's dividends are viewed as distributions of previously recognized income that already has been capitalized in the carrying amount of the investment. The investor must consider investee dividends declared as a reduction in its equity in the investee and, accordingly, reduce the carrying amount of its investment. In effect, all dividends from the investee are treated as liquidating dividends under the equity method. Thus, if ABC Company owns 20 percent of XYZ Company's common stock and XYZ declares a $20,000 dividend, the following entry is recorded on ABC's books to record its share of the dividend:

(6)	Dividends Receivable	4,000	
	Investment in XYZ Company Stock		4,000

Record dividend from XYZ Company ($20,000 × 0.20).

The following T-accounts summarize all of the normal equity-method entries (journal entries 4–6) on the investor's books:

	Investment in XYZ Company			Income from XYZ Company	
Purchase	100,000				
20% of NI	12,000			12,000	20% of NI
		4,000	20% of Dividend		
Ending Balance	108,000			12,000	Ending Balance

While the Investment in XYZ Company account summarizes ABC's ownership of the net assets of XYZ Company, the Income from XYZ account summarizes ABC's share of XYZ Company's income. The Investment in XYZ Company account appears on ABC's balance sheet and the Income from XYZ Company account appears in ABC's income statement.

Differences in the Carrying Amount of the Investment and Investment Income under the Cost and Equity Methods

Because the investment account on the investor's books under the equity method is adjusted for the investor's share of the investee's income or losses and dividends, the carrying amount of the investment usually is not the same as the original cost to the investor. Only if the investee pays dividends in the exact amount of its earnings will the carrying amount of the investment subsequent to acquisition be equal to its original cost.

To compare the change in the carrying amount of the investment under the equity method relative to the cost method, assume the same facts listed previously for ABC's 20 percent acquisition of XYZ's common stock. The carrying amount of the investment using the equity method at the end of the period is $108,000 ($100,000 + $12,000 − $4,000), compared to the original acquisition price of $100,000 under the cost method.

Investment income under the equity method (the balance in the Income from XYZ account) is $12,000 while investment income under the cost method is equal to dividend income, $4,000.

Acquisition at Interim Date

When a company purchases an investment, the investor begins accruing income from the investee under the equity method at the date of acquisition. The investor may not accrue income earned by the investee before the acquisition date of the investment. When the purchase occurs between balance sheet dates, the amount of income earned by the investee from the date of acquisition to the end of the fiscal period may need to be estimated by the investor in recording the equity accrual. However, since "significant influence" is a requirement for using the equity method, it is likely that the investor will be able to simply ask for the actual post purchase financial results from the investee.

To illustrate, assume that ABC acquires 20 percent of XYZ's common stock on October 1 for $100,000. XYZ earns income of $60,000 uniformly throughout the year and declares dividends of $20,000 on December 20 (paid on December 31). The carrying amount of the investment is increased by $3,000, which represents ABC's share of XYZ's net income earned between October 1 and December 31 (1/4 of the year), and is decreased by $4,000 as a result of dividends declared at year-end (resulting in a net *decrease* of $1,000 since the time of the stock purchase).[3]

Changes in the Number of Shares Held

Some changes in the number of common shares held by an investor are handled easily under the equity method, but others require a bit more attention. A change resulting from a stock dividend, split, or reverse split is treated in the same way as under the cost method. No formal accounting recognition is required on the books of the investor. On the other hand, purchases and sales of shares do require formal recognition.

FYI

Figure 2–1 indicates that once a company owns more than 50% of the outstanding voting stock of an investee company, the parent company can account for the investment using the cost method on its own books because the investment account is eliminated in the consolidation process. Berkshire Hathaway's 2010 Form 10-K indicates: "As a result of our acquisition of the remaining outstanding stock of BNSF on February 12, 2010, we discontinued the use of the equity method and since that date, BNSF's accounts have been consolidated in our financial statements."

Purchases of Additional Shares

A purchase of additional shares of a common stock already held by an investor and accounted for using the equity method simply involves adding the cost of the new shares to the investment account and applying the equity method in the normal manner from the date of acquisition forward. The new and old investments in the same stock are combined for financial reporting purposes. Income accruing to the new shares can be recognized by the investor only from the date of acquisition forward.

To illustrate, assume that ABC Company purchases 20 percent of XYZ Company's common stock on January 2, 20X1, for $100,000, and another 10 percent on July 1, 20X1, for $51,500, and that the stock purchases represent 20 percent and 10 percent, respectively, of the book value of XYZ's net assets. If XYZ earns income of $25,000 from January 2 to June 30 and earns $35,000 from July 1 to December 31, the total income recognized in 20X1 by ABC from its investment in XYZ is $15,500, computed as follows:

---

[3] Note that we assume the entire dividend ($20,000) was declared and paid at the end of the year. If dividends had been declared and paid quarterly, we would record dividends declared only after ABC's acquisition of the XYZ shares.

Income, January 2 to June 30: $25,000 × 0.20	$ 5,000
Income, July 1 to December 31: $35,000 × 0.30	10,500
Investment Income, 20X1	$15,500

If XYZ declares and pays a $10,000 dividend on January 15 and again on July 15, ABC reduces its investment account by $2,000 ($10,000 × 0.20) on January 15 and by $3,000 ($10,000 × 0.30) on July 15. Thus, the ending balance in the investment account at the end of the year is $160,500, computed as follows:

	Investment in XYZ Company				Income from XYZ Company	
1/2/X1 Purchase	100,000					
20% NI to 6/30	5,000	2,000	20% Div. to 6/30		5,000	20% NI to 6/30
7/1/X1 Purchase	51,500					
30% NI from 7/1	10,500	3,000	30% Div. from 7/1		10,500	30% NI from 7/1
Ending Balance	162,000				15,500	Ending Balance

When an investment in common stock is carried using the cost method and purchases of additional shares give the investor the ability to significantly influence the investee, a retroactive switch from the cost method to the equity method is required. This change to the equity method must be applied retroactively to the date of the first acquisition of the investee's stock.

To illustrate a change to the equity method, assume that Aron Corporation purchases 15 percent of Zenon Company's common stock on January 2, 20X1, and another 10 percent on January 2, 20X4. Furthermore, assume that Aron switches to the equity method on January 2, 20X4, because it gains the ability to significantly influence Zenon. Given the following income and dividend data for Zenon, and assuming that the purchases of stock are at book value, the investment income figures reported by Aron originally and as restated are as follows:

	Zenon		Aron's Reported Investment Income	
Year	Net Income	Dividends	Originally under Cost[a]	Restated under Equity[b]
20X1	$15,000	$10,000	$1,500	$2,250
20X2	18,000	10,000	1,500	2,700
20X3	22,000	10,000	1,500	3,300
	$55,000	$30,000	$4,500	$8,250

[a]15 percent of Zenon's dividends for the year.
[b]15 percent of Zenon's net income for the year.

Thus, in Aron's 20X4 financial report, the comparative statements for 20X1, 20X2, and 20X3 are restated to include Aron's 15 percent share of Zenon's profit and to exclude from income Aron's share of dividends recognized under the cost method. In addition, Aron's investment account and retained earnings are restated as if the equity method had been applied from the date of the original acquisition. This restatement is accomplished on Aron's books with the following journal entry on January 2, 20X4:

(7)	Investment in Zenon Company Stock	3,750	
	Retained Earnings		3,750
	Restate investment account from cost to equity method:		
	$8,250 − $4,500.		

In 20X4, if Zenon reports net income of $30,000, Aron's investment income is $7,500 (25 percent of Zenon's net income).

FYI

The summary of Berkshire Hathaway's holdings at the beginning of the chapter lists its stake in Moody's at 12.8%. Its holdings had previously exceeded 20%. However, Berkshire's 2009 10-K indicates: "As a result of a reduction in our ownership of Moody's in July of 2009, we discontinued the use of the equity method as of the beginning of the third quarter of 2009."

Sales of Shares

The sale of all or part of an investment in common stock carried using the equity method is treated the same as the sale of any noncurrent asset. First, the investment account is adjusted to the date of sale for the investor's share of the investee's current earnings. Then a gain or loss is recognized for the difference between the proceeds received and the carrying amount of the shares sold.

If only part of the investment is sold, the investor must decide whether to continue using the equity method to account for the remaining shares or to change to the cost method. The choice is based on evidence available after the sale as to whether the investor still is able to exercise significant influence over the investee. If the equity method no longer is appropriate after the date of sale, the carrying value of the remaining investment is treated as the cost of that investment, and the cost method is applied in the normal manner from the date of sale forward. No retroactive restatement of the investment to actual cost is made.

COMPARISON OF THE COST AND EQUITY METHODS[4]

LO 2-4

Understand and explain differences between the cost and equity methods.

Advanced
StudyGuide
.com

Figure 2–2 summarizes some of the key features of the cost and equity methods of accounting for intercorporate investments. The cost method is consistent with the historical cost basis for most other assets. This method is subject to the usual criticisms leveled against historical cost. In particular, questions arise as to the relevance of reporting the purchase price of an investment acquired some years earlier. The cost method conforms more closely to the traditional accounting and legal views of the realization of income in that the investee's earnings are not available to the investor until transferred as dividends. However, income based on dividend distributions can sometimes be manipulated. The significant influence criterion required for the equity method considers that the declaration of dividends by the investee can be influenced by the investor. Recognizing

FIGURE 2–2
Summary Comparison of the Cost and Equity Methods

Item	Cost Method	Equity Method
Recorded amount of investment at date of acquisition	Original cost	Original cost
Usual carrying amount of investment subsequent to acquisition	Original cost	Original cost increased (decreased) by investor's share of investee's income (loss) and decreased by investor's share of investee's dividends
Income recognition by investor	Investor's share of investee's dividends declared from earnings since acquisition	Investor's share of investee's earnings since acquisition, whether distributed or not
Investee dividends from earnings since acquisition by investor	Income	Reduction of investment
Investee dividends in excess of earnings since acquisition by investor	Reduction of investment	Reduction of investment

[4] To view a video explanation of this topic, visit advancedstudyguide.com.

equity-method income from the investee without regard to investee dividends provides protection against manipulating the investor's net income by influencing investee dividend declarations. On the other hand, the equity method is sometimes criticized because the asset valuation departs from historical cost but stops short of a market value approach. Instead, the carrying amount of the investment is composed of a number of components and is not similar to the valuation of any other assets.

Over the years, there has been considerable criticism of the use of the equity method as a substitute for the consolidation of certain types of subsidiaries. Although the equity method has been viewed as a *one-line consolidation,* the amount of detail reported is considerably different under the equity method than with consolidation. For example, an investor would report the same equity-method income from the following two investees even though their income statements are quite different in composition:

	Investee 1	Investee 2
Sales	$ 50,000	$ 500,000
Operating Expenses	(30,000)	(620,000)
Operating Income (Loss)	$ 20,000	$(120,000)
Gain on Sale of Land		140,000
Net Income	$ 20,000	$ 20,000

Similarly, an investment in the stock of another company is reported under the equity method as a single amount in the investor's balance sheet regardless of the investee's asset and capital structure.

THE FAIR VALUE OPTION

LO 2-5

Prepare journal entries using the fair value option.

ASC 825-10-45 permits, but does not require, companies to measure many financial assets and liabilities at fair value. Companies holding investments in the common stock of other companies have this option for investments that are not required to be consolidated. Thus, rather than using the cost or equity method to report unconsolidated investments in common stock, investors may report those investments at fair value.

Under the fair value option, the investor remeasures the investment to its fair value at the end of each period. The change in value is then recognized in income for the period. Although the FASB does not specify how to account for dividends received from the investment, normally the investor recognizes dividend income in the same manner as under the cost method.

To illustrate the use of the fair value method, assume that Ajax Corporation purchases 40 percent of Barclay Company's common stock on January 1, 20X1, for $200,000. Ajax prepares financial statements at the end of each calendar quarter. On March 1, 20X1, Ajax receives a cash dividend of $1,500 from Barclay. On March 31, 20X1, Ajax determines the fair value of its investment in Barclay to be $207,000. During the first quarter of 20X1, Ajax records the following entries on its books in relation to its investment in Barclay:

(8)	Investment in Barclay Stock		200,000	
	Cash			200,000
	Record purchase of Barclay Company stock.			

(9)	Cash	1,500	
	Dividend Income		1,500
	Record dividend income from Barclay Company.		

(10)	Investment in Barclay Stock	7,000	
	Unrealized Gain on Barclay Stock		7,000
	Record increase in fair value of Barclay stock.		

OVERVIEW OF THE CONSOLIDATION PROCESS

LO 2-6

Make calculations and prepare basic consolidation entries for a simple consolidation.

Advanced
StudyGuide
.com

The consolidation process adds together the financial statements of two or more legally separate companies, creating a single set of financial statements. Chapters 2 through 5 discuss the specific procedures used to produce consolidated financial statements in considerable detail. An understanding of the procedures is important because they facilitate the accurate and efficient preparation of consolidated statements. However, the focus should continue to be on the end product—the financial statements. The procedures are intended to produce financial statements that appear as if the consolidated companies are actually a single company.

The separate financial statements of the companies involved serve as the starting point each time consolidated statements are prepared. These separate statements are added together, after some adjustments, to generate consolidated financial statements. The adjustments relate to intercompany transactions and holdings. Although the individual companies within a consolidated entity may legitimately report sales and receivables or payables to one another, the consolidated entity as a whole must report transactions only with parties outside the consolidated entity and receivables from or payables to external parties. Thus, the adjustments required as part of the consolidation process aim at ensuring that the consolidated financial statements are presented as if they were the statements of a single enterprise.

CONSOLIDATION PROCEDURES FOR WHOLLY OWNED SUBSIDIARIES THAT ARE CREATED OR PURCHASED AT BOOK VALUE

We begin preparing consolidated financial statements with the books of the individual companies that are to be consolidated. Because the consolidated entity has no books, all amounts in the consolidated financial statements originate on the books of the parent or a subsidiary or in the consolidation worksheet.

The term *subsidiary* has been defined as "an entity . . . in which another entity, known as its *parent,* holds a controlling financial interest **(ASC 810-10-20)."** A parent company does not need to hold all of a corporate subsidiary's common stock, but at least majority ownership is normally required for the presentation of consolidated financial statements. Most, but not all, corporate subsidiaries are wholly owned by their parents.

Because most subsidiaries are wholly owned, this chapter begins the in-depth examination of consolidation procedures for wholly owned subsidiaries. Moreover, we begin with the most basic consolidation scenario when the subsidiary is either created by the parent or purchased for an amount exactly equal to the book value of the subsidiary's net assets. This assumption simplifies the consolidation because there is no differential. We start with basic consolidation procedures applied to the preparation of a consolidated balance sheet immediately following the establishment of a parent–subsidiary relationship, either through creation or acquisition of the subsidiary. Then we introduce the use of a simple consolidation worksheet for the balance sheet only. The chapter then moves to the preparation of a full set of consolidated financial statements in subsequent periods and the use of a three-part worksheet designed to facilitate the preparation of a consolidated income statement, retained earnings statement, and balance sheet.

CONSOLIDATION WORKSHEETS

LO 2-7

Prepare a consolidation worksheet.

The *consolidation worksheet* provides a mechanism for efficiently combining the accounts of the separate companies involved in the consolidation and for adjusting the combined balances to the amounts that would be reported if all consolidating companies were actually a single company. When consolidated financial statements are prepared, the account balances are taken from the separate books of the parent and each subsidiary and placed in the consolidation worksheet. The consolidated statements are prepared, after adjustments, from the amounts in the consolidation worksheet.

Worksheet Format

In practice, companies use several different worksheet formats for preparing consolidated financial statements. One of the most widely used formats is the three-part worksheet, consisting of one part for each of three financial statements: (1) the income statement, (2) the statement of retained earnings, and (3) the balance sheet. In recent years, the retained earnings statement has been dropped by many companies in favor of the statement of changes in stockholders' equity. Nevertheless, the information normally found in a retained earnings statement is included in the statement of stockholders' equity, along with additional information, and so the three-part worksheet still provides a useful format. Figure 2–3 presents the format for the comprehensive three-part consolidation worksheet. Specifically, Figure 2–3 illustrates the basic form of a consolidation worksheet. The titles of the accounts of the consolidating companies are listed in the first column of the worksheet. The account balances from the books or trial balances of the individual companies are listed in the next set of columns, with a separate column for each company included in the consolidation. Entries are made in the columns labeled *Consolidation Entries* to adjust or eliminate balances so that the resulting amounts are those that would appear in the financial statements if all the consolidating companies actually formed a single company. The balances in the last column are obtained by summing all amounts algebraically across the worksheet by account. These are the balances that appear in the consolidated financial statements.

The top portion of the worksheet is used in preparing the consolidated income statement. All income statement accounts are listed in the order they normally appear in an income

FIGURE 2–3
Format for Consolidation Worksheet

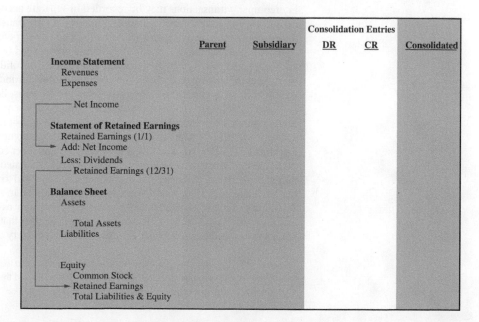

statement.[5] When the income statement portion of the worksheet is completed, a total for each column is entered at the bottom of the income statement portion of the worksheet. The bottom line in this part of the worksheet shows the parent's net income, the subsidiary's net income, the totals of the debit and credit adjustments for this section of the worksheet, and consolidated net income. The entire bottom line is carried down to the "net income" line in the retained earnings statement portion of the worksheet immediately below the income statement.

The retained earnings statement section of the worksheet is in the same format as a retained earnings statement, or the retained earnings section of a statement of stockholders' equity. Net income and the other column totals from the bottom line of the income statement portion of the worksheet are brought down from the income statement above. Similarly, the final line in the retained earnings statement section of the worksheet is carried down in its entirety to the retained earnings line in the balance sheet section.

The bottom portion of the worksheet reflects the balance sheet amounts at the end of the period.[6] The retained earnings amounts appearing in the balance sheet section of the worksheet are the totals carried forward from the bottom line of the retained earnings statement section. The examples in the following sections of this chapter demonstrate the use of the comprehensive three-part consolidation worksheet.

> **! CAUTION**
>
> The most common error students commit in preparing the worksheet is forgetting to carry down the adjustments when they carry down net income from the income statement to the statement of retained earnings and when they carry down the retained earnings ending balance in the statement of retained earnings to the balance sheet.

Nature of Consolidation Entries

Consolidation entries are used in the consolidation worksheet to adjust the totals of the individual account balances of the separate consolidating companies to reflect the amounts that would appear if the legally separate companies were actually a single company. Consolidation entries appear only in the consolidation worksheet and do not affect the books of the separate companies. These worksheet entries are sometimes called "elimination" entries.

For the most part, companies that are to be consolidated record their transactions during the period without regard to the consolidated entity. Transactions with related companies tend to be recorded in the same manner as those with unrelated parties, although intercompany transactions may be recorded in separate accounts or other records may be kept to facilitate the later elimination of intercompany transactions. Each of the consolidating companies also prepares its adjusting and closing entries at the end of the period in the normal manner. The resulting balances are entered in the consolidation worksheet and combined to arrive at the consolidated totals. Consolidation entries are used in the worksheet to increase or decrease the combined totals for individual accounts so that only transactions with external parties are reflected in the consolidated amounts.

Some consolidation entries are required at the end of one period but not at the end of subsequent periods. For example, a loan from a parent to a subsidiary in December 20X1, repaid in February 20X2, requires an entry to eliminate the intercompany receivable and payable on December 31, 20X1, but not at the end of 20X2. Some other consolidation entries need to be placed in the consolidation worksheets each time consolidated statements are prepared for a period of years. For example, if a parent company sells land to a subsidiary for $5,000 above the original cost to the parent, a worksheet entry is needed to reduce the basis of the land by $5,000 each time consolidated statements are prepared for as long as an *affiliate* (an affiliated company) holds the land.[7] It is important to remember that because consolidation entries are not made on the books of any company, they do not carry over from period to period.

---

[5] An optional format lists accounts with credit balance accounts first and those having debit balances listed next.

[6] Optionally, accounts can be separated and listed with debits first and then credits.

[7] An affiliated company is one that is related to the company in question. For example, two corporations controlled by the same parent company would be considered affiliates.

Advanced Financial Accounting, 11th Edition   **63**

Chapter 2   *Reporting Intercorporate Investments and Consolidation of Wholly Owned Subsidiaries with No Differential*   **63**

CONSOLIDATED BALANCE SHEET WITH WHOLLY OWNED SUBSIDIARY

The simplest consolidation setting occurs when the financial statements of related companies are consolidated immediately after a parent–subsidiary relationship is established through a business combination or the creation of a new subsidiary. We present a series of examples to illustrate the preparation of a consolidated balance sheet. Consolidation procedures are the same whether a subsidiary is created or acquired. We use the case of an acquired subsidiary to illustrate the consolidation procedures in the examples that follow. In each example, Peerless Products Corporation purchases all of the common stock of Special Foods Inc. on January 1, 20X1, and immediately prepares a consolidated balance sheet. Figure 2–4 presents the separate balance sheets of the two companies immediately before the combination.

In the following discussion, we present all journal entries and worksheet consolidation entries in the text of the chapter. To avoid confusing the consolidation entries with journal entries that appear on the separate books of the parent or subsidiary, all worksheet consolidation entries appearing in the text are shaded; journal entries recorded in the books of the parent company are not shaded.

100 Percent Ownership Acquired at Book Value

In the first example, Peerless acquires all of Special Foods' outstanding common stock for $300,000, an amount equal to the fair value of Special Foods as a whole. On the date of combination, the fair values of Special Foods' individual assets and liabilities are equal to their book values shown in Figure 2–4. Because Peerless acquires all of Special Foods' common stock and because Special Foods has only the one class of stock outstanding, the total book value of the shares acquired equals the total stockholders' equity of Special Foods ($200,000 + $100,000). The $300,000 of consideration exchanged is equal to the book value of the shares acquired. This ownership situation can be characterized as follows:

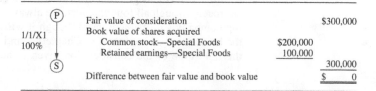

Fair value of consideration		$300,000
Book value of shares acquired		
Common stock—Special Foods	$200,000	
Retained earnings—Special Foods	100,000	
		300,000
Difference between fair value and book value		$ 0

FIGURE 2–4
Balance Sheets of Peerless Products and Special Foods, January 1, 20X1, Immediately before Combination

	Peerless Products	Special Foods
Assets		
Cash	$ 350,000	$ 50,000
Accounts Receivable	75,000	50,000
Inventory	100,000	60,000
Land	175,000	40,000
Buildings & Equipment	800,000	600,000
Accumulated Depreciation	(400,000)	(300,000)
Total Assets	$1,100,000	$500,000
Liabilities & Stockholders' Equity		
Accounts Payable	$ 100,000	$100,000
Bonds Payable	200,000	100,000
Common Stock	500,000	200,000
Retained Earnings	300,000	100,000
Total Liabilities & Equity	$1,100,000	$500,000

Peerless records the stock acquisition on its books with the following entry on the combination date:

(11)	Investment in Special Foods	300,000	
	Cash		300,000

Record the purchase of Special Foods stock.

Figure 2–5 presents the separate financial statements of Peerless and Special Foods immediately after the combination. Special Foods' balance sheet in Figure 2–5 is the same as in Figure 2–4, but Peerless' balance sheet has changed to reflect the $300,000 reduction in cash and the recording of the investment in Special Foods stock for the same amount. Note that the $300,000 of cash was paid to the former stockholders of Special Foods, not to the company itself. Accordingly, that cash is no longer in the consolidated entity. Instead, Peerless' balance sheet now reflects a $300,000 Investment in Special Foods Stock account.

Basic Consolidation Entry

The basic consolidation entry removes the Investment in Special Foods Stock account and the subsidiary's stockholders' equity accounts. Although this consolidation entry is very simple, to be consistent with the discussion of more complicated examples later in the chapter, we illustrate the thought process in developing the worksheet entry.

In this example, Peerless' investment is exactly equal to the book value of equity of Special Foods. Therefore, no goodwill is recorded and all assets and liabilities are simply combined from Special Foods' financial statements at their current book values. In Chapters 4 and 5, we will explore situations in which the acquiring company pays more than the book value of the acquired company's net assets (i.e., when there is a positive differential). However, in Chapters 2 and 3, the excess value of identifiable net assets and goodwill will always be equal to zero. To maintain a consistent approach through all four chapters, we always illustrate the components of the acquiring company's investment, even though it will always be exactly equal to its share of the book value of net assets in Chapters 2 and 3. Therefore, the relationship between the fair value of the consideration given to acquire Special Foods, the fair value of

FIGURE 2–5
Balance Sheets of Peerless Products and Special Foods, January 1, 20X1, Immediately after Combination

	Peerless Products	Special Foods
Assets		
Cash	$ 50,000	$ 50,000
Accounts Receivable	75,000	50,000
Inventory	100,000	60,000
Land	175,000	40,000
Buildings & Equipment	800,000	600,000
Accumulated Depreciation	(400,000)	(300,000)
Investment in Special Foods Stock	300,000	
Total Assets	$1,100,000	$500,000
Liabilities & Stockholders' Equity		
Accounts Payable	$ 100,000	$100,000
Bonds Payable	200,000	100,000
Common Stock	500,000	200,000
Retained Earnings	300,000	100,000
Total Liabilities & Equity	$1,100,000	$500,000

Special Foods' net assets, and the book value of Special Foods' net assets can be illustrated as follows:

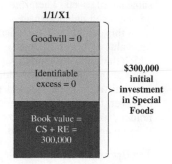

The book value of Special Foods' equity as of the acquisition date is equal to the sum of common stock and retained earnings:

Book Value Calculations:

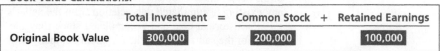

	Total Investment	=	Common Stock	+	Retained Earnings
Original Book Value	300,000		200,000		100,000

Therefore, the consolidation entry simply credits the Investment in Special Foods Stock account (for the acquisition price, $300,000) from Peerless' balance sheet. In this and all future examples, we use blue highlighting with white drop-out lettering to designate the numbers from the book value analysis that appear in the basic consolidation entry:

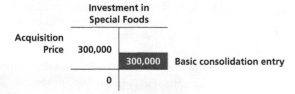

The corresponding debits eliminate the beginning balances in the equity accounts of Special Foods:

Basic Consolidation Entry:

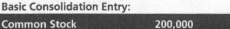

Common Stock	200,000	← Common stock balance
Retained Earnings	100,000	← Beginning balance in ret. earnings
Investment in Special Foods	300,000	← Book value in investment account

Remember that this entry is made in the consolidation worksheet, not on the books of either the parent or the subsidiary, and is presented here in general journal form only for instructional purposes.

The investment account must be eliminated because, from a single entity viewpoint, a company cannot hold an investment in itself. The subsidiary's stockholders' equity accounts must be eliminated because the subsidiary's stock is held entirely within the consolidated entity and none represents claims by outsiders.

From a somewhat different viewpoint, the investment account on the parent's books can be thought of as a single account representing the parent's investment in the net assets of the subsidiary, a so-called *one-line consolidation*. In a full consolidation, the subsidiary's individual assets and liabilities are combined with those of the parent. Including both the net assets of the subsidiary, as represented by the balance in the investment account, and the subsidiary's individual assets and liabilities would double-count the same set of assets. Therefore, the investment account is eliminated and not carried to the consolidated balance sheet.

In this example, the acquisition price of the stock acquired by Peerless is equal to the fair value of Special Foods as a whole. This assumption reflects the normal situation in which the acquisition price paid by the parent is equal to the fair value of its proportionate share of the subsidiary. In addition, this example assumes that the subsidiary's fair value is equal to its book value, a generally unrealistic assumption. Given this assumption, however, the balance of Peerless' investment account is equal to Special Foods' stockholders' equity accounts, so this worksheet entry fully eliminates Peerless' investment account against Special Foods' stockholders' equity accounts.

The Optional Accumulated Depreciation Consolidation Entry

We now introduce a second consolidation entry that is optional but that provides for a more "correct" consolidation. When a company acquires a depreciable asset, it records the asset with a zero balance in accumulated depreciation (i.e., without any accumulated depreciation previously recorded by the seller). Likewise, when a company acquires all of the net assets of another company, the depreciable assets acquired are recorded without any existing accumulated depreciation from the seller's books. The buyer disregards the seller's historical cost and accumulated since they are irrelevant to the acquiring company. For the same reason, when a parent company acquires the stock of a subsidiary, the consolidated financial statements should include the depreciable assets of the subsidiary without the preacquisition accumulated depreciation. However, in a stock acquisition, the consolidation worksheet begins with the book values reflected in the subsidiary's financial statements. Eliminating the old accumulated depreciation of the subsidiary as of the acquisition date and netting it out against the historical cost gives the appearance that the depreciable assets have been newly acquired as of the acquisition date. Special Foods' books indicate accumulated depreciation on the acquisition date of $300,000. Thus, the following consolidation entry will be made to eliminate this acquisition date subsidiary accumulated depreciation.

Optional Accumulated Depreciation Consolidation Entry:

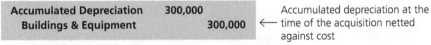

| Accumulated Depreciation | 300,000 | |
| Buildings & Equipment | | 300,000 |

Accumulated depreciation at the ← time of the acquisition netted against cost

Note that this worksheet consolidation entry does not change the net buildings and equipment balance. Netting the preacquisition accumulated depreciation against the cost basis of the corresponding assets merely causes the buildings and equipment to appear in the consolidated financial statements as if they had been acquired without their existing accumulated depreciation.

As explained previously, consolidation entries are not made on the books of any company, so they do not carry over from period to period. Thus, we would make this same accumulated depreciation consolidation entry each succeeding period as long as these depreciable assets remain on Special Foods' books (always based on accumulated depreciation balance as of the acquisition date).

Consolidation Worksheet

We present the worksheet for the preparation of a consolidated balance sheet immediately following the acquisition in Figure 2–6. The first two columns of the worksheet in Figure 2–6 are the account balances taken from the books of Peerless and Special Foods, as shown in Figure 2–5. The balances of like accounts are placed side by side so that they may be added together. If more than two companies were to be consolidated, a separate column would be included in the worksheet for each additional subsidiary.

The accounts are placed in the worksheet in the order they would normally appear in the companies' financial statements. The two columns labeled *Consolidation Entries* in Figure 2–6 are used to adjust the amounts reported by the individual companies to the amounts appropriate for the consolidated statement. All adjustments made in the worksheets are made in double-entry form. Thus, when the worksheet is completed, total debits entered in the Debit Consolidation column must equal total credits entered in the Credit Consolidation column. We highlight all parts of each consolidation entry with the same color so that the reader can identify the individual consolidation entries in the worksheet. After the appropriate consolidation entries have been entered in the Consolidation Entries columns, summing algebraically across the individual accounts provides the consolidated totals.

The consolidated balance sheet presented in Figure 2–7 comes directly from the last column of the consolidation worksheet in Figure 2–6. Because no operations occurred between the date of combination and the preparation of the consolidated balance sheet, the stockholders' equity section of the consolidated balance sheet is identical to that of Peerless in Figure 2–5.

FIGURE 2–6 Worksheet for Consolidated Balance Sheet, January 1, 20X1, Date of Combination; 100 Percent Acquisition at Book Value

	Peerless Products	Special Foods	Consolidation Entries DR	Consolidation Entries CR	Consolidated
Balance Sheet					
Cash	$ 50,000	$ 50,000			$ 100,000
Accounts Receivable	75,000	50,000			125,000
Inventory	100,000	60,000			160,000
Investment in Special Foods	300,000			$300,000	0
Land	175,000	40,000			215,000
Buildings & Equipment	800,000	600,000		300,000	1,100,000
Less: Accumulated Depreciation	(400,000)	(300,000)	300,000		(400,000)
Total Assets	**$1,100,000**	**$500,000**	**$300,000**	**$600,000**	**$1,300,000**
Accounts Payable	100,000	100,000			200,000
Bonds Payable	200,000	100,000			300,000
Common Stock	500,000	200,000	200,000		500,000
Retained Earnings	300,000	100,000	100,000		300,000
Total Liabilities & Equity	**$1,100,000**	**$500,000**	**$300,000**	**$ 0**	**$1,300,000**

FIGURE 2–7 Consolidated Balance Sheet, January 1, 20X1, Date of Combination; 100 Percent Acquisition at Book Value

PEERLESS PRODUCTS CORPORATION AND SUBSIDIARY Consolidated Balance Sheet January 1, 20X1				
Assets			**Liabilities**	
Cash		$ 100,000	Accounts Payable	$ 200,000
Accounts Receivable		125,000	Bonds Payable	300,000
Inventory		160,000		
Land		215,000	Stockholders' Equity	
Buildings & Equipment	$1,100,000		Common Stock	500,000
Accumulated Depreciation	(400,000)	700,000	Retained Earnings	300,000
Total Assets		$1,300,000	Total Liabilities & Equity	$1,300,000

CONSOLIDATION SUBSEQUENT TO ACQUISITION

The preceding section introduced the procedures used to prepare a consolidated balance sheet as of the acquisition date. However, more than a consolidated balance sheet is needed to provide a comprehensive picture of the consolidated entity's activities following acquisition. As with a single company, the set of basic financial statements for a consolidated entity consists of a balance sheet, an income statement, a statement of changes in retained earnings, and a statement of cash flows.

This section of the chapter presents the procedures used to prepare an income statement, statement of retained earnings, and consolidated balance sheet subsequent to the acquisition date. We discuss the preparation of a consolidated statement of cash flows in Chapter 10.

The following discussion first deals with the important concepts of consolidated net income and consolidated retained earnings, followed by a description of the worksheet format used to facilitate the preparation of a full set of consolidated financial statements. We then discuss the specific procedures used to prepare consolidated financial statements subsequent to the date of combination.

This and subsequent chapters focus on procedures for consolidation when the parent company accounts for its investment in subsidiary stock using the equity method. If the parent accounts for its investment using the cost method, the general approach to the preparation of consolidated financial statements is the same, but the specific consolidation entries differ. Appendix 2B summarizes consolidation procedures using the cost method. Regardless of the method the parent uses to account for its subsidiary investment, the consolidated statements will be the same because the investment and related accounts are eliminated in the consolidation process.

The approach followed to prepare a complete set of consolidated financial statements subsequent to a business combination is quite similar to that used to prepare a consolidated balance sheet as of the date of combination. However, in addition to the assets and liabilities, the consolidating companies' revenues and expenses must be combined. As the accounts are combined, adjustments must be made in the consolidation worksheet so that the consolidated financial statements appear as if they are the financial statements of a single company.

When a full set of consolidated financial statements is prepared subsequent to the date of combination, two of the important concepts affecting the statements are those of consolidated net income and consolidated retained earnings.

Consolidated Net Income

All revenues and expenses of the individual consolidating companies arising from transactions with unaffiliated companies are included in the consolidated financial statements. The consolidated income statement includes 100 percent of the revenues and expenses regardless of the parent's percentage ownership. Similar to single-company financial statements, where the difference between revenues and expenses equals net income, revenues minus expenses in the consolidated financial statements equal consolidated net income. *Consolidated net income* is equal to the parent's income from its own operations, excluding any investment income from consolidated subsidiaries, plus the net income from each of the consolidated subsidiaries, adjusted for any differential write-off (which is zero in this chapter). Intercorporate investment income from consolidated subsidiaries included in the parent's net income under either the cost or equity method must be eliminated in computing consolidated net income to avoid double-counting.

Consolidated net income and consolidated net income attributable to the controlling interest are the same when all consolidated subsidiaries are wholly owned. For example, assume that Push Corporation purchases all of the stock of Shove Company at an amount equal to its book value. During 20X1, Shove reports net income of $25,000 while Push reports net income of $125,000, including equity-method income from Shove of $25,000. Consolidated net income for 20X1 is computed as follows:

Push's net income	$125,000
Less: Equity-method income from Shove	(25,000)
Shove's net income	25,000
Consolidated net income	$125,000

Note that when the parent company properly applies the equity method, consolidated net income is always equal to the parent's equity-method net income.

Consolidated Retained Earnings

Consolidated retained earnings, as it appears in the consolidated balance sheet, is that portion of the consolidated enterprise's undistributed earnings accruing to the parent company shareholders. Consolidated retained earnings at the end of the period is equal to the beginning consolidated retained earnings balance, plus consolidated net income attributable to the controlling interest, less dividends declared by the parent company.

Computing Consolidated Retained Earnings

Consolidated retained earnings is computed by adding together the parent's retained earnings from its own operations (excluding any income from consolidated subsidiaries recognized by the parent) and the parent's proportionate share of the net income of each subsidiary since the date of acquisition, adjusted for differential write-off and goodwill impairment. Consolidated retained earnings should be equal to the parent's equity-method retained earnings.

If the parent accounts for subsidiaries using the equity method on its books, the retained earnings of each subsidiary is completely eliminated when the subsidiary is consolidated. This is necessary because (1) retained earnings cannot be purchased, and so subsidiary retained earnings at the date of a business combination cannot be included in the combined company's retained earnings; (2) the parent's share of the subsidiary's income since acquisition is already included in the parent's equity-method retained earnings; and (3) the noncontrolling interest's share (if any) of the subsidiary's retained earnings is not included in consolidated retained earnings.

In the simple example given previously, assume that on the date of combination, January 1, 20X1, Push's retained earnings balance is $400,000 and Shove's is $250,000. During 20X1, Shove reports $25,000 of net income and declares $10,000 of dividends. Push reports $100,000 of separate operating earnings plus $25,000 of equity-method income from its 100 percent interest in Shove; Push declares dividends of $30,000. Based on this information, the retained earnings balances for Push and Shove on December 31, 20X1, are computed as follows:

	Push	Shove
Balance, January 1, 20X1	$400,000	$250,000
Net income, 20X1	125,000	25,000
Dividends declared in 20X1	(30,000)	(10,000)
Balance, December 31, 20X1	$495,000	$265,000

Consolidated retained earnings is computed by first determining the parent's retained earnings from its own operations. This computation involves removing from the parent's retained earnings the $25,000 of subsidiary income since acquisition recognized by the parent, leaving $470,000 ($495,000 − $25,000) of retained earnings resulting from the parent's own operations. The parent's 100 percent share of the subsidiary's net income since the date of acquisition is then added to this number, resulting in consolidated retained earnings of $495,000. We note that because this is the first year since the acquisition, the net income since the date of acquisition is just this year's income. Subsequent examples will illustrate how this calculation differs in later years. We also emphasize that since Push uses the ***fully adjusted equity method,*** this number is the same as the parent's equity-method retained earnings.

CONSOLIDATED FINANCIAL STATEMENTS—100 PERCENT OWNERSHIP, CREATED OR ACQUIRED AT BOOK VALUE

Each of the consolidated financial statements is prepared as if it is taken from a single set of books that is being used to account for the overall consolidated entity. There is, of course, no set of books for the consolidated entity, and as in the preparation of the consolidated balance sheet, the consolidation process starts with the data recorded on the books of the individual consolidating companies. The account balances from the books of the individual companies are placed in the three-part worksheet, and entries are made to eliminate the effects of intercorporate ownership and transactions. The consolidation approach and procedures are the same whether the subsidiary being consolidated was acquired or created.

To understand the process of consolidation subsequent to the start of a parent–subsidiary relationship, assume that on January 1, 20X1, Peerless Products Corporation acquires all of the common stock of Special Foods Inc. for $300,000, an amount equal to Special Foods' book value on that date. At that time, Special Foods has $200,000 of common stock outstanding and retained earnings of $100,000, summarized as follows:

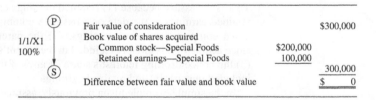

Peerless accounts for its investment in Special Foods stock using the equity method. Information about Peerless and Special Foods as of the date of combination and for the years 20X1 and 20X2 appears in Figure 2–8.

FIGURE 2–8
Selected Information about Peerless Products and Special Foods on January 1, 20X1, and for the Years 20X1 and 20X2

	Peerless Products	Special Foods
Common Stock, January 1, 20X1	$500,000	$200,000
Retained Earnings, January 1, 20X1	300,000	100,000
20X1:		
Separate Operating Income, Peerless	140,000	
Net Income, Special Foods		50,000
Dividends	60,000	30,000
20X2:		
Separate Operating Income, Peerless	160,000	
Net Income, Special Foods		75,000
Dividends	60,000	40,000

Advanced Financial Accounting, 11th Edition   **71**

Chapter 2 *Reporting Intercorporate Investments and Consolidation of Wholly Owned Subsidiaries with No Differential*   **71**

Initial Year of Ownership

On January 1, 20X1, Peerless records its purchase of Special Foods common stock with the following entry:

(12)	Investment in Special Foods	300,000	
	Cash		300,000
	Record the purchase of Special Foods stock.		

During 20X1, Peerless records operating earnings of $140,000, excluding its income from investing in Special Foods, and declares dividends of $60,000. Special Foods reports 20X1 net income of $50,000 and declares dividends of $30,000.

Parent Company Entries

Peerless records its 20X1 income and dividends from Special Foods under the equity method as follows:

(13)	Investment in Special Foods	50,000	
	Income from Special Foods		50,000
	Record Peerless' 100% share of Special Foods' 20X1 income.		

(14)	Cash	30,000	
	Investment in Special Foods		30,000
	Record Peerless' 100% share of Special Foods' 20X1 dividend.		

Advanced
StudyGuide
.com

Consolidation Worksheet—Initial Year of Ownership

After all appropriate entries have been made on the books of Peerless and Special Foods, including year-end adjustments, a consolidation worksheet is prepared as in Figure 2–9. The adjusted account balances from the books of Peerless and Special Foods are placed in the first two columns of the worksheet. Then all amounts that reflect intercorporate transactions or ownership are eliminated in the consolidation process.

The distinction between journal entries recorded on the books of the individual companies and the consolidation entries recorded only on the consolidation worksheet is an important one. Book entries affect balances on the books and the amounts that are carried to the consolidation worksheet; worksheet consolidation entries affect only those balances carried to the consolidated financial statements in that period. As mentioned previously, the consolidation entries presented in this text are shaded both when presented in journal entry form in the text and in the worksheet.

In this example, the accounts that must be eliminated because of intercorporate ownership are the stockholders' equity accounts of Special Foods, including dividends declared, Peerless' investment in Special Foods stock, and Peerless' income from Special Foods. However, unlike previous examples, the book value portion of Peerless' investment has changed because earnings and dividends have adjusted the investment account balance. The book value portion of the investment account can be summarized as follows:

Book Value Calculations:

	Total Investment	=	Common Stock	+	Retained Earnings
Original Book Value	300,000		200,000		100,000
+ Net Income	50,000				50,000
– Dividends	(30,000)				(30,000)
Ending Book Value	320,000		200,000		120,000

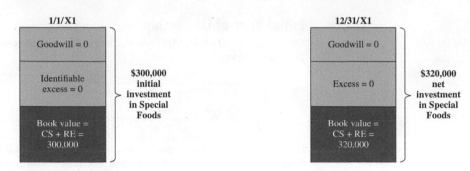

Under the equity method, Peerless recognizes its share (100 percent) of Special Foods' reported income. In the consolidated income statement, however, Special Foods' individual revenue and expense accounts are combined with Peerless' accounts. Peerless' equity method income from Special Foods, therefore, must be eliminated to avoid double-counting. Special Foods' dividends paid to Peerless must be eliminated when consolidated statements are prepared (because the dividend is really just an intercompany cash transfer, not a transfer of wealth to external shareholders) so that only dividend declarations related to the parent's shareholders are reported as dividends of the consolidated entity. Thus, the basic consolidation entry removes both the equity method Income from Special Foods and also all dividends declared by Special Foods during the period:

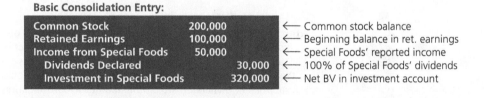

The book value calculations in the chart on the previous page help to facilitate preparation of the basic consolidation entry. Thus, the basic consolidation entry removes (1) Special Foods' equity accounts, (2) Special Foods' dividends declared, (3) Peerless' Income from Special Foods account, and (4) Peerless' Investment in Special Foods account. Note that we use blue highlighting with white drop-out numbers in the book value analysis that appear in the basic consolidation entry. Also note that we eliminate the beginning retained earnings balance since income and dividends are eliminated separately. Because there is no differential in this example, the basic consolidation entry completely eliminates the balance in Peerless' investment account on the balance sheet as well as the Income from Special Foods account on the income statement in the worksheet. Additional consolidation entries will be necessary when there is a differential as illustrated in Chapters 4 and 5.

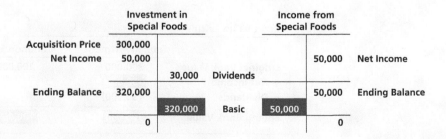

Advanced Financial Accounting, 11th Edition

73

Chapter 2 *Reporting Intercorporate Investments and Consolidation of Wholly Owned Subsidiaries with No Differential* **73**

We show the worksheet entry in these T-accounts only to illustrate how these accounts are eliminated in the consolidation worksheet. Consolidation entries do not affect the actual books of either the parent or the subsidiary.

As explained previously, we repeat the accumulated depreciation worksheet entry in each succeeding period for as long as the subsidiary owns these assets. The purpose of this entry is to appropriately present these assets in the consolidated financial statements as if they had been purchased on the date the subsidiary was acquired at their acquisition date book values with no preacquisition accumulated depreciation.

Optional Accumulated Depreciation Consolidation Entry:

Accumulated Depreciation	300,000	
Buildings & Equipment		300,000

⟵ Accumulated depreciation at the time of the acquisition netted against cost

Worksheet Relationships

Both of the consolidation entries are entered in Figure 2–9 and the amounts are totaled across each row and down each column to complete the worksheet. Some specific points to recognize with respect to the full worksheet are as follows:

1. Because of the normal articulation among the financial statements, the bottom-line number from each of the first two sections of the worksheet carries down to the next

FIGURE 2–9 December 31, 20X1, Equity-Method Worksheet for Consolidated Financial Statements, Initial Year of Ownership; 100 Percent Acquisition at Book Value

	Peerless Products	Special Foods	Consolidation Entries DR	Consolidation Entries CR	Consolidated
Income Statement					
Sales	400,000	200,000			600,000
Less: Cost of Goods Sold (COGS)	(170,000)	(115,000)			(285,000)
Less: Depreciation Expense	(50,000)	(20,000)			(70,000)
Less: Other Expenses	(40,000)	(15,000)			(55,000)
Income from Special Foods	50,000		50,000		0
Net Income	**190,000**	**50,000**	**50,000**	**0**	**190,000**
Statement of Retained Earnings					
Beginning Balance	300,000	100,000	100,000		300,000
Net Income	**190,000**	**50,000**	50,000	0	190,000
Less: Dividends Declared	(60,000)	(30,000)		30,000	(60,000)
Ending Balance	**430,000**	**120,000**	**150,000**	**30,000**	**430,000**
Balance Sheet					
Cash	210,000	75,000			285,000
Accounts Receivable	75,000	50,000			125,000
Inventory	100,000	75,000			175,000
Investment in Special Foods	320,000			320,000	0
Land	175,000	40,000			215,000
Buildings & Equipment	800,000	600,000		300,000	1,100,000
Less: Accumulated Depreciation	(450,000)	(320,000)	300,000		(470,000)
Total Assets	**1,230,000**	**520,000**	**300,000**	**620,000**	**1,430,000**
Accounts Payable	100,000	100,000			200,000
Bonds Payable	200,000	100,000			300,000
Common Stock	500,000	200,000	200,000		500,000
Retained Earnings	**430,000**	**120,000**	150,000	30,000	430,000
Total Liabilities & Equity	**1,230,000**	**520,000**	**350,000**	**30,000**	**1,430,000**

financial statement in a logical progression. As part of the normal accounting cycle, net income is closed to retained earnings, and retained earnings is reflected in the balance sheet. Therefore, in the consolidation worksheet, the net income is carried down to the retained earnings statement section of the worksheet, and the ending retained earnings line is carried down to the balance sheet section of the worksheet. Note that in both cases the entire line, including total adjustments, is carried forward.

2. Double-entry bookkeeping requires total debits to equal total credits for any single consolidation entry and for the worksheet as a whole. Because some consolidation entries extend to more than one section of the worksheet, however, the totals of the debit and credit adjustments are not likely to be equal in either of the first two sections of the worksheet. The totals of all debits and credits at the bottom of the balance sheet section are equal because the cumulative balances from the two upper sections are carried forward to the balance sheet section.

3. In the balance sheet portion of the worksheet, total debit balances must equal total credit balances for each company and the consolidated entity.

4. When the parent uses the full equity method of accounting for the investment, consolidated net income should equal the parent's net income, and consolidated retained earnings should equal the parent's retained earnings. This means the existing balance in subsidiary retained earnings must be eliminated to avoid double-counting.

5. Certain other clerical safeguards are incorporated into the worksheet. The amounts reflected in the bottom line of the income statement section, when summed (algebraically) across, must equal the number reported as consolidated net income. Similarly, the amounts in the last line of the retained earnings statement section must equal consolidated retained earnings when summed across.

Second and Subsequent Years of Ownership

The consolidation procedures employed at the end of the second and subsequent years are basically the same as those used at the end of the first year. Adjusted trial balance data of the individual companies are used as the starting point each time consolidated statements are prepared because no separate books are kept for the consolidated entity. An additional check is needed in each period following acquisition to ensure that the beginning balance of consolidated retained earnings shown in the completed worksheet after consolidation entries equals the balance reported at the end of the prior period. In all other respects, the consolidation entries and worksheet are comparable with those shown for the first year.

Parent Company Entries

We illustrate consolidation after two years of ownership by continuing the example of Peerless Products and Special Foods, based on the data in Figure 2–8. Peerless' separate income from its own operations for 20X2 is $160,000, and its dividends total $60,000. Special Foods reports net income of $75,000 in 20X2 and pays dividends of $40,000. Peerless records the following equity-method entries in 20X2:

(15)	Investment in Special Foods	75,000	
	Income from Special Foods		75,000
	Record Peerless' 100% share of Special Foods' 20X2 income.		

(16)	Cash	40,000	
	Investment in Special Foods		40,000
	Record Peerless' 100% share of Special Foods' 20X2 dividend.		

The balance in the investment account reported by Peerless increases from $320,000 on January 1, 20X2, to $355,000 on December 31, 20X2, and reported net income of Peerless totals $235,000 ($160,000 + $75,000).

Consolidation Worksheet—Second Year of Ownership

Figure 2–10 illustrates the worksheet to prepare consolidated statements for 20X2. The book value of Peerless' investment in Special Foods (which is equal to the book value of Special Foods' equity accounts) can be analyzed and summarized as follows:

Book Value Calculations:

	Total Investment	=	Common Stock	+	Retained Earnings
Beginning Book Value	320,000		200,000		120,000
+ Net Income	75,000				75,000
− Dividends	(40,000)				(40,000)
Ending Book Value	355,000		200,000		155,000

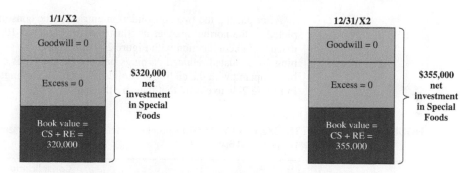

Again, the basic consolidation entry removes (1) Special Foods' equity accounts, (2) Special Foods' dividends declared, (3) Peerless' Income from Special Foods account, and (4) Peerless' Investment in Special Foods account:

Basic Consolidation Entry:

Common Stock	200,000		← Common stock balance
Retained Earnings	120,000		← Beginning balance in RE
Income from Special Foods	75,000		← Special Foods' reported income
Dividends Declared		40,000	← 100% of Special Foods' dividends
Investment in Special Foods		355,000	← Net BV in investment account

Note that the beginning balance in retained earnings in 20X2, $75,000, is different than the balance in 20X1 because of income earned and dividends declared during 20X1. However, it is the beginning balance in retained earnings that is eliminated since income and dividends are eliminated separately. As explained previously, since there is no differential in this example, the basic consolidation entry completely eliminates the balance in Peerless' investment account on the balance sheet as well as the Income from Special Foods account on the income statement in the worksheet.

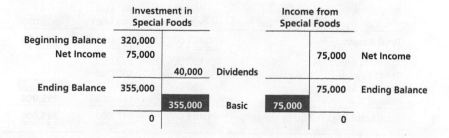

	Investment in Special Foods			Income from Special Foods	
Beginning Balance	320,000				
Net Income	75,000			75,000	Net Income
		40,000	Dividends		
Ending Balance	355,000			75,000	Ending Balance
		355,000	Basic	75,000	
	0			0	

We again show the worksheet entry in these T-accounts only to illustrate how these accounts are eliminated in the consolidation worksheet. Consolidation entries do not affect the actual books of either the parent or the subsidiary.

In this example, Special Foods had accumulated depreciation of $300,000 on the acquisition date. Thus, we repeat the same accumulated depreciation consolidation entry this year (and every year as long as Special Foods owns the assets) that we used in the initial year.

Optional Accumulated Depreciation Consolidation Entry:

Accumulated Depreciation	300,000	
Buildings & Equipment		300,000

Accumulated depreciation at the ← time of the acquisition netted against cost

After placing the two consolidation entries in the consolidation worksheet, it is completed in the normal manner as illustrated in Figure 2–10. All worksheet relationships discussed in conjunction with Figure 2–9 continue in the second year as well. The beginning consolidated retained earnings balance for 20X2, as shown in Figure 2–10, should be compared with the ending consolidated retained earnings balance for 20X1, as shown in Figure 2–9, to ensure that they are the same.

FIGURE 2–10 December 31, 20X2, Equity-Method Worksheet for Consolidated Financial Statements, Second Year of Ownership; 100 Percent Acquisition at Book Value

	Peerless Products	Special Foods	Consolidation Entries DR	Consolidation Entries CR	Consolidated
Income Statement					
Sales	450,000	300,000			750,000
Less: COGS	(180,000)	(160,000)			(340,000)
Less: Depreciation Expense	(50,000)	(20,000)			(70,000)
Less: Other Expenses	(60,000)	(45,000)			(105,000)
Income from Special Foods	75,000		75,000		0
Net Income	**235,000**	**75,000**	**75,000**	**0**	**235,000**
Statement of Retained Earnings					
Beginning Balance	430,000	120,000	120,000		430,000
Net Income	**235,000**	**75,000**	75,000	0	235,000
Less: Dividends Declared	(60,000)	(40,000)		40,000	(60,000)
Ending Balance	**605,000**	**155,000**	**195,000**	**40,000**	**605,000**
Balance Sheet					
Cash	245,000	85,000			330,000
Accounts Receivable	150,000	80,000			230,000
Inventory	180,000	90,000			270,000
Investment in Special Foods	355,000			355,000	0
Land	175,000	40,000			215,000
Buildings & Equipment	800,000	600,000		300,000	1,100,000
Less: Accumulated Depreciation	(500,000)	(340,000)	300,000		(540,000)
Total Assets	**1,405,000**	**555,000**	**300,000**	**655,000**	**1,605,000**
Accounts Payable	100,000	100,000			200,000
Bonds Payable	200,000	100,000			300,000
Common Stock	500,000	200,000	200,000		500,000
Retained Earnings	**605,000**	**155,000**	195,000	40,000	605,000
Total Liabilities & Equity	**1,405,000**	**555,000**	**395,000**	**40,000**	**1,605,000**

Advanced Financial Accounting, 11th Edition

77

Chapter 2 *Reporting Intercorporate Investments and Consolidation of Wholly Owned Subsidiaries with No Differential*   **77**

Consolidated Net Income and Retained Earnings

In the consolidation worksheets illustrated in Figures 2–9 and 2–10, consolidated net income for 20X1 and 20X2 appear as the last numbers in the income statement section of the worksheets in the Consolidated column on the far right. The numbers can be computed as follows:

	20X1	20X2
Peerless' net income	$190,000	$235,000
Peerless' equity income from Special Foods	(50,000)	(75,000)
Special Foods' net income	50,000	75,000
Consolidated net income	$190,000	$235,000

In this simple illustration, consolidated net income is the same as Peerless' equity-method net income.

In Figures 2–9 and 2–10, the ending consolidated retained earnings number is equal to the beginning balance of consolidated retained earnings plus consolidated net income, less dividends declared on the parent's common stock. It also can be computed as follows:

	20X1	20X2
Peerless' beginning retained earnings from its own operations	$300,000	$380,000
Peerless' income from its own operations	140,000	160,000
Peerless' income from Special Foods since acquisition (cumulative)	50,000	125,000
Peerless' dividends declared	(60,000)	(60,000)
Consolidated retained earnings	$430,000	$605,000

 STOP & THINK

Note that Peerless' beginning retained earnings from its own operations in 20X2, $380,000, is calculated as the beginning balance for 20X1 plus Peerless' income from its own operations in 20X1, $140,000, minus its dividends declared in 20X1, $60,000.

As with income, consolidated retained earnings is the same as the parent's equity-method retained earnings if the parent company uses the equity method. We note that the second year of this calculation illustrates how cumulative income from Special Foods (since the acquisition date) can be used to calculate ending retained earnings.

SUMMARY OF KEY CONCEPTS

Companies owning investments in the common stock of other companies generally report those investments by consolidating them or reporting them using the cost method (adjusted to market, if appropriate) or equity method, depending on the circumstances. Consolidation generally is appropriate if one entity controls the investee, usually through majority ownership of the investee's voting stock. The equity method is required when an investor has sufficient stock ownership in an investee to significantly influence the operating and financial policies of the investee but owns less than a majority of the investee's stock. In the absence of other evidence, ownership of 20 percent or more of an investee's voting stock is viewed as giving the investor the ability to exercise significant influence over the investee. The cost method is used when consolidation and the equity method are not appropriate, usually when the investor is unable to exercise significant influence over the investee.

The cost method is similar to the approach used in accounting for other noncurrent assets. The investment is carried at its original cost to the investor. Consistent with the realization concept, income from the investment is recognized when distributed by the investee in the form of dividends.

The equity method is unique in that the carrying value of the investment is adjusted periodically to reflect the investor's changing equity in the underlying investee. Income from the investment is recognized by the investor under the equity method as the investee reports the income rather than when it is distributed.

Companies also have the choice of reporting nonconsolidated investments using the fair value option instead of the cost or equity method. Under the fair value option, the investment is remeasured to fair value at the end of each reporting period and the change in value recognized as an unrealized gain or loss in income.

Consolidated financial statements present the financial position and results of operations of two or more separate legal entities as if they were a single company. A consolidated balance sheet prepared on the date a parent acquires a subsidiary appears the same as if the acquired company had been merged into the parent.

A consolidation worksheet provides a means of efficiently developing the data needed to prepare consolidated financial statements. The worksheet includes a separate column for the trial balance data of each of the consolidating companies, a debit and a credit column for the consolidation entries, and a column for the consolidated totals that appear in the consolidated financial statements. A three-part consolidation worksheet facilitates preparation of a consolidated income statement, retained earnings statement, and balance sheet, and it includes a section for each statement. Consolidation entries are needed in the worksheet to remove the effects of intercompany ownership and intercompany transactions so the consolidated financial statements appear as if the separate companies are actually one.

KEY TERMS

affiliate, *62*	control, *49*	liquidating dividends, *51*
consolidated net income, *68*	corporate joint venture, *53*	modified equity method, *80*
consolidated retained earnings, *69*	cost method, *49*	one-line consolidation, *59*
consolidation, *49*	equity accrual, *54*	parent, *49*
consolidation entries, *62*	equity method, *49*	significant influence, *49*
consolidation worksheet, *61*	fully adjusted equity method, *70*	subsidiary, *49*
		unconsolidated subsidiary, *49*

Appendix 2A   Additional Considerations Relating to the Equity Method

Determination of Significant Influence

The general rule established in **ASC 323-10-15** is that the equity method is appropriate when the investor, by virtue of its common stock interest in an investee, is able to exercise significant influence, but not control, over the operating and financial policies of the investee. In the absence of other evidence, common stock ownership of 20 percent or more is viewed as indicating that the investor is able to exercise significant influence over the investee. However, the APB also stated a number of factors that could constitute other evidence of the ability to exercise significant influence:

1. Representation on board of directors.

2. Participation in policy making.

3. Material intercompany transactions.

4. Interchange of managerial personnel.

5. Technological dependency.

6. Size of investment in relation to concentration of other shareholdings.

Conversely, the FASB provides in **ASC 323-10-15-10** some examples of evidence where an investor is unable to exercise significant influence over an investee. These situations include legal or regulatory challenges to the investor's influence by the investee, agreement by the investor to give up important shareholder rights, concentration of majority ownership among a small group of owners who disregard the views of the investor, and unsuccessful attempts by the investor to obtain information from the investee or to obtain representation on the investee's board of directors.

Advanced Financial Accounting, 11th Edition   **79**

Chapter 2   *Reporting Intercorporate Investments and Consolidation of Wholly Owned Subsidiaries with No Differential*   **79**

Unrealized Intercompany Profits

Only "arms-length" transactions (i.e., those conducted between completely independent parties who act in their own best interests) may be reflected in the consolidated financial statements. Thus, all aspects of intercompany transfers must be eliminated in preparing consolidated financial statements so that the statements appear as if they were those of a single company.

Adjusting for Unrealized Intercompany Profits

An intercompany sale normally is recorded on the books of the selling affiliate in the same manner as any other sale, including the recognition of profit. In applying the equity method, any intercompany profit remaining unrealized at the end of the period must be deducted from the amount of income that otherwise would be reported.

The income recognized from the investment and the carrying amount of the investment are reduced to remove the effects of the unrealized intercompany profits. In future periods when the intercompany profit actually is realized, the entry is reversed.

Unrealized Profit Adjustments Illustrated

To illustrate the adjustment for unrealized intercompany profits under the equity method, assume that Palit Corporation owns 40 percent of the common stock of Label Manufacturing. During 20X1, Palit sells inventory to Label for $10,000; the inventory originally cost Palit $7,000. Label resells one-third of the inventory to outsiders during 20X1 and retains the other two-thirds in its ending inventory. The amount of unrealized profit is computed as follows:

Total intercompany profit	$10,000 − $7,000 = $3,000
Unrealized portion	$3,000 × 2/3 = $2,000

Assuming that Label reports net income of $60,000 for 20X1 and declares no dividends, the following entries are recorded on Palit's books at the end of 20X1:

(17)	Investment in Label Manufacturing	24,000	
	Income from Label Manufacturing		24,000
	Record equity-method income: $60,000 × 0.40.		

(18)	Income from Label Manufacturing	2,000	
	Investment in Label Manufacturing		2,000
	Remove unrealized intercompany profit.		

If all the remaining inventory is sold in 20X2, the following entry is made on Palit's books at the end of 20X2 to record the realization of the previously unrealized intercompany profit:

(19)	Investment in Label Manufacturing Stock	2,000	
	Income from Label Manufacturing		2,000
	Recognize realized intercompany profit.		

Additional Requirements of ASC 323-10

ASC 323-10, the main authoritative guidance on equity-method reporting, includes several additional requirements:

1. The investor's share of the investee's extraordinary items and prior-period adjustments should be reported as such by the investor, if material.

2. If an investor's share of investee losses exceeds the carrying amount of the investment, the equity method should be discontinued once the investment has been reduced to zero. No further losses are to be recognized by the investor unless the investor is committed to provide further financial support for the investee or unless the investee's imminent return to profitability appears assured. If, after the equity method has been suspended, the investee reports net income, the investor again should apply the equity method, but only after the investor's share of net income equals its share of losses not previously recognized.

3. Preferred dividends of the investee should be deducted from the investee's net income if declared or, whether declared or not, if the preferred stock is cumulative, before the investor computes its share of investee earnings.

ASC 323-10-50-3 includes a number of required financial statement disclosures. When using the equity method, the investor must disclose[8] the following:

1. The name and percentage ownership of each investee.

2. The investor's accounting policies with respect to its investments in common stock, including the reasons for any departures from the 20 percent criterion established by **ASC 323-10-15.**

3. The amount and accounting treatment of any differential.

4. The aggregate market value of each identified nonsubsidiary investment where a quoted market price is available.

5. Either separate statements for or summarized information as to assets, liabilities, and results of operations of corporate joint ventures of the investor, if material in the aggregate.

Investor's Share of Other Comprehensive Income

When an investor uses the equity method to account for its investment in another company, the investor's comprehensive income should include its proportionate share of each of the amounts reported as "Other Comprehensive Income" by the investee. For example, assume that Ajax Corporation purchases 40 percent of the common stock of Barclay Company on January 1, 20X1. For the year 20X1, Barclay reports net income of $80,000 and comprehensive income of $115,000, which includes other comprehensive income (in addition to net income) of $35,000. This other comprehensive income (OCI) reflects an unrealized $35,000 gain (net of tax) resulting from an increase in the fair value of an investment in stock classified as available-for-sale under the criteria established by **ASC 320-10-35-1.** In addition to recording the normal equity-method entries, Ajax recognizes its proportionate share of the unrealized gain on available-for-sale securities reported by Barclay during 20X1 with the following entry:

(20)	Investment in Barclay Stock	14,000	
	Unrealized Gain on Investee AFS Investments		14,000

Recognize share of investee's unrealized gain on available-for-sale securities.

Entry (20) has no effect on Ajax's net income for 20X1, but it does increase Ajax's other comprehensive income, and thus its total comprehensive income, by $14,000. Ajax will make a similar entry at the end of each period for its proportionate share of any increase or decrease in Barclay's accumulated unrealized holding gain on the available-for-sale securities.

Alternative Versions of the Equity Method of Accounting for Investments in Consolidated Subsidiaries

Companies are free to adopt whatever procedures they wish in accounting for investments in controlled subsidiaries on their books. Because investments in consolidated subsidiaries are eliminated when consolidated statements are prepared, the consolidated statements are not affected by the procedures used to account for the investments on the parent's books.

In practice, companies follow three different approaches in accounting for their consolidated subsidiaries:

1. Cost method.

2. Fully adjusted equity method.

3. Modified version of the equity method.

Several modified versions of the equity method are found in practice, and all are usually referred to as the ***modified equity method.*** Some companies apply the equity method without

[8] **ASC 825-10-45** requires most of the same disclosures for investments in common stock reported under the fair value option that otherwise would have been reported using the equity method.

making adjustments for unrealized intercompany profits and the amortization of the differential. Others adjust for the amortization of the differential but omit the adjustments for unrealized intercompany profits. Modified versions of the equity method may provide some clerical savings for the parent if used on the books when consolidation of the subsidiary is required.

Appendix 2B Consolidation and the Cost Method

Advanced
StudyGuide
.com

Not all parent companies use the equity method to account for their subsidiary investments that are to be consolidated. The choice of the cost or equity method has no effect on the consolidated financial statements. This is true because the balance in the parent's investment account, the parent's income from the subsidiary, and related items are eliminated in preparing the consolidated statements. Thus, the parent is free to use either the cost method or some version of the equity method on its separate books in accounting for investments in subsidiaries that are to be consolidated.

Because the cost method uses different parent company entries than the equity method, it also requires different consolidation entries in preparing the consolidation worksheet. Keep in mind that the consolidated financial statements appear the same regardless of whether the parent uses the cost or the equity method on its separate books.

CONSOLIDATION—YEAR OF COMBINATION

To illustrate the preparation of consolidated financial statements when the parent company carries its subsidiary investment using the cost method, refer again to the Peerless Products and Special Foods example. Assume that Peerless purchases 100 percent of the common stock of Special Foods on January 1, 20X1, for $300,000. At that date, the book value of Special Foods as a whole is $300,000. All other data are the same as presented in Figures 2–4 and 2–5.

Parent Company Cost-Method Entries

When the parent company uses the cost method, Peerless records only two journal entries during 20X1 related to its investment in Special Foods. Entry (21) records Peerless' purchase of Special Foods stock; entry (22) recognizes dividend income based on the $30,000 ($30,000 × 100%) of dividends received during the period:

(21)	Investment in Special Foods	300,000	
	Cash		300,000
	Record the initial investment in Special Foods.		

(22)	Cash	30,000	
	Dividend Income		30,000
	Record Peerless' 100% share of Special Foods' 20X1 dividend.		

No entries are made on the parent's books with respect to Special Foods income in 20X1, as would be done under the equity method.

Consolidation Worksheet—Year of Combination

Figure 2–11 illustrates the worksheet to prepare consolidated financial statements for December 31, 20X1, using the cost method. The trial balance data for Peerless and Special Foods included in the worksheet in Figure 2–11 differ from those presented in Figure 2–9 only by the effects of using the cost method rather than the equity method on Peerless' books. Note that all of the amounts in the Consolidated column are the same as in Figure 2–9 because the method used by the parent to account for its subsidiary investment on its books has no effect on the consolidated financial statements.

When a company uses the cost method, the basic consolidation entry can be divided into two parts. The first eliminates the investment account. The investment consolidation entry eliminates the balances in the stockholders' equity accounts of Special Foods and the balance in Peerless' investment account as of the date of combination. This consolidation entry is the same each year (assuming there is no impairment of the investment account) because it relates to the original acquisition price and the original balances in Special Foods' equity accounts.

FIGURE 2–11   December 31, 20X1, Cost-Method Worksheet for Consolidated Financial Statements, Initial Year of Ownership; 100 Percent Acquisition at Book Value

	Peerless Products	Special Foods	Consolidation Entries DR	Consolidation Entries CR	Consolidated
Income Statement					
Sales	400,000	200,000			600,000
Less: COGS	(170,000)	(115,000)			(285,000)
Less: Depreciation Expense	(50,000)	(20,000)			(70,000)
Less: Other Expenses	(40,000)	(15,000)			(55,000)
Dividend Income	30,000		30,000		0
Net Income	**170,000**	**50,000**	**30,000**	**0**	**190,000**
Statement of Retained Earnings					
Beginning Balance	300,000	100,000	100,000		300,000
Net Income	**170,000**	**50,000**	30,000	0	190,000
Less: Dividends Declared	(60,000)	(30,000)		30,000	(60,000)
Ending Balance	**410,000**	**120,000**	**130,000**	**30,000**	**430,000**
Balance Sheet					
Cash	210,000	75,000			285,000
Accounts Receivable	75,000	50,000			125,000
Inventory	100,000	75,000			175,000
Investment in Special Foods	300,000			300,000	0
Land	175,000	40,000			215,000
Buildings & Equipment	800,000	600,000		300,000	1,100,000
Less: Accumulated Depreciation	(450,000)	(320,000)	300,000		(470,000)
Total Assets	**1,210,000**	**520,000**	**300,000**	**600,000**	**1,430,000**
Accounts Payable	100,000	100,000			200,000
Bonds Payable	200,000	100,000			300,000
Common Stock	500,000	200,000	200,000		500,000
Retained Earnings	**410,000**	**120,000**	130,000	30,000	430,000
Total Liabilities & Equity	**1,210,000**	**520,000**	**330,000**	**30,000**	**1,430,000**

Investment Consolidation Entry:

Common Stock	200,000	
Retained Earnings	100,000	
Investment in Special Foods		300,000

The dividend consolidation entry eliminates the dividend income recorded by Peerless during the period along with Special Foods' dividend declaration related to the stockholdings of Peerless.

Dividend Consolidation Entry:

Dividend Income	30,000	
Dividends Declared		30,000

Finally, the accumulated depreciation consolidation entry is the same as under the equity method.

Optional Accumulated Depreciation Consolidation Entry:

Accumulated Depreciation	300,000	
Buildings & Equipment		300,000

As mentioned previously, the amounts in the Consolidated column of the worksheet in Figure 2–11 are the same as those in Figure 2–9 because the method used on the parent's books to account for the subsidiary investment does not affect the consolidated financial statements.

CONSOLIDATION—SECOND YEAR OF OWNERSHIP

Consolidation differences between cost-method accounting and equity-method accounting tend to be more evident in the second year of ownership simply because the equity-method entries change every year while the cost-method entries are generally the same (with the exception of recording the initial investment).

Parent Company Cost-Method Entry

Peerless only records a single entry on its books in 20X2 related to its investment in Special Foods:

| (23) | Cash | 40,000 | |
| | Dividend Income | | 40,000 |

Record Peerless' 100% share of Special Foods' 20X2 dividend.

Consolidation Worksheet—Second Year Following Combination

The worksheet consolidation entries are identical to those used in the first year except that the amount of dividends declared by Special Foods in the second year is $40,000 instead of $30,000.

Investment Consolidation Entry:

Common Stock	200,000	
Retained Earnings	100,000	
Investment in Special Foods		300,000

Dividend Consolidation Entry:

| Dividend Income | 40,000 | |
| Dividends Declared | | 40,000 |

Optional Accumulated Depreciation Consolidation Entry:

| Accumulated Depreciation | 300,000 | |
| Buildings & Equipment | | 300,000 |

Under the cost method, Peerless has not recognized any portion of the undistributed earnings of Special Foods on its parent company books. Therefore, Peerless' retained earnings at the beginning of the second year are less than consolidated retained earnings. Also, Peerless' Investment in Special Foods account balance is less than its 100 percent share of Special Foods' net assets at that date. The consolidation worksheet in Figure 2–12 demonstrates how the worksheet entries eliminate the balances reported by Peerless under the cost method.

Note that while the Consolidated column yields identical numbers to those found in Figure 2–10, the cost method does not maintain the favorable properties that exist when the equity method is employed. Specifically, the parent's net income no longer equals consolidated net income, and the parent's retained earnings no longer equals consolidated retained earnings balance. Hence, although the procedures used under the cost method require less work, the parent company does not enjoy some of the favorable relationships among parent and consolidated numbers that exist under the equity method.

QUESTIONS

LO 2-1 **Q2-1** What types of investments in common stock normally are accounted for using *(a)* the equity method and *(b)* the cost method?

LO 2-1 **Q2-2A** How is the ability to significantly influence the operating and financial policies of a company normally demonstrated?

"A" and "B" indicate that the item relates to Appendix 2A and Appendix 2B, respectively.

FIGURE 2–12   December 31, 20X1, Cost-Method Worksheet for Consolidated Financial Statements, Second Year of Ownership; 100 Percent Acquisition at Book Value

	Peerless Products	Special Foods	Consolidation Entries DR	Consolidation Entries CR	Consolidated
Income Statement					
Sales	450,000	300,000			750,000
Less: COGS	(180,000)	(160,000)			(340,000)
Less: Depreciation Expense	(50,000)	(20,000)			(70,000)
Less: Other Expenses	(60,000)	(45,000)			(105,000)
Income from Special Foods	40,000		40,000		0
Net Income	**200,000**	**75,000**	**40,000**	**0**	**235,000**
Statement of Retained Earnings					
Beginning Balance	410,000	120,000	100,000		430,000
Net Income	**200,000**	**75,000**	40,000	0	235,000
Less: Dividends Declared	(60,000)	(40,000)		40,000	(60,000)
Ending Balance	**550,000**	**155,000**	**140,000**	**40,000**	**605,000**
Balance Sheet					
Cash	245,000	85,000			330,000
Accounts Receivable	150,000	80,000			230,000
Inventory	180,000	90,000			270,000
Investment in Special Foods	300,000			300,000	0
Land	175,000	40,000			215,000
Buildings & Equipment	800,000	600,000		300,000	1,100,000
Less: Accumulated Depreciation	(500,000)	(340,000)	300,000		(540,000)
Total Assets	**1,350,000**	**555,000**	**300,000**	**600,000**	**1,605,000**
Accounts Payable	100,000	100,000			200,000
Bonds Payable	200,000	100,000			300,000
Common Stock	500,000	200,000	200,000		500,000
Retained Earnings	**550,000**	**155,000**	140,000	40,000	605,000
Total Liabilities & Equity	**1,350,000**	**555,000**	**340,000**	**40,000**	**1,605,000**

LO 2-1   **Q2-3A**   When is equity-method reporting considered inappropriate even though sufficient common shares are owned to allow the exercise of significant influence?

LO 2-4   **Q2-4**   When will the balance in the intercorporate investment account be the same under the cost method and the equity method?

LO 2-2, 2-3   **Q2-5**   Describe an investor's treatment of an investee's prior-period dividends and earnings when the investor acquires significant influence through a purchase of additional stock.

LO 2-2, 2-3   **Q2-6**   From the point of view of an investor in common stock, what is a liquidating dividend?

LO 2-2, 2-3   **Q2-7**   What effect does a liquidating dividend have on the balance in the investment account under the cost method and the equity method?

LO 2-2, 2-3   **Q2-8**   How is the receipt of a dividend recorded under the equity method? Under the cost method?

LO 2-5   **Q2-9**   How does the fair value method differ from the cost method and equity method in reporting income from nonsubsidiary investments?

LO 2-3   **Q2-10A**   How does the fully adjusted equity method differ from the modified equity method?

LO 2-4   **Q2-11**   Explain the concept of a one-line consolidation.

LO 2-3   **Q2-12A**   What is the modified equity method? When might a company choose to use the modified equity method rather than the fully adjusted equity method?

LO 2-3   **Q2-13A**   How are extraordinary items of the investee disclosed by the investor under equity-method reporting?

LO 2-7	**Q2-14**	How does a consolidation entry differ from an adjusting entry?
LO 2-6, 2-7	**Q2-15**	What portion of the balances of subsidiary stockholders' equity accounts is included in the consolidated balance sheet?
LO 2-7	**Q2-16**	How does the consolidation process change when consolidated statements are prepared after—rather than at—the date of acquisition?
LO 2-7	**Q2-17**	What are the three parts of the consolidation worksheet, and what sequence is used in completing the worksheet parts?
LO 2-7	**Q2-18**	How are a subsidiary's dividend declarations reported in the consolidated retained earnings statement?
LO 2-7	**Q2-19**	How is consolidated net income computed in a consolidation worksheet?
LO 2-7	**Q2-20**	Give a definition of *consolidated retained earnings.*
LO 2-7	**Q2-21**	How is the amount reported as consolidated retained earnings determined?
LO 2-7	**Q2-22**	Why is the beginning retained earnings balance for each company entered in the three-part consolidation worksheet rather than just the ending balance?

CASES

LO 2-2, 2-3	**C2-1A**

Choice of Accounting Method

Understanding

Slanted Building Supplies purchased 32 percent of the voting shares of Flat Flooring Company in March 20X3. On December 31, 20X3, the officers of Slanted Building Supplies indicated they needed advice on whether to use the equity method or cost method in reporting their ownership in Flat Flooring.

Required

a. What factors should be considered in determining whether equity-method reporting is appropriate?

b. Which of the two methods is likely to show the larger reported contribution to Slanted's earnings in 20X4? Explain.

c. Why might the use of the equity method become more appropriate as the percentage of ownership increases?

LO 2-2, 2-3	**C2-2**

Intercorporate Ownership

Research

Most Company purchased 90 percent of the voting common stock of Port Company on January 1, 20X4, and 15 percent of the voting common stock of Adams Company on July 1, 20X4. In preparing the financial statements for Most Company at December 31, 20X4, you discover that Port Company purchased 10 percent of the common stock of Adams Company in 20X2 and continues to hold those shares. Adams Company reported net income of $200,000 for 20X4 and paid a dividend of $70,000 on December 20, 20X4.

Required

Most Company's chief accountant instructs you to review the Accounting Standards Codification and prepare a memo discussing whether the cost or equity method should be used in reporting the investment in Adams Company in Most's consolidated statements prepared at December 31, 20X4. Support your recommendations with citations and quotations from the authoritative financial reporting standards or other literature.

LO 2-2, 2-3	**C2-3A**

Application of the Equity Method

Research

Forth Company owned 85,000 of Brown Company's 100,000 shares of common stock until January 1, 20X2, at which time it sold 70,000 of the shares to a group of seven investors, each of whom purchased 10,000 shares. On December 3, 20X2, Forth received a dividend of $9,000 from Brown. Forth continues to purchase a substantial portion of Brown's output under a contract that runs until the end of 20X9. Because of this arrangement, Forth is permitted to place two of its employees on Brown's board of directors.

Required

Forth Company's controller is not sure whether the company should use the cost or equity method in accounting for its investment in Brown Company. The controller asked you to review the relevant accounting literature and prepare a memo containing your recommendations. Support your recommendations with citations and quotations from the Accounting Standards Codification.

LO 2-6, 2-7 | **C2-4** | ### Need for Consolidation Process

Communication

At a recent staff meeting, the vice president of marketing appeared confused. The controller had assured him that the parent company and each of the subsidiary companies had properly accounted for all transactions during the year. After several other questions, he finally asked, "If it has been done properly, then why must you spend so much time and make so many changes to the amounts reported by the individual companies when you prepare the consolidated financial statements each month? You should be able to just add the reported balances together."

Required

Prepare an appropriate response to help the controller answer the marketing vice president's question.

LO 2-1 | **C2-5** | ### Account Presentation

Research

Prime Company has been expanding rapidly and is now an extremely diversified company for its size. It currently owns three companies with manufacturing facilities, two companies primarily in retail sales, a consumer finance company, and two natural gas pipeline companies. This has led to some conflict between the company's chief accountant and its treasurer. The treasurer advocates presenting no more than five assets and three liabilities on its balance sheet. The chief accountant has resisted combining balances from substantially different subsidiaries and has asked for your assistance.

Required

Research the Accounting Standards Codification to see what guidance is provided and prepare a memo to the chief accountant with your findings. Include citations to and quotations from the most relevant references. Include in your memo at least two examples of situations in which it may be inappropriate to combine similar-appearing accounts of two subsidiaries.

LO 2-6, 2-7 | **C2-6** | ### Consolidating an Unprofitable Subsidiary

Research

Amazing Chemical Corporation's president had always wanted his own yacht and crew and concluded that Amazing Chemical should diversify its investments by purchasing an existing boatyard and repair facility on the lakeshore near his summer home. He could then purchase a yacht and have a convenient place to store it and have it repaired. Although the board of directors was never formally asked to approve this new venture, the president moved forward with optimism and a rather substantial amount of corporate money to purchase full ownership of the boatyard, which had lost rather significant amounts of money each of the five prior years and had never reported a profit for the original owners.

Not surprisingly, the boatyard continued to lose money after Amazing Chemical purchased it, and the losses grew larger each month. Amazing Chemical, a very profitable chemical company, reported net income of $780,000 in 20X2 and $850,000 in 20X3 even though the boatyard reported net losses of $160,000 in 20X2 and $210,000 in 20X3 and was fully consolidated.

Required

Amazing Chemical's chief accountant has become concerned that members of the board of directors or company shareholders will accuse him of improperly preparing the consolidated statements. The president does not plan to tell anyone about the losses, which do not show up in the consolidated income statement that the chief accountant prepared. You have been asked to prepare a memo to the chief accountant indicating the way to include subsidiaries in the consolidated income statement and to provide citations to or quotations from the Accounting Standards Codification that would assist the chief accountant in dealing with this matter. You have also been asked to search the accounting literature to see whether any reporting requirements require disclosure of the boatyard in notes to the financial statements or in management's discussion and analysis.

EXERCISES

LO 2-2, 2-3   **E2-1**   **Multiple-Choice Questions on Use of Cost and Equity Methods [AICPA Adapted]**
Select the correct answer for each of the following questions.

1. Peel Company received a cash dividend from a common stock investment. Should Peel report an **increase** in the investment account if it uses the cost method or equity method of accounting?

	Cost	Equity
a.	No	No
b.	Yes	Yes
c.	Yes	No
d.	No	Yes

2. In 20X0, Neil Company held the following investments in common stock:

   - 25,000 shares of B&K Inc.'s 100,000 outstanding shares. Neil's level of ownership gives it the ability to exercise significant influence over the financial and operating policies of B&K.

   - 6,000 shares of Amal Corporation's 309,000 outstanding shares.

   During 20X0, Neil received the following distributions from its common stock investments:

November 6	$30,000 cash dividend from B&K
November 11	$1,500 cash dividend from Amal
December 26	3 percent common stock dividend from Amal
	The closing price of this stock was $115 per share.

   What amount of dividend revenue should Neil report for 20X0?
   a. $1,500.
   b. $4,200.
   c. $31,500.
   d. $34,200.

3. An investor uses the equity method to account for an investment in common stock. Assume that (1) the investor owns more than 50 percent of the outstanding common stock of the investee, (2) the investee company reports net income and declares dividends during the year, and (3) the investee's net income is more than the dividends it declares. How would the investor's investment in the common stock of the investee company under the equity method differ at year-end from what it would have been if the investor had accounted for the investment under the cost method?

   a. The balance under the equity method is higher than it would have been under the cost method.
   b. The balance under the equity method is lower than it would have been under the cost method.
   c. The balance under the equity method is higher than it would have been under the cost method, but only if the investee company actually paid the dividends before year-end.
   d. The balance under the equity method is lower than it would have been under the cost method, but only if the investee company actually paid the dividends before year-end.

4. A corporation exercises significant influence over an affiliate in which it holds a 40 percent common stock interest. If its affiliate completed a fiscal year profitably but paid no dividends, how would this affect the investor corporation?

   a. Result in an increased current ratio.
   b. Result in increased earnings per share.
   c. Increase asset turnover ratios.
   d. Decrease book value per share.

5. An investor in common stock received dividends in excess of the investor's share of investee's earnings subsequent to the date of the investment. How will the investor's investment account be affected by those dividends under each of the following methods?

	Cost Method	Equity Method
a.	No effect	No effect
b.	Decrease	No effect
c.	No effect	Decrease
d.	Decrease	Decrease

6. An investor uses the cost method to account for an investment in common stock. A portion of the dividends received this year was in excess of the investor's share of the investee's earnings subsequent to the date of investment. The amount of dividend revenue that should be reported in the investor's income statement for this year would be

   a. Zero.

   b. The total amount of dividends received this year.

   c. The portion of the dividends received this year that was in excess of the investor's share of investee's earnings subsequent to the date of investment.

   d. The portion of the dividends received this year that was not in excess of the investor's share of the investee's earnings subsequent to the date of investment.

LO 2-4

E2-2 Multiple-Choice Questions on Intercorporate Investments

Select the correct answer for each of the following questions.

1. Companies often acquire ownership in other companies using a variety of ownership arrangements. The investor should use equity-method reporting whenever

   a. The investor purchases voting common stock of the investee.

   b. The investor has significant influence over the operating and financing decisions of the investee.

   c. The investor purchases goods and services from the investee.

   d. When there is no differential included in an investment, the carrying value of the investment is less than the market value of the investee's shares held by the investor.

2. The carrying amount of an investment in stock correctly accounted for under the equity method is equal to

   a. The original price paid to purchase the investment.

   b. The original price paid to purchase the investment plus cumulative net income plus cumulative dividends declared by the investee since the date the investment was acquired.

   c. The original price paid to purchase the investment plus cumulative net income minus cumulative dividends declared by the investee since the date the investment was acquired.

   d. The original price paid to purchase the investment minus cumulative net income minus cumulative dividends declared by the investee since the date the investment was acquired.

LO 2-3

E2-3 Multiple-Choice Questions on Applying Equity Method [AICPA Adapted]

Select the correct answer for each of the following questions.

1. On January 2, 20X3, Kean Company purchased a 30 percent interest in Pod Company for $250,000. Pod reported net income of $100,000 for 20X3 and declared and paid a dividend of $10,000. Kean accounts for this investment using the equity method. In its December 31, 20X3, balance sheet, what amount should Kean report as its investment in Pod?

   a. $160,000.

   b. $223,000.

   c. $340,000.

   d. $277,000.

2. On January 1, 20X8, Mega Corporation acquired 10 percent of the outstanding voting stock of Penny Inc. On January 2, 20X9, Mega gained the ability to exercise significant influence over Penny's financial and operating decisions by acquiring an additional 20 percent of Penny's outstanding stock. The two purchases were made at prices proportionate to the value assigned to Penny's net assets, which equaled their carrying amounts. For the years ended December 31, 20X8 and 20X9, Penny reported the following:

	20X8	20X9
Dividends Paid	$200,000	$300,000
Net Income	600,000	650,000

In 20X9, what amounts should Mega report as current year investment income and as an adjustment, before income taxes, to 20X8 investment income?

	20X9 Investment Income	Adjustment to 20X8 Investment Income
a.	$195,000	$160,000
b.	195,000	100,000
c.	195,000	40,000
d.	105,000	40,000

3. Investor Inc. owns 40 percent of Alimand Corporation. During the calendar year 20X5, Alimand had net earnings of $100,000 and paid dividends of $10,000. Investor mistakenly recorded these transactions using the cost method rather than the equity method of accounting. What effect would this have on the investment account, net earnings, and retained earnings, respectively?

   a. Understate, overstate, overstate.
   b. Overstate, understate, understate.
   c. Overstate, overstate, overstate.
   d. Understate, understate, understate.

4. A corporation using the equity method of accounting for its investment in a 40 percent–owned investee, which earned $20,000 and paid $5,000 in dividends, made the following entries:

| Investment in Investee | 8,000 | |
| Income from Investee | | 8,000 |

| Cash | 2,000 | |
| Dividend Revenue | | 2,000 |

What effect will these entries have on the investor's statement of financial position?

   a. Financial position will be fairly stated.
   b. Investment in the investee will be overstated, retained earnings understated.
   c. Investment in the investee will be understated, retained earnings understated.
   d. Investment in the investee will be overstated, retained earnings overstated.

LO 2-4

E2-4   Cost versus Equity Reporting

Winston Corporation purchased 40 percent of the stock of Fullbright Company on January 1, 20X2, at underlying book value. The companies reported the following operating results and dividend payments during the first three years of intercorporate ownership:

	Winston Corporation		Fullbright Company	
Year	Operating Income	Dividends	Net Income	Dividends
20X2	$100,000	$ 40,000	$70,000	$30,000
20X3	60,000	80,000	40,000	60,000
20X4	250,000	120,000	25,000	50,000

Required

Compute the net income reported by Winston for each of the three years, assuming it accounts for its investment in Fullbright using (*a*) the cost method and (*b*) the equity method.

LO 2-2, 2-3   **E2-5**   ## Acquisition Price

Phillips Company bought 40 percent ownership in Jones Bag Company on January 1, 20X1, at underlying book value. In 20X1, 20X2, and 20X3, Jones Bag reported the following:

Year	Net Income	Dividends
20X1	$ 8,000	$15,000
20X2	12,000	10,000
20X3	20,000	10,000

The balance in Phillips Company's investment account on December 31, 20X3, was $54,000.

Required

In each of the following independent cases, determine the amount that Phillips paid for its investment in Jones Bag stock assuming that Phillips accounted for its investment using the (*a*) cost method and (*b*) equity method.

LO 2-2, 2-3   **E2-6**   ## Investment Income

Advanced
StudyGuide
.com

Ravine Corporation purchased 30 percent ownership of Valley Industries for $90,000 on January 1, 20X6, when Valley had capital stock of $240,000 and retained earnings of $60,000. The following data were reported by the companies for the years 20X6 through 20X9:

	Operating Income,	Net Income,	Dividends Declared	
Year	Ravine Corporation	Valley Industries	Ravine	Valley
20X6	$140,000	$30,000	$ 70,000	$20,000
20X7	80,000	50,000	70,000	40,000
20X8	220,000	10,000	90,000	40,000
20X9	160,000	40,000	100,000	20,000

Required

a. What net income would Ravine Corporation have reported for each of the years, assuming Ravine accounts for the intercorporate investment using (1) the cost method and (2) the equity method?

b. Give all appropriate journal entries for 20X8 that Ravine made under both the cost and the equity methods.

LO 2-3   **E2-7**   ## Investment Value

Port Company purchased 30,000 of the 100,000 outstanding shares of Sund Company common stock on January 1, 20X2, for $180,000. The purchase price was equal to the book value of the shares purchased. Sund reported the following:

Year	Net Income	Dividends
20X2	$40,000	$25,000
20X3	30,000	
20X4	5,000	

Required

Compute the amounts Port Company should report as the carrying values of its investment in Sund Company at December 31, 20X2, 20X3, and 20X4.

LO 2-2, 2-3   **E2-8A**   **Income Reporting**

Grandview Company purchased 40 percent of the stock of Spinet Corporation on January 1, 20X8, at underlying book value. Spinet recorded the following income for 20X9:

Income before Extraordinary Gain	$60,000
Extraordinary Gain	30,000
Net Income	$90,000

Required

Prepare all journal entries on Grandview's books for 20X9 to account for its investment in Spinet.

LO 2-4, 2-5   **E2-9**   **Fair Value Method**

Small Company reported 20X7 net income of $40,000 and paid dividends of $15,000 during the year. Mock Corporation acquired 20 percent of Small's shares on January 1, 20X7, for $105,000. At December 31, 20X7, Mock determined the fair value of the shares of Small to be $121,000. Mock reported operating income of $90,000 for 20X7.

Required

Compute Mock's net income for 20X7 assuming it uses

a. The cost method in accounting for its investment in Small.

b. The equity method in accounting for its investment in Small.

c. The fair value method in accounting for its investment in Small.

LO 2-3, 2-5   **E2-10**   **Fair Value Recognition**

Kent Company purchased 35 percent ownership of Lomm Company on January 1, 20X8, for $140,000. Lomm reported 20X8 net income of $80,000 and paid dividends of $20,000. At December 31, 20X8, Kent determined the fair value of its investment in Lomm to be $174,000.

Required

Give all journal entries recorded by Kent with respect to its investment in Lomm in 20X8 assuming it uses

a. The equity method.

b. The fair value method.

LO 2-3, 2-5   **E2-11A**   **Investee with Preferred Stock Outstanding**

Reden Corporation purchased 45 percent of Montgomery Company's common stock on January 1, 20X9, at underlying book value of $288,000. Montgomery's balance sheet contained the following stockholders' equity balances:

Preferred Stock ($5 par value, 50,000 shares issued and outstanding)	$250,000
Common Stock ($1 par value, 150,000 shares issued and outstanding)	150,000
Additional Paid-In Capital	180,000
Retained Earnings	310,000
Total Stockholders' Equity	$890,000

Montgomery's preferred stock is cumulative and pays a 10 percent annual dividend. Montgomery reported net income of $95,000 for 20X9 and paid total dividends of $40,000.

Required

Give the journal entries recorded by Reden Corporation for 20X9 related to its investment in Montgomery Company common stock.

LO 2-2, 2-3 **E2-12A** **Other Comprehensive Income Reported by Investee**

Callas Corporation paid $380,000 to acquire 40 percent ownership of Thinbill Company on January 1, 20X9. The amount paid was equal to Thinbill's underlying book value. During 20X9, Thinbill reported operating income of $45,000 and an increase of $20,000 in the market value of available-for-sale securities held for the year. Thinbill paid dividends of $9,000 on December 10, 20X9.

Required

Give all journal entries that Callas Corporation recorded in 20X9, including closing entries at December 31, 20X9, associated with its investment in Thinbill Company.

LO 2-2, 2-3 **E2-13A** **Other Comprehensive Income Reported by Investee**

Advanced
StudyGuide
.com

Baldwin Corporation purchased 25 percent of Gwin Company's common stock on January 1, 20X8, at underlying book value. In 20X8, Gwin reported a net loss of $20,000 and paid dividends of $10,000, and in 20X9, The company reported net income of $68,000 and paid dividends of $16,000. Gwin also purchased marketable securities classified as available-for-sale on February 8, 20X9, and reported an increase of $12,000 in their fair value at December 31, 20X9. Baldwin reported a balance of $67,000 in its investment in Gwin at December 31, 20X9.

Required

Compute the amount paid by Baldwin Corporation to purchase the shares of Gwin Company.

LO 2-7 **E2-14** **Basic Consolidation Entry**

On December 31, 20X3, Broadway Corporation reported common stock outstanding of $200,000, additional paid-in capital of $300,000, and retained earnings of $100,000. On January 1, 20X4, Johe Company acquired control of Broadway in a business combination.

Required

Give the consolidation entry that would be needed in preparing a consolidated balance sheet immediately following the combination if Johe acquired all of Broadway's outstanding common stock for $600,000.

LO 2-6, 2-7 **E2-15** **Balance Sheet Worksheet**

Blank Corporation acquired 100 percent of Faith Corporation's common stock on December 31, 20X2, for $150,000. Data from the balance sheets of the two companies included the following amounts as of the date of acquisition:

Item	Blank Corporation	Faith Corporation
Cash	$ 65,000	$ 18,000
Accounts Receivable	87,000	37,000
Inventory	110,000	60,000
Buildings & Equipment (net)	220,000	150,000
Investment in Faith Corporation Stock	150,000	
Total Assets	$632,000	$265,000
Accounts Payable	$ 92,000	$ 35,000
Notes Payable	150,000	80,000
Common Stock	100,000	60,000
Retained Earnings	290,000	90,000
Total Liabilities & Stockholders' Equity	$632,000	$265,000

At the date of the business combination, the book values of Faith's net assets and liabilities approximated fair value. Assume that Faith Corporation's accumulated depreciation on buildings and equipment on the acquisition date was $30,000.

Advanced Financial Accounting, 11th Edition **93**

Chapter 2 *Reporting Intercorporate Investments and Consolidation of Wholly Owned Subsidiaries with No Differential* **93**

Required

a. Give the consolidation entry or entries needed to prepare a consolidated balance sheet immediately following the business combination.

b. Prepare a consolidated balance sheet worksheet.

LO 2-3, 2-7 **E2-16** ### Consolidation Entries for Wholly Owned Subsidiary

Trim Corporation acquired 100 percent of Round Corporation's voting common stock on January 1, 20X2, for $400,000. At that date, the book values and fair values of Round's assets and liabilities were equal. Round reported the following summarized balance sheet data:

Assets	$700,000	Accounts Payable	$100,000
		Bonds Payable	200,000
		Common Stock	120,000
		Retained Earnings	280,000
Total	$700,000	Total	$700,000

Round reported net income of $80,000 for 20X2 and paid dividends of $25,000.

Required

a. Give the journal entries recorded by Trim Corporation during 20X2 on its books if Trim accounts for its investment in Round using the equity method.

b. Give the consolidation entries needed at December 31, 20X2, to prepare consolidated financial statements.

LO 2-3, 2-7 **E2-17** ### Basic Consolidation Entries for Fully Owned Subsidiary

Amber Corporation reported the following summarized balance sheet data on December 31, 20X6:

Assets	$600,000	Liabilities	$100,000
		Common Stock	300,000
		Retained Earnings	200,000
Total	$600,000	Total	$600,000

On January 1, 20X7, Purple Company acquired 100 percent of Amber's stock for $500,000. At the acquisition date, the book values and fair values of Amber's assets and liabilities were equal. Amber reported net income of $50,000 for 20X7 and paid dividends of $20,000.

Required

a. Give the journal entries recorded by Purple on its books during 20X7 if it accounts for its investment in Amber using the equity method.

b. Give the consolidation entries needed on December 31, 20X7, to prepare consolidated financial statements.

PROBLEMS

LO 2-2, 2-3 **P2-18** ### Retroactive Recognition

Idle Corporation has been acquiring shares of Fast Track Enterprises at book value for the last several years. Fast Track provided data including the following:

	20X2	20X3	20X4	20X5
Net Income	$40,000	$60,000	$40,000	$50,000
Dividends	20,000	20,000	10,000	20,000

Fast Track declares and pays its annual dividend on November 15 each year. Its net book value on January 1, 20X2, was $250,000. Idle purchased shares of Fast Track on three occasions:

Date	Percent of Ownership Purchased	Amount Paid
January 1, 20X2	10%	$25,000
July 1, 20X3	5	15,000
January 1, 20X5	10	34,000

Required

Give the journal entries to be recorded on Idle's books in 20X5 related to its investment in Fast Track.

Advanced
StudyGuide
.com

LO 2-4, 2-5   **P2-19**   **Fair Value Method**

Gant Company purchased 20 percent of the outstanding shares of Temp Company for $70,000 on January 1, 20X6. The following results are reported for Temp Company:

	20X6	20X7	20X8
Net Income	$40,000	$35,000	$60,000
Dividends Paid	15,000	30,000	20,000
Fair Value of Shares Held by Gant:			
January 1	70,000	89,000	86,000
December 31	89,000	86,000	97,000

Required

Determine the amounts reported by Gant as income from its investment in Temp for each year and the balance in Gant's investment in Temp at the end of each year assuming that Gant uses the following methods in accounting for its investment in Temp:

a. Cost method.

b. Equity method.

c. Fair value method.

LO 2-5   **P2-20**   **Fair Value Journal Entries**

Marlow Company acquired 40 percent of the voting shares of Brown Company on January 1, 20X8, for $85,000. The following results are reported for Brown Company:

	20X8	20X9
Net Income	$20,000	$30,000
Dividends Paid	10,000	15,000
Fair Value of Shares Held by Marlow:		
January 1	85,000	97,000
December 31	97,000	92,000

Required

Give all journal entries recorded by Marlow for 20X8 and 20X9 assuming that it uses the fair value method in accounting for its investment in Brown.

LO 2-5   **P2-21A**   **Other Comprehensive Income Reported by Investee**

Dewey Corporation owns 30 percent of the common stock of Jimm Company, which it purchased at underlying book value on January 1, 20X5. Dewey reported a balance of $245,000 for its investment in Jimm Company on January 1, 20X5, and $276,800 at December 31, 20X5. During 20X5, Dewey and Jimm Company reported operating income of $340,000 and $70,000, respectively. Jimm received dividends from investments in marketable equity securities in the amount of $7,000 during 20X5. It also reported an increase of $18,000 in the market value of its portfolio of trading securities and an increase in the value of its portfolio of securities classified as available-for-sale. Jimm paid dividends of $20,000 in 20X5. Ignore income taxes in determining your solution.

Required

a. Assuming that Dewey uses the equity method in accounting for its investment in Jimm, compute the amount of income from Jimm recorded by Dewey in 20X5.

b. Compute the amount reported by Jimm as other comprehensive income in 20X5.

c. If all of Jimm's other comprehensive income arose solely from its investment in available-for-sale securities purchased on March 10, 20X5, for $130,000, what was the market value of those securities at December 31, 20X5?

LO 2-3, 2-7   **P2-22A   Equity-Method Income Statement**

Wealthy Manufacturing Company purchased 40 percent of the voting shares of Diversified Products Corporation on March 23, 20X4. On December 31, 20X8, Wealthy Manufacturing's controller attempted to prepare income statements and retained earnings statements for the two companies using the following summarized 20X8 data:

	Wealthy Manufacturing	Diversified Products
Net Sales	$850,000	$400,000
Cost of Goods Sold	670,000	320,000
Other Expenses	90,000	25,000
Dividends Declared & Paid	30,000	10,000
Retained Earnings, 1/1/X8	420,000	260,000

Wealthy Manufacturing uses the equity method in accounting for its investment in Diversified Products. The controller was also aware of the following specific transactions for Diversified Products in 20X8, which were not included in the preceding data:

1. On June 30, 20X8, Diversified incurred a $5,000 extraordinary loss from a volcanic eruption near its Greenland facility.

2. Diversified sold its entire Health Technologies division on September 30, 20X8, for $375,000. The book value of Health Technologies division's net assets on that date was $331,000. The division incurred an operating loss of $15,000 in the first nine months of 20X8.

3. During 20X8, Diversified sold one of its delivery trucks after it was involved in an accident and recorded a gain of $10,000.

Required

a. Prepare an income statement and retained earnings statement for Diversified Products for 20X8.

b. Prepare an income statement and retained earnings statement for Wealthy Manufacturing for 20X8.

LO 2-3, 2-6, 2-7   **P2-23   Consolidated Worksheet at End of the First Year of Ownership (Equity Method)**

Peanut Company acquired 100 percent of Snoopy Company's outstanding common stock for $300,000 on January 1, 20X8, when the book value of Snoopy's net assets was equal to $300,000. Peanut uses the equity method to account for investments. Trial balance data for Peanut and Snoopy as of December 31, 20X8, are as follows:

Advanced
StudyGuide
.com

	Peanut Company		Snoopy Company	
	Debit	Credit	Debit	Credit
Cash	$ 130,000		$ 80,000	
Accounts Receivable	165,000		65,000	
Inventory	200,000		75,000	
Investment in Snoopy Stock	355,000		0	
Land	200,000		100,000	
Buildings & Equipment	700,000		200,000	
Cost of Goods Sold	200,000		125,000	
Depreciation Expense	50,000		10,000	
S&A Expense	225,000		40,000	
Dividends Declared	100,000		20,000	
Accumulated Depreciation		$ 450,000		$ 20,000
Accounts Payable		75,000		60,000
Bonds Payable		200,000		85,000
Common Stock		500,000		200,000
Retained Earnings		225,000		100,000
Sales		800,000		250,000
Income from Snoopy		75,000		0
Total	$2,325,000	$2,325,000	$715,000	$715,000

Required

a. Prepare the journal entries on Peanut's books for the acquisition of Snoopy on January 1, 20X8, as well as any normal equity-method entry(ies) related to the investment in Snoopy Company during 20X8.

b. Prepare a consolidation worksheet for 20X8 in good form.

LO 2-3, 2-6, 2-7   **P2-24**   **Consolidated Worksheet at End of the Second Year of Ownership (Equity Method)**
Peanut Company acquired 100 percent of Snoopy Company's outstanding common stock for $300,000 on January 1, 20X8, when the book value of Snoopy's net assets was equal to $300,000. Problem 2-23 summarizes the first year of Peanut's ownership of Snoopy. Peanut uses the equity method to account for investments. The following trial balance summarizes the financial position and operations for Peanut and Snoopy as of December 31, 20X9:

Advanced
StudyGuide
.com

	Peanut Company		Snoopy Company	
	Debit	Credit	Debit	Credit
Cash	$ 230,000		$ 75,000	
Accounts Receivable	190,000		80,000	
Inventory	180,000		100,000	
Investment in Snoopy Stock	405,000		0	
Land	200,000		100,000	
Buildings & Equipment	700,000		200,000	
Cost of Goods Sold	270,000		150,000	
Depreciation Expense	50,000		10,000	
Selling & Administrative Expense	230,000		60,000	
Dividends Declared	225,000		30,000	
Accumulated Depreciation		$ 500,000		$ 30,000
Accounts Payable		75,000		35,000
Bonds Payable		150,000		85,000
Common Stock		500,000		200,000
Retained Earnings		525,000		155,000
Sales		850,000		300,000
Income from Snoopy		80,000		0
Total	$2,680,000	$2,680,000	$805,000	$805,000

Required

a. Prepare any equity-method journal entry(ies) related to the investment in Snoopy Company during 20X9.

b. Prepare a consolidation worksheet for 20X9 in good form.

LO 2-3, 2-6, 2-7

P2-25 **Consolidated Worksheet at End of the First Year of Ownership (Equity Method)**

Paper Company acquired 100 percent of Scissor Company's outstanding common stock for $370,000 on January 1, 20X8, when the book value of Scissor's net assets was equal to $370,000. Paper uses the equity method to account for investments. Trial balance data for Paper and Scissor as of December 31, 20X8, are as follows:

	Paper Company		Scissor Company	
	Debit	**Credit**	**Debit**	**Credit**
Cash	$ 122,000		$ 46,000	
Accounts Receivable	140,000		60,000	
Inventory	190,000		120,000	
Investment in Scissor Stock	438,000		0	
Land	250,000		125,000	
Buildings & Equipment	875,000		250,000	
Cost of Goods Sold	250,000		155,000	
Depreciation Expense	65,000		12,000	
Selling & Administrative Expense	280,000		50,000	
Dividends Declared	80,000		25,000	
Accumulated Depreciation		$ 565,000		$ 36,000
Accounts Payable		77,000		27,000
Bonds Payable		250,000		100,000
Common Stock		625,000		250,000
Retained Earnings		280,000		120,000
Sales		800,000		310,000
Income from Scissor		93,000		0
Total	$2,690,000	$2,690,000	$843,000	$843,000

Required

a. Prepare the journal entries on Paper's books for the acquisition of Scissor on January 1, 20X8 as well as any normal equity-method entry(ies) related to the investment in Scissor Company during 20X8.

b. Prepare a consolidation worksheet for 20X8 in good form.

LO 2-3, 2-6, 2-7

P2-26 **Consolidated Worksheet at End of the Second Year of Ownership (Equity Method)**

Paper Company acquired 100 percent of Scissor Company's outstanding common stock for $370,000 on January 1, 20X8, when the book value of Scissor's net assets was equal to $370,000. Problem 2-25 summarizes the first year of Paper's ownership of Scissor. Paper uses the equity method to account for investments. The following trial balance summarizes the financial position and operations for Paper and Scissor as of December 31, 20X9:

	Paper Company		Scissor Company	
	Debit	**Credit**	**Debit**	**Credit**
Cash	$232,000		$116,000	
Accounts Receivable	165,000		97,000	
Inventory	193,000		115,000	
Investment in Scissor Stock	515,000		0	
Land	250,000		125,000	
Buildings & Equipment	875,000		250,000	
Cost of Goods Sold	$278,000		$178,000	
Depreciation Expense	65,000		12,000	
Selling & Administrative Expense	312,000		58,000	
Dividends Declared	90,000		30,000	

(continued)

Accumulated Depreciation		$ 630,000		$ 48,000
Accounts Payable		85,000		40,000
Bonds Payable		150,000		100,000
Common Stock		625,000		250,000
Retained Earnings		498,000		188,000
Sales		880,000		355,000
Income from Scissor		107,000		0
Total		$2,975,000	$2,975,000	$981,000	$981,000

Required

a. Prepare any equity-method journal entry(ies) related to the investment in Scissor Company during 20X9.

b. Prepare a consolidation worksheet for 20X9 in good form.

LO 2-2, 2-6, 2-7 **P2-27B** **Consolidated Worksheet at End of the First Year of Ownership (Cost Method)**

Peanut Company acquired 100 percent of Snoopy Company's outstanding common stock for $300,000 on January 1, 20X8, when the book value of Snoopy's net assets was equal to $300,000. Peanut uses the cost method to account for investments. Trial balance data for Peanut and Snoopy as of December 31, 20X8, are as follows:

	Peanut Company		Snoopy Company	
	Debit	**Credit**	**Debit**	**Credit**
Cash	$ 130,000		$ 80,000	
Accounts Receivable	165,000		65,000	
Inventory	200,000		75,000	
Investment in Snoopy Stock	300,000		0	
Land	200,000		100,000	
Buildings & Equipment	700,000		200,000	
Cost of Goods Sold	200,000		125,000	
Depreciation Expense	50,000		10,000	
Selling & Administrative Expense	225,000		40,000	
Dividends Declared	100,000		20,000	
Accumulated Depreciation		$ 450,000		$ 20,000
Accounts Payable		75,000		60,000
Bonds Payable		200,000		85,000
Common Stock		500,000		200,000
Retained Earnings		225,000		100,000
Sales		800,000		250,000
Dividend Income		20,000		0
Total	$2,270,000	$2,270,000	$715,000	$715,000

Required

a. Prepare the journal entries on Peanut's books for the acquisition of Snoopy on January 1, 20X8 as well as any normal cost-method entry(ies) related to the investment in Snoopy Company during 20X8.

b. Prepare a consolidation worksheet for 20X8 in good form.

LO 2-2, 2-6, 2-7 **P2-28B** **Consolidated Worksheet at End of the Second Year of Ownership (Cost Method)**

Peanut Company acquired 100 percent of Snoopy Company's outstanding common stock for $300,000 on January 1, 20X8, when the book value of Snoopy's net assets was equal to $300,000.

Problem 2-27 summarizes the first year of Peanut's ownership of Snoopy. Peanut uses the cost method to account for investments. The following trial balance summarizes the financial position and operations for Peanut and Snoopy as of December 31, 20X9:

	Peanut Company		Snoopy Company	
	Debit	Credit	Debit	Credit
Cash	$ 230,000		$ 75,000	
Accounts Receivable	190,000		80,000	
Inventory	180,000		100,000	
Investment in Snoopy Stock	300,000		0	
Land	200,000		100,000	
Buildings & Equipment	700,000		200,000	
Cost of Goods Sold	270,000		150,000	
Depreciation Expense	50,000		10,000	
Selling & Administrative Expense	230,000		60,000	
Dividends Declared	225,000		30,000	
Accumulated Depreciation		$ 500,000		$ 30,000
Accounts Payable		75,000		35,000
Bonds Payable		150,000		85,000
Common Stock		500,000		200,000
Retained Earnings		470,000		155,000
Sales		850,000		300,000
Dividend Income		30,000		0
Total	$2,575,000	$2,575,000	$805,000	$805,000

Required

a. Prepare any cost-method journal entry(ies) related to the investment in Snoopy Company during 20X9.

b. Prepare a consolidation worksheet for 20X9 in good form.

KAPLAN CPA REVIEW

Kaplan CPA Review Simulation on Comprehensive Consolidation Procedures

Please visit the *Connect Library* for the online Kaplan CPA Review task-based simulation.

Situation

For each parent–subsidiary relationship, determine the proper accounting treatment.

Topics Covered in the Simulation

a. Consolidation requirements.

b. Consolidation exceptions.

3

The Reporting Entity and the Consolidation of Less-than-Wholly-Owned Subsidiaries with No Differential

Multicorporate Entities

Business Combinations

Consolidation Concepts and Procedures

Intercompany Transfers

Additional Consolidation Issues

Multinational Entities

Reporting Requirements

Partnerships

Governmental and Not-for-Profit Entities

Corporations in Financial Difficulty

THE COLLAPSE OF ENRON AND THE BIRTH OF A NEW PARADIGM

In February 2001, *Fortune* magazine named Enron the most innovative company in America for the sixth year in a row. Ten months later on December 2, 2001, Enron filed for bankruptcy. At that time, it was the largest bankruptcy in history. What was the cause of this drastic turnaround? Did Enron just throw in the towel after six years of "innovation" and decide to call it quits? Sadly, this was not the case; something much more serious caused Enron's historic fall.

Enron came into being in 1985 when InterNorth acquired Houston Natural Gas. Originally, the company was headquartered in Omaha, but shortly after Kenneth Lay took over as CEO of the company, he moved its headquarters to Houston. Enron was originally in the business of transmitting electricity and natural gas throughout the United States, which it accomplished through its extensive network of pipelines and power plants. These types of services made up the bulk of Enron's revenues until management decided to branch out. In 1990, Enron began to serve as an intermediary for gas contracts.

Energy and gas prices have traditionally been extremely volatile. Companies didn't want to sign long-term contracts because of the large fluctuations in these prices. Enron would buy 30-day gas contracts from a variety of suppliers and then bundle these contracts to offer long-term prices to local utility companies. Basically, Enron accepted the price risk in exchange for a fee. Over time, the wholesale trading of energy contracts became an increasingly important part of Enron's business, as illustrated in the figure on the next page. For the 2000 fiscal year, Enron reported revenues of $93 billion from these "wholesale" activities and only $2.7 billion from its traditional piping business.

Even with these extreme revenues, Enron was forced to file for bankruptcy at the end of 2001. How did this happen? Enron used two clever accounting tricks to inflate its performance. First, managers used special-purpose entities (SPEs) to hide losses and move liabilities and impaired assets off Enron's books. We discuss SPEs in detail in this chapter. Second, Enron "grossed up" its revenues to make its performance look better than it actually was. That is, Enron reported the total value of the trades it facilitated, not just its fee for its wholesale services.

Enron

As a result of Enron's bankruptcy and the demise of its auditor, Arthur Andersen, more than 100,000 jobs were lost along with billions of dollars of investors' money. Accounting policies can have a significant influence on the economy. As Enron illustrated, careful manipulation of even a few simple rules can have catastrophic effects on individuals and on the global economy. This chapter introduces accounting rules (resulting from this and other accounting scandals) for determining when a business entity must be consolidated. It also explores how the basic consolidation process differs when a subsidiary is only partially owned instead of wholly owned as discussed in Chapter 2.

LEARNING OBJECTIVES

When you finish studying this chapter, you should be able to:

LO 3-1 Understand and explain the usefulness and limitations of consolidated financial statements.

LO 3-2 Understand and explain how direct and indirect control influence the consolidation of a subsidiary.

LO 3-3 Understand and explain differences in the consolidation process when the subsidiary is not wholly owned.

LO 3-4 Make calculations for the consolidation of a less-than-wholly-owned subsidiary.

LO 3-5 Prepare a consolidation worksheet for a less-than-wholly-owned subsidiary.

LO 3-6 Understand and explain the purpose of combined financial statements and how they differ from consolidated financial statements.

LO 3-7 Understand and explain rules related to the consolidation of variable interest entities.

LO 3-8 Understand and explain differences in consolidation rules under U.S. GAAP and IFRS.

THE USEFULNESS OF CONSOLIDATED FINANCIAL STATEMENTS

LO 3-1

Understand and explain the usefulness and limitations of consolidated financial statements.

Chapter 2 provides an introduction to the consolidation process and introduces an example of a basic consolidation. This chapter expands the consolidation discussion by exploring more complex situations in which the parent company does not have complete ownership of the subsidiary. Companies provide consolidated financial statements primarily for parties having a long-run interest in the parent company, including the parent's shareholders, creditors, and other resource providers. Consolidated statements often provide the only means of obtaining a clear picture of the total resources of the combined entity that are under the parent's control and the results of employing those resources. Especially when the number of related companies is substantial, consolidated statements are the only way to conveniently summarize the vast amount of information relating to the individual companies and how the financial positions and operations of these companies affect the overall consolidated entity.

Current and prospective stockholders of the parent company are usually more interested in the consolidated financial statements than those of the individual companies because the well-being of the parent company is affected by its subsidiaries' operations. When subsidiaries are profitable, profits accrue to the parent. However, the parent cannot escape the ill effects of unprofitable subsidiaries. By examining the consolidated statements, owners and potential owners are better able to assess how effectively management employs all the resources under its control.

The parent's long-term creditors also find the consolidated statements useful because the effects of subsidiary operations on the overall health and future of the parent are relevant to their decisions. In addition, although the parent and its subsidiaries are separate companies, the parent's creditors have an indirect claim on the subsidiaries' assets.

The parent company's management has a continuing need for current information about the combined operations of the consolidated entity in addition to details about the individual companies forming the consolidated entity. For example, some of the individual subsidiaries might have substantial volatility in their operations. As a result, the manager may not be able to fully understand the overall impact of the activities for the period until the operating results and balance sheets are combined into consolidated financial statements. On the other hand, information about individual companies within the consolidated entity also may be useful. For example, it may allow a manager to offset a cash shortfall in one subsidiary with excess cash from another without resorting to costly outside borrowing. The parent company's management may be particularly concerned with the consolidated financial statements because top management generally is evaluated, and sometimes compensated, based on the overall performance of the entity as reflected in the consolidated statements.

LIMITATIONS OF CONSOLIDATED FINANCIAL STATEMENTS

Although consolidated financial statements are useful, their limitations also must be kept in mind. Some information is lost any time data sets are aggregated; this is particularly true when the information involves an aggregation across companies that have substantially different operating characteristics. Some of the more important limitations of consolidated financial statements are:

1. *The masking of poor performance:* Because the operating results and financial position of individual companies included in the consolidation are not disclosed, the poor performance or financial position of one or more companies may be hidden by the good performance and financial position of others.

2. *Limited availability of resources:* Not all of the consolidated retained earnings balance is necessarily available for dividends of the parent because a portion may represent the parent's share of undistributed subsidiary earnings. Similarly, because

Advanced Financial Accounting, 11th Edition   **103**

Chapter 3   *The Reporting Entity and the Consolidation of Less-than-Wholly-Owned Subsidiaries with No Differential*   **103**

the consolidated statements include the subsidiary's assets, not all assets shown are available for dividend distributions of the parent company.

3. *Unrepresentative combined financial ratios:* Because financial ratios based on the consolidated statements are calculated on aggregated information, they are not necessarily representative of any single company in the consolidation, including the parent.

4. *A lack of uniformity:* Similar accounts of different companies that are combined in the consolidation may not be entirely comparable. For example, the length of operating cycles of different companies may vary, causing receivables of similar length to be classified differently.

5. *The lack of detailed disclosures:* Additional information about individual companies or groups of companies included in the consolidation often is necessary for a fair presentation; such additional disclosures may require voluminous footnotes.

SUBSIDIARY FINANCIAL STATEMENTS

Some financial statement users may be interested in the separate financial statements of individual subsidiaries, either instead of or in addition to consolidated financial statements. Although the parent company's management is concerned with the entire consolidated entity as well as individual subsidiaries, the creditors, preferred stockholders, and noncontrolling common stockholders of subsidiary companies are most interested in the separate financial statements of the subsidiaries in which they have an interest. Because subsidiaries are legally separate from their parents, a subsidiary's creditors and stockholders generally have no claim on the parent and the subsidiary's stockholders do not share in the parent's profits unless the parent has provided guarantees or entered into other arrangements for the benefit of the subsidiaries. Therefore, consolidated financial statements usually are of little use to those interested in obtaining information about the assets, capital, or income of individual subsidiaries.

CONSOLIDATED FINANCIAL STATEMENTS: CONCEPTS AND STANDARDS

LO 3-2

Understand and explain how direct and indirect control influence the consolidation of a subsidiary.

Consolidated financial statements are intended to provide a meaningful representation of the overall financial position and activities of a single economic entity comprising a number of related companies. Under current standards, subsidiaries must be consolidated unless the parent is precluded from exercising control. When it is not appropriate to consolidate a subsidiary, it is reported as an intercompany investment (**ASC 810-10-10, 15, 25**).

Traditional View of Control

Over the years, the concept of control has been the single most important criterion for determining when an individual subsidiary should be consolidated. **ASC 810-10-10** indicates that consolidated financial statements normally are appropriate for a group of companies when one company "has a controlling financial interest in the other companies." It also states that "the usual condition for a controlling financial interest is ownership of a majority voting interest. . . ." In practice, control has been determined by the proportion of voting shares of a company's stock owned directly or indirectly by another company. This criterion was formalized by **ASC 810-10-15,** which requires consolidation of all majority-owned subsidiaries unless the parent is unable to exercise control.

Although majority ownership is the most common means of acquiring control, a company may be able to direct the operating and financing policies of another with less than majority ownership, such as when the remainder of the stock is widely held. **ASC 810-10-15** does not preclude consolidation with less than majority ownership, but the consolidation of less-than-majority-owned subsidiaries is very rare in practice.

More directly, **ASC 810-10-55** indicates that control can be obtained without majority ownership of a company's common stock.

Indirect Control[1]

The traditional view of control includes both direct and indirect control. ***Direct control*** typically occurs when one company owns a majority of another company's common stock. ***Indirect control*** or *pyramiding* occurs when a company's common stock is owned by one or more other companies that are all under common control. In each of the following examples, P Company controls Z Company. However, in each case, P Company does not own a direct interest in Z. Instead, P controls Z indirectly through the ownership of other companies.

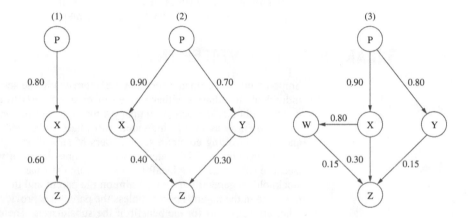

Advanced StudyGuide .com

In (1), P owns 80 percent of X, which owns 60 percent of Z. Because P controls X and X controls Z, P indirectly controls Z. In (2), P owns 90 percent of X and 70 percent of Y; X owns 40 percent of Z; Y owns 30 percent of Z. Because P controls both X and Y and they, in turn, jointly control Z (with a combined ownership of 70 percent), P effectively controls Z through its two subsidiaries. In (3), P owns 90 percent of X and 80 percent of Y; X owns 80 percent of W and 30 percent of Z; Y owns 15 percent of Z; W owns 15 percent of Z. Because P controls both X and Y and they, in turn, jointly control Z (with a combined control of 60 percent—15 percent of which comes through X's subsidiary W), P effectively controls Z through its two subsidiaries. In each case, P controls Z through its subsidiaries.

Ability to Exercise Control

Under certain circumstances, a subsidiary's majority stockholders may not be able to exercise control even though they hold more than 50 percent of its outstanding voting stock. This might occur, for instance, if the subsidiary was in legal reorganization or in bankruptcy; although the parent might hold majority ownership, control would rest with the courts or a court-appointed trustee. Similarly, if the subsidiary were located in a foreign country and that country had placed restrictions on the subsidiary that prevented the remittance of profits or assets back to the parent company, consolidation of that subsidiary would not be appropriate because of the parent's inability to control important aspects of the subsidiary's operations.

---

[1] To view a video explanation of this topic, visit advancedstudyguide.com.

Differences in Fiscal Periods

A difference in the fiscal periods of a parent and subsidiary should not preclude consolidation of that subsidiary. Often the subsidiary's fiscal period, if different from the parent's, is changed to coincide with that of the parent. Another alternative is to adjust the financial statement data of the subsidiary each period to place the data on a basis consistent with the parent's fiscal period. Both the Securities and Exchange Commission and current accounting standards permit the consolidation of a subsidiary's financial statements without adjusting the fiscal period of the subsidiary if that period does not differ from the parent's by more than three months and if recognition is given to intervening events that have a material effect on financial position or results of operations.

Changing Concept of the Reporting Entity

For nearly three decades beginning in the 1960s, little change was observed in the authoritative literature governing consolidation policies. However, during that time, many changes occurred in the business environment, including widespread diversification of companies and the increased emphasis on financial services by manufacturing and merchandising companies (such as General Electric and Harley-Davidson).

In addition, the criteria used in determining whether to consolidate specific subsidiaries were subject to varying interpretations. Companies exercised great latitude in selecting which subsidiaries to consolidate and which to report as intercorporate investments. The lack of consistency in consolidation policy became of increasing concern as many manufacturing and merchandising companies engaged in "off-balance sheet financing" by borrowing heavily through finance subsidiaries and then excluding those subsidiaries from consolidation.

In 1982, the FASB began a project aimed at developing a comprehensive consolidation policy. The guidance in **ASC 810-10-15** was developed in 1987, requiring the consolidation of all majority-owned subsidiaries. The intent was to eliminate the inconsistencies found in practice until a more comprehensive standard could be issued. Unfortunately, the issues have been more difficult to resolve than anticipated. After grappling with these issues for more than two decades, the FASB has still been unable to provide a comprehensive consolidation policy.

Completion of the FASB's consolidation project has been hampered by, among other things, the inability to resolve issues related to two important concepts: (1) control and (2) the reporting entity. Regarding the first issue, the FASB has attempted to move beyond the traditional notion of control based on majority ownership of common stock to requiring consolidation of entities under *effective control.* This idea reflects the ability to direct the policies of another entity even though majority ownership is lacking. Adopting the concept of effective control can lead to the consolidation of companies in which little or even no ownership is held and to the consolidation of entities other than corporations, such as partnerships and trusts. Although the FASB has indicated in **ASC 805-10-55** that control can be achieved without majority ownership, a comprehensive consolidation policy has yet to be achieved.

With respect to the second issue, defining the accounting entity would go a long way toward resolving the issue of when to prepare consolidated financial statements and what entities should be included. Unfortunately, the FASB has found both the entity and control issues so complex that they are not easily resolved and require further study. Accordingly, the FASB issued guidance dealing with selected issues related to consolidated financial statements **(ASC 810),** leaving a comprehensive consolidation policy until a later time.

NONCONTROLLING INTEREST

LO 3-3

Understand and explain differences in the consolidation process when the subsidiary is not wholly owned.

A parent company does not always own 100 percent of a subsidiary's outstanding common stock. The parent may have acquired less than 100 percent of a company's stock in a business combination, or it may originally have held 100 percent but sold or awarded some shares to others. For the parent to consolidate the subsidiary, only a controlling interest is needed. Those shareholders of the subsidiary other than the parent are referred to as "noncontrolling" shareholders. The claim of these shareholders on the income and net assets of the subsidiary is referred to as the ***noncontrolling interest*** (formerly referred to as the ***minority interest***).[2] Throughout this chapter and in subsequent chapters, whenever the acquired company is less than wholly owned, we will frequently refer to the noncontrolling interest shareholders as the "NCI shareholders." The NCI shareholders clearly have a claim on the subsidiary's assets and earnings through their stock ownership. Because 100 percent of a subsidiary's assets, liabilities, and earnings is included in the consolidated financial statements, regardless of the parent's percentage ownership, the NCI shareholders' claim on these items must be reported.

Computation and Presentation of Noncontrolling Interest

In uncomplicated situations, the noncontrolling interest's share of consolidated net income is a simple proportionate share of the subsidiary's net income. For example, if a subsidiary has net income of $150,000 and the NCI shareholders own 10 percent of the subsidiary's common stock, their share of income is $15,000 ($150,000 × 0.10).

The NCI shareholders' claim on the net assets of the subsidiary is based on the acquisition-date fair value of the noncontrolling interest, adjusted over time for a proportionate share of the subsidiary's income and dividends. We discuss the noncontrolling interest in more detail in Chapter 5.

The current standard on reporting noncontrolling interests, **ASC 810-10-50,** requires that the term "consolidated net income" be applied to the income available to all stockholders, with the allocation of that income between the controlling and noncontrolling stockholders included in the consolidated income statement. For example, assume that Parent Company owns 90 percent of Sub Company's stock, acquired without a differential, and that the two companies report revenues and expenses as follows:

	Parent	Sub
Revenues	$300,000	$100,000
Expenses	225,000	65,000

An abbreviated consolidated income statement for Parent and its subsidiary would appear as follows:

Revenues	$ 400,000
Expenses	(290,000)
Consolidated Net Income	$ 110,000
Less: Consolidated Net Income Attributable to the Noncontrolling Interest in Sub Company	(3,500)
Consolidated Net Income Attributable to the Controlling Interest in Sub Company	$ 106,500

Also assume that Parent's beginning retained earnings is $200,500, common stock is $50,000, additional paid-in capital is $700,000, and dividends declared and paid by the parent this period are $27,000. The noncontrolling interest's claim on the net assets of the subsidiary was previously reported in the balance sheet most frequently in the "mezzanine" between liabilities and stockholders' equity. Some companies reported the

---

[2] Although the term "minority interest" was commonly used in the past, **ASC 805-10-20** replaces this term with "noncontrolling interest." The FASB's intent is that the term "noncontrolling interest" be used going forward. Thus, we use this term consistently throughout this and future chapters.

FYI

In Berkshire Hathaway's 2011 consolidated income statement, the company reported total consolidated net income of $10.75 billion, which included $492 million in earnings attributable to noncontrolling interests. Additionally, Berkshire's 2011 consolidated balance sheet reported total noncontrolling interests in net assets of $4.1 billion.

noncontrolling interest as a liability, although it clearly did not meet the definition of a liability. **ASC 810-10-55** is clear that the noncontrolling interest's claim on net assets is an element of equity, not a liability. It requires reporting the noncontrolling interest in equity in the following manner:

Controlling Interest:	
Common Stock	$ 50,000
Additional Paid-In Capital	700,000
Retained Earnings	280,000
Total Controlling Interest	$1,030,000
Noncontrolling Interest in the Net Assets of Sub Company	75,000
Total Stockholders' Equity	$1,105,000

THE EFFECT OF A NONCONTROLLING INTEREST

LO 3-4

Make calculations for the consolidation of a less-than-wholly-owned subsidiary.

When a subsidiary is less than wholly owned, the general approach to consolidation is the same as discussed in Chapter 2, but the consolidation procedures must be modified slightly to recognize the noncontrolling interest. Thus, the difference between the consolidation procedures illustrated in Chapter 2 and what we will demonstrate here is that we now have to account for the NCI shareholders' ownership in the income and net assets of the acquired company. The following two-by-two matrix indicates that the only difference in consolidation in Chapter 3 relative to Chapter 2 is the separate recognition of the NCI shareholder share of income and net assets.

Before examining the specific procedures used in consolidating a less-than-wholly-owned subsidiary, we discuss the computation of consolidated net income, consolidated retained earnings, and the noncontrolling interest's claim on income and net assets. We also discuss modifications to the consolidation worksheet.

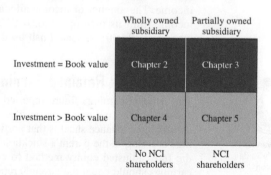

Consolidated Net Income

Consolidated net income, as it appears in the consolidated income statement, is the difference between consolidated revenues and expenses. In the absence of transactions between companies included in the consolidation, *consolidated net income* is equal to the parent's income from its own operations, excluding any investment income from consolidated subsidiaries, plus the net income from each of the consolidated subsidiaries.

When all subsidiaries are wholly owned, all of the consolidated net income accrues to the parent company, or the controlling interest. If one or more of the consolidated subsidiaries is less than wholly owned, a portion of the consolidated net income accrues to the NCI shareholders. In that case, the income attributable to the subsidiary's noncontrolling interest is deducted from consolidated net income on the face of the income statement to arrive at consolidated net income attributable to the controlling interest.

Income attributable to a noncontrolling interest in a subsidiary is based on a proportionate share of that subsidiary's net income. The subsidiary's net income available to common shareholders is divided between the parent and noncontrolling stockholders based on their relative common stock ownership of the subsidiary. Note that the NCI shareholders in a particular subsidiary have a proportionate claim only on the income of that subsidiary and not on the income of the parent or any other subsidiary.

As an example of the computation and allocation of consolidated net income, assume that Push Corporation purchases 80 percent of the stock of Shove Company for an amount equal to 80 percent of Shove's total book value. During 20X1, Shove reports separate net income of $25,000, while Push reports net income of $120,000, including equity-method income from Shove of $20,000 ($25,000 × 0.80). Consolidated net income for 20X1 is computed and allocated as follows:

Push's net income	$120,000
Less: Equity-method income from Shove	(20,000)
Shove's net income	25,000
Consolidated net income	$125,000
Income attributable to noncontrolling interest	(5,000)
Income attributable to controlling interest	$120,000

Consolidated net income is equal to the separate income of Push from its own operations ($100,000) plus Shove's net income ($25,000). The $20,000 of equity-method income from Shove that had been recognized by Push must be excluded from the computation to avoid double-counting the same income. Consolidated net income is allocated to the noncontrolling stockholders based on their 20 percent share of Shove's net income. The amount of income allocated to the controlling interest is equal to Push's income from its own operations ($100,000) and Push's 80 percent share of Shove's income ($20,000) because Push used the equity method of accounting for its investment in Shove.

Consolidated Retained Earnings

Advanced
StudyGuide
.com

The retained earnings figure reported in the consolidated balance sheet is not entirely consistent with the computation of consolidated net income. Retained earnings in the consolidated balance sheet is that portion of the consolidated entity's undistributed earnings accruing to the parent's stockholders. Assuming the parent company correctly uses the fully adjusted equity method to account for its investments, consolidated retained earnings should equal the parent's retained earnings. It is calculated by adding the parent's share of subsidiary cumulative net income since acquisition to the parent's retained earnings from its own operations (excluding any income from the subsidiary included in the parent's retained earnings) and subtracting the parent's share of any differential write-off. Any retained earnings related to subsidiary NCI shareholders is included in the Noncontrolling Interest in Net Assets of Subsidiary amount reported in the equity section of the consolidated balance sheet.

To illustrate the computation of consolidated retained earnings when a noncontrolling interest exists, assume that Push purchases 80 percent of Shove's stock on January 1, 20X1, and accounts for the investment using the equity method. Assume net income and dividends as follows during the two years following the acquisition:

Advanced Financial Accounting, 11th Edition

109

Chapter 3   *The Reporting Entity and the Consolidation of Less-than-Wholly-Owned Subsidiaries with No Differential*   **109**

	Push	Shove
Retained earnings, January 1, 20X1	$400,000	$250,000
Net income, 20X1	120,000	25,000
Dividends, 20X1	(30,000)	(10,000)
Retained earnings, December 31, 20X1	$490,000	$265,000
Net income, 20X2	148,000	35,000
Dividends, 20X2	(30,000)	(10,000)
Retained earnings, December 31, 20X2	$608,000	$290,000

Consolidated retained earnings as of two years after the date of combination is computed as follows:

Push's retained earnings, December 31, 20X2	$608,000
Equity accrual from Shove since acquisition ($25,000 + $35,000) × 0.80	(48,000)
Push's retained earnings from its own operations, December 31, 20X2	$560,000
Push's share of Shove's net income since acquisition ($60,000 × 0.80)	48,000
Consolidated retained earnings, December 31, 20X2	$608,000

We note several important points from the example. First, the subsidiary's retained earnings are not combined with the parent's retained earnings. Only the parent's share of the subsidiary's cumulative net income since the date of combination is included. Second, consolidated retained earnings are equal to the parent's retained earnings because the parent uses the equity method to account for its investment in the subsidiary. If the parent accounted for the investment using the cost method, the parent's retained earnings and consolidated retained earnings would differ. Finally, we note that the consolidated financial statements include the equity accounts of the parent. In the Push and Shove example, Push's shareholders effectively control both Push and Shove. Hence, Push's equity accounts, along with the noncontrolling interest in Shove's net assets, comprise the equity section of the consolidated group of companies. For the same reason, only Push's dividends influence consolidated retained earnings.

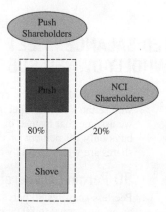

Worksheet Format

The same three-part worksheet described in Chapter 2 can be used when consolidating less-than-wholly-owned subsidiaries, with only minor modifications. The worksheet must allow for including the noncontrolling interest's claim on the income and net assets of the subsidiaries. The noncontrolling interest's claim on the income of a subsidiary is deducted from consolidated net income at the bottom of the worksheet's income statement section in the Consolidated column to arrive at consolidated net income attributable to the controlling interest. The noncontrolling interest's claim on the subsidiary's net assets is placed at the bottom of the worksheet's balance sheet section. The noncontrolling interest's claims on both income and net assets are entered in the worksheet through consolidation entries and then carried over to the Consolidated column. As discussed in Chapter 2, the amounts in the Consolidated column are used to prepare the consolidated financial statements.

| | Parent | Subsidiary | Consolidation Entries | | Consolidated |
			DR	CR	
Income Statement					
Revenues					
Expenses					
Consolidated Net Income					
NCI in Net Income					
Controlling interest in Net Income					
Statement of Retained Earnings					
Retained Earnings (1/1)					
Add: Net Income					
Less: Dividends					
Retained Earnings (12/31)					
Balance Sheet					
Assets					
Total Assets					
Liabilities					
Equity					
Common Stock					
Retained Earnings					
NCI in Net Assets of Subsidiary					
Total Liabilities & Equity					

CONSOLIDATED BALANCE SHEET WITH A LESS-THAN-WHOLLY-OWNED SUBSIDIARY

LO 3-5

Prepare a consolidation worksheet for a less-than-wholly-owned subsidiary.

In order to illustrate the consolidation process for a less-than-wholly-owned subsidiary, we use the Peerless-Special Foods example from Chapter 2. The only difference is that we assume that instead of acquiring all of the common stock of Special Foods, Peerless buys only 80 percent of the shares. Thus, we assume that the other 20 percent of the shares are widely held by other shareholders (the NCI shareholders).

80 Percent Ownership Acquired at Book Value

Peerless acquires 80 percent of Special Foods' outstanding common stock for $240,000, an amount equal to 80 percent of the fair value of Special Foods' net assets on January 1, 20X1. On this date, the fair values of Special Foods' individual assets and liabilities are equal to their book values. Thus, there is no differential. Because Peerless acquires only 80 percent of Special Foods' common stock, the Investment in Special Foods equals 80 percent of the total stockholders' equity of Special Foods ($200,000 + $100,000). We can summarize Special Foods' ownership as follows:

Advanced Financial Accounting, 11th Edition   **111**

Chapter 3   *The Reporting Entity and the Consolidation of Less-than-Wholly-Owned Subsidiaries with No Differential*   **111**

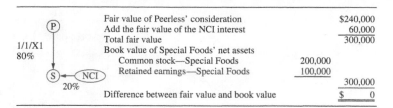

Fair value of Peerless' consideration		$240,000
Add the fair value of the NCI interest		60,000
Total fair value		300,000
Book value of Special Foods' net assets		
Common stock—Special Foods	200,000	
Retained earnings—Special Foods	100,000	
		300,000
Difference between fair value and book value		$ 0

Peerless records the 80 percent stock acquisition on its books with the following entry on January 1, 20X1:

(1)	Investment in Special Foods	240,000	
	Cash		240,000
	Record purchase of Special Foods stock.		

The Basic Investment Consolidation Entry

The basic consolidation entry on the date of acquisition would be the same as the one illustrated in Chapter 2 except that the $300,000 book value of net assets is now jointly owned by Peerless (80 percent) and the NCI shareholders (20 percent). Thus, the original $300,000 credit to the Investment in Special Foods account from the wholly owned example in Chapter 2 is now "shared" with the NCI shareholders as shown in the breakdown of the book value of Special Foods:

Book Value Calculations:

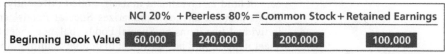

	NCI 20%	+ Peerless 80%	= Common Stock	+ Retained Earnings
Beginning Book Value	60,000	240,000	200,000	100,000

Because the fair value of Special Foods' net assets on the acquisition date is equal to their book value, there is no differential. Thus, the only required consolidation entry (the basic consolidation entry) in the worksheet removes the Investment in Special Foods Stock account and Special Foods' stockholders' equity accounts and records the $60,000 NCI interest in the net assets of Special Foods.

Basic Consolidation Entry:

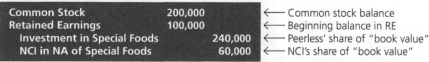

Common Stock	200,000		← Common stock balance
Retained Earnings	100,000		← Beginning balance in RE
Investment in Special Foods		240,000	← Peerless' share of "book value"
NCI in NA of Special Foods		60,000	← NCI's share of "book value"

In this example, Peerless' investment is exactly equal to its 80 percent share of the book value of Special Foods' net assets. Therefore, goodwill is not recorded and all assets and liabilities are simply combined from Special Foods' financial statements at their current book values. Again, in Chapters 4 and 5, we will explore situations in which the acquiring company pays more than the book value of the acquired company's net assets. However, in Chapters 2 and 3, the excess value of identifiable net assets and goodwill will always be equal to zero. To maintain a consistent approach through all four chapters, we always illustrate the components of the acquiring company's investment, even though the acquiring company's investment will always be exactly equal to its share of the book value of net assets in this chapter. Thus, the relationship between the fair value of the consideration given to acquire Special Foods, the fair value of Special Foods' net assets, and the book value of Special Foods' net assets can be illustrated as follows:

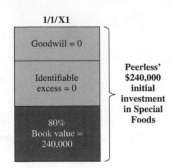

The consolidation entry simply credits the Investment in Special Foods Stock account (for the original acquisition price, $240,000), eliminating this account from Peerless' balance sheet.

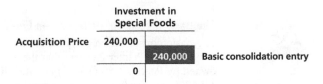

Remember that this entry is made in the consolidation worksheet, not on the books of either the parent or the subsidiary, and is presented here in T-account form for instructional purposes only. The investment account must be eliminated in the consolidation process because, as explained in Chapter 2, from a single-entity viewpoint, a company cannot hold an investment in itself. Stated differently, since the Investment in Special Foods account already summarizes Special Foods' entire balance sheet, adding the individual line items on Special Foods' balance sheet together with Peerless' balance sheet items would be equivalent to double counting Special Foods' balance sheet.

As explained in Chapter 2, we first examine situations where a subsidiary is created (hence the parent's book values of transferred assets carry over) or where the acquisition price is exactly equal to the book value of the target company's net assets. When a parent company acquires a subsidiary, the consolidated financial statements should appear as if all of the subsidiary's assets and liabilities were acquired and recorded at their acquisition prices (equal to their former book values). If Peerless had purchased Special Foods' assets instead of its stock with an acquisition price equal to the book value of net assets, the assets would have been recorded in Peerless' books at their acquisition prices (as if they were new assets with zero accumulated depreciation). Following this logic, because Peerless did acquire Special Foods' stock, the consolidated financial statements should present all of Special Foods' assets and liabilities as if they had been recorded at their acquisition prices and then depreciated from that date forward. Thus, eliminating the old accumulated depreciation of the subsidiary as of the acquisition date and netting it out against the historical cost gives the appearance that the depreciable assets have been newly recorded at their acquisition prices (which happen to be equal to Special Foods' book values). In this example, Special Foods had accumulated depreciation on the acquisition date of $300,000. Thus, as explained in Chapter 2, the following consolidation entry nets this accumulated depreciation out against the cost of the building and equipment.

Optional Accumulated Depreciation Consolidation Entry:

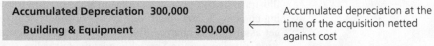

Also as explained in Chapter 2, this worksheet consolidation entry does not change the net buildings and equipment balance. Netting the preacquisition accumulated depreciation out against the cost basis of the corresponding assets merely causes the buildings and equipment to appear in the consolidated financial statements as if they had been recorded as new assets (which coincidentally happen to be equal to their former book values) on the acquisition date. In this chapter and in Chapter 2, we assume that the fair values of all assets and liabilities are equal to their book values on the acquisition date. This same entry would be included in each succeeding consolidation as long as the assets remain on Special Foods' books (always based on the accumulated depreciation balance as of the acquisition date).

Consolidation Worksheet

Figure 3–1 presents the consolidation worksheet. As explained previously in Chapter 2, the investment account on the parent's books can be thought of as a single account representing the parent's investment in the net assets of the subsidiary, a *one-line consolidation.* In a full consolidation, the subsidiary's individual assets and liabilities are combined with those of the parent. Including both the net assets of the subsidiary, as represented by the balance in the investment account, and the subsidiary's individual assets and liabilities would double-count the same set of assets. Therefore, the investment account is eliminated, not carried to the consolidated balance sheet.

Figure 3–2 presents the consolidated balance sheet, prepared from the consolidation worksheet, as of the acquisition date. Because no operations occurred between the date of combination and the preparation of the consolidated balance sheet, there is no income statement or statement of retained earnings.

FIGURE 3–1   January 1, 20X1, Worksheet for Consolidated Balance Sheet, Date of Combination; 80 Percent Acquisition at Book Value

	Peerless Products	Special Foods	Consolidation Entries		Consolidated
			DR	CR	
Balance Sheet					
Cash	110,000	50,000			160,000
Accounts Receivable	75,000	50,000			125,000
Inventory	100,000	60,000			160,000
Investment in Special Foods	240,000			240,000	0
Land	175,000	40,000			215,000
Buildings & Equipment	800,000	600,000		300,000	1,100,000
Less: Accumulated Depreciation	(400,000)	(300,000)	300,000		(400,000)
Total Assets	**1,100,000**	**500,000**	**$300,000**	**$540,000**	**1,360,000**
Accounts Payable	100,000	100,000			200,000
Bonds Payable	200,000	100,000			300,000
Common Stock	500,000	200,000	200,000		500,000
Retained Earnings	300,000	100,000	100,000		300,000
NCI in NA of Special Foods				60,000	60,000
Total Liabilities & Equity	**1,100,000**	**500,000**	**300,000**	**60,000**	**1,360,000**

FIGURE 3–2
Consolidated Balance Sheet, January 1, 20X1, Date of Combination; 80 Percent Acquisition at Book Value

PEERLESS PRODUCTS CORPORATION AND SUBSIDIARY
Consolidated Balance Sheet
January 1, 20X1

Assets			Liabilities	
Cash		160,000	Accounts Payable	200,000
Accounts Receivable		125,000	Bonds Payable	300,000
Inventory		160,000	Stockholders' Equity	
Land		215,000	Common Stock	500,000
Buildings & Equipment	1,100,000		Retained Earnings	300,000
Accumulated Depreciation	(400,000)	700,000	NCI in NA of Special Foods	60,000
Total Assets		1,360,000	Total Liabilities & Equity	1,360,000

CONSOLIDATION SUBSEQUENT TO ACQUISITION— 80 PERCENT OWNERSHIP ACQUIRED AT BOOK VALUE

Chapter 2 explains the procedures used to prepare a consolidated balance sheet as of the acquisition date. More than a consolidated balance sheet, however, is needed to provide a comprehensive picture of the consolidated entity's activities following acquisition. As with a single company, the set of basic financial statements for a consolidated entity consists of an income statement, a statement of changes in retained earnings, a balance sheet, and a statement of cash flows. Each of the consolidated financial statements is prepared as if it is taken from a single set of books that is being used to account for the overall consolidated entity. There is, of course, no set of books for the consolidated entity. Therefore, as in the preparation of the consolidated balance sheet, the consolidation process starts with the data recorded on the books of the individual consolidating companies. The account balances from the books of the individual companies are placed in the three-part worksheet, and entries are made to eliminate the effects of intercorporate ownership and transactions. The consolidation approach and procedures are the same whether the subsidiary being consolidated was acquired or created.

Initial Year of Ownership

Assume that Peerless already recorded the acquisition on January 1, 20X1, and that during 20X1, Peerless records operating earnings of $140,000, excluding its income from investing in Special Foods, and declares dividends of $60,000. Special Foods reports 20X1 net income of $50,000 and declares dividends of $30,000.

Parent Company Entries

Peerless records its 20X1 income and dividends from Special Foods under the equity method as follows:

| (2) | Investment in Special Foods | 40,000 | |
| | Income from Special Foods | | 40,000 |

Record Peerless' 80% share of Special Foods' 20X1 income.

| (3) | Cash | 24,000 | |
| | Investment in Special Foods | | 24,000 |

Record Peerless' 80% share of Special Foods' 20X1 dividend.

Consolidation Worksheet—Initial Year of Ownership

After all appropriate equity method entries have been recorded on Peerless' books, the company can prepare a consolidation worksheet. Peerless begins the worksheet by placing the adjusted account balances from both Peerless' and Special Foods' books in the first two columns of the worksheet. Then all amounts that reflect intercorporate transactions or ownership are eliminated in the consolidation process.

The distinction between journal entries recorded on the books of the individual companies and the consolidation entries recorded only on the consolidation worksheet is an important one. Book entries affect balances on the books and the amounts that are carried to the consolidation worksheet; worksheet consolidation entries affect only those balances carried to the consolidated financial statements in the period. As mentioned previously, the consolidation entries presented in this text are shaded when presented both in journal entry form in the text and in the worksheet.

In this example, the accounts that must be eliminated because of intercorporate ownership are the stockholders' equity accounts of Special Foods, including dividends declared, Peerless' investment in Special Foods stock, and Peerless' income from Special Foods. However, the book value portion of Peerless' investment has changed since the January 1 acquisition date because under the equity method, Peerless has adjusted the investment account balance for its share of earnings and dividends (entries 2 and 3). The book value portion of the investment account can be summarized as follows:

Book Value Calculations:

	NCI 20%	+ Peerless 80%	= Common Stock	+ Retained Earnings
Beginning Book Value	60,000	240,000	200,000	100,000
+ Net Income	10,000	40,000		50,000
− Dividends	(6,000)	(24,000)		(30,000)
Ending Book Value	64,000	256,000	200,000	120,000

Note that we use dark shading with a white drop-out font for the amounts in the book value analysis that appear in the basic consolidation entry.

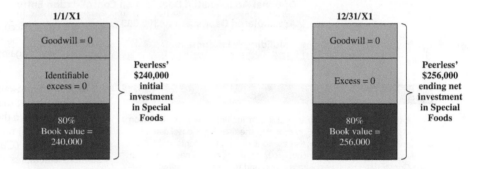

Under the equity method, the parent recognized its share (80 percent) of the subsidiary's income on its separate books. In the consolidated income statement, however, the individual revenue and expense accounts of the subsidiary are combined with those of the parent. Income recognized by the parent from all consolidated subsidiaries, therefore, must be eliminated to avoid double-counting. The subsidiary's dividends must be eliminated when consolidated statements are prepared so that only dividend declarations related to the parent's shareholders are treated as dividends of the consolidated entity. Thus, the basic consolidation entry removes both the investment income reflected in the parent's income statement and any dividends declared by the subsidiary during the period:

Basic Consolidation Entry:

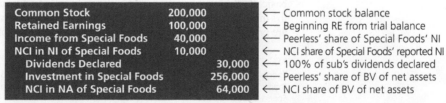

Common Stock	200,000		← Common stock balance
Retained Earnings	100,000		← Beginning RE from trial balance
Income from Special Foods	40,000		← Peerless' share of Special Foods' NI
NCI in NI of Special Foods	10,000		← NCI share of Special Foods' reported NI
Dividends Declared		30,000	← 100% of sub's dividends declared
Investment in Special Foods		256,000	← Peerless' share of BV of net assets
NCI in NA of Special Foods		64,000	← NCI share of BV of net assets

Because there is no differential in this example, the basic consolidation entry completely eliminates the balance in Peerless' investment account on the balance sheet as well as the Income from Special Foods account on the income statement. Note again that the parent's investment in the stock of a consolidated subsidiary never appears in the consolidated balance sheet and the income from subsidiary account never appears on the consolidated income statement.

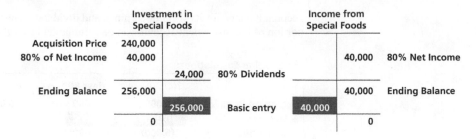

As explained previously, we repeat the accumulated depreciation entry in each succeeding period for as long as the subsidiary owns these assets. The purpose of this entry is to appropriately present these assets in the consolidated financial statements as if they had been purchased on the date the subsidiary was acquired at their acquisition date fair values.

Optional Accumulated Depreciation Consolidation Entry:

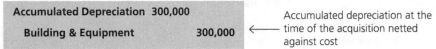

Accumulated depreciation at the time of the acquisition netted against cost

> **! CAUTION**
>
> Note that the $10,000 debit to NCI in Net Income in the Consolidation Entries column of Figure 3–3 is added to the $40,000 Consolidated Net Income debit subtotal to arrive at the total debit adjustments in the Controlling Interest in the Net Income row. Students sometimes forget that the Consolidation Entries columns simply add total debit and credit adjustments (ignoring the "formula" used in the income calculation). The reason the $10,000 NCI in Net Income is listed with brackets in the Consolidated column is because a debit *decreases* income.

Figure 3–3 presents the consolidation worksheet. We note that there are only two changes on the worksheet when the subsidiary is only partially owned (Chapter 3) relative to when the subsidiary is wholly owned (Chapter 2). First, the income statement calculates the consolidated net income ($190,000 in this example) and then deducts the portion attributable to the NCI shareholders (NCI in Net Income) to arrive at the portion attributable to the parent (controlling interest). In this example, the final line of the income statement presents Peerless' share of the consolidated net income, $180,000. This amount should always equal the parent's net income in the first column of the worksheet if the parent properly accounts for the investment in the subsidiary using the equity method on its own books.[3] Second, since the parent company consolidates the entire balance sheet of the subsidiary, it must disclose the portion of the subsidiary's net assets that belong to the noncontrolling interest (NCI in Net Assets).

Second and Subsequent Years of Ownership

The consolidation procedures employed at the end of the second and subsequent years are basically the same as those used at the end of the first year. Adjusted trial balance data of the individual companies are used as the starting point each time consolidated statements are prepared because no separate books are kept for the consolidated entity. An additional

---

[3] Note that the "Consolidated Net Income" line properly adds Peerless' reported net income, $180,000, to Special Foods' net income, $50,000, and eliminates Peerless' share of Special Foods' net income such that the total consolidated net income is equal to Peerless' income from separate operations ($140,000) plus Special Foods' reported net income ($50,000). On the other hand, the "Controlling Interest in Net Income" line indicates that Peerless' true income can be calculated in two ways. Either start with total "Consolidated Net Income" and deduct the portion that belongs to the NCI shareholders in the far right column or simply use Peerless' correctly calculated equity method net income, $180,000, which is its income from separate operations ($140,000), plus its share of Special Foods' net income ($40,000). The controlling interest in the Net Income line starts with this correctly calculated number from Peerless' income statement (in the first column) and adds it to Special Foods' reported income (in the second column), but then eliminates Special Foods' reported income in the Consolidation Entries column. Thus, the controlling interest in net income in the Consolidation column equals Peerless' reported net income under the equity method.

FIGURE 3–3   December 31, 20X1, Equity-Method Worksheet for Consolidated Financial Statements, Initial Year of Ownership; 80 percent Acquisition at Book Value

	Peerless Products	Special Foods	Consolidation Entries DR	Consolidation Entries CR	Consolidated
Income Statement					
Sales	400,000	200,000			600,000
Less: COGS	(170,000)	(115,000)			(285,000)
Less: Depreciation Expense	(50,000)	(20,000)			(70,000)
Less: Other Expenses	(40,000)	(15,000)			(55,000)
Income from Special Foods	40,000		40,000		0
Consolidated Net Income	180,000	50,000	40,000	0	190,000
NCI in Net Income			10,000		(10,000)
Controlling Interest in Net Income	**180,000**	**50,000**	**50,000**	0	**180,000**
Statement of Retained Earnings					
Beginning Balance	300,000	100,000	100,000		300,000
Net Income	**180,000**	**50,000**	50,000	0	180,000
Less: Dividends Declared	(60,000)	(30,000)		30,000	(60,000)
Ending Balance	**420,000**	**120,000**	**150,000**	**30,000**	**420,000**
Balance Sheet					
Cash	264,000	75,000			339,000
Accounts Receivable	75,000	50,000			125,000
Inventory	100,000	75,000			175,000
Investment in Special Foods	256,000			256,000	0
Land	175,000	40,000			215,000
Buildings & Equipment	800,000	600,000		300,000	1,100,000
Less: Accumulated Depreciation	(450,000)	(320,000)	300,000		(470,000)
Total Assets	**1,220,000**	**520,000**	**300,000**	**556,000**	**1,484,000**
Accounts Payable	100,000	100,000			200,000
Bonds Payable	200,000	100,000			300,000
Common Stock	500,000	200,000	200,000		500,000
Retained Earnings	**420,000**	**120,000**	150,000	30,000	420,000
NCI in NA of Special Foods				64,000	64,000
Total Liabilities & Equity	**1,220,000**	**520,000**	**350,000**	**94,000**	**1,484,000**

check is needed in each period following acquisition to ensure that the beginning balance of consolidated retained earnings shown in the completed worksheet equals the balance reported at the end of the prior period. In all other respects, the consolidation entries and worksheet are comparable with those shown for the first year.

Parent Company Entries

Consolidation after two years of ownership is illustrated by continuing the example of Peerless Products and Special Foods. Peerless' separate income from its own operations for 20X2 is $160,000, and its dividends total $60,000. Special Foods reports net income of $75,000 in 20X2 and pays dividends of $40,000. Equity-method entries recorded by Peerless in 20X2 are as follows:

(4)	Investment in Special Foods	60,000	
	Income from Special Foods		60,000
	Record Peerless' 80% share of Special Foods' 20X2 income.		

(5)	Cash	32,000	
	Investment in Special Foods		32,000
	Record Peerless' 80% share of Special Foods' 20X2 dividend.		

Peerless' reported net income totals $220,000 ($160,000 from separate operations + $60,000 from Special Foods).

Consolidation Worksheet—Second Year of Ownership

In order to complete the worksheet, Peerless must calculate the worksheet consolidation entries using the following process. The book value of equity can be analyzed and summarized as follows:

Advanced
StudyGuide
.com

Book Value Calculations:

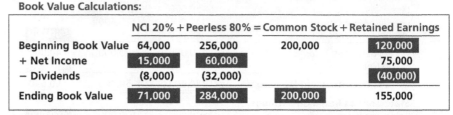

	NCI 20%	+ Peerless 80%	= Common Stock	+ Retained Earnings
Beginning Book Value	64,000	256,000	200,000	120,000
+ Net Income	15,000	60,000		75,000
− Dividends	(8,000)	(32,000)		(40,000)
Ending Book Value	71,000	284,000	200,000	155,000

The book value calculations indicate that the balance in Peerless' Investment in Special Foods account increases from $256,000 to $284,000 in 20X2. Recall that the numbers in the lighter font from the book value calculations appear in the basic consolidation entry. This consolidation entry removes both the investment income reflected in the parent's income statement and any dividends declared by the subsidiary during the period:

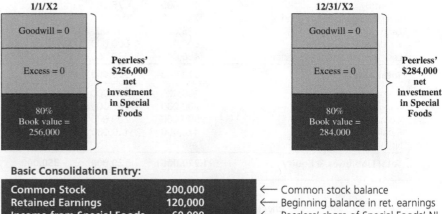

1/1/X2

Goodwill = 0

Excess = 0

80%
Book value =
256,000

Peerless'
$256,000
net
investment
in Special
Foods

12/31/X2

Goodwill = 0

Excess = 0

80%
Book value =
284,000

Peerless'
$284,000
net
investment
in Special
Foods

Basic Consolidation Entry:

Common Stock	200,000		← Common stock balance
Retained Earnings	120,000		← Beginning balance in ret. earnings
Income from Special Foods	60,000		← Peerless' share of Special Foods' NI
NCI in NI of Special Foods	15,000		← NCI share of Special Foods' reported NI
Dividends Declared		40,000	← 100% of sub's dividends declared
Investment in Special Foods		284,000	← Peerless' share of BV of net assets
NCI in NA of Special Foods		71,000	← NCI share of BV of net assets

Because there is no differential in this example, the basic consolidation entry completely eliminates the balance in Peerless' investment account on the balance sheet as well as the Income from Special Foods account on the income statement.

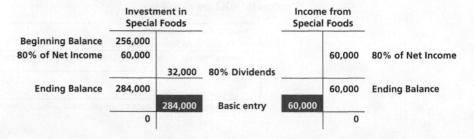

	Investment in Special Foods			Income from Special Foods	
Beginning Balance	256,000				
80% of Net Income	60,000			60,000	80% of Net Income
		32,000	80% Dividends		
Ending Balance	284,000			60,000	Ending Balance
		284,000	Basic entry	60,000	
	0			0	

FIGURE 3–4   December 31, 20X2, Equity-Method Worksheet for Consolidated Financial Statements, Second Year of Ownership; 80 percent Acquisition at Book Value

	Peerless Products	Special Foods	Consolidation Entries DR	Consolidation Entries CR	Consolidated
Income Statement					
Sales	450,000	300,000			750,000
Less: COGS	(180,000)	(160,000)			(340,000)
Less: Depreciation Expense	(50,000)	(20,000)			(70,000)
Less: Other Expenses	(60,000)	(45,000)			(105,000)
Income from Special Foods	60,000		60,000		0
Consolidated Net Income	220,000	75,000	60,000	0	235,000
NCI in Net Income			15,000		(15,000)
Controlling Interest Net Income	**220,000**	**75,000**	**75,000**	**0**	**220,000**
Statement of Retained Earnings					
Beginning Balance	420,000	120,000	120,000		420,000
Net Income	**220,000**	**75,000**	75,000	0	220,000
Less: Dividends Declared	(60,000)	(40,000)		40,000	(60,000)
Ending Balance	**580,000**	**155,000**	195,000	40,000	**580,000**
Balance Sheet					
Cash	291,000	85,000			376,000
Accounts Receivable	150,000	80,000			230,000
Inventory	180,000	90,000			270,000
Investment in Special Foods	284,000			284,000	0
Land	175,000	40,000			215,000
Buildings & Equipment	800,000	600,000		300,000	1,100,000
Less: Accumulated Depreciation	(500,000)	(340,000)	300,000		(540,000)
Total Assets	**1,380,000**	**555,000**	300,000	584,000	**1,651,000**
Accounts Payable	100,000	100,000			200,000
Bonds Payable	200,000	100,000			300,000
Common Stock	500,000	200,000	200,000		500,000
Retained Earnings	**580,000**	**155,000**	195,000	40,000	580,000
NCI in NA of Special Foods				71,000	71,000
Total Liabilities & Equity	**1,380,000**	**555,000**	395,000	111,000	**1,651,000**

In this example, Special Foods had accumulated depreciation on the acquisition date of $300,000. Thus, we repeat the same accumulated depreciation consolidation entry this year (and every year as long as Special Foods owns the assets) that we used in the initial year.

Optional Accumulated Depreciation Consolidation Entry:

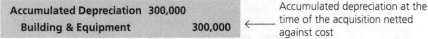

Accumulated Depreciation	300,000	
Building & Equipment		300,000

Accumulated depreciation at the time of the acquisition netted against cost

After placement of the two consolidation entries in the consolidation worksheet, the worksheet is completed in the normal manner as shown in Figure 3–4.

COMBINED FINANCIAL STATEMENTS

LO 3-6

Understand and explain the purpose of combined financial statements and how they differ from consolidated financial statements.

Financial statements are sometimes prepared for a group of companies when no one company in the group owns a majority of the common stock of any other company in the group. Financial statements that include a group of related companies without including the parent company or other owner are referred to as ***combined financial statements.***

Combined financial statements are commonly prepared when an individual, rather than a corporation, owns or controls a number of companies and wishes to include them all in a single set of financial statements. In some cases, a parent company may prepare financial statements that include only its subsidiaries, not the parent. In other cases, a parent may prepare financial statements for its subsidiaries by operating group, with all the subsidiaries engaged in a particular type of operation, or those located in a particular geographical region, reported together.

The procedures used to prepare combined financial statements are essentially the same as those used in preparing consolidated financial statements. All intercompany receivables and payables, intercompany transactions, and unrealized intercompany profits and losses must be eliminated in the same manner as in the preparation of consolidated statements. Although no parent company is included in the reporting entity, any intercompany ownership, and the associated portion of stockholders' equity, must be eliminated in the same way as the parent's investment in a subsidiary is eliminated in preparing consolidated financial statements. The remaining stockholders' equity of the companies in the reporting entity is divided into the portions accruing to the controlling and noncontrolling interests.

SPECIAL-PURPOSE AND VARIABLE INTEREST ENTITIES

LO 3-7

Understand and explain rules related to the consolidation of variable interest entities.

Although consolidation standards pertaining to related corporations have at times lacked clarity and needed updating, consolidation standards relating to partnerships or other types of entities such as trusts have been virtually nonexistent. Even corporate consolidation standards have not been adequate in situations in which other relationships such as guarantees and operating agreements overshadow the lack of a significant ownership element. As a result, companies such as Enron have taken advantage of the lack of standards to avoid reporting debt or losses by hiding them in special entities that were not consolidated. Although many companies have used special entities for legitimate purposes, financial reporting has not always captured the economic substance of the relationships. Only in recent years have consolidation standards for these special entities started to provide some uniformity in the financial reporting for corporations having relationships with such entities.

ASC 810-10-10 establishes consolidation standards in terms of one company controlling another and sets majority voting interest as the usual condition leading to consolidation. Similarly, **ASC 810-10-15** requires consolidation for majority-owned subsidiaries. In recent years, however, new types of relationships have been established between corporations and other entities that often are difficult to characterize in terms of voting, controlling, or ownership interests. Such entities often are structured to provide financing and/or control through forms other than those used by traditional operating companies. Some entities have no governing boards, or they may have boards or managers with only a limited ability to direct the entity's activities. Such entities may be governed instead by their incorporation or partnership documents, or by other agreements or documents. Some entities may have little equity investment, and the equity investors may have little or no control over the entity. For these special types of entities, **ASC 810-10-10** does not provide a clear basis for consolidation.

These special types of entities have generally been referred to as ***special-purpose entities (SPEs).*** In general, SPEs are corporations, trusts, or partnerships created for a single specified purpose. They usually have no substantive operations and are used only for financing purposes. SPEs have been used for several decades for asset securitization, risk sharing, and taking advantage of tax statutes. Prior to 2003, no comprehensive reporting framework had been established for SPEs. Several different pronouncements from various bodies dealt with selected issues or types of SPEs, but the guidance provided by these issuances was incomplete, vague, and not always correctly interpreted in practice.

Variable Interest Entities

In January 2003, the FASB issued guidance on variable interest entities (**ASC 810-10-25**) and updated this guidance later the same year (**ASC 810-10-38C**). For clarification, the interpretation uses the term *variable interest entities* to encompass SPEs and any other entities falling within its conditions.

A *variable interest entity (VIE)* is a legal structure used for business purposes, usually a corporation, trust, or partnership, that either (1) does not have equity investors that have voting rights and share in all of the entity's profits and losses or (2) has equity investors that do not provide sufficient financial resources to support the entity's activities. In a variable interest entity, specific agreements may limit the extent to which the equity investors, if any, share in the entity's profits or losses, and the agreements may limit the control that equity investors have over the entity's activities. For the equity investment to be considered sufficient financial support for the entity's activities (condition 2), it must be able to absorb the entity's expected future losses. A total equity investment that is less than 10 percent of the entity's total assets is, in general, considered to be insufficient by itself to allow the entity to finance its activities, and an investment of more than 10 percent might be needed, depending on the circumstances.

A corporation might create (or sponsor) a typical variable interest entity for a particular purpose, such as purchasing the sponsoring company's receivables or leasing facilities to the sponsoring company. The sponsoring company may acquire little or no stock in the VIE. Instead, the sponsoring company may enlist another party to purchase most or all of the common stock. The majority of the VIE's capital, however, normally comes from borrowing. Because lenders may be reluctant to lend (at least at reasonable interest rates) to an entity with only a small amount of equity, the sponsoring company often guarantees the VIE's loans. Thus, the sponsoring company may have little or no equity investment in the VIE, but the loan guarantees represent a type of interest in the VIE.

A corporation having an interest in a VIE cannot simply rely on its percentage stock ownership, if any, to determine whether to consolidate the entity. Instead each party having a variable interest in the VIE must determine the extent to which it shares in the VIE's expected profits and losses. **ASC 810-10-20** defines a *variable interest* in a VIE as a contractual ownership (with or without voting rights), or other money-related interest in an entity that changes with changes in the fair value of the entity's net assets exclusive of variable interests. In other words, variable interests increase with the VIE's profits and decrease with its losses. The VIE's variable interests will absorb portions of the losses, if they occur, or receive portions of the residual returns.

There are several different types of variable interests, some of which can be summarized as follows:

Type of Interest	Variable Interest?
Common stock, with no special features or provisions	Yes
Common stock, with loss protection or other provisions	Maybe
Senior debt	Usually not
Subordinated debt	Yes
Loan or asset guarantees	Yes

✋ STOP & THINK

The following "red flags" often indicate a variable interest:

- Subordinated loans to a VIE.
- Equity interests in a VIE (50% or less).
- Guarantees to a VIE's lenders or equity holders.
- Guarantees of asset recovery values.
- Written <u>put</u> options on a VIE's assets held by a VIE or its lenders or equity holders.
- Forward contracts on purchases and sales.

Common stock that places the owners' investment at risk is a variable interest. In some cases, common stock may have, by agreement, special provisions that protect the investor against losses or provide a fixed return. These special types of shares may not involve significant risk on the part of the investor and might, depending on the provisions, result in an interest that is not a variable interest. Senior debt usually carries a fixed return and is protected against loss by subordinated

> **! CAUTION**
>
> A pending FASB rule change regarding the determination of the primary beneficiary will involve a more qualitative approach requiring both of the following (810-10-25-38A): (a) The power to direct the activities of a VIE that most significantly impact the VIE's economic performance and (b) The obligation to absorb losses of the VIE that could potentially be significant to the VIE or the right to receive benefits from the VIE that could potentially be significant to the VIE.

interests. Subordinated debt represents a variable interest because, if the entity's cash flows are insufficient to pay off the subordinated debt, the holders of that debt will sustain losses. They do not have the same protection against loss that holders of the senior debt have. Parties that guarantee the value of assets or liabilities can sustain losses if they are called on to make good on their guarantees, and, therefore, the guarantees represent variable interests.

The nature of each party's variable interest determines whether consolidation by that party is appropriate. In recent years, an enterprise that absorbs a majority of the VIE's expected losses, receives a majority of the VIE's expected residual returns, or both, is called the ***primary beneficiary*** of the variable interest entity. The primary beneficiary must consolidate the VIE. If the entity's profits and losses are divided differently, the enterprise absorbing a majority of the losses will consolidate the VIE.

As an example of the financial reporting determinations of parties with an interest in a VIE, suppose that Young Company and Zebra Corporation, both financially stable companies, create YZ Corporation to lease equipment to Young and other companies. Zebra purchases all of YZ's common stock. Young guarantees Zebra a 7 percent dividend on its stock, agrees to absorb all of YZ's losses, and guarantees fixed-rate bank loans that are made to YZ. All profits in excess of the 7 percent payout to Zebra are split evenly between Young and Zebra.

In this case, the bank loans are not variable interests because they carry a fixed interest rate and are guaranteed by Young, a company capable of honoring the guarantee. Common stock of a VIE is a variable interest if the investment is at risk. In this case, Zebra's investment is not at risk, but it does share in the profits of YZ, and the amount of profits is not fixed. Therefore, the common stock is a variable interest. However, Zebra will not consolidate YZ because Zebra does not share in the losses, all of which Young will bear. Young will consolidate YZ because Young's guarantees represent a variable interest, and it will absorb a majority (all) of the losses.

If consolidation of a VIE is appropriate, the amounts to be consolidated with those of the primary beneficiary are based on fair values at the date the enterprise first becomes the primary beneficiary. However, assets and liabilities transferred to a VIE by its primary beneficiary are valued at their book values, with no gain or loss recognized on the transfer. Subsequent to the initial determination of consolidation values, a VIE is accounted for in consolidated financial statements in accordance with **ASC 810-10-10** in the same manner as if it were consolidated based on voting interests. Intercompany balances and transactions are eliminated so the resulting consolidated financial statements appear as if there were just a single entity. These procedures are consistent with those used when consolidating parent and subsidiary corporations. Appendix 3A at the end of the chapter presents a simple illustration of the consolidation of a VIE.

> **FYI**
>
> Disney controls Euro Disney and Hong Kong Disneyland as variable interest entities. Disney follows **ASC 810-10-10** by fully consolidating the financial statements of Euro Disney and Hong Kong Disneyland.

LO 3-8

Understand and explain differences in consolidation rules under U.S. GAAP and IFRS.

IFRS Differences in Determining Control of VIEs and SPEs

Although rules under International Financial Reporting Standards (IFRS) for consolidation are generally very similar to those under U.S. GAAP, there are some important differences. Figure 3–5 provides a summary of the main differences in current standards.

FIGURE 3–5   Summary of Differences between IFRS and U.S. GAAP related to Control and VIEs

Topic	U.S. GAAP	IFRS
Determination of Control	• Normally, control is determined by majority ownership of voting shares. • However, majority ownership may not indicate control of a VIE. • Thus, VIE rules must be evaluated first in all situations. • The primary beneficiary must consolidate a VIE. • The majority shareholder consolidates most non-VIEs. • Control is based on direct or indirect voting interests. • An entity with less than 50 percent ownership may have "effective control" through other contractual arrangements.	• Normally, control is determined by majority ownership of voting shares. • In addition to voting shares, convertible instruments and other contractual rights that could affect control are considered. • A parent with less than 50 percent of the voting shares could have control through contractual arrangements allowing control of votes or the board of directors. • Control over SPEs is determined based on judgment and relevant facts. • Substance over is form considered in determining whether an SPE should be consolidated.
Related Parties	• Interests held by related parties and *de facto* agents may be considered in determining control of a VIE.	• There is no specific provision for related parties or *de facto* agents.
Definitions of VIEs versus SPEs	• SPEs can be VIEs. • Consolidation rules focus on whether an entity is a VIE (regardless of whether or not it is an SPE). • U.S. GAAP guidance applies only to legal entities.	• IFRS considers specific indicators of whether an entity has control of an SPE: (1) whether the SPE conducts activities for the entity, (2) whether the entity has decision-making power to obtain majority of benefits from the SPE, (3) whether the entity has the right to majority of benefits from the SPE, and (4) whether the entity has a majority of the SPE's residual or risks. • IFRS guidance applies whether or not conducted by a legal entity.
Disclosure	• Disclosures are required for determining control of a VIE. • Entities must disclose whether or not they are the primary beneficiary of related VIEs.	• There are no SPE-specific disclosure requirements. • There are specific disclosure requirements related to consolidation in general.
Accounting for Joint Ventures	• Owners typically share control (often with 50-50 ownership). • If the joint venture is a VIE, contracts must be considered to determine whether consolidation is required. • If the joint venture is not a VIE, venturers use the equity method. • Proportional consolidation is generally not permitted.	• Joint ventures can be accounted for using either proportionate consolidation or the equity method. • Proportionate consolidation reports the venturer's share of the assets, liabilities, income, and expenses on a line-by-line basis based on the venturer's financial statement line items.

SUMMARY OF KEY CONCEPTS

Consolidated financial statements present the financial position and operating results of a parent and one or more subsidiaries as if they were actually a single company. As a result, the consolidated financial statements portray a group of legally separate companies as a single economic entity. All indications of intercorporate ownership and the effects of all intercompany transactions are excluded from the consolidated statements. The basic approach to the preparation of consolidated financial statements is to combine the separate financial statements of the individual consolidating companies and then to eliminate or adjust those items that would not appear, or that would appear differently, if the companies actually were one.

Current consolidation standards require that the consolidated financial statements include all companies under common control unless control is questionable. Consolidated financial statements are prepared primarily for those with a long-run interest in the parent company, especially the parent's stockholders and long-term creditors. While consolidated financial statements allow interested parties to view a group of related companies as a single economic entity, such statements have some limitations. In particular, information about the characteristics and operations of the individual companies within the consolidated entity is lost in the process of combining financial statements.

New types of business arrangements have proven troublesome in the past for financial reporting. In particular, special types of entities, called *special-purpose entities* and *variable interest entities,* have been used to hide or transform various types of transactions, in addition to being used for many legitimate purposes such as risk sharing. Often these entities were disclosed only through vague notes to the financial statements. Reporting standards now require that the party that is the primary beneficiary of a variable interest entity consolidate that entity.

KEY TERMS

combined financial statements, *119*	effective control, *105*	special-purpose entities (SPEs), *120*
consolidated net income, *107*	indirect control, *104*	variable interest entity (VIE), *121*
direct control, *104*	minority interest, *106*	
	noncontrolling interest, *106*	
	primary beneficiary, *122*	

Appendix 3A   Consolidation of Variable Interest Entities

The standards for determining whether a party with an interest in a variable interest entity (VIE) should consolidate the VIE were discussed earlier in the chapter. Once a party has determined that it must consolidate a VIE, the consolidation procedures are similar to those used when consolidating a subsidiary. As an illustration, assume that Ignition Petroleum Company joins with Mammoth Financial Corporation to create a special corporation, Exploration Equipment Company, that would lease equipment to Ignition and other companies. Ignition purchases 10 percent of Exploration's stock for $1,000,000, and Mammoth purchases the other 90 percent for $9,000,000. Profits are to be split equally between the two owners, but Ignition agrees to absorb the first $500,000 of annual losses. Immediately after incorporation, Exploration borrows $120,000,000 from a syndicate of banks, and Ignition guarantees the loan. Exploration then purchases plant, equipment, and supplies for its own use and equipment for lease to others. The balance sheets of Ignition and Exploration appear as follows just prior to the start of Exploration's operations:

Item	Ignition	Exploration
Cash and Receivables	$100,000,000	$ 23,500,000
Inventory and Supplies	50,000,000	200,000
Equipment Held for Lease		105,000,000
Investment in Exploration Equipment Co.	1,000,000	
Plant & Equipment (net)	180,000,000	1,350,000
Total Assets	$331,000,000	$130,050,000
Accounts Payable	$ 900,000	$ 50,000
Bank Loans Payable	30,000,000	120,000,000
Common Stock Issued & Outstanding	200,000,000	10,000,000
Retained Earnings	100,100,000	
Total Liabilities & Equity	$331,000,000	$130,050,000

FIGURE 3–6
Balance Sheet
Consolidating a Variable
Interest Entity

IGNITION PETROLEUM COMPANY
Consolidated Balance Sheet

Assets		
Cash & Receivables		$123,500,000
Inventory & Supplies		50,200,000
Equipment Held for Lease		105,000,000
Plant & Equipment (net)		181,350,000
Total Assets		$460,050,000
Liabilities		
Accounts Payable	$ 950,000	
Bank Loans Payable	150,000,000	
Total Liabilities		$150,950,000
Stockholders' Equity		
Common Stock	$200,000,000	
Retained Earnings	100,100,000	
Noncontrolling Interest	9,000,000	
Total Stockholders' Equity		309,100,000
Total Liabilities & Stockholders' Equity		$460,050,000

Both Ignition and Mammoth hold variable interests in Exploration. Ignition's variable interests include both its common stock and its guarantees. Ignition is the primary beneficiary of Exploration because it shares equally in the profits with Mammoth but must absorb a larger share of the expected losses than Mammoth through both its profit-and-loss-sharing agreement with Mammoth and its loan guarantee. Accordingly, Ignition must consolidate Exploration.

Ignition's consolidated balance sheet that includes Exploration appears as in Figure 3–6. The balances in Exploration's asset and liability accounts are added to the balances of Ignition's like accounts. Ignition's $1,000,000 investment in Exploration is eliminated against the common stock of Exploration, and Exploration's remaining $9,000,000 of common stock (owned by Mammoth) is labeled as noncontrolling interest and reported within the equity section of the consolidated balance sheet.

QUESTIONS

LO 3-1	**Q3-1**	What is the basic idea underlying the preparation of consolidated financial statements?
LO 3-1	**Q3-2**	How might consolidated statements help an investor assess the desirability of purchasing shares of the parent company?
LO 3-1	**Q3-3**	Are consolidated financial statements likely to be more useful to the owners of the parent company or to the noncontrolling owners of the subsidiaries? Why?
LO 3-2	**Q3-4**	What is meant by *parent company?* When is a company considered to be a parent?
LO 3-1	**Q3-5**	Are consolidated financial statements likely to be more useful to the creditors of the parent company or the creditors of the subsidiaries? Why?
LO 3-2	**Q3-6**	Why is ownership of a majority of the common stock of another company considered important in consolidation?
LO 3-2	**Q3-7**	What major criteria must be met before a company is consolidated?
LO 3-2	**Q3-8**	When is consolidation considered inappropriate even though the parent holds a majority of the voting common shares of another company?
LO 3-7	**Q3-9**	How has reliance on legal control as a consolidation criterion led to off-balance sheet financing?
LO 3-7	**Q3-10**	What types of entities are referred to as *special-purpose entities,* and how have they generally been used?

LO 3-7   **Q3-11**   How does a variable interest entity typically differ from a traditional corporate business entity?

LO 3-7   **Q3-12**   What characteristics are normally examined in determining whether a company is a primary beneficiary of a variable interest entity?

LO 3-2   **Q3-13**   What is meant by *indirect control?* Give an illustration.

LO 3-2   **Q3-14**   What means other than majority ownership might be used to gain control over a company? Can consolidation occur if control is gained by other means?

LO 3-4   **Q3-15**   Why are subsidiary shares not reported as stock outstanding in the consolidated balance sheet?

LO 3-2   **Q3-16**   What must be done if the fiscal periods of the parent and its subsidiary are not the same?

LO 3-3   **Q3-17**   What is the noncontrolling interest in a subsidiary?

LO 3-4, 3-6   **Q3-18**   What is the difference between consolidated and combined financial statements?

CASES

LO 3-5   **C3-1**   **Computation of Total Asset Values**

A reader of Gigantic Company's consolidated financial statements received from another source copies of the financial statements of the individual companies included in the consolidation. The person is confused by the fact that the total assets in the consolidated balance sheet differ rather substantially from the sum of the asset totals reported by the individual companies.

Required

Will this relationship always be true? What factors may cause this difference to occur?

LO 3-3, 3-7   **C3-2**   **Accounting Entity [AICPA Adapted]**

The concept of the accounting entity often is considered to be the most fundamental of accounting concepts, one that pervades all of accounting. For each of the following, indicate whether the entity concept is applicable; discuss and give illustrations.

Required

  a. A unit created by or under law.
  b. The product-line segment of an enterprise.
  c. A combination of legal units.
  d. All the activities of an owner or a group of owners.
  e. The economy of the United States.

LO 3-3, 3-6   **C3-3**   **Joint Venture Investment**

 Research

Dell Computer Corp. and CIT Group Inc. established Dell Financial Services LP (DFS) as a joint venture to provide financing services for Dell customers. Dell originally purchased 70 percent of the equity of DFS and CIT purchased 30 percent. In the initial agreement, losses were allocated entirely to CIT, although CIT would recoup any losses before any future income was allocated. At the time the joint venture was formed, both Dell and CIT indicated that they had no plans to consolidate DFS.

Required

  a. How could both Dell and CIT avoid consolidating DFS?
  b. Does Dell currently employ off-balance sheet financing? Explain.

LO 3-1   **C3-4**   **What Company Is That?**

 Analysis

Many well-known products and names come from companies that may be less well known or may be known for other reasons. In some cases, an obscure parent company may have well-known subsidiaries, and often familiar but diverse products may be produced under common ownership.

Required

  a. Viacom is not necessarily a common name easily identified because it operates through numerous subsidiaries, but its brand names are seen every day. What are some of the well-known brand names from Viacom's subsidiaries? What changes occurred in its organizational structure in 2006? Who is Sumner Redstone?

b. ConAgra Foods Inc. is one of the world's largest food processors and distributors. Although it produces many products with familiar names, the company's name generally is not well known. What are some of ConAgra's brand names?

c. What type of company is Yum! Brands Inc.? What are some of its well-known brands? What is the origin of the company, and what was its previous name?

LO 3-1

Analysis

C3-5   Subsidiaries and Core Businesses

During previous merger booms, a number of companies acquired many subsidiaries that often were in businesses unrelated to the acquiring company's central operations. In many cases, the acquiring company's management was unable to manage effectively the many diverse types of operations found in the numerous subsidiaries. More recently, many of these subsidiaries have been sold or, in a few cases, liquidated so the parent companies could concentrate on their core businesses.

Required

a. In 1986, General Electric acquired nearly all of the common stock of the large brokerage firm Kidder, Peabody Inc. Unfortunately, the newly acquired subsidiary's performance was very poor. What ultimately happened to this General Electric subsidiary?

b. What major business has Sears Holdings Corporation been in for many decades? What other businesses was it in during the 1980s and early 1990s? What were some of its best-known subsidiaries during that time? Does Sears still own those subsidiaries? What additional acquisitions have occurred?

c. PepsiCo is best known as a soft-drink company. What well-known subsidiaries did PepsiCo own during the mid-1990s? Does PepsiCo still own them?

d. When a parent company and its subsidiaries are in businesses that are considerably different in nature, such as retailing and financial services, how meaningful are their consolidated financial statements in your opinion? Explain. How might financial reporting be improved in such situations?

LO 3-8

Research

C3-6   International Consolidation Issues

The International Accounting Standards Board (IASB) is charged with developing a set of high-quality standards and encouraging their adoption globally. Standards promulgated by the IASB are called International Financial Reporting Standards (IFRS). The European Union (EU) requires statements prepared using IFRS for all companies that list on the EU stock exchanges. Currently, the SEC allows international companies that list on U.S. exchanges to use IFRS for financial reporting in the United States.

The differences between U.S. GAAP and IFRS are described in many different publications. For example, PricewaterhouseCoopers has a publication available for download on its website (http://www.pwc.com/us/en/issues/ifrs-reporting/publications/ifrs-and-us-gaap-similarities-and-differences.jhtml) entitled "IFRS and U.S. GAAP: Similarities and Differences" that provides a topic-based comparison. Based on the information in this publication or others, answer the following questions about the preparation of consolidated financial statements.

Required

a. Under U.S. GAAP, a two-tiered consolidation model is applied, one focused on voting rights and the second based on a party's exposure to risks and rewards associated with the entity's activities (the VIE model). Upon what is the IFRS framework based?

b. U.S. GAAP requires a two-step process to evaluate goodwill for potential impairment (as discussed in Chapter 1). What is required by IFRS with respect to goodwill impairment?

c. Under U.S. GAAP, noncontrolling interests are measured at fair value. What is required by IFRS?

LO 3-7

Understanding

C3-7   Off-Balance Sheet Financing and VIEs

A variable interest entity (VIE) is a structure frequently used for off-balance sheet financing. VIEs have become quite numerous in recent years and have been the subject of some controversy.

Required

a. Briefly explain what is meant by off-balance sheet financing.

b. What are three techniques used to keep debt off the balance sheet?

c. What are some legitimate uses of VIEs?

d. How can VIEs be used to manage earnings to meet financial reporting goals? How does this relate to the importance of following the intent of the guidelines for consolidations?

LO 3-6

C3-8   Consolidation Differences among Major Companies

Research

A variety of organizational structures are used by major companies, and different approaches to consolidation are sometimes found. Two large and familiar U.S. corporations are Union Pacific and ExxonMobil.

Required

a. Many large companies have tens or even hundreds of subsidiaries. List the significant subsidiaries of Union Pacific Corporation.

b. ExxonMobil Corporation is a major energy company. Does ExxonMobil consolidate all of its majority-owned subsidiaries? Explain. Does ExxonMobil consolidate any entities in which it does not hold majority ownership? Explain. What methods does ExxonMobil use to account for investments in the common stock of companies in which it holds less than majority ownership?

EXERCISES

LO 3-1, 3-2

E3-1   Multiple-Choice Questions on Consolidation Overview [AICPA Adapted]

Select the correct answer for each of the following questions.

1. When a parent–subsidiary relationship exists, consolidated financial statements are prepared in recognition of the accounting concept of
   a. Reliability.
   b. Materiality.
   c. Legal entity.
   d. Economic entity.

2. Consolidated financial statements are typically prepared when one company has a controlling interest in another unless
   a. The subsidiary is a finance company.
   b. The fiscal year-ends of the two companies are more than three months apart.
   c. Circumstances prevent the exercise of control.
   d. The two companies are in unrelated industries, such as real estate and manufacturing.

3. Penn Inc., a manufacturing company, owns 75 percent of the common stock of Sell Inc., an investment company. Sell owns 60 percent of the common stock of Vane Inc., an insurance company. In Penn's consolidated financial statements, should Sell and Vane be consolidated or reported as equity method investments (assuming there are no side agreements)?
   a. Consolidation used for Sell and equity method used for Vane.
   b. Consolidation used for both Sell and Vane.
   c. Equity method used for Sell and consolidation used for Vane.
   d. Equity method used for both Sell and Vane.

4. Which of the following is the best theoretical justification for consolidated financial statements?
   a. In form, the companies are one entity; in substance, they are separate.
   b. In form, the companies are separate; in substance, they are one entity.
   c. In form and substance, the companies are one entity.
   d. In form and substance, the companies are separate.

LO 3-7

E3-2   Multiple-Choice Questions on Variable Interest Entities

Select the correct answer for each of the following questions.

1. Special-purpose entities generally
   a. Have a much larger portion of assets financed by equity shareholders than do companies such as General Motors.
   b. Have relatively large amounts of preferred stock and convertible securities outstanding.

Advanced Financial Accounting, 11th Edition   **129**

Chapter 3 *The Reporting Entity and the Consolidation of Less-than-Wholly-Owned Subsidiaries with No Differential*   **129**

   c. Have a much smaller portion of their assets financed by equity shareholders than do companies such as General Motors.

   d. Pay out a relatively high percentage of their earnings as dividends to facilitate the sale of additional shares.

2. Variable interest entities may be established as

   a. Corporations.

   b. Trusts.

   c. Partnerships.

   d. All of the above.

3. An enterprise that will absorb a majority of a variable interest entity's expected losses is called the

   a. Primary beneficiary.

   b. Qualified owner.

   c. Major facilitator.

   d. Critical management director.

4. In determining whether or not a variable interest entity is to be consolidated, the FASB focused on

   a. Legal control.

   b. Share of profits and obligation to absorb losses.

   c. Frequency of intercompany transfers.

   d. Proportionate size of the two entities.

LO 3-5

E3-3   Multiple-Choice Questions on Consolidated Balances [AICPA Adapted]
Select the correct answer for each of the following questions.

Items 1 and 2 are based on the following:

On January 2, 20X8, Pare Company acquired 75 percent of Kidd Company's outstanding common stock at an amount equal to its underlying book value. Selected balance sheet data at December 31, 20X8, are as follows:

	Pare Company	Kidd Company
Total Assets	$420,000	$180,000
Liabilities	$120,000	$ 60,000
Common Stock	100,000	50,000
Retained Earnings	200,000	70,000
	$420,000	$180,000

1. In Pare's December 31, 20X8, consolidated balance sheet, what amount should be reported as minority interest in net assets?

   a. $0.

   b. $30,000.

   c. $45,000.

   d. $105,000.

2. In its consolidated balance sheet at December 31, 20X8, what amount should Pare report as common stock outstanding?

   a. $50,000.

   b. $100,000.

   c. $137,500.

   d. $150,000.

3. Consolidated statements are proper for Neely Inc., Randle Inc., and Walker Inc., if

    a. Neely owns 80 percent of the outstanding common stock of Randle and 40 percent of Walker; Randle owns 30 percent of Walker.

    b. Neely owns 100 percent of the outstanding common stock of Randle and 90 percent of Walker; Neely bought the Walker stock one month before the foreign country in which Walker is based imposed restrictions preventing Walker from remitting profits to Neely.

    c. Neely owns 100 percent of the outstanding common stock of Randle and Walker; Walker is in legal reorganization.

    d. Neely owns 80 percent of the outstanding common stock of Randle and 40 percent of Walker; Reeves Inc. owns 55 percent of Walker.

LO 3-2, 3-3   **E3-4**   **Multiple-Choice Questions on Consolidation Overview [AICPA Adapted]**

Select the correct answer for each of the following questions.

1. Consolidated financial statements are typically prepared when one company has

    a. Accounted for its investment in another company by the equity method.

    b. Accounted for its investment in another company by the cost method.

    c. Significant influence over the operating and financial policies of another company.

    d. The controlling financial interest in another company.

2. Aaron Inc. owns 80 percent of the outstanding stock of Belle Inc. Compare the total consolidated net earnings of Aaron and Belle (X) and Aaron's operating earnings before considering the income from Belle (Y). Assume that neither company incurs a net loss during the period.

    a. X is more than Y.

    b. X is equal to Y.

    c. X is less than Y.

    d. Cannot be determined.

3. On October 1, X Company acquired for cash all of Y Company's outstanding common stock. Both companies have a December 31 year-end and have been in business for many years. Consolidated net income for the year ended December 31 should include net income of

    a. X Company for three months and Y Company for three months.

    b. X Company for 12 months and Y Company for 3 months.

    c. X Company for 12 months and Y Company for 12 months.

    d. X Company for 12 months, but no income from Y Company until Y Company distributes a dividend.

4. Ownership of 51 percent of the outstanding voting stock of a company would usually result in

    a. The use of the cost method.

    b. The use of the lower-of-cost-or-market method.

    c. The use of the equity method.

    d. A consolidation.

LO 3-5   **E3-5**   **Balance Sheet Consolidation**

On January 1, 20X3, Guild Corporation reported total assets of $470,000, liabilities of $270,000, and stockholders' equity of $200,000. At that date, Bristol Corporation reported total assets of $190,000, liabilities of $135,000, and stockholders' equity of $55,000. Following lengthy negotiations, Guild paid Bristol's existing shareholders $44,000 in cash for 80 percent of the voting common shares of Bristol.

Required

Immediately after Guild purchased the Bristol shares

    a. What amount of total assets did Guild report in its individual balance sheet?

    b. What amount of total assets was reported in the consolidated balance sheet?

    c. What amount of total liabilities was reported in the consolidated balance sheet?

    d. What amount of stockholders' equity was reported in the consolidated balance sheet?

LO 3-5

E3-6   Balance Sheet Consolidation with Intercompany Transfer

Potter Company acquired 90 percent of the voting common shares of Stately Corporation by issuing bonds with a par value and fair value of $121,500 to Stately's existing shareholders. Immediately prior to the acquisition, Potter reported total assets of $510,000, liabilities of $320,000, and stockholders' equity of $190,000. At that date, Stately reported total assets of $350,000, liabilities of $215,000, and stockholders' equity of $135,000.

Required
Immediately after Potter acquired Stately's shares

a. What amount of total assets did Potter report in its individual balance sheet?
b. What amount of total assets was reported in the consolidated balance sheet?
c. What amount of total liabilities was reported in the consolidated balance sheet?
d. What amount of stockholders' equity was reported in the consolidated balance sheet?

LO 3-5

E3-7   Subsidiary Acquired for Cash

Fineline Pencil Company acquired 80 percent of Smudge Eraser Corporation's stock on January 2, 20X3, for $72,000 cash. Summarized balance sheet data for the companies on December 31, 20X2, are as follows:

	Fineline Pencil Company		Smudge Eraser Corporation	
	Book Value	Fair Value	Book Value	Fair Value
Cash	$200,000	$200,000	$ 50,000	$ 50,000
Other Assets	400,000	400,000	120,000	120,000
Total Debits	$600,000		$170,000	
Current Liabilities	$100,000	100,000	$ 80,000	80,000
Common Stock	300,000		50,000	
Retained Earnings	200,000		40,000	
Total Credits	$600,000		$170,000	

Required
Prepare a consolidated balance sheet immediately following the acquisition.

LO 3-5

E3-8   Subsidiary Acquired with Bonds

Byte Computer Corporation acquired 75 percent of Nofail Software Company's stock on January 2, 20X3, by issuing bonds with a par value of $50,000 and a fair value of $67,500 in exchange for the shares. Summarized balance sheet data presented for the companies just before the acquisition are as follows:

	Byte Computer Corporation		Nofail Software Company	
	Book Value	Fair Value	Book Value	Fair Value
Cash	$200,000	$200,000	$ 50,000	$ 50,000
Other Assets	400,000	400,000	120,000	120,000
Total Debits	$600,000		$170,000	
Current Liabilities	$100,000	100,000	$ 80,000	80,000
Common Stock	300,000		50,000	
Retained Earnings	200,000		40,000	
Total Credits	$600,000		$170,000	

Required
Prepare a consolidated balance sheet immediately following the acquisition.

LO 3-5

E3-9 Subsidiary Acquired by Issuing Preferred Stock

Byte Computer Corporation acquired 90 percent of Nofail Software Company's common stock on January 2, 20X3, by issuing preferred stock with a par value of $6 per share and a market value of $8.10 per share. A total of 10,000 shares of preferred stock was issued. Balance sheet data for the two companies immediately before the business combination are presented in E3-8.

Required
Prepare a consolidated balance sheet for the companies immediately after Byte obtains ownership of Nofail by issuing the preferred stock.

LO 3-4, 3-7

E3-10 Reporting for a Variable Interest Entity

Gamble Company convinced Conservative Corporation that the two companies should establish Simpletown Corporation to build a new gambling casino in Simpletown Corner. Although chances for the casino's success were relatively low, a local bank loaned $140,000,000 to the new corporation, which built the casino at a cost of $130,000,000. Conservative purchased 100 percent of the initial capital stock offering for $5,600,000, and Gamble agreed to supply 100 percent of the management and guarantee the bank loan. Gamble also guaranteed a 20 percent return to Conservative on its investment for the first 10 years. Gamble will receive all profits in excess of the 20 percent return to Conservative. Immediately after the casino's construction, Gamble reported the following amounts:

Cash	$ 3,000,000
Buildings & Equipment	240,600,000
Accumulated Depreciation	10,100,000
Accounts Payable	5,000,000
Bonds Payable	20,300,000
Common Stock	103,000,000
Retained Earnings	105,200,000

The only disclosure that Gamble currently provides in its financial reports about its relationships to Conservative and Simpletown is a brief footnote indicating that a contingent liability exists on its guarantee of Simpletown Corporation's debt.

Required
Prepare a consolidated balance sheet in good form for Gamble immediately following the casino's construction.

LO 3-4, 3-7

E3-11 Consolidation of a Variable Interest Entity

Teal Corporation is the primary beneficiary of a variable interest entity with total assets of $500,000, liabilities of $470,000, and owners' equity of $30,000. Because Teal owns 25 percent of the VIE's voting stock, it reported a $7,500 investment in the VIE in its balance sheet. Teal reported total assets of $190,000 (including its investment in the VIE), liabilities of $80,000, common stock of $15,000, and retained earnings of $95,000 in its balance sheet.

Required
Prepare a consolidated balance sheet in good form for Teal, taking into consideration that it is the primary beneficiary of the variable interest entity.

LO 3-3

E3-12 Computation of Subsidiary Net Income

Frazer Corporation owns 70 percent of Messer Company's stock. In the 20X9 consolidated income statement, the noncontrolling interest was assigned $18,000 of income. There was no differential in the acquisition.

Required
What amount of net income did Messer Company report for 20X9?

Advanced Financial Accounting, 11th Edition   **133**

Chapter 3   *The Reporting Entity and the Consolidation of Less-than-Wholly-Owned Subsidiaries with No Differential*   **133**

Advanced
StudyGuide
.com

LO 3-3, 3-4   **E3-13**   ### Incomplete Consolidation

Belchfire Motors' accountant was called away after completing only half of the consolidated statements at the end of 20X4. The data left behind included the following:

Item	Belchfire Motors	Premium Body Shop	Consolidated
Cash	$ 40,000	$ 20,000	$ 60,000
Accounts Receivable	180,000	30,000	200,000
Inventory	220,000	50,000	270,000
Buildings & Equipment (net)	300,000	290,000	590,000
Investment in Premium Body Shop	150,000		
Total Debits	$890,000	$390,000	$1,120,000
Accounts Payable	$ 30,000	$ 40,000	
Bonds Payable	400,000	200,000	
Common Stock	200,000	100,000	
Retained Earnings	260,000	50,000	
Total Credits	$890,000	$390,000	

Required

a. Belchfire Motors acquired shares of Premium Body Shop at underlying book value on January 1, 20X1. What portion of the ownership of Premium Body Shop does Belchfire apparently hold?

b. Compute the consolidated totals for each of the remaining balance sheet items.

LO 3-3, 3-4   **E3-14**   ### Noncontrolling Interest

Sanderson Corporation acquired 70 percent of Kline Corporation's common stock on January 1, 20X7, for $294,000 in cash. At the acquisition date, the book values and fair values of Kline's assets and liabilities were equal, and the fair value of the noncontrolling interest was equal to 30 percent of the total book value of Kline. The stockholders' equity accounts of the two companies at the date of purchase are:

	Sanderson Corporation	Kline Corporation
Common Stock ($10 par value)	$400,000	$180,000
Additional Paid-In Capital	222,000	65,000
Retained Earnings	358,000	175,000
Total Stockholders' Equity	$980,000	$420,000

Required

a. What amount will be assigned to the noncontrolling interest on January 1, 20X7, in the consolidated balance sheet?

b. Prepare the stockholders' equity section of Sanderson and Kline's consolidated balance sheet as of January 1, 20X7.

c. Sanderson acquired ownership of Kline to ensure a constant supply of electronic switches, which it purchases regularly from Kline. Why might Sanderson not feel compelled to purchase all of Kline's shares?

LO 3-3, 3-4   **E3-15**   ### Computation of Consolidated Net Income

Ambrose Corporation owns 75 percent of Kroop Company's common stock, acquired at underlying book value on January 1, 20X4. At the acquisition date, the book values and fair values of Kroop's assets and liabilities were equal, and the fair value of the noncontrolling interest was equal to 25 percent of the total book value of Kroop. The income statements for Ambrose and Kroop for 20X4 include the following amounts:

	Ambrose Corporation	Kroop Company
Sales	$528,000	$150,000
Dividend Income	9,000	
Total Income	$537,000	$150,000
Less: Cost of Goods Sold	$380,000	$ 87,000
Depreciation Expense	32,000	20,000
Other Expenses	66,000	23,000
Total Expenses	$478,000	$130,000
Net Income	$ 59,000	$ 20,000

Ambrose uses the cost method in accounting for its ownership of Kroop. Kroop paid dividends of $12,000 in 20X4.

Required

a. What amount would Ambrose report in its income statement as income from its investment in Kroop if Ambrose used equity-method accounting?

b. What amount of income should be assigned to noncontrolling interest in the consolidated income statement for 20X4?

c. What amount should Ambrose report as consolidated net income for 20X4?

d. Why should Ambrose not report consolidated net income of $79,000 ($59,000 + $20,000) for 20X4?

LO 3-4

Advanced StudyGuide .com

E3-16 Computation of Subsidiary Balances

Tall Corporation acquired 75 percent of Light Corporation's voting common stock on January 1, 20X2, at underlying book value. At the acquisition date, the book values and fair values of Light's assets and liabilities were equal, and the fair value of the noncontrolling interest was equal to 25 percent of the total book value of Light. Noncontrolling interest was assigned income of $8,000 in Tall's consolidated income statement for 20X2 and a balance of $65,500 in Tall's consolidated balance sheet at December 31, 20X2. Light reported retained earnings of $70,000 and additional paid-in capital of $40,000 on January 1, 20X2. Light did not pay dividends or issue stock in 20X2.

Required

a. Compute the amount of net income reported by Light for 20X2.

b. Prepare the stockholders' equity section of Light's balance sheet at December 31, 20X2.

LO 3-4, 3-5

E3-17 Subsidiary Acquired at Net Book Value

On December 31, 20X8, Banner Corporation acquired 80 percent of Dwyer Company's common stock for $136,000. At the acquisition date, the book values and fair values of all of Dwyer's assets and liabilities were equal. Banner uses the equity method in accounting for its investment. Balance sheet information provided by the companies at December 31, 20X8, immediately following the acquisition is as follows:

	Banner Corporation	Dwyer Company
Cash	$ 74,000	$ 20,000
Accounts Receivable	120,000	70,000
Inventory	180,000	90,000
Fixed Assets (net)	350,000	240,000
Investment in Dwyer Company Stock	136,000	
Total Debits	$860,000	$420,000
Accounts Payable	$ 65,000	$ 30,000
Notes Payable	350,000	220,000
Common Stock	150,000	90,000
Retained Earnings	295,000	80,000
Total Credits	$860,000	$420,000

Required

Prepare a consolidated balance sheet for Banner at December 31, 20X8.

LO 3-4

E3-18 Acquisition of Majority Ownership

Lang Company reports net assets with a book value and fair value of $200,000. Pace Corporation acquires 75 percent ownership for $150,000. Pace reports net assets with a book value of $520,000 and a fair value of $640,000 at that time, excluding its investment in Lang.

Required

For each of the following, compute the amounts that would be reported immediately after the combination under current accounting practice:

a. Consolidated net identifiable assets.

b. Noncontrolling interest.

PROBLEMS

LO 3-4, 3-6

P3-19 Multiple-Choice Questions on Consolidated and Combined Financial Statements [AICPA Adapted]

Select the correct answer for each of the following questions.

1. What is the theoretically preferred method of presenting a noncontrolling interest in a consolidated balance sheet?

   a. As a separate item within the liability section.

   b. As a deduction from (contra to) goodwill from consolidation, if any.

   c. By means of notes or footnotes to the balance sheet.

   d. As a separate item within the stockholders' equity section.

2. Mr. Cord owns four corporations. Combined financial statements are being prepared for these corporations, which have intercompany loans of $200,000 and intercompany profits of $500,000. What amount of these intercompany loans and profits should be included in the combined financial statements?

	Intercompany	
	Loans	**Profits**
a.	$200,000	$ 0
b.	$200,000	$500,000
c.	$ 0	$ 0
d.	$ 0	$500,000

LO 3-4

P3-20 Determining Net Income of Parent Company

Tally Corporation and its subsidiary reported consolidated net income of $164,300 for 20X2. Tally owns 60 percent of the common shares of its subsidiary, acquired at book value. Noncontrolling interest was assigned income of $15,200 in the consolidated income statement for 20X2.

Required

Determine the amount of separate operating income reported by Tally for 20X2.

LO 3-7

P3-21 Consolidation of a Variable Interest Entity

On December 28, 20X3, Stern Corporation and Ram Company established S&R Partnership, with cash contributions of $10,000 and $40,000, respectively. The partnership's purpose is to purchase from Stern accounts receivable that have an average collection period of 80 days and hold them to collection. The partnership borrows cash from Midtown Bank and purchases the receivables without recourse but at an amount equal to the expected percent to be collected, less a financing fee of 3 percent of the gross receivables. Stern and Ram hold 20 percent and 80 percent of the ownership of the partnership, respectively, and Stern guarantees both the bank loan made to the partnership and a 15 percent annual return on the investment made by Ram. Stern receives any income in excess of the 15 percent return guaranteed to Ram. The partnership agreement provides Stern total control over the partnership's activities. On December 31, 20X3, Stern sold $8,000,000 of accounts receivable to the partnership. The partnership immediately borrowed $7,500,000 from the bank and paid Stern $7,360,000. Prior to the sale, Stern had established a $400,000 allowance for uncollectibles on the receivables sold to the partnership. The balance sheets of Stern and S&R immediately after the sale of receivables to the partnership contained the following:

	Stern Corporation	S&R Partnership
Cash	$7,960,000	$ 190,000
Accounts Receivable	4,200,000	8,000,000
Allowance for Uncollectible Accounts	(210,000)	(400,000)
Other Assets	5,400,000	
Prepaid Finance Charges	240,000	
Investment in S&R Partnership	10,000	
Accounts Payable	950,000	
Deferred Revenue		240,000
Bank Notes Payable		7,500,000
Bonds Payable	9,800,000	
Common Stock	700,000	
Retained Earnings	6,150,000	
Capital, Stern Corporation		10,000
Capital, Ram Company		40,000

Required

Assuming that Stern is S&R's primary beneficiary, prepare a consolidated balance sheet in good form for Stern at January 1, 20X4.

LO 3-7

P3-22   **Reporting for Variable Interest Entities**

Purified Oil Company and Midwest Pipeline Corporation established Venture Company to conduct oil exploration activities in North America to reduce their dependence on imported crude oil. Midwest Pipeline purchased all 20,000 shares of the newly created company for $10 each. Purified Oil agreed to purchase all of Venture's output at market price, guarantee up to $5,000,000 of debt for Venture, and absorb all losses if the company proved unsuccessful. Purified and Midwest agreed to share equally the profits up to $80,000 per year and to allocate 70 percent of those in excess of $80,000 to Purified and 30 percent to Midwest.

Venture immediately borrowed $3,000,000 from Second National Bank and purchased land, drilling equipment, and supplies to start its operations. Following these asset purchases, Venture and Purified Oil reported the following balances:

	Venture Company	Purified Oil Company
Cash	$ 230,000	$ 410,000
Drilling Supplies	420,000	
Accounts Receivable		640,000
Equipment (net)	1,800,000	6,700,000
Land	900,000	4,200,000
Accounts Payable	150,000	440,000
Bank Loans Payable	3,000,000	8,800,000
Common Stock	200,000	560,000
Retained Earnings		2,150,000

The only disclosure that Purified Oil currently provides in its financial statements with respect to its relationship with Midwest Pipeline and Venture is a brief note indicating that a contingent liability exists on the guarantee of Venture Company debt.

Required

Assuming that Venture is considered to be a variable interest entity and Purified Oil is the primary beneficiary, prepare a balance sheet in good form for Purified Oil.

LO 3-4   **P3-23**   ## Parent Company and Consolidated Amounts

Quoton Corporation acquired 80 percent of Tempro Company's common stock on December 31, 20X5, at underlying book value. The book values and fair values of Tempro's assets and liabilities were equal, and the fair value of the noncontrolling interest was equal to 20 percent of the total book value of Tempro. Tempro provided the following trial balance data at December 31, 20X5:

	Debit	Credit
Cash	$ 28,000	
Accounts Receivable	65,000	
Inventory	90,000	
Buildings & Equipment (net)	210,000	
Cost of Goods Sold	105,000	
Depreciation Expense	24,000	
Other Operating Expenses	31,000	
Dividends Declared	15,000	
Accounts Payable		$ 33,000
Notes Payable		120,000
Common Stock		90,000
Retained Earnings		130,000
Sales		195,000
Total	$568,000	$568,000

Required

a. How much did Quoton pay to purchase its shares of Tempro?

b. If consolidated financial statements are prepared at December 31, 20X5, what amount will be assigned to the noncontrolling interest in the consolidated balance sheet?

c. If Quoton reported income of $143,000 from its separate operations for 20X5, what amount of consolidated net income will be reported for 20X5?

d. If Quoton had purchased its ownership of Tempro on January 1, 20X5, at underlying book value and Quoton reported income of $143,000 from its separate operations for 20X5, what amount of consolidated net income would be reported for 20X5?

LO 3-4   **P3-24**   ## Parent Company and Consolidated Balances

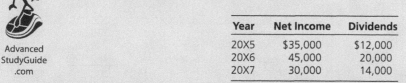

Advanced
StudyGuide
.com

Exacto Company reported the following net income and dividends for the years indicated:

Year	Net Income	Dividends
20X5	$35,000	$12,000
20X6	45,000	20,000
20X7	30,000	14,000

True Corporation acquired 75 percent of Exacto's common stock on January 1, 20X5. On that date, the fair value of Exacto's net assets was equal to the book value. True uses the equity method in accounting for its ownership in Exacto and reported a balance of $259,800 in its investment account on December 31, 20X7.

Required

a. What amount did True pay when it purchased Exacto's shares?

b. What was the fair value of Exacto's net assets on January 1, 20X5?

c. What amount was assigned to the NCI shareholders on January 1, 20X5?

d. What amount will be assigned to the NCI shareholders in the consolidated balance sheet prepared at December 31, 20X7?

LO 3-2, 3-4 **P3-25** **Indirect Ownership**

Purple Corporation recently attempted to expand by acquiring ownership in Green Company. The following ownership structure was reported on December 31, 20X9:

Investor	Investee	Percentage of Ownership Held
Purple Corporation	Green Company	70
Green Company	Orange Corporation	10
Orange Corporation	Blue Company	60
Green Company	Yellow Company	40

The following income from operations (excluding investment income) and dividend payments were reported by the companies during 20X9:

Company	Operating Income	Dividends Paid
Purple Corporation	$ 90,000	$60,000
Green Company	20,000	10,000
Orange Corporation	40,000	30,000
Blue Company	100,000	80,000
Yellow Company	60,000	40,000

Required

Compute the amount reported as consolidated net income for 20X9.

LO 3-4, 3-5 **P3-26** **Consolidated Worksheet and Balance Sheet on the Acquisition Date (Equity Method)**

Advanced
StudyGuide
.com

Peanut Company acquired 90 percent of Snoopy Company's outstanding common stock for $270,000 on January 1, 20X8, when the book value of Snoopy's net assets was equal to $300,000. Peanut uses the equity method to account for investments. Trial balance data for Peanut and Snoopy as of January 1, 20X8, are as follows:

	Peanut Company	Snoopy Company
Assets		
Cash	55,000	20,000
Accounts Receivable	50,000	30,000
Inventory	100,000	60,000
Investment in Snoopy Stock	270,000	
Land	225,000	100,000
Buildings & Equipment	700,000	200,000
Accumulated Depreciation	(400,000)	(10,000)
Total Assets	1,000,000	400,000
Liabilities & Stockholders' Equity		
Accounts Payable	75,000	25,000
Bonds Payable	200,000	75,000
Common Stock	500,000	200,000
Retained Earnings	225,000	100,000
Total Liabilities & Equity	1,000,000	400,000

Required

a. Prepare the journal entry on Peanut's books for the acquisition of Snoopy on January 1, 20X8.

b. Prepare a consolidation worksheet on the acquisition date, January 1, 20X8, in good form.

c. Prepare a consolidated balance sheet on the acquisition date, January 1, 20X8, in good form.

LO 3-4, 3-5   **P3-27**

Advanced
StudyGuide
.com

Consolidated Worksheet at End of the First Year of Ownership (Equity Method)

Peanut Company acquired 90 percent of Snoopy Company's outstanding common stock for $270,000 on January 1, 20X8, when the book value of Snoopy's net assets was equal to $300,000. Peanut uses the equity method to account for investments. Trial balance data for Peanut and Snoopy as of December 31, 20X8, are as follows:

	Peanut Company		Snoopy Company	
	Debit	**Credit**	**Debit**	**Credit**
Cash	158,000		80,000	
Accounts Receivable	165,000		65,000	
Inventory	200,000		75,000	
Investment in Snoopy Stock	319,500		0	
Land	200,000		100,000	
Buildings & Equipment	700,000		200,000	
Cost of Goods Sold	200,000		125,000	
Depreciation Expense	50,000		10,000	
Selling & Administrative Expense	225,000		40,000	
Dividends Declared	100,000		20,000	
Accumulated Depreciation		450,000		20,000
Accounts Payable		75,000		60,000
Bonds Payable		200,000		85,000
Common Stock		500,000		200,000
Retained Earnings		225,000		100,000
Sales		800,000		250,000
Income from Snoopy		67,500		0
Total	2,317,500	2,317,500	715,000	715,000

Required

a. Prepare any equity-method entry(ies) related to the investment in Snoopy Company during 20X8.

b. Prepare a consolidation worksheet for 20X8 in good form.

LO 3-4, 3-5   **P3-28**

Advanced
StudyGuide
.com

Consolidated Worksheet at End of the Second Year of Ownership (Equity Method)

Peanut Company acquired 90 percent of Snoopy Company's outstanding common stock for $270,000 on January 1, 20X8, when the book value of Snoopy's net assets was equal to $300,000. Problem 3-34 summarizes the first year of Peanut's ownership of Snoopy. Peanut uses the equity method to account for investments. The following trial balance summarizes the financial position and operations for Peanut and Snoopy as of December 31, 20X9:

	Peanut Company		Snoopy Company	
	Debit	**Credit**	**Debit**	**Credit**
Cash	255,000		75,000	
Accounts Receivable	190,000		80,000	
Inventory	180,000		100,000	
Investment in Snoopy Stock	364,500		0	
Land	200,000		100,000	
Buildings & Equipment	700,000		200,000	
Cost of Goods Sold	270,000		150,000	
Depreciation Expense	50,000		10,000	
Selling & Administrative Expense	230,000		60,000	
Dividends Declared	225,000		30,000	
Accumulated Depreciation		500,000		30,000
Accounts Payable		75,000		35,000
Bonds Payable		150,000		85,000
Common Stock		500,000		200,000

(continued)

Retained Earnings		517,500		155,000
Sales		850,000		300,000
Income from Snoopy		72,000		0
Total	2,664,500	2,664,500	805,000	805,000

Required

a. Prepare any equity-method journal entry(ies) related to the investment in Snoopy Company during 20X9.

b. Prepare a consolidation worksheet for 20X9 in good form.

LO 3-4, 3-5   P3-29   Consolidated Worksheet and Balance Sheet on the Acquisition Date (Equity Method)

Paper Company acquired 80 percent of Scissor Company's outstanding common stock for $296,000 on January 1, 20X8, when the book value of Scissor's net assets was equal to $370,000. Paper uses the equity method to account for investments. Trial balance data for Paper and Scissor as of January 1, 20X8, are as follows:

	Paper Company	Scissor Company
Assets		
Cash	109,000	25,000
Accounts Receivable	65,000	37,000
Inventory	125,000	87,000
Investment in Scissor Stock	296,000	
Land	280,000	125,000
Buildings & Equipment	875,000	250,000
Accumulated Depreciation	(500,000)	(24,000)
Total Assets	1,250,000	500,000
Liabilities & Stockholders' Equity		
Accounts Payable	95,000	30,000
Bonds Payable	250,000	100,000
Common Stock	625,000	250,000
Retained Earnings	280,000	120,000
Total Liabilities & Equity	1,250,000	500,000

Required

a. Prepare the journal entry on Paper's books for the acquisition of Scissor Co. on January 1, 20X8.

b. Prepare a consolidation worksheet on the acquisition date, January 1, 20X8, in good form.

c. Prepare a consolidated balance sheet on the acquisition date, January 1, 20X8, in good form.

LO 3-4, 3-5   P3-30   Consolidated Worksheet at End of the First Year of Ownership (Equity Method)

Paper Company acquired 80 percent of Scissor Company's outstanding common stock for $296,000 on January 1, 20X8, when the book value of Scissor's net assets was equal to $370,000. Paper uses the equity method to account for investments. Trial balance data for Paper and Scissor as of December 31, 20X8, are as follows:

	Paper Company		Scissor Company	
	Debit	**Credit**	**Debit**	**Credit**
Cash	191,000		46,000	
Accounts Receivable	140,000		60,000	

(continued)

Inventory	190,000		120,000	
Investment in Scissor Stock	350,400		0	
Land	250,000		125,000	
Buildings & Equipment	875,000		250,000	
Cost of Goods Sold	250,000		155,000	
Depreciation Expense	65,000		12,000	
Selling & Administrative Expense	280,000		50,000	
Dividends Declared	80,000		25,000	
Accumulated Depreciation		565,000		36,000
Accounts Payable		77,000		27,000
Bonds Payable		250,000		100,000
Common Stock		625,000		250,000
Retained Earnings		280,000		120,000
Sales		800,000		310,000
Income from Scissor		74,400		0
Total	2,671,400	2,671,400	843,000	843,000

Required

a. Prepare any equity-method entry(ies) related to the investment in Scissor Company during 20X8.

b. Prepare a consolidation worksheet for 20X8 in good form.

LO 3-4, 3-5   **P3-31**   **Consolidated Worksheet at End of the Second Year of Ownership (Equity Method)**

Paper Company acquired 80 percent of Scissor Company's outstanding common stock for $296,000 on January 1, 20X8, when the book value of Scissor's net assets was equal to $370,000. Problem 3-30 summarizes the first year of Paper's ownership of Scissor. Paper uses the equity method to account for investments. The following trial balance summarizes the financial position and operations for Paper and Scissor as of December 31, 20X9:

	Paper Company		Scissor Company	
	Debit	**Credit**	**Debit**	**Credit**
Cash	295,000		116,000	
Accounts Receivable	165,000		97,000	
Inventory	193,000		115,000	
Investment in Scissor Stock	412,000		0	
Land	250,000		125,000	
Buildings & Equipment	875,000		250,000	
Cost of Goods Sold	278,000		178,000	
Depreciation Expense	65,000		12,000	
Selling & Administrative Expense	312,000		58,000	
Dividends Declared	90,000		30,000	
Accumulated Depreciation		630,000		48,000
Accounts Payable		85,000		40,000
Bonds Payable		150,000		100,000
Common Stock		625,000		250,000
Retained Earnings		479,400		188,000
Sales		880,000		355,000
Income from Scissor		85,600		0
Total	2,935,000	2,935,000	981,000	981,000

Required

a. Prepare any equity-method journal entry(ies) related to the investment in Scissor Company during 20X9.

b. Prepare a consolidation worksheet for 20X9 in good form.

4   Consolidation of Wholly Owned Subsidiaries Acquired at More than Book Value

HOW MUCH WORK DOES IT REALLY TAKE TO CONSOLIDATE? ASK THE PEOPLE WHO DO IT AT DISNEY

DISNEY

The Walt Disney Company, whose history goes back to 1923, is parent company to some of the most well-known businesses in the world. While best known for Walt Disney Studios, world-famous parks and resorts, media operations such as the Disney Channel, and its consumer products, Disney is a widely diversified company. For example, did you know that Disney owns the ABC Television Network and is the majority owner of ESPN? While the consolidation examples you're working on in class usually involve a parent company and a single subsidiary, Disney employs a dedicated staff at its Burbank, California, headquarters each quarter to complete the consolidation of its five segments, each comprising many subsidiaries, in preparation for its quarterly 10-Q and annual 10-K filings with the SEC. Preparation for the actual consolidation begins before the end of the fiscal period. Soon after the end of the period, each segment closes its books, including performing its own subsidiary consolidations, works with the independent auditors, and prepares for the roll-up to the overall company consolidation. The work continues as the finance and accounting staff of approximately 100 men and women at the corporate offices review and analyze the results from the individual segments and work with segment financial staff to prepare what becomes the publicly disclosed set of consolidated financial statements.

However, the work doesn't all take place at the end of the fiscal period. The accounting system also tracks intercompany transactions throughout the period. The consolidation process requires the elimination of intercompany sales and asset transfers among others cost allocations (as discussed in Chapters 6 and 7). Tracking these transactions involves ongoing efforts throughout the period.

One of the reasons Disney has grown and become so diversified over the years is that it frequently acquires other companies. Three of the more notable acquisitions in recent years are Lucasfilm in 2012, Marvel Entertainment in 2009, and Pixar Animation Studios in 2006. In these and other well-known acquisitions, Disney paid more than the book value of each acquired company's net assets. Acquisition accounting rules require Disney to account for the full acquisition price—even though the acquired companies may continue to report their assets and liabilities on their separate books at their historical book values. Thus, acquisition accounting requires Disney to essentially revalue the balance sheets of these companies to their amortized fair values in the consolidation process each period. We provide more details on the Pixar and Lucasfilm acquisitions later in the chapter.

The bottom line is that preparation of Disney's publicly disclosed financial statements is the culmination of a lot of work by the segment and corporate accounting and finance staff. The issues mentioned here illustrate the complexity of a process that requires substantial teamwork and effort to produce audited financial statements that are valuable to an investor or interested accounting student. You'll learn in this chapter about the activities during the consolidation process performed by the accounting staff at any well-known public company. This chapter also introduces differences in the consolidation process when there is a differential (i.e., the acquiring company pays something other than the book value of the acquired company's net assets).

LEARNING OBJECTIVES

When you finish studying this chapter, you should be able to:

LO 4-1   Understand and make equity-method journal entries related to the differential.

LO 4-2   Understand and explain how consolidation procedures differ when there is a differential.

LO 4-3   Make calculations and prepare consolidation entries for the consolidation of a wholly owned subsidiary when there is a complex positive differential at the acquisition date.

LO 4-4   Make calculations and prepare consolidation entries for the consolidation of a wholly owned subsidiary when there is a complex bargain-purchase differential.

LO 4-5   Prepare equity-method journal entries, consolidation entries, and the consolidation worksheet for a wholly owned subsidiary when there is a complex positive differential.

LO 4-6   Understand and explain the elimination of basic intercompany transactions.

LO 4-7   Understand and explain the basics of push-down accounting.

DEALING WITH THE DIFFERENTIAL

This chapter continues to build upon the foundation established in Chapters 2 and 3 related to the consolidation of majority-owned subsidiaries. In Chapters 2 and 3, we focus on relatively simple situations when the acquisition price is exactly equal to the parent's share of the book value of the subsidiary's net assets or where the subsidiary is created by the parent. In Chapter 4, we relax this assumption and allow the acquisition price to differ from book value. As explained in Chapter 1, this allows for a "differential."

	Wholly owned subsidiary	Partially owned subsidiary	
Investment = Book value	Chapter 2	Chapter 3	No differential
Investment > Book value	Chapter 4	Chapter 5	Differential
	No NCI shareholders	NCI shareholders	

The Difference between Acquisition Price and Underlying Book Value

When an investor purchases the common stock of another company, the purchase price normally is based on the market value of the shares acquired rather than the book value of the investee's assets and liabilities. Not surprisingly, the acquisition price is usually different from the book value of the investor's proportionate share of the investee's net assets. This difference is referred to as a *differential.* The differential is frequently positive, meaning the acquiring company pays more than its share of the book value of the subsidiary's net assets. Note that in the case of an equity-method investment, the differential on the parent's books relates only to the parent's share of any difference between total investee's fair value and book value. The differential in the case of an equity-method investment is implicit in the investment account on the parent's books and is not recorded separately.

> **FYI**
>
> In 2009, Bank of America reported one of the largest goodwill balances of all time, $86.3 billion. However, due to large goodwill impairment charges in 2010 and 2011, its 2011 goodwill balance decreased to $69.967 billion.

The cost of an investment might exceed the book value of the underlying net assets, giving rise to a positive differential, for any of several reasons. One reason is that the investee's assets may be worth more than their book values. Another reason could be the existence of unrecorded goodwill associated with the excess earning power of the investee. In either case, the portion of the differential pertaining to each asset of the investee, including goodwill, must be ascertained. When the parent company uses the equity method, for reporting purposes (i.e., the subsidiary remains unconsolidated) that portion of the differential pertaining to limited-life assets of the investee, including identifiable intangibles, must be amortized over the remaining economic lives of those assets. Any portion of the differential that represents goodwill (referred to as *equity-method goodwill* or *implicit goodwill*) is not amortized or separately tested for impairment. However, an impairment loss on the investment itself should be recognized if it suffers a material decline in value that is other than temporary (**ASC 323-10-35-32**).

LO 4-1

Understand and make equity-method journal entries related to the differential.

Advanced StudyGuide .com

Amortization or Write-Off of the Differential[1]

When the equity method is used, each portion of the differential must be treated in the same manner that the investee treats the assets or liabilities to which the differential relates. Thus, any portion of the differential related to depreciable or amortizable assets of the investee should be amortized over the remaining time to which the cost of the related asset is being allocated by the investee. Amortization of the differential associated with depreciable or amortizable assets of the investee is necessary on the investor's books to reflect the decline in the future benefits the investor expects from that portion of the investment cost associated with those assets. The investee recognizes the reduction in service potential of assets with limited lives as depreciation or amortization expense based on the amount it has invested in those assets. This reduction, in turn, is recognized by the investor through its share of the investee's net income. When the acquisition price of the investor's interest in the investee's assets is higher than the investee's cost (as reflected in a positive differential), the additional cost must be amortized.

The approach to amortizing the differential that is most consistent with the idea of reflecting all aspects of the investment in just one line on the balance sheet and one line on the income statement is to reduce the income recognized by the investor from the investee and the balance of the investment account:

Income from Investee	XXXX	
Investment in Common Stock of Investee		XXX

[1] To view a video explanation of this topic, visit advancedstudyguide.com.

The differential represents the amount paid by the investor company in excess of the book value of the net assets of the investee company and is included in the original acquisition price. Hence, the amortization or reduction of the differential involves the reduction of the investment account. At the same time, the investor's net income must be reduced by an equal amount to recognize that a portion of the amount paid for the investment has expired.

Treatment of the Differential Illustrated

To illustrate how to apply the equity method when the cost of the investment exceeds the book value of the underlying net assets, assume that Ajax Corporation purchases 40 percent of the common stock of Barclay Company on January 1, 20X1, for $200,000. Barclay has net assets on that date with a book value of $400,000 and fair value of $465,000. The total differential is equal to the market value of Barclay's common stock, $500,000, ($200,000/40%) minus the book value of its net assets, $400,000. Thus, the entire differential is $100,000.

Ajax's share of the book value of Barclay's net assets at acquisition is $160,000 ($400,000 × 0.40). Thus, Ajax's 40 percent share of the differential is computed as follows:

Cost of Ajax's investment in Barclay's stock	$200,000
Book value of Ajax's share of Barclay's net assets	(160,000)
Ajax's share of the differential	$ 40,000

The portion of the total differential that can be directly traced to specific assets that are undervalued on Barclay's books is the $65,000 excess of the fair value over the book value of Barclay's net assets ($465,000 − $400,000), and the remaining $35,000 of the differential is goodwill. Specifically, an appraisal of Barclay's assets indicates that its land is worth $15,000 more than the recorded value on its books and its equipment is worth $50,000 more than its current book value. Ajax's 40 percent share of the differential is as follows:

	Total Increase	Ajax's 40% Share
Land	$ 15,000	6,000
Equipment	50,000	20,000
Goodwill	35,000	14,000
	$100,000	$40,000

Thus, $26,000 of Ajax's share of the differential is assigned to land and equipment, with the remaining $14,000 attributed to goodwill. The allocation of Ajax's share of the differential can be illustrated as shown in the diagram below:

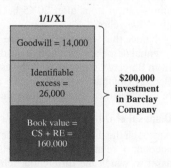

Although the differential relates to Barclay's assets, the additional cost incurred by Ajax to acquire a claim on Barclay's assets is reflected in Ajax's investment in

Barclay. There is no need to establish a separate differential account and separate accounts are not recorded on Ajax's books to reflect the apportionment of the differential to specific assets. Similarly, a separate expense account is not established on Ajax's books. Amortization or write-off of the differential is accomplished by reducing Ajax's investment account and the income Ajax recognizes from its investment in Barclay.

Because land has an unlimited economic life, the portion of the differential related to land is not amortized. Ajax's $20,000 portion of the differential related to Barclay's equipment is amortized over the equipment's remaining life. If the equipment's remaining life is five years, Ajax's annual amortization of the differential is $4,000 ($20,000 ÷ 5) (assuming straight-line depreciation).

Regarding the goodwill in the differential, accounting standards state that equity-method goodwill is not amortized nor is it separately tested for impairment when the equity method is used for reporting purposes. Instead, the entire investment is tested for impairment **(ASC 323-10-35-32)**. In this example, the only amortization of the differential is the $4,000 related to Barclay's equipment.

Barclay reports net income of $80,000 at year end and declares dividends of $20,000 during 20X1. Using the equity-method, Ajax records the following entries on its books during 20X1:

(1)	Investment in Barclay Stock	200,000	
	Cash		200,000
	Record purchase of Barclay stock.		

(2)	Investment in Barclay Stock	32,000	
	Income from Barclay Company		32,000
	Record equity-method income: $80,000 × 0.40.		

(3)	Cash	8,000	
	Investment in Barclay Stock		8,000
	Record dividend from Barclay: $20,000 × 0.40.		

(4)	Income from Barclay Company	4,000	
	Investment in Barclay Stock		4,000
	Amortize differential related to equipment.		

With these entries, Ajax recognizes $28,000 of income from Barclay and adjusts its investment in Barclay to an ending balance of $220,000.

The amortization on Ajax's books of the portion of the differential related to Barclay's equipment is the same ($4,000) for each of the first five years (20X1 through 20X5). This amortization stops after 20X5 because this portion of the differential is fully amortized after five years.

Notice that special accounts are not established on Ajax's books with regard to the differential or the amortization of the differential. The only two accounts involved are "Income from Barclay Company" and "Investment in Barclay Company Stock." As the Investment in Barclay Company Stock account is amortized, the differential between the carrying amount of the investment and the book value of the underlying net assets decreases.

Disposal of Differential-Related Assets

Although the differential is included on the books of the investor as part of the investment account, it relates to specific assets of the investee. Thus, if the investee disposes of any asset to which the differential relates, that portion of the differential must be removed from the investment account on the investor's books. When this is done, the investor's share of the investee's gain or loss on disposal of the asset must be adjusted to reflect the fact that the investor paid more for its proportionate share of that asset than did the investee.

For example, if in the previous illustration Barclay Company sells the land to which $6,000 of Ajax's differential relates, Ajax does not recognize a full 40 percent of the gain or loss on the sale. Assume that Barclay originally had purchased the land in 20X0 for $75,000 and sells the land in 20X2 for $125,000. Barclay recognizes a gain on the sale of $50,000, and Ajax's share of that gain is 40 percent, or $20,000. The portion of the gain actually recognized by Ajax, however, must be adjusted as follows because of the amount in excess of book value paid by Ajax for its investment in Barclay:

Ajax's share of Barclay's reported gain	$20,000
Portion of Ajax's differential related to the land	(6,000)
Gain to be recognized by Ajax	$14,000

Thus, if Barclay reports net income (including the gain on the sale of land) of $150,000 for 20X2, Ajax records the following entries (disregarding dividends and amortization of the differential relating to equipment):

(5)	Investment in Barclay Company	60,000	
	Income from Barclay Company		60,000
	Record equity-method income: $150,000 × 0.40.		

(6)	Income from Barclay Company	6,000	
	Investment in Barclay Stock		6,000
	Remove differential related to Barclay's land that was sold.		

The same approach applies when dealing with a limited-life asset. The unamortized portion of the original differential relating to the asset sold is removed from the investment account, and the investor's share of the investee's income is adjusted by that amount.

Note that the investor does not separately report its share of ordinary gains or losses included in the investee's net income, such as the gain on the sale of the fixed asset or the write-off of the unamortized differential. Consistent with the idea of using only a single line in the income statement to report the impact of the investee's activities on the investor, all such items are included in the Income from Investee account. Current standards require the investor to report its share of an investee's extraordinary gains and losses, discontinued operations, and elements of other comprehensive income, if material to the investor, as separate items in the same manner as the investor reports its own.

Impairment of Investment Value

As with many assets, accounting standards require that equity-method investments be written down if their value is impaired. If the market value of the investment declines materially below its equity-method carrying amount, and the decline in value is considered other than temporary, the carrying amount of the investment should be written down to the market value and a loss should be recognized. The new lower value serves as a starting point for continued application of the equity-method. Subsequent recoveries in the value of the investment may not be recognized.

ADDITIONAL CONSIDERATIONS

Disney's 2006 Pixar Acquisition

On May 5, 2006, Disney completed an all-stock acquisition of Pixar, a digital animation studio. To purchase Pixar, Disney exchanged 2.3 shares of its common stock for each share of Pixar common stock, resulting in the issuance of 279 million shares of Disney common stock, and converted previously issued vested and unvested Pixar equity-based awards into approximately 45 million Disney equity-based awards.

The acquisition purchase price was $7.5 billion ($6.4 billion, net of Pixar's cash and investments of approximately $1.1 billion). The value of the stock issued was calculated based on the market value of the Company's common stock using the average stock price for the five-day period beginning two days before the acquisition announcement date on January 24, 2006. The fair value of the vested equity-based awards issued at the closing was estimated using the Black-Scholes option pricing model, as the information required to use a binomial valuation model was not reasonably available.

The Company allocated the purchase price to the tangible and identifiable intangible assets acquired and liabilities assumed based on their fair values, which were determined primarily through third-party appraisals. The excess of the purchase price over those fair values was recorded as goodwill, which is not amortizable for tax purposes. The fair values set forth below are subject to adjustment if additional information is obtained prior to the one-year anniversary of the acquisition that would change the fair value allocation as of the acquisition date. The following table summarizes the allocation of the purchase price:

	Estimated Fair Value	Weighted Average Useful Lives (years)
Cash and cash equivalents	$ 11	
Investments	1,073	
Prepaid and other assets	45	
Film costs	538	12
Buildings & equipment	225	16
Intangibles	233	17
Goodwill	5,557	
Total assets acquired	$ 7,682	
Liabilities	64	
Deferred income taxes	123	
Total liabilities assumed	$ 187	
Net assets acquired	$ 7,495	

Disney's 2012 Lucasfilm Acquisition

On October 30, 2012, The Walt Disney Company announced the acquisition of Lucasfilm Ltd. in a stock and cash transaction.[*] The press release on that date states:

"For the past 35 years, one of my greatest pleasures has been to see Star Wars passed from one generation to the next," said George Lucas, Chairman and Chief Executive Officer of Lucasfilm. "It's now time for me to pass Star Wars on to a new generation of filmmakers. I've always believed that Star Wars could live beyond me, and I thought it was important to set up the transition during my lifetime ... Disney's reach and experience give Lucasfilm the opportunity to blaze new trails in film, television, interactive media, theme parks, live entertainment, and consumer products."

The acquisition combines two highly compatible family entertainment brands, and strengthens the long-standing beneficial relationship between them that already includes successful integration of Star Wars content into Disney theme parks in Anaheim, Orlando, Paris and Tokyo. Driven by a tremendously talented creative team, Lucasfilm's legendary Star Wars franchise has flourished for more than 35 years, and offers a virtually limitless universe of characters

[*] *The Walt Disney Company,* "Disney to Acquire Lucasfilm LTD." October 30, 2012, http://thewaltdisneycompany.com/disney-news/press-releases/2012/10/disney-acquire-lucasfilm-ltd.

and stories to drive continued feature film releases and franchise growth over the long term. Star Wars resonates with consumers around the world and creates extensive opportunities for Disney to deliver the content across its diverse portfolio of businesses including movies, television, consumer products, games and theme parks. Star Wars feature films have earned a total of $4.4 billion in global box to date, and continued global demand has made Star Wars one of the world's top product brands, and Lucasfilm a leading product licensor in the United States in 2011 … The Lucasfilm acquisition follows Disney's very successful acquisitions of Pixar and Marvel, which demonstrated the company's unique ability to fully develop and expand the financial potential of high quality creative content with compelling characters and storytelling through the application of innovative technology and multiplatform distribution on a truly global basis to create maximum value. Adding Lucasfilm to Disney's portfolio of world class brands significantly enhances the company's ability to serve consumers with a broad variety of the world's highest-quality content and to create additional long-term value for our shareholders.

On December 21, 2012, the Walt Disney Company completed the merger transaction in which the company distributed 37.1 million shares and paid $2.2 billion in cash. Based on the $50 per share closing price of Disney shares on December 21, 2012, the transaction had a value of $4.1 billion. The excess of the purchase price over those fair values of assets was allocated to goodwill.

CONSOLIDATION PROCEDURES FOR WHOLLY OWNED SUBSIDIARIES ACQUIRED AT MORE THAN BOOK VALUE

LO 4-2

Understand and explain how consolidation procedures differ when there is a differential.

Advanced StudyGuide .com

Many factors have an effect on the fair value of a company and its stock price, including its asset values, its earning power, and general market conditions. When one company acquires another, the acquiree's fair value usually differs from its book value (differential), and so the consideration given by the acquirer does as well.

The process of preparing a consolidated balance sheet immediately after a business combination is complicated only slightly when 100 percent of a company's stock is acquired at a price that differs from the acquiree's book value. To illustrate the acquisition of a subsidiary when the consideration given is greater than the book value of the net assets of the acquiree, we use the Peerless-Special Foods example from Chapter 2. We assume that Peerless Products acquires all of Special Foods' outstanding stock on January 1, 20X1, by paying $340,000 cash, an amount equal to Special Foods' fair value as a whole. The consideration given by Peerless is $40,000 in excess of Special Foods' book value of $300,000. The resulting ownership situation can be viewed as follows:

Fair value of consideration		$340,000
Book value of Special Foods' net assets		
Common stock—Special Foods	200,000	
Retained earnings—Special Foods	100,000	
		300,000
Difference between fair value and book value		$ 40,000

1/1/X1 100%

Peerless records the stock acquisition with the following entry:

(7)	Investment in Special Foods	340,000	
	Cash		340,000
	Record purchase of Special Foods stock.		

In a business combination, and therefore in a consolidation following a business combination, the full amount of the consideration given by the acquirer must be assigned to the individual assets and liabilities acquired and to goodwill. In this example, the fair value of consideration given (the acquisition price) includes an extra $40,000 for appreciation in the value of the land since it was originally acquired by Special Foods. The relationship between the fair value of the consideration given for Special Foods, the fair value of Special Foods' net assets, and the book value of Special Foods' net assets can be illustrated as follows:

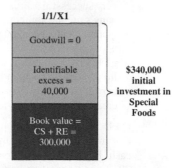

Assume that Peerless prepares a consolidated balance sheet on the date it acquires Special Foods. The consolidation worksheet procedures used in adjusting to the proper consolidated amounts follow a consistent pattern. The first worksheet entry (often referred to as the "basic" consolidation entry) eliminates the book value portion of the parent's investment account and each of the subsidiary's stockholders' equity accounts. It is useful to analyze the investment account and the subsidiary's equity accounts as follows:

Book Value Calculations:

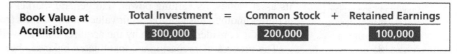

The worksheet entry to eliminate the book value portion of Peerless' investment account and the stockholders' equity accounts of Special Foods is as follows:

Basic Consolidation Entry:

When the acquisition-date fair value of the consideration is more than the acquiree's book value at that date, the second consolidation entry reclassifies the excess acquisition price to the specific accounts on the balance sheet for which the book values are not the same as their fair values on the acquisition date.[2] The differential represents (in simple situations involving a 100 percent acquisition) the total difference between the acquisition-date fair value of the consideration given by the acquirer and the acquiree's

---

[2] Alternatively, a separate clearing account titled "Excess of Acquisition Consideration over Acquiree Book Value" or just "Differential" can be debited for this excess amount. A subsequent entry can be used to reclassify the differential to the various accounts on the balance sheet that need to be revalued to their acquisition date amounts. Note that the Differential account is simply a worksheet clearing account and is not found on the books of the parent or subsidiary and does not appear in the consolidated financial statements.

book value of net assets. In this example, the differential is the additional $40,000 Peerless paid to acquire Special Foods because its land was worth $40,000 more than its book value as of the acquisition date. In preparing a consolidated balance sheet immediately after acquisition (on January 1, 20X1), the second consolidation entry appearing in the consolidation worksheet simply reassigns this $40,000 from the investment account to the land account so that: (*a*) the Land account fully reflects the fair value of this asset as of the acquisition date and (*b*) the investment account is fully eliminated from Peerless' books:

Excess Value Reclassification Entry:

Land	40,000		← Excess value assigned to land
Investment in Special Foods		40,000	← Reclassify excess acquisition price

Thus, these two consolidation entries completely eliminate the balance in Peerless' investment account and the second entry assigns the differential to the land account.

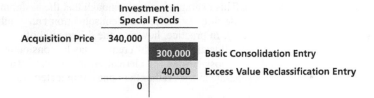

In more complicated examples when the fair values of various balance sheet accounts differ from book values, the excess value reclassification entry reassigns the differential to adjust various account balances to reflect the fair values of the subsidiary's assets and liabilities at the time the parent acquired the subsidiary and to establish goodwill, if appropriate.

Figure 4–1 illustrates the consolidation worksheet reflecting the elimination of Special Foods' equity accounts and the allocation of the differential to the subsidiary's land. As explained previously, the combination of these two worksheet entries also eliminates the investment account.

FIGURE 4–1 January 1, 20X1, Worksheet for Consolidated Balance Sheet, Date of Combination; 100 Percent Acquisition at More than Book Value

	Peerless Products	Special Foods	Consolidation Entries DR	Consolidation Entries CR	Consolidated
Balance Sheet					
Cash	10,000	50,000			60,000
Accounts Receivable	75,000	50,000			125,000
Inventory	100,000	60,000			160,000
Investment in Special Foods	340,000			300,000	0
				40,000	
Land	175,000	40,000	40,000		255,000
Buildings & Equipment	800,000	600,000		300,000	1,100,000
Less: Accumulated Depreciation	(400,000)	(300,000)	300,000		(400,000)
Total Assets	**1,100,000**	**500,000**	**$340,000**	**$640,000**	**1,300,000**
Accounts Payable	100,000	100,000			200,000
Bonds Payable	200,000	100,000			300,000
Common Stock	500,000	200,000	200,000		500,000
Retained Earnings	300,000	100,000	100,000		300,000
Total Liabilities & Equity	**1,100,000**	**500,000**	**300,000**	**0**	**1,300,000**

As usual, we eliminate Special Foods' acquisition date accumulated depreciation against the Buildings and Equipment account balance so that, combined with the excess value reclassification entry it will appear as if these fixed assets were recorded at their acquisition costs.

Optional Accumulated Depreciation Consolidation Entry:

Accumulated Depreciation	300,000		← Accumulated depreciation at the time
Buildings & Equipment		300,000	of the acquisition netted against cost

The amounts reported externally in the consolidated balance sheet are those in the Consolidated column of the worksheet in Figure 4–1. Land would be included in the consolidated balance sheet at $255,000, the amount carried on Peerless' books ($175,000) plus the amount carried on Special Foods' books ($40,000) plus the differential reflecting the increased value of Special Foods' land ($40,000).

This example is simple enough that the assignment of the differential to land could be made directly in the basic consolidation entry rather than through the use of a separate entry. In practice, however, the differential often relates to more than a single asset, and the allocation of the differential may be considerably more complex than in this example. The possibilities for clerical errors are reduced in complex situations by making two separate entries rather than one complicated entry.

Treatment of a Positive Differential

The fair value, and hence acquisition price, of a subsidiary might exceed the book value for several reasons, such as the following:

1. Errors or omissions on the subsidiary's books.
2. Excess of fair value over the book value of the subsidiary's net identifiable assets.
3. Existence of goodwill.

Errors or Omissions on the Books of the Subsidiary

An examination of an acquired company's books may reveal material errors. In some cases, the acquired company may have expensed rather than capitalized assets or, for other reasons, omitted them from the books. An acquired company that previously had been closely held may not have followed generally accepted accounting principles in maintaining its accounting records. In some cases, the recordkeeping may have simply been inadequate.

Where errors or omissions occur, corrections should be made directly on the subsidiary's books as of the date of acquisition. These corrections are treated as prior-period adjustments in accordance with **ASC 250-10-60.** Once the subsidiary's books are stated in accordance with generally accepted accounting principles, that portion of the differential attributable to errors or omissions will no longer exist.

Excess of Fair Value over Book Value of Subsidiary's Net Identifiable Assets

The fair value of a company's assets is an important factor in the overall determination of the company's fair value. In many cases, the fair value of an acquired company's net assets exceeds the book value. Consequently, the consideration given by an acquirer may exceed the acquiree's book value. The procedures used in preparing the consolidated balance sheet should lead to reporting all of the acquired company's assets and liabilities based on their fair values on the date of combination. This valuation may be accomplished in one of two ways: (1) the subsidiary's assets and liabilities may be revalued directly on the books of the subsidiary or (2) the accounting basis of the subsidiary may be maintained and the revaluations made each period in the consolidation worksheet.

Revaluing the assets and liabilities on the subsidiary's books generally is the simplest approach if all of the subsidiary's common stock is acquired. On the other hand, it generally is not appropriate to revalue the assets and liabilities on the subsidiary's books if there is a significant noncontrolling interest in that subsidiary. From a noncontrolling shareholder's point of view, the subsidiary is a continuing company, and the basis of accounting should not change. More difficult to resolve is the situation in which the parent acquires all of the subsidiary's common stock but continues to issue separate financial statements of the subsidiary to holders of the subsidiary's bonds or preferred stock. Revaluing the assets and liabilities of the subsidiary directly on its books is referred to as ***push-down accounting.*** It is discussed later in this chapter and is illustrated in Appendix 4A.

When the assets and liabilities are revalued directly on the subsidiary's books, that portion of the differential then no longer exists. However, if the assets and liabilities are not revalued on the subsidiary's books, an entry to revalue those assets and allocate the differential is needed in the consolidation worksheet each time consolidated financial statements are prepared for as long as the related assets are held.

Existence of Goodwill

If the acquisition-date fair value of the consideration exchanged for an acquired subsidiary is higher than the total fair value of the subsidiary's net identifiable assets, the difference is considered to be related to the future economic benefits associated with other assets of the subsidiary that are not separately identified and recognized and is referred to as ***goodwill.*** Thus, once a subsidiary's identifiable assets and liabilities are revalued to their fair values, any remaining debit differential is normally allocated to goodwill. For example, assuming that in the Peerless Products and Special Foods illustration, the acquisition-date fair values of Special Foods' assets and liabilities are equal to their book values, then the $40,000 difference between the $340,000 consideration exchanged and the $300,000 fair value of the subsidiary's net identifiable assets should be attributed to goodwill. The following entry to assign the differential is needed in the consolidation worksheet prepared immediately after the combination:

Excess Value Reclassification Entry:

Goodwill	40,000		← Excess value assigned to goodwill
Investment in Special Foods		40,000	← Reassign excess acquisition price

The consolidation worksheet is similar to Figure 4–1 except that the debit in the excess value reclassification worksheet entry would be to goodwill instead of land. Goodwill, which does not appear on the books of either Peerless or Special Foods, would appear at $40,000 in the consolidated balance sheet prepared immediately after acquisition.

In the past, some companies have included the fair-value increment related to certain identifiable assets of the subsidiary in goodwill rather than separately recognizing those assets. This treatment is not acceptable, and any fair-value increment related to an intangible asset that arises from a contractual or legal right or that is separable from the entity must be allocated to that asset.

Illustration of Treatment of a Complex Differential

LO 4-3

Make calculations and prepare consolidation entries for the consolidation of a wholly owned subsidiary when there is a complex positive differential at the acquisition date.

In many situations, the differential relates to a number of different assets and liabilities. As a means of illustrating the allocation of the differential to various assets and liabilities, assume that the acquisition-date book values and fair values of Special Foods' assets and liabilities are as shown in Figure 4–2. The inventory and land have fair values in excess of their book values, although the buildings and equipment are worth less than their book values.

Bond prices fluctuate as interest rates change. In this example, the value of Special Foods' bonds payable is higher than the book value. This indicates that the nominal interest rate on the bonds is higher than the current market interest rate and, therefore, investors are willing to

FIGURE 4–2

Differences between Book and Fair Values of Special Foods' Identifiable Assets and Liabilities as of January 1, 20X1, the Date of Combination

		Book Value	Fair Value	Difference between Fair Value and Book Value
Cash		$ 50,000	$ 50,000	
Accounts Receivable		50,000	50,000	
Inventory		60,000	75,000	$15,000
Land		40,000	100,000	60,000
Buildings & Equipment	600,000			
Accumulated Depreciation	(300,000)	300,000	290,000	(10,000)
		$500,000	$565,000	
Accounts Payable		$100,000	$100,000	
Bonds Payable		100,000	135,000	(35,000)
Common Stock		200,000		
Retained Earnings		100,000		
		$500,000	$235,000	$30,000

pay a price higher than par for the bonds. In determining the value of Special Foods, Peerless must recognize that it is assuming a liability that pays an interest rate higher than the current market rate. Accordingly, the fair value of Special Foods' net assets will be less than if the liability had been carried at a lower interest rate. The resulting consolidated financial statements must recognize the acquisition-date fair values of Special Foods' liabilities as well as its assets.

Assume that Peerless Products acquires all of Special Foods' capital stock for $400,000 on January 1, 20X1, by issuing $100,000 of 9 percent bonds, with a fair value of $100,000, and paying cash of $300,000. The resulting ownership situation can be pictured as follows with a $100,000 differential:

(P)	Fair value of consideration		$400,000
1/1/X1 100%	Book value of Special Foods' net assets		
	Common stock—Special Foods	200,000	
	Retained earnings—Special Foods	100,000	
(S)			300,000
	Difference between fair value and book value		$100,000

Peerless records the investment on its books with the following entry:

(8)	Investment in Special Foods	400,000	
	Bonds Payable		100,000
	Cash		300,000
	Record purchase of Special Foods stock.		

The fair value of the consideration that Peerless gave to acquire Special Foods' stock ($400,000) can be divided between the fair value of Special Foods' identifiable net assets ($330,000) and goodwill ($70,000), illustrated as follows:

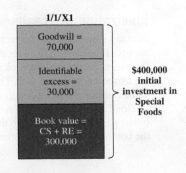

The total $400,000 consideration exceeds the book value of Special Foods' net assets, $300,000 (assets of $500,000 less liabilities of $200,000), by $100,000. Thus, the total differential is $100,000. The total fair value of the net identifiable assets acquired in the combination is $330,000 ($565,000 − $235,000), based on the data in Figure 4–2. The amount by which the total consideration of $400,000 exceeds the $330,000 fair value of the net identifiable assets is $70,000, and that amount is assigned to goodwill in the consolidated balance sheet. Assume that Peerless decides to prepare a consolidated balance sheet as of the date it acquired Special Foods.

The book value portion of the acquisition price is $300,000:

Book Value Calculations:

Book Value at Acquisition	Total Investment	=	Common Stock	+	Retained Earnings
	300,000		200,000		100,000

Thus, the basic consolidation entry is as follows:

Basic Consolidation Entry:

Common Stock	200,000	← Common stock balance
Retained Earnings	100,000	← Beginning balance in RE
Investment in Special Foods	300,000	← Net BV in investment account

The reclassification of the differential to the various accounts that are either over- or undervalued on Special Foods' balance sheet as of the acquisition date is more complicated than in the previous example. Thus, it is helpful to analyze the differential as follows:

Excess Value (Differential) Calculations:

Total Differential	=	Inventory	+	Land	+	Goodwill	+	Building	+	Bonds Payable
100,000		15,000		60,000		70,000		(10,000)		(35,000)

This analysis leads to the following reclassification entry to assign the $100,000 differential to the specific accounts that need to be "revalued" to reflect their fair values as of the acquisition date. Moreover, this entry completes the elimination of the investment account from Peerless' books.

Excess Value (Differential) Reclassification Entry:

Inventory	15,000		← Excess value assigned to inventory
Land	60,000		← Excess value assigned to land
Goodwill	70,000		← Excess value assigned to goodwill
Building		10,000	← Building revalued down to fair value
Bonds Payable		35,000	← Excess liability associated with the bonds
Investment in Special Foods		100,000	← Reassign excess acquisition price

In summary, these two consolidation entries completely eliminate the balance in Peerless' investment account and the second entry assigns the differential to various balance sheet accounts. As in previous examples, it is helpful to visualize how the two consolidation entries "zero out" the investment account:

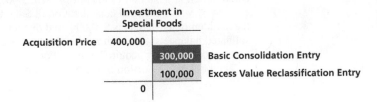

As usual, we eliminate Special Foods' acquisition date accumulated depreciation against the Buildings and Equipment account balance so that, combined with the excess value reclassification entry it will appear as if these fixed assets were recorded at their acquisition costs.

Optional Accumulated Depreciation Consolidation Entry:

Accumulated Depreciation 300,000		← Accumulated depreciation at the time
Buildings & Equipment	**300,000**	of the acquisition netted against cost

These entries are reflected in the worksheet in Figure 4–3. Although the reclassification entry is somewhat more complex than in the previous example, the differential allocation is conceptually the same in both cases. In each case, the end result is a consolidated balance sheet with the subsidiary's assets and liabilities valued at their fair values at the date of combination.

FIGURE 4–3   January 1, 20X1, Worksheet for Consolidated Balance Sheet, Date of Combination; 100 Percent Acquisition at More than Book Value

	Peerless Products	Special Foods	Consolidation Entries DR	Consolidation Entries CR	Consolidated
Balance Sheet					
Cash	50,000	50,000			100,000
Accounts Receivable	75,000	50,000			125,000
Inventory	100,000	60,000	15,000		175,000
Investment in Special Foods	400,000			300,000	0
				100,000	
Land	175,000	40,000	60,000		275,000
Buildings & Equipment	800,000	600,000		10,000	1,090,000
				300,000	
Less: Accumulated Depreciation	(400,000)	(300,000)	300,000		(400,000)
Goodwill			70,000		70,000
Total Assets	**1,200,000**	**500,000**	**$445,000**	**$710,000**	**1,435,000**
Accounts Payable	100,000	100,000			200,000
Bonds Payable	300,000	100,000			400,000
Premium on Bonds Payable				35,000	35,000
Common Stock	500,000	200,000	200,000		500,000
Retained Earnings	300,000	100,000	100,000		300,000
Total Liabilities & Equity	**1,200,000**	**500,000**	**300,000**	**35,000**	**1,435,000**

100 Percent Ownership Acquired at Less than Fair Value of Net Assets

LO 4-4

Make calculations and prepare consolidation entries for the consolidation of a wholly owned subsidiary when there is a complex bargain-purchase differential.

Advanced
StudyGuide
.com

It is not uncommon for companies' stock to trade at prices that are lower than the fair value of their net assets. These companies are often singled out as prime acquisition targets. The acquisition price of an acquired company may be less than the fair value of its net assets because some of the acquiree's assets or liabilities may have been incorrectly valued or because the transaction reflects a forced sale where the seller was required to sell quickly and was unable to fully market the sale.

Obviously, if assets or liabilities acquired in a business combination have been incorrectly valued, the errors must be corrected and the assets and liabilities valued at their fair values. Once this is done, if the fair value of the consideration given is still less than the fair value of the net assets acquired, a gain attributable to the acquirer is recognized for the difference. In general, as discussed in Chapter 1, a business combination in which (1) the sum of the acquisition-date fair values of the consideration given, any equity interest already held by the acquirer, and any noncontrolling interest is less than (2) the amounts at which the identifiable net assets must be valued at the acquisition date (usually fair values) is considered a ***bargain purchase,*** and a gain attributable to the acquirer is recognized for the difference (as specified by **ASC 805-10-20**).

The purpose of the differential is to account for items attributable to the subsidiary company that are not already accounted for by that acquiring entity. Since the gain on bargain purchase is attributed to the parent, it is recorded directly on the records of the parent, in effect increasing the differential, which is the difference between the investment account on the parent records and the book value of the subsidiary. The acquirer will record the gain as part of the acquisition transaction in its individual records.

Illustration of Treatment of Bargain-Purchase

Using the example of Peerless Products and Special Foods, assume that the acquisition-date book values and fair values of Special Foods' assets and liabilities are equal except that the fair value of Special Foods' land is $40,000 more than its book value. On January 1, 20X1, Peerless acquires all of Special Foods' common stock for $310,000, resulting in a bargain purchase. The resulting ownership situation is as follows:

(P)	Fair value of consideration			$310,000
1/1/X1 100%	Book value of Special Foods' net assets			
	Common stock—Special Foods	200,000		
	Retained earnings—Special Foods	100,000		
(S)				300,000
	Difference between fair value and book value			$ 10,000

Peerless records its investment in Special Foods with the following entry on its books:

(9)	Investment in Special Foods	340,000	
	Cash		310,000
	Gain on Bargain Purchase		30,000
	Record purchase of Special Foods stock.		

In this example, the acquisition-date fair value of Special Foods' net assets ($340,000) is higher than its book value by $40,000. However, the purchase price ($310,000) exceeds Special Foods' book value by only $10,000 and, thus, is less than the fair value of the net identifiable assets acquired. This business combination, therefore, represents a bargain purchase. All of the acquiree's assets and liabilities must be valued at fair value, which in this case requires only Special Foods' land to be revalued. This revaluation is accomplished in the consolidation worksheet. Assuming

Peerless wants to prepare a consolidated balance sheet on the acquisition date, the book value portion of the acquisition price is $300,000:

Book Value Calculations:

Book Value at Acquisition	Total Investment	=	Common Stock	+	Retained Earnings
	300,000		200,000		100,000

Thus, the basic consolidation entry is the same as in previous examples:

Basic Consolidation Entry:

Common Stock	200,000		← Common stock balance
Retained Earnings	100,000		← Beginning balance in RE
Investment in Special Foods		300,000	← Net BV in investment account

In this example, the total differential relates to the fair value of Special Foods' land, which is $40,000 more than its book value at acquisition. The reclassification of this total differential can be summarized as follows:

Excess Value (Differential) Calculations:

Total Differential	=	Land
40,000		40,000

This analysis leads to the following reclassification entry to assign the $40,000 net differential to the Land.

Excess Value (Differential) Reclassification Entry:

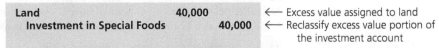

Land	40,000		← Excess value assigned to land
Investment in Special Foods		40,000	← Reclassify excess value portion of the investment account

In summary, these two consolidation entries effectively eliminate the balance in Peerless' investment account and assign the total differential to the Land account. As in previous examples, it is helpful to visualize how the two consolidation entries "zero out" the investment account:

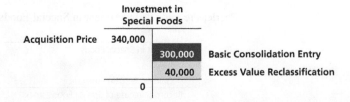

When the consolidation worksheet is prepared at the end of the year, the notion of recognizing a gain for the $30,000 excess of the $340,000 fair value of Special Foods' net assets over the $310,000 fair value of the consideration given by Peerless in the exchange is correct. However, assuming a consolidation worksheet is also prepared on the acquisition date (January 1, 20X1), the gain will already be recorded in the parent's retained earnings account because an income statement is not prepared on the acquisition date, only a balance sheet (because it is the first day of the year).

CONSOLIDATED FINANCIAL STATEMENTS—100 PERCENT OWNERSHIP ACQUIRED AT MORE THAN BOOK VALUE

LO 4-5

Prepare equity-method journal entries, consolidation entries, and the consolidation worksheet for a wholly owned subsidiary when there is a complex positive differential.

Advanced
StudyGuide
.com

When an investor company accounts for an investment using the equity method, as illustrated in Chapter 2, it records the amount of differential viewed as expiring during the period as a reduction of the income recognized from the investee. In consolidation, the differential is assigned to the appropriate asset and liability balances, and consolidated income is adjusted for the amounts expiring during the period by assigning them to the related expense items (e.g., depreciation expense).

Initial Year of Ownership

As an illustration of the acquisition of 100 percent ownership acquired at an amount higher than book value, assume that Peerless Products acquires all of Special Foods' common stock on January 1, 20X1, for $387,500, an amount $87,500 in excess of the book value. The acquisition price includes cash of $300,000 and a 60-day note for $87,500 (paid at maturity during 20X1). At the date of combination, Special Foods holds the assets and liabilities shown in Figure 4–2. The resulting ownership situation is as follows:

Fair value of consideration		$387,500
Book value of Special Foods' net assets		
Common stock—Special Foods	200,000	
Retained earnings—Special Foods	100,000	
		300,000
Difference between fair value and book value		$ 87,500

(P) 1/1/X1 100% (S)

On the acquisition date, all of Special Foods' assets and liabilities have fair values equal to their book values, except as follows:

	Book Value	Fair Value	Fair Value Increment
Inventory	$ 60,000	$ 65,000	$ 5,000
Land	40,000	50,000	10,000
Buildings & Equipment	300,000	360,000	60,000
	$400,000	$475,000	$75,000

Of the $87,500 total differential, $75,000 relates to identifiable assets of Special Foods. The remaining $12,500 is attributable to goodwill. The apportionment of the differential appears as follows: The entire amount of inventory to which the differential relates is sold during 20X1; none is left in ending inventory. The buildings and equipment have a remaining economic life of 10 years from the date of combination, and Special Foods uses straight-line depreciation. At the end of 20X1, in evaluating the Investment in Special Foods account for impairment, Peerless' management determines that the goodwill acquired in the combination with Special Foods has been impaired. Management determines that a $3,000 goodwill impairment loss should be recognized in the consolidated income statement.

For the first year immediately after the date of combination, 20X1, Peerless Products earns income from its own separate operations of $140,000 and pays dividends of $60,000. Special Foods reports net income of $50,000 and pays dividends of $30,000.

Parent Company Entries

During 20X1, Peerless makes the normal equity-method entries on its books to record its purchase of Special Foods stock and its income and dividends from Special Foods:

(10)	Investment in Special Foods	387,500	
	Cash		300,000
	Notes Payable		87,500

Record the initial investment in Special Foods.

(11)	Investment in Special Foods	50,000	
	Income from Special Foods		50,000

Record Peerless' 100% share of Special Foods' 20X1 income.

(12)	Cash	30,000	
	Investment in Special Foods		30,000

Record Peerless' 100% share of Special Foods' 20X1 dividend.

In this case, Peerless paid an amount for its investment that was $87,500 in excess of the book value of the shares acquired. As discussed previously, this difference is a differential that is implicit in the amount recorded in the investment account on Peerless' books. Because Peerless acquired 100 percent of Special Foods' stock, Peerless' differential included in its investment account is equal to the total differential arising from the business combination. However, although the differential arising from the business combination must be allocated to specific assets and liabilities in consolidation, the differential on Peerless' books does not appear separate from the Investment in Special Foods account. A portion of the differential ($5,000) in the investment account on Peerless' books relates to a portion of Special Foods' inventory that is sold during 20X1. Because Special Foods no longer holds the asset to which that portion of the differential relates at year-end, that portion of the differential is written off by reducing the investment account and Peerless' income from Special Foods. An additional $60,000 of the differential is attributable to the excess of the acquisition-date fair value over book value of Special Foods' buildings and equipment. As the service potential of the underlying assets expires, Peerless must amortize the additional cost it incurred because of the higher fair value of those assets. This is accomplished through annual amortization of $6,000 ($60,000 ÷ 10) over the remaining 10-year life beginning in 20X1. Finally, the goodwill is deemed to be impaired by $3,000 and is also adjusted on Peerless' books. Thus, the differential must be written off on Peerless' books to recognize the cost expiration related to the service expiration of Special Foods' assets to which it relates. Under the equity method, the differential is written off periodically from the investment account to Income from Special Foods to reflect these changes in the differential ($5,000 inventory + $6,000 depreciation + $3,000 goodwill impairment = $14,000):

(13)	Income from Special Foods	14,000	
	Investment in Special Foods		14,000

Record amortization of excess acquisition price.

Consolidation Worksheet—Year of Combination

The following diagrams illustrate the breakdown of the book value and excess value components of the investment account at the beginning and end of the year.

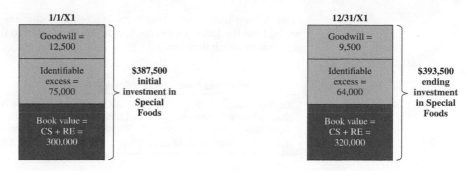

Because a year has passed since the acquisition date, the book value of Special Foods' net assets has changed because it has earned income and declared dividends. The book value component can be summarized as follows:

Book Value Calculations:

	Total Investment	=	Common Stock	+	Retained Earnings
Beginning Book Value	300,000		200,000		100,000
+ Net Income	50,000				50,000
− Dividends	(30,000)				(30,000)
Ending Book Value	320,000		200,000		120,000

This chart leads to the basic consolidation entry. Note that we use a shaded font to distinguish the numbers that appear in the consolidation entry to help the reader see how it should be constructed.

Basic Consolidation Entry:

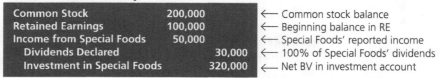

Common Stock	200,000		← Common stock balance
Retained Earnings	100,000		← Beginning balance in RE
Income from Special Foods	50,000		← Special Foods' reported income
Dividends Declared		30,000	← 100% of Special Foods' dividends
Investment in Special Foods		320,000	← Net BV in investment account

We then analyze the differential and its changes during the period:

Excess Value (Differential) Calculations:

	Total	= Inventory +	Land +	Building +	Acc. Depr. +	Goodwill
Beginning Balance	87,500	5,000	10,000	60,000	0	12,500
− Changes	(14,000)	(5,000)			(6,000)	(3,000)
Ending Balance	73,500	0	10,000	60,000	(6,000)	9,500

The entire differential amount assigned to the inventory already passed through cost of goods sold during the year. The only other amortization item—the excess value assigned to the building—is amortized over a 10-year period ($60,000 ÷ 10 = $6,000 per year). Finally, the goodwill is deemed to be impaired and worth only $9,500. Because the amortization of the differential has already been written off on Peerless' books from the investment account against the Income from Special Foods account, the amortized excess value reclassification entry simply reclassifies these changes in the differential during the period from the Income from the Special Foods account to the various income statement accounts to which they apply:

Amortized Excess Value Reclassification Entry:

Cost of Goods Sold	**5,000**	← Extra cost of goods sold
Depreciation Expense	**6,000**	← Depreciation of excess building value
Goodwill Impairment Loss	**3,000**	← Goodwill impairment
Income from Special Foods	**14,000**	← See calculation above

Finally, the remaining unamortized differential of $73,500 is reclassified to the correct accounts based on the ending balances (the bottom row) in the excess value calculations chart:

Excess Value (Differential) Reclassification Entry:

Land	**10,000**	← Excess value at acquisition
Building	**60,000**	← Excess value at acquisition
Goodwill	**9,500**	← Calculated value postimpairment
Accumulated Depreciation	**6,000**	← = 60,000 ÷ 10 years
Investment in Special Foods	**73,500**	← Remaining balance in differential

Recall that Special Foods reports its balance sheet based on the book values of the various accounts. This consolidation entry essentially reclassifies the differential from the Investment in Special Foods account to the individual accounts that need to be revalued to their amortized fair values as of the balance sheet date.

In sum, these worksheet entries (1) eliminate the balances in the Investment in Special Foods and Income from Special Foods accounts, (2) reclassify the amortization of excess

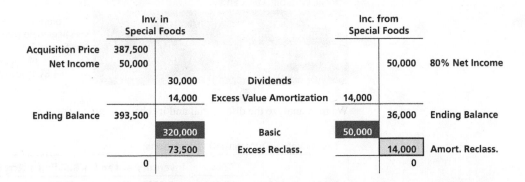

value to the proper income statement accounts, and (3) reclassify the remaining differential to the appropriate balance sheet accounts as of the end of the period.

As usual, we eliminate Special Foods' acquisition date accumulated depreciation against the Buildings and Equipment account balance.

Optional Accumulated Depreciation Consolidation Entry:

Accumulated Depreciation	**300,000**	← Accumulated depreciation at the time
Buildings & Equipment	**300,000**	of the acquisition netted against cost

The following T-accounts illustrate how the excess value reclassification entry combined with the accumulated depreciation consolidation entry make the consolidated balances for the Buildings and Equipment and Accumulated Depreciation accounts appear as if these assets had been purchased at the beginning of the year for their acquisition date fair values ($360,000) and that these "new" assets had then been depreciated $26,000 during the first year of their use by the newly purchased company.

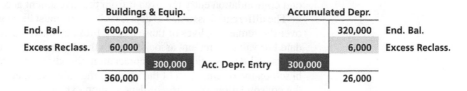

After the subsidiary income accruals are entered on Peerless' books, the adjusted trial balance data of the consolidating companies are entered in the three-part consolidation worksheet as shown in Figure 4–4. We note that because all inventory on hand on the date of combination has been sold during the year, the $5,000 of differential applicable

FIGURE 4–4   December 31, 20X1, Equity-Method Worksheet for Consolidated Financial Statements, Initial Year of Ownership; 100 Percent Acquisition at More than Book Value

	Peerless Products	Special Foods	Consolidation Entries		Consolidated
			DR	CR	
Income Statement					
Sales	400,000	200,000			600,000
Less: COGS	(170,000)	(115,000)	5,000		(290,000)
Less: Depreciation Expense	(50,000)	(20,000)	6,000		(76,000)
Less: Other Expenses	(40,000)	(15,000)			(55,000)
Less: Impairment Loss			3,000		(3,000)
Income from Special Foods	36,000		50,000	14,000	0
Net Income	**176,000**	**50,000**	**64,000**	**14,000**	**176,000**
Statement of Retained Earnings					
Beginning Balance	300,000	100,000	100,000		300,000
Net Income	**176,000**	**50,000**	64,000	14,000	176,000
Less: Dividends Declared	(60,000)	(30,000)		30,000	(60,000)
Ending Balance	**416,000**	**120,000**	**164,000**	**44,000**	**416,000**
Balance Sheet					
Cash	122,500	75,000			197,500
Accounts Receivable	75,000	50,000			125,000
Inventory	100,000	75,000			175,000
Investment in Special Foods	393,500			320,000	0
				73,500	
Land	175,000	40,000	10,000		225,000
Buildings & Equipment	800,000	600,000	60,000	300,000	1,160,000
Less: Accumulated Depreciation	(450,000)	(320,000)	300,000	6,000	(476,000)
Goodwill			9,500		9,500
Total Assets	**1,216,000**	**520,000**	**379,500**	**699,500**	**1,416,000**
Accounts Payable	100,000	100,000			200,000
Bonds Payable	200,000	100,000			300,000
Common Stock	500,000	200,000	200,000		500,000
Retained Earnings	**416,000**	**120,000**	164,000	44,000	416,000
Total Liabilities & Equity	**1,216,000**	**520,000**	**364,000**	**44,000**	**1,416,000**

to inventory is allocated directly to cost of goods sold. The cost of goods sold recorded on Special Foods' books is correct for that company's separate financial statements. However, the cost of the inventory to the consolidated entity is viewed as being $5,000 higher, and this additional cost must be included in consolidated cost of goods sold. No worksheet entry is needed in future periods with respect to the inventory because it has been expensed and no longer is on the subsidiary's books. The portion of the differential related to the inventory no longer exists on Peerless' books after 20X1 because the second consolidation entry removed it from the investment account.

The differential assigned to depreciable assets must be charged to depreciation expense over the remaining lives of those assets. From a consolidated viewpoint, the acquisition-date fair value increment associated with the depreciable assets acquired becomes part of the assets' depreciation base. Depreciation already is recorded on the subsidiary's books based on the original cost of the assets to the subsidiary, and these amounts are carried to the consolidation worksheet as depreciation expense.

The difference between the $387,500 fair value of the consideration exchanged and the $375,000 fair value of Special Foods' net identifiable assets is assumed to be related to the excess earning power of Special Foods. This difference is entered in the worksheet in Figure 4–4. A distinction must be made between journal entries recorded on the parent's books under equity-method reporting and the consolidation entries needed in the worksheet to prepare the consolidated financial statements. Again, we distinguish between actual equity-method journal entries on the parent's books (not shaded) and worksheet consolidation entries (shaded).

Consolidated Net Income and Retained Earnings

As can be seen from the worksheet in Figure 4–4, consolidated net income for 20X1 is $176,000 and consolidated retained earnings on December 31, 20X1, is $416,000. These amounts can be computed as shown in Figure 4–5.

Second Year of Ownership

The consolidation procedures employed at the end of the second year, and in periods thereafter, are basically the same as those used at the end of the first year. Consolidation two years after acquisition is illustrated by continuing the example used for 20X1. During 20X2, Peerless Products earns income of $160,000 from its own separate operations and pays dividends of $60,000; Special Foods reports net income of $75,000 and pays dividends of $40,000. No further impairment of the goodwill from the business combination occurs during 20X2.

FIGURE 4–5
Consolidated Net Income and Retained Earnings, 20X1; 100 Percent Acquisition at More than Book Value

Consolidated net income, 20X1:	
Peerless' separate operating income	$140,000
Special Foods' net income	50,000
Write-off of differential related to inventory sold during 20X1	(5,000)
Amortization of differential related to buildings & equipment in 20X1	(6,000)
Goodwill impairment loss	(3,000)
Consolidated net income, 20X1	$176,000
Consolidated retained earnings, December 31, 20X1:	
Peerless' retained earnings on date of combination, January 1, 20X1	$300,000
Peerless' separate operating income, 20X1	140,000
Special Foods' 20X1 net income	50,000
Write-off of differential related to inventory sold during 20X1	(5,000)
Amortization of differential related to buildings & equipment in 20X1	(6,000)
Goodwill impairment loss	(3,000)
Dividends declared by Peerless, 20X1	(60,000)
Consolidated retained earnings, December 31, 20X1	$416,000

Parent Company Entries

Peerless Products records the following entries on its separate books during 20X2:

(14)	Investment in Special Foods	75,000	
	Income from Special Foods		75,000
	Record Peerless' 100% share of Special Foods' 20X2 income.		

(15)	Cash	40,000	
	Investment in Special Foods		40,000
	Record Peerless' 100% share of Special Foods' 20X2 dividend.		

(16)	Income from Special Foods	6,000	
	Investment in Special Foods		6,000
	Record amortization of excess acquisition price.		

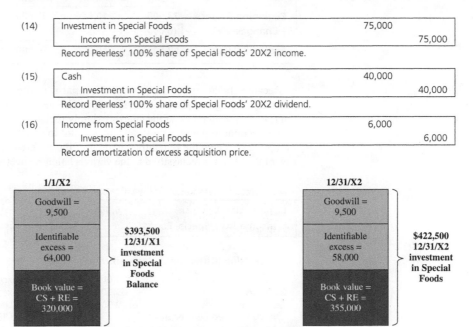

The book value component can be summarized as follows:

Book Value Calculations:

	Total Investment	=	Common Stock	+	Retained Earnings
Beginning Book Value	320,000		200,000		120,000
+ Net Income	75,000				75,000
– Dividends	(40,000)				(40,000)
Ending Book Value	355,000		200,000		155,000

The numbers in this chart in the shaded font determine the basic consolidation entry:

Basic Consolidation Entry:

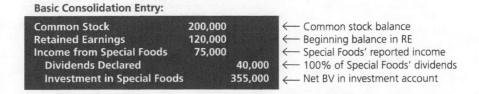

Common Stock	200,000		← Common stock balance
Retained Earnings	120,000		← Beginning balance in RE
Income from Special Foods	75,000		← Special Foods' reported income
Dividends Declared		40,000	← 100% of Special Foods' dividends
Investment in Special Foods		355,000	← Net BV in investment account

The entire differential amount assigned to the inventory already passed through cost of goods sold during the prior year period. The only other amortization item is the excess value assigned to the building, which continues to be written off over a 10-year period ($60,000 ÷ 10 = $6,000) as illustrated in the following chart. Again, the goodwill is deemed not to be further impaired this year.

Excess Value (Differential) Calculations:

	Total	=	Land	+	Building	+	Acc. Depr.	+	Goodwill
Beginning Balance	73,500		10,000		60,000		(6,000)		9,500
– Changes	(6,000)						(6,000)		
Ending Balance	67,500		10,000		60,000		(12,000)		9,500

Because the amortization of the differential was already written off from the investment account against the Income from Special Foods account, the change to the differential (i.e., the middle row of the chart) is simply reclassified from the Income from Special Foods account to the income statement account to which it applies during the consolidation process. Then, the remaining amount of the differential at year end (i.e., the bottom row of the chart) is reclassified to the various balance sheet accounts to which they apply:

Amortized Excess Value Reclassification Entry:

Depreciation Expense	6,000		← Extra depreciation expense
Income from Special Foods		6,000	← See calculation above.

Excess Value (Differential) Reclassification Entry:

Land	10,000		← Excess value at acquisition
Building	60,000		← Excess value at acquisition
Goodwill	9,500		← Calculated value postimpairment
Accumulated Depreciation		12,000	← = (60,000 ÷ 10 years) × 2 years
Investment in Special Foods		67,500	← Remaining balance in differential

These consolidation entries (1) eliminate the balances in the Investment in Special Foods and Income from Special Foods accounts, (2) reclassify the amortization of excess value to the proper income statement accounts, and (3) reclassify the remaining differential to the appropriate balance sheet accounts as of the end of the accounting period. The following T-accounts illustrate how the three consolidation entries "zero out" the equity-method investment and income accounts:

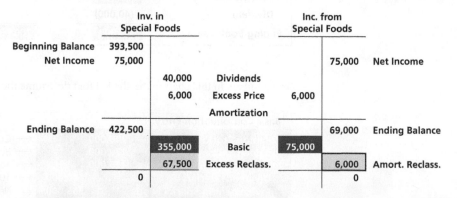

Again, we repeat the same accumulated depreciation consolidation entry this year (and every year as long as Special Foods owns the assets) that we used in the initial year.

Optional Accumulated Depreciation Consolidation Entry:

Accumulated Depreciation	300,000		← Accumulated depreciation at the time
Building and Equipment		300,000	of the acquisition netted against cost

FIGURE 4–6   December 31, 20X2, Equity-Method Worksheet for Consolidated Financial Statements, Second Year of Ownership; 100 Percent Acquisition at More than Book Value

	Peerless Products	Special Foods	Consolidation Entries DR	Consolidation Entries CR	Consolidated
Income Statement					
Sales	450,000	300,000			750,000
Less: COGS	(180,000)	(160,000)			(340,000)
Less: Depreciation Expense	(50,000)	(20,000)	6,000		(76,000)
Less: Other Expenses	(60,000)	(45,000)			(105,000)
Less: Impairment Loss					0
Income from Special Foods	69,000		75,000	6,000	0
Net Income	**229,000**	**75,000**	81,000	6,000	**229,000**
Statement of Retained Earnings					
Beginning Balance	416,000	120,000	120,000		416,000
Net Income	**229,000**	**75,000**	81,000	6,000	229,000
Less: Dividends Declared	(60,000)	(40,000)		40,000	(60,000)
Ending Balance	**585,000**	**155,000**	201,000	46,000	**585,000**
Balance Sheet					
Cash	157,500	85,000			242,500
Accounts Receivable	150,000	80,000			230,000
Inventory	180,000	90,000			270,000
Investment in Special Foods	422,500			355,000	0
				67,500	
Land	175,000	40,000	10,000		225,000
Buildings & Equipment	800,000	600,000	60,000	300,000	1,160,000
Less: Accumulated Depreciation	(500,000)	(340,000)	300,000	12,000	(552,000)
Goodwill			9,500		9,500
Total Assets	**1,385,000**	**555,000**	379,500	734,500	**1,585,000**
Accounts Payable	100,000	100,000			200,000
Bonds Payable	200,000	100,000			300,000
Common Stock	500,000	200,000	200,000		500,000
Retained Earnings	**585,000**	**155,000**	201,000	46,000	585,000
Total Liabilities & Equity	**1,385,000**	**555,000**	401,000	46,000	**1,585,000**

Consolidation Worksheet—Second Year Following Combination

The worksheet for the second year, 20X2, completes the two-year cycle as illustrated in Figure 4–6. Moreover, as can be seen from the worksheet, consolidated net income for 20X2 is $229,000 and consolidated retained earnings on December 31, 20X2, is $585,000 as illustrated in Figure 4–7.

FIGURE 4–7
Consolidated Net Income and Retained Earnings, 20X2; 100 Percent Acquisition at More than Book Value

Consolidated net income, 20X2:	
Peerless' separate operating income	$160,000
Special Foods' net income	75,000
Amortization of differential related to buildings & equipment in 20X2	(6,000)
Consolidated net income, 20X2	$229,000
Consolidated retained earnings, December 31, 20X2:	
Consolidated retained earnings, December 31, 20X1	$416,000
Peerless' separate operating income, 20X2	160,000
Special Foods' 20X2 net income	75,000
Amortization of differential related to buildings & equipment in 20X2	(6,000)
Dividends declared by Peerless, 20X2	(60,000)
Consolidated retained earnings, December 31, 20X2	$585,000

INTERCOMPANY RECEIVABLES AND PAYABLES

LO 4-6

Understand and explain the elimination of basic intercompany transactions.

All forms of intercompany receivables and payables need to be eliminated when consolidated financial statements are prepared. From a single-company viewpoint, a company cannot owe itself money. If a company owes an affiliate $1,000 on account, one company carries a $1,000 receivable on its separate books and the other has a payable for the same amount. When consolidated financial statements are prepared, the following consolidation entry is needed in the consolidation worksheet:

Accounts Payable	1,000	
Accounts Receivable		1,000

Eliminate intercompany receivable/payable.

If no consolidation entry is made, both the consolidated assets and liabilities are overstated by an equal amount.

If the intercompany receivable/payable bears interest, all accounts related to the intercompany claim must be eliminated in the preparation of consolidated statements, including the receivable/payable, interest income, interest expense, and any accrued interest on the intercompany claim. Other forms of intercorporate claims, such as bonds, are discussed in subsequent chapters. In all cases, failure to eliminate these claims can distort consolidated balances. As a result, the magnitude of debt of the combined entity may appear to be greater than it is, working capital ratios may be incorrect, and other types of comparisons may be distorted.

PUSH-DOWN ACCOUNTING

LO 4-7

Understand and explain the basics of push-down accounting.

The term **push-down accounting** refers to the practice of revaluing an acquired subsidiary's assets and liabilities to their fair values directly on that subsidiary's books at the date of acquisition. If this practice is followed, the revaluations are recorded once on the subsidiary's books at the date of acquisition and, therefore, are not made in the consolidation worksheets each time consolidated statements are prepared.

Those who favor push-down accounting argue that the change in the subsidiary's ownership in an acquisition is reason for adopting a new basis of accounting for the subsidiary's assets and liabilities, and this new basis of accounting should be reflected directly on the subsidiary's books. This argument is most persuasive when the subsidiary is wholly owned, is consolidated, or has its separate financial statements included with the parent's statements.

On the other hand, when a subsidiary has a significant noncontrolling interest or the subsidiary has bonds or preferred stock held by the public, push-down accounting may be inappropriate. Its use in the financial statements issued to the noncontrolling shareholders or to those holding bonds or preferred stock results in a new basis of accounting even though, from the perspective of those statement users, the entity has not changed. From their viewpoint, push-down accounting results in the revaluation of the assets and liabilities of a continuing enterprise, a practice that normally is not acceptable.

ASC 805-50-S99-2 requires push-down accounting whenever a business combination results in the acquired subsidiary becoming substantially wholly owned, i.e., greater than 95 percent ownership, (but only if it issues separate financial statements). It encourages but does not require the use of push-down accounting in situations in which the subsidiary is less than wholly owned (80 to 95 percent ownership) or the subsidiary has outstanding debt or preferred stock held by the public. Push-down accounting is prohibited when the subsidiary is less than 80 percent owned.

The revaluation of assets and liabilities on a subsidiary's books involves making an entry to debit or credit each asset and liability account to be revalued, with the balancing entry to a revaluation capital account (this amount is usually a credit). The revaluation capital account is part of the subsidiary's stockholders' equity. Once the revaluations are made on the books of the subsidiary, the new book values of the subsidiary's assets, including goodwill, are equal to the acquisition cost of the subsidiary.

Thus, no differential arises in the consolidation process. The investment consolidation entry in a consolidation worksheet prepared immediately after acquisition of a subsidiary and revaluation of its assets on its books might appear as follows:

Capital Stock—Subsidiary	XXX	
Retained Earnings	XXX	
Revaluation Capital	XXX	
Investment in Subsidiary Stock		XXX

Eliminate investment balance.

Note that the Revaluation Capital account, as part of the subsidiary's stockholders' equity, is eliminated in preparing consolidated statements. We provide a more detailed example of push-down accounting in Appendix 4A.

SUMMARY OF KEY CONCEPTS

Worksheet consolidation entries are needed to remove the effects of intercompany ownership and intercompany transactions so the consolidated financial statements appear as if the separate companies are actually one. These worksheet entries are needed to (1) eliminate the book value portion of the parent's subsidiary investment and the subsidiary's stockholders' equity accounts, (2) reclassify the amortization of excess value from the parent's income from subsidiary account to the correct income statement line items, (3) assign any remaining differential to specific assets and liabilities, and (4) net the subsidiary's accumulated depreciation as of the acquisition date against the historical cost of property, plant, and equipment.

Consolidated net income is computed in simple cases for a parent and a wholly owned subsidiary as the total of the parent's income from its own operations and the subsidiary's net income, adjusted for the write-off of differential, if appropriate. In this situation, consolidated retained earnings is computed as the total of the parent's retained earnings, excluding any income from the subsidiary, plus the subsidiary's cumulative net income since acquisition adjusted for the differential amount.

When a subsidiary is acquired for an amount higher than its book value, some parent companies may prefer to assign the differential to individual assets and liabilities directly on the subsidiary's books at the time of acquisition, thereby eliminating the need for revaluation entries in the consolidation worksheet each period. This procedure is called push-down accounting.

KEY TERMS

bargain purchase, *157*	goodwill, *153*	push-down
differential, *144*		accounting, *153, 168*

Appendix 4A   Push-Down Accounting Illustrated

When a subsidiary is acquired in a business combination, its assets and liabilities must be revalued to their fair values as of the date of combination for consolidated reporting. If *push-down accounting* is employed, the revaluations are made as of the date of combination directly on the books of the subsidiary and no consolidation entries related to the differential are needed in the consolidation worksheets.

The following example illustrates the consolidation process when assets and liabilities are revalued directly on a subsidiary's books rather than using consolidation worksheet entries to accomplish the revaluation. Assume that Peerless Products purchases all of Special Foods' common stock on January 1, 20X1, for $370,000 cash. The purchase price is $70,000 in excess of Special Foods' book value. Of the $70,000 total differential, $10,000 is related to land held by Special Foods and $60,000 is related to buildings and equipment having a 10-year remaining life. Accumulated depreciation on Special Foods' books at the acquisition date is $300,000. Peerless accounts for its investment in Special Foods stock using the equity method.

Peerless records the acquisition of stock on its books with the following entry:

(17)	Investment in Special Foods	370,000	
	Cash		370,000

Record the initial investment in Special Foods.

In contrast to a worksheet revaluation, the use of push-down accounting involves the revaluation of the assets on the separate books of Special Foods and alleviates the need for revaluation entries in the consolidation worksheet each period. If push-down accounting is used to revalue Special Foods' assets, the following entry is made directly on its books:

(18)	Land	10,000	
	Buildings & Equipment	60,000	
	Revaluation Capital		70,000

Record the increase in fair value of land and buildings.

This entry increases the amount at which the land and the buildings and equipment are shown in Special Foods' separate financial statements and gives rise to a revaluation capital account that is shown in the stockholders' equity section of Special Foods' balance sheet. Special Foods records $6,000 additional depreciation on its books to reflect the amortization over 10 years of the $60,000 write-up of buildings and equipment.

Entry (19) removes the accumulated depreciation on the acquisition date so that the buildings and equipment appear at their acquisition date fair value with zero accumulated depreciation.

| (19) | Accumulated Depreciation | 300,000 | |
| | Buildings & Equipment | | 300,000 |

Assuming Special Foods recorded net income of $44,000 and paid dividends of $30,000 during 20X1, Peerless records the following entries on its parent-company books:

| (20) | Investment in Special Foods | 44,000 | |
| | Income from Special Foods | | 44,000 |

Record Peerless' 100% share of Special Foods' 20X1 income.

| (21) | Cash | 30,000 | |
| | Investment in Special Foods | | 30,000 |

Record Peerless' 100% share of Special Foods' 20X1 dividend.

Because the revaluation is recorded on the subsidiary's books, Special Foods' book value is then equal to the fair value of the consideration given in the combination. Therefore, no differential exists, and Peerless need not record any amortization associated with the investment. The net amount of income from Special Foods recorded by Peerless is the same regardless of whether or not push-down accounting is employed. The book value portion of the investment account can be summarized as follows:

Book Value Calculations:

	Total Investment	=	Common Stock	+	Retained Earnings	+	Revaluation Capital
Beginning Book Value	370,000		200,000		100,000		70,000
+ Net Income	44,000				44,000		
− Dividends	(30,000)				(30,000)		
Ending Book Value	384,000		200,000		114,000		70,000

The basic consolidation entry is very similar to the original example presented previously except that it must also eliminate Special Foods' revaluation capital account:

Basic Consolidation Entry:

Common Stock	200,000	
Retained Earnings	100,000	
Revaluation Capital	70,000	
Income from Special Foods	44,000	
Dividends Declared		30,000
Investment in Special Foods		384,000

Again, because there is no differential with push-down accounting, the basic consolidation entry completely eliminates the balance in Peerless' investment account on the balance sheet as well as the Income from Special Foods account on the income statement.

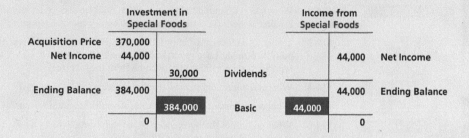

Figure 4–8 shows the consolidation worksheet prepared at the end of 20X1 and includes the effects of revaluing Special Foods' assets. Note that Special Foods' Land and Buildings and Equipment have been increased by $10,000 and $60,000, respectively. Also note the Revaluation Capital account in Special Foods' stockholders' equity. Because the revaluation was accomplished directly on the books of Special Foods, only the basic consolidation entry is needed in the worksheet illustrated in Figure 4–8.

FIGURE 4–8   December 31, 20X1, Equity-Method Worksheet for Consolidated Financial Statements, Initial Year of Ownership; 100 Percent Acquisition at More than Book Value; Push-Down Accounting

	Peerless Products	Special Foods	Consolidation Entries DR	Consolidation Entries CR	Consolidated
Income Statement					
Sales	400,000	200,000			600,000
Less: COGS	(170,000)	(115,000)			(285,000)
Less: Depreciation Expense	(50,000)	(26,000)			(76,000)
Less: Other Expenses	(40,000)	(15,000)			(55,000)
Income from Special Foods	44,000		44,000		0
Net Income	**184,000**	**44,000**	**44,000**	**0**	**184,000**
Statement of Retained Earnings					
Beginning Balance	300,000	100,000	100,000		300,000
Net Income	**184,000**	**44,000**	44,000	0	184,000
Less: Dividends Declared	(60,000)	(30,000)		30,000	(60,000)
Ending Balance	**424,000**	**114,000**	**144,000**	**30,000**	**424,000**
Balance Sheet					
Cash	140,000	75,000			215,000
Accounts Receivable	75,000	50,000			125,000
Inventory	100,000	75,000			175,000
Investment in Special Foods	384,000			384,000	0
Land	175,000	50,000			225,000
Buildings & Equipment	800,000	360,000			1,160,000
Less: Accumulated Depreciation	(450,000)	(26,000)			(476,000)
Total Assets	**1,224,000**	**584,000**	**0**	**384,000**	**1,424,000**
Accounts Payable	100,000	100,000			200,000
Bonds Payable	200,000	100,000			300,000
Common Stock	500,000	200,000	200,000		500,000
Retained Earnings	**424,000**	**114,000**	144,000	30,000	424,000
Revaluation Capital		70,000	70,000		0
Total Liabilities & Equity	**1,224,000**	**584,000**	**414,000**	**30,000**	**1,424,000**

QUESTIONS

LO 4-1   **Q4-1**   When is the carrying value of the investment account reduced under equity-method reporting?

LO 4-1   **Q4-2**   What is a differential? How is a differential treated by an investor in computing income from an investee under (*a*) cost-method and (*b*) equity-method reporting?

LO 4-1   **Q4-3**   Turner Manufacturing Corporation owns 100 percent of the common shares of Straight Lace Company. If Straight Lace reports net income of $100,000 for 20X5, what factors may cause Turner to report less than $100,000 of income from the investee?

LO 4-1   **Q4-4**   What is the term *differential* used to indicate?

LO 4-1   **Q4-5**   What conditions must exist for a negative differential to occur?

LO 4-2   **Q4-6**   What portion of the book value of the net assets held by a subsidiary at acquisition is included in the consolidated balance sheet?

LO 4-2   **Q4-7**   What portion of the fair value of a subsidiary's net assets normally is included in the consolidated balance sheet following a business combination?

LO 4-3   **Q4-8**   What happens to the differential in the consolidation worksheet prepared as of the date of combination? How is it reestablished so that the proper balances can be reported the following year?

LO 4-2   **Q4-9**   Explain why consolidated financial statements become increasingly important when the differential is very large.

LO 4-3   **Q4-10**   Give a definition of *consolidated net income*.

LO 4-5   **Q4-11**   When Ajax was preparing its consolidation worksheet, the differential was properly assigned to buildings and equipment. What additional entry generally must be made in the worksheet?

LO 4-3, 4-4   **Q4-12**   What determines whether the balance assigned to the differential remains constant or decreases each period?

LO 4-7   **Q4-13**   What does the term *push-down accounting* mean?

LO 4-7   **Q4-14**   Under what conditions is push-down accounting considered appropriate?

LO 4-7   **Q4-15**   What happens to the differential when push-down accounting is used following a business combination?

CASES

LO 4-1   **C4-1**   **Reporting Significant Investments in Common Stock**

Analysis   The reporting treatment for investments in common stock depends on the level of ownership and the ability to influence the investee's policies. The reporting treatment may even change over time as ownership levels or other factors change. When investees are not consolidated, the investments typically are reported in the Investments section of the investor's balance sheet. However, the investor's income from those investments is not always easy to find in the investor's income statement.

Required

a. Harley-Davidson Inc. holds an investment in the common stock of Buell Motorcycle Company. How did Harley-Davidson report this investment before 1998? How does it report the investment now? Why did Harley change its method of reporting its investment in Buell?

b. How does Chevron Corporation account for its investments in affiliated companies? How does the company account for issuances of additional stock by affiliates that change the company's proportionate dollar share of the affiliates' equity? How does Chevron treat a differential associated with an equity-method investment? How does Chevron account for the impairment of an equity investment?

c. Does Sears have any investments in companies that it accounts for using the equity method? Where are these investments reported in the balance sheet, and where is the income from these investments reported in the income statement?

LO 4-2

Analysis

C4-2 Assigning an Acquisition Differential

Ball Corporation's owners recently offered to sell 100 percent of their ownership to Timber Corporation for $450,000. Timber's business manager was told that Ball's book value was $300,000, and she estimates the fair value of its net assets at approximately $600,000. Ball has relatively old equipment and manufacturing facilities and uses a LIFO basis for inventory valuation of some items and a FIFO basis for others.

Required

If Timber accepts the offer and acquires a controlling interest in Ball, what difficulties are likely to be encountered in assigning the differential?

LO 4-2, 4-3

Understanding

C4-3 Negative Retained Earnings

Although Sloan Company had good earnings reports in 20X5 and 20X6, it had a negative retained earnings balance on December 31, 20X6. Jacobs Corporation purchased 100 percent of Sloan's common stock on January 1, 20X7.

Required

a. Explain how Sloan's negative retained earnings balance is reflected in the consolidated balance sheet immediately following the acquisition.

b. Explain how the existence of negative retained earnings changes the consolidation worksheet entries.

c. Can goodwill be recorded if Jacobs pays more than book value for Sloan's shares? Explain.

LO 4-1, 4-3

Judgment

C4-4 Balance Sheet Reporting Issues

Crumple Car Rentals is planning to expand into the western part of the United States and needs to acquire approximately 400 additional automobiles for rental purposes. Because Crumple's cash reserves were substantially depleted in replacing the bumpers on existing automobiles with new "fashion plate" bumpers, the expansion funds must be acquired through other means. Crumple's management has identified two options:

1. Issue additional debt.

2. Create a wholly owned leasing subsidiary that would borrow the money with a guarantee for payment from Crumple. The subsidiary would then lease the cars to the parent.

The acquisition price of the cars is approximately the same under both alternatives.

Required

a. You have been asked to compare and contrast the two alternatives from the perspective of

    (1) The impact on Crumple's consolidated balance sheet.

    (2) Their legal ramifications.

    (3) The ability to control the maintenance, repair, and replacement of automobiles.

b. What other alternatives might be used in acquiring the required automobiles?

c. Select your preferred alternative and show why it is the better choice.

LO 4-1, 4-2

Research

C4-5 Subsidiary Ownership: AMR Corporation and International Lease

Most subsidiaries are wholly owned, although only majority ownership is usually all that is required for consolidation. The parent's ownership may be direct or indirect. Frequently, a parent's direct subsidiaries have subsidiaries of their own, thus providing the parent with indirect ownership of the subsidiary's subsidiaries.

Required

International Lease Finance Corporation is a very large leasing company. It leases equipment that everyone is familiar with and many have used.

(1) Specifically, what is the principal business of International Lease Finance Corporation?

(2) Who are the direct owners of International Lease?

(3) In what city is International Lease headquartered?

(4) In what state is International Lease incorporated?

(5) Where is International Lease's common stock traded?

(6) What company is the parent in the consolidated financial statements in which International Lease is included, and what is that company's principal business?

EXERCISES

LO 4-1

E4-1 Cost versus Equity Reporting

Roller Corporation purchased 100 percent ownership of Steam Company on January 1, 20X5, for $270,000. On that date, the book value of Steam's reported net assets was $200,000. The excess over book value paid is attributable to depreciable assets with a remaining useful life of 10 years. Net income and dividend payments of Steam in the following periods were

Year	Net Income	Dividends
20X5	$20,000	$ 5,000
20X6	40,000	15,000
20X7	20,000	35,000

Required
Prepare journal entries on Roller Corporation's books relating to its investment in Steam Company for each of the three years, assuming it accounts for the investment using (*a*) the cost method and (*b*) the equity method.

LO 4-1

E4-2 Differential Assigned to Patents

Power Corporation purchased 100 percent of the common stock of Snow Corporation on January 1, 20X2, by issuing 45,000 shares of its $6 par value common stock. The market price of Power's shares at the date of issue was $24. Snow reported net assets with a book value of $980,000 on that date. The amount paid in excess of the book value of Snow's net assets was attributed to the increased value of patents held by Snow with a remaining useful life of eight years. Snow reported net income of $56,000 and paid dividends of $20,000 in 20X2 and reported a net loss of $44,000 and paid dividends of $10,000 in 20X3.

Required
Assuming that Power Corporation uses the equity method in accounting for its investment in Snow Corporation, prepare all journal entries for Power for 20X2 and 20X3.

LO 4-1

E4-3 Differential Assigned to Copyrights

Best Corporation acquired 100 percent of the voting common stock of Flair Company on January 1, 20X7, by issuing bonds with a par value and fair value of $670,000 and making a cash payment of $24,000. At the date of acquisition, Flair reported assets of $740,000 and liabilities of $140,000. The book values and fair values of Flair's net assets were equal except for land and copyrights. Flair's land had a fair value $16,000 higher than its book value. All of the remaining purchase price was attributable to the increased value of Flair's copyrights with a remaining useful life of eight years. Flair Company reported a loss of $88,000 in 20X7 and net income of $120,000 in 20X8. Flair paid dividends of $24,000 each year.

Required
Assuming that Best Corporation uses the equity method in accounting for its investment in Flair Company, prepare all journal entries for Best for 20X7 and 20X8.

LO 4-1

Advanced
StudyGuide
.com

E4-4 Differential Attributable to Depreciable Assets

Capital Corporation purchased 100 percent of Cook Company's stock on January 1, 20X4, for $340,000. On that date, Cook reported net assets with a historical cost of $300,000 and a fair value of $340,000. The difference was due to the increased value of buildings with a remaining life of 10 years. During 20X4 and 20X5 Cook reported net income of $10,000 and $20,000 and paid dividends of $6,000 and $9,000, respectively.

Required

Assuming that Capital Corporation uses (*a*) the equity method and (*b*) the cost method in accounting for its ownership of Cook Company, give the journal entries that Capital recorded in 20X4 and 20X5.

LO 4-1

E4-5 Investment Income

Brindle Company purchased 100 percent of Monroe Company's voting common stock for $648,000 on January 1, 20X4. At that date, Monroe reported assets of $690,000 and liabilities of $230,000. The book values and fair values of Monroe's assets were equal except for land, which had a fair value $108,000 more than book value, and equipment, which had a fair value $80,000 more than book value. The remaining economic life of all depreciable assets at January 1, 20X4, was five years. Monroe reported net income of $68,000 and paid dividends of $34,000 in 20X4.

Required

Compute the amount of investment income to be reported by Brindle for 20X4.

LO 4-1

E4-6 Determination of Purchase Price

Branch Corporation purchased 100 percent of Hardy Company's common stock on January 1, 20X5, and paid $28,000 above book value. The full amount of the additional payment was attributed to amortizable assets with a life of eight years remaining at January 1, 20X5. During 20X5 and 20X6, Hardy reported net income of $33,000 and $6,000 and paid dividends of $15,000 and $12,000, respectively. Branch uses the equity method in accounting for its investment in Hardy and reported a balance in its investment account of $161,000 on December 31, 20X6.

Required

Compute the amount paid by Branch to purchase Hardy shares.

LO 4-1, 4-2

E4-7 Correction of Error

During review of the adjusting entries to be recorded on December 31, 20X8, Grand Corporation discovered that it had inappropriately been using the cost method in accounting for its investment in Case Products Corporation. Grand purchased 100 percent ownership of Case Products on January 1, 20X6, for $56,000, at which time Case Products reported retained earnings of $10,000 and capital stock outstanding of $30,000. The differential was attributable to patents with a life of eight years. Income and dividends of Case Products were:

Year	Net Income	Dividends
20X6	$16,000	$6,000
20X7	24,000	8,000
20X8	32,000	8,000

Required

Give the correcting entry required on December 31, 20X8, to properly report the investment under the equity method, assuming the books have not been closed. Case Products' dividends were declared in early November and paid in early December each year.

LO 4-1

E4-8 Differential Assigned to Land and Equipment

Rod Corporation purchased 100 percent ownership of Stafford Corporation on January 1, 20X4, for $65,000, which was $10,000 above the underlying book value. Half the additional amount was attributable to an increase in the value of land held by Stafford, and half was due to an increase in the value of equipment. The equipment had a remaining economic life of five years on January 1, 20X4. During 20X4, Stafford reported net income of $12,000 and paid dividends of $4,500.

Required

Give the journal entries that Rod Corporation recorded during 20X4 related to its investment in Stafford Corporation, assuming Rod uses the equity method in accounting for its investment.

176 Chapter 4 *Consolidation of Wholly Owned Subsidiaries Acquired at More than Book Value*

LO 4-1, 4-2   **E4-9**   **Equity Entries with Goodwill**

Turner Corporation reported the following balances at January 1, 20X9:

Advanced
StudyGuide
.com

Item	Book Value	Fair Value
Cash	$ 45,000	$ 45,000
Accounts Receivable	60,000	60,000
Inventory	120,000	130,000
Buildings & Equipment	300,000	240,000
Less: Accumulated Depreciation	(150,000)	
Total Assets	$375,000	$475,000
Accounts Payable	$ 75,000	$ 75,000
Common Stock ($10 par value)	100,000	
Additional Paid-In Capital	30,000	
Retained Earnings	170,000	
Total Liabilities & Equities	$375,000	

On January 1, 20X9, Gross Corporation purchased 100 percent of Turner's stock. All tangible assets had a remaining economic life of 10 years at January 1, 20X9. Both companies use the FIFO inventory method. Turner reported net income of $16,000 in 20X9 and paid dividends of $3,200. Gross uses the equity method in accounting for its investment in Turner.

Required

Give all journal entries that Gross recorded during 20X9 with respect to its investment assuming Gross paid $437,500 for the ownership of Turner on January 1, 20X9. The amount of the differential assigned to goodwill is not impaired.

LO 4-1, 4-2,   **E4-10**   **Multiple-Choice Questions on Consolidation Process**
4-6

Select the most appropriate answer for each of the following questions.

1. Goodwill is

    a. Seldom reported because it is too difficult to measure.

    b. Reported when more than book value is paid in purchasing another company.

    c. Reported when the fair value of the acquiree is higher than the fair value of the net identifiable assets acquired.

    d. Generally smaller for small companies and increases in amount as the companies acquired increase in size.

2. [AICPA Adapted] Wright Corporation includes several subsidiaries in its consolidated financial statements. In its December 31, 20X2, trial balance, Wright had the following intercompany balances before consolidation entries:

	Debit	Credit
Current receivable due from Main Company	$ 32,000	
Noncurrent receivable from Main Company	114,000	
Cash advance to Corn Corporation	6,000	
Cash advance from King Company		$ 15,000
Intercompany payable to King Company		101,000

In its December 31, 20X2, consolidated balance sheet, what amount should Wright report as intercompany receivables?

    a. $152,000.

    b. $146,000.

    c. $36,000.

    d. $0.

3. Beni Corporation acquired 100 percent of Carr Corporation's outstanding capital stock for $430,000 cash. Immediately before the purchase, the balance sheets of both corporations reported the following:

	Beni	Carr
Assets	$2,000,000	$750,000
Liabilities	$ 750,000	$400,000
Common Stock	1,000,000	310,000
Retained Earnings	250,000	40,000
Liabilities & Stockholders' Equity	$2,000,000	$750,000

At the date of purchase, the fair value of Carr's assets was $50,000 more than the aggregate carrying amounts. In the consolidated balance sheet prepared immediately after the purchase, the consolidated stockholders' equity should amount to

  a. $1,680,000.

  b. $1,650,000.

  c. $1,600,000.

  d. $1,250,000.

Note: Questions 4 and 5 are based on the following information:
Nugget Company's balance sheet on December 31, 20X6, was as follows:

Assets		Liabilities & Stockholders' Equity	
Cash	$ 100,000	Current Liabilities	$ 300,000
Accounts Receivable	200,000	Long-Term Debt	500,000
Inventories	500,000	Common Stock (par $1 per share)	100,000
Property, Plant & Equipment (net)	900,000	Additional Paid-In Capital	200,000
		Retained Earnings	600,000
Total Assets	$1,700,000	Total Liabilities & Stockholders' Equity	$1,700,000

On December 31, 20X6, Gold Company acquired all of Nugget's outstanding common stock for $1,500,000 cash. On that date, the fair (market) value of Nugget's inventories was $450,000, and the fair value of Nugget's property, plant, and equipment was $1,000,000. The fair values of all other assets and liabilities of Nugget were equal to their book values.

4. As a result of Gold's acquisition of Nugget, the consolidated balance sheet of Gold and Nugget should reflect goodwill in the amount of

  a. $500,000.

  b. $550,000.

  c. $600,000.

  d. $650,000.

5. Assuming Gold uses the equity method to account for investments and that Gold's (unconsolidated) balance sheet on December 31, 20X6, reflected retained earnings of $2,000,000, what amount of retained earnings should be shown in the December 31, 20X6, consolidated balance sheet of Gold and its new subsidiary, Nugget?

  a. $2,000,000.

  b. $2,600,000.

  c. $2,800,000.

  d. $3,150,000.

LO 4-3, 4-6 | **E4-11** | **Multiple-Choice Questions on Consolidation [AICPA Adapted]**

Select the correct answer for each of the following questions.

1. On January 1, 20X1, Prim Inc. acquired all of Scrap Inc.'s outstanding common shares for cash equal to the stock's book value. The carrying amounts of Scrap's assets and liabilities approximated their fair values, except that the carrying amount of its building was more than fair value. In preparing Prim's 20X1 consolidated income statement, which of the following adjustments would be made?

   a. Decrease depreciation expense and recognize goodwill amortization.

   b. Increase depreciation expense and recognize goodwill amortization.

   c. Decrease depreciation expense and recognize no goodwill amortization.

   d. Increase depreciation expense and recognize no goodwill amortization.

2. The first examination of Rudd Corporation's financial statements was made for the year ended December 31, 20X8. The auditor found that Rudd had acquired another company on January 1, 20X8, and had recorded goodwill of $100,000 in connection with this acquisition. Although a friend of the auditor believes the goodwill will last no more than five years, Rudd's management has found no impairment of goodwill during 20X8. In its 20X8 financial statements, Rudd should report

	Amortization Expense	Goodwill
a.	$ 0	$100,000
b.	$100,000	$ 0
c.	$ 20,000	$ 80,000
d.	$ 0	$ 0

3. Consolidated financial statements are being prepared for a parent and its four wholly owned subsidiaries that have intercompany loans of $100,000 and intercompany profits of $300,000. How much of these intercompany loans and profits should be eliminated?

	Intercompany Loans	Profits
a.	$ 0	$ 0
b.	$ 0	$300,000
c.	$100,000	$ 0
d.	$100,000	$300,000

4. On April 1, 20X8, Plum Inc. paid $1,700,000 for all of Long Corp.'s issued and outstanding common stock. On that date, the costs and fair values of Long's recorded assets and liabilities were as follows:

	Cost	Fair Value
Cash	$ 160,000	$ 160,000
Inventory	480,000	460,000
Property, plant & equipment (net)	980,000	1,040,000
Liabilities	(360,000)	(360,000)
Net assets	$1,260,000	$1,300,000

In Plum's March 31, 20X9, consolidated balance sheet, what amount of goodwill should be reported as a result of this business combination?

   a. $360,000.

   b. $396,000.

   c. $400,000.

   d. $440,000.

LO 4-3

E4-12 Consolidation Entries with Differential

On June 10, 20X8, Tower Corporation acquired 100 percent of Brown Company's common stock. Summarized balance sheet data for the two companies immediately after the stock acquisition are as follows:

Item	Tower Corp.	Brown Company Book Value	Fair Value
Cash	$ 15,000	$ 5,000	$ 5,000
Accounts Receivable	30,000	10,000	10,000
Inventory	80,000	20,000	25,000
Buildings & Equipment (net)	120,000	50,000	70,000
Investment in Brown Stock	100,000		
Total	$345,000	$85,000	$110,000
Accounts Payable	$ 25,000	$ 3,000	$ 3,000
Bonds Payable	150,000	25,000	25,000
Common Stock	55,000	20,000	
Retained Earnings	115,000	37,000	
Total	$345,000	$85,000	$ 28,000

Advanced StudyGuide .com

Required

a. Give the consolidation entries required to prepare a consolidated balance sheet immediately after the acquisition of Brown Company shares.

b. Explain how consolidation entries differ from other types of journal entries recorded in the normal course of business.

LO 4-5

E4-13 Balance Sheet Consolidation

Reed Corporation acquired 100 percent of Thorne Corporation's voting common stock on December 31, 20X4, for $395,000. At the date of combination, Thorne reported the following:

Cash	$120,000	Current Liabilities	$ 80,000
Inventory	100,000	Long-Term Liabilities	200,000
Buildings (net)	420,000	Common Stock	120,000
		Retained Earnings	240,000
Total	$640,000	Total	$640,000

At December 31, 20X4, the book values of Thorne's net assets and liabilities approximated their fair values, except for buildings, which had a fair value of $20,000 less than book value, and inventories, which had a fair value $36,000 more than book value.

Required

Reed Corporation wishes to prepare a consolidated balance sheet immediately following the business combination. Give the consolidation entry or entries needed to prepare a consolidated balance sheet at December 31, 20X4.

LO 4-2, 4-3

E4-14 Acquisition with Differential

Road Corporation acquired all of Conger Corporation's voting shares on January 1, 20X2, for $470,000. At that time Conger reported common stock outstanding of $80,000 and retained earnings of $130,000. The book values of Conger's assets and liabilities approximated fair values, except for land, which had a book value of $80,000 and a fair value of $100,000, and buildings, which had a book value of $220,000 and a fair value of $400,000. Land and buildings are the only noncurrent assets that Conger holds.

Required

a. Compute the amount of goodwill at the date of acquisition.

b. Give the consolidation entry or entries required immediately following the acquisition to prepare a consolidated balance sheet.

LO 4-5   **E4-15**   ### Balance Sheet Worksheet with Differential

Blank Corporation acquired 100 percent of Faith Corporation's common stock on December 31, 20X2, for $189,000. Data from the balance sheets of the two companies included the following amounts as of the date of acquisition:

Item	Blank Corporation	Faith Corporation
Cash	$ 26,000	$ 18,000
Accounts Receivable	87,000	37,000
Inventory	110,000	60,000
Buildings & Equipment (net)	220,000	150,000
Investment in Faith Corporation Stock	189,000	
Total Assets	$632,000	$265,000
Accounts Payable	$ 92,000	$ 35,000
Notes Payable	150,000	80,000
Common Stock	100,000	60,000
Retained Earnings	290,000	90,000
Total Liabilities & Stockholders' Equity	$632,000	$265,000

At the date of the business combination, Faith's net assets and liabilities approximated fair value except for inventory, which had a fair value of $84,000, and buildings and equipment (net), which had a fair value of $165,000.

Required

a. Give the consolidation entry or entries needed to prepare a consolidated balance sheet immediately following the business combination.

b. Prepare a consolidation balance sheet worksheet.

LO 4-5   **E4-16**   ### Worksheet for Wholly Owned Subsidiary

Gold Enterprises acquired 100 percent of Premium Builders' stock on December 31, 20X4. Balance sheet data for Gold and Premium on January 1, 20X5, are as follows:

	Gold Enterprises	Premium Builders
Cash & Receivables	$ 80,000	$ 30,000
Inventory	150,000	350,000
Buildings & Equipment (net)	430,000	80,000
Investment in Premium Stock	167,000	
Total Assets	$827,000	$460,000
Current Liabilities	$100,000	$110,000
Long-Term Debt	400,000	200,000
Common Stock	200,000	140,000
Retained Earnings	127,000	10,000
Total Liabilities & Stockholders' Equity	$827,000	$460,000

At the date of the business combination, Premium's cash and receivables had a fair value of $28,000, inventory had a fair value of $357,000, and buildings and equipment had a fair value of $92,000.

Required

a. Give all consolidation entries needed to prepare a consolidated balance sheet on January 1, 20X5.

b. Complete a consolidated balance sheet worksheet.

c. Prepare a consolidated balance sheet in good form.

LO 4-3, 4-5 **E4-17** **Computation of Consolidated Balances**

Astor Corporation's balance sheet at January 1, 20X7, reflected the following balances:

Cash & Receivables	$ 80,000	Accounts Payable	$ 40,000
Inventory	120,000	Income Taxes Payable	60,000
Land	70,000	Bonds Payable	200,000
Buildings & Equipment (net)	480,000	Common Stock	250,000
		Retained Earnings	200,000
Total Assets	$750,000	Total Liabilities & Stockholders' Equity	$750,000

Phel Corporation, which had just entered into an active acquisition program, acquired 100 percent of Astor's common stock on January 2, 20X7, for $576,000. A careful review of the fair value of Astor's assets and liabilities indicated the following:

	Book Value	Fair Value
Inventory	$120,000	$140,000
Land	70,000	60,000
Buildings & Equipment (net)	480,000	550,000

Assume the book values of Phel's Inventory, Land, and Buildings and Equipment accounts are $300,000, $85,000, and $1,200,000, respectively.

Required

Compute the appropriate amount to be included in the consolidated balance sheet immediately following the acquisition for each of the following items:

a. Inventory.

b. Land.

c. Buildings and Equipment (net).

d. Goodwill.

e. Investment in Astor Corporation.

LO 4-3 **E4-18** **Multiple-Choice Questions on Balance Sheet Consolidation**

Top Corporation acquired 100 percent of Sun Corporation's common stock on December 31, 20X2. Balance sheet data for the two companies immediately following the acquisition follow:

Item	Top Corporation	Sun Corporation
Cash	$ 49,000	$ 30,000
Accounts Receivable	110,000	45,000
Inventory	130,000	70,000
Land	80,000	25,000
Buildings & Equipment	500,000	400,000
Less: Accumulated Depreciation	(223,000)	(165,000)
Investment in Sun Corporation Stock	198,000	
Total Assets	$844,000	$405,000
Accounts Payable	$ 61,500	$ 28,000
Taxes Payable	95,000	37,000
Bonds Payable	280,000	200,000
Common Stock	150,000	50,000
Retained Earnings	257,500	90,000
Total Liabilities & Stockholders' Equity	$844,000	$405,000

At the date of the business combination, the book values of Sun's net assets and liabilities approximated fair value except for inventory, which had a fair value of $85,000, and land, which had a fair value of $45,000.

Required

For each question, indicate the appropriate total that should appear in the consolidated balance sheet prepared immediately after the business combination.

1. What amount of inventory will be reported?

    a. $70,000.
    b. $130,000.
    c. $200,000.
    d. $215,000.

2. What amount of goodwill will be reported?

    a. $0.
    b. $23,000.
    c. $43,000.
    d. $58,000.

3. What amount of total assets will be reported?

    a. $84,400.
    b. $1,051,000.
    c. $1,109,000.
    d. $1,249,000.

4. What amount of total liabilities will be reported?

    a. $265,000.
    b. $436,500.
    c. $701,500.
    d. $1,249,000.

5. What amount of consolidated retained earnings will be reported?

    a. $547,500.
    b. $397,500.
    c. $347,500.
    d. $257,500.

6. What amount of total stockholders' equity will be reported?

    a. $407,500.
    b. $547,500.
    c. $844,000.
    d. $1,249,000.

LO 4-3   **E4-19**   ### Wholly Owned Subsidiary with Differential

Canton Corporation is a wholly owned subsidiary of Winston Corporation. Winston acquired ownership of Canton on January 1, 20X3, for $28,000 above Canton's reported net assets. At that date, Canton reported common stock outstanding of $60,000 and retained earnings of $90,000. The differential is assigned to equipment with an economic life of seven years at the date of the business combination. Canton reported net income of $30,000 and paid dividends of $12,000 in 20X3.

Required

a. Give the journal entries recorded by Winston Corporation during 20X3 on its books if Winston accounts for its investment in Canton using the equity method.

b. Give the consolidation entries needed at December 31, 20X3, to prepare consolidated financial statements.

LO 4-5

E4-20   Basic Consolidation Worksheet

Blake Corporation acquired 100 percent of Shaw Corporation's voting shares on January 1, 20X3, at underlying book value. At that date, the book values and fair values of Shaw's assets and liabilities were equal. Blake uses the equity method in accounting for its investment in Shaw. Adjusted trial balances for Blake and Shaw on December 31, 20X3, are as follows:

	Blake Corporation		Shaw Corporation	
Item	Debit	Credit	Debit	Credit
Current Assets	$145,000		$105,000	
Depreciable Assets (net)	325,000		225,000	
Investment in Shaw Corporation Stock	170,000			
Depreciation Expense	25,000		15,000	
Other Expenses	105,000		75,000	
Dividends Declared	40,000		10,000	
Current Liabilities		$ 50,000		$ 40,000
Long-Term Debt		100,000		120,000
Common Stock		200,000		100,000
Retained Earnings		230,000		50,000
Sales		200,000		120,000
Income from Subsidiary		30,000		
	$810,000	$810,000	$430,000	$430,000

Required

a. Give all consolidation entries required on December 31, 20X3, to prepare consolidated financial statements.

b. Prepare a three-part consolidation worksheet as of December 31, 20X3.

LO 4-5

E4-21   Basic Consolidation Worksheet for Second Year

Blake Corporation acquired 100 percent of Shaw Corporation's voting shares on January 1, 20X3, at underlying book value. At that date, the book values and fair values of Shaw's assets and liabilities were equal. Blake uses the equity method in accounting for its investment in Shaw. Adjusted trial balances for Blake and Shaw on December 31, 20X4, are as follows:

	Blake Corporation		Shaw Corporation	
Item	Debit	Credit	Debit	Credit
Current Assets	$210,000		$150,000	
Depreciable Assets (net)	300,000		210,000	
Investment in Shaw Corporation Stock	190,000			
Depreciation Expense	25,000		15,000	
Other Expenses	150,000		90,000	
Dividends Declared	50,000		15,000	
Current Liabilities		$ 70,000		$ 50,000
Long-Term Debt		100,000		120,000
Common Stock		200,000		100,000
Retained Earnings		290,000		70,000
Sales		230,000		140,000
Income from Subsidiary		35,000		
	$925,000	$925,000	$480,000	$480,000

Required

a. Give all consolidation entries required on December 31, 20X4, to prepare consolidated financial statements.

b. Prepare a three-part consolidation worksheet as of December 31, 20X4.

LO 4-5

E4-22 **Consolidation Worksheet with Differential**

Kennelly Corporation acquired all of Short Company's common shares on January 1, 20X5, for $180,000. On that date, the book value of the net assets reported by Short was $150,000. The entire differential was assigned to depreciable assets with a six-year remaining economic life from January 1, 20X5.

The adjusted trial balances for the two companies on December 31, 20X5, are as follows:

Item	Kennelly Corporation Debit	Kennelly Corporation Credit	Short Company Debit	Short Company Credit
Cash	$ 15,000		$ 5,000	
Accounts Receivable	30,000		40,000	
Inventory	70,000		60,000	
Depreciable Assets (net)	325,000		225,000	
Investment in Short Company Stock	195,000			
Depreciation Expense	25,000		15,000	
Other Expenses	105,000		75,000	
Dividends Declared	40,000		10,000	
Accounts Payable		$ 50,000		$ 40,000
Notes Payable		100,000		120,000
Common Stock		200,000		100,000
Retained Earnings		230,000		50,000
Sales		200,000		120,000
Income from Subsidiary		25,000		
	$805,000	$805,000	$430,000	$430,000

Kennelly uses the equity method in accounting for its investment in Short. Short declared and paid dividends on December 31, 20X5.

Required

a. Prepare the consolidation entries needed as of December 31, 20X5, to complete a consolidation worksheet.

b. Prepare a three-part consolidation worksheet as of December 31, 20X5.

LO 4-5

E4-23 **Consolidation Worksheet for Subsidiary**

Land Corporation acquired 100 percent of Growth Company's voting stock on January 1, 20X4, at underlying book value. Land uses the equity method in accounting for its ownership of Growth. On December 31, 20X4, the trial balances of the two companies are as follows:

Item	Land Corporation Debit	Land Corporation Credit	Growth Company Debit	Growth Company Credit
Current Assets	$ 238,000		$150,000	
Depreciable Assets	500,000		300,000	
Investment in Growth Company Stock	190,000			
Depreciation Expense	25,000		15,000	
Other Expenses	150,000		90,000	
Dividends Declared	50,000		15,000	
Accumulated Depreciation		$ 200,000		$ 90,000
Current Liabilities		70,000		50,000
Long-Term Debt		100,000		120,000
Common Stock		200,000		100,000
Retained Earnings		318,000		70,000
Sales		230,000		140,000
Income from Subsidiary		35,000		
	$1,153,000	$1,153,000	$570,000	$570,000

Required

a. Give all consolidation entries required on December 31, 20X4, to prepare consolidated financial statements.

b. Prepare a three-part consolidation worksheet as of December 31, 20X4.

LO 4-7 **E4-24A** **Push-Down Accounting**

Jefferson Company acquired all of Louis Corporation's common shares on January 2, 20X3, for $789,000. At the date of combination, Louis's balance sheet appeared as follows:

Assets		Liabilities	
Cash & Receivables	$ 34,000	Current Payables	$ 25,000
Inventory	165,000	Notes Payable	100,000
Land	60,000	Stockholders' Equity	
Buildings (net)	250,000	Common Stock	200,000
Equipment (net)	320,000	Additional Capital	425,000
		Retained Earnings	79,000
Total	$829,000	Total	$829,000

The fair values of all of Louis's assets and liabilities were equal to their book values except for its fixed assets. Louis's land had a fair value of $75,000; the buildings, a fair value of $300,000; and the equipment, a fair value of $340,000.

Jefferson Company decided to employ push-down accounting for the acquisition of Louis Corporation. Subsequent to the combination, Louis continued to operate as a separate company.

Required

a. Record the acquisition of Louis's stock on Jefferson's books.

b. Present any entries that would be made on Louis's books related to the business combination, assuming push-down accounting is used.

c. Present, in general journal form, all consolidation entries that would appear in a consolidation worksheet for Jefferson and its subsidiary prepared immediately following the combination.

PROBLEMS

LO 4-5 **P4-25** **Assignment of Differential in Worksheet**

Teresa Corporation acquired all the voting shares of Sally Enterprises on January 1, 20X4. Balance sheet amounts for the companies on the date of acquisition were as follows:

	Teresa Corporation	Sally Enterprises
Cash & Receivables	$ 40,000	$ 20,000
Inventory	95,000	40,000
Land	80,000	90,000
Buildings & Equipment	400,000	230,000
Investment in Sally Enterprises	290,000	
Total Debits	$905,000	$380,000
Accumulated Depreciation	$175,000	$ 65,000
Accounts Payable	60,000	15,000
Notes Payable	100,000	50,000
Common Stock	300,000	100,000
Retained Earnings	270,000	150,000
Total Credits	$905,000	$380,000

Sally Enterprises' buildings and equipment were estimated to have a market value of $175,000 on January 1, 20X4. All other items appeared to have market values approximating current book values.

Required

a. Complete a consolidated balance sheet worksheet for January 1, 20X4.

b. Prepare a consolidated balance sheet in good form.

LO 4-3

P4-26   ## Computation of Consolidated Balances

Retail Records Inc. acquired all of Decibel Studios' voting shares on January 1, 20X2, for $280,000. Retail's balance sheet immediately after the combination contained the following balances:

RETAIL RECORDS INC. Balance Sheet January 1, 20X2			
Cash & Receivables	$120,000	Accounts Payable	$ 75,000
Inventory	110,000	Taxes Payable	50,000
Land	70,000	Notes Payable	300,000
Buildings & Equipment (net)	350,000	Common Stock	400,000
Investment in Decibel Stock	280,000	Retained Earnings	105,000
Total Assets	$930,000	Total Liabilities & Stockholders' Equity	$930,000

Decibel's balance sheet at acquisition contained the following balances:

DECIBEL STUDIOS Balance Sheet January 1, 20X2			
Cash & Receivables	$ 40,000	Accounts Payable	$ 90,000
Inventory	180,000	Notes Payable	250,000
Buildings & Equipment (net)	350,000	Common Stock	100,000
Goodwill	30,000	Additional Paid-In Capital	200,000
		Retained Earnings	(40,000)
Total Assets	$600,000	Total Liabilities & Stockholders' Equity	$600,000

On the date of combination, the inventory held by Decibel had a fair value of $170,000, and its buildings and recording equipment had a fair value of $375,000. Goodwill reported by Decibel resulted from a purchase of Sound Stage Enterprises in 20X1. Sound Stage was liquidated and its assets and liabilities were brought onto Decibel's books.

Required

Compute the balances to be reported in the consolidated balance sheet immediately after the acquisition for:

a. Inventory.

b. Buildings and Equipment (net).

c. Investment in Decibel Stock.

d. Goodwill.

e. Common Stock.

f. Retained Earnings.

LO 4-5

P4-27   ## Balance Sheet Consolidation [AICPA Adapted]

Case Inc. acquired all Frey Inc.'s outstanding $25 par common stock on December 31, 20X3, in exchange for 40,000 shares of its $25 par common stock. Case's common stock closed at

$56.50 per share on a national stock exchange on December 31, 20X3. Both corporations continued to operate as separate businesses maintaining separate accounting records with years ending December 31.

On December 31, 20X4, after year-end adjustments and the closing of nominal accounts, the companies had condensed balance sheet accounts (below).

Additional Information

1. Case uses the equity method of accounting for its investment in Frey.

2. On December 31, 20X3, Frey's assets and liabilities had fair values equal to the book balances with the exception of land, which had a fair value of $550,000. Frey had no land transactions in 20X4.

3. On June 15, 20X4, Frey paid a cash dividend of $4 per share on its common stock.

4. On December 10, 20X4, Case paid a cash dividend totaling $256,000 on its common stock.

5. On December 31, 20X3, immediately before the combination, the stockholders' equity balance was:

	Case Inc.	Frey Inc.
Common Stock	$2,200,000	$1,000,000
Additional Paid-In Capital	1,660,000	190,000
Retained Earnings	3,166,000	820,000
	$7,026,000	$2,010,000

6. The 20X4 net income amounts according to the separate books of Case and Frey were $890,000 (exclusive of equity in Frey's earnings) and $580,000, respectively.

	Case Inc.	Frey Inc.
Assets		
Cash	$ 825,000	$ 330,000
Accounts & Other Receivables	2,140,000	835,000
Inventories	2,310,000	1,045,000
Land	650,000	300,000
Depreciable Assets (net)	4,575,000	1,980,000
Investment in Frey Inc.	2,680,000	
Long-Term Investments & Other Assets	865,000	385,000
Total Assets	$14,045,000	$4,875,000
Liabilities & Stockholders' Equity		
Accounts Payable & Other Current Liabilities	$ 2,465,000	$1,145,000
Long-Term Debt	1,900,000	1,300,000
Common Stock, $25 Par Value	3,200,000	1,000,000
Additional Paid-In Capital	2,100,000	190,000
Retained Earnings	4,380,000	1,240,000
Total Liabilities & Stockholders' Equity	$14,045,000	$4,875,000

Required

Prepare a consolidated balance sheet worksheet for Case and its subsidiary, Frey, for December 31, 20X4. A formal consolidated balance sheet is not required.

LO 4-5   **P4-28**   **Consolidated Balance Sheet**

Thompson Company spent $240,000 to acquire all of Lake Corporation's stock on January 1, 20X2. The balance sheets of the two companies on December 31, 20X3, showed the following amounts:

	Thompson Company	Lake Corporation
Cash	$ 30,000	$ 20,000
Accounts Receivable	100,000	40,000
Land	60,000	50,000
Buildings & Equipment	500,000	350,000
Less: Accumulated Depreciation	(230,000)	(75,000)
Investment in Lake Corporation	252,000	
	$712,000	$385,000
Accounts Payable	$ 80,000	$ 10,000
Taxes Payable	40,000	70,000
Notes Payable	100,000	85,000
Common Stock	200,000	100,000
Retained Earnings	292,000	120,000
	$712,000	$385,000

Lake reported retained earnings of $100,000 at the date of acquisition. The difference between the acquisition price and underlying book value is assigned to buildings and equipment with a remaining economic life of 10 years from the date of acquisition. Assume Lake's accumulated depreciation on the acquisition date was $25,000.

Required

a. Give the appropriate consolidation entry or entries needed to prepare a consolidated balance sheet as of December 31, 20X3.

b. Prepare a consolidated balance sheet worksheet as of December 31, 20X3.

LO 4-5, 4-6   **P4-29**   **Comprehensive Problem: Consolidation in Subsequent Period**

Thompson Company spent $240,000 to acquire all of Lake Corporation's stock on January 1, 20X2. On December 31, 20X4, the trial balances of the two companies were as follows:

	Thompson Company		Lake Corporation	
Item	Debit	Credit	Debit	Credit
Cash	$ 74,000		$ 42,000	
Accounts Receivable	130,000		53,000	
Land	60,000		50,000	
Buildings & Equipment	500,000		350,000	
Investment in Lake Corporation Stock	268,000			
Cost of Services Provided	470,000		130,000	
Depreciation Expense	35,000		18,000	
Other Expenses	57,000		60,000	
Dividends Declared	30,000		12,000	
Accumulated Depreciation		$ 265,000		$ 93,000
Accounts Payable		71,000		17,000
Taxes Payable		58,000		60,000
Notes Payable		100,000		85,000
Common Stock		200,000		100,000
Retained Earnings		292,000		120,000
Service Revenue		610,000		240,000
Income from Subsidiary		28,000		
	$1,624,000	$1,624,000	$715,000	$715,000

Lake Corporation reported retained earnings of $100,000 at the date of acquisition. The difference between the acquisition price and underlying book value is assigned to buildings and equipment with a remaining economic life of 10 years from the date of acquisition. Lake's accumulated depreciation on the acquisition date was $25,000. At December 31, 20X4, Lake owed Thompson $2,500.

Required

a. Give all journal entries recorded by Thompson with regard to its investment in Lake during 20X4.

b. Give all consolidation entries required on December 31, 20X4, to prepare consolidated financial statements.

c. Prepare a three-part consolidation worksheet as of December 31, 20X4.

LO 4-3, 4-4   **P4-30**   ## Acquisition at Other than Fair Value of Net Assets

Mason Corporation acquired 100 percent ownership of Best Company on February 12, 20X9. At the date of acquisition, Best Company reported assets and liabilities with book values of $420,000 and $165,000, respectively, common stock outstanding of $80,000, and retained earnings of $175,000. The book values and fair values of Best's assets and liabilities were identical except for land, which had increased in value by $20,000, and inventories, which had decreased by $7,000.

Required

Give the consolidation entries required to prepare a consolidated balance sheet immediately after the business combination assuming Mason acquired its ownership of Best for:

a. $280,000.

b. $251,000.

LO 4-5, 4-6   **P4-31**   ## Intercorporate Receivables and Payables

Kim Corporation acquired 100 percent of Normal Company's outstanding shares on January 1, 20X7. Balance sheet data for the two companies immediately after the purchase follow:

	Kim Corporation	Normal Company
Cash	$ 70,000	$ 35,000
Accounts Receivable	90,000	65,000
Inventory	84,000	80,000
Buildings & Equipment	400,000	300,000
Less: Accumulated Depreciation	(160,000)	(75,000)
Investment in Normal Company Stock	305,000	
Investment in Normal Company Bonds	50,000	
Total Assets	$839,000	$405,000
Accounts Payable	$ 50,000	$ 20,000
Bonds Payable	200,000	100,000
Common Stock	300,000	150,000
Capital in Excess of Par		140,000
Retained Earnings	289,000	(5,000)
Total Liabilities & Equities	$839,000	$405,000

As indicated in the parent company balance sheet, Kim purchased $50,000 of Normal's bonds from the subsidiary at par value immediately after it acquired the stock. An analysis of intercompany receivables and payables also indicates that the subsidiary owes the parent $10,000. On the date of combination, the book values and fair values of Normal's assets and liabilities were the same.

Required

a. Give all consolidation entries needed to prepare a consolidated balance sheet for January 1, 20X7.

b. Complete a consolidated balance sheet worksheet.

c. Prepare a consolidated balance sheet in good form.

LO 4-5 **P4-32** **Balance Sheet Consolidation**

On January 2, 20X8, Primary Corporation acquired 100 percent of Street Company's outstanding common stock. In exchange for Street's stock, Primary issued bonds payable with a par and fair value of $650,000 directly to the selling stockholders of Street. The two companies continued to operate as separate entities subsequent to combination.

Immediately prior to the combination, the book values and fair values of the companies' assets and liabilities were as follows:

	Primary Corporation		Street Company	
	Book Value	Fair Value	Book Value	Fair Value
Cash	$ 12,000	$ 12,000	$ 9,000	$ 9,000
Receivables	41,000	39,000	31,000	30,000
Allowance for Bad Debts	(2,000)		(1,000)	
Inventory	86,000	89,000	68,000	72,000
Land	55,000	200,000	50,000	70,000
Buildings & Equipment	960,000	650,000	670,000	500,000
Accumulated Depreciation	(411,000)		(220,000)	
Patent				40,000
Total Assets	$741,000	$990,000	$607,000	$721,000
Current Payables	$ 38,000	$ 38,000	$ 29,000	$ 29,000
Bonds Payable	200,000	210,000	100,000	90,000
Common Stock	300,000		200,000	
Additional Paid-In Capital	100,000		130,000	
Retained Earnings	103,000		148,000	
Total Liabilities & Equity	$741,000		$607,000	

At the date of combination, Street owed Primary $6,000 plus accrued interest of $500 on a short-term note. Both companies have properly recorded these amounts.

Required

a. Record the business combination on the books of Primary Corporation.

b. Present in general journal form all consolidation entries needed in a worksheet to prepare a consolidated balance sheet immediately following the business combination on January 2, 20X8.

c. Prepare and complete a consolidated balance sheet worksheet as of January 2, 20X8, immediately following the business combination.

d. Present a consolidated balance sheet for Primary and its subsidiary as of January 2, 20X8.

LO 4-5 **P4-33** **Consolidation Worksheet at End of First Year of Ownership**

Advanced
StudyGuide
.com

Mill Corporation acquired 100 percent ownership of Roller Company on January 1, 20X8, for $128,000. At that date, the fair value of Roller's buildings and equipment was $20,000 more than the book value. Buildings and equipment are depreciated on a 10-year basis. Although goodwill is not amortized, Mill's management concluded at December 31, 20X8, that goodwill involved in its acquisition of Roller shares had been impaired and the correct carrying value was $2,500.

Trial balance data for Mill and Roller on December 31, 20X8, are as follows:

Item	Mill Corporation		Roller Company	
	Debit	**Credit**	**Debit**	**Credit**
Cash	$ 19,500		$ 21,000	
Accounts Receivable	70,000		12,000	
Inventory	90,000		25,000	
Land	30,000		15,000	
Buildings & Equipment	350,000		150,000	
Investment in Roller Co. Stock	128,500			
Cost of Goods Sold	125,000		110,000	
Wage Expense	42,000		27,000	
Depreciation Expense	25,000		10,000	
Interest Expense	12,000		4,000	
Other Expenses	13,500		5,000	
Dividends Declared	30,000		16,000	
Accumulated Depreciation		$145,000		$ 40,000
Accounts Payable		45,000		16,000
Wages Payable		17,000		9,000
Notes Payable		150,000		50,000
Common Stock		200,000		60,000
Retained Earnings		102,000		40,000
Sales		260,000		180,000
Income from Subsidiary		16,500		
	$935,500	$935,500	$395,000	$395,000

Required

a. Give all consolidation entries needed to prepare a three-part consolidation worksheet as of December 31, 20X8.

b. Prepare a three-part consolidation worksheet for 20X8 in good form.

Advanced
StudyGuide
.com

P4-34

Consolidation Worksheet at End of Second Year of Ownership

Mill Corporation acquired 100 percent ownership of Roller Company on January 1, 20X8, for $128,000. At that date, the fair value of Roller's buildings and equipment was $20,000 more than the book value. Buildings and equipment are depreciated on a 10-year basis. Although goodwill is not amortized, Mill's management concluded at December 31, 20X8, that goodwill involved in its acquisition of Roller shares had been impaired and the correct carrying value was $2,500. No additional impairment occurred in 20X9.

Trial balance data for Mill and Roller on December 31, 20X9, are as follows:

Item	Mill Corporation		Roller Company	
	Debit	**Credit**	**Debit**	**Credit**
Cash	$ 45,500		$ 32,000	
Accounts Receivable	85,000		14,000	
Inventory	97,000		24,000	
Land	50,000		25,000	
Buildings & Equipment	350,000		150,000	
Investment in Roller Co. Stock	142,500			
Cost of Goods Sold	145,000		114,000	
Wage Expense	35,000		20,000	
Depreciation Expense	25,000		10,000	
Interest Expense	12,000		4,000	
Other Expenses	23,000		16,000	
Dividends Declared	30,000		20,000	

(continued)

LO 4-5

Accumulated Depreciation		$ 170,000		$ 50,000
Accounts Payable		51,000		15,000
Wages Payable		14,000		6,000
Notes Payable		150,000		50,000
Common Stock		200,000		60,000
Retained Earnings		131,000		48,000
Sales		290,000		200,000
Income from Subsidiary		34,000		
	$1,040,000	$1,040,000	$429,000	$429,000

Required

a. Give all consolidation entries needed to prepare a three-part consolidation worksheet as of December 31, 20X9.

b. Prepare a three-part consolidation worksheet for 20X9 in good form.

c. Prepare a consolidated balance sheet, income statement, and retained earnings statement for 20X9.

LO 4-5

P4-35 **Comprehensive Problem: Wholly Owned Subsidiary**

Power Corporation acquired 100 percent ownership of Upland Products Company on January 1, 20X1, for $200,000. On that date, Upland reported retained earnings of $50,000 and had $100,000 of common stock outstanding. Power has used the equity method in accounting for its investment in Upland.

The trial balances for the two companies on December 31, 20X5, appear below.

Additional Information

1. On the date of combination (five years ago), the fair value of Upland's depreciable assets was $50,000 more than the book value. Accumulated depreciation at that date was $10,000. The differential assigned to depreciable assets should be written off over the following 10-year period.

2. There was $10,000 of intercorporate receivables and payables at the end of 20X5.

Required

a. Give all journal entries that Power recorded during 20X5 related to its investment in Upland.

b. Give all consolidation entries needed to prepare consolidated statements for 20X5.

c. Prepare a three-part worksheet as of December 31, 20X5.

Item	Power Corporation		Upland Products Company	
	Debit	**Credit**	**Debit**	**Credit**
Cash & Receivables	$ 43,000		$ 65,000	
Inventory	260,000		90,000	
Land	80,000		80,000	
Buildings & Equipment	500,000		150,000	
Investment in Upland Products Stock	235,000			
Cost of Goods Sold	120,000		50,000	
Depreciation Expense	25,000		15,000	
Inventory Losses	15,000		5,000	
Dividends Declared	30,000		10,000	
Accumulated Depreciation		$ 205,000		$105,000
Accounts Payable		60,000		20,000
Notes Payable		200,000		50,000
Common Stock		300,000		100,000
Retained Earnings		318,000		90,000
Sales		200,000		100,000
Income from Subsidiary		25,000		
	$1,308,000	$1,308,000	$465,000	$465,000

LO 4-5 **P4-36** ## Comprehensive Problem: Differential Apportionment

Jersey Corporation acquired 100 percent of Lime Company on January 1, 20X7, for $203,000. The trial balances for the two companies on December 31, 20X7, included the following amounts:

Item	Jersey Corporation Debit	Jersey Corporation Credit	Lime Company Debit	Lime Company Credit
Cash	$ 82,000		$ 25,000	
Accounts Receivable	50,000		55,000	
Inventory	170,000		100,000	
Land	80,000		20,000	
Buildings & Equipment	500,000		150,000	
Investment in Lime Company Stock	240,000			
Cost of Goods Sold	500,000		250,000	
Depreciation Expense	25,000		15,000	
Other Expenses	75,000		75,000	
Dividends Declared	50,000		20,000	
Accumulated Depreciation		$ 155,000		$ 75,000
Accounts Payable		70,000		35,000
Mortgages Payable		200,000		50,000
Common Stock		300,000		50,000
Retained Earnings		290,000		100,000
Sales		700,000		400,000
Income from Subsidiary		57,000		
	$1,772,000	$1,772,000	$710,000	$710,000

Additional Information

1. On January 1, 20X7, Lime reported net assets with a book value of $150,000. A total of $20,000 of the acquisition price is applied to goodwill, which was not impaired in 20X7.

2. Lime's depreciable assets had an estimated economic life of 11 years on the date of combination. The difference between fair value and book value of tangible assets is related entirely to buildings and equipment.

3. Jersey used the equity method in accounting for its investment in Lime.

4. Detailed analysis of receivables and payables showed that Lime owed Jersey $16,000 on December 31, 20X7.

Required

a. Give all journal entries recorded by Jersey with regard to its investment in Lime during 20X7.
b. Give all consolidation entries needed to prepare a full set of consolidated financial statements for 20X7.
c. Prepare a three-part consolidation worksheet as of December 31, 20X7.

LO 4-7 **P4-37A** ## Push-Down Accounting

On December 31, 20X6, Greenly Corporation and Lindy Company entered into a business combination in which Greenly acquired all of Lindy's common stock for $935,000. At the date of combination, Lindy had common stock outstanding with a par value of $100,000, additional paid-in capital of $400,000, and retained earnings of $175,000. The fair values and book values of all Lindy's assets and liabilities were equal at the date of combination, except for the following:

	Book Value	Fair Value
Inventory	$ 50,000	$ 55,000
Land	75,000	160,000
Buildings	400,000	500,000
Equipment	500,000	570,000

"A" indicates that the item relates to Appendix 4A.

The buildings had a remaining life of 20 years, and the equipment was expected to last another 10 years. In accounting for the business combination, Greenly decided to use push-down accounting on Lindy's books.

During 20X7, Lindy earned net income of $88,000 and paid a dividend of $50,000. All of the inventory on hand at the end of 20X6 was sold during 20X7. During 20X8, Lindy earned net income of $90,000 and paid a dividend of $50,000.

Required

a. Record the acquisition of Lindy's stock on Greenly's books on December 31, 20X6.

b. Record any entries that would be made on December 31, 20X6, on Lindy's books related to the business combination if push-down accounting is employed.

c. Present all consolidation entries that would appear in the worksheet to prepare a consolidated balance sheet immediately after the combination.

d. Present all entries that Greenly would record during 20X7 related to its investment in Lindy if Greenly uses the equity method of accounting for its investment.

e. Present all consolidation entries that would appear in the worksheet to prepare a full set of consolidated financial statements for the year 20X7.

f. Present all consolidation entries that would appear in the worksheet to prepare a full set of consolidated financial statements for the year 20X8.

5

Consolidation of Less-than-Wholly-Owned Subsidiaries Acquired at More than Book Value

CISCO ACQUIRES A CONTROLLING INTEREST IN NUOVA

In many of the examples of corporate acquisitions discussed so far, the acquiring company has purchased 100 percent of the outstanding stock of the acquired company. However, the buyer doesn't always acquire 100 percent ownership of the target company. For example, in 2006 Cisco Systems Inc. acquired 80 percent of Nuova Systems in order to take advantage of Nuova's innovative data center technology. Individual investors still held the remaining 20 percent of the company. Cisco's initial investment in Nuova was $50 million. Accounting for this type of investment can be very complicated. First, Cisco's $50 million investment was not intended solely to purchase Nuova's tangible assets. Cisco also paid for Nuova's potential future earnings capability, for its innovation, and for the fair value (FV) of assets in excess of their book values as of the acquisition date. Because Cisco did not purchase 100 percent of Nuova, the Cisco consolidated financial statements in future years would have to account for the portion of the company owned by the noncontrolling interest (NCI) shareholders. This chapter explores the consolidation of less-than-wholly-owned subsidiaries when there is a positive differential.

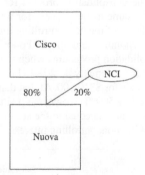

LEARNING OBJECTIVES

When you finish studying this chapter, you should be able to:

LO 5-1   Understand and explain how the consolidation process differs when the subsidiary is less-than-wholly-owned and there is a differential.

LO 5-2   Make calculations and prepare consolidation entries for the consolidation of a partially owned subsidiary when there is a complex positive differential.

LO 5-3   Understand and explain what happens when a parent company ceases to consolidate a subsidiary.

LO 5-4   Make calculations and prepare consolidation entries for the consolidation of a partially owned subsidiary when there is a complex positive differential and other comprehensive income.

A NONCONTROLLING INTEREST IN CONJUNCTION WITH A DIFFERENTIAL

LO 5-1

Understand and explain how the consolidation process differs when the subsidiary is less-than-wholly-owned and there is a differential.

This chapter continues to build upon the foundation established in Chapters 2 through 4 related to the consolidation of majority-owned subsidiaries. In fact, Chapter 5 represents the culmination of our learning process related to procedures associated with the consolidation process. Chapter 5 combines the complexities introduced in Chapters 3 and 4. Specifically, Chapter 5 examines situations in which the acquiring company purchases less than 100 percent of the outstanding stock of the acquired company (similar to Chapter 3) and pays an amount higher than its proportionate share of the book value of net assets (resulting in a differential as introduced in Chapter 4). Once you master Chapter 5, you can handle virtually any consolidation problem!

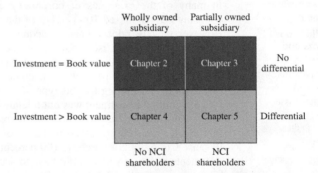

	Wholly owned subsidiary	Partially owned subsidiary	
Investment = Book value	Chapter 2	Chapter 3	No differential
Investment > Book value	Chapter 4	Chapter 5	Differential
	No NCI shareholders	NCI shareholders	

CONSOLIDATED BALANCE SHEET WITH MAJORITY-OWNED SUBSIDIARY

The consolidation process for a less-than-wholly-owned subsidiary with a differential is the same as the process for a wholly owned subsidiary with a differential except that the claims of the noncontrolling interest must be considered. The example of Peerless Products Corporation and Special Foods Inc. from Chapter 4 will serve as a basis for illustrating consolidation procedures when the parent has less than full ownership of a subsidiary. Assume that on January 1, 20X1, Peerless acquires 80 percent of the common stock of Special Foods for $310,000. At that date, the fair value of the noncontrolling interest is estimated to be $77,500. The ownership situation can be viewed as follows, when Special Foods' total fair value is equal to the sum of the fair value of the consideration given and the fair value of the noncontrolling interest:

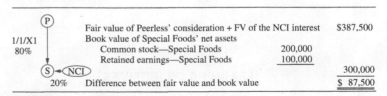

	Fair value of Peerless' consideration + FV of the NCI interest		$387,500
1/1/X1	Book value of Special Foods' net assets		
80%	Common stock—Special Foods	200,000	
	Retained earnings—Special Foods	100,000	
			300,000
20%	Difference between fair value and book value		$ 87,500

Peerless records the acquisition on its books with the following entry:

(1)	Investment in Special Foods	310,000	
	Cash		310,000

Record purchase of Special Foods stock.

FIGURE 5–1   Balance Sheets of Peerless Products and Special Foods, January 1, 20X1, Immediately after Combination and Values of Select Assets of Special Foods

	Peerless Products	Special Foods	Special Foods' Fair Value	Fair Value Increment
Assets				
Cash	$ 40,000	$ 50,000		
Accounts Receivable	75,000	50,000		
Inventory	100,000	60,000	$ 65,000	$ 5,000
Land	175,000	40,000	50,000	10,000
Buildings & Equipment	800,000	600,000	360,000	60,000
Accumulated Depreciation	(400,000)	(300,000)		
Net Book Value	400,000	300,000		
Investment in Special Foods Stock	310,000			
Total Assets	$1,100,000	$500,000	$475,000	$75,000
Liabilities & Stockholders' Equity				
Accounts Payable	$ 100,000	$100,000		
Bonds Payable	200,000	100,000		
Common Stock	500,000	200,000		
Retained Earnings	300,000	100,000		
Total Liabilities & Equity	$1,100,000	$500,000		

The balance sheets of Peerless and Special Foods appear immediately after acquisition in Figure 5–1. On the acquisition date, the fair values of all of Special Foods' assets and liabilities are equal to their book values except as shown in Figure 5–1.

The excess of the $387,500 total fair value of the consideration given and the noncontrolling interest on the date of combination over the $300,000 book value of Special Foods is $87,500. Of this total $87,500 differential, $75,000 relates to the excess of the acquisition-date fair value over the book value of Special Foods' net identifiable assets, as presented in Figure 5–1. The remaining $12,500 of the differential, the excess of the consideration given and the noncontrolling interest over the fair value of Special Foods' net identifiable assets, is assigned to goodwill. Because Peerless acquires only 80 percent of Special Foods' outstanding common stock, Peerless' share of the total differential is $70,000 ($87,500 × 0.80). Specifically, Peerless' share of the excess fair value over book value of identifiable net assets (NA) is $60,000 ($75,000 × 0.80) and its share of the goodwill is $10,000 ($12,500 × 0.80). Peerless' share of the book value of Special Foods' net assets is $240,000 (0.80 × [CS $200,000 + RE $100,000]). As a result, Peerless' acquisition price of $310,000 applies to the book value and differential components of Special Foods' fair value as follows:

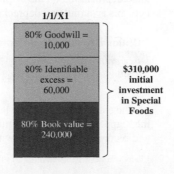

Assuming that Peerless decides to prepare a consolidated balance sheet on the acquisition date, the book value component of the acquisition price is divided between Peerless and the noncontrolling interest as follows:

Book Value Calculations:

	NCI 20%	+ Peerless 80%	= Common Stock	+ Retained Earnings
Book Value at Acquisition	60,000	240,000	200,000	100,000

This analysis leads to the following basic consolidation entry:

Basic Consolidation Entry:[1]

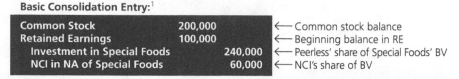

Common Stock	200,000		← Common stock balance
Retained Earnings	100,000		← Beginning balance in RE
Investment in Special Foods		240,000	← Peerless' share of Special Foods' BV
NCI in NA of Special Foods		60,000	← NCI's share of BV

The basic consolidation entry here is identical to the entry in Chapter 4 with one small exception: The credit to Investment in Special Foods was $300,000 in Chapter 4 when Peerless purchased 100 percent of Special Foods' common stock. In this example, Peerless purchased only 80 percent of the common stock, so the $300,000 book value of net assets is shared with the NCI shareholders. The differential can be allocated between Peerless and the noncontrolling interest as follows:

Excess Value (Differential) Calculations:

	NCI 20%	+ Peerless 80%	= Inventory	+ Land	+ Building	+ Acc. Depr.	+ Goodwill
Beginning Balance	17,500	70,000	5,000	10,000	60,000	0	12,500

From this analysis, we can construct the excess value reclassification entry:

Excess Value (Differential) Reclassification Entry:

Inventory	5,000		← Excess value at acquisition
Land	10,000		← Excess value at acquisition
Building	60,000		← Excess value at acquisition
Goodwill	12,500		← Calculated value from acquisition
Investment in Special Foods		70,000	← Peerless' share of differential
NCI in NA of Special Foods		17,500	← NCI's share of differential

Again, this entry is identical to the one in the 100 percent owned Chapter 4 example except that the credit to Investment in Special Foods from the Chapter 4 example is now shared with the NCI shareholders. As explained in Chapter 4, Special Foods had accumulated depreciation on the acquisition date of $300,000. The following consolidation entry nets this accumulated depreciation out against the cost of the buildings and equipment.

Optional Accumulated Depreciation Consolidation Entry:

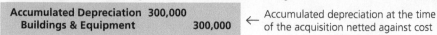

Accumulated Depreciation	300,000		← Accumulated depreciation at the time
Buildings & Equipment		300,000	of the acquisition netted against cost

The combination of these last two consolidation entries makes the buildings and equipment appear as if they were purchased on the acquisition date for their fair market values and recorded as new assets with zero accumulated depreciation as of that date.

---

[1] To view a video explanation of this topic, visit advancedstudyguide.com.

FIGURE 5–2   January 1, 20X1, Worksheet for Consolidated Balance Sheet, Date of Combination; 80 Percent Acquisition at More than Book Value

Balance Sheet	Peerless Products	Special Foods	Consolidation Entries DR	Consolidation Entries CR	Consolidated
Cash	40,000	50,000			90,000
Accounts Receivable	75,000	50,000			125,000
Inventory	100,000	60,000	5,000		165,000
Investment in Special Foods	310,000			240,000	0
				70,000	
Land	175,000	40,000	10,000		225,000
Buildings & Equipment	800,000	600,000	60,000	300,000	1,160,000
Less: Accumulated Depreciation	(400,000)	(300,000)	300,000		(400,000)
Goodwill			12,500		12,500
Total Assets	**1,100,000**	**500,000**	**387,500**	**610,000**	**1,377,500**
Accounts Payable	100,000	100,000			200,000
Bonds Payable	200,000	100,000			300,000
Common Stock	500,000	200,000	200,000		500,000
Retained Earnings	300,000	100,000	100,000		300,000
NCI in NA of Special Foods				60,000	77,500
				17,500	
Total Liabilities & Equity	**1,100,000**	**500,000**	**300,000**	**77,500**	**1,377,500**

Advanced
StudyGuide
.com

Figure 5–2 illustrates Peerless' consolidation worksheet on the date of acquisition at January 1, 20X1. Once the consolidation entries are placed in the worksheet, each row is summed across to get the consolidated totals. Note that the asset amounts included in the Consolidated column, and thus in the consolidated balance sheet, consist of book values for Peerless' assets and liabilities plus acquisition-date fair values for Special Foods' assets and liabilities plus goodwill.

CONSOLIDATED FINANCIAL STATEMENTS WITH A MAJORITY-OWNED SUBSIDIARY

LO 5-2

Make calculations and prepare consolidation entries for the consolidation of a partially owned subsidiary when there is a complex positive differential.

Consolidation subsequent to acquisition involves the preparation of a complete set of consolidated financial statements, as discussed in Chapter 4. To continue the illustration from the previous section beyond the date of acquisition, assume Peerless Products and Special Foods report the income and dividends during 20X1 and 20X2 shown in Figure 5–3. With respect to the assets to which the $87,500 differential relates, assume that the entire inventory is sold during 20X1, the buildings and equipment have a remaining economic life of 10 years from the date of combination, and Special Foods uses straight-line depreciation. Furthermore, assume that management determines at the end of 20X1 that the goodwill is impaired and should be written down by $3,125. Management has determined that the goodwill arising in the acquisition of Special Foods relates proportionately to the controlling and noncontrolling interests, as does the impairment. Finally, assume that Peerless accounts for its investment in Special Foods using the equity method.

Initial Year of Ownership

The business combination of Peerless Products and Special Foods occurs at the beginning of 20X1. Accordingly, Peerless records the acquisition on January 1, 20X1, as illustrated previously.

Advanced
StudyGuide
.com

Parent Company Entries

During 20X1, Peerless makes the usual equity-method entries to record income and dividends from its subsidiary (see Figure 5–3). Unlike Chapter 4, because Peerless

FIGURE 5–3
Income and Dividend Information about Peerless Products and Special Foods for the Years 20X1 and 20X2

	Peerless Products	Special Foods
20X1:		
Separate operating income, Peerless	$140,000	
Net income, Special Foods		$50,000
Dividends	60,000	30,000
20X2:		
Separate operating income, Peerless	160,000	
Net income, Special Foods		75,000
Dividends	60,000	40,000

purchased only 80 percent of the voting stock, it must share Special Foods' income and dividends with the subsidiary's noncontrolling stockholders. Accordingly, Peerless recognizes only its proportionate share of Special Foods' net income and dividends. Peerless records the following entries during 20X1:

(2)	Investment in Special Foods	40,000	
	Income from Special Foods		40,000

Record Peerless' 80% share of Special Foods' 20X1 income.

(3)	Cash	24,000	
	Investment in Special Foods		24,000

Record Peerless' 80% share of Special Foods' 20X1 dividend.

In addition, Peerless must write off a portion of the differential with the following entry:

(4)	Income from Special Foods	11,300	
	Investment in Special Foods		11,300

Record amortization of excess acquisition price.

Special Foods' undervalued inventory, comprising $5,000 of the total differential, was sold during the year. Therefore, Peerless' $4,000 portion ($5,000 × 80%) must be written off by reducing both the investment account and the parent's income from the subsidiary. Also, Peerless' portion of the excess fair value of Special Foods' buildings and equipment must be amortized at $4,800 per year [($60,000 ÷ 10) × 0.80] over the remaining 10-year life. Finally, Peerless' portion of the goodwill impairment, 2,500 ($3,125 × 0.80), is also included in this adjustment. Thus, the entire write-off of the differential is $11,300 ($4,000 + $4,800 + $2,500). A more detailed calculation of Peerless' share of the differential amortization is illustrated below in the "Excess Value (Differential) Calculations."

The following diagrams illustrate the breakdown of the book value and excess value components of the investment account at the beginning and end of the year.

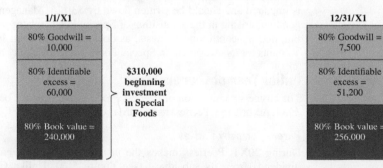

The book value component can be summarized as follows:

Book Value Calculations:

	NCI 20%	+ Peerless 80%	= Common Stock	+ Retained Earnings
Original Book Value	60,000	240,000	200,000	100,000
+ Net Income	10,000	40,000		50,000
− Dividends	(6,000)	(24,000)		(30,000)
Ending Book Value	64,000	256,000	200,000	120,000

The boxed numbers in the chart above comprise the basic consolidation entry:

Basic Consolidation Entry:

Common Stock	200,000		← Common stock balance
Retained Earnings	100,000		← Beginning balance in RE
Income from Special Foods	40,000		← Peerless' share of Special Foods' NI
NCI in NI of Special Foods	10,000		← NCI's share of Special Foods' NI
Dividends Declared		30,000	← 100% of Special Foods' dividends
Investment in Special Foods		256,000	← Peerless' share of Special Foods' BV
NCI in NA of Special Foods		64,000	← NCI's share of net amount of BV

We then analyze the differential and its changes during the period:

Excess Value (Differential) Calculations:

	NCI 20%	+ Peerless 80%	= Inventory	+ Land	+ Building	+ Acc. Depr.	+ Goodwill
Beginning Balance	17,500	70,000	5,000	10,000	60,000	0	12,500
Amortization	(2,825)	(11,300)	(5,000)			(6,000)	(3,125)
Ending Balance	14,675	58,700	0	10,000	60,000	(6,000)	9,375

The entire differential amount assigned to the inventory already passed through cost of goods sold during the year. Thus, there is no longer a differential related to inventory at the end of the year. The only other amortization item is the excess value assigned to the building, amortized over a 10-year period ($60,000 ÷ 10 = $6,000 per year). Finally, the goodwill is deemed to be impaired and worth only $9,375.

Because Peerless' share of the amortization of the differential was already written off from the investment account against the Income from Special Foods account on its books, the changes shown in the middle row of this chart are simply reclassified from the Income from Special Foods account to the various income statement accounts to which they apply using the following worksheet entry:

Amortized Excess Value Reclassification Entry:

Cost of Goods Sold	5,000		← Extra cost of goods sold
Depreciation Expense	6,000		← Depreciation of excess building value
Goodwill Impairment Loss	3,125		← Goodwill impairment
Income from Special Foods		11,300	← Peerless' share of amortization
NCI in NI of Special Foods		2,825	← NCI's share of amortization

Finally, the remaining unamortized differential shown in the bottom row of the Excess Value calculations chart is reclassified to the accounts that need to be revalued to their amortized acquisition-date fair values:

Excess Value (Differential) Reclassification Entry:

Land	10,000		← Remaining excess value
Building	60,000		← Remaining excess value
Goodwill	9,375		← Calculated value from acquisition
Accumulated Depreciation		6,000	← Excess building value ÷ 10 years
Investment in Special Foods		58,700	← Peerless' share of differential
NCI in NA of Special Foods		14,675	← NCI's share of differential

In sum, these worksheet entries (1) eliminate the balances in the Investment in Special Foods and Income from Special Foods accounts, (2) reclassify the amortization of excess value to the proper income statement accounts, and (3) reclassify the remaining differential to the appropriate balance sheet accounts as of the end of the accounting period. The following T-accounts illustrate how Peerless' equity method investment-related accounts are eliminated.

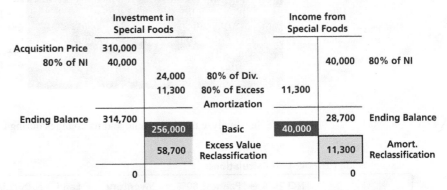

Again, we repeat the same accumulated depreciation consolidation entry this year (and every year as long as Special Foods owns the assets) that we used in the initial year.

Optional Accumulated Depreciation Consolidation Entry:

Accumulated Depreciation	300,000		← Accumulated depreciation at the time
Buildings & Equipment		300,000	of the acquisition netted against cost

Consolidation Worksheet—Initial Year of Ownership

After the subsidiary income accruals are entered on Peerless' books, the adjusted trial balance data of the consolidating companies are entered in the three-part consolidation worksheet as shown in Figure 5–4. The last column in the worksheet will serve as a basis for preparing consolidated financial statements at the end of 20X1.

Once the appropriate consolidation entries are placed in the consolidation worksheet in Figure 5–4, the worksheet is completed by summing each row across, taking into consideration the debit or credit effect of the consolidation entries.

Consolidated Net Income and Retained Earnings

As can be seen from the worksheet in Figure 5–4, total consolidated net income for 20X1 is $175,875 and the amount of that income accruing to the controlling interest, presented as the last number in the income statement section of the worksheet in the Consolidated column, is $168,700. The amount of retained earnings reported in the consolidated balance sheet at December 31, 20X1, shown as the last number in the retained earnings section of the worksheet in the Consolidated column, is $408,700. Figure 5–5 on page 204 illustrates the computation of these amounts.

Advanced
StudyGuide
.com

FIGURE 5–4   December 31, 20X1, Equity-Method Worksheet for Consolidated Financial Statements, Initial Year of Ownership; 80 Percent Acquisition at More than Book Value

	Peerless Products	Special Foods	Consolidation Entries DR	Consolidation Entries CR	Consolidated
Income Statement					
Sales	400,000	200,000			600,000
Less: COGS	(170,000)	(115,000)	5,000		(290,000)
Less: Depreciation Expense	(50,000)	(20,000)	6,000		(76,000)
Less: Other Expenses	(40,000)	(15,000)			(55,000)
Less: Impairment Loss			3,125		(3,125)
Income from Special Foods	28,700		40,000	11,300	0
Consolidated Net Income	168,700	50,000	54,125	11,300	175,875
NCI in Net Income			10,000	2,825	(7,175)
Controlling Interest in Net Income	**168,700**	**50,000**	64,125	14,125	**168,700**
Statement of Retained Earnings					
Beginning Balance	300,000	100,000	100,000		300,000
Net Income	**168,700**	**50,000**	64,125	14,125	168,700
Less: Dividends Declared	(60,000)	(30,000)		30,000	(60,000)
Ending Balance	**408,700**	**120,000**	164,125	44,125	**408,700**
Balance Sheet					
Cash	194,000	75,000			269,000
Accounts Receivable	75,000	50,000			125,000
Inventory	100,000	75,000			175,000
Investment in Special Foods	314,700			256,000	0
				58,700	
Land	175,000	40,000	10,000		225,000
Buildings & Equipment	800,000	600,000	60,000	300,000	1,160,000
Less: Accumulated Depreciation	(450,000)	(320,000)	300,000	6,000	(476,000)
Goodwill			9,375		9,375
Total Assets	**1,208,700**	**520,000**	379,375	620,700	**1,487,375**
Accounts Payable	100,000	100,000			200,000
Bonds Payable	200,000	100,000			300,000
Common Stock	500,000	200,000	200,000		500,000
Retained Earnings	**408,700**	**120,000**	164,125	44,125	408,700
NCI in NA of Special Foods				64,000	78,675
				14,675	
Total Liabilities & Equity	**1,208,700**	**520,000**	364,125	122,800	**1,487,375**

Second Year of Ownership

The equity-method and consolidation procedures employed during the second and subsequent years of ownership are the same as those used during the first year and are illustrated by continuing the Peerless Products and Special Foods example through 20X2. No further impairment of the goodwill arising from the business combination occurs in 20X2.

Parent Company Entries

Given the income and dividends as shown in Figure 5–3, Peerless Products records the following entries on its separate books during 20X2:

(5)	Investment in Special Foods	60,000	
	Income from Special Foods		60,000
	Record Peerless' 80% share of Special Foods' 20X2 income.		

FIGURE 5–5
Consolidated Net Income and Retained Earnings, 20X1; 80 Percent Acquisition at More than Book Value

Consolidated net income, 20X1:	
Peerless' separate operating income	$140,000
Special Foods' net income	50,000
Write-off of differential related to inventory sold in 20X1	(5,000)
Amortization of differential related to buildings and equipment in 20X1	(6,000)
Goodwill impairment loss	(3,125)
Consolidated net income	$175,875
Income to controlling interest, 20X1:	
Consolidated net income	$175,875
Income to noncontrolling interest	(7,175)
Income to controlling interest	$168,700
Consolidated retained earnings, December 31, 20X1:	
Peerless' retained earnings on date of combination, January 1, 20X1	$300,000
Income to controlling interest, 20X1	168,700
Dividends declared by Peerless, 20X1	(60,000)
Consolidated retained earnings	$408,700

(6)	Cash	32,000	
	Investment in Special Foods		32,000
	Record Peerless' 80% share of Special Foods' 20X2 dividend.		

(7)	Income from Special Foods	4,800	
	Investment in Special Foods		4,800
	Record amortization of excess acquisition price.		

Consolidation Worksheet—Second Year Following Combination

The consolidation procedures in the second year following the acquisition are very similar to those in the first year. Consistent with the process illustrated in 20X1, we follow the same process for 20X2. In order to determine the worksheet entries for 20X2, we first summarize the changes in the parent's investment account during 20X2 as follows:

Advanced
StudyGuide
.com

The book value component can be summarized as follows:

Book Value Calculations:

	NCI 20%	+ Peerless 80%	= Common Stock	+ Retained Earnings
Beginning Book Value	64,000	256,000	200,000	120,000
+ Net Income	15,000	60,000		75,000
− Dividends	(8,000)	(32,000)		(40,000)
Ending Book Value	71,000	284,000	200,000	155,000

The boxed numbers in the preceding chart comprise the basic consolidation entry:

Basic Consolidation Entry:

Common Stock	200,000		← Common stock balance
Retained Earnings	120,000		← Beginning RE from trial balance
Income from Special Foods	60,000		← Peerless' share of reported income
NCI in NI of Special Foods	15,000		← NCI's share of reported income
Dividends Declared		40,000	← 100% of sub's dividends declared
Investment in Special Foods		284,000	← Peerless' share of Special Foods' BV
NCI in NA of Special Foods		71,000	← NCI's share of net amount of BV

The entire differential amount assigned to the inventory already passed through cost of goods sold during the prior year period. The only other amortization item is the excess value assigned to the building, which continues to be written off over a 10-year period ($60,000 \div 10 = \$6,000$).

Excess Value (Differential) Calculations:

	NCI 20%	+ Peerless 80%	= Land	+ Building	+ Acc. Depr.	+ Goodwill
Beginning Balances	14,675	58,700	10,000	60,000	(6,000)	9,375
Amortization	(1,200)	(4,800)			(6,000)	
Ending Balance	13,475	53,900	10,000	60,000	(12,000)	9,375

Because the amortization of the differential was already written off from the investment account against the Income from Special Foods account, the change to the differential presented in the middle row of this chart is simply reclassified from the Income from Special Foods account to the income statement account to which it applies during the consolidation process. Then, the remaining amount of the differential from the last row of this chart is reclassified to the various balance accounts that need to be revalued to their amortized acquisition-date fair values:

Amortized Excess Value Reclassification Entry:

Depreciation Expense	6,000		← Depreciation of excess building value
Income from Special Foods		4,800	← Peerless' share of amortization of diff.
NCI in NI of Special Foods		1,200	← NCI's share of amortization of differential

Excess Value (Differential) Reclassification Entry:

Land	10,000		← Remaining excess value
Building	60,000		← Remaining excess value
Goodwill	9,375		← Calculated value from acquisition
Accumulated Depreciation		12,000	← = (Excess value ÷ 10 years) × 2 years
Investment in Special Foods		53,900	← Peerless' share of excess value
NCI in NA of Special Foods		13,475	← NCI's share of excess value

Again, these worksheet entries (1) eliminate the balances in the Investment in Special Foods and Income from Special Foods accounts, (2) reclassify the amortization of excess value to the proper income statement accounts, and (3) reclassify the remaining differential to the appropriate balance sheet accounts at the end of the accounting period. The following T-accounts illustrate how Peerless' Investment in Special Foods and Income from Special Foods accounts are eliminated.

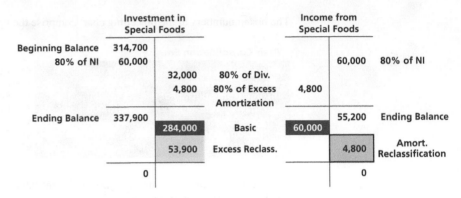

Again, we repeat the same accumulated depreciation consolidation entry this year (and every year as long as Special Foods owns the assets) that we used in the initial year.

Optional Accumulated Depreciation Consolidation Entry:

Accumulated Depreciation	300,000	
Buildings & Equipment		300,000

← Accumulated depreciation at the time of the acquisition netted against cost

Figure 5–6 illustrates the worksheet to prepare a complete set of consolidated financial statements for the year 20X2. Figure 5–7 shows the computation of 20X2 consolidated net income and consolidated retained earnings at the end of 20X2.

Consolidated Financial Statements

Figure 5–8 on page 208 presents a consolidated income statement and retained earnings statement for the year 20X2 and a consolidated balance sheet as of December 31, 20X2.

DISCONTINUANCE OF CONSOLIDATION

LO 5-3

Understand and explain what happens when a parent company ceases to consolidate a subsidiary.

A parent that has been consolidating a subsidiary in its financial statements should exclude that company from future consolidation if the parent can no longer exercise control over it. Control might be lost for a number of reasons, such as (1) the parent sells some or all of its interest in the subsidiary, (2) the subsidiary issues additional common stock, (3) the parent enters into an agreement to relinquish control, or (4) the subsidiary comes under the control of the government or other regulator.

If a parent loses control of a subsidiary and no longer holds an equity interest in the former subsidiary, it recognizes a gain or loss for the difference between any proceeds received from the event leading to loss of control (e.g., sale of interest, expropriation of subsidiary) and the carrying amount of the parent's equity interest. If the parent loses control but maintains a noncontrolling equity interest in the former subsidiary, it must recognize a gain or loss for the difference, at the date control is lost, between (1) the sum of any proceeds received by the parent and the fair value of its remaining equity interest in the former subsidiary and (2) the carrying amount of the parent's total interest in the subsidiary.

As an example, assume that Peerless Products sells three-quarters of its 80 percent interest in Special Foods to an unrelated entity on January 1, 20X2, for $246,000, leaving it holding 20 percent of Special Foods' outstanding stock. On that date, assume that the fair value of Special Foods as a whole is $410,000 and the carrying amount of Peerless' 80 percent share of Special Foods is $314,700 (as shown earlier in the chapter). Assume

FIGURE 5–6   December 31, 20X2, Equity-Method Worksheet for Consolidated Financial Statements, Second Year of Ownership; 80 Percent Acquisition at More than Book Value

	Peerless Products	Special Foods	Consolidation Entries DR	Consolidation Entries CR	Consolidated
Income Statement					
Sales	450,000	300,000			750,000
Less: COGS	(180,000)	(160,000)			(340,000)
Less: Depreciation Expense	(50,000)	(20,000)	6,000		(76,000)
Less: Other Expenses	(60,000)	(45,000)			(105,000)
Less: Impairment Loss					0
Income from Special Foods	55,200		60,000	4,800	0
Consolidated Net Income	215,200	75,000	66,000	4,800	229,000
NCI in Net Income			15,000	1,200	(13,800)
Controlling Interest Net Income	**215,200**	**75,000**	81,000	6,000	**215,200**
Statement of Retained Earnings					
Beginning Balance	408,700	120,000	120,000		408,700
Net Income	**215,200**	**75,000**	81,000	6,000	215,200
Less: Dividends Declared	(60,000)	(40,000)		40,000	(60,000)
Ending Balance	**563,900**	**155,000**	201,000	46,000	**563,900**
Balance Sheet					
Cash	221,000	85,000			306,000
Accounts Receivable	150,000	80,000			230,000
Inventory	180,000	90,000			270,000
Investment in Special Foods	337,900			284,000	0
				53,900	
Land	175,000	40,000	10,000		225,000
Buildings & Equipment	800,000	600,000	60,000	300,000	1,160,000
Less: Accumulated Depreciation	(500,000)	(340,000)	300,000	12,000	(552,000)
Goodwill			9,375		9,375
Total Assets	**1,363,900**	**555,000**	379,375	649,900	**1,648,375**
Accounts Payable	100,000	100,000			200,000
Bonds Payable	200,000	100,000			300,000
Common Stock	500,000	200,000	200,000		500,000
Retained Earnings	**563,900**	**155,000**	201,000	46,000	563,900
NCI in NA of Special Foods				71,000	84,475
				13,475	
Total Liabilities & Equity	**1,363,900**	**555,000**	401,000	130,475	**1,648,375**

FIGURE 5–7

Consolidated Net Income and Retained Earnings, 20X2; 80 Percent Acquisition at More than Book Value

Consolidated net income, 20X2:	
Peerless' separate operating income	$160,000
Special Foods' net income	75,000
Amortization of differential related to buildings & equipment in 20X2	(6,000)
Consolidated net income	$229,000
Income to controlling interest, 20X2:	
Consolidated net income	$229,000
Income to noncontrolling interest	(13,800)
Income to controlling interest	$215,200
Consolidated retained earnings, December 31, 20X2:	
Peerless' retained earnings on date of combination, January 1, 20X1	$300,000
Income to controlling interest, 20X1	168,700
Dividends declared by Peerless, 20X1	(60,000)
Consolidated retained earnings, December 31, 20X1	$408,700
Income to controlling interest, 20X2	215,200
Dividends declared by Peerless, 20X2	(60,000)
Consolidated retained earnings, December 31, 20X2	$563,900

FIGURE 5–8   Consolidated Financial Statements for Peerless Products Corporation and Special Foods Inc., 20X2

PEERLESS PRODUCTS CORPORATION AND SUBSIDIARY
Consolidated Income Statement
For the Year Ended December 31, 20X2

Sales		$750,000
Cost of Goods Sold		(340,000)
Gross Margin		$410,000
Expenses:		
Depreciation & Amortization	$ 76,000	
Other Expenses	105,000	
Total Expenses		(181,000)
Consolidated Net Income		$229,000
Income to Noncontrolling Interest		(13,800)
Income to Controlling Interest		$215,200

PEERLESS PRODUCTS CORPORATION AND SUBSIDIARY
Consolidated Retained Earnings Statement
For the Year Ended December 31, 20X2

Retained Earnings, January 1, 20X2	$408,700
Income to Controlling Interest, 20X2	215,200
Dividends Declared, 20X2	(60,000)
Retained Earnings, December 31, 20X2	$563,900

PEERLESS PRODUCTS CORPORATION AND SUBSIDIARY
Consolidated Balance Sheet
December 31, 20X2

Assets			Liabilities		
Cash		$ 306,000	Accounts Payable	$200,000	
Accounts Receivable		230,000	Bonds Payable	300,000	
Inventory		270,000			$500,000
Land		225,000	Stockholders' Equity		
Buildings & Equipment	$1,160,000		Controlling Interest		
Accumulated Depreciation	(552,000)		Common Stock	$500,000	
		608,000	Retained Earnings	563,900	
Goodwill		9,375	Total Controlling Interest		1,063,900
			Noncontrolling Interest		84,475
Total Assets		$1,648,375	Total Liabilities & Equity		$1,648,375

the fair value of Peerless' remaining 20 percent interest in Special Foods is $82,000. Peerless' gain on the sale of Special Foods stock is computed as follows:

Cash proceeds received	$246,000
Fair value of Peerless' remaining equity interest in Special Foods	82,000
	$328,000
Peerless' total interest in Special Foods at date of sale	314,700
Gain on sale of 60 percent interest in Special Foods	$ 13,300

Peerless reports the $13,300 gain in 20X2 income as follows:

(8)	Cash	246,000	
	Investment in Special Foods Stock		232,700
	Gain on sale of investment.		13,300

Record the sale of 75% of the investment in Special Foods Stock.

Note that because Peerless no longer has a significant influence, the investment will be accounted for using the cost basis ($82,000) going forward.[2]

---

[2] As noted in Chapter 2, the cost basis for this type of investment would entail classifying these shares either as trading or available-for-sale securities.

TREATMENT OF OTHER COMPREHENSIVE INCOME

LO 5-4

Make calculations and prepare consolidation entries for the consolidation of a partially owned subsidiary when there is a complex positive differential and other comprehensive income.

ASC 220-10-55 requires that companies separately report *other comprehensive income (OCI),* which includes all revenues, expenses, gains, and losses that under generally accepted accounting principles are excluded from net income.[3] *Comprehensive income* is the sum of net income and other comprehensive income. **ASC 220-10-55** permits several different options for reporting comprehensive income, but the consolidation process is the same regardless of the reporting format.

Other comprehensive income accounts are temporary accounts that are closed at the end of each period. However, other comprehensive income accounts are closed to a special stockholders' equity account, *Accumulated Other Comprehensive Income (AOCI),* not to Retained Earnings as with typical temporary accounts like revenues and expenses.

FYI

Levi Strauss & Co. reported a $69.1 million loss in other comprehensive income (OCI) in 2012. The portion of this loss that accrued to the NCI shareholders was $457,000; the remaining $68.6 million was attributable to the parent company's shareholders.

Modification of the Consolidation Worksheet

When a parent or subsidiary has recorded other comprehensive income, the consolidation worksheet normally includes an additional section for other comprehensive income. This section of the worksheet facilitates computation of the amount of other comprehensive income to be reported; the portion, if any, of other comprehensive income to be assigned to the noncontrolling interest; and the amount of accumulated other comprehensive income to be reported in the consolidated balance sheet. Although this extra section of the worksheet for comprehensive income could be placed after the income statement section of the standard worksheet, the format used here is to place it at the bottom of the worksheet. If neither the parent nor any subsidiary reports other comprehensive income, the section can be omitted from the worksheet. When other comprehensive income is reported, the worksheet is prepared in the normal manner, with the additional section added to the bottom. The only modification within the standard worksheet is an additional stockholders' equity account included in the balance sheet portion of the worksheet for the cumulative effects of the other comprehensive income.

To illustrate the consolidation process when a subsidiary reports other comprehensive income, assume that during 20X2 Special Foods purchases $20,000 of investments classified as available-for-sale. By December 31, 20X2, the fair value of the securities increases to $30,000. Other than the effects of accounting for Special Foods' investment in securities, the financial statement information reported by Peerless Products and Special Foods at December 31, 20X2, is identical to that presented in Figure 5–7.

Adjusting Entry Recorded by Subsidiary

At December 31, 20X2, Special Foods, the subsidiary, recognizes the increase in the fair value of its available-for-sale securities by recording the following adjusting entry:

(9)	Investment in Available-for-Sale Securities	10,000	
	Unrealized Gain on Investments (OCI)		10,000
	Record the increase in fair value of available-for sale securities.		

The unrealized gain is not included in the subsidiary's net income but is reported by the subsidiary as an element of OCI.

[3] Other comprehensive income elements include foreign currency translation adjustments, unrealized gains and losses on certain derivatives and investments in certain types of securities, and certain minimum pension liability adjustments.

Adjusting Entry Recorded by Parent Company

In 20X2, Peerless records all its normal entries relating to its investment in Special Foods as if the subsidiary had not reported other comprehensive income. In addition, at December 31, 20X2, Peerless Products separately recognizes its proportionate share of the subsidiary's unrealized gain from the increase in the value of the available-for-sale securities:

(10)	Investment in Special Foods	8,000	
	Other Comprehensive Income from Special Foods		8,000

Record share of the increase in value of available-for-sale securities held by subsidiary.

Consolidation Worksheet—Second Year Following Combination

The worksheet to prepare a complete set of consolidated financial statements for the year 20X2 is illustrated in Figure 5–9. In the worksheet, Peerless' balance in the Investment in Special Foods Stock account is more than the balance in Figure 5–6. Specifically, because of the adjusting entry just mentioned, Peerless' $8,000 proportionate share of Special Foods' unrealized gain is included in the separate section of the worksheet for comprehensive income (Other Comprehensive Income from Subsidiary—Unrealized Gain on Investments). Special Foods' trial balance has been changed to reflect (1) the reduction in the cash balance resulting from the investment acquisition, (2) the investment in available-for-sale securities, and (3) an unrealized gain of $10,000 on the investment.

Consolidation Procedures

The normal consolidation entries (the basic consolidation entry, the amortized excess cost reclassification entry, the differential reclassification entry, and the accumulated depreciation consolidation entry) were used in preparing the consolidation worksheet for 20X2 presented in Figure 5–6.

One additional entry is needed for the treatment of the subsidiary's other comprehensive income. First, the proportionate share of the subsidiary's other comprehensive income recorded by the parent in the adjusting entry previously mentioned must be eliminated to avoid double-counting the subsidiary's other comprehensive income. Thus, the adjusting entry is reversed in the worksheet. Moreover, a proportionate share of the subsidiary's other comprehensive income must be allocated to the noncontrolling interest:

Other Comprehensive Income Entry:

OCI from Special Foods	8,000	
OCI to the NCI	2,000	
Investment in Special Foods		8,000
NCI in NA of Subsidiary		2,000

The amount of consolidated other comprehensive income reported in the consolidated financial statements is equal to the subsidiary's $10,000 amount. The noncontrolling interest's $2,000 proportionate share of the subsidiary's other comprehensive income is deducted to arrive at the $8,000 other comprehensive income allocated to the controlling interest.

Although consolidated net income is the same in Figure 5–9 as in Figure 5–6, the other comprehensive income section of the worksheet in Figure 5–9 gives explicit recognition to the unrealized gain on available-for-sale securities held by Special Foods. This permits recognition in the consolidated financial statements under any of the alternative formats permitted by the FASB. Note that the *Accumulated Other Comprehensive Income* row of the balance sheet in the consolidation worksheet is simply carried up from the last row of the separate *Other Comprehensive Income* section at the bottom of the worksheet.

FIGURE 5–9   December 31, 20X2, Comprehensive Income Illustration, Second Year of Ownership; 80 Percent Acquisition at More than Book Value

	Peerless Products	Special Foods	Consolidation Entries DR	Consolidation Entries CR	Consolidated
Income Statement					
Sales	450,000	300,000			750,000
Less: COGS	(180,000)	(160,000)			(340,000)
Less: Depreciation Expense	(50,000)	(20,000)	6,000		(76,000)
Less: Other Expenses	(60,000)	(45,000)			(105,000)
Less: Impairment Loss					0
Income from Special Foods	55,200		60,000	4,800	0
Consolidated Net Income	215,200	75,000	66,000	4,800	**229,000**
NCI in Net Income			15,000	1,200	(13,800)
Controlling Interest in Net Income	**215,200**	**75,000**	**81,000**	**6,000**	**215,200**
Statement of Retained Earnings					
Beginning Balance	408,700	120,000	120,000		408,700
Add Net Income	**215,200**	**75,000**	81,000	6,000	215,200
Less: Dividends Declared	(60,000)	(40,000)		40,000	(60,000)
Ending Balance	**563,900**	**155,000**	**201,000**	**46,000**	**563,900**
Balance Sheet					
Cash	221,000	65,000			286,000
Accounts Receivable	150,000	80,000			230,000
Inventory	180,000	90,000			270,000
Investment in Subsidiary	345,900			284,000	0
				53,900	
				8,000	
Investment in AFS Securities		30,000			30,000
Land	175,000	40,000	10,000		225,000
Buildings & Equipment	800,000	600,000	60,000	300,000	1,160,000
Less: Accumulated Depreciation	(500,000)	(340,000)	300,000	12,000	(552,000)
Goodwill			9,375		9,375
Total Assets	**1,371,900**	**565,000**	**379,375**	**657,900**	**1,658,375**
Accounts Payable	100,000	100,000			200,000
Bonds Payable	200,000	100,000			300,000
Common Stock	500,000	200,000	200,000		500,000
Retained Earnings	**563,900**	**155,000**	201,000	46,000	563,900
Accumulated Other Comprehensive Income, 12/31/X2	8,000	10,000	10,000	0	8,000
NCI in NA of Special Foods				71,000	86,475
				13,475	
				2,000	
Total Liabilities & Equity	**1,371,900**	**565,000**	**411,000**	**132,475**	**1,658,375**
Other Comprehensive Income					
Accumulated Other Comprehensive Income, 1/1/X2	0	0			0
Other Comprehensive Income from Special Foods	8,000		8,000		0
Unrealized Gain on Investments		10,000			10,000
Other Comprehensive Income to NCI			2,000		(2,000)
Accumulated Other Comprehensive Income, 12/31/X2	**8,000**	**10,000**	**10,000**	**0**	**8,000**

Consolidated financial statements for the other comprehensive income example are presented in Figure 5–10. Note that consolidated other comprehensive income includes the full $10,000 unrealized gain. The noncontrolling interest's share, $15,800 ($13,800

FIGURE 5–10

Consolidated Financial Statements for Peerless Products Corporation and Special Foods Inc., 20X2, Including Other Comprehensive Income

PEERLESS PRODUCTS CORPORATION AND SUBSIDIARY
Consolidated Income Statement
For the Year Ended December 31, 20X2

Sales		$750,000
Cost of Goods Sold		(340,000)
Gross Margin		$410,000
Expenses:		
Depreciation & Amortization	$ 76,000	
Other Expenses	105,000	
Total Expenses		(181,000)
Consolidated Net Income		$229,000
Income to Noncontrolling Interest		(13,800)
Income to Controlling Interest		$215,200

PEERLESS PRODUCTS CORPORATION AND SUBSIDIARY
Consolidated Statement of Comprehensive Income
For the Year Ended December 31, 20X2

Consolidated Net Income	$229,000
Other Comprehensive Income:	
Unrealized Gain on Investments	10,000
Total Consolidated Comprehensive Income	$239,000
Less: Comprehensive Income Attribute to Noncontrolling Interest	(15,800)
Comprehensive Income Attribute to Controlling Interest	$223,200

PEERLESS PRODUCTS CORPORATION AND SUBSIDIARY
Consolidated Statement of Financial Position
December 31, 20X2

Assets		
Cash		$ 286,000
Accounts Receivable		230,000
Inventory		270,000
Investment in Available-for-Sale Securities		30,000
Land		225,000
Buildings & Equipment	$1,160,000	
Accumulated Depreciation	(552,000)	
		608,000
Goodwill		9,375
Total Assets		$1,658,375
Liabilities		
Accounts Payable	$ 200,000	
Bonds Payable	300,000	
Total Liabilities		$ 500,000
Stockholders' Equity		
Controlling Interest:		
Common Stock	$ 500,000	
Retained Earnings	563,900	
Accumulated Other Comprehensive Income	8,000	
Total Controlling Interest	$1,071,900	
Noncontrolling Interest	86,475	
Total Stockholders' Equity		1,158,375
Total Liabilities & Stockholders' Equity		$1,658,375

income + $2,000 OCI), is then deducted, along with its share of consolidated net income, to arrive at the consolidated comprehensive income allocated to the controlling interest. The amount of other comprehensive income allocated to the controlling interest is carried to the Accumulated Other Comprehensive Income that is reported in the consolidated balance sheet, and the noncontrolling interest's share is included in the Noncontrolling Interest amount in the consolidated balance sheet. The FASB requires that the amount of each other comprehensive income element allocated to the controlling and noncontrolling interests be disclosed in the consolidated statements or notes.

Consolidation Worksheet—Comprehensive Income in Subsequent Years

Each year following 20X2, Special Foods will adjust the unrealized gain on investments on its books for the change in fair value of the available-for-sale securities. For example, if Special Foods' investment increased in value by an additional $5,000 during 20X3, Special Foods would increase by $5,000 the carrying amount of its investment in securities and recognize as an element of 20X3's other comprehensive income an unrealized gain of $5,000. Under equity-method recording, Peerless would increase its Investment in Special Foods Stock account and record its $4,000 share of the subsidiary's other comprehensive income.

The consolidation entries required to prepare the consolidation worksheet at December 31, 20X3, would include the normal consolidation entries (the basic consolidation entry, the amortized excess cost reclassification entry, the differential reclassification entry, and the accumulated depreciation consolidation entry). In addition, the basic consolidation entry would be expanded to eliminate the subsidiary's $10,000 beginning Accumulated Other Comprehensive Income balance and to increase the noncontrolling interest by its proportionate share of the subsidiary's beginning Accumulated Other Comprehensive Income amount ($10,000 × 0.20). The Other Comprehensive Income consolidation entry allocates the 20X3 other comprehensive income to the noncontrolling interest:

Other Comprehensive Income Entry:

OCI from Special Foods	4,000	
OCI to the NCI	1,000	
Investment in Special Foods		4,000
NCI in NA of Subsidiary		1,000

SUMMARY OF KEY CONCEPTS

The procedures and worksheet for consolidating less-than-wholly-owned subsidiaries are the same as discussed in Chapter 4 for wholly owned subsidiaries, with several modifications. The worksheet consolidation entries are modified to include the noncontrolling shareholders' claim on the income and assets of the subsidiary. The noncontrolling interest has a claim on subsidiary assets based on its acquisition-date fair value. If the acquisition-date fair value of the consideration given in a business combination, plus the fair value of any noncontrolling interest, exceeds the book value of the subsidiary, the difference is referred to as a *differential* and increases both the controlling and noncontrolling interests. The subsidiary's assets and liabilities are valued in consolidation based on their full acquisition-date fair values, with goodwill recognized at acquisition for the difference between (1) the sum of the fair value of the consideration given in the combination and the fair value of the noncontrolling interest and (2) the fair value of the subsidiary's net identifiable assets. Any subsequent write-off of the differential reduces both the controlling and noncontrolling interests.

Consolidated net income is equal to the parent's income from its own operations plus the subsidiary's net income adjusted for any amortization or write-off of the differential. The amount of consolidated net income attributable to the noncontrolling interest is equal to the noncontrolling interest's proportionate share of the subsidiary's net income less a proportionate share of any differential write-off. The income attributable to the controlling interest is equal to consolidated net income less the income attributable to the noncontrolling interest.

A subsidiary's other comprehensive income for the period must be recognized in consolidated other comprehensive income and allocated between the controlling and noncontrolling interests. The consolidation worksheet is modified to accommodate the other comprehensive income items by adding a special section at the bottom.

KEY TERMS

accumulated other comprehensive income (AOCI), *209, 210*
comprehensive income, *209*
other comprehensive income (OCI), *209, 210*

Appendix **5A**	Additional Consolidation Details

Chapters 3, 4, and 5 provide a conceptual foundation for preparing consolidated financial statements and a description of the basic procedures used in preparing consolidated statements. Before moving on to intercompany transactions in Chapters 6 through 8, several additional items should be considered to provide completeness and clarity.

NEGATIVE RETAINED EARNINGS OF SUBSIDIARY AT ACQUISITION

A parent company may acquire a subsidiary with a negative or debit balance in its retained earnings account. An accumulated deficit of a subsidiary at acquisition causes no special problems in the consolidation process. The basic investment account consolidation entry is the same in the consolidation worksheet except that the debit balance in the subsidiary's Retained Earnings account is eliminated with a credit entry. Thus, the basic investment account consolidation entry appears as follows:

Basic Investment Account Consolidation Entry:

Common Stock	XX	
Income from Special Foods	XX	
NCI in NI of Special Foods	XX	
Retained Earnings (Accumulated deficit)		XX
Dividends Declared		XX
Investment in Special Foods		XX
NCI in NA of Special Foods		XX

OTHER STOCKHOLDERS' EQUITY ACCOUNTS

The discussion of consolidated statements up to this point has dealt with companies having stockholders' equity consisting only of retained earnings and a single class of capital stock issued at par. Typically, companies have more complex stockholders' equity structures, often including preferred stock and various types of additional contributed capital. In general, all stockholders' equity accounts accruing to the common shareholders receive the same treatment as common stock and are eliminated at the time common stock is eliminated. The treatment of preferred stock in the consolidation process is discussed in Chapter 9.

SUBSIDIARY'S DISPOSAL OF DIFFERENTIAL-RELATED ASSETS

The disposal of an asset usually has income statement implications. If the asset is held by a subsidiary and is one to which a differential is assigned in the consolidation worksheet, both the parent's equity-method income and consolidated net income are affected. On the parent's books, the portion of the differential included in the subsidiary investment account that relates to the asset sold must be written off by the parent under the equity method as a reduction in both the income from the subsidiary and the investment account. In consolidation, the portion of the differential related to the asset sold is treated as an adjustment to consolidated income.

Inventory

Any inventory-related differential is assigned to inventory for as long as the subsidiary holds the inventory units. In the period in which the inventory units are sold, the inventory-related differential is assigned to Cost of Goods Sold, as illustrated previously in Figure 5–4.

The inventory costing method used by the subsidiary determines the period in which the differential cost of goods sold is recognized. When the subsidiary uses FIFO inventory costing, the inventory units on hand on the date of combination are viewed as being the first units sold after the combination. Therefore, the differential normally is assigned to cost of goods sold in the period immediately after the combination. When the subsidiary uses LIFO inventory costing, the inventory units on the date of combination are viewed as remaining in the subsidiary's inventory. Thus, when the subsidiary uses LIFO inventory costing, the differential is not assigned to cost of goods sold unless the inventory level drops below its level at the date of combination.

Fixed Assets

A differential related to land held by a subsidiary is added to the Land balance in the consolidation worksheet each time a consolidated balance sheet is prepared. If the subsidiary sells the land to which the differential relates, the differential is treated in the consolidation worksheet as an adjustment to the gain or loss on the sale of the land in the period of the sale.

To illustrate, assume that on January 1, 20X1, Pluto purchases all the common stock of Star at $10,000 more than book value. All the differential relates to land that Star had purchased earlier for $25,000. So long as Star continues to hold the land, the $10,000 differential is assigned to Land in the consolidation worksheet. If Star sells the land to an unrelated company for $40,000, the following entry is recorded on Star's books:

(11)	Cash	40,000	
	Land		25,000
	Gain on Sale of Land		15,000
	Record sale of land.		

While a gain of $15,000 is appropriate for Star to report, the accounting basis of the land to the consolidated entity is $35,000 ($25,000 + $10,000). Therefore, the consolidated enterprise must report a gain of only $5,000. To reduce the $15,000 gain reported by Star to the $5,000 gain that should be reported by the consolidated entity, the following consolidation entry is included in the worksheet for the year of the sale:

Eliminate Gain on Sale of Land:

| Gain on Sale of Land | 10,000 | |
| Income from Star | | 10,000 |

If, instead, Star sells the land for $32,000, the $7,000 ($32,000 − $25,000) gain recorded by Star is eliminated, and a loss of $3,000 ($32,000 − $35,000) is recognized in the consolidated income statement. The consolidation entry in this case is

Eliminate Gain and Record Loss on Sale of Land:

Gain on Sale of Land	7,000	
Loss on Sale of Land	3,000	
Income from Star		10,000

When the equity method is used on the parent's books, the parent must adjust the carrying amount of the investment and its equity-method income in the period of the sale to write off the differential, as discussed in Chapter 2. Thereafter, the $10,000 differential no longer exists.

The sale of differential-related equipment is treated in the same manner as land except that the amortization for the current and previous periods must be considered as well as any accumulated depreciation that may have existed at the acquisition date that is being removed from the records. If all of the assets associated with that accumulated depreciation are sold, there is no need for the optional entry after the sale of those assets.

QUESTIONS

LO 5-1	**Q5-1**	Where is the balance assigned to the noncontrolling interest reported in the consolidated balance sheet?
LO 5-1	**Q5-2**	Why must a noncontrolling interest be reported in the consolidated balance sheet?
LO 5-1	**Q5-3**	How does the introduction of noncontrolling shareholders change the consolidation worksheet?
LO 5-1	**Q5-4**	How is the amount assigned to the noncontrolling interest normally determined when a consolidated balance sheet is prepared immediately after a business combination?
LO 5-2	**Q5-5**	What portion of consolidated retained earnings is assigned to the noncontrolling interest in the consolidated balance sheet?
LO 5-2	**Q5-6**	When majority ownership is acquired, what portion of the fair value of assets held by the subsidiary at acquisition is reported in the consolidated balance sheet?
LO 5-2	**Q5-7**	When majority ownership is acquired, what portion of the goodwill reported in the consolidated balance sheet is assigned to the noncontrolling interest?
LO 5-2	**Q5-8**	How is the income assigned to the noncontrolling interest normally computed?
LO 5-2	**Q5-9**	How is income assigned to the noncontrolling interest shown in the consolidation worksheet?
LO 5-2	**Q5-10**	How are dividends paid by a subsidiary to noncontrolling shareholders treated in the consolidation worksheet?
LO 5-3	**Q5-11**	Under what circumstances would a parent company cease consolidation of a subsidiary? Explain.
LO 5-4	**Q5-12**	How do other comprehensive income elements reported by a subsidiary affect the consolidated financial statements?
LO 5-4	**Q5-13**	What portion of other comprehensive income reported by a subsidiary is included in the consolidated statement of comprehensive income as accruing to parent company shareholders?
	Q5-14A	What effect does a negative retained earnings balance on the subsidiary's books have on consolidation procedures?
	Q5-15A	What type of adjustment must be made in the consolidation worksheet if a differential is assigned to land and the subsidiary disposes of the land in the current period?

CASES

LO 5-2	**C5-1**	**Consolidation Worksheet Preparation**

The newest clerk in the accounting office recently entered trial balance data for the parent company and its subsidiaries in the company's consolidation program. After a few minutes of additional work needed to eliminate the intercompany investment account balances, he expressed his satisfaction at having completed the consolidation worksheet for 20X5. In reviewing the printout of the consolidation worksheet, other employees raised several questions, and you are asked to respond.

Analysis

Required

Indicate whether each of the following questions can be answered by looking at the data in the consolidation worksheet (indicate why or why not):

a. Is it possible to tell if the parent is using the equity method in recording its ownership of each subsidiary?

b. Is it possible to tell if the correct amount of consolidated net income has been reported?

c. One of the employees thought the parent company had paid well above the fair value of net assets for a subsidiary purchased on January 1, 20X5. Is it possible to tell by reviewing the consolidation worksheet?

d. Is it possible to determine from the worksheet the percentage ownership of a subsidiary held by the parent?

"A" indicates that the item relates to Appendix 5A.

LO 5-2

C5-2   Consolidated Income Presentation

Research

Standard Company has a relatively high profit margin on its sales, and Jewel Company has a substantially lower profit margin. Standard holds 55 percent of Jewel's common stock and includes Jewel in its consolidated statements. Standard and Jewel reported sales of $100,000 and $60,000, respectively, in 20X4. Sales increased to $120,000 and $280,000 for the two companies in 20X5. The average profit margins of the two companies remained constant over the two years at 60 percent and 10 percent, respectively.

Standard's treasurer was aware that the subsidiary was awarded a major new contract in 20X5 and anticipated a substantial increase in net income for the year. She was disappointed to learn that consolidated net income allocated to the controlling interest had increased by only 38 percent even though sales were 2.5 times higher than in 20X4. She is not trained in accounting and does not understand the fundamental processes used in preparing Standard's consolidated income statement. She does know, however, that the earnings per share figures reported in the consolidated income statement are based on income allocated to the controlling interest and she wonders why that number isn't higher.

Required

As a member of the accounting department, you have been asked to prepare a memo to the treasurer explaining how consolidated net income is computed and the procedures used to allocate income to the parent company and to the subsidiary's noncontrolling shareholders. Include in your memo citations to or quotations from the authoritative literature. To assist the treasurer in gaining a better understanding, prepare an analysis showing the income statement amounts actually reported for 20X4 and 20X5.

LO 5-1

C5-3   Pro Rata Consolidation

Research

Rose Corporation and Krome Company established a joint venture to manufacture components for both companies' use on January 1, 20X1, and have operated it quite successfully for the past four years. Rose and Krome both contributed 50 percent of the equity when the joint venture was created. Rose purchases roughly 70 percent of the output of the joint venture and Krome purchases 30 percent. Rose and Krome have equal numbers of representatives on the joint venture's board of directors and participate equally in its management. Joint venture profits are distributed at year-end on the basis of total purchases by each company.

Required

Rose has been using the equity method to report its investment in the joint venture; however, Rose's financial vice president believes that each company should use pro rata consolidation. As a senior accountant at Rose, you have been asked to prepare a memo discussing those situations in which pro rata consolidation may be appropriate and to offer your recommendation as to whether Rose should continue to use the equity method or switch to pro rata consolidation. Include in your memo citations of and quotations from the authoritative literature to support your arguments.

LO 5-1

C5-4   Consolidation Procedures

Communication

A new employee has been given responsibility for preparing the consolidated financial statements of Sample Company. After attempting to work alone for some time, the employee seeks assistance in gaining a better overall understanding of the way in which the consolidation process works.

Required

You have been asked to provide assistance in explaining the consolidation process.

a. Why must the consolidation entries be entered in the consolidation worksheet each time consolidated statements are prepared?

b. How is the beginning-of-period noncontrolling interest balance determined?

c. How is the end-of-period noncontrolling interest balance determined?

d. Which of the subsidiary's account balances must always be eliminated?

e. Which of the parent company's account balances must always be eliminated?

LO 5-1

C5-5   Changing Accounting Standards: Monsanto Company

Research

Monsanto Company, a St. Louis–based company, is a leading provider of agricultural products for farmers. It sells seeds, biotechnology trait products, and herbicides worldwide.

Required

a. How did Monsanto Company report its income to noncontrolling (minority) shareholders of consolidated subsidiaries in its 2007 consolidated income statement?

b. How did Monsanto Company report its subsidiary noncontrolling (minority) interest in its 2007 consolidated balance sheet?

c. Comment on Monsanto's treatment of its subsidiary noncontrolling interest.

d. In 2007, Monsanto had several affiliates that were special-purpose or variable interest entities. What level of ownership did Monsanto have in these entities? Were any of these consolidated? Why?

EXERCISES

LO 5-1, 5-2 | **E5-1** **Multiple-Choice Questions on Consolidation Process**

Select the most appropriate answer for each of the following questions.

1. If A Company acquires 80 percent of the stock of B Company on January 1, 20X2, immediately after the acquisition, which of the following is correct?

    a. Consolidated retained earnings will be equal to the combined retained earnings of the two companies.

    b. Goodwill will always be reported in the consolidated balance sheet.

    c. A Company's additional paid-in capital may be reduced to permit the carryforward of B Company retained earnings.

    d. Consolidated retained earnings and A Company retained earnings will be the same.

2. Which of the following is correct?

    a. The noncontrolling shareholders' claim on the subsidiary's net assets is based on the book value of the subsidiary's net assets.

    b. Only the parent's portion of the difference between book value and fair value of the subsidiary's assets is assigned to those assets.

    c. Goodwill represents the difference between the book value of the subsidiary's net assets and the amount paid by the parent to buy ownership.

    d. Total assets reported by the parent generally will be less than total assets reported on the consolidated balance sheet.

3. Which of the following statements is correct?

    a. Foreign subsidiaries do not need to be consolidated if they are reported as a separate operating group under segment reporting.

    b. Consolidated retained earnings do not include the noncontrolling interest's claim on the subsidiary's retained earnings.

    c. The noncontrolling shareholders' claim should be adjusted for changes in the fair value of the subsidiary assets but should not include goodwill.

    d. Consolidation is expected any time the investor holds significant influence over the investee.

4. [AICPA Adapted] At December 31, 20X9, Grey Inc. owned 90 percent of Winn Corporation, a consolidated subsidiary, and 20 percent of Carr Corporation, an investee in which Grey cannot exercise significant influence. On the same date, Grey had receivables of $300,000 from Winn and $200,000 from Carr. In its December 31, 20X9, consolidated balance sheet, Grey should report accounts receivable from its affiliates of

    a. $500,000.

    b. $340,000.

    c. $230,000.

    d. $200,000.

LO 5-1, 5-2   **E5-2**   **Multiple-Choice Questions on Consolidation [AICPA Adapted]**

Select the correct answer for each of the following questions.

1. A 70 percent owned subsidiary company declares and pays a cash dividend. What effect does the dividend have on the retained earnings and noncontrolling interest balances in the parent company's *consolidated* balance sheet?

    a. No effect on either retained earnings or noncontrolling interest.

    b. No effect on retained earnings and a decrease in noncontrolling interest.

    c. Decreases in both retained earnings and noncontrolling interest.

    d. A decrease in retained earnings and no effect on noncontrolling interest.

2. How is the portion of consolidated earnings to be assigned to the noncontrolling interest in consolidated financial statements determined?

    a. The parent's net income is subtracted from the subsidiary's net income to determine the noncontrolling interest.

    b. The subsidiary's net income is extended to the noncontrolling interest.

    c. The amount of the subsidiary's earnings recognized for consolidation purposes is multiplied by the noncontrolling interest's percentage of ownership.

    d. The amount of consolidated earnings on the consolidated worksheets is multiplied by the noncontrolling interest percentage on the balance sheet date.

3. On January 1, 20X5, Post Company acquired an 80 percent investment in Stake Company. The acquisition cost was equal to Post's equity in Stake's net assets at that date. On January 1, 20X5, Post and Stake had retained earnings of $500,000 and $100,000, respectively. During 20X5, Post had net income of $200,000, which included its equity in Stake's earnings, and declared dividends of $50,000; Stake had net income of $40,000 and declared dividends of $20,000. There were no other intercompany transactions between the parent and subsidiary. On December 31, 20X5, what should the consolidated retained earnings be?

    a. $650,000.

    b. $666,000.

    c. $766,000.

    d. $770,000.

Note: Items 4 and 5 are based on the following information:

On January 1, 20X8, Ritt Corporation acquired 80 percent of Shaw Corporation's $10 par common stock for $956,000. On this date, the fair value of the noncontrolling interest was $239,000, and the carrying amount of Shaw's net assets was $1,000,000. The fair values of Shaw's identifiable assets and liabilities were the same as their carrying amounts except for plant assets (net) with a remaining life of 20 years, which were $100,000 in excess of the carrying amount. For the year ended December 31, 20X8, Shaw had net income of $190,000 and paid cash dividends totaling $125,000.

4. In the January 1, 20X8, consolidated balance sheet, the amount of goodwill reported should be

    a. $0.

    b. $76,000.

    c. $95,000.

    d. $156,000.

5. In the December 31, 20X8, consolidated balance sheet, the amount of noncontrolling interest reported should be

    a. $200,000.

    b. $239,000.

    c. $251,000.

    d. $252,000.

LO 5-2

Advanced
StudyGuide
.com

E5-3 Consolidation Entries with Differential

On June 10, 20X8, Game Corporation acquired 60 percent of Amber Company's common stock. The fair value of the noncontrolling interest was $32,800 on that date. Summarized balance sheet data for the two companies immediately after the stock purchase are as follows:

Item	Game Corp. Book Value	Amber Company Book Value	Fair Value
Cash	$ 25,800	$ 5,000	$ 5,000
Accounts Receivable	30,000	10,000	10,000
Inventory	80,000	20,000	25,000
Buildings & Equipment (net)	120,000	50,000	70,000
Investment in Amber Stock	49,200		
Total	$305,000	$85,000	$110,000
Accounts Payable	$ 25,000	$ 3,000	$ 3,000
Bonds Payable	150,000	25,000	25,000
Common Stock	55,000	20,000	
Retained Earnings	75,000	37,000	
Total	$305,000	$85,000	$ 28,000

Required

a. Give the consolidation entries required to prepare a consolidated balance sheet immediately after the purchase of Amber Company shares.

b. Explain how consolidation entries differ from other types of journal entries recorded in the normal course of business.

LO 5-2

E5-4 Computation of Consolidated Balances

Slim Corporation's balance sheet at January 1, 20X7, reflected the following balances:

Cash & Receivables	$ 80,000	Accounts Payable	$ 40,000
Inventory	120,000	Income Taxes Payable	60,000
Land	70,000	Bonds Payable	200,000
Buildings & Equipment (net)	480,000	Common Stock	250,000
		Retained Earnings	200,000
Total Assets	$750,000	Total Liabilities & Stockholders' Equity	$750,000

Ford Corporation entered into an active acquisition program and acquired 80 percent of Slim's common stock on January 2, 20X7, for $470,000. The fair value of the noncontrolling interest at that date was determined to be $117,500. A careful review of the fair value of Slim's assets and liabilities indicated the following:

	Book Value	Fair Value
Inventory	$120,000	$140,000
Land	70,000	60,000
Buildings & Equipment (net)	480,000	550,000

Goodwill is assigned proportionately to Ford and the noncontrolling shareholders.

Required

Compute the appropriate amount related to Slim to be included in the consolidated balance sheet immediately following the acquisition for each of the following items:

a. Inventory.

b. Land.

  c. Buildings and Equipment (net).

  d. Goodwill.

  e. Investment in Slim Corporation.

  f. Noncontrolling Interest.

LO 5-2

E5-5   Balance Sheet Worksheet

Power Company owns 90 percent of Pleasantdale Dairy's stock. The balance sheets of the two companies immediately after the Pleasantdale acquisition showed the following amounts:

	Power Company	Pleasantdale Dairy
Cash & Receivables	$ 130,000	$ 70,000
Inventory	210,000	90,000
Land	70,000	40,000
Buildings & Equipment (net)	390,000	220,000
Investment in Pleasantdale Stock	270,000	
Total Assets	$1,070,000	$420,000
Current Payables	$ 80,000	$ 40,000
Long-Term Liabilities	200,000	100,000
Common Stock	400,000	60,000
Retained Earnings	390,000	220,000
Total Liabilities & Stockholders' Equity	$1,070,000	$420,000

The fair value of the noncontrolling interest at the date of acquisition was determined to be $30,000. The full amount of the increase over book value is assigned to land held by Pleasantdale. At the date of acquisition, Pleasantdale owed Power $8,000 plus $900 accrued interest. Pleasantdale had recorded the accrued interest, but Power had not.

Required

Prepare and complete a consolidated balance sheet worksheet.

LO 5-2

E5-6   Majority-Owned Subsidiary Acquired at Higher than Book Value

Zenith Corporation acquired 70 percent of Down Corporation's common stock on December 31, 20X4, for $102,200. The fair value of the noncontrolling interest at that date was determined to be $43,800. Data from the balance sheets of the two companies included the following amounts as of the date of acquisition:

Item	Zenith Corporation	Down Corporation
Cash	$ 50,300	$ 21,000
Accounts Receivable	90,000	44,000
Inventory	130,000	75,000
Land	60,000	30,000
Buildings & Equipment	410,000	250,000
Less: Accumulated Depreciation	(150,000)	(80,000)
Investment in Down Corporation Stock	102,200	
Total Assets	$692,500	$340,000
Accounts Payable	$152,500	$ 35,000
Mortgage Payable	250,000	180,000
Common Stock	80,000	40,000
Retained Earnings	210,000	85,000
Total Liabilities & Stockholders' Equity	$692,500	$340,000

At the date of the business combination, the book values of Down's assets and liabilities approximated fair value except for inventory, which had a fair value of $81,000, and buildings and equipment, which had a fair value of $185,000. At December 31, 20X4, Zenith reported accounts payable of $12,500 to Down, which reported an equal amount in its accounts receivable.

Required

a. Give the consolidation entry or entries needed to prepare a consolidated balance sheet immediately following the business combination.

b. Prepare a consolidated balance sheet worksheet.

c. Prepare a consolidated balance sheet in good form.

LO 5-2

E5-7   Consolidation with Noncontrolling Interest

Temple Corporation acquired 75 percent of Dynamic Corporation's voting common stock on December 31, 20X4, for $390,000. At the date of combination, Dynamic reported the following:

Current Assets	$220,000	Current Liabilities	$ 80,000
Long-Term Assets (net)	420,000	Long-Term Liabilities	200,000
		Common Stock	120,000
		Retained Earnings	240,000
Total	$640,000	Total	$640,000

At December 31, 20X4, the book values of Dynamic's net assets and liabilities approximated their fair values, except for buildings, which had a fair value of $80,000 more than book value, and inventories, which had a fair value of $36,000 more than book value. The fair value of the noncontrolling interest was determined to be $130,000 at that date.

Required

Temple Corporation wishes to prepare a consolidated balance sheet immediately following the business combination. Give the consolidation entry or entries needed to prepare a consolidated balance sheet at December 31, 20X4.

LO 5-2

E5-8   Multiple-Choice Questions on Balance Sheet Consolidation

Power Corporation acquired 70 percent of Silk Corporation's common stock on December 31, 20X2. Balance sheet data for the two companies immediately following the acquisition follow:

Item	Power Corporation	Silk Corporation
Cash	$ 44,000	$ 30,000
Accounts Receivable	110,000	45,000
Inventory	130,000	70,000
Land	80,000	25,000
Buildings & Equipment	500,000	400,000
Less: Accumulated Depreciation	(223,000)	(165,000)
Investment in Silk Corporation Stock	150,500	
Total Assets	$ 791,500	$405,000
Accounts Payable	$ 61,500	$ 28,000
Taxes Payable	95,000	37,000
Bonds Payable	280,000	200,000
Common Stock	150,000	50,000
Retained Earnings	205,000	90,000
Total Liabilities & Stockholders' Equity	$ 791,500	$405,000

At the date of the business combination, the book values of Silk's net assets and liabilities approximated fair value except for inventory, which had a fair value of $85,000, and land, which had a fair value of $45,000. The fair value of the noncontrolling interest was $64,500 on December 31, 20X2.

Required

For each question below, indicate the appropriate total that should appear in the consolidated balance sheet prepared immediately after the business combination.

1. What amount of inventory will be reported?

    a. $179,000.

    b. $200,000.

    c. $210,500.

    d. $215,000.

2. What amount of goodwill will be reported?

    a. $0.

    b. $28,000.

    c. $40,000.

    d. $52,000.

3. What amount of total assets will be reported?

    a. $1,081,000.

    b. $1,121,000.

    c. $1,196,500.

    d. $1,231,500.

4. What amount of total liabilities will be reported?

    a. $265,000.

    b. $436,500.

    c. $622,000.

    d. $701,500.

5. What amount will be reported as noncontrolling interest?

    a. $42,000.

    b. $52,500.

    c. $60,900.

    d. $64,500.

6. What amount of consolidated retained earnings will be reported?

    a. $295,000.

    b. $268,000.

    c. $232,000.

    d. $205,000.

7. What amount of total stockholders' equity will be reported?

    a. $355,000.

    b. $397,000.

    c. $419,500.

    d. $495,000.

LO 5-2   **E5-9**   ### Majority-Owned Subsidiary with Differential

Canton Corporation is a majority-owned subsidiary of West Corporation. West acquired 75 percent ownership on January 1, 20X3, for $133,500. At that date, Canton reported common stock outstanding of $60,000 and retained earnings of $90,000, and the fair value of the noncontrolling interest was $44,500. The differential is assigned to equipment, which had a fair value $28,000 more than book value and a remaining economic life of seven years at the date of the business combination. Canton reported net income of $30,000 and paid dividends of $12,000 in 20X3.

Required

a. Give the journal entries recorded by West during 20X3 on its books if it accounts for its investment in Canton using the equity method.

b. Give the consolidation entries needed at December 31, 20X3, to prepare consolidated financial statements.

LO 5-1, 5-2 **E5-10** **Differential Assigned to Amortizable Asset**

Major Corporation acquired 90 percent of Lancaster Company's voting common stock on January 1, 20X1, for $486,000. At the time of the combination, Lancaster reported common stock outstanding of $120,000 and retained earnings of $380,000, and the fair value of the noncontrolling interest was $54,000. The book value of Lancaster's net assets approximated market value except for patents that had a market value of $40,000 more than their book value. The patents had a remaining economic life of five years at the date of the business combination. Lancaster reported net income of $60,000 and paid dividends of $20,000 during 20X1.

Required

a. What balance did Major report as its investment in Lancaster at December 31, 20X1, assuming Major uses the equity method in accounting for its investment?

b. Give the consolidation entry or entries needed to prepare consolidated financial statements at December 31, 20X1.

LO 5-2 **E5-11** **Consolidation after One Year of Ownership**

Pioneer Corporation purchased 80 percent of Lowe Corporation's stock on January 1, 20X2. At that date, Lowe reported retained earnings of $80,000 and had $120,000 of stock outstanding. The fair value of its buildings was $32,000 more than the book value.

Pioneer paid $190,000 to acquire the Lowe shares. At that date, the noncontrolling interest had a fair value of $47,500. The remaining economic life for all Lowe's depreciable assets was eight years on the date of combination. The amount of the differential assigned to goodwill is not impaired. Lowe reported net income of $40,000 in 20X2 and declared no dividends.

Required

a. Give the consolidation entries needed to prepare a consolidated balance sheet immediately after Pioneer purchased Lowe stock.

b. Give all consolidation entries needed to prepare a full set of consolidated financial statements for 20X2.

LO 5-1, 5-2 **E5-12** **Consolidation Following Three Years of Ownership**

Knox Corporation purchased 60 percent of Conway Company ownership on January 1, 20X7, for $277,500. Conway reported the following net income and dividend payments:

Year	Net Income	Dividends Paid
20X7	$45,000	$25,000
20X8	55,000	35,000
20X9	30,000	10,000

Advanced
StudyGuide
.com

On January 1, 20X7, Conway had $250,000 of $5 par value common stock outstanding and retained earnings of $150,000, and the fair value of the noncontrolling interest was $185,000. Conway held land with a book value of $22,500 and a market value of $30,000 and equipment with a book value of $320,000 and a market value of $360,000 at the date of combination. The remainder of the differential at acquisition was attributable to an increase in the value of patents, which had a remaining useful life of 10 years. All depreciable assets held by Conway at the date of acquisition had a remaining economic life of eight years.

Required

a. Compute the increase in the fair value of patents held by Conway.

b. Prepare the consolidation entries needed at January 1, 20X7, to prepare a consolidated balance sheet.

c. Compute the balance reported by Knox as its investment in Conway at December 31, 20X8.

d. Prepare the journal entries recorded by Knox with regard to its investment in Conway during 20X9.

e. Prepare the consolidation entries needed at December 31, 20X9, to prepare a three-part consolidation worksheet.

LO 5-2

E5-13 Consolidation Worksheet for Majority-Owned Subsidiary

Proud Corporation acquired 80 percent of Stergis Company's voting stock on January 1, 20X3, at underlying book value. The fair value of the noncontrolling interest was equal to 20 percent of the book value of Stergis at that date. Assume that the accumulated depreciation on depreciable assets was $60,000 on the acquisition date. Proud uses the equity method in accounting for its ownership of Stergis during 20X3. On December 31, 20X3, the trial balances of the two companies are as follows:

Item	Proud Corporation		Stergis Company	
	Debit	Credit	Debit	Credit
Current Assets	$173,000		$105,000	
Depreciable Assets	500,000		300,000	
Investment in Stergis Company Stock	136,000			
Depreciation Expense	25,000		15,000	
Other Expenses	105,000		75,000	
Dividends Declared	40,000		10,000	
Accumulated Depreciation		$175,000		$ 75,000
Current Liabilities		50,000		40,000
Long-Term Debt		100,000		120,000
Common Stock		200,000		100,000
Retained Earnings		230,000		50,000
Sales		200,000		120,000
Income from Subsidiary		24,000		
	$979,000	$979,000	$505,000	$505,000

Required

a. Give all consolidation entries required as of December 31, 20X3, to prepare consolidated financial statements.

b. Prepare a three-part consolidation worksheet.

c. Prepare a consolidated balance sheet, income statement, and retained earnings statement for 20X3.

LO 5-2

E5-14 Consolidation Worksheet for Majority-Owned Subsidiary for Second Year

This exercise is a continuation of E5-13. Proud Corporation acquired 80 percent of Stergis Company's voting stock on January 1, 20X3, at underlying book value. The fair value of the noncontrolling interest was equal to 20 percent of the book value of Stergis at that date. Assume that the accumulated depreciation on depreciable assets was $60,000 on the acquisition date. Proud uses the equity method in accounting for its ownership of Stergis. On December 31, 20X4, the trial balances of the two companies are as follows:

Item	Proud Corporation		Stergis Company	
	Debit	Credit	Debit	Credit
Current Assets	$ 235,000		$150,000	
Depreciable Assets	500,000		300,000	
Investment in Stergis Company Stock	152,000			
Depreciation Expense	25,000		15,000	
Other Expenses	150,000		90,000	
Dividends Declared	50,000		15,000	

(continued)

Item	Proud Corporation		Stergis Company	
	Debit	Credit	Debit	Credit
Accumulated Depreciation		$ 200,000		$ 90,000
Current Liabilities		70,000		50,000
Long-Term Debt		100,000		120,000
Common Stock		200,000		100,000
Retained Earnings		284,000		70,000
Sales		230,000		140,000
Income from Subsidiary		28,000		
	$1,112,000	$1,112,000	$570,000	$570,000

Required

a. Give all consolidation entries required on December 31, 20X4, to prepare consolidated financial statements.

b. Prepare a three-part consolidation worksheet as of December 31, 20X4.

LO 5-4

E5-15 **Preparation of Stockholders' Equity Section with Other Comprehensive Income**

Advanced
StudyGuide
.com

Broadmore Corporation acquired 75 percent of Stem Corporation's common stock on January 1, 20X8, for $435,000. At that date, Stem reported common stock outstanding of $300,000 and retained earnings of $200,000, and the fair value of the noncontrolling interest was $145,000. The book values and fair values of Stem's assets and liabilities were equal, except for other intangible assets, which had a fair value $80,000 more than book value and a 10-year remaining life. Broadmore and Stem reported the following data for 20X8 and 20X9:

	Stem Corporation			Broadmore Corporation	
Year	Net Income	Comprehensive Income	Dividends Paid	Operating Income	Dividends Paid
20X8	$40,000	$50,000	$15,000	$120,000	$70,000
20X9	60,000	65,000	30,000	140,000	70,000

Required

a. Compute consolidated comprehensive income for 20X8 and 20X9.

b. Compute comprehensive income attributable to the controlling interest for 20X8 and 20X9.

c. Assuming that Broadmore reported capital stock outstanding of $320,000 and retained earnings of $430,000 at January 1, 20X8, prepare the stockholders' equity section of the consolidated balance sheet at December 31, 20X8 and 20X9.

LO 5-4

E5-16 **Consolidation Entries for Subsidiary with Other Comprehensive Income**

Palmer Corporation acquired 70 percent of Krown Corporation's ownership on January 1, 20X8, for $140,000. At that date, Krown reported capital stock outstanding of $120,000 and retained earnings of $80,000, and the fair value of the noncontrolling interest was equal to 30 percent of the book value of Krown. During 20X8, Krown reported net income of $30,000 and comprehensive income of $36,000 and paid dividends of $25,000.

Required

a. Present all equity-method entries that Palmer would have recorded in accounting for its investment in Krown during 20X8.

b. Present all consolidation entries needed at December 31, 20X8, to prepare a complete set of consolidated financial statements for Palmer Corporation and its subsidiary.

E5-17A **Consolidation of Subsidiary with Negative Retained Earnings**

General Corporation acquired 80 percent of Strap Company's voting common stock on January 1, 20X4, for $138,000. At that date, the fair value of the noncontrolling interest was $34,500. Strap's balance sheet at the date of acquisition contained the following balances:

STRAP COMPANY
Balance Sheet
January 1, 20X4

Cash	$ 20,000	Accounts Payable	$ 35,000
Accounts Receivable	35,000	Notes Payable	180,000
Land	90,000	Common Stock	100,000
Building & Equipment	300,000	Additional Paid-in Capital	75,000
Less: Accumulated Depreciation	(85,000)	Retained Earnings	(30,000)
Total Assets	$360,000	Total Liabilities & Stockholders' Equity	$360,000

At the date of acquisition, the reported book values of Strap's assets and liabilities approximated fair value.

Required
Give the consolidation entry or entries needed to prepare a consolidated balance sheet immediately following the business combination.

E5-18A Complex Assignment of Differential
On December 31, 20X4, Worth Corporation acquired 90 percent of Brinker Inc.'s common stock for $864,000. At that date, the fair value of the noncontrolling interest was $96,000. Of the $240,000 differential, $5,000 related to the increased value of Brinker's inventory, $75,000 related to the increased value of its land, $60,000 related to the increased value of its equipment, and $50,000 was associated with a change in the value of its notes payable due to increasing interest rates. Brinker's equipment had a remaining life of 15 years from the date of combination. Brinker sold all inventory it held at the end of 20X4 during 20X5; the land to which the differential related also was sold during the year for a large gain. The amortization of the differential relating to Brinker's notes payable was $7,500 for 20X5.

At the date of combination, Brinker reported retained earnings of $120,000, common stock outstanding of $500,000, and premium on common stock of $100,000. For the year 20X5, it reported net income of $150,000 but paid no dividends. Worth accounts for its investment in Brinker using the equity method.

Required
a. Present all entries that Worth would have recorded during 20X5 with respect to its investment in Brinker.
b. Present all consolidation entries that would have been included in the worksheet to prepare a full set of consolidated financial statements for the year 20X5.

PROBLEMS

LO 5-1

P5-19 Reported Balances
Roof Corporation acquired 80 percent of the stock of Gable Company by issuing shares of its common stock with a fair value of $192,000. At that time, the fair value of the noncontrolling interest was estimated to be $48,000, and the fair values of Gable's identifiable assets and liabilities were $310,000 and $95,000, respectively. Gable's assets and liabilities had book values of $220,000 and $95,000, respectively.

Required
Compute the following amounts to be reported immediately after the combination

a. Investment in Gable reported by Roof.
b. Goodwill for the combined entity.
c. Noncontrolling interest reported in the consolidated balance sheet.

LO 5-1

P5-20 Acquisition Price
Darwin Company holds assets with a fair value of $120,000 and a book value of $90,000 and liabilities with a book value and fair value of $25,000.

Required

Compute the following amounts if Brad Corporation acquires 60 percent ownership of Darwin:

a. What amount did Brad pay for the shares if no goodwill and no gain on a bargain purchase are reported?

b. What amount did Brad pay for the shares if the fair value of the noncontrolling interest at acquisition is $54,000 and goodwill of $40,000 is reported?

c. What balance will be assigned to the noncontrolling interest in the consolidated balance sheet if Brad pays $73,200 to acquire its ownership and goodwill of $27,000 is reported?

LO 5-1   **P5-21**   ## Multiple-Choice Questions on Applying the Equity Method [AICPA Adapted]

Select the correct answer for each of the following questions.

1. On July 1, 20X3, Barker Company purchased 20 percent of Acme Company's outstanding common stock for $400,000 when the fair value of Acme's net assets was $2,000,000. Barker does not have the ability to exercise significant influence over Acme's operating and financial policies. The following data concerning Acme are available for 20X3:

	Twelve Months Ended December 31, 20X3	Six Months Ended December 31, 20X3
Net income	$300,000	$160,000
Dividends declared and paid	190,000	100,000

In its income statement for the year ended December 31, 20X3, how much income should Barker report from this investment?

a. $20,000.

b. $32,000.

c. $38,000.

d. $60,000.

2. On January 1, 20X3, Miller Company purchased 25 percent of Wall Corporation's common stock; no differential resulted from the purchase. Miller appropriately uses the equity method for this investment, and the balance in Miller's investment account was $190,000 on December 31, 20X3. Wall reported net income of $120,000 for the year ended December 31, 20X3, and paid dividends on its common stock totaling $48,000 during 20X3. How much did Miller pay for its 25 percent interest in Wall?

a. $172,000.

b. $202,000.

c. $208,000.

d. $232,000.

3. On January 1, 20X7, Robohn Company purchased for cash 40 percent of Lowell Company's 300,000 shares of voting common stock for $1,800,000 when 40 percent of the underlying equity in Lowell's net assets was $1,740,000. The payment in excess of underlying equity was assigned to amortizable assets with a remaining life of six years. As a result of this transaction, Robohn has the ability to exercise significant influence over Lowell's operating and financial policies. Lowell's net income for the year ended December 31, 20X7, was $600,000. During 20X7, Lowell paid $325,000 in dividends to its shareholders. The income reported by Robohn for its investment in Lowell should be

a. $120,000.

b. $130,000.

c. $230,000.

d. $240,000.

4. In January 20X0, Farley Corporation acquired 20 percent of Davis Company's outstanding common stock for $800,000. This investment gave Farley the ability to exercise significant influence over Davis. The book value of the acquired shares was $600,000. The excess of cost over book

value was attributed to an identifiable intangible asset, which was undervalued on Davis' balance sheet and had a remaining economic life of 10 years. For the year ended December 31, 20X0, Davis reported net income of $180,000 and paid cash dividends of $40,000 on its common stock. What is the proper carrying value of Farley's investment in Davis on December 31, 20X0?

   a. $772,000.

   b. $780,000.

   c. $800,000.

   d. $808,000.

LO 5-1

P5-22 Amortization of Differential

Ball Corporation purchased 30 percent of Krown Company's common stock on January 1, 20X5, by issuing preferred stock with a par value of $50,000 and a market price of $120,000. The following amounts relate to Krown's balance sheet items at that date:

	Book Value	Fair Value
Cash & Receivables	$ 200,000	$200,000
Buildings & Equipment	400,000	360,000
Less: Accumulated Depreciation	(100,000)	
Total Assets	$ 500,000	
Accounts Payable	$ 50,000	50,000
Bonds Payable	200,000	200,000
Common Stock	100,000	
Retained Earnings	150,000	
Total Liabilities & Equities	$ 500,000	

Krown purchased buildings and equipment on January 1, 20X0, with an expected economic life of 20 years. No change in overall expected economic life occurred as a result of the acquisition of Ball's stock. The amount paid in excess of the fair value of Krown's reported net assets is attributed to unrecorded copyrights with a remaining useful life of eight years. During 20X5, Krown reported net income of $40,000 and paid dividends of $10,000.

Required

Give all journal entries to be recorded on Ball Corporation's books during 20X5, assuming it uses the equity method in accounting for its ownership of Krown Company.

LO 5-1

P5-23 Computation of Account Balances

Easy Chair Company purchased 40 percent ownership of Stuffy Sofa Corporation on January 1, 20X1, for $150,000. Stuffy Sofa's balance sheet at the time of acquisition was as follows:

STUFFY SOFA CORPORATION
Balance Sheet
January 1, 20X1

Cash		$ 30,000	Current Liabilities	$ 40,000
Accounts Receivable		120,000	Bonds Payable	200,000
Inventory		80,000	Common Stock	200,000
Land		150,000	Additional Paid-In Capital	40,000
Buildings & Equipment	$ 300,000			
Less: Accumulated Depreciation	(120,000)	180,000	Retained Earnings	80,000
Total Assets		$560,000	Total Liabilities & Equities	$560,000

During 20X1 Stuffy Sofa Corporation reported net income of $30,000 and paid dividends of $9,000. The fair values of Stuffy Sofa's assets and liabilities were equal to their book values at the date of acquisition, with the exception of buildings and equipment, which had a fair value $35,000 above book value.

All buildings and equipment had remaining lives of five years at the time of the business combination. The amount attributed to goodwill as a result of its purchase of Stuffy Sofa shares is not impaired.

Required

a. What amount of investment income will Easy Chair Company record during 20X1 under equity-method accounting?

b. What amount of income will be reported under the cost method?

c. What will be the balance in the investment account on December 31, 20X1, under (1) cost-method and (2) equity-method accounting?

LO 5-1, 5-2   **P5-24**   ### Complex Differential

Essex Company issued common shares with a par value of $50,000 and a market value of $165,000 in exchange for 30 percent ownership of Tolliver Corporation on January 1, 20X2. Tolliver reported the following balances on that date:

TOLLIVER CORPORATION
Balance Sheet
January 1, 20X2

	Book Value	Fair Value
Assets		
Cash	$ 40,000	$ 40,000
Accounts Receivable	80,000	80,000
Inventory (FIFO basis)	120,000	150,000
Land	50,000	65,000
Buildings & Equipment	500,000	320,000
Less: Accumulated Depreciation	(240,000)	
Patent		25,000
Total Assets	$550,000	$680,000
Liabilities & Equities		
Accounts Payable	$ 30,000	$ 30,000
Bonds Payable	100,000	100,000
Common Stock	150,000	
Additional Paid-In Capital	20,000	
Retained Earnings	250,000	
Total Liabilities & Equities	$550,000	

The estimated economic life of the patents held by Tolliver is 10 years. The buildings and equipment are expected to last 12 more years on average. Tolliver paid dividends of $9,000 during 20X2 and reported net income of $80,000 for the year.

Required

Compute the amount of investment income (loss) reported by Essex from its investment in Tolliver for 20X2 and the balance in the investment account on December 31, 20X2, assuming the equity method is used in accounting for the investment.

LO 5-1   **P5-25**   ### Equity Entries with Differential

On January 1, 20X0, Hunter Corporation issued 6,000 of its $10 par value shares to acquire 45 percent of the shares of Arrow Manufacturing. Arrow Manufacturing's balance sheet immediately before the acquisition contained the following items:

ARROW MANUFACTURING
Balance Sheet
January 1, 20X0

	Book Value	Fair Value
Assets		
Cash & Receivables	$ 30,000	$ 30,000
Land	70,000	80,000

(continued)

Buildings & Equipment (net)	120,000	150,000
Patent	80,000	80,000
Total Assets	$300,000	
Liabilities & Equities		
Accounts Payable	$ 90,000	90,000
Common Stock	150,000	
Retained Earnings	60,000	
Total Liabilities & Equities	$300,000	

On the date of the stock acquisition, Hunter's shares were selling at $35, and Arrow Manufacturing's buildings and equipment had a remaining economic life of 10 years. The amount of the differential assigned to goodwill is not impaired.

In the two years following the stock acquisition, Arrow Manufacturing reported net income of $80,000 and $50,000 and paid dividends of $20,000 and $40,000, respectively. Hunter used the equity method in accounting for its ownership of Arrow Manufacturing.

Required

a. Give the entry recorded by Hunter Corporation at the time of acquisition.

b. Give the journal entries recorded by Hunter during 20X0 and 20X1 related to its investment in Arrow Manufacturing.

c. What balance will be reported in Hunter's investment account on December 31, 20X1?

LO 5-1   **P5-26**   **Equity Entries with Differential**

Ennis Corporation acquired 35 percent of Jackson Corporation's stock on January 1, 20X8, by issuing 25,000 shares of its $2 par value common stock. Jackson Corporation's balance sheet immediately before the acquisition contained the following items:

JACKSON CORPORATION Balance Sheet January 1, 20X8		
	Book Value	**Fair Value**
Assets		
Cash & Receivables	$ 40,000	$ 40,000
Inventory (FIFO basis)	80,000	100,000
Land	50,000	70,000
Buildings & Equipment (net)	240,000	320,000
Total Assets	$410,000	$530,000
Liabilities & Equities		
Accounts Payable	$ 70,000	$ 70,000
Common Stock	130,000	
Retained Earnings	210,000	
Total Liabilities & Equities	$410,000	

Shares of Ennis were selling at $8 at the time of the acquisition. On the date of acquisition, the remaining economic life of buildings and equipment held by Jackson was 20 years. The amount of the differential assigned to goodwill is not impaired. For the year 20X8, Jackson reported net income of $70,000 and paid dividends of $10,000.

Required

a. Give the journal entries recorded by Ennis Corporation during 20X8 related to its investment in Jackson Corporation.

b. What balance will Ennis report as its investment in Jackson at December 31, 20X8?

LO 5-1   **P5-27**   ## Additional Ownership Level

Balance sheet, income, and dividend data for Amber Corporation, Blair Corporation, and Carmen Corporation at January 1, 20X3, were as follows:

Account Balances	Amber Corporation	Blair Corporation	Carmen Corporation
Cash	$ 70,000	$ 60,000	$ 20,000
Accounts Receivable	120,000	80,000	40,000
Inventory	100,000	90,000	65,000
Fixed Assets (net)	450,000	350,000	240,000
Total Assets	$740,000	$580,000	$365,000
Accounts Payable	$105,000	$110,000	$ 45,000
Bonds Payable	300,000	200,000	120,000
Common Stock	150,000	75,000	90,000
Retained Earnings	185,000	195,000	110,000
Total Liabilities & Equity	$740,000	$580,000	$365,000
Income from Operations in 20X3	$220,000	$100,000	
Net Income for 20X3			$ 50,000
Dividends Declared & Paid	60,000	30,000	25,000

On January 1, 20X3, Amber Corporation purchased 40 percent of the voting common stock of Blair Corporation by issuing common stock with a par value of $40,000 and fair value of $130,000. Immediately after this transaction, Blair purchased 25 percent of the voting common stock of Carmen Corporation by issuing bonds payable with a par value and market value of $51,500.

On January 1, 20X3, the book values of Blair's net assets were equal to their fair values except for equipment that had a fair value $30,000 more than book value and patents that had a fair value $25,000 more than book value. At that date, the equipment had a remaining economic life of eight years, and the patents had a remaining economic life of five years. The book values of Carmen's assets were equal to their fair values except for inventory that had a fair value $6,000 in excess of book value and was accounted for on a FIFO basis.

Required

a. Compute the net income reported by Amber Corporation for 20X3, assuming Amber and Blair used the equity method in accounting for their intercorporate investments.

b. Give all journal entries recorded by Amber relating to its investment in Blair during 20X3.

LO 5-1   **P5-28**   ## Correction of Error

Hill Company paid $164,000 to acquire 40 percent ownership of Dale Company on January 1, 20X2. Net book value of Dale's assets on that date was $300,000. Book values and fair values of net assets held by Dale were the same except for equipment and patents. Equipment held by Dale had a book value of $70,000 and fair value of $120,000. All of the remaining purchase price was attributable to the increased value of patents with a remaining useful life of eight years. The remaining economic life of all depreciable assets held by Dale was five years.

Dale Company's net income and dividends for the three years immediately following the purchase of shares were

Year	Net Income	Dividends
20X2	$40,000	$15,000
20X3	60,000	20,000
20X4	70,000	25,000

The computation of Hill's investment income for 20X4 and entries in its investment account since the date of purchase were as follows:

20X4 Investment Income

Pro rata income accrual ($70,000 × 0.40)		$28,000
Amortize patents ($44,000 ÷ 8 years)	$5,500	
Dividends received ($25,000 × 0.40)		10,000
20X4 investment income		$32,500

Investment in Dale Company

1/1/X2 purchase price	$164,000	
20X2 income accrual	16,000	
Amortize patents		$5,500
20X3 income accrual	24,000	
Amortize patents		5,500
20X4 income accrual	28,000	
Amortize patents		5,500
12/31/X4 balance	$215,500	

Before making closing entries at the end of 20X4, Hill's new controller reviewed the reports and was convinced that both the balance in the investment account and the investment income that Hill reported for 20X4 were in error.

Required
Prepare a correcting entry, along with supporting computations, to properly state the balance in the investment account and all related account balances at the end of 20X4.

LO 5-2

P5-29 **Majority-Owned Subsidiary Acquired at More Than Book Value**
Porter Corporation acquired 70 percent of Darla Corporation's common stock on December 31, 20X4, for $102,200. At that date, the fair value of the noncontrolling interest was $43,800. Data from the balance sheets of the two companies included the following amounts as of the date of acquisition:

Item	Porter Corporation	Darla Corporation
Cash	$ 50,300	$ 21,000
Accounts Receivable	90,000	44,000
Inventory	130,000	75,000
Land	60,000	30,000
Buildings & Equipment	410,000	250,000
Less: Accumulated Depreciation	(150,000)	(80,000)
Investment in Darla Corporation Stock	102,200	
Total Assets	$692,500	$340,000
Accounts Payable	$152,500	$ 35,000
Mortgage Payable	250,000	180,000
Common Stock	80,000	40,000
Retained Earnings	210,000	85,000
Total Liabilities & Stockholders' Equity	$692,500	$340,000

At the date of the business combination, the book values of Darla's assets and liabilities approximated fair value except for inventory, which had a fair value of $81,000, and buildings and equipment, which had a fair value of $185,000. At December 31, 20X4, Porter reported accounts payable of $12,500 to Darla, which reported an equal amount in its accounts receivable.

Required

a. Give the consolidation entry or entries needed to prepare a consolidated balance sheet immediately following the business combination.

b. Prepare a consolidated balance sheet worksheet.

c. Prepare a consolidated balance sheet in good form.

LO 5-2   **P5-30**   **Balance Sheet Consolidation of Majority-Owned Subsidiary**

On January 2, 20X8, Total Corporation acquired 75 percent of Ticken Tie Company's outstanding common stock. In exchange for Ticken Tie's stock, Total issued bonds payable with a par value of $500,000 and fair value of $510,000 directly to the selling stockholders of Ticken Tie. At that date, the fair value of the noncontrolling interest was $170,000. The two companies continued to operate as separate entities subsequent to the combination.

Immediately prior to the combination, the book values and fair values of the companies' assets and liabilities were as follows:

	Total		Ticken Tie	
	Book Value	**Fair Value**	**Book Value**	**Fair Value**
Cash	$ 12,000	$ 12,000	$ 9,000	$ 9,000
Receivables	41,000	39,000	31,000	30,000
Allowance for Bad Debts	(2,000)		(1,000)	
Inventory	86,000	89,000	68,000	72,000
Land	55,000	200,000	50,000	70,000
Buildings & Equipment	960,000	650,000	670,000	500,000
Accumulated Depreciation	(411,000)		(220,000)	
Patent				40,000
Total Assets	$741,000	$990,000	$607,000	$721,000
Current Payables	$ 38,000	$ 38,000	$ 29,000	$ 29,000
Bonds Payable	200,000	210,000	100,000	100,000
Common Stock	300,000		200,000	
Additional Paid-in Capital	100,000		130,000	
Retained Earnings	103,000		148,000	
Total Liabilities & Equity	$741,000		$607,000	

At the date of combination, Ticken Tie owed Total $6,000 plus accrued interest of $500 on a short-term note. Both companies have properly recorded these amounts.

Required

a. Record the business combination on the books of Total Corporation.

b. Present in general journal form all consolidation entries needed in a worksheet to prepare a consolidated balance sheet immediately following the business combination on January 2, 20X8.

c. Prepare and complete a consolidated balance sheet worksheet as of January 2, 20X8, immediately following the business combination.

d. Present a consolidated balance sheet for Total and its subsidiary as of January 2, 20X8.

LO 5-1, 5-2   **P5-31**   **Incomplete Data**

Blue Corporation acquired controlling ownership of Skyler Corporation on December 31, 20X3, and a consolidated balance sheet was prepared immediately. Partial balance sheet data for the two companies and the consolidated entity at that date follow:

BLUE CORPORATION AND SKYLER CORPORATION
Balance Sheet Data
December 31, 20X3

Item	Blue Corporation	Skyler Corporation	Consolidated Entity
Cash	$ 63,650	$ 35,000	$ 98,650
Accounts Receivable	98,000	?	148,000

(continued)

Inventory	105,000	80,000	195,000
Buildings & Equipment	400,000	340,000	640,000
Less: Accumulated Depreciation	(215,000)	(140,000)	(215,000)
Investment in Skyler Corporation Stock	?		
Goodwill			9,000
Total Assets	$620,000	$380,000	$875,650
Accounts Payable	$115,000	$ 46,000	$146,000
Wages Payable	?	?	94,000
Notes Payable	200,000	110,000	310,000
Common Stock	120,000	75,000	?
Retained Earnings	115,000	125,000	?
Noncontrolling Interest			90,650
Total Liabilities & Equities	$?	$380,000	$875,650

During 20X3, Blue provided engineering services to Skyler and has not yet been paid for them. There were no other receivables or payables between Blue and Skyler at December 31, 20X3.

Required

a. What is the amount of unpaid engineering services at December 31, 20X3, on work done by Blue for Skyler?

b. What balance in accounts receivable did Skyler report at December 31, 20X3?

c. What amounts of wages payable did Blue and Skyler report at December 31, 20X3?

d. What was the fair value of Skyler as a whole at the date of acquisition?

e. What percentage of Skyler's shares were purchased by Blue?

f. What amounts of capital stock and retained earnings must be reported in the consolidated balance sheet?

LO 5-2

P5-32   Income and Retained Earnings

Quill Corporation acquired 70 percent of North Company's stock on January 1, 20X9, for $105,000. At that date, the fair value of the noncontrolling interest was equal to 30 percent of the book value of North Company. The companies reported the following stockholders' equity balances immediately after the acquisition:

	Quill Corporation	North Company
Common Stock	$120,000	$ 30,000
Additional Paid-in Capital	230,000	80,000
Retained Earnings	290,000	40,000
Total	$640,000	$150,000

Quill and North reported 20X9 operating incomes of $90,000 and $35,000 and dividend payments of $30,000 and $10,000, respectively.

Required

a. Compute the amount reported as net income by each company for 20X9, assuming Quill uses equity-method accounting for its investment in North.

b. Compute consolidated net income for 20X9.

c. Compute the reported balance in retained earnings at December 31, 20X9, for both companies.

d. Compute consolidated retained earnings at December 31, 20X9.

e. How would the computation of consolidated retained earnings at December 31, 20X9, change if Quill uses the cost method in accounting for its investment in North?

LO 5-2

P5-33   Consolidation Worksheet at End of First Year of Ownership

Power Corporation acquired 75 percent of Best Company's ownership on January 1, 20X8, for $96,000. At that date, the fair value of the noncontrolling interest was $32,000. The book

Advanced
StudyGuide
.com

value of Best's net assets at acquisition was $100,000. The book values and fair values of Best's assets and liabilities were equal, except for Best's buildings and equipment, which were worth $20,000 more than book value. Accumulated depreciation on the buildings and equipment was $30,000 on the acquisition date. Buildings and equipment are depreciated on a 10-year basis.

Although goodwill is not amortized, the management of Power concluded at December 31, 20X8, that goodwill from its purchase of Best shares had been impaired and the correct carrying amount was $2,500. Goodwill and goodwill impairment were assigned proportionately to the controlling and noncontrolling shareholders.

Trial balance data for Power and Best on December 31, 20X8, are as follows:

Item	Power Corporation		Best Company	
	Debit	Credit	Debit	Credit
Cash	$ 47,500		$ 21,000	
Accounts Receivable	70,000		12,000	
Inventory	90,000		25,000	
Land	30,000		15,000	
Buildings & Equipment	350,000		150,000	
Investment in Best Co. Stock	96,375			
Cost of Goods Sold	125,000		110,000	
Wage Expense	42,000		27,000	
Depreciation Expense	25,000		10,000	
Interest Expense	12,000		4,000	
Other Expenses	13,500		5,000	
Dividends Declared	30,000		16,000	
Accumulated Depreciation		$145,000		$ 40,000
Accounts Payable		45,000		16,000
Wages Payable		17,000		9,000
Notes Payable		150,000		50,000
Common Stock		200,000		60,000
Retained Earnings		102,000		40,000
Sales		260,000		180,000
Income from Subsidiary		12,375		
	$931,375	$931,375	$395,000	$395,000

Required

a. Give all consolidation entries needed to prepare a three-part consolidation worksheet as of December 31, 20X8.

b. Prepare a three-part consolidation worksheet for 20X8 in good form.

LO 5-2   **P5-34   Consolidation Worksheet at End of Second Year of Ownership**

Advanced
StudyGuide
.com

This problem is a continuation of P5-33. Power Corporation acquired 75 percent of Best Company's ownership on January 1, 20X8, for $96,000. At that date, the fair value of the noncontrolling interest was $32,000. The book value of Best's net assets at acquisition was $100,000. The book values and fair values of Best's assets and liabilities were equal, except for Best's buildings and equipment, which were worth $20,000 more than book value. Accumulated depreciation on the buildings and equipment was $30,000 on the acquisition date. Buildings and equipment are depreciated on a 10-year basis.

Although goodwill is not amortized, the management of Power concluded at December 31, 20X8, that goodwill from its purchase of Best shares had been impaired and the correct carrying amount was $2,500. Goodwill and goodwill impairment were assigned proportionately to the controlling and noncontrolling shareholders. No additional impairment occurred in 20X9.

Trial balance data for Power and Best on December 31, 20X9, are as follows:

Item	Power Corporation Debit	Power Corporation Credit	Best Company Debit	Best Company Credit
Cash	$ 68,500		$ 32,000	
Accounts Receivable	85,000		14,000	
Inventory	97,000		24,000	
Land	50,000		25,000	
Buildings & Equipment	350,000		150,000	
Investment in Best Co. Stock	106,875			
Cost of Goods Sold	145,000		114,000	
Wage Expense	35,000		20,000	
Depreciation Expense	25,000		10,000	
Interest Expense	12,000		4,000	
Other Expenses	23,000		16,000	
Dividends Declared	30,000		20,000	
Accumulated Depreciation		$ 170,000		$ 50,000
Accounts Payable		51,000		15,000
Wages Payable		14,000		6,000
Notes Payable		150,000		50,000
Common Stock		200,000		60,000
Retained Earnings		126,875		48,000
Sales		290,000		200,000
Income from Subsidiary		25,500		
	$1,027,375	$1,027,375	$429,000	$429,000

Required

a. Give all consolidation entries needed to prepare a three-part consolidation worksheet as of December 31, 20X9.

b. Prepare a three-part consolidation worksheet for 20X9 in good form.

c. Prepare a consolidated balance sheet, income statement, and retained earnings statement for 20X9.

LO 5-2

P5-35 **Comprehensive Problem: Differential Apportionment**

Mortar Corporation acquired 80 percent ownership of Granite Company on January 1, 20X7, for $173,000. At that date, the fair value of the noncontrolling interest was $43,250. The trial balances for the two companies on December 31, 20X7, included the following amounts:

Item	Mortar Corporation Debit	Mortar Corporation Credit	Granite Company Debit	Granite Company Credit
Cash	$ 38,000		$ 25,000	
Accounts Receivable	50,000		55,000	
Inventory	240,000		100,000	
Land	80,000		20,000	
Buildings & Equipment	500,000		150,000	
Investment in Granite Company Stock	202,000			
Cost of Goods Sold	500,000		250,000	
Depreciation Expense	25,000		15,000	
Other Expenses	75,000		75,000	
Dividends Declared	50,000		20,000	
Accumulated Depreciation		$ 155,000		$ 75,000
Accounts Payable		70,000		35,000
Mortgages Payable		200,000		50,000
Common Stock		300,000		50,000
Retained Earnings		290,000		100,000
Sales		700,000		400,000
Income from Subsidiary		45,000		
	$1,760,000	$1,760,000	$710,000	$710,000

Additional Information

1. On January 1, 20X7, Granite reported net assets with a book value of $150,000 and a fair value of $191,250. Accumulated depreciation on Buildings and Equipment was $60,000 on the acquisition date.

2. Granite's depreciable assets had an estimated economic life of 11 years on the date of combination. The difference between fair value and book value of Granite's net assets is related entirely to buildings and equipment.

3. Mortar used the equity method in accounting for its investment in Granite.

4. Detailed analysis of receivables and payables showed that Granite owed Mortar $16,000 on December 31, 20X7.

Required

a. Give all journal entries recorded by Mortar with regard to its investment in Granite during 20X7.

b. Give all consolidation entries needed to prepare a full set of consolidated financial statements for 20X7.

c. Prepare a three-part consolidation worksheet as of December 31, 20X7.

LO 5-2   **P5-36**   **Comprehensive Problem: Differential Apportionment in Subsequent Period**

This problem is a continuation of P5-35. Mortar Corporation acquired 80 percent ownership of Granite Company on January 1, 20X7, for $173,000. At that date, the fair value of the noncontrolling interest was $43,250. The trial balances for the two companies on December 31, 20X8, included the following amounts:

Item	Mortar Corporation		Granite Company	
	Debit	**Credit**	**Debit**	**Credit**
Cash	$ 59,000		$ 31,000	
Accounts Receivable	83,000		71,000	
Inventory	275,000		118,000	
Land	80,000		30,000	
Buildings & Equipment	500,000		150,000	
Investment in Granite Company Stock	206,200			
Cost of Goods Sold	490,000		310,000	
Depreciation Expense	25,000		15,000	
Other Expenses	62,000		100,000	
Dividends Declared	45,000		25,000	
Accumulated Depreciation		$ 180,000		$ 90,000
Accounts Payable		86,000		30,000
Mortgages Payable		200,000		70,000
Common Stock		300,000		50,000
Retained Earnings		385,000		140,000
Sales		650,000		470,000
Income from Subsidiary		24,200		
	$1,825,200	$1,825,200	$850,000	$850,000

Additional Information

1. On January 1, 20X7, Granite reported net assets with a book value of $150,000 and a fair value of $191,250. The difference between fair value and book value of Granite's net assets is related entirely to Buildings and Equipment. Accumulated depreciation on Buildings and Equipment was $60,000 on the acquisition date. Granite's depreciable assets had an estimated economic life of 11 years on the date of combination.

2. At December 31, 20X8, Mortar's management reviewed the amount attributed to goodwill and concluded goodwill was impaired and should be reduced to $14,000. Goodwill and goodwill impairment were assigned proportionately to the controlling and noncontrolling shareholders.

3. Mortar used the equity method in accounting for its investment in Granite.

4. Detailed analysis of receivables and payables showed that Mortar owed Granite $9,000 on December 31, 20X8.

Required

a. Give all journal entries recorded by Mortar with regard to its investment in Granite during 20X8.

b. Give all consolidation entries needed to prepare a full set of consolidated financial statements for 20X8.

c. Prepare a three-part consolidation worksheet as of December 31, 20X8.

LO 5-4

P5-37   **Subsidiary with Other Comprehensive Income in Year of Acquisition**

Amber Corporation acquired 60 percent ownership of Sparta Company on January 1, 20X8, at underlying book value. At that date, the fair value of the noncontrolling interest was equal to 40 percent of the book value of Sparta Company. Accumulated depreciation on Buildings and Equipment was $75,000 on the acquisition date. Trial balance data at December 31, 20X8, for Amber and Sparta are as follows:

Item	Amber Corporation Debit	Amber Corporation Credit	Sparta Company Debit	Sparta Company Credit
Cash	$ 27,000		$ 8,000	
Accounts Receivable	65,000		22,000	
Inventory	40,000		30,000	
Buildings & Equipment	500,000		235,000	
Investment in Row Company Securities			40,000	
Investment in Sparta Company	108,000			
Cost of Goods Sold	150,000		110,000	
Depreciation Expense	30,000		10,000	
Interest Expense	8,000		3,000	
Dividends Declared	24,000		15,000	
Accumulated Depreciation		$140,000		$ 85,000
Accounts Payable		63,000		20,000
Bonds Payable		100,000		50,000
Common Stock		200,000		100,000
Retained Earnings		208,000		60,000
Other Comprehensive Income from Subsidiary (OCI)—Unrealized Gain on Investments		6,000		
Unrealized Gain on Investments (OCI)				10,000
Sales		220,000		148,000
Income from Subsidiary		15,000		
	$952,000	$952,000	$473,000	$473,000

Additional Information

Sparta purchased stock of Row Company on January 1, 20X8, for $30,000 and classified the investment as available-for-sale securities. The value of Row's securities increased to $40,000 at December 31, 20X8.

Required

a. Give all consolidation entries needed to prepare a three-part consolidation worksheet as of December 31, 20X8.

b. Prepare a three-part consolidation worksheet for 20X8 in good form.

c. Prepare a consolidated balance sheet, income statement, and statement of comprehensive income for 20X8.

LO 5-4

P5-38 **Subsidiary with Other Comprehensive Income in Year Following Acquisition**

This problem is a continuation of P5-37. Amber Corporation acquired 60 percent ownership of Sparta Company on January 1, 20X8, at underlying book value. At that date, the fair value of the noncontrolling interest was equal to 40 percent of the book value of Sparta Company. Accumulated depreciation on Buildings and Equipment was $75,000 on the acquisition date. Trial balance data at December 31, 20X9, for Amber and Sparta are as follows:

Item	Amber Corporation		Sparta Company	
	Debit	**Credit**	**Debit**	**Credit**
Cash	$ 18,000		$ 11,000	
Accounts Receivable	45,000		21,000	
Inventory	40,000		30,000	
Buildings & Equipment	585,000		257,000	
Investment in Row Company Securities			44,000	
Investment in Sparta Company	116,400			
Cost of Goods Sold	170,000		97,000	
Depreciation Expense	30,000		10,000	
Interest Expense	8,000		3,000	
Dividends Declared	40,000		20,000	
Accumulated Depreciation		$ 170,000		$ 95,000
Accounts Payable		75,000		24,000
Bonds Payable		100,000		50,000
Common Stock		200,000		100,000
Retained Earnings		231,000		70,000
Accumulated Other Comprehensive Income		6,000		10,000
Other Comprehensive Income from Subsidiary (OCI)—Unrealized Gain on Investments		2,400		
Unrealized Gain on Investments (OCI)				4,000
Sales		250,000		140,000
Income from Subsidiary		18,000		
	$1,052,400	$1,052,400	$493,000	$493,000

Additional Information

Sparta purchased stock of Row Company on January 1, 20X8, for $30,000 and classified the investment as available-for-sale securities. The value of Row's securities increased to $40,000 and $44,000, respectively, at December 31, 20X8, and 20X9.

Required

a. Give all consolidation entries needed to prepare a three-part consolidation worksheet as of December 31, 20X9.

b. Prepare a three-part consolidation worksheet for 20X9 in good form.

LO 5-2

P5-39 **Comprehensive Problem: Majority-Owned Subsidiary**

Master Corporation acquired 80 percent ownership of Stanley Wood Products Company on January 1, 20X1, for $160,000. On that date, the fair value of the noncontrolling interest was $40,000, and Stanley reported retained earnings of $50,000 and had $100,000 of common stock outstanding. Master has used the equity method in accounting for its investment in Stanley.

Trial balance data for the two companies on December 31, 20X5, are as follows:

Item	Master Corporation		Stanley Wood Products Company	
	Debit	Credit	Debit	Credit
Cash & Receivables	$ 81,000		$ 65,000	
Inventory	260,000		90,000	
Land	80,000		80,000	
Buildings & Equipment	500,000		150,000	
Investment in Stanley Wood Products Stock	188,000			
Cost of Goods Sold	120,000		50,000	
Depreciation Expense	25,000		15,000	
Inventory Losses	15,000		5,000	
Dividends Declared	30,000		10,000	
Accumulated Depreciation		$ 205,000		$105,000
Accounts Payable		60,000		20,000
Notes Payable		200,000		50,000
Common Stock		300,000		100,000
Retained Earnings		314,000		90,000
Sales		200,000		100,000
Income from Subsidiary		20,000		
	$1,299,000	$1,299,000	$465,000	$465,000

Additional Information

1. On the date of combination, the fair value of Stanley's depreciable assets was $50,000 more than book value. The accumulated depreciation on these assets was $10,000 on the acquisition date. The differential assigned to depreciable assets should be written off over the following 10-year period.

2. There was $10,000 of intercorporate receivables and payables at the end of 20X5.

Required

a. Give all journal entries that Master recorded during 20X5 related to its investment in Stanley.

b. Give all consolidation entries needed to prepare consolidated statements for 20X5.

c. Prepare a three-part worksheet as of December 31, 20X5.

6

Intercompany Inventory Transactions

INVENTORY TRANSFERS AT SAMSUNG ELECTRONICS

Most people are familiar with Samsung's products, from cell phones to tablets and flat screens. Samsung was formed in Korea in 1938 as a trading company. However, over the years, the company expanded into various industries, including textiles, food processing, insurance, securities, and retail. It wasn't until the 1960s that Samsung launched into electronics, and in the 1970s it also moved into construction and shipbuilding. While Samsung Heavy Industries is the world's second-largest shipbuilder, the best-known of Samsung's segments is clearly its electronics business.

Samsung Electronics is the world's largest manufacturer of LCD panels, televisions, mobile phones, and memory chips. It is also well known for digital cameras, camcorders, batteries, and storage media. The company has many wholly owned subsidiaries such as World Cyber Games, Samsung Semiconductor, Samsung Electronics Digital Printing, and Samsung Telecommunications America, as well as other majority-owned subsidiaries such as Samsung Display and STECO. While each of its many subsidiaries operates as a stand-alone company, technologies and components are often exchanged via intercompany transactions. For example, Samsung Electronics' 2013 annual report indicates that approximately 59 percent of its total revenues result from intercompany sales transactions. The reason Samsung Electronics sells so much inventory to affiliated companies is because of its vertical integration strategy. According to *Forbes* magazine, "Samsung's strategy underscores a competitive advantage: The South Korean company is able to bring products to the market more quickly than [competitors] because it controls the entire manufacturing process for its smartphones. Samsung makes everything from chips to screens at its own factories, allowing it to change designs and pump out new products at a rapid pace."[1]

Transactions between the affiliated companies are not considered *arm's-length*. These transactions are sometimes called *related-party transactions*. Generally Accepted Accounting Principles only allow companies to recognize sales to third-party buyers outside the consolidated entity. Hence, Samsung Electronics eliminates all within-group sales in calculating consolidated sales revenues. This elimination is required because all companies owned or controlled by Samsung Electronics are, in essence, parts of the same company and a company cannot make a profit by selling inventory to itself. This chapter examines intercompany inventory transactions and the consolidation procedures associated with them.

LEARNING OBJECTIVES

When you finish studying this chapter, you should be able to:

LO 6-1 Understand and explain intercompany transfers and why they must be eliminated.

LO 6-2 Understand and explain concepts associated with inventory transfers and transfer pricing.

[1] Tim Worstall, "Why Samsung Beats Apple or Perhaps Vice Versa," *Forbes*, September 9, 2013; Ian Sherr, Eva Dou, and Lorraine Luk, "Apple Tests iPhone Screens as Large as Six Inches," The *Wall Street Journal*, September 5, 2013.

LO 6-3 Prepare equity-method journal entries and consolidation entries for the consolidation of a subsidiary following downstream inventory transfers.

LO 6-4 Prepare equity-method journal entries and consolidation entries for the consolidation of a subsidiary following upstream inventory transfers.

LO 6-5 Understand and explain additional considerations associated with consolidation.

OVERVIEW OF THE CONSOLIDATED ENTITY AND INTERCOMPANY TRANSACTIONS

LO 6-1

Understand and explain intercompany transfers and why they must be eliminated.

The consolidated entity is an aggregation of a number of different companies. The financial statements prepared by the individual affiliates are consolidated into a single set of financial statements representing the financial position and operating results of the entire economic entity as if it were a single company.

A parent company and its subsidiaries often engage in a variety of transactions among themselves. For example, manufacturing companies often have subsidiaries that develop raw materials or produce components to be included in the products of affiliated companies. Some companies sell consulting or other services to affiliated companies. United States Steel Corporation and its subsidiaries engage in numerous transactions with one another, including sales of raw materials, fabricated products, and transportation services. Such transactions often are critical to the operations of the overall consolidated entity. These transactions between related companies are referred to as *intercompany* or *intercorporate transfers.*

Figure 6–1 illustrates a consolidated entity with each of the affiliated companies engaging in both intercompany transfers and transactions with external parties. From a consolidated viewpoint, only transactions with parties outside the economic entity are included in the income statement. Thus, the arrows crossing the perimeter of the consolidated entity in Figure 6–1 represent transactions that are included in the operating

FIGURE 6–1
Transactions of
Affiliated Companies

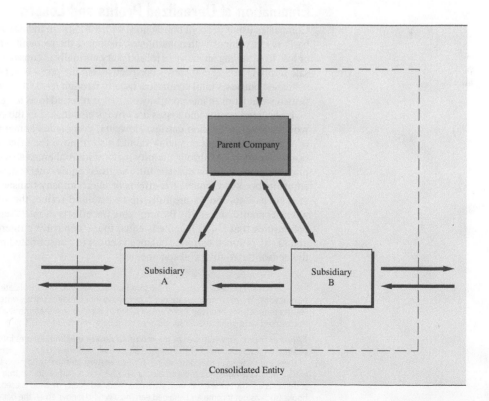
Consolidated Entity

results of the consolidated entity for the period. Transfers between the affiliated companies, shown in Figure 6–1 as those arrows not crossing the boundary of the consolidated entity, are equivalent to transfers between operating divisions of a single company and are not reported in the consolidated statements.

The central idea of consolidated financial statements is that they report on the activities of the consolidating affiliates as if the separate affiliates actually constitute a single company. Because single companies are not permitted to reflect internal transactions in their financial statements, consolidated entities also must exclude the effects of transactions that are totally within the consolidated entity from their financial statements. Building on the basic consolidation procedures presented in earlier chapters, this chapter and the next two deal with the effects of intercompany transfers. This chapter deals with intercompany inventory sales, and Chapters 7 and 8 discuss intercompany services, fixed asset sales, and intercompany debt transfers.

Elimination of Intercompany Transfers

Only *arm's-length* transactions (i.e., those conducted between completely independent parties who act in their own best interests) may be reflected in the consolidated financial statements.[2] Thus, all aspects of intercompany transfers must be eliminated in preparing consolidated financial statements so that the statements appear as if they were those of a single company. **ASC 810-10-45-1** mentions open account balances, security holdings, sales and purchases, and interest and dividends as examples of the intercompany balances and transactions that must be eliminated.

No distinction is made between wholly owned and less-than-wholly-owned subsidiaries with regard to the elimination of intercompany transfers. The focus in consolidation is on the single-entity concept rather than on the percentage of ownership. Once the conditions for consolidation are met, a company becomes part of a single economic entity, and all transactions with consolidated companies become internal transfers that must be eliminated fully, regardless of the level of ownership held.

Elimination of Unrealized Profits and Losses

Companies usually record transactions with affiliates in their accounting records on the same basis as transactions with nonaffiliates, including the recognition of profits and losses. Profit or loss from selling an item to a related party normally is considered realized at the time of the sale from the selling company's perspective, but the profit is not considered realized for consolidation purposes until confirmed, usually through resale to an unrelated party. This unconfirmed profit from an intercompany transfer is referred to as *unrealized intercompany profit.*

Unrealized profits and losses are always eliminated in the consolidation process using worksheet consolidation entries. However, companies sometimes differ on the question of whether the parent company should also remove the effects of intercompany transactions from its books through equity method journal entries. To maintain consistency with prior chapters, we advocate the fully adjusted equity method, which requires the parent to adjust its books to remove the effects of intercompany transactions. This method ensures that the parents' books are fully up-to-date and reflect the results of operations for the whole consolidated entity. By removing the effects of intercompany transactions, the parent ensures that (1) its income is equal to the controlling interest in consolidated income and (2) its retained earnings balance is equal to consolidated retained earnings amount in the consolidated financial statements.[3]

---

[2] Special rules require companies to disclose transactions with unconsolidated affiliates as related-party transactions. These companies are not "completely independent parties who act in their own best interests," yet the transactions between them are included in the financial statements. The key difference is that all transactions with consolidated subsidiaries must be eliminated.

[3] Another approach, which we call the *modified equity method,* ignores intercompany transactions on the parents' books. Proponents of this method argue that worksheet consolidation entries remove the effects of these transactions in the consolidation process anyway, so there is no need for the parent to record the extra entries to ensure that its books are always up-to-date. Although it is true that the consolidated financial statements are the same either way, when the modified equity method is used, key numbers in the parents' books (such as net income and retained earnings) will no longer equal the balances in the consolidated financial statements. We present this alternative approach in Appendix A.

INVENTORY TRANSACTIONS

LO 6-2

Understand and explain concepts associated with inventory transfers and transfer pricing.

Inventory transactions are the most common form of intercompany exchange. All revenue and expense items recorded by the participants must be eliminated fully in preparing the consolidated income statement, and the recorded value of transferred assets must be adjusted so that they appear in the consolidated balance sheet at the original owner's cost. Moreover, under the fully adjusted equity method, unrealized profits and losses on intercompany transfers are deferred until the items are sold to a nonaffiliate.

The recordkeeping process for intercompany inventory transfers may be more complex than for other forms of transfers. Companies often have many different types of inventory items, and some may be transferred from affiliate to affiliate. Also, the problems of keeping tabs on which items have been resold and which items are still on hand are greater in the case of inventory transactions because part of a shipment may be sold immediately by the purchasing company and other units may remain on hand for one or more accounting periods.[4]

Worksheet Consolidation Entries

The worksheet entries ensure that only the cost of the inventory to the consolidated entity is (1) included in the consolidated balance sheet when the inventory is still on hand and (2) charged to cost of goods sold in the period the inventory is resold to nonaffiliates.

Transfers at Cost

Merchandise is sometimes sold to related companies at the seller's cost or carrying value. When an intercorporate sale includes no profit or loss, the balance sheet inventory amounts at the end of the period require no adjustment for consolidation because the purchasing affiliate's inventory carrying amount is the same as the cost to the transferring affiliate and the consolidated entity. At the time the inventory is resold to a nonaffiliate, the amount recognized as cost of goods sold by the affiliate making the outside sale is the cost to the consolidated entity.

Even when the intercorporate sale includes no profit or loss, however, a worksheet consolidation entry is needed to remove both the revenue and the cost of goods sold recorded by the seller from the intercorporate sale and any unpaid payable or receivable balance that may remain. This worksheet consolidation entry avoids overstating these accounts. The consolidation entry does not affect consolidated net income when the transfer is made at cost because both revenue and cost of goods sold are reduced by the same amount.

Transfers at a Profit or Loss

Companies use many different approaches in setting intercorporate transfer prices. In some companies, the sale price to an affiliate is the same as the price to any other customer. Some companies routinely mark up inventory transferred to affiliates by a certain percentage of cost. Other companies have elaborate transfer pricing policies designed to encourage internal sales. Regardless of the method used in setting intercorporate transfer prices, the consolidation process must remove the effects of such sales from the consolidated statements.

Calculating Unrealized Profit or Loss

The calculation of unrealized intercompany profit or loss is an important step in eliminating the effects of intercompany transfers. In order to illustrate this calculation, it

---

[4] Inventory is not typically held for multiple years. However, many companies prepare quarterly consolidated financial statements and each quarter would be considered a unique period. Also, some companies sell large items (like cars, boats, or recreational vehicles) or expensive items (like jewelry), which may remain in inventory for more than one quarterly or annual period. Finally, when companies report LIFO inventories, they may build up LIFO layers, which create a fictional accounting notion that inventory items (long since sold) are still in stock.

FIGURE 6–2

Two Types of Intercompany Inventory Transfers

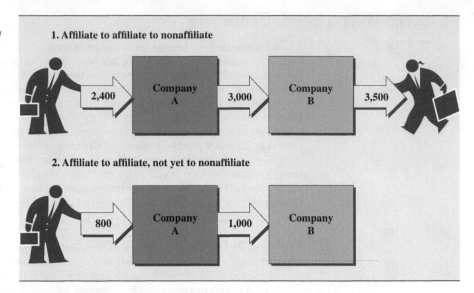

is important to first understand that there are two types of intercompany inventory transfers: (1) a transfer from one affiliate to another, which is then sold to an independent nonaffiliate and (2) a transfer from one affiliate to another, which has not yet been sold to an independent nonaffiliate. Figure 6–2 presents examples of each type of transfer.

In each case, Company A purchases inventory in an arm's-length transaction from an independent party. Company A then transfers the inventory to Company B (an affiliate) at a profit. In case 1, Company B eventually sells the inventory to an unrelated party. However, in case 2, Company B still holds the inventory at the end of the reporting period. The gross profit on the case 2 transfer from Company A to Company B represents unrealized intercompany profit because the inventory has not yet been sold to an independent party. When companies sell to affiliated companies on a regular basis, at the end of a reporting period, some of the inventory is often still on hand awaiting the sale to an independent party. Thus, the two cases in Figure 6–2 could represent intercompany sales between the same two companies (1) during the period and (2) just prior to the end of the period. The following chart summarizes these intercompany inventory transactions:

	Total Intercompany Sales	(1) Resold to Nonaffiliate	(2) Inventory on Hand
Sales	$4,000	$3,000	$1,000
– COGS	3,200	2,400	800
Gross Profit	800	600	200
GP%	20%		

! CAUTION

Note that all numbers in this chart are stated from Company A's perspective. Columns 2 and 3 simply break out the portion of the total column that was (1) resold or (2) still on hand in Company B's ending inventory. For example, the inventory in case 1 was eventually resold to a nonaffiliate for $3,500. However, this chart reports only what happened to Company A's sales.

Company A has total intercompany sales of $4,000 to Company B with total gross profit on these sales of $800. These sales can be divided into two categories: (1) those that Company B eventually resells during the current period, $3,000, and (2) those that are still in Company B's inventory at the end of the accounting period, $1,000. The gross profit on the intercompany sales that have not yet been realized through a sale to an independent third party, $200, should be deferred until this inventory is eventually resold to a nonaffiliate. Under the fully adjusted equity method, this unrealized gross profit is deferred on the parent company's books through an equity method entry (discussed in more detail later). All intercompany sales are eliminated in the consolidated financial statements through a worksheet consolidation entry(ies).

It is sometimes necessary to use the gross profit percentage to estimate the unrealized gross profit on intercompany transfers, assuming that the selling company uses a constant markup percentage on all intercompany transfers. For example, assume that Company A transfers inventory costing $9,000 to Company B, an affiliated company, for $10,000. At the end of the accounting period, Company B still has $3,000 of this inventory on hand in its warehouse. To calculate the unrealized profit given this limited information, first calculate gross profit and gross profit percentage on total intercompany sales.

	Total Intercompany Sales	(1) Resold to Nonaffiliate	(2) Inventory on Hand
Sales	$10,000		$3,000
– COGS	9,000		
Gross Profit			???

Gross profit is $1,000. Thus, the gross profit percentage is 10 percent ($1,000 ÷ $10,000). If we assume the gross profit percentage is the same across all intercompany sales, we can estimate the unrealized gross profit on intercompany sales (lower right-hand corner of the chart) by multiplying the balance on hand in intercompany inventory by the gross profit percentage to calculate the unrealized gross profit of $300 ($3,000 × 10%).

	Total Intercompany Sales	(1) Resold to Nonaffiliate	(2) Inventory on Hand
Sales	$10,000		$3,000
– COGS	9,000		
Gross Profit	1,000		300
GP%	10%		

> **! CAUTION**
>
> Students are sometimes confused when given information about markup on cost. Obviously, markup on cost is not the same ratio as the markup on transfer price. Nevertheless, students often mix them up. Be careful to ensure that you use the markup on transfer price (gross profit percentage) to calculate unrealized gross profit!
> *Hint:*
> Markup on cost = Gross Profit / COGS
> Markup on transfer price = Gross Profit / Sales = GP%

Inventory transfer problems often use terminology that is unfamiliar. For example, the selling price of the inventory is sometimes called the ***transfer price*** and the gross profit on intercompany sales is often referred to simply as the ***markup***. Based on these definitions, another term for gross profit percentage is simply ***markup on sales***. Similarly, ***markup on cost*** is the ratio of gross profit divided by cost of goods sold. When provided with information about markup on cost, this information must first be used to calculate cost of goods sold. Then calculate gross profit and gross profit percentage to determine unrealized gross profit on intercompany inventory transfers.

As an example, assume that Company A transfers inventory to an affiliate, Company B, for $5,000 with a 25 percent markup on cost and that Company B resells $3,500 of this inventory to nonaffiliates during the accounting period. How much unrealized gross profit from Company A's intercompany sales should be deferred at the end of the period? This information can be summarized as follows:

	Total Intercompany Sales	(1) Resold to Nonaffiliate	(2) Inventory on Hand
Sales	$5,000	$3,500	
– COGS			
Gross Profit			???
GP%			

When the information is given in terms of markup on cost, we must first calculate the cost of goods sold. Because the markup on cost is given as 25 percent, we can express this relationship by defining cost of goods sold as C and then expressing the markup (gross profit) as 0.25C.

	Total Intercompany Sales	(1) Resold to Nonaffiliate	(2) Inventory on Hand
Sales	$5,000	$3,500	
– COGS	C		
Gross Profit	0.25 C		???
GP%			

Thus, we can solve for cost of goods sold algebraically as follows:

$$Sales - COGS = Gross\ Profit$$
$$\$5,000 - C = 0.25C$$
$$\$5,000 = 1.25C$$
$$C = \$4,000$$

We can then calculate gross profit percentage (markup on transfer price) of 20 percent ($1,000 ÷ $5,000). Moreover, we can solve for Company B's ending inventory balance of $1,500 ($5,000 − $3,500 resold).

	Total Intercompany Sales	(1) Resold to Nonaffiliate	(2) Inventory on Hand
Sales	$5,000	$3,500	$1,500
– COGS	4,000		
Gross Profit	1,000		???
GP%	20%		

Finally, we can calculate the unrealized gross profit of $300 ($1,500 × 20%).

The chart above provides valuable information for two important accounting tasks. First, the number in the lower right-hand corner represents the unrealized profit or loss that must be deferred. The parent company makes an equity method journal entry to defer the portion of the unrealized profits that accrue to the controlling interest. After all the missing numbers in the chart are filled in, it can then be used to prepare consolidation entries to defer unrealized profit and to adjust the recorded value of inventory to reflect the actual purchase price when it was purchased from a nonaffiliate.

Deferring Unrealized Profit or Loss on the Parent's Books

For consolidation purposes, profits recorded on an intercorporate inventory sale are recognized in the period in which the inventory is resold to an unrelated party. Until the point of resale, all intercorporate profits must be deferred. When a parent company sells inventory to a subsidiary, referred to as a ***downstream sale,*** any profit or loss on the transfer accrues to the parent company's stockholders. When a subsidiary sells inventory to its parent, an ***upstream sale,*** any profit or loss accrues to the subsidiary's stockholders. If the subsidiary is wholly owned, all profit or loss ultimately accrues to the parent company as the sole stockholder. If, however, the selling subsidiary is not wholly owned, the profit or loss on the upstream sale is apportioned between the parent company and the noncontrolling shareholders.

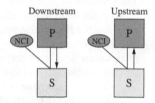

In addition to deferring unrealized profits and losses on the consolidation worksheet, under the fully adjusted equity method, an unrealized profit or loss on intercompany inventory transfers is deferred on the parent's books to ensure that the parent company's (1) net income equals the controlling interest in consolidated income and (2) retained earnings equals consolidated retained earnings. The only question is whether *all* (with downstream transactions) or *the parent's proportionate share* (with upstream transactions) of the unrealized gross profit should be deferred on the parent's books.[5] The journal entry on the parent's books to defer unrealized gross profit follows:

Income from Subsidiary	XXX	
Investment in Subsidiary		XXX

> **! CAUTION**
>
> On downstream transactions, the parent defers *all* (i.e.,100% of) unrealized profits and losses, whether the parent owns 100% or less than 100% of the subsidiary. On upstream transactions, the parent always defers its ownership percentage of unrealized profits and losses.

The unrealized gross profit is calculated as demonstrated in the previous subsection. In downstream transactions, the parent company uses this journal entry to defer the entire amount. In upstream transactions, the parent defers only its proportional share of the unrealized gross profit.

Unrealized profits or losses are deferred only until they are realized. In most cases, inventory on hand at the end of one period is sold in the next period. Once the inventory is sold to an unaffiliated party, the previously deferred amount is recognized in the period of the arm's-length sale by reversing the deferral on the parent's books as follows:

Investment in Subsidiary	XXX	
Income from Subsidiary		XXX

[5] Under the equity method, the parent accounts for all transactions related to its ownership in a subsidiary through the Investment in Subsidiary and Income from Subsidiary accounts. Even though the transaction giving rise to the unrealized profit or loss in this situation relates to an inventory transfer, the parent defers the unrealized profit or loss by making adjustments to the investment and Income from Subsidiary accounts.

Deferring Unrealized Profit or Loss in the Consolidation

When intercompany sales include unrealized profits or losses, the worksheet entry(ies) needed for consolidation in the period of transfer must adjust accounts in both the consolidated income statement and balance sheet:

> **Income statement: Sales and cost of goods sold.** All sales revenue from intercompany transfers and the related cost of goods sold recorded by the transferring affiliate must be removed.

> **Balance sheet: Inventory.** The entire unrealized profit or loss on intercompany transfers must be removed from inventory so that it will be reported at the cost to the consolidated entity.

The resulting financial statements appear as if the intercompany transfer had not occurred.

To understand how to eliminate the effects of intercompany inventory transfers in the consolidated financial statements, we refer to the examples illustrated in Figure 6–2 and assume a perpetual inventory system. One way to eliminate intercompany inventory profits or losses is to separately eliminate the effects of (1) sales from one affiliate to another that have subsequently been sold to a nonaffiliated party(ies) and (2) sales from one affiliate to another that have not yet been sold to a nonaffiliated person(s) or entity(ies). To explain how to separately eliminate the effects of these types of inventory transfers, we repeat the summary of the transactions from Figure 6–2 here:

	Total Intercompany Sales	(1) Resold to Nonaffiliate	(2) Inventory on Hand
Sales	$4,000	$3,000	$1,000
– COGS	3,200	2,400	800
Gross Profit	800	600	200

We first focus on Column (1), which summarizes all sales of inventory from Company A to Company B that have eventually been sold to a nonaffiliated party. The inventory was originally purchased in an arm's-length transaction for $2,400. It was then transferred from Company A to Company B for $3,000. Finally, this inventory was sold to an unrelated party for $3,500. The only portion of this transaction that does not involve an unaffiliated party is the $3,000 internal transfer, which needs to be eliminated. In this transaction, it turns out that Company A's transfer price (sales revenue) is $3,000. Company B originally records its inventory at this same amount, but when it is sold, $3,000 is removed from inventory and recorded as cost of goods sold. Thus, the worksheet consolidation entry to remove the effects of this transfer removes Company A's sales revenue and Company B's cost of goods sold related to this intercompany transfer as follows:

Sales	3,000	
Cost of Goods Sold		3,000

We next turn our attention to Column (2), which summarizes all inventory sales from Company A to Company B that are not yet sold to a nonaffiliated party. Company A originally purchased the inventory from an unaffiliated party for $800 and then transferred it to Company B for $1,000. The unrealized gross profit on this transfer is $200. Two problems are associated with this transaction. First, Company A's income is overstated by $200. Second, Company B's inventory is overstated by $200. Although the inventory was purchased in an arm's-length transaction for $800, the intercompany transfer resulted in the recorded value of the inventory being increased by $200. To ensure that the consolidated financial statements will appear as if the inventory had stayed on Company A's books (as if it had not been transferred), we prepare the following worksheet consolidation entry:

Sales	1,000	
Cost of Goods Sold		800
Inventory		200

These two consolidation entries could also be combined. The combined entry would appear as follows:

Sales	4,000	
Cost of Goods Sold		3,800
Inventory		200

After preparing the three-by-three internal inventory transfer summary chart, this elimination "combined" entry can be taken directly from the chart. The debit to sales is always the number in the upper left-hand corner (total intercompany sales). The credit to cost of goods sold is always the sum of the numbers in the middle column of the top row (intercompany sales that are eventually resold to nonaffiliates) and the middle row of the third column (intercompany cost of goods sold on inventory still on hand). Finally, the credit to inventory is the unrealized gross profit number in the lower right column. The purpose of this credit to inventory is to ensure that inventory appears in the consolidated financial statements at the original cost from an arm's-length transaction.

	Total Intercompany Sales	(1) Resold to Nonaffiliate	(2) Inventory on Hand
Sales	$ 4,000	$3,000	$1,000
− COGS	3,200	2,400	800
Gross Profit	800	600	200

The net effect of this combined worksheet consolidation entry is to remove the gross profit on *all* intercompany sales and to adjust the ending intercompany-transferred inventory back to its original cost. Thus, one consolidation entry can remove the effects of all intercompany inventory transfers during the accounting period.

We note that the basic consolidation entry is modified slightly when intercompany profits associated with inventory transfers result in unrealized profits. We illustrate this modification later in several examples.

Assuming the inventory in Column (2), which is still on hand at the end of the first year, is subsequently sold in the following year, recognizing the deferred gross profit from the first year in the second year would then be appropriate. The worksheet entry to essentially force this now realized gross profit to be recognized in the consolidated financial statements in year 2 is to credit Cost of Goods Sold and debit the Investment in Subsidiary account as follows:

Investment in Subsidiary	200	
Cost of Goods Sold		200

Because the overvalued intercompany inventory in beginning inventory is charged to cost of goods sold at the time of the inventory's sale to an unrelated party during the period, the cost of the goods sold is overstated. Thus, a credit to Cost of Goods Sold corrects this account balance and increases income by the amount of gross profit that was deferred in the prior year. The debit goes to Investment in Subsidiary. Note that we prepared an equity-method adjustment in the previous year to defer the unrealized gross profit. We can say that essentially this entry artificially decreased the investment account, so we debit that amount back into the investment account so that the account essentially increases back to its correct balance so that it can be eliminated by the basic consolidation entry. We demonstrate how this works later in the chapter.

Why Adjust the Parent's Books and Make Worksheet Entries?

We defer unrealized intercompany profit or loss to ensure that the parent's books are completely up-to-date. To be consistent with prior chapters, the fully adjusted equity method requires a journal entry to defer intercompany profit/loss to ensure that the parent's net income equals the controlling interest in consolidated net income and that the parent's retained earnings is equal to consolidated retained earnings. However, even though we "fix" the parent's books through an equity-method journal entry, the Investment in Subsidiary account and the Income from Subsidiary accounts are eliminated in the consolidation process. However, without a worksheet consolidation entry, sales and cost of goods sold would be overstated on the income statement, and inventory would be overstated on the balance sheet. Thus, even though we ensure that the parent's books are up-to-date, we still need to remove the effects of intercompany inventory transfers from the consolidated financial statements.

DOWNSTREAM SALE OF INVENTORY[6]

LO 6-3

Prepare equity-method journal entries and consolidation entries for the consolidation of a subsidiary following downstream inventory transfers.

Advanced
StudyGuide
.com

Consolidated net income must be based on realized income. Because intercompany profits from downstream sales are on the parent's books, consolidated net income and the overall claim of parent company shareholders must be reduced by the full amount of the unrealized profits.

When a company sells an inventory item to an affiliate, one of three situations results: (1) the item is resold to a nonaffiliate during the same period, (2) the item is resold to a nonaffiliate during the next period, or (3) the item is held for two or more periods by the purchasing affiliate.[7] We use the continuing example of Peerless Products Corporation and Special Foods Inc. to illustrate the consolidation process under each of the alternatives. Picking up with the example in Chapter 3, to illustrate more fully the treatment of unrealized intercompany profits, assume the following with respect to the Peerless and Special Foods example used previously:

1. Peerless Products Corporation purchases 80 percent of Special Foods Inc.'s stock on December 31, 20X0, at the stock's book value of $240,000. The fair value of Special Foods' noncontrolling interest on that date is $60,000, the book value of those shares.

2. During 20X1, Peerless reports separate income of $140,000 income from regular operations and declares dividends of $60,000. Special Foods reports net income of $50,000 and declares dividends of $30,000.

3. Peerless accounts for its investment in Special Foods using the equity method under which it records its share of Special Foods' net income and dividends and also adjusts for unrealized intercompany profits using the fully adjusted equity method.

As an illustration of the effects of a downstream inventory sale, assume that on March 1, 20X1, Peerless buys inventory for $7,000 and resells it to Special Foods for $10,000 on April 1. Peerless records the following entries on its books:

	March 1, 20X1		
(1)	Inventory	7,000	
	Cash		7,000
	Record inventory purchase.		

	April 1, 20X1		
(2)	Cash	10,000	
	Sales		10,000
	Record sale of inventory to Special Foods.		

---

[6] To view a video explanation of this topic, visit advancedstudyguide.com.

[7] As explained previously, inventory is not typically held for multiple periods, but some companies prepare quarterly consolidated financial statements, and some companies sell large or expensive items, which may remain in inventory for more than one period. Moreover, when companies report LIFO inventories, they may build up LIFO layers, which create a fictional accounting notion that inventory items (long since sold) are still in stock.

| (3) | Cost of Goods Sold | 7,000 | |
| | Inventory | | 7,000 |

Record cost of inventory sold to Special Foods.

Special Foods records the purchase of the inventory from Peerless with the following entry:

April 1, 20X1

| (4) | Inventory | 10,000 | |
| | Cash | | 10,000 |

Record purchase of inventory from Peerless.

Resale in Period of Intercorporate Transfer

To illustrate consolidation when inventory is sold to an affiliate and then resold to a nonaffiliate during the same period, assume that on November 5, 20X1, Special Foods sells the inventory purchased from Peerless to a nonaffiliated party for $15,000, as follows:

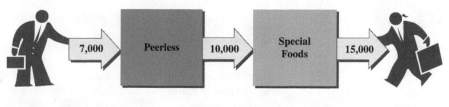

March 1, 20X1   **April 1, 20X1**   **November 5, 20X1**

This inventory transfer can be summarized as follows:

	Total Intercompany Sales	(1) Resold to Nonaffiliate	(2) Inventory on Hand
Sales	$10,000	$10,000	0
– COGS	7,000	7,000	0
Gross Profit	3,000	3,000	0

Peerless does not need to defer any intercompany profit on its books because all the intercompany profit has been realized through resale of the inventory to the external party during the current period. Stated differently, the summary chart indicates that there is no intercompany inventory on hand at the end of the period. Thus, there are no unrealized profits to defer.

Special Foods records the sale to a nonaffiliated party with the following entries:

November 5, 20X1

| (5) | Cash | 15,000 | |
| | Sales | | 15,000 |

Record sale of inventory.

| (6) | Cost of Goods Sold | 10,000 | |
| | Inventory | | 10,000 |

Record cost of inventory sold.

A review of all entries recorded by the individual companies indicates that incorrect balances will be reported in the consolidated income statement if the effects of the intercorporate sale are not removed:

Item	Peerless Products	+	Special Foods	=	Unadjusted Totals	≠	Consolidated Amounts
Sales	$10,000		$15,000		$25,000		$15,000
Cost of Goods Sold	(7,000)		(10,000)		(17,000)		(7,000)
Gross Profit	$ 3,000		$ 5,000		$ 8,000		$ 8,000

Although consolidated gross profit is correct even if no adjustments are made, the totals for sales and cost of goods sold derived by simply adding the amounts on the books of Peerless and Special Foods are overstated for the consolidated entity. The selling price of the inventory in an arm's-length transaction is $15,000, and the original cost to Peerless Products is $7,000. Thus, gross profit of $8,000 is correct from a consolidated viewpoint, but consolidated sales and cost of goods sold should be $15,000 and $7,000, respectively, rather than $25,000 and $17,000. In the consolidation worksheet, the amount of the intercompany sale must be eliminated from both sales and cost of goods sold to correctly state the consolidated totals:

Sales	10,000	
Cost of Goods Sold		10,000

Note that this worksheet entry does not affect consolidated net income because both sales and cost of goods sold are reduced by the same amount.

Resale in Period Following Intercorporate Transfer

When inventory is sold to an affiliate at a profit but is not resold during the same period, appropriate adjustments are needed to prepare consolidated financial statements in the period of the intercompany sale and in each subsequent period until the inventory is sold to a nonaffiliate. By way of illustration, assume that Peerless Products purchases inventory on March 1, 20X1, for $7,000 and sells the inventory during the year (on April 1) to Special Foods for $10,000. Special Foods sells the inventory to a nonaffiliated party for $15,000 on January 2, 20X2, as follows:

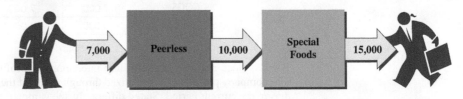

	March 1, 20X1	April 1, 20X1	January 2, 20X2

This inventory transfer can be summarized as follows:

	Total Intercompany Sales	(1) Resold to Nonaffiliate	(2) Inventory on Hand
Sales	$ 10,000	0	$ 10,000
− COGS	7,000	0	7,000
Gross Profit	3,000	0	3,000

As of the end of 20X1, the entire intercompany inventory is still on hand in Special Foods' warehouse. In this case, all the intercompany gross profit is unrealized at December 31, 20X1. Thus, Peerless needs to defer the entire intercompany gross profit on its books because none of the intercompany profit has been realized through resale of the inventory to an external party during the current period. In other words, the summary chart indicates that there is $10,000 of intercompany inventory on hand at the end of the period and the unrealized profit of $3,000 must be deferred on Peerless' books as shown in entry (9). During 20X1, Peerless records the purchase of the inventory and the sale to Special Foods with journal entries (1) through (3), given previously; Special Foods records the purchase of the inventory from Peerless with entry (4). In 20X2, Special Foods records the sale of the inventory to Nonaffiliated with entries (5) and (6).

Equity-Method Entries—20X1

Under the equity method, Peerless records its share of Special Foods' income and dividends for 20X1:

(7)	Investment in Special Foods	40,000	
	Income from Special Foods		40,000
	Record Peerless' 80% share of Special Foods' 20X1 income.		

(8)	Cash	24,000	
	Investment in Special Foods		24,000
	Record Peerless' 80% share of Special Foods' 20X1 dividend.		

As a result of these entries, the ending balance in the investment account is currently $256,000 ($240,000 + $40,000 − $24,000). However, because the downstream sale of inventory to Special Foods results in $3,000 of unrealized profits, Peerless defers the unrealized gross profit by making an adjustment in the equity method investment and income accounts to reduce the income from Special Foods on the income statement and Investment in Special Foods on the balance sheet by its share of the unrealized gross profit. Because this is a downstream transaction, the sale (and associated unrealized gross

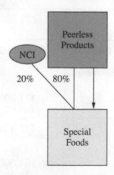

profit) resides on Peerless' income statement. Because we assume the NCI shareholders do not own Peerless stock, they do not share in the deferral of the unrealized profit. Under the fully adjusted equity method, Peerless defers the entire $3,000 using the following equity-method entry:

(9)	Income from Special Foods	3,000	
	Investment in Special Foods		3,000
	Defer unrealized gross profit on inventory sales to Special Foods not yet resold.		

Note that this entry accomplishes two important objectives. First, because Peerless' income is overstated by $3,000, the adjustment to Income from Special Foods offsets this overstatement so that Peerless' bottom-line net income is now correct. Second, Special Foods' inventory is currently overstated by $3,000. Because the Investment in Special Foods account summarizes Peerless' investment in Special Foods' balance sheet, this reduction to the investment account offsets the fact that Special Foods' inventory (and thus entire balance sheet) is overstated by $3,000. Thus, after making this equity-method adjustment to defer the unrealized gross profit, Peerless' financial statements are now correctly stated. Therefore, Peerless' reported income will be exactly equal to the controlling interest in net income on the consolidated financial statements.

Consolidation Worksheet—20X1

We present the consolidation worksheet prepared at the end of 20X1 in Figure 6–3. The first two consolidation entries are the same as we calculated in Chapter 3 with one minor exception. Under the fully adjusted equity method, there is one difference in preparing the basic consolidation entry when unrealized intercompany profits exist. Although the analysis of the "book value" portion of the investment account is the same, in preparing the basic consolidation entry, we reduce the amounts in the Income from Special Foods and Investment in Special Foods by the $3,000 unrealized gross profit deferral.

FIGURE 6–3   December 31, 20X1, Consolidation Worksheet, Period of Intercompany Sale; Downstream Inventory Sale

	Peerless Products	Special Foods	Consolidation Entries DR	Consolidation Entries CR	Consolidated
Income Statement					
Sales	400,000	200,000	10,000		590,000
Less: COGS	(170,000)	(115,000)		7,000	(278,000)
Less: Depreciation Expense	(50,000)	(20,000)			(70,000)
Less: Other Expenses	(40,000)	(15,000)			(55,000)
Income from Special Foods	37,000		37,000		0
Consolidated Net Income	177,000	50,000	47,000	7,000	187,000
NCI in Net Income			10,000		(10,000)
Controlling Interest Net Income	**177,000**	**50,000**	**57,000**	**7,000**	**177,000**
Statement of Retained Earnings					
Beginning Balance	300,000	100,000	100,000		300,000
Net Income	**177,000**	**50,000**	57,000	7,000	177,000
Less: Dividends Declared	(60,000)	(30,000)		30,000	(60,000)
Ending Balance	**417,000**	**120,000**	**157,000**	**37,000**	**417,000**
Balance Sheet					
Cash	264,000	75,000			339,000
Accounts Receivable	75,000	50,000			125,000
Inventory	100,000	75,000		3,000	172,000
Investment in Special Foods	253,000			253,000	0
Land	175,000	40,000			215,000
Buildings & Equipment	800,000	600,000		300,000	1,100,000
Less: Accumulated Depreciation	(450,000)	(320,000)	300,000		(470,000)
Total Assets	**1,217,000**	**520,000**	**300,000**	**556,000**	**1,481,000**
Accounts Payable	100,000	100,000			200,000
Bonds Payable	200,000	100,000			300,000
Common Stock	500,000	200,000	200,000		500,000
Retained Earnings	**417,000**	**120,000**	157,000	37,000	417,000
NCI in NA of Special Foods				64,000	64,000
Total Liabilities & Equity	**1,217,000**	**520,000**	**357,000**	**101,000**	**1,481,000**

Calculations for Basic Consolidation Entry:

Book Value Calculations:

	NCI 20% +	Peerless 80%	=	Common Stock	+	Retained Earnings
Original Book Value	60,000	240,000		200,000		100,000
+ Net Income	10,000	40,000				50,000
– Dividends	(6,000)	(24,000)				(30,000)
Ending Book Value	64,000	256,000		200,000		120,000

Adjustment to Basic Consolidation Entry:

	NCI 20%	Peerless 80%
Net Income	10,000	40,000
– Gross profit deferral		(3,000)
Income to be eliminated	10,000	37,000
Ending Book Value	64,000	256,000
– Gross profit deferral		(3,000)
Adjusted Book Value	64,000	253,000

Basic Consolidation Entry:

Common Stock	200,000		← Common stock balance
Retained Earnings	100,000		← Beginning balance in RE
Income from Special Foods	37,000		← Peerless' % of NI with Adjustment
NCI in NI of Special Foods	10,000		← NCI share of Special Foods' NI
Dividends Declared		30,000	← 100% of sub's dividends declared
Investment in Special Foods		253,000	← Net BV in investment with Adjustment
NCI in NA of Special Foods		64,000	← NCI share of net amount of BV

The accumulated depreciation entry is the same as in previous chapters. It is always the amount of the subsidiary's accumulated depreciation on the acquisition date.

Optional Accumulated Depreciation Consolidation Entry:

Accumulated Depreciation	300,000		Accumulated depreciation at
Buildings & Equipment		300,000	← the time of the acquisition netted against cost

Moreover, although Peerless recorded an equity-method entry to defer the unrealized gross profit, both the Income from Special Foods and Investment in Special Foods accounts are eliminated with the basic consolidation entry. Peerless' Sales and Cost of Goods Sold amounts are still overstated (by $10,000 and $7,000, respectively). Moreover, Special Foods' ending inventory is still overstated by $3,000. Simply adding up the Peerless and Special Foods columns of the consolidation worksheet will result in overstated consolidated net income, total assets, and retained earnings. Therefore, we also record a new consolidation entry to correct the unadjusted totals to the appropriate consolidated amounts. In doing so, consolidated income is reduced by $3,000 ($10,000 − $7,000). In addition, ending inventory reported on Special Foods' books is stated at the intercompany exchange price rather than the historical cost to the consolidated entity. Until Special Foods resells it to an external party, the inventory must be reduced by the amount of unrealized intercompany profit each time consolidated statements are prepared.

Elimination of Intercompany Sales to Special Foods (still on hand in ending inventory):

Sales	10,000	
Cost of Goods Sold		7,000
Inventory		3,000

This consolidation entry removes the effects of the intercompany inventory sale. The journal entries recorded by Peerless Products and Special Foods in 20X1 on their separate books will result in an overstatement of consolidated gross profit for 20X1 and the consolidated inventory balance at year-end unless the amounts are adjusted in the consolidation worksheet. The amounts resulting from the intercompany inventory transactions from the separate books of Peerless Products and Special Foods, and the appropriate consolidated amounts, are as follows:

Item	Peerless Products	+	Special Foods	=	Unadjusted Totals	∓	Consolidated Amounts
Sales	$10,000		$ 0		$10,000		$ 0
Cost of Goods Sold	(7,000)		0		(7,000)		0
Gross Profit	$ 3,000		$ 0		$ 3,000		$ 0
Inventory	$ 0		$10,000		$10,000		$7,000

The following T-accounts summarize the effects of all equity-method entries on Peerless' books as well as the basic consolidation entry:

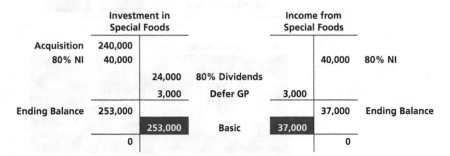

Consolidated Net Income—20X1

Consolidated net income for 20X1 is shown as $187,000 in the Figure 6–3 worksheet. This amount is computed and allocated as follows:

Peerless' separate income	$140,000
Less: Unrealized intercompany profit on downstream inventory sale	(3,000)
Peerless' separate realized income	$137,000
Special Foods' net income	50,000
Consolidated net income, 20X1	$187,000
Income to noncontrolling interest ($50,000 × 0.20)	(10,000)
Income to controlling interest	$177,000

Equity-Method Entries—20X2

During 20X2, Special Foods receives $15,000 when it sells to an unaffiliated party the inventory that it had purchased for $10,000 from Peerless in 20X1. Also, Peerless records its pro rata portion of Special Foods' net income ($75,000) and dividends ($40,000) for 20X2 with the normal equity-method entries:

(10)	Investment in Special Foods	60,000	
	Income from Special Foods		60,000

Record Peerless' 80% share of Special Foods' 20X2 income.

(11)	Cash	32,000	
	Investment in Special Foods		32,000

Record Peerless' 80% share of Special Foods' 20X2 dividend.

Under the fully adjusted equity method, once the inventory is sold to an unaffiliated party, the deferral in the equity-method accounts is no longer necessary (see entry (9) from 20X1) and is reversed as follows:

(12)	Investment in Special Foods	3,000	
	Income from Special Foods		3,000

Reverse the 20X1 gross profit deferral on inventory sold to unaffiliated customers.

Consolidation Worksheet—20X2

Figure 6–4 illustrates the consolidation worksheet at the end of 20X2. The first two consolidation entries are the same as those presented in Chapter 3 with one exception to the basic consolidation entry. Whereas we subtracted the deferral of unrealized gross profit in 20X1, we now add back this deferral in the basic consolidation entry for 20X2.

Calculations for Basic Consolidation Entry:

Book Value Calculations:

	NCI 20% +	Peerless 80% =	Common Stock +	Retained Earnings
Original Book Value	64,000	256,000	200,000	120,000
+ Net Income	15,000	60,000		75,000
− Dividends	(8,000)	(32,000)		(40,000)
Ending Book Value	71,000	284,000	200,000	155,000

Adjustment to Basic Consolidation Entry:

	NCI 20%	Peerless 80%
Net Income	15,000	60,000
+ Reverse GP deferral		3,000
Income to be eliminated	15,000	63,000
Ending Book Value	71,000	284,000
+ Reverse GP deferral		3,000
Adjusted Book Value	71,000	287,000

Basic Consolidation Entry:

Common Stock	200,000		← Common stock balance
Retained Earnings	120,000		← Beginning balance in RE
Income from Special Foods	63,000		← Peerless' % of NI with Adjustments
NCI in NI of Special Foods	15,000		← NCI share of Special Foods' NI
Dividends Declared		40,000	← 100% of sub's dividends declared
Investment in Special Foods		287,000	← Net investment with Adjustments
NCI in NA of Special Foods		71,000	← NCI share of ending book value

Optional Accumulated Depreciation Consolidation Entry:

Accumulated Depreciation	300,000		Accumulated depreciation at
Buildings & Equipment		300,000	← the time of the acquisition
			netted against cost

FIGURE 6–4   December 31, 20X2, Consolidation Worksheet, Next Period Following Intercompany Sale; Downstream Inventory Sale

	Peerless Products	Special Foods	Consolidation Entries DR	Consolidation Entries CR	Consolidated
Income Statement					
Sales	450,000	300,000			750,000
Less: COGS	(180,000)	(160,000)		3,000	(337,000)
Less: Depreciation Expense	(50,000)	(20,000)			(70,000)
Less: Other Expenses	(60,000)	(45,000)			(105,000)
Income from Special Foods	63,000		63,000		0
Consolidated Net Income	223,000	75,000	63,000	3,000	238,000
NCI in Net Income			15,000		(15,000)
Controlling Interest Net Income	**223,000**	**75,000**	78,000	3,000	**223,000**
Statement of Retained Earnings					
Beginning Balance	417,000	120,000	120,000		417,000
Net Income	**223,000**	**75,000**	78,000	3,000	223,000
Less: Dividends Declared	(60,000)	(40,000)		40,000	(60,000)
Ending Balance	**580,000**	**155,000**	198,000	43,000	**580,000**
Balance Sheet					
Cash	291,000	85,000			376,000
Accounts Receivable	150,000	80,000			230,000
Inventory	180,000	90,000			270,000
Investment in Special Foods	284,000		3,000	287,000	0
Land	175,000	40,000			215,000
Buildings & Equipment	800,000	600,000		300,000	1,100,000
Less: Accumulated Depreciation	(500,000)	(340,000)	300,000		(540,000)
Total Assets	**1,380,000**	**555,000**	303,000	587,000	**1,651,000**
Accounts Payable	100,000	100,000			200,000
Bonds Payable	200,000	100,000			300,000
Common Stock	500,000	200,000	200,000		500,000
Retained Earnings	**580,000**	**155,000**	198,000	43,000	580,000
NCI in NA of Special Foods				71,000	71,000
Total Liabilities & Equity	**1,380,000**	**555,000**	398,000	114,000	**1,651,000**

An additional consolidation entry is needed to recognize the $3,000 of income that was deferred in 20X1. Whereas the inventory had not yet been sold to an unaffiliated customer in 20X1 and needed to be deferred, that inventory has now been sold in 20X2 and should be recognized in the consolidated financial statements.

Reversal of the 20X1 Gross Profit Deferral:

Investment in Special Foods	**3,000**	
Cost of Goods Sold		**3,000**

Special Foods' unrealized intercompany profit included in beginning inventory was charged to Cost of Goods Sold when Special Foods sold the inventory during the period. Thus, consolidated cost of goods sold will be overstated for 20X2 if it is based on the unadjusted totals from the books of Peerless and Special Foods:

Item	Peerless Products	+	Special Foods	=	Unadjusted Totals	≠	Consolidated Amounts
Sales	$ 0		$ 15,000		$ 15,000		$15,000
Cost of Goods Sold	0		(10,000)		(10,000)		(7,000)
Gross Profit	$ 0		$ 5,000		$ 5,000		$ 8,000

Unlike the period in which the intercompany transfer occurs, no adjustment to sales is required in a subsequent period when the inventory is sold to a nonaffiliate. The amount reported by Special Foods reflects the sale outside the economic entity and is the appropriate amount to be reported for consolidation. By removing the $3,000 of intercorporate profit from Cost of Goods Sold with this consolidation entry, the original acquisition price paid by Peerless Products is reported in Cost of Goods Sold, and $8,000 of gross profit is correctly reported in the consolidated income statement.

Once the sale is made to an external party, the transaction is complete and no adjustments or consolidation entries related to the intercompany transaction are needed in future periods. The following T-accounts illustrate the effects of all equity-method journal entries on Peerless' books as well as the worksheet entries on the consolidation worksheet.

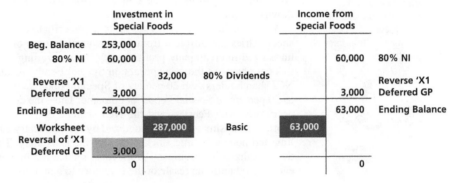

Consolidated Net Income—20X2

Consolidated net income for 20X2 is shown as $238,000 in the Figure 6–4 worksheet. This amount is verified and allocated as follows:

Peerless' separate income	$160,000
Realization of deferred intercompany profit on downstream inventory sale	3,000
Peerless' separate realized income	$163,000
Special Foods' net income	75,000
Consolidated net income, 20X2	$238,000
Income to noncontrolling interest ($75,000 × 0.20)	(15,000)
Income to controlling interest	$223,000

Inventory Held for Two or More Periods

Companies may carry the cost of inventory purchased from an affiliate for more than one accounting period. For example, the cost of an item may be in a LIFO inventory layer and would be included as part of the inventory balance until the layer is liquidated. Prior to liquidation, a consolidation entry is needed in the consolidation worksheet each time consolidated statements are prepared to restate the inventory to its cost to the consolidated entity. For example, if Special Foods continues to hold the inventory purchased from Peerless Products, the following consolidation entry is needed in the consolidation worksheet each time a consolidated balance sheet is prepared for years following the year of intercompany sale, for as long as the inventory is held:

Investment in Special Foods	3,000	
Inventory		3,000

This consolidation entry simply corrects the balance in both the Inventory and Investment in Special Foods accounts. Whereas Peerless recorded an equity-method adjustment to defer the $3,000 of unrealized gross profit in the year of the intercompany inventory transfer by artificially decreasing the Investment in Special Foods to offset the overstated inventory balance on Special Foods' books, this entry simply corrects both accounts. No income statement adjustments are needed in the periods following the intercorporate sale until the inventory is resold to parties external to the consolidated entity.

UPSTREAM SALE OF INVENTORY

LO 6-4

Prepare equity-method journal entries and consolidation entries for the consolidation of a subsidiary following upstream inventory transfers.

Advanced
StudyGuide
.com

When an upstream inventory sale occurs and the parent resells the inventory to a nonaffiliate during the same period, all the parent's equity-method entries and the consolidation entries in the consolidation worksheet are identical to those in the downstream case.

When the inventory is not resold to a nonaffiliate before the end of the period, worksheet entries are different from the downstream case only by the apportionment of the unrealized intercompany profit to both the controlling and noncontrolling interests. In this case because the sale appears on Special Foods' income statement and because the NCI shareholders own 20 percent of Special Foods' outstanding shares, they are entitled to 20 percent of Special Foods' net income. Thus, the deferral of unrealized gross profits accrues to both Peerless and the NCI shareholders. In other words, the intercompany profit in an upstream sale is recognized by the subsidiary and shared between the controlling and noncontrolling stockholders of the subsidiary. Therefore, the consolidation of the unrealized intercompany profit must reduce the interests of both ownership groups each period until the resale of the inventory to a nonaffiliated party confirms the profit.

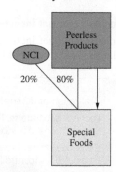

We illustrate an upstream sale using the same example as used for the downstream sale except that Special Foods sells the inventory to Peerless. Assume Special Foods purchases the inventory on March 1, 20X1, for $7,000 and sells it to Peerless for $10,000 during the same year. Peerless holds the inventory until January 2, 20X2, at which time Peerless sells it to a nonaffiliated party for $15,000.

Equity-Method Entries—20X1

Peerless Products records the following equity-method entries in 20X1:

(13)	Investment in Special Foods	40,000	
	Income from Special Foods		40,000
	Record Peerless' 80% share of Special Foods' 20X1 income.		

(14)	Cash	24,000	
	Investment in Special Foods		24,000
	Record Peerless' 80% share of Special Foods' 20X1 dividend.		

These entries are the same as in the illustration of the downstream sale. The only difference is that the fully adjusted equity-method entry to defer the unrealized gross profit is only for Peerless' ownership percentage of Special Foods (80 percent). Thus, the deferral of Peerless' relative share of the unrealized gross profit is $2,400 ($3,000 × 80%).

| (15) | Income from Special Foods | 2,400 | |
| | Investment in Special Foods | | 2,400 |

Eliminate unrealized gross profit on inventory purchases from Special Foods.

Consolidation Worksheet—20X1

Advanced
StudyGuide
.com

We present the worksheet for the preparation of the 20X1 consolidated financial statements in Figure 6–5. The first two consolidation entries are the same as we calculated in Chapter 3 with one minor exception. Although the analysis of the book value portion of the investment account is the same, in preparing the basic consolidation entry, we reduce the amounts in Peerless' Income from Special Foods and Investment in Special Foods accounts by Peerless' share of the deferral, $2,400 ($3,000 × 80%). We also reduce the NCI in Net Income of Special Foods and NCI in Net Assets of Special Foods by the NCI share of the deferral, $600 ($3,000 × 20%).

FIGURE 6–5   December 31, 20X1, Consolidation Worksheet, Period of Intercompany Sale; Upstream Inventory Sale

	Peerless Products	Special Foods	Consolidation Entries DR	Consolidation Entries CR	Consolidated
Income Statement					
Sales	400,000	200,000	10,000		590,000
Less: COGS	(170,000)	(115,000)		7,000	(278,000)
Less: Depreciation Expense	(50,000)	(20,000)			(70,000)
Less: Other Expenses	(40,000)	(15,000)			(55,000)
Income from Special Foods	37,600		37,600		0
Consolidated Net Income	177,600	50,000	47,600	7,000	187,000
NCI in Net Income			9,400		(9,400)
Controlling Interest Net Income	**177,600**	**50,000**	**57,000**	**7,000**	**177,600**
Statement of Retained Earnings					
Beginning Balance	300,000	100,000	100,000		300,000
Net Income	**177,600**	**50,000**	57,000	7,000	177,600
Less: Dividends Declared	(60,000)	(30,000)		30,000	(60,000)
Ending Balance	**417,600**	**120,000**	**157,000**	**37,000**	**417,600**
Balance Sheet					
Cash	264,000	75,000			339,000
Accounts Receivable	75,000	50,000			125,000
Inventory	100,000	75,000		3,000	172,000
Investment in Special Foods	253,600			253,600	0
Land	175,000	40,000			215,000
Buildings & Equipment	800,000	600,000		300,000	1,100,000
Less: Accumulated Depreciation	(450,000)	(320,000)	300,000		(470,000)
Total Assets	**1,217,600**	**520,000**	**300,000**	**556,600**	**1,481,000**
Accounts Payable	100,000	100,000			200,000
Bonds Payable	200,000	100,000			300,000
Common Stock	500,000	200,000	200,000		500,000
Retained Earnings	**417,600**	**120,000**	157,000	37,000	417,600
NCI in NA of Special Foods				63,400	63,400
Total Liabilities & Equity	**1,217,600**	**520,000**	**357,000**	**100,400**	**1,481,000**

Calculations for Basic Consolidation Entry:

Book Value Calculations:

	NCI 20% +	Peerless 80%	=	Common Stock	+	Retained Earnings
Original Book Value	60,000	240,000		200,000		100,000
+ Net Income	10,000	40,000				50,000
− Dividends	(6,000)	(24,000)				(30,000)
Ending Book Value	64,000	256,000		200,000		120,000

Adjustment to Basic Consolidation Entry:

	NCI 20%	Peerless 80%
Net Income	10,000	40,000
− Gross profit deferral	(600)	(2,400)
Income to be eliminated	9,400	37,600
Ending Book Value	64,000	256,000
− Gross profit deferral	(600)	(2,400)
Adjusted Book Value	63,400	253,600

Basic Consolidation Entry:

Common Stock	200,000		← Common stock balance
Retained Earnings	100,000		← Beginning balance in RE
Income from Special Foods	37,600		← Peerless' % of NI with Adjustment
NCI in NI of Special Foods	9,400		← NCI share of NI with Adjustment
Dividends Declared		30,000	← 100% of sub's dividends declared
Investment in Special Foods		253,600	← Net book value with Adjustment
NCI in NA of Special Foods		63,400	← NCI share of BV with Adjustment

Optional Accumulated Depreciation Consolidation Entry:

Accumulated Depreciation	300,000	
Buildings & Equipment		300,000

← Accumulated depreciation at the time of the acquisition netted against cost

The consolidation worksheet entry to remove the effects of the intercompany sale is identical to the downstream case. The only difference is that the overstated Sales and Cost of Goods Sold numbers are now in the Special Foods' column of the consolidation worksheet and the overstated inventory is now in the Peerless column.

Eliminate Inventory Purchases from Special Foods (still on hand):

Sales	10,000	
Cost of Goods Sold		7,000
Inventory		3,000

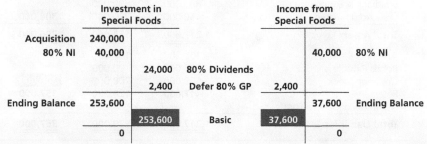

Consolidated Net Income—20X1

We note that because the unrealized profit consolidation is allocated proportionately between the controlling and noncontrolling interests in the upstream case, the income assigned to the noncontrolling shareholders is $600 ($3,000 × 0.20) less in Figure 6–5 for the upstream case than in Figure 6–3 for the downstream case. Accordingly, the amount of income assigned to the controlling interest is $600 higher. Note that consolidated net income and all other income statement amounts are the same whether the sale is upstream or downstream. The worksheet indicates that consolidated net income for 20X1 is $187,000. Consolidated net income is computed and allocated to the controlling and noncontrolling stockholders as follows:

Peerless' separate income		$140,000
Special Foods' net income	$50,000	
Less: Unrealized intercompany profit on upstream inventory sale	(3,000)	
Special Foods' realized net income		47,000
Consolidated net income, 20X1		$187,000
Income to noncontrolling interest ($47,000 × 0.20)		(9,400)
Income to controlling interest		$177,600

Equity-Method Entries—20X2

Peerless recognizes its share of Special Foods' income ($75,000) and dividends ($40,000) for 20X2 with the normal equity-method entries:

(16)	Investment in Special Foods	60,000	
	Income from Special Foods		60,000
	Record Peerless' 80% share of Special Foods' 20X2 income.		

(17)	Cash	32,000	
	Investment in Special Foods		32,000
	Record Peerless' 80% share of Special Foods' 20X2 dividend.		

Under the fully adjusted equity method, Peerless reverses the deferred gross profit from 20X1 because this inventory has now been sold.

(18)	Investment in Special Foods	2,400	
	Income from Special Foods		2,400
	Reverse the 20X1 gross profit deferral on inventory sold to unaffiliated customers.		

Consolidation Worksheet—20X2

Figure 6–6 illustrates the consolidation worksheet used to prepare consolidated financial statements at the end of 20X2. The first two consolidation entries are the same as we prepared in Chapter 3 with the previously explained exception. Although the analysis of the book value portion of the investment account is the same, in preparing the basic consolidation entry and because the inventory sold to Peerless by Special Foods last year has now been sold to an unaffiliated party, we must now increase the amounts in Peerless' Income from Special Foods and Investment in Special Foods accounts by Peerless' share of the deferral, $2,400 ($3,000 × 80%). We also increase the NCI in Net Income of Special Foods and NCI in Net Assets of Special Foods by the NCI share of the deferral, $600 ($3,000 × 20%).

FIGURE 6–6 December 31, 20X2, Consolidation Worksheet, Next Period following Intercompany Sale; Upstream Inventory Sale

	Peerless Products	Special Foods	Consolidation Entries DR	Consolidation Entries CR	Consolidated
Income Statement					
Sales	450,000	300,000			750,000
Less: COGS	(180,000)	(160,000)		3,000	(337,000)
Less: Depreciation Expense	(50,000)	(20,000)			(70,000)
Less: Other Expenses	(60,000)	(45,000)			(105,000)
Income from Special Foods	62,400		62,400		0
Consolidated Net Income	222,400	75,000	62,400	3,000	238,000
NCI in Net Income			15,600		(15,600)
Controlling Interest Net Income	**222,400**	**75,000**	78,000	3,000	**222,400**
Statement of Retained Earnings					
Beginning Balance	417,600	120,000	120,000		417,600
Net Income	**222,400**	**75,000**	78,000	3,000	222,400
Less: Dividends Declared	(60,000)	(40,000)		40,000	(60,000)
Ending Balance	**580,000**	**155,000**	198,000	43,000	**580,000**
Balance Sheet					
Cash	291,000	85,000			376,000
Accounts Receivable	150,000	80,000			230,000
Inventory	180,000	90,000			270,000
Investment in Special Foods	284,000		2,400	286,400	0
Land	175,000	40,000			215,000
Buildings & Equipment	800,000	600,000		300,000	1,100,000
Less: Accumulated Depreciation	(500,000)	(340,000)	300,000		(540,000)
Total Assets	**1,380,000**	**555,000**	302,400	586,400	**1,651,000**
Accounts Payable	100,000	100,000			200,000
Bonds Payable	200,000	100,000			300,000
Common Stock	500,000	200,000	200,000		500,000
Retained Earnings	**580,000**	**155,000**	198,000	43,000	580,000
NCI in NA of Special Foods			600	71,600	71,000
Total Liabilities & Equity	**1,380,000**	**555,000**	398,600	114,600	**1,651,000**

Calculations for Basic Consolidation Entry:

Book Value Calculations:

	NCI 20% +	Peerless 80% =	Common Stock +	Retained Earnings
Original Book Value	64,000	256,000	200,000	120,000
+ Net Income	15,000	60,000		75,000
− Dividends	(8,000)	(32,000)		(40,000)
Ending Book Value	71,000	284,000	200,000	155,000

Adjustment to Basic Consolidation Entry:

	NCI 20%	Peerless 80%
Net Income	15,000	60,000
+ Reverse GP deferral	600	2,400
Income to be eliminated	15,600	62,400
Ending Book Value	71,000	284,000
+ Reverse GP deferral	600	2,400
Adjusted Book Value	71,600	286,400

Advanced
StudyGuide
.com

Basic Consolidation Entry:

Common Stock	200,000	←— Common stock balance
Retained Earnings	120,000	←— Beginning balance in RE
Income from Special Foods	62,400	←— Peerless' % of NI with Adjustment
NCI in NI of Special Foods	15,600	←— NCI % of NI with Adjustment
Dividends Declared	40,000	←— 100% of sub's dividends declared
Investment in Special Foods	286,400	←— Net book value with Adjustment
NCI in NA of Special Foods	71,600	←— NCI % of BV with Adjustment

Optional Accumulated Depreciation Consolidation Entry:

Accumulated Depreciation	300,000	Accumulated depreciation at the
Buildings & Equipment	300,000	←— time of the acquisition netted against cost

FYI

Recall that Peerless deferred 80 percent of the unrealized gross profit on the upstream inventory sale last year on its books through an equity-method journal entry. Thus, the beginning balance in the Investment account ($253,600) is not equal to Peerless' 80 percent share of Special Foods' equity accounts in the beginning balance line of the Book Value Calculations box above ($256,000). This is why the basic consolidation entry to the Investment in Special Foods account is increased by the amount of last year's deferral.

Similar to the downstream example, the unrealized intercompany profit included in Peerless' beginning inventory was charged to Cost of Goods Sold when Peerless sold the inventory during 20X2. Thus, consolidated cost of goods sold will be overstated for 20X2 if it is reported in the consolidated income statement at the unadjusted total from the books of Peerless and Special Foods. The following consolidation entry corrects Cost of Goods Sold and splits this adjustment proportionately between Peerless' investment account and the NCI in Net Assets of Special Foods.

Reversal of 20X1 Gross Profit Deferral:

Investment in Special Foods	2,400	
NCI in NA of Special Foods	600	
Cost of Goods Sold		3,000

The following T-accounts illustrate the effects of all equity-method journal entries on Peerless' books as well as the worksheet consolidation entries.

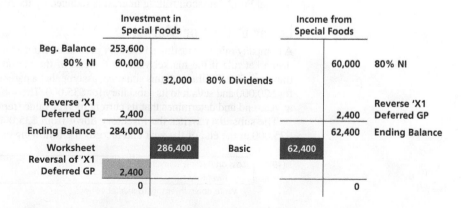

Consolidated Net Income—20X2

Consolidated net income for 20X2 is shown as $238,000 in the Figure 6–6 worksheet. This amount is computed and allocated as follows:

Peerless' separate income		$160,000
Special Foods' net income	$75,000	
Realization of deferred intercompany profit on upstream inventory sale	3,000	
Special Foods' realized net income		78,000
Consolidated net income, 20X2		$238,000
Income to noncontrolling interest ($78,000 × 0.20)		(15,600)
Income to controlling interest		$222,400

ADDITIONAL CONSIDERATIONS

LO 6-5

Understand and explain additional considerations associated with consolidation.

The frequency of intercompany inventory transfers and the varied circumstances under which they may occur raise a number of additional implementation issues. We discuss several of these briefly in this section.

Sale from One Subsidiary to Another

Inventory transfers often occur between companies that are under common control or ownership. When one subsidiary sells merchandise to another subsidiary, the consolidation entries are identical to those presented earlier for sales from a subsidiary to its parent. The full amount of any unrealized intercompany profit is eliminated, with the profit elimination allocated proportionately against the selling subsidiary's ownership interests.

As an illustration, assume that Peerless Products owns 90 percent of the outstanding stock of Super Industries in addition to its 80 percent interest in Special Foods. If Special Foods sells inventory at a $3,000 profit to Super Industries for $10,000 and Super Industries holds all of the inventory at the end of the period, the following consolidation entry is among those needed in the consolidation worksheet prepared at the end of the period:

Eliminate Intercompany Inventory Sales (still on hand):

Sales	10,000	
Cost of Goods Sold		7,000
Inventory		3,000

The two shareholder groups of the selling affiliate allocate proportionately the $3,000 deferral of unrealized intercompany profit. Consolidated net income is reduced by the full $3,000 unrealized intercompany profit. The income allocated to the controlling interest is reduced by Peerless' 80 percent share of the intercompany profit, or $2,400, and Special Foods' noncontrolling interest is reduced by its 20 percent share, or $600.

Lower of Cost or Market

A company might write down inventory purchased from an affiliate under the lower-of-cost-or-market rule if the market value at the end of the period is less than the intercompany transfer price. To illustrate this situation, assume that a parent company purchases inventory for $20,000 and sells it to its subsidiary for $35,000. The subsidiary still holds the inventory at year-end and determines that its current market value (replacement cost) is $25,000.

The subsidiary writes the inventory down from $35,000 to its lower market value of $25,000 at the end of the year and records the following entry:

(19)	Loss on Decline in Inventory Value	10,000	
	Inventory		10,000
	Write down inventory to market value.		

Although this entry revalues the inventory to $25,000 on the subsidiary's books, the appropriate valuation from a consolidated viewpoint is the $20,000 original cost of the inventory to the parent. Therefore, the following consolidation entry is needed in the worksheet:

Eliminate Intercompany Inventory Sales (still on hand):

Sales	35,000	
Cost of Goods Sold		20,000
Inventory		5,000
Loss on Decline in Inventory Value		10,000

The inventory loss recorded by the subsidiary must be eliminated because the $20,000 inventory valuation for consolidation purposes is below the $25,000 market value of the inventory.

Sales and Purchases before Affiliation

Sometimes companies that have sold inventory to one another later join together in a business combination. The consolidation treatment of profits on inventory transfers that occurred before the business combination depends on whether the companies were at that time independent and the sale transaction was the result of arm's-length bargaining. As a general rule, the effects of transactions that are not the result of arm's-length bargaining must be eliminated. However, the combining of two companies does not necessarily mean that their prior transactions with one another were not conducted at arm's length. The circumstances surrounding the prior transactions, such as the price and quantity of units transferred, would have to be examined.

In the absence of evidence to the contrary, companies that have joined together in a business combination are viewed as having been separate and independent prior to the combination. Thus, if the prior sales were the result of arm's-length bargaining, they are viewed as transactions between unrelated parties. Accordingly, no consolidation entry or adjustment is needed in preparing consolidated statements subsequent to the combination, even if an affiliate still holds the inventory.

SUMMARY OF KEY CONCEPTS

Consolidated financial statements are prepared for the consolidated entity as if it were a single company. Therefore, the effects of all transactions between companies within the entity must be eliminated in preparing consolidated financial statements.

Each time consolidated statements are prepared, all effects of intercompany transactions occurring during that period and the effects of unrealized profits from transactions in prior periods must be eliminated. For intercompany inventory transactions, the intercompany sale and cost of goods sold must be eliminated. In addition, the intercompany profit may not be recognized in consolidation until it is confirmed by resale of the inventory to an external party. Unrealized intercompany profits must be eliminated fully and are allocated proportionately against the stockholder groups of the selling affiliate. If inventory containing unrealized intercompany profits is sold during the period, consolidated cost of goods sold must be adjusted to reflect the actual cost to the consolidated entity of the inventory sold; if the inventory is still held at the end of the period, it must be adjusted to its actual cost to the consolidated entity.

KEY TERMS

downstream sale, *249*
intercompany transfers, *243*
intercorporate transfers, *243*
markup, *247*

markup on cost, *247*
markup on sales, *247*
modified equity method, *244*
transfer price, *247*

unrealized intercompany
   profit, *244*
upstream sale, *249*

Appendix 6A — Intercompany Inventory Transactions—Modified Equity Method and Cost Method

This appendix illustrates consolidation procedures under the modified (or sometimes called the basic) equity method and then the cost method. We use the upstream sale example presented earlier to illustrate these alternative methods. Assume that Special Foods purchases inventory for $7,000 in 20X1 and, in the same year, sells the inventory to Peerless Products for $10,000. Peerless Products sells the inventory to external parties in 20X2. Both companies use perpetual inventory control systems.

MODIFIED EQUITY METHOD

The journal entries on Peerless' books and the consolidation entries in the consolidation worksheet are the same under the modified equity method as under the fully adjusted method except for differences related to unrealized intercompany profits. When using the fully adjusted equity method, the parent reduces its income and the balance of the investment account for its share of unrealized intercompany profits that arise during the period. Subsequently, the parent increases its income and the carrying amount of the investment account when the intercompany profits are realized through transactions with external parties. These adjustments related to unrealized gross profit on intercompany sales are omitted under the modified equity method. As a result, the worksheet entry in the second year to recognize the deferred gross profit from the first year is slightly different. Instead of recording a debit to the investment account, this debit goes to beginning retained earnings.

Modified Equity-Method Entries—20X1

In 20X1, Peerless Products records the normal equity-method entries reflecting its share of Special Foods' income and dividends but omits the additional entry to reduce income and the investment account by the parent's share of the unrealized intercompany profit arising during the year:

(20)	Investment in Special Foods	40,000	
	Income from Special Foods		40,000
	Record Peerless' 80% share of Special Foods' 20X1 income.		

(21)	Cash	24,000	
	Investment in Special Foods		24,000
	Record Peerless' 80% share of Special Foods' 20X1 dividend.		

Consolidation Entries—20X1

Figure 6–7 illustrates the consolidation worksheet for 20X1 under the modified equity method. The consolidation entries are the same as we presented for the fully adjusted equity method with one minor exception. We do not reduce the amounts in Peerless' Income from Special Foods and Investment in Special Foods accounts by Peerless' share of the deferral, because no adjustment was made to the investment account or income from subsidiary account under the modified equity method, $2,400 ($3,000 \times 80\%$), but we do reduce the NCI in Net Income of Special Foods and NCI in Net Assets of Special Foods by the NCI share of the deferral, $600 ($3,000 \times 20\%$). Thus, the only adjustments to the book value calculations for the basic consolidation entry are made to the NCI amounts for the deferral of unrealized gross profit.

Calculations for Basic Consolidation Entry:

Book Value Calculations:				
	NCI 20% +	Peerless 80%	= Common Stock +	Retained Earnings
Original Book Value	60,000	240,000	200,000	100,000
+ Net Income	10,000	40,000		50,000
− Dividends	(6,000)	(24,000)		(30,000)
Ending Book Value	64,000	256,000	200,000	120,000

Adjustment to Basic Consolidation Entry:

	NCI	Peerless
Net Income	10,000	40,000
– Gross profit deferral	(600)	(2,400)
Income to be eliminated	9,400	37,600
Ending Book value	64,000	256,000
– Gross profit deferral	(600)	(2,400)
Ending Book Value	63,400	253,600

Basic Consolidation Entry:

Common Stock	200,000		← Common stock balance
Retained Earnings	100,000		← Beginning balance in RE
Income from Special Foods	40,000		← Peerless' % of NI
NCI in NI of Special Foods	9,400		← NCI share of NI with Adjustment
Dividends Declared		30,000	← 100% of sub's dividends declared
Investment in Special Foods		256,000	← Net book value
NCI in NA of Special Foods		63,400	← NCI share BV with Adjustment

FIGURE 6–7 December 31, 20X1, Modified Equity-Method Consolidation Worksheet, Period of Intercompany Sale; Upstream Inventory Sale

	Peerless Products	Special Foods	Consolidation Entries DR	Consolidation Entries CR	Consolidated
Income Statement					
Sales	400,000	200,000	10,000		590,000
Less: COGS	(170,000)	(115,000)		7,000	(278,000)
Less: Depreciation Expense	(50,000)	(20,000)			(70,000)
Less: Other Expenses	(40,000)	(15,000)			(55,000)
Income from Special Foods	40,000		40,000		0
Consolidated Net Income	180,000	50,000	50,000	7,000	187,000
NCI in Net Income			9,400		(9,400)
Controlling Interest Net Income	180,000	50,000	59,400	7,000	177,600
Statement of Retained Earnings					
Beginning Balance	300,000	100,000	100,000		300,000
Net Income	180,000	50,000	59,400	7,000	177,600
Less: Dividends Declared	(60,000)	(30,000)		30,000	(60,000)
Ending Balance	420,000	120,000	159,400	37,000	417,600
Balance Sheet					
Cash	264,000	75,000			339,000
Accounts Receivable	75,000	50,000			125,000
Inventory	100,000	75,000		3,000	172,000
Investment in Special Foods	256,000			256,000	0
Land	175,000	40,000			215,000
Buildings & Equipment	800,000	600,000		300,000	1,100,000
Less: Accumulated Depreciation	(450,000)	(320,000)	300,000		(470,000)
Total Assets	1,220,000	520,000	300,000	559,000	1,481,000
Accounts Payable	100,000	100,000			200,000
Bonds Payable	200,000	100,000			300,000
Common Stock	500,000	200,000	200,000		500,000
Retained Earnings	420,000	120,000	159,400	37,000	417,600
NCI in NA of Special Foods				63,400	63,400
Total Liabilities & Equity	1,220,000	520,000	359,400	100,400	1,481,000

Optional Accumulated Depreciation Consolidation Entry:

Accumulated Depreciation	300,000	
Buildings & Equipment		300,000

← Accumulated depreciation at the time of the acquisition netted against cost

Eliminate Inventory Purchases from Special Foods (still on hand):

Sales	10,000	
Cost of Goods Sold		7,000
Inventory		3,000

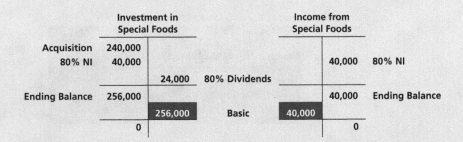

Modified Equity-Method Entries—20X2

The equity-method journal entries on Peerless' books are the same as illustrated previously, except that the adjustment for Peerless' share of the deferral is omitted:

(22)	Investment in Special Foods	60,000	
	Income from Special Foods		60,000

Record Peerless' 80% share of Special Foods' 20X2 income.

(23)	Cash	32,000	
	Investment in Special Foods		32,000

Record Peerless' 80% share of Special Foods' 20X2 dividend.

Consolidation Entries—20X2

Figure 6–8 illustrates the consolidation worksheet for 20X2 under the modified equity method. The first two consolidation entries are the same with one exception. Because the inventory sold to Peerless by Special Foods last year has now been sold to an unaffiliated party, we now increase the NCI in Net Income of Special Foods and NCI in Net Assets of Special Foods by the NCI share of the deferral, $600 ($3,000 × 20%). However, we do not increase the amounts in Peerless' Income from Special Foods and Investment in Special Foods accounts by Peerless' share of the deferral, $2,400 ($3,000 × 80%), because no adjustment was made to the investment account or income account under the modified equity method. Again, the only adjustments to the book value calculations for the basic consolidation entry are made to the NCI amounts for the reversal of last year's unrealized gross profit.

Calculations for Basic Consolidation Entry:

Book Value Calculations:					
	NCI 20% +	Peerless 80% =	Common Stock	+	Retained Earnings
Original Book Value	64,000	256,000	200,000		120,000
+ Net Income	15,000	60,000			75,000
− Dividends	(8,000)	(32,000)			(40,000)
Ending Book Value	71,000	284,000	200,000		155,000

Adjustment to Basic Consolidation Entry:

	NCI	Peerless
Net Income	15,000	60,000
+ Reverse GP deferral	(600)	(2,400)
Income to be eliminated	15,600	62,400
Ending Book Value	71,000	284,000
+ Reverse GP deferral	(600)	(2,400)
Ending Book Value	71,600	286,400

Basic Consolidation Entry:

Common Stock	200,000	← Common stock balance
Retained Earnings	120,000	← Beginning balance in RE
Income from Special Foods	60,000	← Peerless' % of NI
NCI in NI of Special Foods	15,600	← NCI % of NI with Adjustment
Dividends Declared	40,000	← 100% of sub's dividends declared
Investment in Special Foods	284,000	← Net book value
NCI in NA of Special Foods	71,600	← NCI % of BV with Adjustment

FIGURE 6–8   December 31, 20X2, Modified Equity-Method Consolidation Worksheet, Next Period Following Intercompany Sale; Upstream Inventory Sale

	Peerless Products	Special Foods	Consolidation Entries DR	Consolidation Entries CR	Consolidated
Income Statement					
Sales	450,000	300,000			750,000
Less: COGS	(180,000)	(160,000)		3,000	(337,000)
Less: Depreciation Expense	(50,000)	(20,000)			(70,000)
Less: Other Expenses	(60,000)	(45,000)			(105,000)
Income from Special Foods	60,000		60,000		0
Consolidated Net Income	220,000	75,000	60,000	3,000	238,000
NCI in Net Income			15,600		(15,600)
Controlling Interest Net Income	**220,000**	**75,000**	**75,600**	**3,000**	**222,400**
Statement of Retained Earnings					
Beginning Balance	420,000	120,000	120,000		417,600
			2,400		
Net Income	**220,000**	**75,000**	**75,600**	**3,000**	222,400
Less: Dividends Declared	(60,000)	(40,000)		40,000	(60,000)
Ending Balance	**580,000**	**155,000**	**198,000**	**43,000**	**580,000**
Balance Sheet					
Cash	291,000	85,000			376,000
Accounts Receivable	150,000	80,000			230,000
Inventory	180,000	90,000			270,000
Investment in Special Foods	284,000			284,000	0
Land	175,000	40,000			215,000
Buildings & Equipment	800,000	600,000		300,000	1,100,000
Less: Accumulated Depreciation	(500,000)	(340,000)	300,000		(540,000)
Total Assets	**1,380,000**	**555,000**	**300,000**	**584,000**	**1,651,000**
Accounts Payable	100,000	100,000			200,000
Bonds Payable	200,000	100,000			300,000
Common Stock	500,000	200,000	200,000		500,000
Retained Earnings	**580,000**	**155,000**	198,000	43,000	580,000
NCI in NA of Special Foods			600	71,600	71,000
Total Liabilities & Equity	**1,380,000**	**555,000**	**398,600**	**114,600**	**1,651,000**

Similar to 20X1, the unrealized intercompany profit included in Peerless' beginning inventory was charged to Cost of Goods Sold when Peerless sold the inventory during 20X2. Thus, consolidated cost of goods sold will be overstated for 20X2 if it is reported in the consolidated income statement at the unadjusted total from the books of Peerless and Special Foods. The following consolidation entry corrects Cost of Goods Sold and splits this adjustment proportionately between beginning Retained Earnings and the NCI in Net Assets of Special Foods.

Reversal of 20X1 Gross Profit Deferral:

Retained Earnings	2,400	
NCI in NA of Special Foods	600	
Cost of Goods Sold		3,000

Optional Accumulated Depreciation Consolidation Entry:

Accumulated Depreciation	300,000	
Buildings & Equipment		300,000

← Accumulated depreciation at the time of the acquisition netted against cost

COST METHOD

When using the cost method, the parent records dividends received from the subsidiary as income but makes no adjustments with respect to undistributed income of the subsidiary or unrealized intercompany profits. As an example of consolidation following an upstream intercompany sale of inventory when the parent accounts for its investment in the subsidiary using the cost method, assume the same facts as in previous illustrations dealing with an upstream sale.

Consolidation Entries—20X1

Figure 6–9 illustrates the consolidation worksheet for 20X1 under the cost method. The following consolidation entries are needed in the worksheet used to prepare consolidated financial statements for 20X1 using the cost method:

Investment Consolidation Entry:

Common Stock	200,000		← Common stock balance
Retained Earnings	100,000		← RE on acquisition date
Investment in Special Foods		240,000	← Original cost of investment
NCI in NA of Special Foods		60,000	← NCI share of acquisition date BV

Dividend Consolidation Entry:

Dividend Income	24,000		← Peerless' 80% share of dividends
NCI in NI of Special Foods	6,000		← NCI's 20% share of dividends declared
Dividends Declared		30,000	← 100% of Special Foods' dividends

The amount of undistributed net income assigned to the NCI is adjusted for the NCI's share of the gross profit deferral.

NCI in NI and NCI in NA of Special Foods:

	NCI 20%
Net Income	10,000
− Dividend	(6,000)
− Gross profit deferral	(600)
NCI in NI of Special Foods	**3,400**

Assign Special Foods' Undistributed Income to NCI:

NCI in NI of Special Foods	3,400	
NCI in NA of Special Foods		3,400

← NCI's 20% share of undistributed NI with Adjustment
← NCI's 20% share of undistributed NI with Adjustment

FIGURE 6–9 December 31, 20X1, Cost Method Consolidation Worksheet, Period of Intercompany Sale; Upstream Inventory Sale

	Peerless Products	Special Foods	Consolidation Entries DR	Consolidation Entries CR	Consolidated
Income Statement					
Sales	400,000	200,000	10,000		590,000
Less: COGS	(170,000)	(115,000)		7,000	(278,000)
Less: Depreciation Expense	(50,000)	(20,000)			(70,000)
Less: Other Expenses	(40,000)	(15,000)			(55,000)
Dividend Income	24,000		24,000		0
Consolidated Net Income	164,000	50,000	34,000	7,000	187,000
NCI in Net Income			6,000		(9,400)
			3,400		
Controlling Interest Net Income	**164,000**	**50,000**	43,400	7,000	**177,600**
Statement of Retained Earnings					
Beginning Balance	300,000	100,000	100,000		300,000
Net Income	**164,000**	**50,000**	43,400	7,000	177,600
Less: Dividends Declared	(60,000)	(30,000)		30,000	(60,000)
Ending Balance	**404,000**	**120,000**	143,400	37,000	**417,600**
Balance Sheet					
Cash	264,000	75,000			339,000
Accounts Receivable	75,000	50,000			125,000
Inventory	100,000	75,000		3,000	172,000
Investment in Special Foods	240,000			240,000	0
Land	175,000	40,000			215,000
Buildings & Equipment	800,000	600,000		300,000	1,100,000
Less: Accumulated Depreciation	(450,000)	(320,000)	300,000		(470,000)
Total Assets	**1,204,000**	**520,000**	300,000	543,000	**1,481,000**
Accounts Payable	100,000	100,000			200,000
Bonds Payable	200,000	100,000			300,000
Common Stock	500,000	200,000	200,000		500,000
Retained Earnings	**404,000**	**120,000**	143,400	37,000	417,600
NCI in NA of Special Foods				60,000	63,400
				3,400	
Total Liabilities & Equity	**1,204,000**	**520,000**	343,400	100,400	**1,481,000**

Optional Accumulated Depreciation Consolidation Entry:

Accumulated Depreciation	300,000	
Buildings & Equipment		300,000

← Accumulated depreciation at the time of the acquisition netted against cost

Eliminate Inventory Purchases from Special Foods (still on hand):

Sales	10,000	
Cost of Goods Sold		7,000
Inventory		3,000

The investment consolidation entry eliminates the original balances in Special Foods' equity section accounts as of the acquisition date. It simultaneously eliminates the Investment in Special Foods account and establishes the NCI in Net Assets account (for the NCI share of the Special Foods' net assets as of the acquisition date). The dividend consolidation entry eliminates Special Foods' declared dividends and Peerless' dividend income and establishes the NCI in net income with the NCI share of dividends declared. Although Peerless uses the cost method to account for its investment, the consolidated financial statements still must report the NCI shareholders' share of Special Foods' reported net income, and a portion of that income is allocated in the form of a dividend. Nevertheless, the NCI in net income should report the NCI share of reported income (adjusted for the deferred gross profit on upstream intercompany sales). Thus, the third consolidation entry assigns the NCI shareholders' 20 percent of the undistributed income (adjusted for 20 percent of the deferred gross profit) to both the NCI in Net Income of Special Foods and NCI in Net Assets of Special Foods. The optional accumulated depreciation and deferred gross profit consolidation entries are the same as those explained for the fully adjusted equity method.

Consolidation Entries—20X2

Figure 6–10 illustrates the consolidation worksheet for 20X2 under the cost method. Consolidation entries needed in the consolidation worksheet prepared at the end of 20X2 are as follows:

Investment Consolidation Entry:

Common Stock	200,000		← Common stock balance
Retained Earnings	100,000		← RE on acquisition date
Investment in Special Foods		240,000	← Original cost of investment
NCI in NA of Special Foods		60,000	← NCI share of acquisition date BV

Dividend Consolidation Entry:

Dividend Income	32,000		← Peerless' 80% share of dividends
NCI in NI of Special Foods	8,000		← NCI's 20% share of dividends declared
Dividends Declared		40,000	← 100% of Special Foods' dividends

NCI in NI and NCI in NA of Special Foods:

	NCI 20%
Net Income	15,000
− Dividend	(8,000)
+ Reverse GP deferral	(600)
NCI in NI of Special Foods	7,600
Undistributed from prior year	4,000
NCI in NA of Special Foods	11,600

Assign Special Foods' Undistributed Income to NCI:

NCI in NI of Special Foods	7,600		← NCI's 20% share of 20X2 undistributed NI with Adjustment
Retained Earnings*	4,000		← NCI's 20% share of undistributed 20X1 income from Special Foods
NCI in NA of Special Foods		11,600	← NCI's 20% share of cumulative undistributed NI with Adjustment

*Note that these entries adjust for the subsidiary's retained earnings balance. The subsidiary does not adjust for the deferral of unrealized gross profit because this adjustment is made on the consolidation worksheet, not in the records of the subsidiary.

Optional Accumulated Depreciation Consolidation Entry:

Accumulated Depreciation	300,000		← Accumulated depreciation at the time of the acquisition netted against cost
Buildings & Equipment		300,000	

The investment and dividend consolidation entries are the same as in 20X1. The third entry assigns cumulative undistributed net income from Special Foods. It assigns 20 percent of the 20X2 net income to the NCI shareholders and 20 percent of the 20X1 net income to retained earnings for the prior year. The accumulated depreciation consolidation entry is the same as in 20X1. However, the last entry is identical to the entry under the modified equity method.

Similar to 20X1, the unrealized intercompany profit included in Peerless' beginning inventory was charged to Cost of Goods Sold when Peerless sold the inventory during 20X2. Thus, consolidated cost of goods sold will be overstated for 20X2 if it is reported in the consolidated income statement at the unadjusted total from the books of Peerless and Special Foods. The following

FIGURE 6–10   December 31, 20X2, Cost Method Consolidation Worksheet, Next Period Following Intercompany Sale; Upstream Inventory Sale

	Peerless Products	Special Foods	Consolidation Entries DR	Consolidation Entries CR	Consolidated
Income Statement					
Sales	450,000	300,000			750,000
Less: COGS	(180,000)	(160,000)		3,000	(337,000)
Less: Depreciation Expense	(50,000)	(20,000)			(70,000)
Less: Other Expenses	(60,000)	(45,000)			(105,000)
Dividend Income	32,000		32,000		0
Consolidated Net Income	192,000	75,000	32,000	3,000	238,000
			8,000		
NCI in Net Income			7,600		(15,600)
Controlling Interest Net Income	**192,000**	**75,000**	**47,600**	**3,000**	**222,400**
Statement of Retained Earnings					
Beginning Balance	404,000	120,000	100,000		417,600
			4,000		
			2,400		
Net Income	**192,000**	**75,000**	47,600	3,000	222,400
Less: Dividends Declared	(60,000)	(40,000)		40,000	(60,000)
Ending Balance	**536,000**	**155,000**	**154,000**	**43,000**	**580,000**
Balance Sheet					
Cash	291,000	85,000			376,000
Accounts Receivable	150,000	80,000			230,000
Inventory	180,000	90,000			270,000
Investment in Special Foods	240,000			240,000	0
Land	175,000	40,000			215,000
Buildings & Equipment	800,000	600,000		300,000	1,100,000
Less: Accumulated Depreciation	(500,000)	(340,000)	300,000		(540,000)
Total Assets	**1,336,000**	**555,000**	**300,000**	**540,000**	**1,651,000**
Accounts Payable	100,000	100,000			200,000
Bonds Payable	200,000	100,000			300,000
Common Stock	500,000	200,000	200,000		500,000
Retained Earnings	**536,000**	**155,000**	154,000	43,000	580,000
NCI in NA of Special Foods			600	60,000	71,000
				11,600	
Total Liabilities & Equity	**1,336,000**	**555,000**	**354,600**	**114,600**	**1,651,000**

consolidation entry corrects Cost of Goods Sold and splits this adjustment proportionately between beginning Retained Earnings and the NCI in Net Assets of Special Foods.

Reversal of 20X1 Gross Profit Deferral:

Retained Earnings*	2,400	
NCI in NA of Special Foods	600	
Cost of Goods Sold		3,000

*Note that these entries adjust for the subsidiary's retained earnings balance. The subsidiary does not adjust for the deferral of unrealized gross profit because this adjustment is made in the consolidation worksheet, not in the records of the subsidiary.

QUESTIONS

LO 6-1   **Q6-1**   Why must inventory transfers to related companies be eliminated in preparing consolidated financial statements?

LO 6-2   **Q6-2**   Why is there a need for a consolidation entry when an intercompany inventory transfer is made at cost?

LO 6-3	**Q6-3**	Distinguish between an upstream sale of inventory and a downstream sale. Why is it important to know whether a sale is upstream or downstream?
LO 6-3	**Q6-4**	How do unrealized intercompany profits on a downstream sale of inventory made during the current period affect the computation of consolidated net income and income to the controlling interest?
LO 6-4	**Q6-5**	How do unrealized intercompany profits on an upstream sale of inventory made during the current period affect the computation of consolidated net income and income to the controlling interest?
LO 6-3, 6-4	**Q6-6**	Will the consolidation of unrealized intercompany profits on an upstream sale or on a downstream sale in the current period have a greater effect on income assigned to the noncontrolling interest? Why?
LO 6-3	**Q6-7**	What consolidation entry is needed when inventory is sold to an affiliate at a profit and is resold to an unaffiliated party before the end of the reporting period? (Assume both affiliates use perpetual inventory systems.)
LO 6-3	**Q6-8**	What consolidation entry is needed when inventory is sold to an affiliate at a profit and is not resold before the end of the period? (Assume both affiliates use perpetual inventory systems.)
LO 6-3, 6-4	**Q6-9**	How is the amount to be reported as cost of goods sold by the consolidated entity determined when there have been intercorporate sales during the period?
LO 6-3, 6-4	**Q6-10**	How is the amount to be reported as consolidated retained earnings determined when there have been intercorporate sales during the period?
LO 6-3, 6-4	**Q6-11**	How is the amount of consolidated retained earnings assigned to the noncontrolling interest affected by unrealized inventory profits at the end of the year?
LO 6-3, 6-4	**Q6-12**	How do unrealized intercompany inventory profits from a prior period affect the computation of consolidated net income when the inventory is resold in the current period? Is it important to know whether the sale was upstream or downstream? Why, or why not?
LO 6-3, 6-4	**Q6-13**	How will the elimination of unrealized intercompany inventory profits recorded on the parent's books affect consolidated retained earnings?
LO 6-3, 6-4	**Q6-14**	How will the elimination of unrealized intercompany inventory profits recorded on the subsidiary's books affect consolidated retained earnings?
LO 6-5	**Q6-15***	Is an inventory sale from one subsidiary to another treated in the same manner as an upstream sale or a downstream sale? Why?
LO 6-5	**Q6-16***	Par Company regularly purchases inventory from Eagle Company. Recently, Par Company purchased a majority of the voting shares of Eagle Company. How should Par Company treat inventory profits recorded by Eagle Company before the day of acquisition? Following the day of acquisition?

CASES

| LO 6-2 | **C6-1** | **Measuring Cost of Goods Sold** |

Judgment

Shortcut Charlie usually manages to develop some simple rule to handle even the most complex situations. In providing for the elimination of the effects of inventory transfers between the parent company and a subsidiary or between subsidiaries, Shortcut started with the following rules:

1. When the buyer continues to hold the inventory at the end of the period, credit Cost of Goods Sold for the amount recorded as cost of goods sold by the company that made the intercompany sale.

2. When the buyer resells the inventory before the end of the period, credit Cost of Goods Sold for the amount recorded as cost of goods sold by the company that made the intercompany sale plus the profit recorded by that company.

3. Debit Sales for the total amount credited in rule 1 or 2 above.

One of the new employees is seeking some assistance in understanding how the rules work and why.

Required

a. Explain why rule 1 is needed when consolidated statements are prepared.

b. Explain what is missing from rule 1, and prepare an alternative or additional statement for the elimination of unrealized profit when the purchasing affiliate does not resell to an unaffiliated company in the period in which it purchases inventory from an affiliate.

*Indicates that the item relates to "Additional Considerations."

c. Does rule 2 lead to the correct result? Explain your answer.

d. The rules do not provide assistance in determining how much profit either of the two companies recorded. Where should the employee look to determine the amount of profit referred to in rule 2?

LO 6-1, 6-2 **C6-2**

Research

Inventory Values and Intercompany Transfers

Water Products Corporation has been supplying high-quality bathroom fixtures to its customers for several decades and uses a LIFO inventory system. Rapid increases in the cost of fixtures have resulted in inventory values substantially below current replacement cost. To bring its inventory carrying costs up to more reasonable levels, Water Products sold its entire inventory to Plumbers Products Corporation and purchased an entirely new supply of inventory items from Growinkle Manufacturing. Water Products owns common stock of both Growinkle and Plumbers Products.

Water Products' external auditor immediately pointed out that under some ownership levels of these two companies, Water Products could accomplish its goal and under other levels it could not.

Required

Prepare a memo to Water Products' president describing the effects of intercompany transfers on the valuation of inventories and discuss the effects that different ownership levels of Growinkle and Plumbers Products would have on the success of Water Products' plan. Include citations to or quotations from the authoritative accounting literature to support your position.

LO 6-1 **C6-3**

Understanding

Unrealized Inventory Profits

Morrison Company owns 80 percent of Bloom Corporation's stock, acquired when Bloom's fair value as a whole was equal to its book value. The companies frequently engage in intercompany inventory transactions.

Required

Name the conditions that would make it possible for each of the following statements to be true. Treat each statement independently.

a. Income assigned to the noncontrolling interest in the consolidated income statement for 20X3 is higher than a pro rata share of Bloom's reported net income.

b. Income assigned to the noncontrolling interest in the consolidated income statement for 20X3 is higher than a pro rata share of Bloom's reported net income, but consolidated net income is reduced as a result of the elimination of intercompany inventory transfers.

c. Cost of goods sold reported in the income statement of Morrison is higher than consolidated cost of goods sold for 20X3.

d. Consolidated inventory is higher than the amounts reported by the separate companies.

LO 6-3, 6-4 **C6-4**

Analysis

Eliminating Inventory Transfers

Ready Building Products has six subsidiaries that sell building materials and supplies to the public and to the parent and other subsidiaries. Because of the invoicing system Ready uses, it is not possible to keep track of which items have been purchased from related companies and which have been bought from outside sources. Due to the nature of the products purchased, there are substantially different profit margins on different product groupings.

Required

a. If no effort is made to eliminate intercompany sales for the period or unrealized profits at year-end, what elements of the financial statements are likely to be misstated?

b. What type of control system would you recommend to Ready's controller to provide the information needed to make the required consolidation entries?

c. Would it matter if the buyer and seller used different inventory costing methods (FIFO, LIFO, or weighted average)? Explain.

d. Assume you believe that the adjustments for unrealized profit would be material. How would you go about determining what amounts must be eliminated at the end of the current period?

LO 6-1, 6-2 **C6-5**

Analysis

Intercompany Profits and Transfers of Inventory

Many companies transfer inventories from one affiliate to another. Often the companies have integrated operations in which one affiliate provides the raw materials, another manufactures finished products, another distributes the products, and perhaps another sells the products at retail. In other cases, various affiliates may be established for selling the company's products in different geographic locations, especially in different countries. Often tax considerations also have an effect on intercompany transfers.

Required

a. Are Xerox Corporation's intercompany transfers significant? How does Xerox treat intercompany transfers for consolidation purposes?

b. How does ExxonMobil Corporation price its products for intercompany transfers? Are these transfers significant? How does ExxonMobil treat intercompany profits for consolidation purposes?

c. What types of intercompany and intersegment sales does Ford Motor Company have? Are they significant? How are they treated for consolidation?

EXERCISES

LO 6-3, 6-4   **E6-1**   **Multiple-Choice Questions on Intercompany Inventory Transfers [AICPA Adapted]**
Select the correct answer for each of the following questions:

1. Perez Inc. owns 80 percent of Senior Inc. During 20X2, Perez sold goods with a 40 percent gross profit to Senior. Senior sold all of these goods in 20X2. For 20X2 consolidated financial statements, how should the summation of Perez and Senior income statement items be adjusted?

    a. Sales and Cost of Goods Sold should be reduced by the intercompany sales amount.

    b. Sales and Cost of Goods Sold should be reduced by 80 percent of the intercompany sales amount.

    c. Net income should be reduced by 80 percent of the gross profit on intercompany sales amount.

    d. No adjustment is necessary.

2. Parker Corporation owns 80 percent of Smith Inc.'s common stock. During 20X1, Parker sold inventory to Smith for $250,000 on the same terms as sales made to third parties. Smith sold all of the inventory purchased from Parker in 20X1. The following information pertains to Smith's and Parker's sales for 20X1:

	Parker	Smith
Sales	$1,000,000	$ 700,000
Cost of Sales	(400,000)	(350,000)
Gross Profit	$ 600,000	$ 350,000

    What amount should Parker report as cost of sales in its 20X1 consolidated income statement?

    a. $750,000.

    b. $680,000.

    c. $500,000.

    d. $430,000.

Note: Items 3 and 4 are based on the following information:
Nolan owns 100 percent of the capital stock of both Twill Corporation and Webb Corporation. Twill purchases merchandise inventory from Webb at 140 percent of Webb's cost. During 20X0, Webb sold merchandise that had cost it $40,000 to Twill. Twill sold all of this merchandise to unrelated customers for $81,200 during 20X0. In preparing combined financial statements for 20X0, Nolan's bookkeeper disregarded the common ownership of Twill and Webb.

3. What amount should be eliminated from cost of goods sold in the combined income statement for 20X0?

    a. $56,000.

    b. $40,000.

    c. $24,000.

    d. $16,000.

4. By what amount was unadjusted revenue overstated in the combined income statement for 20X0?

   a. $16,000.

   b. $40,000.

   c. $56,000.

   d. $81,200.

5. Clark Company had the following transactions with affiliated parties during 20X2:

   • Sales of $60,000 to Dean Inc., with $20,000 gross profit. Dean had $15,000 of this inventory on hand at year-end. Clark owns a 15 percent interest in Dean and does not exert significant influence.

   • Purchases of raw materials totaling $240,000 from Kent Corporation, a wholly owned subsidiary. Kent's gross profit on the sales was $48,000. Clark had $60,000 of this inventory remaining on December 31, 20X2.

   Before consolidation entries, Clark had consolidated current assets of $320,000. What amount should Clark report in its December 31, 20X2, consolidated balance sheet for current assets?

   a. $320,000.

   b. $317,000.

   c. $308,000.

   d. $303,000.

6. Selected data for two subsidiaries of Dunn Corporation taken from the December 31, 20X8, preclosing trial balances are as follows:

	Banks Co. (Debits)	Lamm Co. (Credits)
Shipments to Banks		$150,000
Shipments from Lamm	$ 200,000	
Intercompany Inventory Profit on Total Shipments		50,000

Additional data relating to the December 31, 20X8, inventory are as follows:

Inventory acquired by Banks from outside parties	$175,000
Inventory acquired by Lamm from outside parties	250,000
Inventory acquired by Banks from Lamm	60,000

At December 31, 20X8, the inventory reported on the combined balance sheet of the two subsidiaries should be:

   a. $425,000.

   b. $435,000.

   c. $470,000.

   d. $485,000.

LO 6-3

E6-2   Multiple-Choice Questions on the Effects of Inventory Transfers [AICPA Adapted]
Select the correct answer for each of the following questions.

1. During 20X3, Park Corporation recorded sales of inventory for $500,000 to Small Company, its wholly owned subsidiary, on the same terms as sales made to third parties. At December 31, 20X3, Small held one-fifth of these goods in its inventory. The following information pertains to Park's and Small's sales for 20X3:

	Park	Small
Sales	$2,000,000	$1,400,000
Cost of Sales	(800,000)	(700,000)
Gross Profit	$1,200,000	$ 700,000

In its 20X3 consolidated income statement, what amount should Park report as cost of sales?

a. $1,000,000.

b. $1,060,000.

c. $1,260,000.

d. $1,500,000.

Note: Items 2 through 6 are based on the following information:
Selected information from the separate and consolidated balance sheets and income statements of Power Inc. and its subsidiary, Spin Company, as of December 31, 20X8, and for the year then ended is as follows:

	Power	Spin	Consolidated
Balance Sheet Accounts			
Accounts Receivable	$ 26,000	$ 19,000	$ 39,000
Inventory	30,000	25,000	52,000
Investment in Spin	53,000		
Patents			20,000
NCI in NA of Spin			14,000
Stockholders' Equity	154,000	50,000	154,000
Income Statement Accounts			
Revenues	$200,000	$140,000	$308,000
Cost of Goods Sold	150,000	110,000	231,000
Gross Profit	$ 50,000	$ 30,000	$ 77,000
Income from Spin	7,400		
Amortization of Patents			2,000
Net Income	$ 33,000	$ 15,000	$ 40,000

Additional Information

During 20X8, Power sold goods to Spin at the same markup that Power uses for all sales. At December 31, 20X8, Spin had not paid for all of these goods and still held 37.5 percent of them in inventory.

Power acquired its interest in Spin on January 2, 20X5, when the book values and fair values of the assets and liabilities of Spin were equal, except for patents, which had a fair value of $28,000. The fair value of the noncontrolling interest was equal to a proportionate share of fair value of Spin's net assets.

2. What was the amount of intercompany sales from Power to Spin during 20X8?

a. $3,000.

b. $6,000.

c. $29,000.

d. $32,000.

3. At December 31, 20X8, what was the amount of Spin's payable to Power for intercompany sales?

a. $3,000.

b. $6,000.

c. $29,000.

d. $32,000.

4. In Power's consolidated balance sheet, what was the carrying amount of the inventory that Spin purchased from Power?

a. $3,000.

b. $6,000.

c. $9,000.

d. $12,000.

5. What is the percent of noncontrolling interest ownership of Spin?

a. 10 percent.

b. 20 percent.

c. 25 percent.

d. 45 percent.

6. Over how many years has Power chosen to amortize patents?

    a. 10 years.

    b. 14 years.

    c. 23 years.

    d. 40 years.

LO 6-3

E6-3 Multiple-Choice Questions—Consolidated Income Statement

Select the correct answer for each of the following questions.

Blue Company purchased 60 percent ownership of Kelly Corporation in 20X1. On May 10, 20X2, Kelly purchased inventory from Blue for $60,000. Kelly sold all of the inventory to an unaffiliated company for $86,000 on November 10, 20X2. Blue produced the inventory sold to Kelly for $47,000. The companies had no other transactions during 20X2.

1. What amount of sales will be reported in the 20X2 consolidated income statement?

    a. $51,600.

    b. $60,000.

    c. $86,000.

    d. $146,000.

2. What amount of cost of goods sold will be reported in the 20X2 consolidated income statement?

    a. $36,000.

    b. $47,000.

    c. $60,000.

    d. $107,000.

3. What amount of consolidated net income will be assigned to the controlling shareholders for 20X2?

    a. $13,000.

    b. $26,000.

    c. $28,600.

    d. $39,000.

LO 6-4

E6-4 Multiple-Choice Questions—Consolidated Balances

Select the correct answer for each of the following questions.

Lorn Corporation purchased inventory from Dresser Corporation for $120,000 on September 20, 20X1, and resold 80 percent of the inventory to unaffiliated companies prior to December 31, 20X1, for $140,000. Dresser produced the inventory sold to Lorn for $75,000. Lorn owns 70 percent of Dresser's voting common stock. The companies had no other transactions during 20X1.

1. What amount of sales will be reported in the 20X1 consolidated income statement?

    a. $98,000.

    b. $120,000.

    c. $140,000.

    d. $260,000.

2. What amount of cost of goods sold will be reported in the 20X1 consolidated income statement?

    a. $60,000.

    b. $75,000.

    c. $96,000.

    d. $120,000.

    e. $171,000.

3. What amount of consolidated net income will be assigned to the controlling interest for 20X1?

    a. $20,000.

    b. $30,800.

    c. $44,000.

    d. $45,000.

 e. $69,200.

 f. $80,000.

4. What inventory balance will be reported by the consolidated entity on December 31, 20X1?

 a. $15,000.

 b. $16,800.

 c. $24,000.

 d. $39,000.

LO 6-3

E6-5 Multiple-Choice Questions—Consolidated Income Statement

Select the correct answer for each of the following questions.

Amber Corporation holds 80 percent of the stock of Movie Productions Inc. During 20X4, Amber purchased an inventory of snack bar items for $40,000 and resold $30,000 to Movie Productions for $48,000. Movie Productions Inc. reported sales of $67,000 in 20X4 and had inventory of $16,000 on December 31, 20X4. The companies held no beginning inventory and had no other transactions in 20X4.

1. What amount of cost of goods sold will be reported in the 20X4 consolidated income statement?

 a. $20,000.

 b. $30,000.

 c. $32,000.

 d. $52,000.

 e. $62,000.

2. What amount of net income will be reported in the 20X4 consolidated income statement?

 a. $12,000.

 b. $18,000.

 c. $40,000.

 d. $47,000.

 e. $53,000.

3. What amount of income will be assigned to the noncontrolling interest in the 20X4 consolidated income statement?

 a. $7,000.

 b. $8,000.

 c. $9,400.

 d. $10,200.

 e. $13,400.

LO 6-3

E6-6 Realized Profit on Intercompany Sale

Nordway Corporation acquired 90 percent of Olman Company's voting shares of stock in 20X1. During 20X4, Nordway purchased 40,000 Playday doghouses for $24 each and sold 25,000 of them to Olman for $30 each. Olman sold all of the doghouses to retail establishments prior to December 31, 20X4, for $45 each. Both companies use perpetual inventory systems.

Required

a. Give the journal entries Nordway recorded for the purchase of inventory and resale to Olman Company in 20X4.

b. Give the journal entries Olman recorded for the purchase of inventory and resale to retail establishments in 20X4.

c. Give the worksheet consolidation entry(ies) needed in preparing consolidated financial statements for 20X4 to remove all effects of the intercompany sale.

LO 6-3

E6-7 Sale of Inventory to Subsidiary

Nordway Corporation acquired 90 percent of Olman Company's voting shares of stock in 20X1. During 20X4, Nordway purchased 40,000 Playday doghouses for $24 each and sold 25,000 of them to Olman for $30 each. Olman sold 18,000 of the doghouses to retail establishments prior to December 31, 20X4, for $45 each. Both companies use perpetual inventory systems.

Required

a. Give all journal entries Nordway recorded for the purchase of inventory and resale to Olman Company in 20X4.

b. Give the journal entries Olman recorded for the purchase of inventory and resale to retail establishments in 20X4.

c. Give the worksheet consolidation entry(ies) needed in preparing consolidated financial statements for 20X4 to remove the effects of the intercompany sale.

LO 6-3

Advanced
StudyGuide
.com

E6-8 Inventory Transfer between Parent and Subsidiary

Karlow Corporation owns 60 percent of Draw Company's voting shares. During 20X3, Karlow produced 25,000 computer desks at a cost of $82 each and sold 10,000 of them to Draw for $94 each. Draw sold 7,000 of the desks to unaffiliated companies for $130 each prior to December 31, 20X3, and sold the remainder in early 20X4 for $140 each. Both companies use perpetual inventory systems.

Required

a. What amounts of cost of goods sold did Karlow and Draw record in 20X3?

b. What amount of cost of goods sold must be reported in the consolidated income statement for 20X3?

c. Give the worksheet consolidation entry or entries needed in preparing consolidated financial statements at December 31, 20X3, relating to the intercorporate sale of inventory.

d. Give the worksheet consolidation entry or entries needed in preparing consolidated financial statements at December 31, 20X4, relating to the intercorporate sale of inventory.

e. Give the worksheet consolidation entry or entries needed in preparing consolidated financial statements at December 31, 20X4, relating to the intercorporate sale of inventory if the sales were upstream. Assume that Draw produced the computer desks at a cost of $82 each and sold 10,000 desks to Karlow for $94 each in 20X3, with Karlow selling 7,000 desks to unaffiliated companies in 20X3 and the remaining 3,000 in 20X4.

LO 6-4

E6-9 Income Statement Effects of Unrealized Profit

Holiday Bakery owns 60 percent of Farmco Products Company's stock. During 20X8, Farmco produced 100,000 bags of flour, which it sold to Holiday Bakery for $900,000. On December 31, 20X8, Holiday had 20,000 bags of flour purchased from Farmco Products on hand. Farmco prices its sales at cost plus 50 percent of cost for profit. Holiday, which purchased all its flour from Farmco in 20X8, had no inventory on hand on January 1, 20X8.

Holiday Bakery reported income from its baking operations of $400,000, and Farmco Products reported net income of $150,000 for 20X8.

Required

a. Compute the amount reported as cost of goods sold in the 20X8 consolidated income statement.

b. Give the worksheet consolidation entry or entries required to remove the effects of the intercompany sale in preparing consolidated statements at the end of 20X8.

c. Compute the amounts reported as consolidated net income and income assigned to the controlling interest in the 20X8 consolidated income statement.

LO 6-4

E6-10 Prior-Period Unrealized Inventory Profit

Holiday Bakery owns 60 percent of Farmco Products Company's stock. On January 1, 20X9, inventory reported by Holiday included 20,000 bags of flour purchased from Farmco at $9 per bag. By December 31, 20X9, all the beginning inventory purchased from Farmco Products had been baked into products and sold to customers by Holiday. There were no transactions between Holiday and Farmco during 20X9.

Both Holiday Bakery and Farmco Products price their sales at cost plus 50 percent markup for profit. Holiday reported income from its baking operations of $300,000, and Farmco reported net income of $250,000 for 20X9.

Required

a. Compute the amount reported as cost of goods sold in the 20X9 consolidated income statement for the flour purchased from Farmco in 20X8.

b. Give the consolidation entry or entries required to remove the effects of the unrealized profit in beginning inventory in preparing the consolidation worksheet as of December 31, 20X9.

c. Compute the amounts reported as consolidated net income and income assigned to the controlling interest in the 20X9 consolidated income statement.

LO 6-3, 6-4 **E6-11**

Advanced
StudyGuide
.com

Computation of Consolidated Income Statement Data

Prem Company acquired 60 percent ownership of Cooper Company's voting shares on January 1, 20X2. During 20X5, Prem purchased inventory for $20,000 and sold the full amount to Cooper Company for $30,000. On December 31, 20X5, Cooper's ending inventory included $6,000 of items purchased from Prem. Also in 20X5, Cooper purchased inventory for $50,000 and sold the units to Prem for $80,000. Prem included $20,000 of its purchase from Cooper in ending inventory on December 31, 20X5.

Summary income statement data for the two companies revealed the following:

	Prem Company	Cooper Company
Sales	$ 400,000	$ 200,000
Income from Cooper	20,500	
	$ 420,500	$ 200,000
Cost of Goods Sold	$ 250,000	$ 120,000
Other Expenses	70,000	35,000
Total Expenses	$(320,000)	$(155,000)
Net Income	$ 100,500	$ 45,000

Required

a. Compute the amount to be reported as sales in the 20X5 consolidated income statement.

b. Compute the amount to be reported as cost of goods sold in the 20X5 consolidated income statement.

c. What amount of income will be assigned to the noncontrolling shareholders in the 20X5 consolidated income statement?

d. What amount of income will be assigned to the controlling interest in the 20X5 consolidated income statement?

LO 6-3, 6-4 **E6-12**

Intercompany Sales

Hollow Corporation acquired 70 percent of Surg Corporation's voting stock on May 18, 20X1. The companies reported the following data with respect to intercompany sales in 20X4 and 20X5:

Year	Purchased by	Purchase Price	Sold to	Sale Price	Unsold at End of Year	Year Sold to Unaffiliated Co.
20X4	Surg Corp.	$120,000	Hollow Corp.	$180,000	$ 45,000	20X5
20X5	Surg Corp.	90,000	Hollow Corp.	135,000	30,000	20X6
20X5	Hollow Corp.	140,000	Surg Corp.	280,000	110,000	20X6

Hollow reported operating income (excluding income from its investment in Surg) of $160,000 and $220,000 in 20X4 and 20X5, respectively. Surg reported net income of $90,000 and $85,000 in 20X4 and 20X5, respectively.

Required

a. Compute consolidated net income for 20X4.

b. Compute the inventory balance reported in the consolidated balance sheet at December 31, 20X5, for the transactions shown.

c. Compute the amount included in consolidated cost of goods sold for 20X5 relating to the transactions shown.

d. Compute the amount of income assigned to the controlling interest in the 20X5 consolidated income statement.

LO 6-3, 6-4 | E6-13 | Consolidated Balance Sheet Worksheet

The December 31, 20X8, balance sheets for Doorst Corporation and its 70 percent-owned subsidiary Hingle Company contained the following summarized amounts:

DOORST CORPORATION AND HINGLE COMPANY
Balance Sheets
December 31, 20X8

	Doorst Corporation	Hingle Company
Cash & Receivables	$ 98,000	$ 40,000
Inventory	150,000	100,000
Buildings & Equipment (net)	310,000	280,000
Investment in Hingle Company Stock	242,000	
Total Assets	$800,000	$420,000
Accounts Payable	$ 70,000	$ 20,000
Common Stock	200,000	150,000
Retained Earnings	530,000	250,000
Total Liabilities & Equity	$800,000	$420,000

Doorst acquired the shares of Hingle Company on January 1, 20X7. On December 31, 20X8, assume Doorst sold inventory to Hingle during 20X8 for $100,000 and Hingle sold inventory to Doorst for $300,000. Doorst's balance sheet contains inventory items purchased from Hingle for $95,000. The items cost Hingle $55,000 to produce. In addition, Hingle's inventory contains goods it purchased from Doorst for $25,000 that Doorst had produced for $15,000. Assume Hingle reported net income of $70,000 and dividends of $14,000.

Required

a. Prepare all consolidation entries needed to complete a consolidated balance sheet worksheet as of December 31, 20X8.

b. Prepare a consolidated balance sheet worksheet as of December 31, 20X8.

LO 6-5 | E6-14* | Multiple Transfers between Affiliates

Klon Corporation owns 70 percent of Brant Company's stock and 60 percent of Torkel Company's stock. During 20X8, Klon sold inventory purchased in 20X7 for $100,000 to Brant for $150,000. Brant then sold the inventory at its cost of $150,000 to Torkel. Prior to December 31, 20X8, Torkel sold $90,000 of inventory to a nonaffiliate for $120,000 and held $60,000 in inventory at December 31, 20X8.

Required

a. Give the journal entries recorded by Klon, Brant, and Torkel during 20X8 relating to the intercorporate sale and resale of inventory.

b. What amount should be reported in the 20X8 consolidated income statement as cost of goods sold?

c. What amount should be reported in the December 31, 20X8, consolidated balance sheet as inventory?

d. Give the consolidation entry needed at December 31, 20X8, to remove the effects of the inventory transfers.

LO 6-4 | E6-15 | Inventory Sales

Herb Corporation holds 60 percent ownership of Spice Company. Each year, Spice purchases large quantities of a gnarl root used in producing health drinks. Spice purchased $150,000 of roots in 20X7 and sold $40,000 of these purchases to Herb for $60,000. By the end of 20X7, Herb had resold all but $15,000 of its purchase from Spice. Herb generated $90,000 on the sale of roots to various health stores during the year.

Required

a. Give the journal entries recorded by Herb and Spice during 20X7 relating to the initial purchase, intercorporate sale, and resale of gnarl roots.

b. Give the worksheet consolidation entries needed as of December 31, 20X7, to remove all effects of the intercompany transfer in preparing the 20X7 consolidated financial statements.

LO 6-4   **E6-16**   **Prior-Period Inventory Profits**

Home Products Corporation, which sells a broad line of home detergent products, owns 75 percent of the stock of Level Brothers Soap Company. During 20X8, Level Brothers sold soap products to Home Products for $180,000, which it had produced for $120,000. Home Products sold $150,000 of its purchase from Level Brothers in 20X8 and the remainder in 20X9. In addition, Home Products purchased $240,000 of inventory from Level Brothers in 20X9 and resold $90,000 of the items before year-end. Level Brothers' cost to produce the items sold to Home Products in 20X9 was $160,000.

Required

a. Give all worksheet consolidation entries needed for December 31, 20X9, to remove the effects of the intercompany inventory transfers in 20X8 and 20X9.

b. Compute the amount of income assigned to noncontrolling shareholders in the 20X8 and 20X9 consolidated income statements if Level Brothers reported net income of $350,000 for 20X8 and $420,000 for 20X9.

PROBLEMS

LO 6-4   **P6-17**   **Consolidated Income Statement Data**

Sweeny Corporation owns 60 percent of Bitner Company's shares. Partial 20X2 financial data for the companies and consolidated entity were as follows:

	Sweeny Corporation	Bitner Company	Consolidated Totals
Sales	$550,000	$450,000	$820,000
Cost of Goods Sold	310,000	300,000	420,000
Inventory, Dec. 31	180,000	210,000	375,000

On January 1, 20X2, Sweeny's inventory contained items purchased from Bitner for $75,000. The cost of the units to Bitner was $50,000. All intercorporate sales during 20X2 were made by Bitner to Sweeny.

Required

a. What amount of intercorporate sales occurred in 20X2?

b. How much unrealized intercompany profit existed on January 1, 20X2? On December 31, 20X2?

c. Give the worksheet consolidation entries relating to inventory and cost of goods sold needed to prepare consolidated financial statements for 20X2.

d. If Bitner reports net income of $90,000 for 20X2, what amount of income is assigned to the noncontrolling interest in the 20X2 consolidated income statement?

LO 6-4   **P6-18**   **Unrealized Profit on Upstream Sales**

Carroll Company sells all its output at 25 percent above cost. Pacific Corporation purchases all its inventory from Carroll. Selected information on the operations of the companies over the past three years is as follows:

	Carroll Company		Pacific Corporation	
Year	Sales to Pacific Corp.	Net Income	Inventory, Dec. 31	Operating Income
20X2	$200,000	$100,000	$ 70,000	$150,000
20X3	175,000	90,000	105,000	240,000
20X4	225,000	160,000	120,000	300,000

Pacific acquired 60 percent of the ownership of Carroll on January 1, 20X1, at underlying book value.

Required

Compute consolidated net income and income assigned to the controlling interest for 20X2, 20X3, and 20X4.

LO 6-3, 6-4   **P6-19**   ### Net Income of Consolidated Entity

Master Corporation acquired 70 percent of Crown Corporation's voting stock on January 1, 20X2, for $416,500. The fair value of the noncontrolling interest was $178,500 at the date of acquisition. Crown reported common stock outstanding of $200,000 and retained earnings of $350,000. The differential is assigned to buildings with an expected life of 15 years at the date of acquisition.

On December 31, 20X4, Master had $25,000 of unrealized profits on its books from inventory sales to Crown, and Crown had $40,000 of unrealized profit on its books from inventory sales to Master. All inventory held at December 31, 20X4, was sold during 20X5.

On December 31, 20X5, Master had $14,000 of unrealized profit on its books from inventory sales to Crown, and Crown had unrealized profit on its books of $55,000 from inventory sales to Master.

Master reported income from its separate operations (excluding income on its investment in Crown and amortization of purchase differential) of $118,000 in 20X5, and Crown reported net income of $65,000.

Required

Compute consolidated net income and income assigned to the controlling interest in the 20X5 consolidated income statement.

LO 6-4   **P6-20**   ### Correction of Consolidation Entries

In preparing the consolidation worksheet for Bolger Corporation and its 60 percent–owned subsidiary, Feldman Company, the following consolidation entries were proposed by Bolger's bookkeeper:

Cash	80,000	
Accounts Payable		80,000

To eliminate the unpaid balance for intercorporate inventory sales in 20X5.

Cost of Goods Sold	12,000	
Income from Subsidiary		12,000

To eliminate unrealized inventory profits at December 31, 20X5.

Income from Subsidiary	140,000	
Sales		140,000

To eliminate intercompany sales for 20X5.

Bolger's bookkeeper recently graduated from Oddball University, and although the dollar amounts recorded are correct, he had some confusion in determining which accounts needed adjustment. All intercorporate sales in 20X5 were from Feldman to Bolger, and Feldman sells inventory at cost plus 40 percent of cost. Bolger uses the fully adjusted equity method in accounting for its ownership in Feldman.

Required

a. What percentage of the intercompany inventory transfer was resold prior to the end of 20X5?

b. Give the appropriate consolidation entries needed at December 31, 20X5, to prepare consolidated financial statements.

LO 6-3, 6-4   **P6-21**   ### Incomplete Data

Lever Corporation acquired 75 percent of the ownership of Tropic Company on January 1, 20X1. The fair value of the noncontrolling interest at acquisition was equal to its proportionate share of the fair value of the net assets of Tropic. The full amount of the differential at acquisition was attributable to buildings and equipment, which had a remaining useful life of eight years.

Financial statement data for the two companies and the consolidated entity at December 31, 20X6, are as follows:

LEVER CORPORATION AND TROPIC COMPANY
Balance Sheet Data
December 31, 20X6

Item	Lever Corporation	Tropic Company	Consolidated Entity
Cash	$ 67,000	$ 45,000	$112,000
Accounts Receivable	?	55,000	145,000
Inventory	125,000	90,000	211,000
Buildings & Equipment	400,000	240,000	680,000
Less: Accumulated Depreciation	(180,000)	(110,000)	(?)
Investment in Tropic Company	?		
Total Assets	$?	$320,000	$?
Accounts Payable	$ 86,000	$ 20,000	$ 89,000
Other Payables	?	8,000	?
Notes Payable	250,000	120,000	370,000
Common Stock	120,000	60,000	120,000
Retained Earnings	172,500	112,000	172,500
Noncontrolling Interest			44,500
Total Liabilities & Equity	$?	$320,000	$?

LEVER CORPORATION AND TROPIC COMPANY
Income Statement Data
For the Year Ended December 31, 20X6

Item	Lever Corporation	Tropic Company	Consolidated Entity
Sales	$420,000	$260,000	$650,000
Income from Subsidiary	32,250		
Total Income	$452,250	$260,000	$650,000
Cost of Goods Sold	$310,000	$170,000	$445,000
Depreciation Expense	20,000	25,000	50,000
Interest Expense	25,000	9,500	34,500
Other Expenses	22,000	15,500	37,500
Total Expenses	($377,000)	($220,000)	($567,000)
Consolidated Net Income			$ 83,000
Income to Noncontrolling Interest			(7,750)
Controlling Interest in Net Income	$ 75,250	$ 40,000	$ 75,250

All unrealized profit on intercompany inventory sales on January 1, 20X6, were eliminated on Lever's books. All unrealized inventory profits at December 31, 20X6, were eliminated on Tropic's books. Assume Lever uses the fully adjusted equity method and that Lever does not make the optional depreciation consolidation worksheet entry.

Required

a. For the buildings and equipment held by Tropic when Lever acquired it and still on hand on December 31, 20X6, by what amount had buildings and equipment increased in value from their acquisition to the date of combination with Lever?

b. What amount should be reported as accumulated depreciation for the consolidated entity at December 31, 20X6 (assuming Lever does not make the optional accumulated depreciation consolidation entry)?

c. If Tropic reported capital stock outstanding of $60,000 and retained earnings of $30,000 on January 1, 20X1, what amount did Lever pay to acquire its ownership of Tropic?

d. What balance does Lever report as its investment in Tropic at December 31, 20X6?

e. What amount of intercorporate sales of inventory occurred in 20X6?

f. What amount of unrealized inventory profit exists at December 31, 20X6?

g. Give the consolidation entry used in eliminating intercompany inventory sales during 20X6.

h. What was the amount of unrealized inventory profit at January 1, 20X6?

i. What balance in accounts receivable did Lever report at December 31, 20X6?

Advanced
StudyGuide
.com

LO 6-4   **P6-22**   **Eliminations for Upstream Sales**

Clean Air Products owns 80 percent of the stock of Superior Filter Company, which it acquired at underlying book value on August 30, 20X6. At that date, the fair value of the noncontrolling interest was equal to 20 percent of the book value of Superior Filter. Summarized trial balance data for the two companies as of December 31, 20X8, are as follows:

	Clean Air Products		Superior Filter Company	
	Debit	Credit	Debit	Credit
Cash and Accounts Receivable	$ 145,000		$ 90,000	
Inventory	220,000		110,000	
Buildings & Equipment (net)	270,000		180,000	
Investment in Superior Filter Stock	268,000			
Cost of Goods Sold	175,000		140,000	
Depreciation Expense	30,000		20,000	
Current Liabilities		$ 150,000		$ 30,000
Common Stock		200,000		90,000
Retained Earnings		472,000		220,000
Sales		250,000		200,000
Income from Subsidiary		36,000		
Total	$1,108,000	$1,108,000	$540,000	$540,000

On January 1, 20X8, Clean Air's inventory contained filters purchased for $60,000 from Superior Filter, which had produced the filters for $40,000. In 20X8, Superior Filter spent $100,000 to produce additional filters, which it sold to Clean Air for $150,000. By December 31, 20X8, Clean Air had sold all filters that had been on hand January 1, 20X8, but continued to hold in inventory $45,000 of the 20X8 purchase from Superior Filter.

Required

a. Prepare all consolidation entries needed to complete a consolidation worksheet for 20X8.

b. Compute consolidated net income and income assigned to the controlling interest in the 20X8 consolidated income statement.

c. Compute the balance assigned to the noncontrolling interest in the consolidated balance sheet as of December 31, 20X8.

LO 6-3, 6-4   **P6-23**   **Multiple Inventory Transfers**

Ajax Corporation purchased at book value 70 percent of Beta Corporation's ownership and 90 percent of Cole Corporation's ownership in 20X5. At the dates the ownership was acquired, the fair value of the noncontrolling interest was equal to a proportionate share of book value. There are frequent intercompany transfers among the companies. Activity relevant to 20X8 follows:

Year	Producer	Production Cost	Buyer	Transfer Price	Unsold at End of Year	Year Sold
20X7	Beta Corporation	$24,000	Ajax Corporation	$30,000	$10,000	20X8
20X7	Cole Corporation	60,000	Beta Corporation	72,000	18,000	20X8
20X8	Ajax Corporation	15,000	Beta Corporation	35,000	7,000	20X9
20X8	Beta Corporation	63,000	Cole Corporation	72,000	12,000	20X9
20X8	Cole Corporation	27,000	Ajax Corporation	45,000	15,000	20X9

For the year ended December 31, 20X8, Ajax reported $80,000 of income from its separate operations (excluding income from intercorporate investments), Beta reported net income of $37,500, and Cole reported net income of $20,000.

Required

a. Compute the amount to be reported as consolidated net income for 20X8.

b. Compute the amount to be reported as inventory in the December 31, 20X8, consolidated balance sheet for the preceding items.

c. Compute the amount to be reported as income assigned to noncontrolling shareholders in the 20X8 consolidated income statement.

LO 6-3, 6-4   **P6-24**   ## Consolidation with Inventory Transfers and Other Comprehensive Income

On January 1, 20X1, Priority Corporation purchased 90 percent of Tall Corporation's common stock at underlying book value. At that date, the fair value of the noncontrolling interest was equal to 10 percent of Tall Corporation's book value. Priority uses the equity method in accounting for its investment in Tall. The stockholders' equity section of Tall at January 1, 20X5, contained the following balances:

Common Stock ($5 par)	$ 400,000
Additional Paid-in Capital	200,000
Retained Earnings	790,000
Accumulated Other Comprehensive Income	10,000
Total	$1,400,000

During 20X4, Tall sold goods costing $30,000 to Priority for $45,000, and Priority resold 60 percent of them prior to year-end. It sold the remainder in 20X5. Also in 20X4, Priority sold inventory items costing $90,000 to Tall for $108,000. Tall resold $60,000 of its purchases in 20X4 and the remaining $48,000 in 20X5.

In 20X5, Priority sold additional inventory costing $30,000 to Tall for $36,000, and Tall resold $24,000 of it prior to year-end. Tall sold inventory costing $60,000 to Priority in 20X5 for $90,000, and Priority resold $48,000 of its purchase by December 31, 20X5.

Priority reported 20X5 income of $240,000 from its separate operations and paid dividends of $150,000. Tall reported 20X5 net income of $90,000 and comprehensive income of $110,000. Tall reported other comprehensive income of $10,000 in 20X4. In both years, other comprehensive income arose from an increase in the market value of securities classified as available-for-sale. Tall paid dividends of $60,000 in 20X5.

Required

a. Compute the balance in the investment account reported by Priority at December 31, 20X5.

b. Compute the amount of investment income reported by Priority on its investment in Tall for 20X5.

c. Compute the amount of income assigned to noncontrolling shareholders in the 20X5 consolidated income statement.

d. Compute the balance assigned to noncontrolling shareholders in the consolidated balance sheet prepared at December 31, 20X5.

e. Priority and Tall report inventory balances of $120,000 and $100,000, respectively, at December 31, 20X5. What amount should be reported as inventory in the consolidated balance sheet at December 31, 20X5?

f. Compute the amount reported as consolidated net income for 20X5.

g. Prepare the consolidation entries needed to complete a consolidation worksheet as of December 31, 20X5.

LO 6-3, 6-4   **P6-25**   ## Multiple Inventory Transfers between Parent and Subsidiary

Proud Company and Slinky Company both produce and purchase equipment for resale each period and frequently sell to each other. Since Proud Company holds 60 percent ownership of Slinky Company, Proud's controller compiled the following information with regard to intercompany transactions between the two companies in 20X5 and 20X6:

Year	Produced by	Sold to	Percent Resold to Nonaffiliate in		Cost to Produce	Sale Price to Affiliate
			20X5	**20X6**		
20X5	Proud Company	Slinky Company	60%	40%	$100,000	$150,000
20X5	Slinky Company	Proud Company	30	50	70,000	100,000
20X6	Proud Company	Slinky Company		90	40,000	60,000
20X6	Slinky Company	Proud Company		25	200,000	240,000

Required

a. Give the consolidation entries required at December 31, 20X6, to eliminate the effects of the inventory transfers in preparing a full set of consolidated financial statements.

b. Compute the amount of cost of goods sold to be reported in the consolidated income statement for 20X6.

LO 6-3, 6-4   **P6-26**   **Consolidation Following Inventory Transactions**

Bell Company purchased 60 percent ownership of Troll Corporation on January 1, 20X1, for $82,800. On that date, the noncontrolling interest had a fair value of $55,200 and Troll reported common stock outstanding of $100,000 and retained earnings of $20,000. The full amount of the differential is assigned to land to be used as a future building site. Bell uses the fully adjusted equity method in accounting for its ownership of Troll. On December 31, 20X2, the trial balances of the two companies are as follows:

Item	Bell Company		Troll Corporation	
	Debit	**Credit**	**Debit**	**Credit**
Cash and Accounts Receivable	$ 69,400		$ 51,200	
Inventory	60,000		55,000	
Land	40,000		30,000	
Buildings & Equipment	520,000		350,000	
Investment in Troll Corporation Stock	103,780			
Cost of Goods Sold	99,800		61,000	
Depreciation Expense	25,000		15,000	
Interest Expense	6,000		14,000	
Dividends Declared	40,000		10,000	
Accumulated Depreciation		$175,000		$ 75,000
Accounts Payable		68,800		41,200
Bonds Payable		80,000		200,000
Bond Premium		1,200		
Common Stock		200,000		100,000
Retained Earnings		227,960		50,000
Sales		200,000		120,000
Income from Subsidiary		11,020		
	$963,980	$963,980	$586,200	$586,200

Troll sold inventory costing $25,500 to Bell for $42,500 in 20X1. Bell resold 80 percent of the purchase in 20X1 and the remainder in 20X2. Troll sold inventory costing $21,000 to Bell in 20X2 for $35,000, and Bell resold 70 percent of it prior to December 31, 20X2. In addition, Bell sold inventory costing $14,000 to Troll for $28,000 in 20X2, and Troll resold all but $13,000 of its purchase prior to December 31, 20X2.

Assume both companies use straight-line depreciation and that no property, plant, and equipment has been purchased since the acquisition.

Required

a. Record the journal entry or entries for 20X2 on Bell's books related to its investment in Troll Corporation, using the equity method.

b. Prepare the consolidation entries needed to complete a consolidated worksheet for 20X2.

c. Prepare a three-part consolidation worksheet for 20X2.

LO 6-3, 6-4 **P6-27** **Consolidation Worksheet**

Crow Corporation purchased 70 percent of West Company's voting common stock on January 1, 20X5, for $291,200. On that date, the noncontrolling interest had a fair value of $124,800 and the book value of West's net assets was $380,000. The book values and fair values of West's assets and liabilities were equal except for land that had a fair value $14,000 higher than book value. The amount attributed to goodwill as a result of the acquisition is not amortized and has not been impaired.

CROW CORPORATION AND WEST COMPANY
Trial Balance Data
December 31, 20X9

Item	Crow Corporation		West Company	
	Debit	Credit	Debit	Credit
Cash and Receivables	$ 81,300		$ 85,000	
Inventory	200,000		110,000	
Land, Buildings, & Equipment (net)	270,000		250,000	
Investment in West Company Stock	290,200			
Cost of Goods & Services	200,000		150,000	
Depreciation Expense	40,000		30,000	
Dividends Declared	35,000		5,000	
Sales & Service Revenue		$ 300,000		$200,000
Income from Subsidiary		24,500		
Accounts Payable		60,000		30,000
Common Stock		200,000		150,000
Retained Earnings		532,000		250,000
Total	$1,116,500	$1,116,500	$630,000	$630,000

On January 1, 20X9, Crow's inventory contained $30,000 of unrealized intercompany profits recorded by West. West's inventory on that date contained $15,000 of unrealized intercompany profits recorded on Crow's books. Both companies sold their ending 20X8 inventories to unrelated companies in 20X9.

During 20X9, West sold inventory costing $37,000 to Crow for $62,000. Crow held all inventory purchased from West during 20X9 on December 31, 20X9. Also during 20X9, Crow sold goods costing $54,000 to West for $90,000. West continues to hold $20,000 of its purchase from Crow on December 31, 20X9. Assume Crow uses the fully adjusted equity method.

Required

a. Prepare all consolidation entries needed to complete a consolidation worksheet as of December 31, 20X9.

b. Prepare a consolidation worksheet as of December 31, 20X9.

LO 6-3, 6-4 **P6-28** **Computation of Consolidated Totals**

Bunker Corporation owns 80 percent of Harrison Company's stock. At the end of 20X8, Bunker and Harrison reported the following partial operating results and inventory balances:

Advanced
StudyGuide
.com

	Bunker Corporation	Harrison Company
Total sales	$660,000	$510,000
Sales to Harrison Company	140,000	
Sales to Bunker Corporation		240,000
Net income		20,000
Operating income (excluding investment income from Harrison)	70,000	
Inventory on hand, December 31, 20X8, purchased from:		
Harrison Company	48,000	
Bunker Corporation		42,000

Bunker regularly prices its products at cost plus a 40 percent markup for profit. Harrison prices its sales at cost plus a 20 percent markup. The total sales reported by Bunker and Harrison include both intercompany sales and sales to nonaffiliates.

Required

a. What amount of sales will be reported in the consolidated income statement for 20X8?

b. What amount of cost of goods sold will be reported in the 20X8 consolidated income statement?

c. What amount of consolidated net income and income to controlling interest will be reported in the 20X8 consolidated income statement?

d. What balance will be reported for inventory in the consolidated balance sheet for December 31, 20X8?

LO 6-3, 6-4   **P6-29**   **Intercompany Transfer of Inventory**

Pine Corporation acquired 70 percent of Bock Company's voting common shares on January 1, 20X2, for $108,500. At that date, the noncontrolling interest had a fair value of $46,500 and Bock reported $70,000 of common stock outstanding and retained earnings of $30,000. The differential is assigned to buildings and equipment, which had a fair value $20,000 higher than book value and a remaining 10-year life, and to patents, which had a fair value $35,000 higher than book value and a remaining life of five years at the date of the business combination. Trial balances for the companies as of December 31, 20X3, are as follows:

Item	Pine Corporation Debit	Pine Corporation Credit	Bock Company Debit	Bock Company Credit
Cash & Accounts Receivable	$ 15,400		$ 21,600	
Inventory	165,000		35,000	
Land	80,000		40,000	
Buildings & Equipment	340,000		260,000	
Investment in Bock Company Stock	109,600			
Cost of Goods Sold	186,000		79,800	
Depreciation Expense	20,000		15,000	
Interest Expense	16,000		5,200	
Dividends Declared	30,000		15,000	
Accumulated Depreciation		$140,000		$ 80,000
Accounts Payable		92,400		35,000
Bonds Payable		200,000		100,000
Bond Premium				1,600
Common Stock		120,000		70,000
Retained Earnings		127,900		60,000
Sales		260,000		125,000
Other Income		13,600		
Income from Subsidiary		8,100		
	$962,000	$962,000	$471,600	$471,600

On December 31, 20X2, Bock purchased inventory for $32,000 and sold it to Pine for $48,000. Pine resold $27,000 of the inventory (i.e., $27,000 of the $48,000 acquired from Bock) during 20X3 and had the remaining balance in inventory at December 31, 20X3.

During 20X3, Bock sold inventory purchased for $60,000 to Pine for $90,000, and Pine resold all but $24,000 of its purchase. On March 10, 20X3, Pine sold inventory purchased for $15,000 to Bock for $30,000. Bock sold all but $7,600 of the inventory prior to December 31, 20X3. Assume Pine uses the fully adjusted equity method, that both companies use straight-line depreciation, and that no property, plant, and equipment has been purchased since the acquisition.

Required

a. Give all consolidation entries needed to prepare a full set of consolidated financial statements at December 31, 20X3, for Pine and Bock.

b. Prepare a three-part consolidation worksheet for 20X3.

LO 6-3, 6-4   **P6-30**   **Consolidation Using Financial Statement Data**

Bower Corporation acquired 60 percent of Concerto Company's stock on January 1, 20X3, for $24,000 in excess of book value. On that date, the book values and fair values of Concerto's assets and liabilities were equal and the fair value of the noncontrolling interest was $16,000 in excess of book value. The full amount of the differential at acquisition was assigned to goodwill of $40,000. At December

31, 20X6, Bower management reviewed the amount assigned to goodwill and concluded it had been impaired. They concluded the correct carrying value at that date should be $30,000 and the impairment loss should be assigned proportionately between the controlling and noncontrolling interests.

Balance sheet data for January 1, 20X6, and December 31, 20X6, and income statement data for 20X6 for the two companies are as follows:

BOWER CORPORATION AND CONCERTO COMPANY
Balance Sheet Data
January 1, 20X6

Item	Bower Corporation		Concerto Company	
Cash	$ 9,800		$ 10,000	
Accounts Receivable	60,000		50,000	
Inventory	100,000		80,000	
Total Current Assets		$169,800		$140,000
Land		70,000		20,000
Buildings & Equipment	$300,000		$200,000	
Less: Accumulated Depreciation	(140,000)	160,000	(70,000)	130,000
Investment in Concerto Company Stock		135,200		
Total Assets		$535,000		$290,000
Accounts Payable		$ 30,000		$ 20,000
Bonds Payable		120,000		70,000
Common Stock	$100,000		$ 50,000	
Retained Earnings	285,000	385,000	150,000	200,000
Total Liabilities & Stockholders' Equity		$535,000		$290,000

BOWER CORPORATION AND CONCERTO COMPANY
Balance Sheet Data
December 31, 20X6

Item	Bower Corporation		Concerto Company	
Cash	$ 26,800		$ 35,000	
Accounts Receivable	80,000		40,000	
Inventory	120,000		90,000	
Total Current Assets		$226,800		$165,000
Land		70,000		20,000
Buildings & Equipment	$340,000		$200,000	
Less: Accumulated Depreciation	(165,000)	175,000	(85,000)	115,000
Investment in Concerto Company Stock		139,600		
Total Assets		$611,400		$300,000
Accounts Payable		$ 80,000		$ 15,000
Bonds Payable		120,000		70,000
Common Stock	$100,000		$ 50,000	
Retained Earnings	311,400	411,400	165,000	215,000
Total Liabilities & Stockholders' Equity		$611,400		$300,000

BOWER CORPORATION AND CONCERTO COMPANY
Income Statement Data
Year Ended December 31, 20X6

Item	Bower Corporation		Concerto Company	
Sales		$400,000		$200,000
Income from Subsidiary		16,400		
		$416,400		$200,000
Cost of Goods Sold	$280,000		$120,000	
Depreciation & Amortization Expense	25,000		15,000	
Other Expenses	35,000	(340,000)	30,000	(165,000)
Net Income		$ 76,400		$ 35,000

On January 1, 20X6, Bower held inventory purchased from Concerto for $48,000. During 20X6, Bower purchased an additional $90,000 of goods from Concerto and held $54,000 of its purchases on December 31, 20X6. Concerto sells inventory to the parent at 20 percent above cost.

Concerto also purchases inventory from Bower. On January 1, 20X6, Concerto held inventory purchased from Bower for $14,000, and on December 31, 20X6, it held inventory purchased from Bower for $7,000. Concerto's total purchases from Bower were $22,000 in 20X6. Bower sells items to Concerto at 40 percent above cost.

During 20X6, Bower paid dividends of $50,000, and Concerto paid dividends of $20,000. Assume that Bower uses the fully adjusted equity method that both companies use straight-line depreciation, and that no property, plant, and equipment has been purchased since the acquisition.

Required

a. Prepare all consolidation entries needed to complete a consolidation worksheet as of December 31, 20X6.

b. Prepare a three-part consolidation worksheet as of December 31, 20X6.

LO 6-3, 6-4 **P6-31** ### Intercorporate Transfer of Inventory

Block Corporation was created on January 1, 20X0, to develop computer software. On January 1, 20X5, Foster Company purchased 90 percent of Block's common stock at underlying book value. At that date, the fair value of the noncontrolling interest was equal to 10 percent of Block's book value. Trial balances for Foster and Block on December 31, 20X9, are as follows:

| | 20X9 Trial Balance Data | | | |
| | Foster Company | | Block Corporation | |
Item	Debit	Credit	Debit	Credit
Cash	$ 187,000		$ 57,400	
Accounts Receivable	80,000		90,000	
Other Receivables	40,000		10,000	
Inventory	137,000		130,000	
Land	80,000		60,000	
Buildings & Equipment	500,000		250,000	
Investment in Block Corporation Stock	234,900			
Cost of Goods Sold	593,000		270,000	
Depreciation Expense	45,000		15,000	
Other Expenses	95,000		75,000	
Dividends Declared	40,000		20,000	
Accumulated Depreciation		$ 155,000		$ 75,000
Accounts Payable		63,000		35,000
Other Payables		95,000		20,000
Bonds Payable		250,000		200,000
Bond Premium				2,400
Common Stock		210,000		50,000
Additional Paid-in Capital		110,000		
Retained Earnings		235,000		165,000
Sales		815,000		415,000
Other Income		26,000		15,000
Income from Subsidiary		72,900		
Total	$2,031,900	$2,031,900	$977,400	$977,400

During 20X9, Block produced inventory for $20,000 and sold it to Foster for $30,000. Foster resold 60 percent of the inventory in 20X9. Also in 20X9, Foster sold inventory purchased from Block in 20X8. It had cost Block $60,000 to produce the inventory, and Foster purchased it for $75,000. Assume Foster uses the fully adjusted equity method.

Required

a. What amount of cost of goods sold will be reported in the 20X9 consolidated income statement?

b. What inventory balance will be reported in the December 31, 20X9, consolidated balance sheet?

c. What amount of income will be assigned to noncontrolling shareholders in the 20X9 consolidated income statement?

d. What amount will be assigned to noncontrolling interest in the consolidated balance sheet prepared at December 31, 20X9?

  e. What amount of retained earnings will be reported in the consolidated balance sheet at December 31, 20X9?

  f. Give all consolidation entries required to prepare a three-part consolidation worksheet at December 31, 20X9.

  g. Prepare a three-part consolidation worksheet at December 31, 20X9.

LO 6-3

P6-32 Consolidated Balance Sheet Worksheet [AICPA Adapted]

The December 31, 20X6, condensed balance sheets of Pine Corporation and its 90 percent–owned subsidiary, Slim Corporation, are presented in the accompanying worksheet.

Additional Information

1. Pine's investment in Slim was acquired for $1,170,000 cash on January 1, 20X6, and is accounted for by the equity method. The fair value of the noncontrolling interest at that date was $130,000.

2. At January 1, 20X6, Slim's retained earnings amounted to $600,000, and its common stock amounted to $200,000.

3. Slim declared a $1,000 cash dividend in December 20X6, payable in January 20X7.

4. Slim borrowed $100,000 from Pine on June 30, 20X6, with the note maturing on June 30, 20X7, at 10 percent interest. Correct interest accruals have been recorded by both companies.

5. During 20X6, Pine sold merchandise to Slim at an aggregate invoice price of $300,000, which included a profit of $60,000. At December 31, 20X6, Slim had not paid Pine for $90,000 of these purchases, and 5 percent of the total merchandise purchased from Pine still remained in Slim's inventory. Assume Pine uses the fully adjusted equity method.

6. Pine's excess cost over book value of its investment in Slim has appropriately been identified as goodwill. At December 31, 20X6, Pine's management reviewed the amount attributed to goodwill and found no evidence of impairment.

Required

Complete the accompanying worksheet for Pine and its subsidiary, Slim, at December 31, 20X6.

PINE CORPORATION AND SUBSIDIARY
Consolidated Balance Sheet Worksheet
December 31, 20X6

	Pine Corporation	Slim Corporation	Consolidation Entries Debit	Consolidation Entries Credit	Consolidated
Assets					
Cash	$ 105,000	$ 15,000			
Accounts & Other Current Receivables	410,000	120,000			
Merchandise Inventory	920,000	670,000			
Plant & Equipment, Net	1,000,000	400,000			
Investment in Slim	1,257,000				
Totals	$3,692,000	$1,205,000			
Liabilities & Stockholders' Equity:					
Accounts Payable & Other Current Liabilities	$ 140,000	$ 305,000			
Common Stock ($10 par)	500,000	200,000			
Retained Earnings	3,052,000	700,000			
Totals	$3,692,000	$1,205,000			

LO 6-4

P6-33 Comprehensive Consolidation Worksheet; Fully Adjusted Equity Method [AICPA Adapted]

Fran Corporation acquired all outstanding $10 par value voting common stock of Brey Inc. on January 1, 20X9, in exchange for 25,000 shares of its $20 par value voting common stock. On December 31, 20X8, Fran's common stock had a closing market price of $30 per share on a national stock exchange. The acquisition was appropriately accounted for under the acquisition method. Both companies continued to operate as separate business entities maintaining separate accounting records with years ending December 31. Fran accounts for its investment in Brey stock using the fully adjusted equity method (i.e., adjusting for unrealized intercompany profits).

On December 31, 20X9, the companies had condensed financial statements as follows:

	Fran Corporation		Brey Inc.	
Income Statement	Dr	(Cr)	Dr	(Cr)
Net Sales		$(3,800,000)		$(1,500,000)
Income from Brey		(128,000)		
Gain on Sale of Warehouse		(30,000)		
Cost of Goods Sold	2,360,000		870,000	
Operating Expenses (including depreciation)	1,100,000		440,000	
Net Income		$ (498,000)		$ (190,000)
Retained Earnings Statement				
Balance, 1/1/X9		$ (440,000)		$ (156,000)
Net Income		(498,000)		(190,000)
Dividends Paid			40,000	
Balance, 12/31/X9		$ (938,000)		$ (306,000)
Balance Sheet				
Assets:				
Cash	$ 570,000		$ 150,000	
Accounts Receivable (net)	860,000		350,000	
Inventories	1,060,000		410,000	
Land, Plant, & Equipment	1,320,000		680,000	
Accumulated Depreciation	(370,000)		(210,000)	
Investment in Brey	838,000			
Total Assets	$ 4,278,000		$ 1,380,000	
Liabilities & Stockholders' Equity:				
Accounts Payable & Accrued Expenses		$(1,340,000)		$ (594,000)
Common Stock		(1,700,000)		(400,000)
Additional Paid-in Capital		(300,000)		(80,000)
Retained Earnings		(938,000)		(306,000)
Total Liabilities & Equity		$(4,278,000)		$(1,380,000)

Additional Information

No changes occurred in the Common Stock and Additional Paid-in Capital accounts during 20X9 except the one necessitated by Fran's acquisition of Brey.

At the acquisition date, the fair value of Brey's machinery exceeded its book value by $54,000. The excess cost will be amortized over the estimated average remaining life of six years. The fair values of all of Brey's other assets and liabilities were equal to their book values. At December 31, 20X9, Fran's management reviewed the amount attributed to goodwill as a result of its purchase of Brey's common stock and concluded an impairment loss of $35,000 should be recognized in 20X9.

During 20X9, Fran purchased merchandise from Brey at an aggregate invoice price of $180,000, which included a 100 percent markup on Brey's cost. At December 31, 20X9, Fran owed Brey $86,000 on these purchases, and $36,000 of this merchandise remained in Fran's inventory.

Required

Develop and complete a consolidation worksheet that would be used to prepare a consolidated income statement and a consolidated retained earnings statement for the year ended December 31, 20X9, and a consolidated balance sheet as of December 31, 20X9. List the accounts in the worksheet in the same order as they are listed in the financial statements provided. Formal consolidated statements are not required. Ignore income tax considerations. Supporting computations should be in good form.

LO 6-3, 6-4 **P6-34** **Comprehensive Worksheet Problem**

Randall Corporation acquired 80 percent of Sharp Company's voting shares on January 1, 20X4, for $280,000 in cash and marketable securities. At that date, the noncontrolling interest had a fair value of $70,000 and Sharp reported net assets of $300,000. Assume Randall uses the fully adjusted equity method. Trial balances for the two companies on December 31, 20X7, are as follows:

Item	Randall Corporation Debit	Randall Corporation Credit	Sharp Company Debit	Sharp Company Credit
Cash	$ 130,300		$ 10,000	
Accounts Receivable	80,000		70,000	
Inventory	170,000		110,000	
Buildings & Equipment	600,000		400,000	
Investment in Sharp Company Stock	293,000			
Cost of Goods Sold	416,000		202,000	
Depreciation Expense	30,000		20,000	
Other Expenses	24,000		18,000	
Dividends Declared	50,000		25,000	
Accumulated Depreciation		$ 310,000		$120,000
Accounts Payable		100,000		15,200
Bonds Payable		300,000		100,000
Bond Premium				4,800
Common Stock		200,000		100,000
Additional Paid-in Capital				20,000
Retained Earnings		337,500		215,000
Sales		500,000		250,000
Other Income		20,400		30,000
Income from Sharp Company		25,400		
	$1,793,300	$1,793,300	$855,000	$855,000

Additional Information

1. The full amount of the differential at acquisition was assigned to buildings and equipment with a remaining 10-year economic life.

2. Randall and Sharp regularly purchase inventory from each other. During 20X6, Sharp Company sold inventory costing $40,000 to Randall Corporation for $60,000, and Randall resold 60 percent of the inventory in 20X6 and 40 percent in 20X7. Also in 20X6, Randall sold inventory costing $20,000 to Sharp for $26,000. Sharp resold two-thirds of the inventory in 20X6 and one-third in 20X7.

3. During 20X7, Sharp sold inventory costing $30,000 to Randall for $45,000, and Randall sold items purchased for $9,000 to Sharp for $12,000. Before the end of the year, Randall resold one-third of the inventory it purchased from Sharp in 20X7. Sharp continues to hold all the units purchased from Randall during 20X7.

4. Sharp owes Randall $10,000 on account on December 31, 20X7.

5. Assume that both companies use straight-line depreciation and that no property, plant, and equipment has been purchased since the acquisition.

Required

a. Prepare the 20X7 journal entries recorded on Randall's books related to its investment in Sharp if Randall uses the equity method.

b. Prepare all consolidation entries needed to complete a consolidation worksheet as of December 31, 20X7.

c. Prepare a three-part consolidation worksheet as of December 31, 20X7.

d. Prepare, in good form, a consolidated income statement, balance sheet, and retained earnings statement for 20X7.

P6-35A **Modified Equity Method**

On December 31, 20X7, Randall Corporation recorded the following entry on its books to adjust from the fully adjusted equity method to the modified equity method for its investment in Sharp Company stock:

Investment in Sharp Company Stock	11,000	
Retained Earnings		8,400
Income from Sharp Company		2,600

Required

a. Adjust the data reported by Randall in the trial balance contained in P6-33 for the effects of the preceding adjusting entry.

b. Prepare the journal entries that would have been recorded on Randall's books during 20X7 under the modified equity method.

c. Prepare all consolidation entries needed to complete a consolidation worksheet at December 31, 20X7, assuming Randall has used the modified equity method.

d. Complete a three-part consolidation worksheet as of December 31, 20X7.

P6-36A **Cost Method**

The trial balance data presented in Problem P6-34 can be converted to reflect use of the cost method by inserting the following amounts in place of those presented for Randall Corporation:

Investment in Sharp Company Stock	$280,000
Retained Earnings	329,900
Income from Subsidiary	0
Dividend Income	20,000

Required

a. Prepare the journal entries that would have been recorded on Randall's books during 20X7 under the cost method.

b. Prepare all consolidation entries needed to complete a consolidation worksheet as of December 31, 20X7, assuming Randall uses the cost method.

c. Complete a three-part consolidation worksheet as of December 31, 20X7.

"A" indicates that the item relates to Appendix 6A.

7

Intercompany Transfers of Services and Noncurrent Assets

MICRON'S INTERCOMPANY FIXED ASSET SALE

Micron Technology Inc., ranked number 318 in the 2013 Fortune 500 listing, was founded in Boise, Idaho, in 1978 and specializes in the fabrication of DRAM, SDRAM, flash memory, SSD, and CMOS semiconductor chips. Through a long series of acquisitions, Micron now owns many subsidiaries both in the United States and internationally. Micron also has several joint ventures with other companies. For example, in January 2006, Micron and Intel Corporation formed a new company called IM Flash Technologies LLC, located in Lehi, Utah. A few years earlier in 2002, Micron acquired Toshiba's commodity DRAM operations located in Manassas, Virginia. This wholly owned subsidiary is now called Micron Technology Virginia.

In June 2009, IM Flash Technologies sold underutilized semiconductor manufacturing equipment to Micron Technology Virginia. The equipment originally cost $3,673,962 and had been assigned a five-year useful life. Because it had been depreciated for only approximately 25 months of its expected 60-month useful life, IM Flash Technologies determined that the equipment had a book value of $2,439,888 at the time of the transfer. Given the agreed-upon fair market value and selling price of $1,500,000, IM Flash Technologies realized a loss of $939,888 on this intercompany asset sale. Because Micron Technology Inc. owns more than 50 percent of IM Flash Technologies and 100 percent of Micron Technology Virginia, it consolidates both companies. Therefore, the loss on this sale between affiliated companies had to be eliminated in the consolidation process. This chapter explores the accounting for both depreciable and nondepreciable asset transfers among affiliated companies.

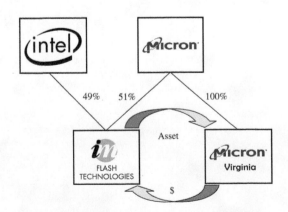

LEARNING OBJECTIVES

When you finish studying this chapter, you should be able to:

LO 7-1 Understand and explain concepts associated with transfers of services and long-term assets.

LO 7-2 Prepare simple equity-method journal entries related to an intercompany land transfer.

LO 7-3 Prepare equity-method journal entries and consolidation entries for the consolidation of a subsidiary following a downstream land transfer.

LO 7-4 Prepare equity-method journal entries and consolidation entries for the consolidation of a subsidiary following an upstream land transfer.

LO 7-5 Prepare equity-method journal entries and consolidation entries for the consolidation of a subsidiary following a downstream depreciable asset transfer.

LO 7-6 Prepare equity-method journal entries and consolidation entries for the consolidation of a subsidiary following an upstream depreciable asset transfer.

INTERCOMPANY TRANSFERS OF SERVICES

LO 7-1

Understand and explain concepts associated with transfers of services and long-term assets.

Related companies frequently purchase services from one another. These services may be of many different types; intercompany purchases of consulting, engineering, marketing, and maintenance services are common.

When one company purchases services from a related company, the purchaser typically records an expense and the seller records revenue. When consolidated financial statements are prepared, both the revenue and the expense must be eliminated. For example, if the parent sells consulting services to the subsidiary for $50,000, the parent would recognize $50,000 of consulting revenue on its books and the subsidiary would recognize $50,000 of consulting expense. In the consolidation worksheet, a consolidation entry would be needed to reduce both consulting revenue (debit) and consulting expense (credit) by $50,000. Because the revenue and expense are equal and both are eliminated, income is unaffected by the consolidation. Even though income is not affected, the consolidation is still important, however, because otherwise both revenues and expenses are overstated.

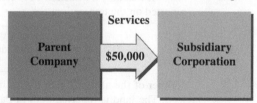

Generally, a simplistic approach is appropriate in eliminating intercompany transfers of services by assuming that the services benefit the current period and, therefore, any intercompany profit on the services becomes realized within the period of transfer. Accordingly, no consolidation entries relating to the current period's transfer of services are needed in future periods because the intercompany profit is considered realized in the transfer period.

Usually the assumption that the profit on intercompany sales of services is realized in the period of sale is realistic. In some cases, however, realization of intercompany profit on the services does not occur in the period the services are provided, and the amounts are significant. For example, if the parent company charges a subsidiary for architectural services to design a new manufacturing facility for the subsidiary, the subsidiary would include that cost in the capitalized cost of the new facility. From a consolidated point of view, however, any profit the parent recognized on the intercompany sale of services (revenue over the cost of providing the service) would have to be eliminated from the reported cost of the new facility until the intercompany profit became realized. Realization would be viewed as occurring over the life of the facility. Thus, consolidation entries would be needed each year similar to those illustrated later in the chapter for intercompany fixed asset transfers.

INTERCOMPANY LONG-TERM ASSET TRANSFERS

The following illustrations provide an overview of the intercompany sale process using land as an example. Figure 7–1 presents a series of transactions involving a parent company and its subsidiary. First, Parent Company purchases land from an unrelated party. Then Parent Company sells the land to a subsidiary. Finally, the subsidiary sells the land to an unrelated party. The three transactions, and the amounts, are

T1—Parent Company purchases land from an independent third party for $10,000.

T2—Parent Company sells the land to Subsidiary Corporation for $15,000.

T3—Subsidiary Corporation sells the land to an independent third party for $25,000.

As illustrated in the following independent cases, the amount of gain reported by each of the individual companies and by the consolidated entity in each accounting period depends on which transactions actually occur during that period.

Case A

Assume that all three transactions are completed in the same accounting period. The gain amounts reported on the transactions are

Parent Company	$ 5,000 ($15,000 − $10,000)
Subsidiary Corporation	10,000 ($25,000 − $15,000)
Consolidated Entity	15,000 ($25,000 − $10,000)

The gain on the sale of the land is considered to be realized because it is resold to an unrelated party during the period. The total gain that the consolidated entity reports is the difference between the $10,000 price it paid to an unaffiliated seller and the $25,000 price at which it sells the land to an unaffiliated buyer. This $15,000 gain is reported in the consolidated income statement. From a consolidated viewpoint, the sale from Parent Company to Subsidiary Corporation, transaction T2, is an internal transaction and is not reported in the consolidated financial statements.

Case B

Assume that only transaction T1 is completed during the current period. The gain amounts reported on the transactions are

Parent Company	$0
Subsidiary Corporation	0
Consolidated Entity	0

Neither of the affiliated companies has made a sale, and no gains are reported or realized. The land is reported both in Parent Company's balance sheet and in the consolidated balance sheet at its cost to Parent, which also is the cost to the consolidated entity.

FIGURE 7–1
Intercompany Sales

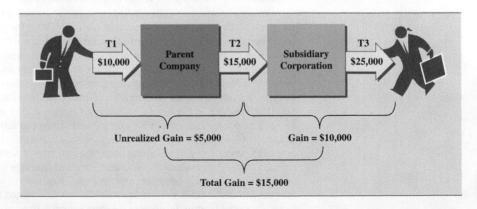

Case C

Assume that only transactions T1 and T2 are completed during the current period. The gain amounts reported on the transactions are

Parent Company	$5,000	($15,000 − $10,000)
Subsidiary Corporation	0	
Consolidated Entity	0	

The $5,000 gain reported by Parent Company is considered unrealized from a consolidated point of view and is not reported in the consolidated income statement because the land has not been resold to a party outside the consolidated entity. Subsidiary Corporation's books carry the land at $15,000, the cost to Subsidiary. From a consolidated viewpoint, the land is overvalued by $5,000 and must be reduced to its $10,000 cost to the consolidated entity.

Case D

Assume that only transaction T3 is completed during the current period and that T1 and T2 occurred in a prior period. The gain amounts reported on the transactions in the current period are

Parent Company	$ 0	
Subsidiary Corporation	10,000	($25,000 − $15,000)
Consolidated Entity	15,000	($25,000 − $10,000)

Subsidiary recognizes a gain equal to the difference between its selling price, $25,000, and cost, $15,000, and the consolidated entity reports a gain equal to the difference between its selling price of $25,000 and the cost to the consolidated entity from an outsider of $10,000.

From a consolidated viewpoint, the sale of an asset wholly within the consolidated entity involves only a change in the technical owner of the asset and possibly its location and does not represent the culmination of the earning process. To culminate the earning process with respect to the consolidated entity, it must make a sale to a party external to the consolidated entity. The key to deciding when to report a transaction in the consolidated financial statements is to visualize the consolidated entity and determine whether a particular transaction (1) occurs totally within the consolidated entity, in which case its effects must be excluded from the consolidated statements or (2) involves outsiders and thus constitutes a transaction of the consolidated entity.

INTERCOMPANY LAND TRANSFERS[1]

LO 7-2

Prepare simple equity-method journal entries related to an intercompany land transfer.

When intercompany transfers of noncurrent assets occur, the parent company must make adjustments in the preparation of consolidated financial statements for as long as the acquiring company holds the assets. The simplest example of an intercompany asset transfer is the intercompany sale of land.

Overview of the Profit Consolidation Process

When related companies transfer land at book value, no special adjustments are needed in preparing the consolidated statements. If, for example, a company purchases land for $10,000 and sells it to its subsidiary for $10,000, the asset continues to be valued at the $10,000 original cost to the consolidated entity:

Parent			Subsidiary		
Cash	10,000		Land	10,000	
Land		10,000	Cash		10,000

Advanced
StudyGuide
.com

[1] To view a video explanation of this topic, visit advancedstudyguide.com.

Because the seller records no gain or loss, both income and assets are stated correctly from a consolidated viewpoint.

Land transfers at more or less than book value require special treatment. Under the fully adjusted equity method, the parent company must defer any unrealized gains or losses until the assets are eventually sold to unrelated parties. Moreover, in the consolidation process, the selling entity's gain or loss must be eliminated because the consolidated entity still holds the land, and no gain or loss may be reported in the consolidated financial statements until the land is sold to a party outside the consolidated entity. Likewise, the land must be reported at its original cost in the consolidated financial statements as long as it is held within the consolidated entity, regardless of which affiliate holds the land.

As an illustration, assume that Peerless Products Corporation acquires land for $20,000 on January 1, 20X1, and sells the land to its subsidiary, Special Foods Incorporated, on July 1, 20X1, for $35,000, as follows:

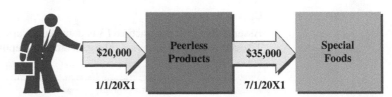

Peerless records the purchase of the land and its sale to Special Foods with the following entries:

January 1, 20X1

(1)	Land	20,000	
	Cash		20,000
	Record land purchase.		

July 1, 20X1

(2)	Cash	35,000	
	Land		20,000
	Gain on Sale of Land		15,000
	Record sale of land to Special Foods.		

Special Foods records the purchase of the land from Peerless as follows:

July 1, 20X1

(3)	Land	35,000	
	Cash		35,000
	Record purchase of land from Peerless.		

The intercompany transfer leads to a $15,000 gain on Peerless' books, and the carrying value of the land increases by the same amount on Special Foods' books. Neither of these amounts may be reported in the consolidated financial statements because the $15,000 intercompany gain is unrealized from a consolidated viewpoint. The land has not been sold to a party outside the consolidated entity but has only been transferred within it; consequently, the land must still be reported in the consolidated financial statements at its original cost to the consolidated entity.

When intercompany gains or losses on asset transfers occur, the parent company can choose to use the fully adjusted equity method, which requires it to adjust its investment and income from subsidiary accounts to remove the unrealized gain.

July 1, 20X1

(4)	Income from Special Foods	15,000	
	Investment in Special Foods Stock		15,000
	Defer gain on intercompany land sale to Special Foods.		

This equity-method entry ensures that the parent company's income is exactly equal to the controlling interest in consolidated income on the consolidated financial statements. Chapter 6 explains that the deferral of unrealized gross profit on intercompany inventory transfers is reversed in the subsequent accounting period if the inventory is sold to an outside party. Similarly, the deferral of gain on an intercompany asset transfer is reversed in the period in which the asset is sold to an outsider (which may or may not be in the very next period).

We use the fully adjusted equity method in all subsequent examples in the chapter. Another option is to ignore this unrealized gain on the parent company's books and adjust for it in the consolidation worksheet only under the modified equity method. We illustrate this approach in the appendix.

In the consolidation process, the gain should be eliminated and the land restated from the $35,000 recorded on Special Foods' books to its original cost of $20,000. This is accomplished with the following entry in the consolidation worksheet prepared at the end of 20X1:

Gain on Sale of Land	15,000	
Land		15,000

Assignment of Unrealized Profit Consolidation

Unrealized intercompany gains and losses must be eliminated fully when preparing consolidated financial statements. Regardless of the parent's percentage ownership of a subsidiary, the full amount of any unrealized gains and losses must be eliminated and must be excluded from consolidated net income. Although the full amount of an unrealized gain or loss is excluded from consolidated net income, a question arises when the parent owns less than 100 percent of a subsidiary as to whether the unrealized profit consolidation should reduce the controlling or noncontrolling interest, or both.

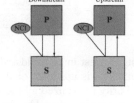

A gain or loss on an intercompany transfer is recognized by the selling affiliate and ultimately accrues to the stockholders of that affiliate. When a parent sells to a subsidiary, referred to as a *downstream sale,* any gain or loss on the transfer accrues to the parent company's stockholders. When a subsidiary sells to its parent, an *upstream sale,* any gain or loss accrues to the subsidiary's stockholders. If the subsidiary is wholly owned, all gain or loss ultimately accrues to the parent company as the sole stockholder. If, however, the selling subsidiary is not wholly owned, the gain or loss on the upstream sale is apportioned between the parent company and the noncontrolling shareholders.

Generally, the consolidated entity does not consider gains and losses realized until a sale is made to an unrelated, external party. Unrealized gains and losses are eliminated in preparing consolidated financial statements against the interests of those shareholders who recognized the gains and losses in the first place: the shareholders of the selling affiliate. Therefore, the direction of the sale determines which shareholder group absorbs the consolidation of unrealized intercompany gains and losses. Thus, unrealized intercompany gains and losses are eliminated in consolidation in the following ways:

Sale	Consolidation
Downstream (parent to subsidiary)	Against controlling interest
Upstream (subsidiary to parent):	
Wholly owned subsidiary	Against controlling interest
Majority-owned subsidiary	Proportionately against controlling and noncontrolling interests

As an illustration, assume that Purity Company owns 75 percent of the common stock of Southern Corporation. Purity reports operating income of $100,000 from its own activities, excluding any investment income from or transactions with Southern; Southern reports operating income of $50,000, exclusive of any gains or losses on asset transfers. In each example, assume the selling affiliate has a separate unrealized gain of $10,000 on the intercompany transfer of an asset. In the case of a downstream transfer, all unrealized profit is eliminated from the controlling interest's share of income when consolidated statements are prepared. Thus, the controlling interest in consolidated net income is computed as follows:

Southern's reported net income	$ 50,000
Purity's ownership percentage	× 0.75
Purity's share of Southern's reported income	37,500
Less: Purity's 100% deferral of the unrealized downstream intercompany gain	(10,000)
Purity's income from Southern	27,500
Purity's separate income (including downstream intercompany gain)	110,000
Income to controlling interest	$137,500

If, instead, the intercompany transfer is upstream from subsidiary to parent, the unrealized profit on the upstream sale is eliminated proportionately from the interests of the controlling and noncontrolling shareholders. In this situation, the controlling interest in consolidated net income is computed as follows:

Southern's operating income	$ 50,000
Upstream intercompany gain	10,000
Southern's reported net income	60,000
Purity's ownership percentage	× 0.75
Purity's share of Southern's reported income	45,000
Less: Purity's 75% deferral of the upstream unrealized intercompany gain	(7,500)
Purity's income from Southern	37,500
Purity's separate income	100,000
Income to controlling interest	$137,500

Consolidated net income ($150,000) and the controlling interest in consolidated net income ($137,500) are the same whether the intercompany sale is upstream or downstream, but the allocation of the deferral differs. Because Purity recognized all the gain in the downstream case, the controlling interest's share of income is reduced by the full unrealized gain consolidation. In the upstream case, the intercompany gain was recognized by Southern and shared proportionately by Southern's controlling and noncontrolling interests. Therefore, the consolidation is made proportionately against the controlling and noncontrolling interests' share of income.

Note that unrealized intercompany gains and losses are always fully eliminated in preparing consolidated financial statements. The existence of a noncontrolling interest in a selling subsidiary only affects the allocation of the deferral of the unrealized gain or loss, not the amount deferred.

Income to the Noncontrolling Interest

The income assigned to the noncontrolling interest is the noncontrolling interest's proportionate share of the subsidiary's reported net income realized in transactions with parties external to the consolidated entity. Income assigned to the noncontrolling interest in the downstream example is computed as follows:

Southern's reported net income	$50,000
NCI's percentage	× 0.25
Income to NCI	$12,500

Income assigned to the noncontrolling interest in the upstream example is computed as follows:

Southern's reported income (including intercompany gain)	$60,000
NCI's ownership percentage	× 0.25
NCI's share of Southern's reported income	$15,000
Less: NCI's 25% deferral of the upstream unrealized intercompany gain	(2,500)
Income to NCI	$12,500

In the downstream example, the $10,000 of unrealized intercompany profit is recognized on the parent company's books; therefore, the noncontrolling interest is not affected by the unrealized gain on the downstream intercompany transaction. The entire $50,000 of the subsidiary's income is realized in transactions with parties external to the consolidated entity. In the upstream example, the subsidiary's income includes $10,000 of unrealized intercompany profit. The amount of the subsidiary's income realized in transactions with external parties is only $50,000 ($60,000 less $10,000 of unrealized intercompany profit).

Downstream Sale of Land (Year of Sale)

As in Chapter 6, assume that Peerless Products purchases 80 percent of the common stock of Special Foods on December 31, 20X0, for its book value of $240,000, and that the fair value of Special Foods' noncontrolling interest on that date is equal to its book value of $60,000. Assume that during 20X1, Peerless reports separate income of $140,000 income from regular operations and declares dividends of $60,000. Special Foods reports net income of $50,000 and declares dividends of $30,000. In addition, on July 1, 20X1, Peerless sells land to Special Foods for $35,000. Peerless had originally purchased the land on January 1, 20X1, for $20,000, resulting in an unrealized gain of $15,000. Special Foods continues to hold the land through 20X1 and subsequent years.

Fully Adjusted Equity-Method Entries—20X1

During 20X1, Peerless records its share of Special Foods' income and dividends with the usual fully adjusted equity-method entries:

(5)	Investment in Special Foods	40,000	
	Income from Special Foods		40,000

Record Peerless' 80% share of Special Foods' 20X1 income.

(6)	Cash	24,000	
	Investment in Special Foods		24,000

Record Peerless' 80% share of Special Foods' 20X1 dividend.

Under the fully adjusted equity method, because the downstream sale of land to Special Foods results in a $15,000 unrealized gain, Peerless makes an adjustment in the equity-method accounts to reduce Income from Special Foods on the income statement and Investment in Special Foods on the balance sheet by its share of the unrealized gain. Because this is a downstream transaction, the sale (and associated

unrealized gain) resides on Peerless' income statement. Because we assume the NCI shareholders do not own Peerless stock, they do not share in the deferral of the unrealized gain.

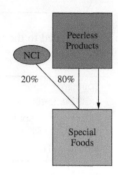

Under the fully adjusted equity method, Peerless Inc. defers the entire $15,000 using the following equity-method entry:

(7)	Income from Special Foods	15,000	
	Investment in Special Foods		15,000

Defer gain on intercompany land sale to Special Foods.

Note that this entry accomplishes two important objectives. First, because Peerless' income is overstated by $15,000, the adjustment to Income from Special Foods offsets this overstatement so that Peerless' bottom-line net income is now correct. Second, Special Foods' land account is currently overstated by $15,000 (because the land was originally acquired by Peerless for $20,000, but it is now recorded at $35,000 on Special Foods' books). Because the Investment in Special Foods account summarizes Peerless' investment in Special Foods' balance sheet, this reduction to the investment account offsets the fact that Special Foods' land (and thus entire balance sheet) is overstated by $15,000. Thus, after making this equity-method adjustment to defer the unrealized gain on the sale of land, Peerless' financial statements are now correctly stated. Therefore, Peerless' reported income will be exactly equal to the controlling interest in net income on the consolidated financial statements.

On December 31, 20X1, the Peerless' equity-method accounts appear as follows:

	Investment in Special Foods				Income from Special Foods	
Acquisition	240,000					
80% of NI	40,000				40,000	80% of NI
		24,000	80% of Dividends			
		15,000	Defer Gain	15,000		
Ending Balance	241,000				25,000	Ending Balance

In summary, when Peerless defers the unrealized gain in the equity method accounts, the $15,000 decrease in the Income from Special Foods account offsets the gain on Peerless' books so that Peerless' income is correct (and equal to the controlling interest in consolidated net income). Moreover, because the Investment in Special Foods account summarizes the entire balance sheet of Special Foods, the $15,000 decrease in the investment account offsets the fact that the land account is overstated by $15,000 on Special Foods' books. The following illustration shows how the internal sale of the land and the deferral on Peerless' books affect the accounting equation.

	Peerless Products				Special Foods		
	Assets	=	Liabilities	+ Equity	Assets	=	Liabilities + Equity
	Investment −15,000			Gain +15,000 — Income from Sub −15,000	Land +15,000		

Consolidation Worksheet—20X1

We present the consolidation worksheet prepared at the end of 20X1 in Figure 7–2. The first two consolidation entries are the same as originally presented in Chapter 3 with one minor exception. Although the analysis of the "book value" portion of the investment account is the same, in preparing the basic consolidation entry, we reduce the amounts in the Income from Special Foods and Investment in Special Foods accounts by the $15,000 gain deferral.

FIGURE 7–2   December 31, 20X1, Consolidation Worksheet, Period of Intercompany Sale; Downstream Sale of Land

	Peerless Products	Special Foods	Consolidation Entries		Consolidated
			DR	**CR**	
Income Statement					
Sales	400,000	200,000			600,000
Less: COGS	(170,000)	(115,000)			(285,000)
Less: Depreciation Expense	(50,000)	(20,000)			(70,000)
Less: Other Expenses	(40,000)	(15,000)			(55,000)
Gain on Sale of Land	15,000		15,000		0
Income from Special Foods	25,000		25,000		0
Consolidated Net Income	180,000	50,000	40,000	0	190,000
NCI in Net Income			10,000		(10,000)
Controlling Interest Net Income	**180,000**	**50,000**	**50,000**	**0**	**180,000**
Statement of Retained Earnings					
Beginning Balance	300,000	100,000	100,000		300,000
Net Income	**180,000**	**50,000**	50,000	0	180,000
Less: Dividends Declared	(60,000)	(30,000)		30,000	(60,000)
Ending Balance	**420,000**	**120,000**	**150,000**	**30,000**	**420,000**
Balance Sheet					
Cash	299,000	40,000			339,000
Accounts Receivable	75,000	50,000			125,000
Inventory	100,000	75,000			175,000
Investment in Special Foods	241,000			241,000	0
Land	155,000	75,000		15,000	215,000
Buildings & Equipment	800,000	600,000		300,000	1,100,000
Less: Accumulated Depreciation	(450,000)	(320,000)	300,000		(470,000)
Total Assets	**1,220,000**	**520,000**	**300,000**	**556,000**	**1,484,000**
Accounts Payable	100,000	100,000			200,000
Bonds Payable	200,000	100,000			300,000
Common Stock	500,000	200,000	200,000		500,000
Retained Earnings	420,000	120,000	150,000	30,000	420,000
NCI in NA of Special Foods				64,000	64,000
Total Liabilities & Equity	**1,220,000**	**520,000**	**350,000**	**94,000**	**1,484,000**

Calculations for Basic Consolidation Entry:

Book Value Calculations:

	NCI 20% +	Peerless 80% =	Common Stock +	Retained Earnings
Original Book Value	60,000	240,000	200,000	100,000
+ Net Income	10,000	40,000		50,000
– Dividends	(6,000)	(24,000)		(30,000)
Ending Book Value	64,000	256,000	200,000	120,000

Adjustment to Basic Consolidation Entry:

	NCI 20%	Peerless 80%
Net Income	10,000	40,000
– Gain on Land Deferral		(15,000)
Income to be Eliminated	10,000	25,000
Ending Book Value	64,000	256,000
– Gain on Land Deferral		(15,000)
Adjusted Book Value	64,000	241,000

Basic Consolidation Entry:

Common Stock	200,000		← Common stock balance
Retained Earnings	100,000		← Beginning RE from trial balance
Income from Special Foods	25,000		← Peerless' % of NI with Adjustments
NCI in NI of Special Foods	10,000		← NCI share of reported NI
Dividends Declared		30,000	← 100% of sub's dividends declared
Investment in Special Foods		241,000	← Net BV with Adjustments
NCI in NA of Special Foods		64,000	← NCI share of net book value

Optional Accumulated Depreciation Consolidation Entry:

Accumulated Depreciation	300,000		Accumulated depreciation at the
Buildings & Equipment		300,000	← time of the acquisition netted against cost

Moreover, although Peerless recorded an equity-method entry to defer the unrealized gain on the sale of land, both the Income from Special Foods and Investment in Special Foods accounts are eliminated with the basic consolidation entry. Therefore, based on the remaining numbers appearing in the trial balance, Peerless' income is overstated by the gain ($15,000). Moreover, Special Foods' land account is still overstated by $15,000. Simply adding up the Peerless and Special Foods columns of the consolidation worksheet will result in overstated consolidated net income, total assets, and retained earnings. Therefore, we also record an entry to correct the unadjusted totals to the appropriate consolidated amounts. In doing so, consolidated income is reduced by $15,000 when the gain is eliminated. In addition, land reported on Special Foods' books is stated at the intercompany sale price rather than the historical cost to the consolidated entity. Until the land is resold to an external party by Special Foods, its carrying value must be reduced by the amount of unrealized intercompany gain each time consolidated statements are prepared.

Eliminate Gain on Sale of Land to Special Foods:

Gain on Sale of Land	15,000	
Land		15,000

In sum, because the land is still held within the consolidated entity, the $15,000 gain recognized on Peerless' books must be eliminated in the consolidation worksheet so that it does not appear in the consolidated income statement. Similarly, the land must appear in the consolidated balance sheet at its $20,000 original cost to the consolidated entity and, therefore, must be reduced from the $35,000 amount carried on Special Foods' books.

Consolidated Net Income

The 20X1 consolidated net income is computed and allocated as follows:

Peerless' separate income	$155,000
Less: Unrealized intercompany gain on downstream land sale	(15,000)
Peerless' separate realized income	$140,000
Special Foods' net income	50,000
Consolidated net income, 20X1	$190,000
Income to noncontrolling interest ($50,000 × 0.20)	(10,000)
Income to controlling interest	$180,000

Noncontrolling Interest

The noncontrolling stockholders' share of consolidated net income is limited to their proportionate share of the subsidiary's income. Special Foods' net income for 20X1 is $50,000, and the noncontrolling stockholders' ownership interest is 20 percent. Therefore, income of $10,000 ($50,000 × 0.20) is allocated to the noncontrolling interest.

As shown in Figure 7–2, the total noncontrolling interest in net assets at the end of 20X1 is $64,000. Normally the noncontrolling interest's claim on the subsidiary's net assets at a particular date is equal to a proportionate share of the subsidiary's book value and remaining differential at that date. In this example, the subsidiary's acquisition-date fair value and book value are equal, and, thus, no differential is associated with the combination. Accordingly, the noncontrolling interest on December 31, 20X1, is equal to a proportionate share of Special Foods' book value:

Book value of Special Foods, December 31, 20X1:	
Common stock	$200,000
Retained earnings	120,000
Total book value	$320,000
Noncontrolling stockholders' proportionate share	× 0.20
Noncontrolling interest, December 31, 20X1	$ 64,000

The noncontrolling interest is unaffected by the unrealized gain on the downstream sale.

Downstream Sale of Land

Eliminating the Downstream Unrealized Gain after the First Year

In the period in which unrealized profits arise from an intercompany sale, worksheet entries are used in the consolidation process to remove the gain or loss recorded by the seller and to adjust the reported amount of the asset back to the price the selling affiliate originally paid.

When Peerless deferred the gain on its books in the year of the internal asset sale, the decrease in Income from Special Foods offset the gain on sale on its own books. When the gain and the Income from Special Foods accounts were closed out to retained earnings, the gain was offset against the artificially low Income from Special Foods balance. Hence, Peerless' retained earnings at the end of the year of the internal land sale is correct. The following illustration shows that Special Foods' land account is still overvalued and Peerless' investment account is still artificially low by the $15,000 deferral.

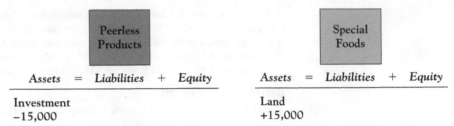

Peerless Products				Special Foods			
Assets	=	Liabilities	+ Equity	Assets	=	Liabilities	+ Equity
Investment −15,000				Land +15,000			

Each period thereafter while the purchasing affiliate holds the asset, the reported asset balance and the shareholder claims of the selling affiliate are adjusted to remove the effects of the unrealized gain or loss. Income in those subsequent periods is not affected. For example, if Special Foods continues to hold the land purchased from Peerless Products, the following consolidation entry is needed in the consolidation worksheet each time a consolidated balance sheet is prepared for years following the year of intercompany sale, for as long as the land is held:

Investment in Special Foods	15,000	
Land		15,000

This consolidation entry simply corrects the balance in both the Land and Investment in Special Foods accounts. Whereas Peerless recorded an equity-method adjustment to defer the $15,000 of unrealized gain on the sale of land in the year of the intercompany land transfer by artificially decreasing the Investment in Special Foods to offset the overstated land balance on Special Foods' books, this entry simply corrects both accounts. No income statement adjustments are needed in the periods following the intercompany sale until the land is resold to parties external to the consolidated entity.

Subsequent Disposition of the Asset

Unrealized profits on intercompany sales of assets are viewed as being realized at the time the assets are resold to external parties. When a transferred asset is subsequently sold to an external party, the gain or loss recognized by the affiliate selling to the external party must be adjusted for consolidated reporting by the amount of the previously unrealized (and deferred) intercompany gain or loss. Although the seller's reported profit on the external sale is based on that affiliate's cost, the gain or loss reported by the consolidated entity is based on the cost of the asset to the consolidated entity, which is the cost incurred by the affiliate that purchased the asset originally from an outside party.

When previously unrealized intercompany profits are realized, the effects of the profit deferral must be reversed. At the time of realization, the full amount of the deferred intercompany profit is added back into the consolidated income computation and assigned to the shareholder interests from which it originally was eliminated.

To illustrate the treatment of unrealized intercompany profits once the transferred asset is resold, assume that Peerless purchases land from an outside party for $20,000 on January 1, 20X1, and sells the land to Special Foods on July 1, 20X1, for $35,000. Special Foods subsequently sells the land to an outside party on March 1, 20X5, for $45,000, as follows:

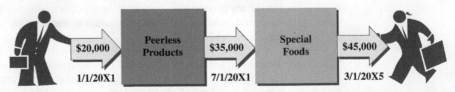

Special Foods recognizes a gain on the sale to the outside party of $10,000 ($45,000 − $35,000). From a consolidated viewpoint, however, the gain is $25,000, the difference between the price at which the land left the consolidated entity ($45,000) and the price at which the land entered the consolidated entity ($20,000) when it was originally purchased by Peerless. Peerless would record an equity-method entry on its books to reverse the original deferral entry (7).

(8)	Investment in Special Foods	15,000	
	Income from Special Foods		15,000

Reverse the deferred profit on the sale of land.

In the consolidation worksheet, the land no longer needs to be reduced by the unrealized intercompany gain because the gain now is realized and the consolidated entity no longer holds it. Instead, the $10,000 gain recognized by Special Foods on the sale of the land to an outsider must be adjusted to reflect a total gain for the consolidated entity of $25,000. Thus, the following consolidation entry is made in the consolidation worksheet prepared at the end of 20X5:

Investment in Special Foods	15,000	
Gain on Sale of Land		15,000

All other consolidation entries are the same as if there were no unrealized intercompany profits at the beginning of the period. No additional consideration need be given to the intercompany transfer in periods subsequent to the external sale. From a consolidated viewpoint, all aspects of the transaction are complete, and the profit is realized once the sale to an external party occurs.

Upstream Sale of Land (Year of Sale)

LO 7-4

Prepare equity-method journal entries and consolidation entries for the consolidation of a subsidiary following an upstream land transfer.

Advanced
StudyGuide
.com

Assume an upstream sale of land results in the recording of an intercompany gain on the subsidiary's books. If the gain is unrealized from a consolidated viewpoint, it must not be included in the consolidated financial statements. Unrealized intercompany gains are eliminated from the consolidation worksheet in the same manner as in the downstream case. However, the gain consolidation reduces both the controlling and the noncontrolling interests in proportion to their ownership.

When an upstream asset sale occurs and the parent resells the asset to a nonaffiliate during the same period, all the parent's equity-method entries and the consolidation entries in the consolidation worksheet are identical to those in the downstream case. When the asset is not resold to a nonaffiliate before the end of the period, worksheet consolidation entries are different from the downstream case only by the apportionment of the unrealized intercompany gain to both the controlling and noncontrolling interests. In this case, because the sale appears on Special Foods' income statement and because the NCI shareholders own 20 percent of Special Foods' outstanding shares, they are entitled to 20 percent of Special Foods' net income. Thus, the deferral of the unrealized gain accrues to both the Peerless and the NCI shareholders. In other words,

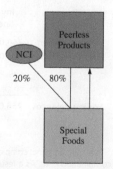

the intercompany gain on an upstream sale is recognized by the subsidiary and shared between the controlling and noncontrolling stockholders of the subsidiary. Therefore, the consolidation of the unrealized intercompany profit must reduce the interests of both ownership groups each period until the profit is realized by resale of the asset to a nonaffiliated party.

The treatment of an upstream sale may be illustrated with the same example used to illustrate a downstream sale. In this case, Special Foods recognizes a $15,000[2] gain from selling the land to Peerless in addition to the $50,000 of income earned from its regular operations; thus, Special Foods' net income for 20X1 is $65,000. Peerless' separate income is $140,000 and comes entirely from its normal operations.

The upstream sale from Special Foods to Peerless is as follows:

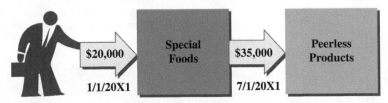

Fully Adjusted Equity-Method Entries—20X1

During 20X1, Peerless records the normal entries under the fully adjusted equity method, reflecting its share of Special Foods' income and dividends:

(9)	Investment in Special Foods	52,000	
	Income from Special Foods		52,000
	Record Peerless' 80% share of Special Foods' 20X1 income.		

(10)	Cash	24,000	
	Investment in Special Foods		24,000
	Record Peerless' 80% share of Special Foods' 20X1 dividend.		

These entries are the same as in the illustration of the downstream sale. The only difference is in the fully adjusted equity-method entry to defer the unrealized gain. The difference is that deferral is only for Peerless' ownership percentage of Special Foods (80 percent). Thus, the deferral of Peerless' relative share of the unrealized gross profit is $12,000 ($15,000 × 0.80).

(11)	Income from Special Foods	12,000	
	Investment in Special Foods		12,000
	Defer Peerless' 80% share of the unrealized gain on the sale of land to Peerless.		

Peerless' equity-method accounts appear as follows at the end of 20X1:

	Investment in Special Foods				Income from Special Foods	
Acquisition	240,000					
80% of NI	52,000				52,000	80% of NI
		24,000	80% of Dividends			
		12,000	Defer 80% of Gain	12,000		
Ending Balance	256,000				40,000	Ending Balance

[2] To avoid additional complexity, we assume the land's fair value is equal to its book value on the business combination date. As a result, there is no differential related to the land.

In summary, when Peerless defers its 80 percent share of Special Foods' unrealized gain in the equity-method accounts, the $12,000 decrease in the Income from Special Foods' account offsets Peerless' 80 percent share of the $15,000 gain on Special Foods' income statement so that Peerless' income is correct (and equal to the controlling interest in consolidated net income). Moreover, the $12,000 decrease in the investment account offsets the fact that its land account is overstated.

Consolidation Worksheet—20X1

Figure 7–3 illustrates the consolidation worksheet prepared at the end of 20X1. The first two consolidation entries are the same as we prepared in Chapter 3 with one minor exception. Although the analysis of the "book value" portion of the investment account is the same, in preparing the basic consolidation entry, we reduce the amounts in Peerless' Income from Special Foods and Investment in Special Foods accounts by Peerless' share of the gain deferral, $12,000 ($15,000 × 0.80). We also reduce the NCI in Net Income of Special Foods and NCI in Net Assets of Special Foods by the NCI's share of the deferral, $3,000 ($15,000 × 0.20).

FIGURE 7–3   December 31, 20X1, Consolidation Worksheet, Period of Intercompany Sale; Upstream Sale of Land

	Peerless Products	Special Foods	Consolidation Entries DR	Consolidation Entries CR	Consolidated
Income Statement					
Sales	400,000	200,000			600,000
Less: COGS	(170,000)	(115,000)			(285,000)
Less: Depreciation Expense	(50,000)	(20,000)			(70,000)
Less: Other Expenses	(40,000)	(15,000)			(55,000)
Gain on Sale of Land		15,000	15,000		0
Income from Special Foods	40,000		40,000		0
Consolidated Net Income	180,000	65,000	55,000	0	190,000
NCI in Net Income			10,000		(10,000)
Controlling Interest Net Income	**180,000**	**65,000**	65,000	0	**180,000**
Statement of Retained Earnings					
Beginning Balance	300,000	100,000	100,000		300,000
Net Income	**180,000**	**65,000**	65,000	0	180,000
Less: Dividends Declared	(60,000)	(30,000)		30,000	(60,000)
Ending Balance	**420,000**	**135,000**	165,000	30,000	**420,000**
Balance Sheet					
Cash	229,000	110,000			339,000
Accounts Receivable	75,000	50,000			125,000
Inventory	100,000	75,000			175,000
Investment in Special Foods	256,000			256,000	0
Land	210,000	20,000		15,000	215,000
Buildings & Equipment	800,000	600,000		300,000	1,100,000
Less: Accumulated Depreciation	(450,000)	(320,000)	300,000		(470,000)
Total Assets	**1,220,000**	**535,000**	300,000	571,000	**1,484,000**
Accounts Payable	100,000	100,000			200,000
Bonds Payable	200,000	100,000			300,000
Common Stock	500,000	200,000	200,000		500,000
Retained Earnings	**420,000**	**135,000**	165,000	30,000	420,000
NCI in NA of Special Foods				64,000	64,000
Total Liabilities & Equity	**1,220,000**	**535,000**	365,000	94,000	**1,484,000**

Calculations for Basic Consolidation Entry:

Book Value Calculations:

	NCI 20% +	Peerless 80% =	Common Stock +	Retained Earnings
Original Book Value	60,000	240,000	200,000	100,000
+ Net Income	13,000	52,000		65,000
− Dividends	(6,000)	(24,000)		(30,000)
Ending Book Value	67,000	268,000	200,000	135,000

Adjustment to Basic Consolidation Entry:

	NCI 20%	Peerless 80%
Net Income	13,000	52,000
− Gain on Land Deferral	(3,000)	(12,000)
Income to be Eliminated	10,000	40,000
Ending Book Value	67,000	268,000
− Gain on Land Deferral	(3,000)	(12,000)
Adjusted Book Value	64,000	256,000

Basic Consolidation Entry:

Common Stock	200,000		← Common stock balance
Retained Earnings	100,000		← Beginning RE from trial balance
Income from Special Foods	40,000		← Peerless' % of NI with Adjustments
NCI in NI of Special Foods	10,000		← NCI share of NI with Adjustments
Dividends Declared		30,000	← 100% of sub's dividends declared
Investment in Special Foods		256,000	← Net BV with Adjustments
NCI in NA of Special Foods		64,000	← NCI share of BV with Adjustments

Optional Accumulated Depreciation Consolidation Entry:

Accumulated Depreciation	300,000		Accumulated depreciation at the
Buildings & Equipment		300,000	← time of the acquisition netted against cost

The consolidation worksheet entry to correct for the intercompany sale is identical to the downstream case. The only difference is that the unrealized gain (and overstated income) is now in Special Foods' column of the consolidation worksheet and the overstated land is now in Peerless' column.

Eliminate Gain on Purchase of Land from Special Foods:

Gain on Sale of Land	15,000	
Land		15,000

Consolidated Net Income

When intercompany profits that are unrealized from a consolidated point of view are included in a subsidiary's income, both consolidated net income and the noncontrolling stockholders' share of income must be adjusted for the unrealized profits. Consolidated net income for 20X1 is computed and allocated as follows:

Peerless' separate income		$140,000
Special Foods' net income	$65,000	
Less: Unrealized intercompany gain on upstream land sale	(15,000)	
Special Foods' realized net income		50,000
Consolidated net income, 20X1		$190,000
Income to noncontrolling interest ($50,000 × 0.20)		(10,000)
Income to controlling interest		$180,000

Consolidated net income in this year is the same whether or not there is an intercompany sale because the gain is unrealized. The unrealized gain must be eliminated fully, with consolidated net income based only on the realized income of the two affiliates.

Noncontrolling Interest

The income assigned to the noncontrolling shareholders is computed as their proportionate share of the realized income of Special Foods, as follows:

Special Foods' net income	$65,000
Less: Unrealized intercompany profit on upstream land sale	(15,000)
Special Foods' realized income	$50,000
Proportionate share to noncontrolling interest	× 0.20
Income to noncontrolling interest	$10,000

The total noncontrolling interest in the net assets of Special Foods is computed, in the absence of a differential, as the noncontrolling stockholders' proportionate share of the stockholders' equity of Special Foods, excluding unrealized gains and losses. On December 31, 20X1, the noncontrolling interest totals $64,000, computed as follows:

Book value of Special Foods, December 31, 20X1:	
Common stock	$200,000
Retained earnings	135,000
Total book value	$335,000
Unrealized intercompany gain on upstream land sale	(15,000)
Realized book value of Special Foods	$320,000
Noncontrolling stockholders' proportionate share	× 0.20
Noncontrolling interest, December 31, 20X1	$ 64,000

Eliminating the Upstream Unrealized Gain after the First Year

As explained previously, in the period in which unrealized profits arise from an intercompany sale, worksheet entries remove the gain or loss recorded by the seller and adjust the reported amount of the asset back to the price the selling affiliate originally paid. Each period thereafter while the purchasing affiliate holds the asset, the reported asset balance and the shareholder claims are adjusted to remove the effects of the unrealized gain or loss. Income in those subsequent periods is not affected. For example, if Peerless continues to hold the land purchased from Special Foods, the unrealized intercompany gain is eliminated from the reported balance of the land and proportionately from the subsidiary ownership interests with the following entry:

Investment in Special Foods	12,000	
NCI in NA of Special Foods	3,000	
Land		15,000

Recall that in the upstream case, Peerless deferred only its 80 percent share of the unrealized gain. As a result, the Investment in Special Foods account is "artificially low" by $12,000. Thus, it make sense that the consolidation entry can only increase the investment account by the amount that was deferred. All other consolidation entries are made as if there is no unrealized intercompany gain.

Subsequent Disposition of the Asset

As explained earlier, when previously unrealized intercompany profits are realized, the effects of the profit deferral must be reversed. At the time of realization, the full amount of the deferred intercompany profit is added back into the consolidated income computation and assigned to the shareholder interests from which it originally was eliminated. In this example, if Peerless had sold the land to the external party following an upstream intercompany transfer from Special Foods, the worksheet treatment would be the same as in the case of the downstream transfer except that the debit would be prorated between Investment in Special Foods ($12,000) and NCI in Net Assets of Special Foods ($3,000) based on the relative ownership interests.

Investment in Special Foods	12,000	
NCI in NA of Special Foods	3,000	
Gain on Sale of Land		15,000

INTERCOMPANY TRANSFERS OF DEPRECIABLE ASSETS

Unrealized intercompany profits on a depreciable or amortizable asset are viewed as being realized gradually over the remaining economic life of the asset as it is used by the purchasing affiliate in generating revenue from unaffiliated parties. In effect, a portion of the unrealized gain or loss is realized each period as benefits are derived from the asset and its service potential expires.

The amount of depreciation recognized on a company's books each period on an asset purchased from an affiliate is based on the intercompany transfer price. From a consolidated viewpoint, however, depreciation must be based on the cost of the asset to the consolidated entity, which is the asset's cost to the affiliate company that originally purchased it from an outsider. Consolidation entries are needed in the consolidation worksheet to restate the asset, the associated accumulated depreciation, and the depreciation expense to the amounts that would have appeared in the financial statements if there had been no intercompany transfer. Because the intercompany sale takes place totally within the consolidated entity, the consolidated financial statements must appear as if the intercompany transfer had never occurred.

Downstream Sale

LO 7-5

Prepare equity-method journal entries and consolidation entries for the consolidation of a subsidiary following a downstream depreciable asset transfer.

Advanced
StudyGuide
.com

We now modify the Peerless Products and Special Foods example to illustrate the downstream sale of a depreciable asset. Assume that Peerless sells equipment to Special Foods on December 31, 20X1, for $7,000, as follows:

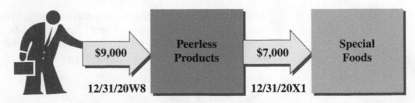

The equipment originally cost Peerless $9,000 when purchased on December 31, 20W8, three years before the December 31, 20X1, sale to Special Foods. Assume that the equipment has been depreciated based on an estimated useful life of 10 years using the straight-line method with no residual value. The book value of the equipment immediately before the sale by Peerless is computed as follows:

Original cost to Peerless		$9,000
Accumulated depreciation on December 31, 20X1:		
Annual depreciation ($9,000 ÷ 10 years)	$900	
Number of years	× 3	
		(2,700)
Book value on December 31, 20X1		$6,300

Buildings & Equipment		Accumulated Depreciation	
9,000			2,700

Book Value = 6,300

The gain recognized by Peerless on the intercompany sale of the equipment is

Sale price of the equipment	$7,000
Less: Book value of the equipment	(6,300)
Gain on sale of the equipment	$ 700

Separate-Company Entries—20X1

Special Foods records the purchase of the equipment at its cost:

December 31, 20X1

(12)	Equipment	7,000	
	Cash		7,000

Record purchase of equipment.

Special Foods does not depreciate the equipment during 20X1 because it purchased the equipment at the very end of 20X1. However, Peerless does record depreciation expense on the equipment for 20X1 because it holds the asset until the end of the year (and the 20X1 depreciation expense is recorded prior to calculating the gain on sale shown above):

December 31, 20X1

(13)	Depreciation Expense	900	
	Accumulated Depreciation		900

Record 20X1 depreciation expense on equipment sold.

Peerless also records the sale of the equipment at the end of 20X1 and recognizes the $700 ($7,000 − $6,300) gain on the sale:

December 31, 20X1

(14)	Cash	7,000	
	Accumulated Depreciation	2,700	
	Equipment		9,000
	Gain on Sale of Equipment		700

Record sale of equipment.

In addition, Peerless records the normal fully adjusted equity-method entries to recognize its share of Special Foods' income and dividends for 20X1:

(15)	Investment in Special Foods Stock	40,000	
	Income from Special Foods		40,000

Record equity-method income: $50,000 × 0.80.

| (16) | Cash | 24,000 | |
| | Investment in Special Foods Stock | | 24,000 |

Record dividends from Special Foods: $30,000 \times 0.80$.

To ensure that its income for 20X1 is correct, under the fully adjusted equity method, Peerless also defers 100 percent of the gain on the downstream intercompany sale of equipment as follows:

| (17) | Income from Special Foods | 700 | |
| | Investment in Special Foods | | 700 |

Defer unrealized gain on asset sale to Special Foods.

Thus, Peerless' equity-method accounts appear as follows at the end of 20X1:

	Investment in Special Foods				Income from Special Foods	
Acquisition	240,000					
80% of NI	40,000				40,000	80% of NI
		24,000	80% of Dividends			
		700	Defer Gain	700		
Ending Balance	255,300				39,300	Ending Balance

Consolidation Worksheet—20X1

Figure 7–4 illustrates the worksheet to prepare consolidated financial statements at the end of 20X1. To prepare the basic consolidation entry, we first analyze the book value of Special Foods and allocate each component to Peerless and the NCI shareholders:

Calculations for Basic Consolidation Entry:

Book Value Calculations:

	NCI 20% +	Peerless 80%	= Common Stock	+ Retained Earnings
Original Book Value	60,000	240,000	200,000	100,000
+ Net Income	10,000	40,000		50,000
− Dividends	(6,000)	(24,000)		(30,000)
Ending Book Value	64,000	256,000	200,000	120,000

Adjustment to Basic Consolidation Entry:

	NCI 20%	Peerless 80%
Net Income	10,000	40,000
− Gain on Equipment Deferral		(700)
Income to be Eliminated	10,000	39,300
Ending Book Value	64,000	256,000
− Gain on Equipment Deferral		(700)
Adjusted Book Value	64,000	255,300

The basic consolidation entry is the same as illustrated in Chapter 3 except that we adjust the entries to the Investment in Special Foods and Income from Special Foods accounts for the gain that has been deferred on the intercompany asset sale ($700):

FIGURE 7–4 December 31, 20X1, Consolidation Worksheet, Period of Intercompany Sale; Downstream

	Peerless Products	Special Foods	Consolidation Entries DR	Consolidation Entries CR	Consolidated
Income Statement					
Sales	400,000	200,000			600,000
Less: COGS	(170,000)	(115,000)			(285,000)
Less: Depreciation Expense	(50,000)	(20,000)			(70,000)
Less: Other Expenses	(40,000)	(15,000)			(55,000)
Gain on sale of fixed asset	700		700		0
Income from Special Foods	39,300		39,300		0
Consolidated Net Income	180,000	50,000	40,000	0	190,000
NCI in Net Income			10,000		(10,000)
Controlling Interest Net Income	**180,000**	**50,000**	**50,000**	**0**	**180,000**
Statement of Retained Earnings					
Beginning Balance	300,000	100,000	100,000		300,000
Net Income	**180,000**	**50,000**	50,000	0	180,000
Less: Dividends Declared	(60,000)	(30,000)		30,000	(60,000)
Ending Balance	**420,000**	**120,000**	**150,000**	**30,000**	**420,000**
Balance Sheet					
Cash	271,000	68,000			339,000
Accounts Receivable	75,000	50,000			125,000
Inventory	100,000	75,000			175,000
Investment in Special Foods	255,300			255,300	0
Land	175,000	40,000			215,000
Buildings & Equipment	791,000	607,000	2,000	300,000	1,100,000
Less: Accumulated Depreciation	(447,300)	(320,000)	300,000	2,700	(470,000)
Total Assets	**1,220,000**	**520,000**	**302,000**	**558,000**	**1,484,000**
Accounts Payable	100,000	100,000			200,000
Bonds Payable	200,000	100,000			300,000
Common Stock	500,000	200,000	200,000		500,000
Retained Earnings	**420,000**	**120,000**	150,000	30,000	420,000
NCI in NA of Special Foods				64,000	64,000
Total Liabilities & Equity	**1,220,000**	**520,000**	**350,000**	**94,000**	**1,484,000**

Basic Consolidation Entry:

Common Stock	200,000		← Common stock balance
Retained Earnings	100,000		← Beginning RE from trial balance
Income from Special Foods	39,300		← Peerless' % of NI with Adjustments
NCI in NI of Special Foods	10,000		← NCI share of reported NI
Dividends Declared		30,000	← 100% of sub's dividends declared
Investment in Special Foods		255,300	← Net BV with Adjustments
NCI in NA of Special Foods		64,000	← NCI share of net amount of BV

Optional Accumulated Depreciation Consolidation Entry:

Accumulated Depreciation	300,000		Accumulated depreciation at the
Buildings & Equipment		300,000	← time of the acquisition netted against cost

Although Peerless recorded an equity-method entry to defer the unrealized gain on the equipment sale, both the Income from Special Foods and Investment in Special Foods accounts are eliminated with the basic consolidation entry. Peerless' income is overstated by the gain ($700). Moreover, Special Foods' Buildings and Equipment account is overstated by the same amount. Therefore, we need an additional consolidation entry to remove the gain that appears in Peerless' income statement and to correct the basis of the equipment on Special Foods' books to make it appear as if the asset had not been sold within the consolidated group. One way to calculate this consolidation entry is to compare what actually happened (as recorded on the individual financial statements of the two companies) with how the accounts would have appeared in the consolidated financial statements if the transfer had not occurred. Whereas the equipment currently resides on Special Foods' books (valued at the acquisition price of $7,000 with no accumulated depreciation), we want it to appear in the consolidated financial statements as if it had not been transferred from Peerless to Special Foods (historical cost of $9,000 with accumulated depreciation of $2,700 as explained previously). The following T-accounts illustrate how to determine the correct consolidation entry to defer the gain and correct the basis of the asset:

	Buildings & Equipment		Accumulated Depreciation		Gain on Sale	
Actual (Special Foods):	7,000			0		700
	2,000			2,700	700	
As if (Peerless):	9,000			2,700		0

Note that the consolidation entry comprises the adjustments to convert each account from "actual" to "as if" the transfer had not taken place.

Eliminate Gain on the Equipment Sold to Special Foods and Correct the Asset's Basis:

Gain on Sale	700	
Buildings & Equipment	2,000	
Accumulated Depreciation		2,700

Separate-Company Entries—20X2

During 20X2, Special Foods begins depreciating its $7,000 cost of the equipment acquired from Peerless Products over its remaining life of seven years using straight-line depreciation. The resulting depreciation is $1,000 per year ($7,000 ÷ 7 years):

(18)	Depreciation Expense	1,000	
	Accumulated Depreciation		1,000

Record depreciation expense for 20X2.

Peerless records its normal equity-method entries for 20X2 to reflect its share of Special Foods' $74,000 income and dividends of $40,000. Note that Special Foods' net income is only $74,000 in 20X2 because it has been reduced by the $1,000 of depreciation on the transferred asset. Accordingly, Peerless' share of that income is $59,200 ($74,000 × 0.80).

(19)	Investment in Special Foods	59,200	
	Income from Subsidiary		59,200

Record equity-method income: $74,000 × 0.80.

(20)	Cash	32,000	
	Investment in Special Foods		32,000

Record dividends from Special Foods: $40,000 × 0.80.

Peerless must record one additional equity-method entry related to the transferred asset. Because the equipment was recorded at the time of the December 31, 20X1, sale on Special

Foods' balance sheet at $7,000 (rather than the $6,300 book value at which it had been recorded on Peerless' books), Special Foods will record "extra" depreciation expense each year over the asset's seven-year life. Special Foods' annual depreciation ($7,000 ÷ 7 years = $1,000 per year) is $100 higher per year than it would have been if Peerless had kept the equipment ($900 per year).

Gain = 700	÷ 7 =	100	Extra depreciation	
BV = 6,300	÷ 7 =	900	Peerless' depreciation	
		1,000	Special Foods' total depreciation	

Special Foods' extra depreciation essentially cancels out one-seventh of the unrealized gain. As a result, over the asset's seven-year life, the unrealized gain is offset by the $700 of extra depreciation expense. Thus, in 20X2 (and each of the next six years) Peerless adjusts for the "extra depreciation" by reversing one-seventh of the gain deferral in its equity-method accounts as follows:

(21)	Investment in Special Foods	100	
	Income from Special Foods		100

Reverse one-seventh of the deferred gain on fixed asset sold to Special Foods.

Consolidation Worksheet—20X2

Figure 7–5 presents the consolidation worksheet for 20X2. The trial balance amounts from the Chapter 3 example have been adjusted to reflect the intercompany asset sale. To prepare the basic consolidation entry, we again analyze the updated book value of Special Foods and examine the allocation of each component to Peerless and the NCI shareholders. Thus, to present the consolidated financial statements as if the equipment had not been transferred to Special Foods, we need to decrease depreciation expense to the amount Peerless would have recorded had the equipment stayed on its books.

Calculations for Basic Consolidation Entry:

Book Value Calculations:

	NCI 20% +	Peerless 80%	= Common Stock	+ Retained Earnings
Original Book Value	64,000	256,000	200,000	120,000
+ Net Income	14,800	59,200		74,000
− Dividends	(8,000)	(32,000)		(40,000)
Ending Book Value	70,800	283,200	200,000	154,000

Adjustment to Basic Consolidation Entry:

	NCI 20%	Peerless 80%
Net Income	14,800	59,200
+ Extra Depreciation		100
Income to be Eliminated	14,800	59,300
Ending Book Value	70,800	283,200
+ Extra Depreciation		100
Adjusted Book Value	70,800	283,300

326   Chapter 7   *Intercompany Transfers of Services and Noncurrent Assets*

FIGURE 7–5   December 31, 20X2, Consolidation Worksheet, Next Period Following Intercompany Sale; Downstream
Sale of Equipment

	Peerless Products	Special Foods	Consolidation Entries		Consolidated
			DR	CR	
Income Statement					
Sales	450,000	300,000			750,000
Less: COGS	(180,000)	(160,000)			(340,000)
Less: Depreciation Expense	(49,100)	(21,000)		100	(70,000)
Less: Other Expenses	(60,000)	(45,000)			(105,000)
Income from Special Foods	59,300		59,300		0
Consolidated Net Income	220,200	74,000	59,300	100	235,000
NCI in Net Income			14,800		(14,800)
Controlling Interest Net Income	**220,200**	**74,000**	74,100	100	**220,200**
Statement of Retained Earnings					
Beginning Balance	420,000	120,000	120,000		420,000
Net Income	**220,200**	**74,000**	74,100	100	220,200
Less: Dividends Declared	(60,000)	(40,000)		40,000	(60,000)
Ending Balance	**580,200**	**154,000**	194,100	40,100	**580,200**
Balance Sheet					
Cash	298,000	78,000			376,000
Accounts Receivable	150,000	80,000			230,000
Inventory	180,000	90,000			270,000
Investment in Special Foods	282,600		700	283,300	0
Land	175,000	40,000			215,000
Buildings & Equipment	791,000	607,000	2,000	300,000	1,100,000
Less: Accumulated Depreciation	(496,400)	(341,000)	300,000	2,700	(540,000)
			100		
Total Assets	**1,380,200**	**554,000**	302,800	586,000	**1,651,000**
Accounts Payable	100,000	100,000			200,000
Bonds Payable	200,000	100,000			300,000
Common Stock	500,000	200,000	200,000		500,000
Retained Earnings	**580,200**	**154,000**	194,100	40,100	580,200
NCI in NA of Special Foods				70,800	70,800
Total Liabilities & Equity	**1,380,200**	**554,000**	394,100	110,900	**1,651,000**

The basic consolidation entry is the same as illustrated in Chapter 3 except that
we adjust the entries to the Investment in Special Foods and Income from Special
Foods accounts for the extra $100 of depreciation for 20X2 associated with the asset
transfer:

Basic Consolidation Entry:

Common Stock	200,000		← Common stock balance
Retained Earnings	120,000		← Beginning RE from trial balance
Income from Special Foods	59,300		← Peerless' % of NI with Adjustments
NCI in NI of Special Foods	14,800		← NCI share of reported NI
Dividends Declared		40,000	← 100% of sub's dividends declared
Investment in Special Foods		283,300	← Net BV with Adjustments
NCI in NA of Special Foods		70,800	← NCI share of net amount of BV

Optional Accumulated Depreciation Consolidation Entry:

Accumulated Depreciation	300,000	
Buildings & Equipment		300,000

← Accumulated depreciation at the time of the acquisition netted against cost

In the 20X2 worksheet, two consolidation entries are necessary. The first corrects depreciation expense by adjusting it to what it would have been if the asset had stayed on Peerless' books. The second revalues the asset from its current book value on Special Foods' books to what its book value would have been if it had stayed on Peerless' books. Again, T-accounts can be a helpful tool in figuring out the consolidation entries. We find it useful to calculate the consolidation of the extra depreciation expense first because the debit to Accumulated Depreciation affects the calculation of the credit to this account in the second entry.

	Buildings & Equipment		Accumulated Depreciation	
Actual (Special Foods):	7,000			1,000
	2,000		100	2,700
As if (Peerless):	9,000			3,600

The actual amounts in these accounts are based on Special Foods' acquisition price ($7,000) and its first year's accumulated depreciation ($1,000). The "as if" amounts are Peerless' original cost when it acquired the equipment from an unrelated party and the accumulated depreciation it would have reflected had the asset stayed on Peerless' books in the absence of the transfer, $3,600 ($2,700 prior year's accumulated depreciation + $900 current year's depreciation). The second consolidation entry is calculated as the amounts needed to adjust from actual to as if the asset had stayed on Peerless' books (after entering the debit to Accumulated Depreciation from the first consolidation entry).

Entries to Adjust Equipment and Accumulated Depreciation as if Still on Parent's Books:

Accumulated Depreciation	100	
Depreciation Expense		100

Investment in Special Foods	700	
Buildings & Equipment	2,000	
Accumulated Depreciation		2,700

Note that the first consolidation entry backs out the extra depreciation expense from Special Foods' income statement. Again, the debit to the investment account in the second consolidation entry is equal to the amount of unrealized gain at the beginning of the year. Given the gain deferral entry in 20X1 under the fully adjusted equity method, the investment account is "artificially low" by $700. Thus, the basic consolidation entry would "overeliminate" this account. Therefore, the debit of $700 helps to eliminate the investment account. The debit to Buildings and Equipment in this consolidation entry is simply the difference between Special Foods' cost ($7,000) and peerless' historical cost ($9,000). The credit to accumulated depreciation in this consolidation entry represents the difference between what accumulated depreciation would have been if the asset had stayed on Peerless' books, $3,600 ($900 × 4 years), and the amount Special Foods actually recorded, $1,000, plus the extra depreciation.

The following T-accounts illustrate how the worksheet entries eliminate the Investment in Special Foods and Income from Special Foods accounts:

328   Chapter 7   *Intercompany Transfers of Services and Noncurrent Assets*

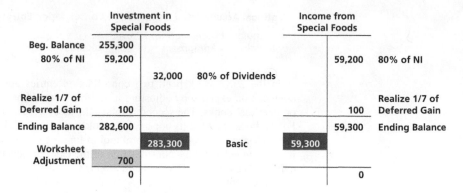

Once all the consolidation entries have been made in the worksheet, the adjusted balances exclude the effects of the intercompany transfer:

	Subsidiary Trial Balance	Consolidation	Consolidated Amounts
Buildings & Equipment	$7,000	$2,000	$9,000
Accumulated Depreciation	(1,000)	(2,600)	(3,600)
Depreciation Expense	1,000	(100)	900

Consolidated Net Income and Retained Earnings

Computation of consolidated net income for 20X2 must include an adjustment for the realization of profit on the 20X1 sale of equipment to Special Foods:

Peerless' separate income	$160,900
Partial realization of intercompany gain on downstream sale of equipment	100
Peerless' separate realized income	$161,000
Special Foods' net income	74,000
Consolidated net income, 20X2	$235,000
Income to noncontrolling interest ($74,000 × 0.20)	(14,800)
Income to controlling interest	$220,200

Because Peerless adjusts its investment income from Special Foods for unrealized gains and losses under the fully adjusted equity method, Peerless' Retained Earnings account equals the amount that should be reported as consolidated retained earnings. This is one of the advantages of using the fully adjusted equity method. Appendix 7A illustrates procedures for the modified equity method.

Noncontrolling Interest

Income allocated to the noncontrolling stockholders in 20X2 is equal to their proportionate share of the subsidiary's realized and reported income. Special Foods' net income for 20X2 is $74,000, and the noncontrolling interest's 20 percent share is $14,800 ($74,000 × 0.20).

The total noncontrolling interest in the net assets of Special Foods at the end of 20X2 is $70,800, equal to the noncontrolling stockholders' proportionate share of the total book value of the subsidiary:

Book value of Special Foods, December 31, 20X2:	
Common stock	$200,000
Retained earnings	154,000
Total book value	$354,000
Noncontrolling stockholders' proportionate share	× 0.20
Noncontrolling interest, December 31, 20X2	$ 70,800

Normally the noncontrolling interest at a particular date is equal to a proportionate share of the subsidiary's book value plus the noncontrolling interest's share of the remaining differential at that date. In this example, however, no differential was recognized at the date of combination.

Consolidation in Subsequent Years

The consolidation procedures in subsequent years are quite similar to those in 20X2. As long as Special Foods continues to hold and depreciate the equipment (i.e., until the asset is fully depreciated), consolidation procedures include two objectives each year:

1. Restating the asset and accumulated depreciation balances from actual to as if the asset had stayed on Peerless' books.
2. Adjusting depreciation expense for the year from actual to as if the asset had stayed on Peerless' books.

Figure 7–6 summarizes the worksheet consolidation entries at December 31 of each year from 20X1 to 20X8. Observation of the consolidation entries from 20X2–20X8 illustrates a clear pattern. The first consolidation entry to back out the extra depreciation is the same each year. Because the extra depreciation recorded each year by Special Foods effectively cancels out one-seventh of the unrealized gain and because Peerless continues to record an equity method adjustment to recognize this "canceling" of the unrealized gain as shown in entry (21), the debit to the Investment in Special Foods account and the credit to Accumulated Depreciation in the second consolidation entry each decreases by $100 each year until the asset is fully depreciated and the intercompany gain is fully recognized. After 20X8, once the transferred asset is fully depreciated no further equity-method entries are required on Peerless' books and only one consolidation entry is required in consolidation related to this asset transfer. The consolidation entry in all subsequent years (for as long as Special Foods owns the transferred asset) would simply debit Buildings and Equipment for $2,000 (to increase the basis from Special Foods acquisition price of $7,000 to Peerless' original purchase price of $9,000) and credit Accumulated Depreciation for $2,000.

Change in Estimated Life of Asset upon Transfer

When a depreciable asset is transferred between companies, a change in the remaining estimated economic life may be appropriate. For example, the acquiring company may use the asset in a different type of production process, or the frequency of use may change. When a change in the estimated life of a depreciable asset occurs at the time of an intercompany transfer, the treatment is no different than if the change had occurred while the asset remained on the books of the transferring affiliate. The new remaining useful life is used as a basis for depreciation both by the purchasing affiliate and for purposes of preparing consolidated financial statements. Thus, the as if calculation assumes the asset stayed on the transferring company's books but that the transferring company decided to revise its depreciation estimate to the useful life adopted by the new asset owner.

Upstream Sale

LO 7-6

Prepare equity-method journal entries and consolidation entries for the consolidation of a subsidiary following an upstream depreciable asset transfer.

The treatment of unrealized profits arising from upstream intercompany sales is identical to that of downstream sales except that the unrealized profit, and subsequent realization, must be allocated between the controlling and noncontrolling interests. We illustrate an upstream sale using the same example we demonstrated previously for the downstream sale. Assume that Special Foods sells equipment to Peerless Products for $7,000 on December 31, 20X1, and reports total income for 20X1 of $50,700 ($50,000 + $700), including the $700 gain on the sale of the equipment. Special Foods originally purchased the equipment for $9,000 three years before the intercompany sale.[3]

[3] To avoid additional complexity, we assume the equipment's fair value is equal to its book value on the business combination date. As a result, there is no differential related to the equipment.

FIGURE 7–6   Summary of Worksheet Consolidation Entries over the Life of the Transferred Asset (Downstream Transfer)

20X1:

Gain on Sale	700	
Buildings & Equipment	2,000	
Accumulated Depreciation		2,700

Note: This is the acquisition date, so Special Foods has not recorded any depreciation.

	Build. & Equip.		Acc. Depr.	
Actual (Special Foods):	7,000			0
	2,000			2,700
As if (Peerless):	9,000			2,700

20X2:

| Accumulated Depreciation | 100 | |
| Depreciation Expense | | 100 |

Investment in Special Foods	700	
Buildings & Equipment	2,000	
Accumulated Depreciation		2,700

	Build. & Equip.		Acc. Depr.	
Actual (Special Foods):	7,000			1,000
	2,000		100	2,700
As if (Peerless):	9,000			3,600

20X3:

| Accumulated Depreciation | 100 | |
| Depreciation Expense | | 100 |

Investment in Special Foods	600	
Buildings & Equipment	2,000	
Accumulated Depreciation		2,600

	Build. & Equip.		Acc. Depr.	
Actual (Special Foods):	7,000			2,000
	2,000		100	2,600
As if (Peerless):	9,000			4,500

20X4:

| Accumulated Depreciation | 100 | |
| Depreciation Expense | | 100 |

Investment in Special Foods	500	
Buildings & Equipment	2,000	
Accumulated Depreciation		2,500

	Build. & Equip.		Acc. Depr.	
Actual (Special Foods):	7,000			3,000
	2,000		100	2,500
As if (Peerless):	9,000			5,400

20X5:

| Accumulated Depreciation | 100 | |
| Depreciation Expense | | 100 |

Investment in Special Foods	400	
Buildings & Equipment	2,000	
Accumulated Depreciation		2,400

	Build. & Equip.		Acc. Depr.	
Actual (Special Foods):	7,000			4,000
	2,000		100	2,400
As if (Peerless):	9,000			6,300

20X6:

| Accumulated Depreciation | 100 | |
| Depreciation Expense | | 100 |

Investment in Special Foods	300	
Buildings & Equipment	2,000	
Accumulated Depreciation		2,300

	Build. & Equip.		Acc. Depr.	
Actual (Special Foods):	7,000			5,000
	2,000		100	2,300
As if (Peerless):	9,000			7,200

20X7:

| Accumulated Depreciation | 100 | |
| Depreciation Expense | | 100 |

Investment in Special Foods	200	
Buildings & Equipment	2,000	
Accumulated Depreciation		2,200

	Build. & Equip.		Acc. Depr.	
Actual (Special Foods):	7,000			6,000
	2,000		100	2,200
As if (Peerless):	9,000			8,100

20X8:

| Accumulated Depreciation | 100 | |
| Depreciation Expense | | 100 |

Investment in Special Foods	100	
Buildings & Equipment	2,000	
Accumulated Depreciation		2,100

	Build. & Equip.		Acc. Depr.	
Actual (Special Foods):	7,000			
	2,000		100	2,100
As if (Peerless):	9,000			9,000

After 20X8:

| Buildings & Equipment | 2,000 | |
| Accumulated Depreciation | | 2,000 |

	Build. & Equip.		Acc. Depr.	
Actual (Special Foods):	7,000			7,000
	2,000			2,000
As if (Peerless):	9,000			9,000

The book value of the equipment at the date of sale is as follows:

Original cost to Special Foods		$9,000
Accumulated depreciation on December 31, 20X1:		
Annual depreciation ($9,000 ÷ 10 years)	$900	
Number of years	× 3	
		(2,700)
Book value on December 31, 20X1		$6,300

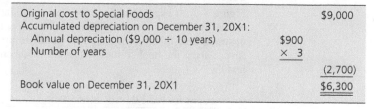

Separate-Company Entries—20X1

Special Foods records depreciation on the equipment for the year and the sale of the equipment to Peerless on December 31, 20X1, with the following entries:

December 31, 20X1

(22)	Depreciation Expense	900	
	Accumulated Depreciation		900
	Record 20X1 depreciation expense on equipment sold.		

December 31, 20X1

(23)	Cash	7,000	
	Accumulated Depreciation	2,700	
	Equipment		9,000
	Gain on Sale of Equipment		700
	Record sale of equipment.		

Peerless records the purchase of the equipment from Special Foods with the following entry:

December 31, 20X1

(24)	Equipment	7,000	
	Cash		7,000
	Record purchase of equipment.		

In addition, Peerless records the following equity-method entries on December 31, 20X1, to recognize its share of Special Foods' reported income and dividends:

(25)	Investment in Special Foods	40,560	
	Income from Special Foods		40,560
	Record Peerless' 80% share of Special Foods' 20X1 income: $50,700 × 0.80		

(26)	Cash	24,000	
	Investment in Special Foods		24,000
	Record Peerless' 80% share of Special Foods' 20X1 dividend: $30,000 × 0.80		

Finally, under the fully adjusted equity method, Peerless records its share of the gain deferral from the purchase of the equipment from Special Foods:

(27)	Income from Special Foods	560	
	Investment in Special Foods		560
	Defer 80% of the unrealized gain on equipment purchase from Special Foods: $700 × 0.80.		

These entries result in the following balances in the Investment in Special Foods and Income from Special Foods equity-method accounts:

	Investment in Special Foods				Income from Special Foods	
Acquisition	240,000					
80% of NI	40,560				40,560	80% of NI
		24,000	80% of Dividends			
		560	Defer 80% Gain	560		
Ending Balance	256,000				40,000	Ending Balance

Consolidation Worksheet—20X1

Figure 7–7 on page 334 illustrates the consolidation worksheet for 20X1. It is the same as the worksheet presented in Figure 7–5 except for minor modifications to reflect the upstream sale of the equipment. As usual, to prepare the basic consolidation entry, we first analyze the book value of Special Foods and allocate each component to Peerless and the NCI shareholders:

Calculations for Basic Consolidation Entry:

Book Value Calculations:

	NCI 20% +	Peerless 80%	=	Common Stock	+	Retained Earnings
Original Book Value	60,000	240,000		200,000		100,000
+ Net Income	10,140	40,560				50,700
− Dividends	(6,000)	(24,000)				(30,000)
Ending Book Value	64,140	256,560		200,000		120,700

Adjustment to Basic Consolidation Entry:

	NCI 20%	Peerless 80%
Net Income	10,140	40,560
− Gain on Equipment Deferral	(140)	(560)
Income to be Eliminated	10,000	40,000
Ending Book Value	64,140	256,560
− Gain on Equipment Deferral	(140)	(560)
Adjusted Book Value	64,000	256,000

The basic consolidation entry is the same as illustrated in Chapter 3 except that we adjust both the controlling and noncontrolling interests in Special Foods' income and net assets by their respective shares of the gain that has been deferred on the intercompany asset sale:

Basic Consolidation Entry:

Common Stock	200,000		← Common stock balance
Retained Earnings	100,000		← Beginning RE from trial balance
Income from Special Foods	40,000		← Peerless' % of NI with Adjustments
NCI in NI of Special Foods	10,000		← NCI share of NI with Adjustments
Dividends Declared		30,000	← 100% of sub's dividends declared
Investment in Special Foods		256,000	← Net BV with Adjustments
NCI in NA of Special Foods		64,000	← NCI share of net BV with Adjustments

Optional Accumulated Depreciation Consolidation Entry:

Accumulated Depreciation	300,000		Accumulated depreciation at the
Buildings & Equipment		300,000	← time of the acquisition netted against cost

As illustrated previously, one way to calculate the gain consolidation entry is to compare what actually happened (as recorded on the individual financial statements of the two companies) with how the transaction would appear in the consolidated financial statements if the asset transfer had not taken place. Whereas the equipment currently resides on Peerless' books (valued at the acquisition price of $7,000 with no accumulated depreciation), we want it to appear in the consolidated financial statements as if it had not been transferred from Special Foods to Peerless (historical cost of $9,000 with accumulated depreciation of $2,700, as explained previously). The following T-accounts illustrate how to determine the correct consolidation entry to defer the gain and correct the basis of the asset:

	Buildings & Equipment		Accumulated Depreciation		Gain on Sale	
Actual (Peerless):	7,000			0		700
	2,000			2,700	700	
As if (Special Foods):	9,000			2,700		0

Eliminate Gain on the Equipment Sold to Peerless and Correct the Asset's Basis:

Gain on Sale	700	
Buildings & Equipment	2,000	
Accumulated Depreciation		2,700

As it turns out, the consolidation entry for the upstream sale is exactly the same as the downstream example for 20X1.

As illustrated in Figure 7–7, the income assigned to the noncontrolling shareholders based on their share of Special Foods' realized income is computed as follows:

Net income of Special Foods for 20X1	$50,700
Unrealized gain on intercompany sale	(700)
Realized net income of Special Foods for 20X1	$50,000
Noncontrolling stockholders' proportionate share	× 0.20
Income to noncontrolling interest, 20X1	$10,000

In the upstream case, as in the downstream case, consolidated net income is reduced by the amount of the current period's unrealized gain on the intercompany transfer. However, in the upstream case, the unrealized gain reduces both the controlling and noncontrolling interests proportionately because both are owners of Special Foods and share in the gain. The allocation of Special Foods' income to the controlling and noncontrolling interests is based on Special Foods' realized net income after having deducted the unrealized gain. The computation and allocation of 20X1 consolidated net income is as follows:

Peerless' separate income		$140,000
Special Foods' net income	$50,700	
Less: Unrealized intercompany gain on upstream sale of equipment	(700)	
Special Foods' realized net income		50,000
Consolidated net income, 20X1		$190,000
Income to noncontrolling interest ($50,000 × 0.20)		(10,000)
Income to controlling interest		$180,000

Separate-Company Books—20X2

In the year following the intercompany transfer, Special Foods reports net income of $75,900 (because the $900 of depreciation expense on the transferred asset is now on

FIGURE 7–7   December 31, 20X1, Consolidation Worksheet, Period of Intercompany Sale; Upstream Sale of Equipment

	Peerless Products	Special Foods	Consolidation Entries DR	Consolidation Entries CR	Consolidated
Income Statement					
Sales	400,000	200,000			600,000
Less: COGS	(170,000)	(115,000)			(285,000)
Less: Depreciation Expense	(50,000)	(20,000)			(70,000)
Less: Other Expenses	(40,000)	(15,000)			(55,000)
Gain on Sale of Fixed Asset		700	700		0
Income from Special Foods	40,000		40,000		0
Consolidated Net Income	180,000	50,700	40,700	0	190,000
NCI in Net Income			10,000		(10,000)
Controlling Interest Net Income	**180,000**	**50,700**	**50,700**	**0**	**180,000**
Statement of Retained Earnings					
Beginning Balance	300,000	100,000	100,000		300,000
Net Income	**180,000**	**50,700**	50,700	0	180,000
Less: Dividends Declared	(60,000)	(30,000)		30,000	(60,000)
Ending Balance	**420,000**	**120,700**	**150,700**	**30,000**	**420,000**
Balance Sheet					
Cash	257,000	82,000			339,000
Accounts Receivable	75,000	50,000			125,000
Inventory	100,000	75,000			175,000
Investment in Special Foods	256,000			256,000	0
Land	175,000	40,000			215,000
Buildings & Equipment	807,000	591,000	2,000	300,000	1,100,000
Less: Accumulated Depreciation	(450,000)	(317,300)	300,000	2,700	(470,000)
Total Assets	**1,220,000**	**520,700**	**302,000**	**558,700**	**1,484,000**
Accounts Payable	100,000	100,000			200,000
Bonds Payable	200,000	100,000			300,000
Common Stock	500,000	200,000	200,000		500,000
Retained Earnings	**420,000**	**120,700**	150,700	30,000	420,000
NCI in NA of Special Foods				64,000	64,000
Total Liabilities & Equity	**1,220,000**	**520,700**	**350,700**	**94,000**	**1,484,000**

Peerless' income statement). In the upstream example, the extra $100 of depreciation expense now appears in Peerless' income statement:

Gain = 700	÷ 7 =	100	Extra depreciation
BV = 6,300	÷ 7 =	900	Special Foods' depreciation
		1,000	Peerless' total depreciation

Peerless records the normal fully adjusted equity-method entries on its books to recognize its share of Special Foods' 20X2 income and dividends. Moreover, it recognizes 80 percent of the deferred gain, $80 (($700 ÷ 7 years) × 0.80).

Peerless' extra depreciation essentially cancels out one-seventh of the unrealized gain. As a result, over the seven-year life of the asset, Peerless recognizes one-seventh of the gain deferral each year in its equity-method accounts:

(28)	Investment in Special Foods	80	
	Income from Special Foods		80

Recognize 80% of 1/7 of the deferred gain on fixed asset purchased from Special Foods.

At the end of 20X2, the Investment in Special Foods and Income from Special Foods accounts on Peerless' books appear as follows:

	Investment in Special Foods		Income from Special Foods	
Beg. Balance	256,000			
80% of NI	60,720		60,720	**80% of NI**
Realize		32,000 **80% of Dividends**		**Realize**
80% of 1/7	80		80	**80% of 1/7**
Deferred Gain				**Deferred Gain**
Ending Balance	284,800		60,800	**Ending Balance**

Consolidation Entries—20X2

Figure 7–8 presents the consolidation worksheet for 20X2. We again analyze the updated book value of Special Foods and examine the allocation of each component to Peerless and the NCI shareholders. Also, to present the consolidated financial statements as if the equipment had not been transferred to Peerless, we need to decrease depreciation expense to the amount Special Foods would have recorded had the equipment stayed on its books.

Calculations for Basic Consolidation Entry:

Book Value Calculations:				
	NCI 20% +	Peerless 80% =	Common Stock +	Retained Earnings
Original Book Value	64,140	256,560	200,000	120,700
+ Net Income	15,180	60,720		75,900
− Dividends	(8,000)	(32,000)		(40,000)
Ending Book Value	71,320	285,280	200,000	156,600

Adjustment to Basic Consolidation Entry:		
	NCI 20%	Peerless 80%
Net Income	15,180	60,720
+ Excess Depreciation	20	80
Income to be Eliminated	15,200	60,800
Ending Book Value	71,320	285,280
+ Excess Depreciation	20	80
Adjusted Book Value	71,340	285,360

The basic consolidation entry is the same as illustrated in Chapter 3 except that we adjust the entries to the Investment in Special Foods and Income from Special Foods accounts for their 80 percent share of the extra $100 of depreciation for 20X2 associated with the asset transfer. Moreover, we add back 20 percent of the $100 of extra depreciation to the NCI in NI of Special Foods and NCI in NA of Special Foods:

FIGURE 7–8   December 31, 20X2, Consolidation Worksheet, Next Period Following Intercompany Sale; Upstream Sale of Equipment

	Peerless Products	Special Foods	Consolidation Entries DR	Consolidation Entries CR	Consolidated
Income Statement					
Sales	450,000	300,000			750,000
Less: COGS	(180,000)	(160,000)			(340,000)
Less: Depreciation Expense	(51,000)	(19,100)		100	(70,000)
Less: Other Expenses	(60,000)	(45,000)			(105,000)
Income from Special Foods	60,800		60,800		0
Consolidated Net Income	219,800	75,900	60,800	100	235,000
NCI in Net Income			15,200		(15,200)
Controlling Interest Net Income	**219,800**	**75,900**	**76,000**	**100**	**219,800**
Statement of Retained Earnings					
Beginning Balance	420,000	120,700	120,700		420,000
Net Income	**219,800**	**75,900**	76,000	100	219,800
Less: Dividends Declared	(60,000)	(40,000)		40,000	(60,000)
Ending Balance	**579,800**	**156,600**	**196,700**	**40,100**	**579,800**
Balance Sheet					
Cash	284,000	92,000			376,000
Accounts Receivable	150,000	80,000			230,000
Inventory	180,000	90,000			270,000
Investment in Special Foods	284,800		560	285,360	0
Land	175,000	40,000			215,000
Buildings & Equipment	807,000	591,000	2,000	300,000	1,100,000
Less: Accumulated Depreciation	(501,000)	(336,400)	300,000	2,700	(540,000)
			100		
Total Assets	**1,379,800**	**556,600**	**302,660**	**588,060**	**1,651,000**
Accounts Payable	100,000	100,000			200,000
Bonds Payable	200,000	100,000			300,000
Common Stock	500,000	200,000	200,000		500,000
Retained Earnings	**579,800**	**156,600**	196,700	40,100	579,800
NCI in NA of Special Foods			140	71,340	71,200
Total Liabilities & Equity	**1,379,800**	**556,600**	**396,840**	**111,440**	**1,651,000**

Basic Consolidation Entry:

Common Stock	200,000	← Common stock balance
Retained Earnings	120,700	← Beginning RE from trial balance
Income from Special Foods	60,800	← Peerless' % of NI with Adjustments
NCI in NI of Special Foods	15,200	← NCI share of NI with Adjustments
Dividends Declared	40,000	← 100% of sub's dividends declared
Investment in Special Foods	285,360	← Net BV with Adjustments
NCI in NA of Special Foods	71,340	← NCI share of BV with Adjustments

Optional Accumulated Depreciation Consolidation Entry:

Accumulated Depreciation	300,000	← Accumulated depreciation at the time of the acquisition netted against cost
Buildings & Equipment		300,000	

In the 20X2 worksheet, the same two consolidation entries discussed in the downstream example are necessary. The only difference from the downstream example is that the amount of deferred gain on Special Foods' equipment sale to Peerless at the beginning of the period ($700) is allocated between Peerless and the NCI shareholders based on their relative ownership percentages. Again, T-accounts can be a helpful tool in figuring out the consolidation entries. It is helpful to calculate the consolidation of the extra depreciation expense first because the debit to Accumulated Depreciation affects the calculation of the credit to this account in the second entry.

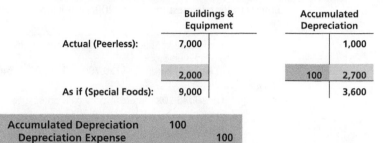

The actual amounts in these accounts are based on Peerless' acquisition price ($7,000) and its first year's accumulated depreciation ($1,000). The *as if* amounts are Special Foods' original cost when it acquired the equipment from an unrelated party and the accumulated depreciation it would have reflected had the asset stayed on Special Foods' books in the absence of the transfer, $3,600 ($2,700 prior-year accumulated depreciation + $900 current-year depreciation). The second consolidation entry is calculated as the amounts needed to adjust from actual to *as if* the asset had stayed on Special Foods' books.

Entries to Adjust Equipment and Accumulated Depreciation as if Still on Subsidiary's Books:

Investment in Special Foods	560	
NCI in NA of Special Foods	140	
Buildings & Equipment	2,000	
Accumulated Depreciation		2,700

As explained in the downstream example, the key to understanding these consolidation entries is that the debit to the investment account in the first consolidation entry is equal to Peerless' share of the unrealized gain at the beginning of the year. Given the gain deferral entry in 20X1 under the fully adjusted equity method, the investment account is "artificially low" by $560. Thus, the basic consolidation entry would "over-eliminate" this account. For this reason, the debit of $560 helps to eliminate the investment account. The rest of the deferral, $140, is allocated to the noncontrolling interest.

Consolidated Net Income

Peerless Products' separate income for 20X2 is $159,000 after deducting an additional $1,000 for the depreciation on the transferred asset. Consolidated net income for 20X2 is computed and allocated as follows:

Peerless' separate income		$159,000
Special Foods' net income	$75,900	
Partial realization of intercompany gain on upstream sale of equipment	100	
Special Foods' realized net income		76,000
Consolidated net income, 20X2		$235,000
Income to noncontrolling interest ($76,000 × 0.20)		(15,200)
Income to controlling interest		$219,800

Note that the partial realization of intercompany gain on the asset transfer is the extra depreciation recorded this year by Peerless.

Noncontrolling Interest

The noncontrolling interest's share of income is $15,200 for 20X2, computed as the noncontrolling stockholders' proportionate share of the realized income of Special Foods ($76,000 × 0.20). Total noncontrolling interest in the absence of a differential is computed as the noncontrolling stockholders' proportionate share of the stockholders' equity of Special Foods, excluding unrealized gains and losses. On December 31, 20X2, the noncontrolling interest totals $71,200, computed as follows:

Book value of Special Foods, December 31, 20X2:	
Common Stock	$200,000
Retained earnings ($120,700 + $75,900 − $40,000)	156,600
Total book value	$356,600
Unrealized 20X1 intercompany gain on upstream sale	(700)
Intercompany gain realized in 20X2	100
Realized book value of Special Foods	$356,000
Noncontrolling stockholders' share	× 0.20
Noncontrolling interest, December 31, 20X2	$ 71,200

Consolidation in Subsequent Years

The consolidation procedures in subsequent years are quite similar to those in 20X2. Figure 7–9 summarizes the worksheet consolidation entries at December 31 of each year from 20X2 to 20X8. We omit 20X1 because it is identical to the downstream entry reported in Figure 7–6. Observation of the consolidation entries from 20X2–20X8 again illustrates a clear pattern. The first consolidation entry to back out the extra depreciation is the same each year. Because the extra depreciation recorded each year by Peerless effectively cancels out one-seventh of the unrealized gain and because Peerless continues to record an equity-method adjustment to recognize this acknowledgment of the unrealized gain (entry 28), the sum of the debits to the Investment and NCI in NA of Special Foods accounts, and the credit to accumulated depreciation in the second consolidation entry each decreases by $100 each year until the asset is fully depreciated and the intercompany gain is fully recognized. After 20X8, no further equity-method entries are required on Peerless' books, and only one consolidation entry is required in consolidation related to this asset transfer. The consolidation entry in all subsequent years (for as long as Peerless owns the transferred asset) would simply debit Buildings and Equipment for $2,000 (to increase the basis from Peerless' acquisition price of $7,000 to Special Foods' original purchase price of $9,000) and credit Accumulated Depreciation for $2,000.

Asset Transfers before Year-End

In cases in which an intercompany asset transfer occurs during a period rather than at its end, a portion of the intercompany gain or loss is considered to be realized in the period of the transfer. When this occurs, the worksheet consolidation entries at year-end must include an adjustment of depreciation expense and accumulated depreciation. The amount of this adjustment is equal to the difference between the depreciation recorded by the purchaser and that which would have been recorded by the seller during the portion of the year elapsing after the intercompany sale.

For example, if the upstream equipment sale from Special Foods to Peerless had occurred on January 1, 20X1, rather than on December 31, 20X1, an additional consolidation entry (the second entry listed for every other year) would be needed in the consolidation worksheet on December 31, 20X1, to eliminate the "extra" depreciation.

FIGURE 7–9   Summary of Worksheet Consolidation Entries over the Life of the Transferred Asset (Upstream Transfer)

					Build. & Equip.		Acc. Depr.	
20X2:	Accumulated Depreciation	100						
	Depreciation Expense		100	Actual (Peerless):	7,000			1,000
	Investment in Special Foods	560			2,000		100	2,700
	NCI in NA of Special Foods	140						
	Buildings & Equipment	2,000		As if (Special Foods):	9,000			3,600
	Accumulated Depreciation		2,700					

					Build. & Equip.		Acc. Depr.	
20X3:	Accumulated Depreciation	100						
	Depreciation Expense		100	Actual (Peerless):	7,000			2,000
	Investment in Special Foods	480			2,000		100	2,600
	NCI in NA of Special Foods	120						
	Buildings & Equipment	2,000		As if (Special Foods):	9,000			4,500
	Accumulated Depreciation		2,600					

					Build. & Equip.		Acc. Depr.	
20X4:	Accumulated Depreciation	100						
	Depreciation Expense		100	Actual (Peerless):	7,000			3,000
	Investment in Special Foods	400			2,000		100	2,500
	NCI in NA of Special Foods	100						
	Buildings & Equipment	2,000		As if (Special Foods):	9,000			5,400
	Accumulated Depreciation		2,500					

					Build. & Equip.		Acc. Depr.	
20X5:	Accumulated Depreciation	100						
	Depreciation Expense		100	Actual (Peerless):	7,000			4,000
	Investment in Special Foods	320			2,000		100	2,400
	NCI in NA of Special Foods	80						
	Buildings & Equipment	2,000		As if (Special Foods):	9,000			6,300
	Accumulated Depreciation		2,400					

					Build. & Equip.		Acc. Depr.	
20X6:	Accumulated Depreciation	100						
	Depreciation Expense		100	Actual (Peerless):	7,000			5,000
	Investment in Special Foods	240			2,000		100	2,300
	NCI in NA of Special Foods	60						
	Buildings & Equipment	2,000		As if (Special Foods):	9,000			7,200
	Accumulated Depreciation		2,300					

					Build. & Equip.		Acc. Depr.	
20X7:	Accumulated Depreciation	100						
	Depreciation Expense		100	Actual (Peerless):	7,000			6,000
	Investment in Special Foods	160			2,000		100	2,200
	NCI in NA of Special Foods	40						
	Buildings & Equipment	2,000		As if (Special Foods):	9,000			8,100
	Accumulated Depreciation		2,200					

					Build. & Equip.		Acc. Depr.	
20X8:	Accumulated Depreciation	100						
	Depreciation Expense		100	Actual (Peerless):	7,000			7,000
	Investment in Special Foods	80			2,000		100	2,100
	NCI in NA of Special Foods	20						
	Buildings & Equipment	2,000		As if (Special Foods):	9,000			9,000
	Accumulated Depreciation		2,100					

					Build. & Equip.		Acc. Depr.	
After 20X8:	Buildings & Equipment	2,000						
	Accumulated Depreciation		2,000	Actual (Peerless):	7,000			7,000
					2,000			2,000
				As if (Special Foods):	9,000			9,000

INTERCOMPANY TRANSFERS OF AMORTIZABLE ASSETS

Production rights, patents, and other types of intangible assets may be sold to affiliated enterprises. Accounting for intangible assets usually differs from accounting for tangible assets in that amortizable intangibles normally are reported at the remaining unamortized balance without the use of a contra account for accumulated amortization. Other than netting the accumulated amortization on an intangible asset against the asset cost, the intercompany sale of intangibles is treated in the same way in consolidation as the intercompany sale of tangible assets.

SUMMARY OF KEY CONCEPTS

Transactions between affiliated companies within a consolidated entity must be viewed as if they occurred within a single company. Under generally accepted accounting principles, the effects of transactions that are internal to an enterprise may not be included in external accounting reports. Therefore, the effects of all transactions between companies within the consolidated entity must be eliminated in preparing consolidated financial statements.

The treatment of intercompany noncurrent asset transfers is similar to the treatment of intercompany inventory transfers discussed in Chapter 6. The consolidation of intercompany transactions must include the removal of unrealized intercompany profits. When one company sells an asset to an affiliate within the consolidated entity, any intercompany profit is not considered realized until confirmed by subsequent events. If the asset has an unlimited life, as with land, the unrealized intercompany gain or loss is realized at the time the asset is resold to a party outside the consolidated entity. If the asset has a limited life, the unrealized intercompany gain or loss is considered to be realized over the remaining life of the asset as the asset is used and depreciated or amortized.

Consolidation procedures relating to unrealized gains and losses on intercompany transfers of assets involve worksheet adjustments to restate the assets and associated accounts, such as accumulated depreciation, to the balances that would be reported if there had been no intercompany transfer. In the period of transfer, the income assigned to the shareholders of the selling affiliate must be reduced by their share of the unrealized intercompany profit. If the sale is a downstream sale, the unrealized intercompany gain or loss is eliminated against the controlling interest. When an upstream sale occurs, the unrealized intercompany gain or loss is eliminated proportionately against the controlling and noncontrolling interests.

KEY TERMS

downstream sale, *307*   upstream sale, *307*

Appendix **7A**	Intercompany Noncurrent Asset Transactions—Modified Equity Method and Cost Method

A parent company may account for a subsidiary using any of several methods. So long as the subsidiary is to be consolidated, the method of accounting for it on the parent's books will have no impact on the consolidated financial statements. Although the primary focus of this chapter is on consolidation using the fully adjusted equity method on the parent's books, two other methods are used in practice with some frequency as well. These methods are the modified equity method and the cost method.

MODIFIED EQUITY METHOD

A company that chooses to account for an investment using the modified equity method records its proportionate share of subsidiary income and dividends in the same manner as under the fully adjusted equity method. However, it does not defer its share of any unrealized profits from intercompany transactions using equity-method entries. Instead, these unrealized gains and losses are removed from the parent's retained earnings in the period after the intercompany sale. In the absence of these equity-method adjustments, the parent's net income is usually not equal to the amount of consolidated net income allocated to the controlling interest.

As an illustration, assume the same facts as in the upstream sale of equipment discussed previously and reflected in the worksheets presented in Figures 7–7 and 7–8. Special Foods sells equipment to Peerless Products for $7,000 on December 31, 20X1, and reports total income of $50,700 for 20X1, including the $700 gain on the sale of the equipment. Special Foods originally purchased the equipment for $9,000 three years before the intercompany sale. Both companies use straight-line depreciation.

As illustrated previously, Special Foods records 20X1 depreciation on the equipment and the gain on the December 31, 20X1, sale of the equipment to Peerless with the following entries:

	December 31, 20X1		
(29)	Depreciation Expense	900	
	Accumulated Depreciation		900
	Record 20X1 depreciation expense on equipment sold.		

	December 31, 20X1		
(30)	Cash	7,000	
	Accumulated Depreciation	2,700	
	Equipment		9,000
	Gain on Sale of Equipment		700
	Record sale of equipment.		

Peerless records the purchase of the equipment from Special Foods with the following entry:

	December 31, 20X1		
(31)	Equipment	7,000	
	Cash		7,000
	Record purchase of equipment.		

Modified Equity-Method Entries—20X1

In addition, Peerless records the following modified equity-method entries on December 31, 20X1, to recognize its share of Special Foods' reported income and dividends:

(32)	Investment in Special Foods	40,560	
	Income from Special Foods		40,560
	Record Peerless' 80% share of Special Foods' 20X1 income: $50,700 × 0.80.		

(33)	Cash	24,000	
	Investment in Special Foods		24,000
	Record Peerless' 80% share of Special Foods' 20X1 dividend: $30,000 × 0.80.		

However, Peerless does not record an equity-method entry for its share of the gain deferral from the purchase of the asset from Special Foods.

Consolidation Entries—20X1

The consolidation worksheet consolidation entries under the modified equity method are almost identical to those used under the fully adjusted equity method for 20X1 with one minor exception. We go through the exact same analysis of the book value of Special Foods and allocate each component to Peerless and the NCI shareholders:

Calculations for Basic Consolidation Entry:

Book Value Calculations:				
	NCI 20% +	Peerless 80%	= Common Stock	+ Retained Earnings
Original Book Value	60,000	240,000	200,000	100,000
+ Net Income	10,140	40,560		50,700
− Dividends	(6,000)	(24,000)		(30,000)
Ending Book Value	64,140	256,560	200,000	120,700

(continued)

Adjustment to Basic Consolidation Entry:

	NCI	Peerless
Net Income	10,140	40,560
– Gain Deferral	(140)	(560)
Income to be Eliminated	10,000	40,000
Ending Book Value	64,140	256,560
– Gain Deferral	(140)	(560)
Adjusted Book Value	64,000	256,000

The basic consolidation entry under the modified equity method is almost identical to the basic consolidation entry under the fully adjusted equity method with one minor exception. Because we don't make equity-method adjustments for the unrealized gain in Peerless' books, we no longer adjust the entries to the Investment in Special Foods and Income from Special Foods accounts for the gain that has been deferred on the intercompany asset sale. Note that we continue to adjust the NCI shareholders' share of Special Foods' income and their share of Special Foods' book value of net assets:

Basic Consolidation Entry:

Common Stock	200,000		← Common stock balance
Retained Earnings	100,000		← Beginning RE from trial balance
Income from Special Foods	40,560		← Peerless' % of reported NI
NCI in NI of Special Foods	10,000		← NCI share of NI with Adjustments
Dividends Declared		30,000	← 100% of sub's dividends declared
Investment in Special Foods		256,560	← Net BV left in the invest. acct.
NCI in NA of Special Foods		64,000	← NCI share of net BV with Adjustments

Optional Accumulated Depreciation Consolidation Entry:

Accumulated depreciation	300,000		Accumulated depreciation at the
Buildings & equipment		300,000	← time of the acquisition netted against cost

The following T-accounts illustrate that we arrive at the exact same answer in 20X1 for eliminating the intercompany gain on the sale of equipment from Special Foods to Peerless Products:

	Buildings & Equipment		Accumulated Depreciation		Gain on Sale	
Actual (Special Foods):	7,000			0		700
	2,000			2,700	700	
As if (Peerless):	9,000			2,700		0

Eliminate Gain on the Equipment Sold to Special Foods and Correct the Assets' Basis:

Gain on Sale	700	
Buildings & Equipment	2,000	
Accumulated Depreciation		2,700

Figure 7–10 illustrates the consolidation worksheet for 20X1.

Modified Equity-Method Entries—20X2

In 20X2, Peerless records its share of Special Foods' $75,900 income and $40,000 of dividends as follows:

(34)	Investment in Special Foods	60,720	
	Income from Special Foods		60,720

Record Peerless' 80% share of Special Foods' 20X2 income: $75,900 × 0.80.

(35)	Cash	32,000	
	Investment in Special Foods		32,000

Record Peerless' 80% share of Special Foods' 20X2 dividend: $40,000 × 0.80.

Peerless does not make an entry under the modified equity method to increase income for the partial realization of the unrealized intercompany gain.

Consolidation Entries—20X2

To derive the consolidation entries for the 20X2 worksheet, we again analyze the updated book value of Special Foods and examine the allocation of each component to Peerless and the NCI shareholders. Also, to present the consolidated financial statements as if the equipment had not been transferred to Peerless, we need to decrease depreciation expense to the amount Special Foods would have recorded had the equipment stayed on its books.

FIGURE 7–10 December 31, 20X1, Modified Equity Method Consolidation Worksheet, Period of Intercompany Sale; Upstream Sale of Equipment

	Peerless Products	Special Foods	Consolidation Entries DR	Consolidation Entries CR	Consolidated
Income Statement					
Sales	400,000	200,000			600,000
Less: COGS	(170,000)	(115,000)			(285,000)
Less: Depreciation Expense	(50,000)	(20,000)			(70,000)
Less: Other Expenses	(40,000)	(15,000)			(55,000)
Gain on Sale of Fixed Asset		700	700		0
Income from Special Foods	40,560		40,560		0
Consolidated Net Income	180,560	50,700	41,260	0	190,000
NCI in Net Income			10,000		(10,000)
Controlling Interest Net Income	**180,560**	**50,700**	**51,260**	**0**	**180,000**
Statement of Retained Earnings					
Beginning Balance	300,000	100,000	100,000		300,000
Net Income	**180,560**	**50,700**	51,260	0	180,000
Less: Dividends Declared	(60,000)	(30,000)		30,000	(60,000)
Ending Balance	**420,560**	**120,700**	**151,260**	**30,000**	**420,000**
Balance Sheet					
Cash	257,000	82,000			339,000
Accounts Receivable	75,000	50,000			125,000
Inventory	100,000	75,000			175,000
Investment in Special Foods	256,560			256,560	0
Land	175,000	40,000			215,000
Buildings & Equipment	807,000	591,000	2,000	300,000	1,100,000
Less: Accumulated Depreciation	(450,000)	(317,300)	300,000	2,700	(470,000)
Total Assets	**1,220,560**	**520,700**	**302,000**	**559,260**	**1,484,000**
Accounts Payable	100,000	100,000			200,000
Bonds Payable	200,000	100,000			300,000
Common Stock	500,000	200,000	200,000		500,000
Retained Earnings	**420,560**	**120,700**	151,260	30,000	420,000
NCI in NA of Special Foods				64,000	64,000
Total Liabilities & Equity	**1,220,560**	**520,700**	**351,260**	**94,000**	**1,484,000**

Calculations for Basic Consolidation Entry:

Book Value Calculations:

	NCI 20% +	Peerless 80% =	Common Stock +	Retained Earnings
Original Book Value	64,140	256,560	200,000	120,700
+ Net Income	15,180	60,720		75,900
− Dividends	(8,000)	(32,000)		(40,000)
Ending Book Value	71,320	285,280	200,000	156,600

Adjustment to Basic Consolidation Entry:

	NCI	Peerless
Net Income	15,180	60,720
+ Excess Depreciation	20	80
Income to be Eliminated	15,200	60,800
Ending Book Value	71,320	285,280
+ Excess Depreciation	20	80
Adjusted Book Value	71,340	285,360

The basic consolidation entry is the same as illustrated for the fully adjusted equity method except that we no longer adjust the entries to the Investment in Special Foods and Income from Special Foods accounts for their 80 percent share of the extra $100 of depreciation for 20X2 associated with the asset transfer. However, we continue to add back 20 percent of the $100 of extra depreciation to the NCI in NI of Special Foods and NCI in NA of Special Foods:

Basic Consolidation Entry:

Common Stock	200,000		← Common stock balance
Retained Earnings	120,700		← Beginning RE from trial balance
Income from Special Foods	60,720		← Peerless' share of reported NI
NCI in NI of Special Foods	15,200		← NCI share of NI with Adjustments
Dividends Declared		40,000	← 100% of sub's dividends declared
Investment in Special Foods		285,280	← Net BV left in the invest. acct.
NCI in NA of Special Foods		71,340	← NCI share of BV with Adjustments

Optional Accumulated Depreciation Consolidation Entry:

Accumulated Depreciation	300,000	
Buildings & Equipment		300,000

← Accumulated depreciation at the time of the acquisition netted against cost

In the 20X2 worksheet, the only difference from the fully adjusted equity-method example is that although the amount of deferred gain on Special Foods' equipment sale to Peerless at the beginning of the period ($700) is still allocated between Peerless and the NCI shareholders based on their relative ownership percentages, the amount accruing to Peerless is recorded as a decrease to beginning Retained Earnings rather than as a debit to the Investment in Special Foods account. The reason the consolidation entry affects the Retained Earnings account instead of the Investment in Special Foods account is that no adjustments have been made under the equity method to ensure that Peerless' books are up-to-date. T-accounts can be a helpful tool in figuring out the consolidation entries:

	Buildings & Equipment		Accumulated Depreciation	
Actual (Special Foods):	7,000			1,000
	2,000		100	2,700
As if (Peerless):	9,000			3,600

| Accumulated Depreciation | 100 | |
| Depreciation Expense | | 100 |

Entries to Adjust Equipment and Accumulated Depreciation as if Still on Parent's Books:

Retained Earnings	560	
NCI in NA of Special Foods	140	
Buildings & Equipment	2,000	
Accumulated Depreciation		2,700

Again, these consolidation entries related to the intercompany asset sale are identical to those used under the fully adjusted equity method with the one exception that the debit for $560 in the second consolidation entry goes to Retained Earnings rather than the Investment in Special Foods account. In all cases, the entries under the modified equity method are identical to those illustrated in Figure 7-9 except that the entries to the Investment in Special Foods account are replaced with entries to Retained Earnings.

Figure 7-11 illustrates the consolidation worksheet for 20X2.

FIGURE 7–11   December 31, 20X2, Modified Equity-Method Consolidation Worksheet, Next Period Following Intercompany Sale; Upstream Sale of Equipment

	Peerless Products	Special Foods	Consolidation Entries		Consolidated
			DR	CR	
Income Statement					
Sales	450,000	300,000			750,000
Less: COGS	(180,000)	(160,000)			(340,000)
Less: Depreciation Expense	(51,000)	(19,100)		100	(70,000)
Less: Other Expenses	(60,000)	(45,000)			(105,000)
Income from Special Foods	60,720		60,720		0
Consolidated Net Income	219,720	75,900	60,720	100	235,000
NCI in Net Income			15,200		(15,200)
Controlling Interest Net Income	**219,720**	**75,900**	**75,920**	**100**	**219,800**
Statement of Retained Earnings					
Beginning Balance	420,560	120,700	120,700		420,000
			560		
Net Income	**219,720**	**75,900**	75,920	100	219,800
Less: Dividends Declared	(60,000)	(40,000)		40,000	(60,000)
Ending Balance	**580,280**	**156,600**	**197,180**	**40,100**	**579,800**
Balance Sheet					
Cash	284,000	92,000			376,000
Accounts Receivable	150,000	80,000			230,000
Inventory	180,000	90,000			270,000
Investment in Special Foods	285,280			285,280	0
Land	175,000	40,000			215,000
Buildings & Equipment	807,000	591,000	2,000	300,000	1,100,000
Less: Accumulated Depreciation	(501,000)	(336,400)	300,000	2,700	(540,000)
			100		
Total Assets	**1,380,280**	**556,600**	**302,100**	**587,980**	**1,651,000**
Accounts Payable	100,000	100,000			200,000
Bonds Payable	200,000	100,000			300,000
Common Stock	500,000	200,000	200,000		500,000
Retained Earnings	**580,280**	**156,600**	197,180	40,100	579,800
NCI in NA of Special Foods			140	71,340	71,200
Total Liabilities & Equity	**1,380,280**	**556,600**	**397,320**	**111,440**	**1,651,000**

COST METHOD

When using the cost method of accounting for an investment in a subsidiary, the parent records dividends received from the subsidiary during the period as income. No entries are made under the cost method to record the parent's share of undistributed subsidiary earnings, amortize differential, or remove unrealized intercompany profits.

To illustrate consolidation following an intercompany sale of equipment when the parent accounts for its subsidiary investment using the cost method, assume the same facts as in the previous illustrations of an upstream sale.

Consolidation Entries—20X1

The following consolidation entries would appear in the worksheet used to consolidate Peerless and Special Foods at the end of 20X1, assuming Peerless uses the cost method to account for its investment:

Investment Consolidation Entry:

Common Stock	200,000	
Retained Earnings	100,000	
Investment in Special Foods		240,000
NCI in NA of Special Foods		60,000

Dividend Consolidation Entry:

Dividend Income	24,000	
NCI in NI of Special Foods	6,000	
Dividends Declared		30,000

The amount of undistributed net income assigned to the NCI is adjusted for the NCI's share of the gain deferral.

NCI in NI and NCI in NA of Special Foods:

	NCI 20%
Net Income	10,140
+ Dividend	(6,000)
− Gain on Equipment Deferral	(140)
NCI in NI of Special Foods	4,000

Assign Undistributed Income to NCI:

NCI in NI of Special Foods	4,000	
NCI in NA of Special Foods		4,000

← NCI's 20% share of undistributed NI with Adjustments

← NCI's 20% share of undistributed NI with Adjustments

Optional Accumulated Depreciation Consolidation Entry:

Accumulated Depreciation	300,000	
Buildings & Equipment		300,000

← Accumulated depreciation at the time of the acquisition netted against cost

Eliminate Asset Purchase from Special Foods:

Buildings & Equipment	2,000	
Gain on Sale	700	
Accumulated Depreciation		2,700

The first four consolidation entries are identical to those illustrated in Appendix 6A. They (1) eliminate the book value of Special Foods' equity accounts against the original investment account, (2) eliminate Special Foods' 20X1 dividends declared, (3) assign undistributed realized income to the NCI shareholders, and (4) eliminate accumulated depreciation recorded by Special Foods on fixed assets prior to Peerless' acquisition. Finally, the consolidation entry related to the fixed asset transfer is identical to the one used under both the fully adjusted and modified equity methods.

Figure 7–12 illustrates the consolidation worksheet for 20X1.

Consolidation Entries—20X2

The following consolidation entries would appear in the worksheet used to consolidate Peerless and Special Foods at the end of 20X2, assuming Peerless uses the cost method to account for its investment:

Investment Consolidation Entry:

Common Stock	200,000	
Retained Earnings	100,000	
Investment in Special Foods		240,000
NCI in NA of Special Foods		60,000

FIGURE 7–12   December 31, 20X1, Cost Method Consolidation Worksheet, Period of Intercompany Sale; Upstream Sale of Equipment

	Peerless Products	Special Foods	Consolidation Entries DR	Consolidation Entries CR	Consolidated
Income Statement					
Sales	400,000	200,000			600,000
Less: COGS	(170,000)	(115,000)			(285,000)
Less: Depreciation Expense	(50,000)	(20,000)			(70,000)
Less: Other Expenses	(40,000)	(15,000)			(55,000)
Gain on Sale of Fixed Asset		700	700		0
Dividend Income	24,000		24,000		0
Consolidated Net Income	164,000	50,700	24,700	0	190,000
NCI in Net Income			6,000		(10,000)
			4,000		
Controlling Interest Net Income	**164,000**	**50,700**	**34,700**	**0**	**180,000**
Statement of Retained Earnings					
Beginning Balance	300,000	100,000	100,000		300,000
Net Income	**164,000**	**50,700**	34,700	0	180,000
Less: Dividends Declared	(60,000)	(30,000)		30,000	(60,000)
Ending Balance	**404,000**	**120,700**	**134,700**	**30,000**	**420,000**
Balance Sheet					
Cash	257,000	82,000			339,000
Accounts Receivable	75,000	50,000			125,000
Inventory	100,000	75,000			175,000
Investment in Special Foods	240,000			240,000	0
Land	175,000	40,000			215,000
Buildings & Equipment	807,000	591,000	2,000	300,000	1,100,000
Less: Accumulated Depreciation	(450,000)	(317,300)	300,000	2,700	(470,000)
Total Assets	**1,204,000**	**520,700**	**302,000**	**542,700**	**1,484,000**
Accounts Payable	100,000	100,000			200,000
Bonds Payable	200,000	100,000			300,000
Common Stock	500,000	200,000	200,000		500,000
Retained Earnings	**404,000**	**120,700**	134,700	30,000	420,000
NCI in NA of Special Foods				60,000	64,000
				4,000	
Total Liabilities & Equity	**1,204,000**	**520,700**	**334,700**	**94,000**	**1,484,000**

Dividend Consolidation Entry:

Dividend Income	32,000	
NCI in NI of Special Foods	8,000	
Dividends Declared		40,000

NCI in NI and NCI in NA of Special Foods

	NCI 20%
Net Income	15,180
− Dividend	(8,000)
+ Reverse GP Deferral	20
NCI in NI of Special Foods	7,200
Undistributed from Prior Years	4,140
NCI in NA of Special Foods	11,340

Assign Prior Undistributed Income to NCI:

NCI in NI of Special Foods	7,200	← NCI's 20% share of 20X2 undistributed NI with Adjustments
Retained Earnings*	4,140	← NCI's 20% share of 20X1 undistributed NI
NCI in NA of Special Foods		11,340 ← NCI's 20% share of cumulative undistributed NI with Adjustments

Optional Accumulated Depreciation Consolidation Entry:

Accumulated Depreciation	300,000	← Accumulated depreciation at the time of the acquisition netted against cost
Buildings & Equipment		300,000

Entries to Adjust Equipment and Accumulated Depreciation as if Still on Subsidiary's Books:

Accumulated Depreciation	100	
Depreciation Expense		100

Retained Earnings†	560	
NCI in NA of Special Foods	140	
Buildings & Equipment	2,000	
Accumulated Depreciation		2,700

Again, the first four consolidation entries are essentially identical to those illustrated in Appendix 6A. They (1) eliminate the book value of Special Foods' equity accounts against the original investment account, (2) eliminate Special Foods' 20X1 dividends declared, (3) assign undistributed income to the NCI shareholders, and (4) eliminate accumulated depreciation recorded by Special Foods on fixed assets prior to Peerless' acquisition. Finally, the consolidation entries related to the fixed asset transfer is identical to the one used under the modified equity method.

Figure 7–13 illustrates the consolidation worksheet for 20X2.

---

* Note that this is the subsidiary's retained earnings balance. The subsidiary does not adjust for the deferral of unrealized gain because this adjustment is made on the consolidation worksheet, not in the records of the subsidiary.

† Note that this is the subsidiary's retained earnings balance. The subsidiary does not adjust for the deferral of the remaining unrealized gain because this adjustment is made on the consolidation worksheet, not in the records of the subsidiary.

FIGURE 7–13 December 31, 20X2, Cost Method Consolidation Worksheet, Next Period Following Intercompany Sale; Upstream Sale of Equipment

	Peerless Products	Special Foods	Consolidation Entries		Consolidated
			DR	CR	
Income Statement					
Sales	450,000	300,000			750,000
Less: COGS	(180,000)	(160,000)			(340,000)
Less: Depreciation Expense	(51,000)	(19,100)		100	(70,000)
Less: Other Expenses	(60,000)	(45,000)			(105,000)
Dividend Income	32,000		32,000		0
Consolidated Net Income	191,000	75,900	32,000	100	235,000
			8,000		
NCI in Net Income			7,200		(15,200)
Controlling Interest Net Income	**191,000**	**75,900**	47,200	100	**219,800**
Statement of Retained Earnings					
Beginning Balance	404,000	120,700	100,000		420,000
			4,140		
			560		
Net Income	**191,000**	**75,900**	47,200	100	219,800
Less: Dividends Declared	(60,000)	(40,000)		40,000	(60,000)
Ending Balance	**535,000**	**156,600**	151,900	40,100	**579,800**
Balance Sheet					
Cash	284,000	92,000			376,000
Accounts Receivable	150,000	80,000			230,000
Inventory	180,000	90,000			270,000
Investment in Special Foods	240,000			240,000	0
Land	175,000	40,000			215,000
Buildings & Equipment	807,000	591,000	2,000	300,000	1,100,000
Less: Accumulated Depreciation	(501,000)	(336,400)	300,000	2,700	(540,000)
			100		
Total Assets	**1,335,000**	**556,600**	302,100	542,700	**1,651,000**
Accounts Payable	100,000	100,000			200,000
Bonds Payable	200,000	100,000			300,000
Common Stock	500,000	200,000	200,000		500,000
Retained Earnings	**535,000**	**156,600**	151,900	40,100	579,800
NCI in NA of Special Foods			140	60,000	71,200
				11,340	
Total Liabilities & Equity	**1,335,000**	**556,600**	352,040	111,440	**1,651,000**

QUESTIONS

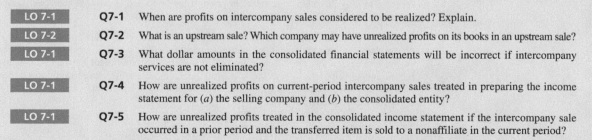

LO 7-1	**Q7-1**	When are profits on intercompany sales considered to be realized? Explain.
LO 7-2	**Q7-2**	What is an upstream sale? Which company may have unrealized profits on its books in an upstream sale?
LO 7-1	**Q7-3**	What dollar amounts in the consolidated financial statements will be incorrect if intercompany services are not eliminated?
LO 7-1	**Q7-4**	How are unrealized profits on current-period intercompany sales treated in preparing the income statement for (*a*) the selling company and (*b*) the consolidated entity?
LO 7-1	**Q7-5**	How are unrealized profits treated in the consolidated income statement if the intercompany sale occurred in a prior period and the transferred item is sold to a nonaffiliate in the current period?

LO 7-1	**Q7-6**	How are unrealized intercompany profits treated in the consolidated statements if the intercompany sale occurred in a prior period and the profits have not been realized by the end of the current period?
LO 7-2	**Q7-7**	What is a downstream sale? Which company may have unrealized profits on its books in a downstream sale?
LO 7-2, 7-3, 7-4	**Q7-8**	What portion of the unrealized intercompany profit is eliminated in a downstream sale? In an upstream sale?
LO 7-2	**Q7-9**	How is the effect of unrealized intercompany profits on consolidated net income different between an upstream and a downstream sale?
LO 7-4	**Q7-10**	Unrealized profits from a prior-year upstream sale were realized in the current period. What effect will this event have on income assigned to the noncontrolling interest in the consolidated income statement for the current period?
LO 7-6	**Q7-11**	A subsidiary sold a depreciable asset to the parent company at a gain in the current period. Will the income assigned to the noncontrolling interest in the consolidated income statement for the current period be more than, less than, or equal to a proportionate share of the reported net income of the subsidiary? Why?
LO 7-6	**Q7-12**	A subsidiary sold a depreciable asset to the parent company at a profit of $1,000 in the current period. Will the income assigned to the noncontrolling interest in the consolidated income statement for the current period be more if the intercompany sale occurs on January 1 or on December 31? Why?
LO 7-5	**Q7-13**	If a company sells a depreciable asset to its subsidiary at a profit on December 31, 20X3, what account balances must be eliminated or adjusted in preparing the consolidated income statement for 20X3?
LO 7-5	**Q7-14**	If the sale in the preceding question occurs on January 1, 20X3, what additional account will require adjustment in preparing the consolidated income statement?
LO 7-5, 7-6	**Q7-15**	In the period in which an intercompany sale occurs, how do the consolidation entries differ when unrealized profits pertain to an intangible asset rather than a tangible asset?
LO 7-3, 7-5	**Q7-16**	When is unrealized profit on an intercompany sale of land considered realized? When is profit on an intercompany sale of equipment considered realized? Why do the treatments differ?
LO 7-5, 7-6	**Q7-17**	In the consolidation of a prior-period unrealized intercompany gain on depreciable assets, why does the debit to the Investment account decrease over time?
LO 7-2, 7-5, 7-6	**Q7-18A**	A parent company may use on its books one of several different methods of accounting for its ownership of a subsidiary: (*a*) cost method, (*b*) modified equity method, or (*c*) fully adjusted equity method. How will the choice of method affect the reported balance in the investment account when there are unrealized intercompany profits on the parent's books at the end of the period?

CASES

LO 7-6	**C7-1**	### Correction of Consolidation Procedures

Plug Corporation purchased 60 percent of Coy Company's common stock approximately 10 years ago. On January 1, 20X2, Coy sold equipment to Plug for $850,000 and recorded a $150,000 loss on the sale. Coy had purchased the equipment for $1,200,000 on January 1, 20X0, and was depreciating it on a straight-line basis over 12 years with no assumed residual value.

Research

In preparing Plug's consolidated financial statements for 20X2, its chief accountant increased the reported amount of the equipment by $150,000 and eliminated the loss on the sale of equipment recorded by Coy. No other consolidations or adjustments related to the equipment were made.

Required

As a member of the audit firm Gotcha and Gotcha, you have been asked, after reviewing Plug's consolidated income statement, to prepare a memo to Plug's controller detailing the consolidation procedures that should be followed in transferring equipment between subsidiary and parent. Include citations to or quotations from the authoritative literature to support your recommendations. Your memo should include the correct consolidation entry and explain why each debit and credit is needed.

"A" indicates that the item relates to Appendix 7A.

LO 7-1, 7-2   **C7-2**   ## Consolidation of Intercompany Services

Research

Dream Corporation owns 90 percent of Classic Company's common stock and 70 percent of Plain Company's stock. Dream provides legal services to each subsidiary and bills it for 150 percent of the cost of the services provided. During 20X3, Classic recorded legal expenses of $80,000 when it paid Dream for legal assistance in an unsuccessful patent infringement suit against another company, and Plain recorded legal expenses of $150,000 when it paid Dream for legal work associated with the purchase of additional property in Montana to expand an existing strip mine owned by Plain. In preparing the consolidated statements at December 31, 20X3, no consolidation entries were made for intercompany services. When asked why no entries had been made to eliminate the intercompany services, Dream's chief accountant replied that intercompany services are not mentioned in the company accounting manual and can be ignored.

Required

Prepare a memo detailing the appropriate treatment of legal services provided by Dream to Plain and Classic during 20X3. Include citations to or quotations from authoritative accounting standards to support your recommendations. In addition, provide the consolidation entries at December 31, 20X3 and 20X4, needed as a result of the services provided in 20X3, and explain why each debit or credit is necessary.

LO 7-2, 7-5   **C7-3**   ## Noncontrolling Interest

Understanding

Current reporting standards require the consolidated entity to include all the revenues, expenses, assets, and liabilities of the parent and its subsidiaries in the consolidated financial statements. When the parent does not own all of a subsidiary's shares, various rules and procedures exist with regard to the assignment of income and net assets to noncontrolling shareholders and the way in which the noncontrolling interest is to be reported.

Required

a. How is the amount of income assigned to noncontrolling shareholders in the consolidated income statement computed if there are no unrealized intercompany profits on the subsidiary's books?

b. How is the amount reported for the noncontrolling interest in the consolidated balance sheet computed if there are no unrealized intercompany profits on the subsidiary's books?

c. What effect do unrealized intercompany profits have on the computation of income assigned to the noncontrolling interest if the profits arose from a transfer of (1) land or (2) equipment?

d. Are the noncontrolling shareholders of a subsidiary likely to find the amounts assigned to them in the consolidated financial statements useful? Explain.

LO 7-1, 7-4   **C7-4**   ## Intercompany Sale of Services

Analysis

Diamond Manufacturing Company regularly purchases janitorial and maintenance services from its wholly owned subsidiary, Schwartz Maintenance Services Inc. Schwartz bills Diamond monthly at its regular rates for the services provided, with the services consisting primarily of cleaning, grounds keeping, and small repairs. The cost of providing the services that Schwartz sells consists mostly of salaries and associated labor costs that total about 60 percent of the amount billed. Diamond issues consolidated financial statements annually.

Required

a. When Diamond prepares consolidated financial statements, what account balances of Diamond and Schwartz related to the intercompany sale of services must be adjusted or eliminated in the consolidation worksheet? What impact do these adjustments have on consolidated net income?

b. In the case of intercompany sales of services at a profit, at what point in time are the intercompany profits considered to be realized? Explain.

LO 7-1   **C7-5**   ## Intercompany Profits

Analysis

Companies have many different practices for pricing transfers of goods and services from one affiliate to another. Regardless of the approaches used for internal decision making and performance evaluation or for tax purposes, all intercompany profits, unless immaterial, are supposed to be eliminated when preparing consolidated financial statements until confirmed through transactions with external parties.

Required

Verizon Communications is in the telephone business, although it is larger and more diversified than many smaller telecommunications companies. How does it treat intercompany profits for consolidation?

EXERCISES

LO 7-5, 7-6   **E7-1**   **Multiple-Choice Questions on Intercompany Transfers [AICPA Adapted]**

For each question, select the single best answer.

1. Water Company owns 80 percent of Fire Company's outstanding common stock. On December 31, 20X9, Fire sold equipment to Water at a price in excess of Fire's carrying amount but less than its original cost. On a consolidated balance sheet at December 31, 20X9, the carrying amount of the equipment should be reported at

   a. Water's original cost.

   b. Fire's original cost.

   c. Water's original cost less Fire's recorded gain.

   d. Water's original cost less 80 percent of Fire's recorded gain.

2. Company J acquired all of Company K's outstanding common stock in exchange for cash. The acquisition price exceeds the fair value of net assets acquired. How should Company J determine the amounts to be reported for the plant and equipment and long-term debt acquired from Company K?

	Plant and Equipment	Long-Term Debt
a.	K's carrying amount	K's carrying amount
b.	K's carrying amount	Fair value
c.	Fair value	K's carrying amount
d.	Fair value	Fair value

3. Port Inc. owns 100 percent of Salem Inc. On January 1, 20X2, Port sold delivery equipment to Salem at a gain. Port had owned the equipment for two years and used a five-year straight-line depreciation rate with no residual value. Salem is using a three-year straight-line depreciation rate with no residual value for the equipment. In the consolidated income statement, Salem's recorded depreciation expense on the equipment for 20X2 will be decreased by

   a. 20 percent of the gain on the sale.

   b. $33\frac{1}{3}$ percent of the gain on the sale.

   c. 50 percent of the gain on the sale.

   d. 100 percent of the gain on the sale.

4. On January 1, 20X0, Poe Corporation sold a machine for $900,000 to Saxe Corporation, its wholly owned subsidiary. Poe paid $1,100,000 for this machine, which had accumulated depreciation of $250,000. Poe estimated a $100,000 salvage value and depreciated the machine using the straight-line method over 20 years, a policy that Saxe continued. In Poe's December 31, 20X0, consolidated balance sheet, this machine should be included in fixed-asset cost and accumulated depreciation as

	Cost	Accumulated Depreciation
a.	$1,100,000	$300,000
b.	$1,100,000	$290,000
c.	$ 900,000	$ 40,000
d.	$ 850,000	$ 42,500

5. Scroll Inc., a wholly owned subsidiary of Pirn Inc., began operations on January 1, 20X1. The following information is from the condensed 20X1 income statements of Pirn and Scroll:

	Pirn	Scroll
Sales	$500,000	$300,000
Cost of Goods Sold	(350,000)	(270,000)
Gross Profit	$150,000	$ 30,000
Depreciation	(40,000)	(10,000)
Other Expenses	(60,000)	(15,000)
Income from Operations	$ 50,000	$ 5,000
Gain on Sale of Equipment to Scroll	12,000	
Income before Taxes	$ 62,000	$ 5,000

Scroll purchased equipment from Pirn for $36,000 on January 1, 20X1, that is depreciated using the straight-line method over four years. What amount should be reported as depreciation expense in Pirn's 20X1 consolidated income statement?

a. $50,000.

b. $47,000.

c. $44,000.

d. $41,000.

LO 7-2, 7-6 **E7-2** **Multiple-Choice Questions on Intercompany Transactions**

Select the correct answer for each of the following questions.

1. Upper Company holds 60 percent of Lower Company's voting shares. During the preparation of consolidated financial statements for 20X5, the following consolidation entry was made:

Investment in Lower	10,000	
Land		10,000

Which of the following statements is correct?

a. Upper Company purchased land from Lower Company during 20X5.

b. Upper Company purchased land from Lower Company before January 1, 20X5.

c. Lower Company purchased land from Upper Company during 20X5.

d. Lower Company purchased land from Upper Company before January 1, 20X5.

2. Middle Company holds 60 percent of Bottom Corporation's voting shares. Bottom has developed a new type of production equipment that appears to be quite marketable. It spent $40,000 in developing the equipment; however, Middle agreed to purchase the production rights for the machine for $100,000. If the intercompany sale occurred on January 1, 20X2, and the production rights are expected to have value for five years, at what amount should the rights be reported in the consolidated balance sheet for December 31, 20X2?

a. $0.

b. $32,000.

c. $80,000.

d. $100,000.

Note: Questions 3 through 6 are based on the following information:

On January 1, 20X4, Gold Company purchased a computer with an expected economic life of five years. On January 1, 20X6, Gold sold the computer to TLK Corporation and recorded the following entry:

Cash	39,000	
Accumulated Depreciation	16,000	
Computer Equipment		40,000
Gain on Sale of Equipment		15,000

TLK Corporation holds 60 percent of Gold's voting shares. Gold reported net income of $45,000 including the gain on the sale of equipment, and TLK reported income from its own operations of $85,000 for 20X6. There is no change in the estimated economic life of the equipment as a result of the intercompany transfer.

3. In the preparation of the 20X6 consolidated income statement, depreciation expense will be

a. Debited for $5,000 in the consolidation entries.

b. Credited for $5,000 in the consolidation entries.

c. Debited for $13,000 in the consolidation entries.

d. Credited for $13,000 in the consolidation entries.

4. In the preparation of the 20X6 consolidated balance sheet, computer equipment will be

a. Debited for $1,000.

b. Debited for $15,000.

c. Credited for $24,000.

d. Debited for $40,000.

5. Income assigned to the noncontrolling interest in the 20X6 consolidated income statement will be
   a. $12,000.
   b. $14,000.
   c. $18,000.
   d. $52,000.

6. Consolidated net income for 20X6 will be
   a. $106,000.
   b. $112,000.
   c. $120,000.
   d. $130,000.

LO 7-3

E7-3 Consolidation Entries for Land Transfer

Huckster Corporation purchased land on January 1, 20X1, for $20,000. On June 10, 20X4, it sold the land to its subsidiary, Lowly Corporation, for $30,000. Huckster owns 60 percent of Lowly's voting shares.

Required

a. Give the worksheet consolidation entries needed to remove the effects of the intercompany sale of land in preparing the consolidated financial statements for 20X4 and 20X5.

b. Give the worksheet consolidation entries needed on December 31, 20X4 and 20X5, if Lowly had initially purchased the land for $20,000 and then sold it to Huckster on June 10, 20X4, for $30,000.

LO 7-1, 7-2

E7-4 Intercompany Services

Power Corporation owns 75 percent of Swift Company's stock. Swift provides health care services to its employees and those of Power. During 20X2, Power recorded $45,000 as health care expense for medical care given to its employees by Swift. Swift's costs incurred in providing the services to Power were $32,000.

Required

a. By what amount will consolidated net income change when the intercompany services are eliminated in preparing Power's consolidated statements for 20X2?

b. What would be the impact of eliminating the intercompany services on consolidated net income if Power owned 100 percent of Swift's stock rather than 75 percent? Explain.

c. If in its consolidated income statement for 20X2 Power had reported total health care costs of $70,000, what was the cost to Swift of providing health care services to its own employees?

LO 7-1, 7-2

E7-5 Consolidation Entries for Intercompany Services

On January 1, 20X5, Block Corporation started using a wholly owned subsidiary to deliver all its sales overnight to its customers. During 20X5, Block recorded delivery service expense of $76,000 and made payments of $58,000 to the subsidiary.

Required

Give the worksheet consolidation entries related to the intercompany services needed on December 31, 20X5, to prepare consolidated financial statements.

LO 7-6

E7-6 Consolidation Entries for Depreciable Asset Transfer: Year-End Sale

Pam Corporation holds 70 percent ownership of Northern Enterprises. On December 31, 20X6, Northern paid Pam $40,000 for a truck that Pam had purchased for $45,000 on January 1, 20X2. The truck was considered to have a 15-year life from January 1, 20X2, and no residual value. Both companies depreciate equipment using the straight-line method.

Required

a. Give the worksheet consolidation entry or entries needed on December 31, 20X6, to remove the effects of the intercompany sale.

b. Give the worksheet consolidation entry or entries needed on December 31, 20X7, to remove the effects of the intercompany sale.

LO 7-4   **E7-7   Transfer of Land**

Bowen Corporation owns 70 percent of Roan Corporation's voting common stock. On March 12, 20X2, Roan sold land it had purchased for $140,000 to Bowen for $185,000. Bowen plans to build a new warehouse on the property in 20X3.

Required

a. Give the worksheet consolidation entries to remove the effects of the intercompany sale of land in preparing the consolidated financial statements at December 31, 20X2 and 20X3.

b. Give the worksheet consolidation entries needed at December 31, 20X3 and 20X4, if Bowen had initially purchased the land for $150,000 and sold it to Roan on March 12, 20X2, for $180,000.

LO 7-5   **E7-8   Transfer of Depreciable Asset at Year-End**

Frazer Corporation purchased 60 percent of Minnow Corporation's voting common stock on January 1, 20X1. On December 31, 20X5, Frazer received $210,000 from Minnow for a truck Frazer had purchased on January 1, 20X2, for $300,000. The truck is expected to have a 10-year useful life and no salvage value. Both companies depreciate trucks on a straight-line basis.

Required

a. Give the worksheet consolidation entry or entries needed at December 31, 20X5, to remove the effects of the intercompany sale.

b. Give the worksheet consolidation entry or entries needed at December 31, 20X6, to remove the effects of the intercompany sale.

LO 7-5   **E7-9   Transfer of Depreciable Asset at Beginning of Year**

Frazer Corporation purchased 60 percent of Minnow Corporation's voting common stock on January 1, 20X1. On January 1, 20X5, Frazer received $245,000 from Minnow for a truck Frazer had purchased on January 1, 20X2, for $300,000. The truck is expected to have a 10-year useful life and no salvage value. Both companies depreciate trucks on a straight-line basis.

Required

a. Give the worksheet consolidation entry or entries needed at December 31, 20X5, to remove the effects of the intercompany sale.

b. Give the worksheet consolidation entry or entries needed at December 31, 20X6, to remove the effects of the intercompany sale.

LO 7-5   **E7-10   Sale of Equipment to Subsidiary in Current Period**

On January 1, 20X7, Wainwrite Corporation sold to Lance Corporation equipment it had purchased for $150,000 and used for eight years. Wainwrite recorded a gain of $14,000 on the sale. The equipment has a total useful life of 15 years and is depreciated on a straight-line basis. Wainwrite holds 70 percent of Lance's voting common shares.

Required

a. Give the journal entry made by Wainwrite on January 1, 20X7, to record the sale of equipment.

b. Give the journal entries recorded by Lance during 20X7 to record the purchase of equipment and year-end depreciation expense.

c. Give the consolidation entry or entries related to the intercompany sale of equipment needed at December 31, 20X7, to prepare a full set of consolidated financial statements.

d. Give the consolidation entry or entries related to the equipment required at January 1, 20X8, to prepare a consolidated balance sheet only.

LO 7-6   **E7-11   Upstream Sale of Equipment in Prior Period**

Baywatch Industries has owned 80 percent of Tubberware Corporation for many years. On January 1, 20X6, Baywatch paid Tubberware $270,000 to acquire equipment that Tubberware had purchased on January 1, 20X3, for $300,000. The equipment is expected to have no scrap value and is depreciated over a 15-year useful life.

Baywatch reported operating earnings of $100,000 for 20X8 and paid dividends of $40,000. Tubberware reported net income of $40,000 and paid dividends of $20,000 in 20X8.

Required

a. Compute the amount reported as consolidated net income for 20X8.

b. By what amount would consolidated net income change if the equipment sale had been a downstream sale rather than an upstream sale?

c. Give the consolidation entry or entries required to eliminate the effects of the intercompany sale of equipment in preparing a full set of consolidated financial statements at December 31, 20X8.

LO 7-5   **E7-12**   **Consolidation Entries for Midyear Depreciable Asset Transfer**

Kline Corporation holds 90 percent ownership of Andrews Company. On July 1, 20X3, Kline sold equipment that it had purchased for $30,000 on January 1, 20X1, to Andrews for $28,000. The equipment's original six-year estimated total economic life remains unchanged. Both companies use straight-line depreciation. The equipment's residual value is considered negligible.

Required

a. Give the consolidation entry or entries in the consolidation worksheet prepared as of December 31, 20X3, to remove the effects of the intercompany sale.

b. Give the consolidation entry or entries in the consolidation worksheet prepared as of December 31, 20X4, to remove the effects of the intercompany sale.

LO 7-2   **E7-13**   **Consolidated Net Income Computation**

Verry Corporation owns 75 percent of Spawn Corporation's voting common stock. Verry reported income from its separate operations of $90,000 and $110,000 in 20X4 and 20X5, respectively. Spawn reported net income of $60,000 and $40,000 in 20X4 and 20X5, respectively.

Required

a. Compute consolidated net income and the income assigned to the controlling interest for 20X4 and 20X5 if Verry sold land with a book value of $95,000 to Spawn for $120,000 on June 30, 20X4.

b. Compute consolidated net income and the amount of income assigned to the controlling interest in the consolidated statements for 20X4 and 20X5 if Spawn sold land with a book value of $95,000 to Verry for $120,000 on June 30, 20X4.

LO 7-2, 7-3,   **E7-14**   **Consolidation Entries for Intercompany Transfers**
7-4

Advanced
StudyGuide
.com

Grand Delivery Service acquired at book value 80 percent of the voting shares of Acme Real Estate Company. On that date, the fair value of the noncontrolling interest was equal to 20 percent of Acme's book value. Acme Real Estate reported common stock of $300,000 and retained earnings of $100,000. During 20X3 Grand Delivery provided courier services for Acme Real Estate in the amount of $15,000. Also during 20X3, Acme Real Estate purchased land for $1,000. It sold the land to Grand Delivery Service for $26,000 so that Grand Delivery could build a new transportation center. Grand Delivery reported $65,000 of operating income from its delivery operations in 20X3. Acme Real Estate reported net income of $40,000 and paid dividends of $10,000 in 20X3.

Required

a. Compute consolidated net income for 20X3.

b. Give all journal entries recorded by Grand Delivery Service related to its investment in Acme Real Estate assuming Grand uses the fully adjusted equity method in accounting for the investment.

c. Give all consolidation entries required in preparing a consolidation worksheet as of December 31, 20X3.

LO 7-6   **E7-15**   **Sale of Building to Parent in Prior Period**

Turner Company purchased 70 percent of Split Company's stock approximately 20 years ago. On December 31, 20X8, Turner purchased a building from Split for $300,000. Split had purchased the building on January 1, 20X1, at a cost of $400,000 and used straight-line depreciation on an expected life of 20 years. The asset's total estimated economic life is unchanged as a result of the intercompany sale.

Required

a. What amount of depreciation expense on the building will Turner report for 20X9?

b. What amount of depreciation expense would Split have reported for 20X9 if it had continued to own the building?

c. Give the consolidation entry or entries needed to eliminate the effects of the intercompany building transfer in preparing a full set of consolidated financial statements at December 31, 20X9.

d. What amount of income will be assigned to the noncontrolling interest in the consolidated income statement for 20X9 if Split reports net income of $40,000 for 20X9?

e. Split reports assets with a book value of $350,000 and liabilities of $150,000 at January 1, 20X9, and reports net income of $40,000 and dividends of $15,000 for 20X9. What amount will be assigned to the noncontrolling interest in the consolidated balance sheet at December 31, 20X9, assuming the fair value of the noncontrolling interest at the date of acquisition was equal to 30 percent of Split Company's book value?

LO 7-5

E7-16   Intercompany Sale at a Loss

Parent Company holds 90 percent of Sunway Company's voting common shares. On December 31, 20X8, Parent recorded a loss of $16,000 on the sale of equipment to Sunway. At the time of the sale, the equipment's estimated remaining economic life was eight years.

Required

a. Will consolidated net income be increased or decreased when consolidation entries associated with the sale of equipment are made at December 31, 20X8? By what amount?

b. Will consolidated net income be increased or decreased when consolidation entries associated with the sale of equipment are made at December 31, 20X9? By what amount?

LO 7-6

E7-17   Consolidation Entries Following Intercompany Sale at a Loss

Brown Corporation holds 70 percent of Transom Company's voting common stock. On January 1, 20X2, Transom paid $300,000 to acquire a building with a 15-year expected economic life. Transom uses straight-line depreciation for all depreciable assets. On December 31, 20X7, Brown purchased the building from Transom for $144,000. Brown reported income, excluding investment income from Transom, of $125,000 and $150,000 for 20X7 and 20X8, respectively. Transom reported net income of $15,000 and $40,000 for 20X7 and 20X8, respectively.

Required

a. Give the appropriate consolidation entry or entries needed to eliminate the effects of the intercompany sale of the building in preparing consolidated financial statements for 20X7.

b. Compute the amount to be reported as consolidated net income for 20X7 and the income to be allocated to the controlling interest.

c. Give the appropriate consolidation entry or entries needed to eliminate the effects of the intercompany sale of the building in preparing consolidated financial statements for 20X8.

d. Compute consolidated net income and the amount of income assigned to the controlling shareholders in the consolidated income statement for 20X8.

LO 7-4

E7-18   Multiple Transfers of Asset

Swanson Corporation purchased land from Clayton Corporation for $240,000 on December 20, 20X3. This purchase followed a series of transactions between Swanson-controlled subsidiaries. On February 7, 20X3, Sullivan Corporation purchased the land from a nonaffiliate for $145,000. It sold the land to Kolder Company for $130,000 on October 10, 20X3, and Kolder sold the land to Clayton for $180,000 on November 27, 20X3. Swanson has control of the following companies:

Subsidiary	Level of Ownership	20X3 Net Income
Sullivan Corporation	80 percent	$120,000
Kolder Company	70 percent	60,000
Clayton Corporation	90 percent	80,000

Swanson reported income from its separate operations of $150,000 for 20X3.

Required

a. At what amount should the land be reported in the consolidated balance sheet as of December 31, 20X3?

b. What amount of gain or loss on sale of land should be reported in the consolidated income statement for 20X3?

c. What amount of income should be assigned to the controlling shareholders in the consolidated income statement for 20X3?

d. Give any consolidation entry related to the land that should appear in the worksheet used to prepare consolidated financial statements for 20X3.

LO 7-6

E7-19 Consolidation Entry in Period of Transfer

Blank Corporation owns 60 percent of Grand Corporation's voting common stock. On December 31, 20X4, Blank paid Grand $276,000 for dump trucks Grand had purchased on January 1, 20X2. Both companies use straight-line depreciation. The consolidation entry included in preparing consolidated financial statements at December 31, 20X4, was

Trucks	24,000	
Gain on Sale of Trucks	36,000	
Accumulated Depreciation		60,000

Required

a. What amount did Grand pay to purchase the trucks on January 1, 20X2?

b. What was the economic life of the trucks on January 1, 20X2?

c. Give the worksheet consolidation entry needed in preparing the consolidated financial statements at December 31, 20X5.

LO 7-6

E7-20 Consolidation Entry Computation

Stern Manufacturing purchased an ultrasound drilling machine with a remaining 10-year economic life from a 70 percent-owned subsidiary for $360,000 on January 1, 20X6. Both companies use straight-line depreciation. The subsidiary recorded the following entry when it sold the machine to Stern:

Cash	360,000	
Accumulated Depreciation	150,000	
Equipment		450,000
Gain on Sale of Equipment		60,000

Required

Give the worksheet consolidation entry or entries needed to remove the effects of the intercompany sale of equipment when consolidated financial statements are prepared as of (*a*) December 31, 20X6, and (*b*) December 31, 20X7.

LO 7-6

E7-21 Using the Consolidation Entry to Determine Account Balances

Pastel Corporation acquired a controlling interest in Somber Corporation in 20X5 for an amount equal to its underlying book value. At the date of acquisition, the fair value of the noncontrolling interest was equal to its proportionate share of the book value of Somber Corporation. In preparing a consolidated balance sheet worksheet at January 1, 20X9, Pastel's controller included the following consolidation entry:

Equipment	53,500	
Investment in Somber Corp.	9,450	
NCI in NA of Somber	1,050	
Accumulated Depreciation		64,000

A note at the bottom of the consolidation worksheet at January 1, 20X9, indicates the equipment was purchased from a nonaffiliate on January 1, 20X1, for $120,000 and was sold to an affiliate on December 31, 20X8. The equipment is being depreciated on a 15-year straight-line basis. Somber reported stock outstanding of $300,000 and retained earnings of $200,000 at January 1, 20X9. Somber reported net income of $25,000 and paid dividends of $6,000 for 20X9.

Required

a. What percentage ownership of Somber Corporation does Pastel hold?

b. Was the parent or subsidiary the owner prior to the intercompany sale of equipment? Explain.

c. What was the intercompany transfer price of the equipment on December 31, 20X8?

d. What amount of income will be assigned to the noncontrolling interest in the consolidated income statement for 20X9?

e. Assuming Pastel and Somber report depreciation expense of $15,000 and $9,000, respectively, for 20X9, what depreciation amount will be reported in the consolidated income statement for 20X9?

f. Give all remaining consolidation entries needed at December 31, 20X9, to prepare a complete set of consolidated financial statements.

LO 7-1, 7-2 **E7-22** ### Intercompany Sale of Services

Norgaard Corporation purchased management consulting services from its 75 percent–owned subsidiary, Bline Inc. During 20X3, Norgaard paid Bline $123,200 for its services. For the year 20X4, Bline billed Norgaard $138,700 for such services and collected all but $6,600 by year-end. Bline's labor cost and other associated costs for the employees providing services to Norgaard totaled $91,000 in 20X3 and $112,000 in 20X4. Norgaard reported $2,342,000 of income from its own separate operations for 20X4, and Bline reported net income of $631,000.

Required

a. Present all consolidation entries related to the intercompany sale of services that would be needed in the consolidation worksheet used to prepare a complete set of consolidated financial statements for 20X4.

b. Compute consolidated net income for 20X4 and the amount of income assigned to the controlling interest.

LO 7-3, 7-6 **E7-23A** ### Modified Equity Method and Cost Method

Newtime Products purchased 65 percent of TV Sales Company's stock at underlying book value on January 1, 20X3. At that date, the fair value of the noncontrolling interest was equal to 35 percent of the book value of TV Sales. TV Sales reported shares outstanding of $300,000 and retained earnings of $100,000. During 20X3, TV Sales reported net income of $50,000 and paid dividends of $5,000. In 20X4, TV Sales reported net income of $70,000 and paid dividends of $20,000.

The following transactions occurred between Newtime Products and TV Sales in 20X3 and 20X4:

1. TV Sales sold camera equipment to Newtime for a $40,000 profit on December 31, 20X3. The equipment had a five-year estimated economic life remaining at the time of intercompany transfer and is depreciated on a straight-line basis.

2. Newtime sold land costing $30,000 to TV Sales on June 30, 20X4, for $41,000.

Required

a. Assuming that Newtime uses the modified equity method to account for its investment in TV Sales:

(1) Give the journal entries recorded on Newtime's books in 20X4 related to its investment in TV Sales.

(2) Give all consolidation entries needed to prepare a consolidation worksheet for 20X4.

b. Assuming that Newtime uses the cost method to account for its investment in TV Sales:

(1) Give the journal entries recorded on Newtime's books in 20X4 related to its investment in TV Sales.

(2) Give all consolidation entries needed to prepare a consolidation worksheet for 20X4.

PROBLEMS

LO 7-3, 7-4 **P7-24** ### Computation of Consolidated Net Income

Petime Corporation acquired 90 percent ownership of United Grain Company on January 1, 20X4, for $108,000 when the fair value of United's net assets was $10,000 higher than its $110,000 book value. The increase in value was attributed to amortizable assets with a remaining life of 10 years. At that date, the fair value of the noncontrolling interest was equal to $12,000.

During 20X4, United sold land to Petime at a $7,000 profit. United Grain reported net income of $19,000 and paid dividends of $4,000 in 20X4. Petime reported income, exclusive of its income from United Grain, of $34,000 and paid dividends of $15,000 in 20X4.

Required

a. Compute the amount of income assigned to the controlling interest in the consolidated income statement for 20X4.

b. By what amount will the 20X4 income assigned to the controlling interest increase or decrease if the sale of land had been from Petime to United Grain, the gain on the sale of land had been included in Petime's $34,000 income, and the $19,000 was income from operations of United Grain?

LO 7-6   **P7-25**   **Subsidiary Net Income**

Bold Corporation acquired 75 percent of Toll Corporation's voting common stock on January 1, 20X4, for $348,000, when the fair value of its net identifiable assets was $464,000 and the fair value of the noncontrolling interest was $116,000. Toll reported common stock outstanding of $150,000 and retained earnings of $270,000. The excess of fair value over book value of Toll's net assets was attributed to amortizable assets with a remaining life of 10 years. On December 31, 20X4, Toll sold a building to Bold and recorded a gain of $20,000. Income assigned to the noncontrolling shareholders in the 20X4 consolidated income statement was $17,500.

Required

a. Compute the amount of net income Toll reported for 20X4.

b. Compute the amount reported as consolidated net income if Bold reported operating income of $234,000 for 20X4.

c. Compute the amount of income assigned to the controlling interest in the 20X4 consolidated income statement.

LO 7-6   **P7-26**   **Transfer of Asset from One Subsidiary to Another**

Pelts Company holds a total of 70 percent of Bugle Corporation and 80 percent of Cook Products Corporation stock. Bugle purchased a warehouse with an expected life of 20 years on January 1, 20X1, for $40,000. On January 1, 20X6, it sold the warehouse to Cook Products for $45,000.

Required

Complete the following table showing selected information that would appear in the separate 20X6 income statements and balance sheets of Bugle Corporation and Cook Products Corporation and in the 20X6 consolidated financial statements.

	Bugle Corporation	Cook Products Corporation	Consolidated Entity
Depreciation expense			
Fixed assets—warehouse			
Accumulated depreciation			
Gain on sale of warehouse			

LO 7-6   **P7-27**   **Consolidation Entry**

In preparing its consolidated financial statements at December 31, 20X7, the following consolidation entries were included in the consolidation worksheet of Master Corporation:

Buildings	140,000	
Gain on Sale of Building	28,000	
Accumulated Depreciation		168,000

Accumulated Depreciation	2,000	
Depreciation Expense		2,000

Master owns 60 percent of Rakel Corporation's voting common stock. On January 1, 20X7, Rakel sold Master a building it had purchased for $600,000 on January 1, 20X1, and depreciated on a 20-year straight-line basis. Master recorded depreciation for 20X7 using straight-line depreciation and the same useful life and residual value as Rakel.

Required

a. What amount did Master pay Rakel for the building?

b. What amount of accumulated depreciation did Rakel report at January 1, 20X7, prior to the sale?

c. What annual depreciation expense did Rakel record prior to the sale?

d. What expected residual value did Rakel use in computing its annual depreciation expense?

e. What amount of depreciation expense did Master record in 20X7?

f. If Rakel reported net income of $80,000 for 20X7, what amount of income will be assigned to the noncontrolling interest in the consolidated income statement for 20X7?

g. If Rakel reported net income of $65,000 for 20X8, what amount of income will be assigned to the noncontrolling interest in the consolidated income statement for 20X8?

LO 7-4, 7-6   **P7-28**   **Multiple-Choice Questions**

Select the correct answer for each of the following questions.

1. In the preparation of a consolidated income statement:

    a. Income assigned to noncontrolling shareholders always is computed as a pro rata portion of the reported net income of the consolidated entity.

    b. Income assigned to noncontrolling shareholders always is computed as a pro rata portion of the reported net income of the subsidiary.

    c. Income assigned to noncontrolling shareholders in the current period is likely to be less than a pro rata portion of the reported net income of the subsidiary in the current period if the subsidiary had an unrealized gain on an intercompany sale of depreciable assets in the preceding period. Assume the depreciable asset was subsequently sold in the current period.

    d. Income assigned to noncontrolling shareholders in the current period is likely to be more than a pro rata portion of the reported net income of the subsidiary in the current period if the subsidiary had an unrealized gain on an intercompany sale of depreciable assets in the preceding period. Assume the depreciable asset was subsequently sold in the current period.

2. When a 90 percent-owned subsidiary records a gain on the sale of land to an affiliate during the current period and the land is not resold before the end of the period:

    a. Ninety percent of the gain will be excluded from consolidated net income.

    b. Consolidated net income will be increased by the full amount of the gain.

    c. A proportionate share of the unrealized gain will be excluded from income assigned to noncontrolling interest.

    d. The full amount of the unrealized gain will be excluded from income assigned to noncontrolling interest.

3. Minor Company sold land to Major Company on November 15, 20X4, and recorded a gain of $30,000 on the sale. Major owns 80 percent of Minor's common shares. Which of the following statements is correct?

    a. A proportionate share of the $30,000 must be treated as a reduction of income assigned to the noncontrolling interest in the consolidated income statement unless the land is resold to a nonaffiliate in 20X4.

    b. The $30,000 will not be treated as an adjustment in computing income assigned to the noncontrolling interest in the consolidated income statement in 20X4 unless the land is resold to a nonaffiliate in 20X4.

    c. In computing consolidated net income, it does not matter whether the land is or is not resold to a nonaffiliate before the end of the period; the $30,000 will not affect the computation of consolidated net income in 20X4 because the profits are on the subsidiary's books.

    d. Minor's trial balance as of December 31, 20X4, should be adjusted to remove the $30,000 gain because the gain is not yet realized.

4. Lewis Company owns 80 percent of Tomassini Corporation's stock. You are told that Tomassini has sold equipment to Lewis and that the following consolidation entries are needed to prepare consolidated statements for 20X9:

Equipment	20,000	
Gain on Sale of Equipment	40,000	
Accumulated Depreciation		60,000

Accumulated Depreciation	5,000	
Depreciation Expense		5,000

Which of the following is incorrect?

a. The parent paid $40,000 in excess of the subsidiary's carrying amount to acquire the asset.

b. From a consolidated viewpoint, depreciation expense as Lewis recorded it is overstated.

c. The asset transfer occurred in 20X9 before the end of the year.

d. Consolidated net income will be reduced by $40,000 when these consolidation entries are made.

LO 7-1, 7-2   **P7-29**   ### Intercompany Services Provided to Subsidiary

During 20X4, Plate Company paid its employees $80,000 for work done in helping its wholly owned subsidiary build a new office building that was completed on December 31, 20X4. Plate recorded the $110,000 payment from the subsidiary for the work done as service revenue. The subsidiary included the payment in the cost of the building and is depreciating the building over 25 years with no assumed residual value. Plate uses the fully adjusted equity method.

Required

Present the consolidation entries needed at December 31, 20X4 and 20X5, to prepare Plate's consolidated financial statements.

LO 7-4, 7-5   **P7-30**   ### Consolidated Net Income with Intercompany Transfers

Advanced
StudyGuide
.com

In its 20X7 consolidated income statement, Bower Development Company reported consolidated net income of $961,000 and $39,000 of income assigned to the 30 percent noncontrolling interest in its only subsidiary, Subsidence Mining Inc. During the year, Subsidence had sold a previously mined parcel of land to Bower for a new housing development; the sales price to Bower was $500,000, and the land had a carrying amount at the time of sale of $560,000. At the beginning of the previous year, Bower had sold excavation and grading equipment to Subsidence for $240,000; the equipment had a remaining life of six years as of the date of sale and a book value of $210,000. The equipment originally had cost $350,000 when Bower purchased it on January 2, 20X2. The equipment never was expected to have any salvage value.

Bower had acquired 70 percent of the voting shares of Subsidence eight years earlier when the fair value of its net assets was $200,000 higher than book value, and the fair value of the noncontrolling interest was $60,000 more than a proportionate share of the book value of Subsidence's net assets. All the excess over the book value was attributable to intangible assets with a remaining life of 10 years from the date of combination. Both parent and subsidiary use straight-line amortization and depreciation. Assume Bower uses the fully adjusted equity method.

Required

a. Present the journal entry made by Bower to record the sale of equipment in 20X6 to Subsidence.

b. Present all consolidation entries related to the intercompany transfers of land and equipment that should appear in the consolidation worksheet used to prepare a complete set of consolidated financial statements for 20X7.

c. Compute Subsidence's 20X7 reported net income.

d. Compute Bower's 20X7 income from its own separate operations, excluding any investment income from its investment in Subsidence Mining.

LO 7-4, 7-5   **P7-31**   ### Preparation of Consolidated Balance Sheet

Lofton Company owns 60 percent of Temple Corporation's voting shares, purchased on May 17, 20X1, at book value. At that date, the fair value of the noncontrolling interest was equal to 40 percent of the book value of Temple Corporation. The companies' permanent accounts on December 31, 20X6, contained the following balances:

	Lofton Company	Temple Corporation
Cash and Receivables	$101,000	$ 20,000
Inventory	80,000	40,000
Land	150,000	90,000
Buildings & Equipment	400,000	300,000
Investment in Temple Corporation Stock	141,000	
	872,000	$450,000
Accumulated Depreciation	$135,000	$ 85,000
Accounts Payable	90,000	25,000
Notes Payable	200,000	90,000
Common Stock	100,000	200,000
Retained Earnings	347,000	50,000
	$872,000	$450,000

On January 1, 20X2, Lofton paid $100,000 for equipment with a 10-year expected total economic life. The equipment was depreciated on a straight-line basis with no residual value. Temple purchased the equipment from Lofton on December 31, 20X4, for $91,000. Assume Temple did not change the remaining estimated useful life of the equipment.

Temple sold land it had purchased for $30,000 on February 23, 20X4, to Lofton for $20,000 on October 14, 20X5. Assume Lofton uses the fully adjusted equity method.

Required

a. Prepare a consolidated balance sheet worksheet in good form as of December 31, 20X6.

b. Prepare a consolidated balance sheet as of December 31, 20X6.

LO 7-4, 7-5   **P7-32**   **Consolidation Worksheet in Year of Intercompany Transfer**

Prime Company holds 80 percent of Lane Company's stock, acquired on January 1, 20X2, for $160,000. On the acquisition date, the fair value of the noncontrolling interest was $40,000. Lane reported retained earnings of $50,000 and had $100,000 of common stock outstanding. Prime uses the fully adjusted equity method in accounting for its investment in Lane.

Trial balance data for the two companies on December 31, 20X6, are as follows:

Advanced
StudyGuide
.com

Item	Prime Company Debit	Prime Company Credit	Lane Company Debit	Lane Company Credit
Cash & Accounts Receivable	$ 113,000		$ 35,000	
Inventory	260,000		90,000	
Land	80,000		80,000	
Buildings & Equipment	500,000		150,000	
Investment in Lane Company Stock	191,600			
Cost of Goods Sold	140,000		60,000	
Depreciation & Amortization	25,000		15,000	
Other Expenses	15,000		5,000	
Dividends Declared	30,000		5,000	
Accumulated Depreciation		$ 205,000		$ 45,000
Accounts Payable		60,000		20,000
Bonds Payable		200,000		50,000
Common Stock		300,000		100,000
Retained Earnings		322,000		95,000
Sales		240,000		130,000
Gain on Sale of Equipment		20,000		
Income from Subsidiary		7,600		
Total	$1,354,600	$1,354,600	$440,000	$440,000

Additional Information

1. At the date of combination, the book values and fair values of all separately identifiable assets and liabilities of Lane were the same. At December 31, 20X6, the management of Prime reviewed the amount attributed to goodwill as a result of its purchase of Lane stock and concluded an impairment loss of $18,000 should be recognized in 20X6 and shared proportionately between the controlling and noncontrolling shareholders.

2. On January 1, 20X5, Lane sold land that had cost $8,000 to Prime for $18,000.

3. On January 1, 20X6, Prime sold to Lane equipment that it had purchased for $75,000 on January 1, 20X1. The equipment has a total economic life of 15 years and was sold to Lane for $70,000. Both companies use straight-line depreciation.

4. There was $7,000 of intercompany receivables and payables on December 31, 20X6.

Required

a. Give all consolidation entries needed to prepare a consolidation worksheet for 20X6.

b. Prepare a three-part worksheet for 20X6 in good form.

c. Prepare a consolidated balance sheet, income statement, and retained earnings statement for 20X6.

LO 7-4, 7-5 **P7-33** **Consolidation Worksheet in Year Following Intercompany Transfer**

Prime Company holds 80 percent of Lane Company's stock, acquired on January 1, 20X2, for $160,000. On the date of acquisition, Lane reported retained earnings of $50,000 and $100,000 of common stock outstanding, and the fair value of the noncontrolling interest was $40,000. Prime uses the fully adjusted equity method in accounting for its investment in Lane.

Trial balance data for the two companies on December 31, 20X7, are as follows:

Item	Prime Company Debit	Prime Company Credit	Lane Company Debit	Lane Company Credit
Cash & Accounts Receivable	$ 151,000		$ 55,000	
Inventory	240,000		100,000	
Land	100,000		80,000	
Buildings & Equipment	500,000		150,000	
Investment in Lane Company Stock	201,600			
Cost of Goods Sold	160,000		80,000	
Depreciation & Amortization	25,000		15,000	
Other Expenses	20,000		10,000	
Dividends Declared	60,000		35,000	
Accumulated Depreciation		$ 230,000		$ 60,000
Accounts Payable		60,000		25,000
Bonds Payable		200,000		50,000
Common Stock		300,000		100,000
Retained Earnings		379,600		140,000
Sales		250,000		150,000
Income from Subsidiary		38,000		
Total	$1,457,600	$1,457,600	$525,000	$525,000

Additional Information

1. At the date of combination, the book values and fair values of Lane's separately identifiable assets and liabilities were equal. The full amount of the increased value of the entity was attributed to goodwill. At December 31, 20X6, the management of Prime reviewed the amount attributed to goodwill as a result of its purchase of Lane stock and recognized an impairment loss of $18,000. No further impairment occurred in 20X7.

2. On January 1, 20X5, Lane sold land for $18,000 that had cost $8,000 to Prime.

3. On January 1, 20X6, Prime sold to Lane equipment that it had purchased for $75,000 on January 1, 20X1. The equipment has a total 15-year economic life and was sold to Lane for $70,000. Both companies use straight-line depreciation.

4. Intercompany receivables and payables total $4,000 on December 31, 20X7.

Required

a. Prepare a reconciliation between the balance in Prime's Investment in Lane Company Stock account reported on December 31, 20X7, and Lane's book value.

b. Prepare all worksheet consolidation entries needed as of December 31, 20X7, and complete a three-part consolidation worksheet for 20X7.

LO 7-4, 7-5   **P7-34**   ### Intercompany Sales in Prior Years

On January 1, 20X5, Pond Corporation acquired 80 percent of Skate Company's stock by issuing common stock with a fair value of $180,000. At that date, Skate reported net assets of $150,000. The fair value of the noncontrolling interest was $45,000. Assume Pond uses the fully adjusted equity method. The balance sheets for Pond and Skate at January 1, 20X8, and December 31, 20X8, and income statements for 20X8 were reported as follows:

	20X8 Balance Sheet Data			
	Pond Corporation		**Skate Company**	
	January 1	**December 31**	**January 1**	**December 31**
Cash	$ 40,400	$ 68,400	$ 10,000	$ 47,000
Accounts Receivable	120,000	130,000	60,000	65,000
Interest & Other Receivables	40,000	45,000	8,000	10,000
Inventory	100,000	140,000	50,000	50,000
Land	50,000	50,000	22,000	22,000
Buildings & Equipment	400,000	400,000	240,000	240,000
Accumulated Depreciation	(150,000)	(185,000)	(70,000)	(94,000)
Investment in Skate Company Stock	185,600	200,100		
Investment in Tin Co. Bonds	135,000	134,000		
Total Assets	921,000	982,500	$320,000	$340,000
Accounts Payable	$ 60,000	$ 65,000	$ 16,500	$ 11,000
Interest & Other Payables	40,000	45,000	7,000	12,000
Bonds Payable	300,000	300,000	100,000	100,000
Bond Discount			(3,500)	(3,000)
Common Stock	150,000	150,000	30,000	30,000
Additional Paid-in Capital	155,000	155,000	20,000	20,000
Retained Earnings	216,000	267,500	150,000	170,000
Total Liabilities & Equities	921,000	982,500	$320,000	$340,000

	20X8 Income Statement Data			
	Pond Corporation		**Skate Company**	
Sales		$450,000		$250,000
Income from Subsidiary		22,500		
Interest Income		14,900		
Total Revenue		487,400		$250,000
Cost of Goods Sold	$285,000		$136,000	
Other Operating Expenses	50,000		40,000	
Depreciation Expense	35,000		24,000	
Interest Expense	24,000		10,500	
Miscellaneous Expenses	11,900	(405,900)	9,500	(220,000)
Net Income		$ 81,500		$ 30,000

Additional Information

1. In 20X2, Skate developed a patent for a high-speed drill bit that Pond planned to market extensively. In accordance with generally accepted accounting standards, Skate charges all research and development costs to expense in the year the expenses are incurred. At January 1, 20X5, the market value of the patent rights was estimated to be $50,000. Pond believes the patent will

be of value for the next 20 years. The remainder of the differential is assigned to buildings and equipment, which also had a 20-year estimated economic life at January 1, 20X5. All of Skate's other assets and liabilities identified by Pond at the date of acquisition had book values and fair values that were relatively equal.

2. On December 31, 20X7, Pond sold a building to Skate for $65,000 that it had purchased for $125,000 and depreciated on a straight-line basis over 25 years. At the time of sale, Pond reported accumulated depreciation of $75,000 and a remaining life of 10 years.

3. On July 1, 20X6, Skate sold land that it had purchased for $22,000 to Pond for $35,000. Pond is planning to build a new warehouse on the property prior to the end of 20X9.

4. Both Pond and Skate paid dividends in 20X8.

Required

a. Give all consolidation entries required to prepare a three-part consolidation working paper at December 31, 20X8.

b. Prepare a three-part worksheet for 20X8 in good form.

LO 7-3, 7-6 **P7-35** **Intercompany Sale of Land and Depreciable Asset**

Topp Corporation acquired 70 percent of Morris Company's voting common stock on January 1, 20X3, for $158,900. Morris reported common stock outstanding of $100,000 and retained earnings of $85,000. The fair value of the noncontrolling interest was $68,100 at the date of acquisition. Buildings and equipment held by Morris had a fair value $25,000 higher than book value. The remainder of the differential was assigned to a copyright held by Morris. Buildings and equipment had a 10-year remaining life and the copyright had a 5-year life at the date of acquisition.

Trial balances for Topp and Morris on December 31, 20X5, are as follows:

	Topp Corporation		Morris Company	
	Debit	**Credit**	**Debit**	**Credit**
Cash	$ 15,850		$ 58,000	
Accounts Receivable	65,000		70,000	
Interest & Other Receivables	30,000		10,000	
Inventory	150,000		180,000	
Land	80,000		60,000	
Buildings & Equipment	315,000		240,000	
Bond Discount			15,000	
Investment in Morris Company Stock	157,630			
Cost of Goods Sold	375,000		110,000	
Depreciation Expense	25,000		10,000	
Interest Expense	24,000		33,000	
Other Expense	28,000		17,000	
Dividends Declared	30,000		5,000	
Accumulated Depreciation—Buildings & Equipment		$ 120,000		$ 60,000
Accounts Payable		61,000		28,000
Other Payables		30,000		20,000
Bonds Payable		250,000		300,000
Common Stock		150,000		100,000
Additional Paid-in Capital		30,000		
Retained Earnings		165,240		100,000
Sales		450,000		190,400
Other Income		28,250		
Gain on Sale of Equipment				9,600
Income from Subsidiary		10,990		
Total	$1,295,480	$1,295,480	$808,000	$808,000

Topp sold land it had purchased for $21,000 to Morris on September 20, 20X4, for $32,000. Morris plans to use the land for future plant expansion. On January 1, 20X5, Morris sold equipment to Topp for $91,600. Morris purchased the equipment on January 1, 20X3, for $100,000 and depreciated it on a 10-year basis, including an estimated residual value of $10,000. The residual value and estimated economic life of the equipment remained unchanged as a result of the transfer and both companies use straight-line depreciation. Assume Topp uses the fully adjusted equity method.

Required

a. Compute the amount of income assigned to the noncontrolling interest in the consolidated income statement for 20X5.

b. Prepare a reconciliation between the balance in the Investment in Morris Company Stock account reported by Topp at December 31, 20X5, and the underlying book value of net assets reported by Morris at that date.

c. Give all consolidation entries needed to prepare a full set of consolidated financial statements at December 31, 20X5, for Topp and Morris.

d. Prepare a three-part worksheet for 20X5 in good form.

LO 7-3, 7-6 **P7-36** **Incomplete Data**

Partial trial balance data for Mound Corporation, Shadow Company, and the consolidated entity at December 31, 20X7, are as follows:

Item	Mound Corporation	Shadow Company	Consolidated Entity
Cash	$ 65,300	$ 25,000	$ 90,300
Accounts Receivable	(d)	35,000	126,000
Inventory	160,000	75,000	235,000
Buildings & Equipment	345,000	150,000	(i)
Land	70,000	90,000	153,000
Investment in Shadow Company Stock	(f)		
Cost of Goods Sold	230,000	195,000	425,000
Depreciation Expense	45,000	10,000	52,000
Amortization Expense			(e)
Miscellaneous Expense	18,000	15,000	33,000
Dividends Declared	25,000	20,000	25,000
Income to Noncontrolling Interest			(l)
Copyrights			9,000
Total Debits	$1,180,900	$615,000	$1,674,200
Accumulated Depreciation	$ 180,000	$ 80,000	$ (j)
Accounts Payable	25,000	85,000	101,000
Common Stock	100,000	50,000	(a)
Additional Paid-in Capital	(b)	70,000	140,000
Retained Earnings	375,800	80,000	(k)
Income from Subsidiary	10,100		
Sales	343,000	(c)	593,000
Gain on Sale of Land	(g)		(h)
Noncontrolling Interest			86,400
Total Credits	$1,180,900	$615,000	$1,674,200

Additional Information

1. Mound Corporation acquired 60 percent ownership of Shadow Company on January 1, 20X4, for $106,200. Shadow reported net assets of $150,000 at that date, and the fair value of the noncontrolling interest was estimated to be $70,800. The full amount of the differential at acquisition is assigned to copyrights that are being amortized over a six-year life.

2. On August 13, 20X7, Mound sold land to Shadow for $28,000. Mound also has accounts receivable from Shadow on services performed prior to the end of 20X7.

3. Shadow sold equipment it had purchased for $60,000 on January 1, 20X4, to Mound on for $45,000 January 1, 20X6. The equipment is depreciated on a straight-line basis and had a total expected useful life of five years when Shadow purchased it. No change in life expectancy resulted from the intercompany transfer. Assume Mound uses the fully adjusted equity method.

4. Assume Mound Corp. does not use the optional accumulation depreciation consolidation entry.

Required
Compute the dollar amount for each of the balances identified by a letter.

LO 7-6

P7-37 Intercompany Sale of Equipment at a Loss in Prior Period

Block Corporation was created on January 1, 20X0, to develop computer software. On January 1, 20X5, Foster Company acquired 90 percent of Block's common stock at its underlying book value. At that date, the fair value of the noncontrolling interest was equal to 10 percent of the book value of Block Corporation. Trial balances for Foster and Block on December 31, 20X9, follow:

	Foster Company		Block Corporation	
	Debit	**Credit**	**Debit**	**Credit**
Cash	$ 82,000		$ 32,400	
Accounts Receivable	80,000		90,000	
Other Receivables	40,000		10,000	
Inventory	200,000		130,000	
Land	80,000		60,000	
Buildings & Equipment	500,000		250,000	
Investment in Block Corporation Stock	229,500			
Cost of Goods Sold	500,000		250,000	
Depreciation Expense	45,000		15,000	
Other Expense	95,000		75,000	
Dividends Declared	40,000		20,000	
Accumulated Depreciation		$ 155,000		$ 75,000
Accounts Payable		63,000		35,000
Other Payables		95,000		20,000
Bonds Payable		250,000		200,000
Bond Premium				2,400
Common Stock		210,000		50,000
Additional Paid-in Capital		110,000		
Retained Earnings		251,200		150,000
Sales		680,000		385,000
Other Income		26,000		15,000
Income from Subsidiary		51,300		
Total	$1,891,500	$1,891,500	$932,400	$932,400

On January 1, 20X7, Block sold equipment to Foster for $48,000. Block had purchased the equipment for $90,000 on January 1, 20X5, and was depreciating it on a straight-line basis with a 10-year expected life and no anticipated scrap value. The equipment's total expected life is unchanged as a result of the intercompany sale. Assume Foster uses the fully adjusted equity method.

Required

a. Give all consolidation entries required to prepare a three-part consolidated working paper at December 31, 20X9.

b. Prepare a three-part worksheet for 20X9 in good form.

LO 7-1, 7-2, 7-3, 7-6

P7-38 Comprehensive Problem: Intercompany Transfers

Rossman Corporation holds 75 percent of the common stock of Schmid Distributors Inc., purchased on December 31, 20X1, for $2,340,000. At the date of acquisition, Schmid reported common stock with a par value of $1,000,000, additional paid-in capital of $1,350,000, and retained earnings of $620,000. The fair value of the noncontrolling interest at acquisition was $780,000. The differential at acquisition was attributable to the following items:

Inventory (sold in 20X2)	$ 30,000
Land	56,000
Goodwill	64,000
Total Differential	$150,000

During 20X2, Rossman sold a plot of land that it had purchased several years before to Schmid at a gain of $23,000; Schmid continues to hold the land. In 20X6, Rossman and Schmid entered into a five-year contract under which Rossman provides management consulting services to Schmid on a continuing basis; Schmid pays Rossman a fixed fee of $80,000 per year for these services. At December 31, 20X8, Schmid owed Rossman $20,000 as the final 20X8 quarterly payment under the contract.

On January 2, 20X8, Rossman paid $250,000 to Schmid to purchase equipment that Schmid was then carrying at $290,000. Schmid had purchased that equipment on December 27, 20X2, for $435,000. The equipment is expected to have a total 15-year life and no salvage value. The amount of the differential assigned to goodwill has not been impaired.

At December 31, 20X8, trial balances for Rossman and Schmid appeared as follows:

	Rossman Corporation		Schmid Distributors Inc.	
Item	Debit	Credit	Debit	Credit
Cash	$ 50,700		$ 38,000	
Current Receivables	101,800		89,400	
Inventory	286,000		218,900	
Investment in Schmid Stock	2,974,000			
Land	400,000		1,200,000	
Buildings & Equipment	2,400,000		2,990,000	
Cost of Goods Sold	2,193,000		525,000	
Depreciation & Amortization	202,000		88,000	
Other Expenses	1,381,000		227,000	
Dividends Declared	50,000		20,000	
Accumulated Depreciation		$ 1,105,000		$ 420,000
Current Payables		86,200		76,300
Bonds Payable		1,000,000		200,000
Common Stock		100,000		1,000,000
Additional Paid-in Capital		1,272,000		1,350,000
Retained Earnings, January 1		1,474,800		1,400,000
Sales		4,801,000		985,000
Other Income or Loss		90,000	35,000	
Income from Schmid		109,500		
Total	$10,038,500	$10,038,500	$5,431,300	$5,431,300

As of December 31, 20X8, Schmid had declared but not yet paid its fourth-quarter dividend of $5,000. Both companies use straight-line depreciation and amortization. Rossman uses the fully adjusted equity method to account for its investment in Schmid.

Required

a. Compute the amount of the differential as of January 1, 20X8.

b. Verify the balance in Rossman's Investment in Schmid Stock account as of December 31, 20X8.

c. Present all consolidation entries that would appear in a three-part consolidation worksheet as of December 31, 20X8.

d. Prepare and complete a three-part worksheet for the preparation of consolidated financial statements for 20X8.

LO 7-4, 7-5 | **P7-39A** | ### Modified Equity Method Computation of Retained Earnings Following Multiple Transfers

Great Company acquired 80 percent of Meager Corporation's common stock on January 1, 20X4, for $280,000. The fair value of the noncontrolling interest was $70,000 at the date of acquisition. Great's corporate controller has lost the consolidation files for the past three years and has asked you to compute the proper retained earnings balances for the consolidated entity at January 1, 20X8, and December 31, 20X8. The controller has been able to determine the following:

1. The book value of Meager's net assets at January 1, 20X4, was $290,000, and the fair value of its net assets was $325,000. This difference was due to an increase in the value of equipment. All depreciable assets had a remaining life of 10 years at the date of combination. At December 31, 20X8, Great's management reviewed the amount attributed to goodwill as a result of its purchase

of Meager common stock and concluded that an impairment loss of $17,500 should be recognized in 20X8 and shared proportionately between the controlling and noncontrolling shareholders.

2. Great uses the modified equity method in accounting for its investment in Meager.

3. Meager has reported net income of $30,000 and paid dividends of $20,000 each year since Great purchased its ownership.

4. Great reported retained earnings of $450,000 in its December 31, 20X7, balance sheet. For 20X8, Great reported operating income of $65,000 and paid dividends of $45,000.

5. Meager sold land costing $40,000 to Great for $56,000 on December 31, 20X7.

6. On January 1, 20X6, Great sold depreciable assets with a remaining useful life of 10 years to Meager and recorded a $22,000 gain on the sale.

Required
Compute the appropriate amounts to be reported as consolidated retained earnings at January 1, 20X8, and December 31, 20X8.

LO 7-1, 7-3, 7-6   **P7-40A**   **Consolidation Worksheet with Intercompany Transfers (Modified Equity Method)**

Mist Company acquired 65 percent of Blank Corporation's voting common stock on June 20, 20X2, at underlying book value. At that date, the fair value of the noncontrolling interest was equal to 35 percent of the book value of Blank Corporation. The balance sheets and income statements for the companies at December 31, 20X4, are as follows:

MIST COMPANY AND BLANK CORPORATION
Balance Sheets
December 31, 20X4

Item	Mist Company	Blank Corp.
Cash	$ 32,500	$ 22,000
Accounts Receivable	62,000	37,000
Inventory	95,000	71,000
Land	40,000	15,000
Buildings & Equipment (net)	200,000	125,000
Investment in Blank Corp. Stock	110,500	
Total Assets	$540,000	$270,000
Accounts Payable	$ 35,000	$ 20,000
Bonds Payable	180,000	80,000
Common Stock, $5 par value	100,000	60,000
Retained Earnings	225,000	110,000
Total Liabilities & Stockholders' Equity	$540,000	$270,000

MIST COMPANY AND BLANK CORPORATION
Combined Income and Retained Earnings Statements
Year Ended December 31, 20X4

Item	Mist Company		Blank Corp.	
Sales and Service Revenue		$286,500		$128,500
Gain on Sale of Land		4,000		
Gain on Sale of Building				13,200
Income from Subsidiary		19,500		
		$310,000		$141,700
Cost of Goods & Services Sold	$160,000		$75,000	
Depreciation Expense	22,000		19,000	
Other Expenses	76,000	(258,000)	17,700	(111,700)
Net Income		$ 52,000		$ 30,000
Dividends Paid		(25,000)		(5,000)
Change in Retained Earnings		$ 27,000		$ 25,000

Additional Information

1. Mist uses the modified equity method in accounting for its investment in Blank.

2. During 20X4, Mist charged Blank $24,000 for consulting services provided to Blank during the year. The services cost Mist $17,000.

3. On January 1, 20X4, Blank sold Mist a building for $13,200 above its carrying value on Blank's books. The building had a 12-year remaining economic life at the time of transfer.

4. On June 14, 20X4, Mist sold land it had purchased for $3,000 to Blank for $7,000. Blank continued to hold the land at December 31, 20X4.

Required

a. Give all consolidation entries needed to prepare a full set of consolidated financial statements for 20X4.

b. Prepare a consolidation worksheet for 20X4.

c. Prepare the 20X4 consolidated balance sheet, income statement, and retained earnings statement.

LO 7-6

P7-41A Modified Equity Method

Using the data in P7-33, on December 31, 20X7, Prime Company recorded the following entry on its books to adjust its investment in Lane Company from the fully adjusted equity method to the modified equity method:

Income from Lane Company	2,000	
Investment in Lane Company Stock	38,400	
Retained Earnings		40,400

Required

a. Adjust the data reported by Prime in the trial balance in Problem P7-33 for the effects of the adjusting entry presented above.

b. Prepare the journal entries that would have been recorded on Prime's books during 20X7 if it had always used the modified equity method.

c. Prepare all consolidation entries needed to complete a consolidation worksheet as of December 31, 20X7, assuming Prime has used the modified equity method.

d. Complete a three-part consolidation worksheet as of December 31, 20X7.

LO 7-6

P7-42A Cost Method

The trial balance data presented in P7-33 can be converted to reflect use of the cost method by inserting the following amounts in place of those presented for Prime Company:

Investment in Lane Company Stock	$160,000
Beginning Retained Earnings	348,000
Income from Subsidiary	0
Dividend Income	28,000

Required

a. Prepare the journal entries that would have been recorded on Prime's books during 20X7 under the cost method.

b. Prepare all consolidation entries needed to complete a consolidation worksheet as of December 31, 20X7, assuming Prime has used the cost method.

c. Complete a three-part consolidation worksheet as of December 31, 20X7.